ontents

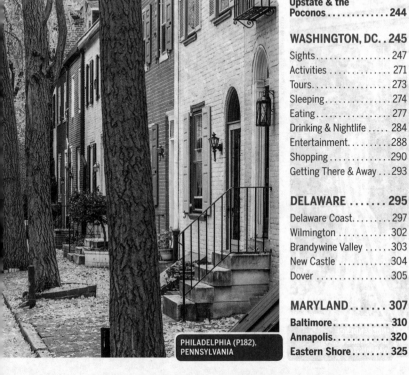

PHILADELPHIA (P182),
PENNSYLVANIA

ON THE ROAD

SHENANDOAH VALLEY,
(P368) VIRGINIA

INDEPENDENCE
DAY PARADE (P274),
WASHINGTON, DC

New York & the Mid-Atlantic

New York State
p122

Pennsylvania
p218

New York City
p48

Philadelphia
p182

New Jersey
p157

Maryland
p307

West Virginia
p377

Washington, DC
p245

Delaware p295

Virginia
p339

Robert B   l, Ali Lemer,
Virginia   immerman

C334344345

PLAN YOUR TRIP

ON THE ROAD

BLUE CRAB, CHESAPEAKE
BAY (P331), MARYLAND

MARTIN LUTHER KING
JR MEMORIAL (P256),
WASHINGTON, DC

Contents

NEW YORK CITY (P48)

Welcome to New York & the Mid-Atlantic

A compelling mix of adventure awaits: monuments and museums, beaches and battlefields, woods and white water. Oyster shooters and bluegrass jams bring the party.

The USA's Story

With museums now acknowledging the accomplishments and struggles of a diverse mix of historic players – from Native Americans to slaves to Founding Fathers – it's a compelling time to study the past in the Mid-Atlantic. Events elemental to the US political system and cultural norms took root here. Whether studying the Jamestown ruins, touring Independence Hall or following the Underground Railroad, this is where the story of the modern USA unfolded. If you time it right, you can experience history in real time by watching legislators in action from the galleries of centuries-old state houses.

Outdoor Fun

Don't let the boring moniker 'Mid-Atlantic' throw you: from Assateague Island to the Appalachian Mountains, the region is chock-full of adventures with gorgeous backdrops. Here you can paddle coastal salt marshes, cycle past historic locks, hike scenic rail trails and scramble to rock-covered peaks. And we saved the best for last: you may not have time for scenery in West Virginia as you plunge over Class V rapids on what might be the wildest white water in America. Hold tight for Pillow Roooooock – ahhhh! Bam! Yeah!

Cultural Bonanza

New York City and Washington, DC, are regional anchors for the arts: from the Big Apple's grand Metropolitan Museum of Art to the 19 museums comprising the Smithsonian Institution in the nation's capital. For live performances, take your pick of prestigious venues: Carnegie Hall, the Kennedy Center, the Folger Theatre and more. But culture doesn't end at big-city borders. Art gets visionary in Baltimore, MD, while Richmond, VA, and Philadelphia, PA, showcase eclectic murals. To the west, traditional arts and crafts reflect long-honed skills, while old-time mountain music wins new fans with catchy modern interpretations.

Good Eats

From biscuits and gravy for breakfast to ramen at lunch and goulash at dinner, you can travel the world in a day in NYC or DC. Both cities dazzle with choice: chow down in a 60-year-old diner or in a hip industrial space with the chef du jour. Salty hams, jumbo peanuts and farm-to-table fare are Virginia specialties, while cracking steamed crabs and slurping oysters in Maryland is heaven for seafood lovers. Delaware's seafood shines too. Cheesesteaks rule in Philly, while fluffy biscuits and pepperoni rolls are winners in West Virginia.

Why I Love New York & the Mid-Atlantic

By Amy C Balfour, Writer

My great-grandfather led hikes to the summit of Sharp Top Mountain in Virginia as a boy, imparting his knowledge of the Blue Ridge Mountains to curious visitors. I understand why he did it – it was a love of place he couldn't help but share. Today, I love the easy accessibility of outdoor adventures from the region's vibrant big and midsized cities, where culinary and cultural attractions shine. History – now refreshingly open to reinterpretation – is also on your doorstep here. And the microbreweries and wineries? Gorgeous views complement great libations.

For more about our writers, see p448

Above: Blue Ridge Highlands (p374), Virginia

New York & the Mid-Atlantic

Niagara Falls
North America's most voluminous cascade (p154)

Pittsburgh
Food, architecture, big energy (p232)

Washington, DC
National Mall: cultural epicenter (p245)

Shenandoah National Park
Skyline Drive, wildlife, big views (p356)

Appalachian Trail
Cross-country mountain trail (p381)

Blue Ridge Parkway
Sublime drive through the Appalachians (p376)

Alpena

Cadillac

Tawas City

Kincardine

MICHIGAN

Bay City

Saginaw

Grand Rapids

Flint

⊙Lansing

Jackson

Detroit

Fort Wayne

Toledo

Georgian Bay

Lake Huron

Midland

Collingwood

Barrie

ONTARIO

Oshawa

Toronto ⊙

CANADA
USA

Lake Ontario

Hamilton

Niagara Falls

Buffalo

Medina

Brockport

Rochester

Batavia

Letchworth State Park

East Aurora

Dunkirk

Dansville

Bath

Fredonia

Erie

Jamestown

Salamanca

Wellsville

Corning

Lake Erie

Conneaut

Corry

Warren

Bradford

Mansfield

Cleveland

Meadville

Titusville

Allegheny National Forest

Galeton

Wellsboro

Franklin

St Marys

PENNSYLVANIA

Williamsport

Akron

Youngstown

DuBois

Clearfield

Punxsutawney

State College

OHIO

East Liverpool

McCandless

Indiana

Tyrone

Steubenville

Pittsburgh

Altoona

Lewistown

Columbus

Wheeling

Washington

Harrisburg

Moundsville

Bedford

Chambersburg

Uniontown

Somerset

Gettysburg

Morgantown

Cumberland

Hagerstown

Westminster

Cincinnati

Martinsburg

Frederick

Winchester

Rockville

Shenandoah National Park

Front Royal

WEST VIRGINIA

Franklin

WASHINGTON, DC

Frankfort

KENTUCKY

Huntington

Monongahela National Forest

Harrisonburg

Culpeper

La Plata

Lexington

⊙Charleston

Monterey

Shenandoah National Park

Fayetteville

Staunton

Fredericksburg

Oak Hill

New River Gorge National River

Lewisburg

Waynesboro

Charlottesville

Jefferson National Forest

Lexington

James River

Princeton

Roanoke

Lynchburg

Richmond

Blacksburg

Bedford

Farmville

Wytheville

Appomattox

Petersburg

Floyd

VIRGINIA

South Hill

Kingsport

Martinsville

South Boston

Franklin

TENNESSEE

Knoxville

NORTH CAROLINA

0 200 km
0 100 miles

★ OTTAWA ⊙ Montréal QUEBEC

Cornwall

MAINE

Appalachian Trail

Kingston

VERMONT NEW HAMPSHIRE

⊙ Montpelier

⊙ Augusta

Catskills
Beautiful mountain
getaway (p132)

New York City
Loud, fast, pulsating, dizzying
metropolis (p48)

Portland

⊙ Concord

Keene

Syracuse Oneida Utica
Oneida
Lake
Auburn NEW
Geneva YORK
Amsterdam
Schenectady
⊙ Troy
Albany ⊙
Pittsfield MASSACHUSETTS
⊙ Salem
Cortland
Norwich
Oneonta
Hudson
Northampton
⊙ Boston
Ithaca
Finger
Lakes
Roxbury
Catskill
Springfield
Elmira Binghamton
Catskill
Park
Kingston
Sayre
Margaretville
Kingston
⊙ Providence
Towanda
Carbondale
Monticello New
Paltz
Poughkeepsie
Hartford
Newport
Wilkes-Barre
Scranton
Port
Jervis
Newburgh
CONNECTICUT
New Haven RHODE
ISLAND

Princeton
Ivy League campus,
600-acre woods (p161)

Bloomsburg
Delaware Water
Gap National
Recreation Area
Stroudsburg
Paterson
Tarrytown
Stamford
Bridgeport
Greenport
Sunbury
Easton
Yonkers
Pottsville
⊙ New York
Southampton
Allentown
Princeton
New Brunswick
40°N
Hershey
Reading
NEW
JERSEY
Long Branch
Ephrata
Asbury Park
York
Lancaster
Trenton
Point
Hanover
Philadelphia
Willingboro
Pleasant

Philadelphia
A delight for chowhounds
and history buffs (p182)

Wilmington
Long Beach
Island
Havre de
Grace
Newark
Hammonton
Baltimore
Smyrna
Millville
⊙ Atlantic City
Annapolis
⊙ Dover
Ocean City
St Michaels Easton
Milford
Wildwoods
Cambridge
Lewes
Cape May
Rehoboth
Seaford Beach

Cape May
Bird-watching, wine on
Jersey Shore (p179)

MARYLAND
Salisbury
⊙ Ocean City
Assateague Island
National Seashore
Leonardtown
Rappahannock
Crisfield
Chincoteague
Island
Saluda
Chesapeake
Bay
Williamsburg
Yorktown
Newport News
⊙ Norfolk
Virginia
Beach
Suffolk

ATLANTIC
OCEAN

Rehoboth Beach
Boardwalk, good eats,
craft beer (p299)

ELEVATION

6000ft
5000ft
4000ft
3000ft
2000ft
1000ft
500ft
0

St Michaels
Crabs, sailing, Eastern shore
fun (p325)

75°W 70°W

New York & the Mid-Atlantic's
Top 22

National Mall

1 Nearly 2 miles long and lined with iconic monuments and hallowed marble buildings, the National Mall (p247) is the epicenter of Washington, DC's political and cultural life. America's finest museums line the green, welcoming visitors year-round; in summer, massive music and food festivals are staged here. For exploring American history, there's no better place to ruminate, whether you're tracing your hand along the Vietnam Veterans Memorial or ascending the steps of the Lincoln Memorial, where Dr Martin Luther King Jr gave his famous 'I Have a Dream' speech.

Below left: Jefferson Memorial (p257)

New York City

2 Home to striving artists, hedge-fund moguls and immigrants from every corner of the globe, New York City (p48) is constantly reinventing itself. It remains one of the world centers of fashion, theater, food, music, publishing, advertising, and finance. A staggering number of museums, parks and ethnic neighborhoods are scattered through the five boroughs. Do as every New Yorker does, and hit the streets: every block reflects the character and history of this dizzying kaleidoscope, and in a short walk you can cross continents.

Below: Brooklyn Bridge (p60)

FLIPHOTO/GETTY IMAGES ©

ALLARD ONE/SHUTTERSTOCK ©

Shenandoah National Park

3 The view of rolling mountains and the lush Shenandoah Valley will take your breath away at the Hawksbill Mountain summit. We mean that literally; at 4050ft, it's the highest peak in the park (p356). You have to hike to get there, but the 360-degree panorama is worth the burn. The park is only 75 miles from Washington, DC. Overlooks, trails and campgrounds hug the lofty Skyline Drive, a 105-mile byway that traverses the whole shebang from north to south. As for wildlife, there's plenty; we guarantee you'll see a white-tailed deer.

Delaware Beaches

4 The First State may be small in size, but its gorgeous beaches punch above their weight. Not only are they easy to access from Washington, DC, and Baltimore, MD – both are 120 miles away – but they each offer a different experience. History buffs and cyclists may prefer Lewes, where the quaint downtown and a woodsy state park border the golden strands. Rehoboth (p299) welcomes fun-seeking families and beachgoers in search of a civilized meal. Dewey (p301) gets wild while Bethany (p301; pictured above) is a quiet spot for sitting on the beach and relaxing.

5

6

Adirondacks

5 Majestic and wild, the Adirondacks (p144), a mountain range with 42 peaks over 4000ft high, rival any of the nation's wilderness areas for sheer awe-inspiring beauty. The 9375 sq miles of protected parklands and forest preserve, which climb from central New York State to the Canadian border, include towns, mountains, glacial lakes, rivers, and more than 2000 miles of hiking trails.

Blue Ridge Parkway

6 There's not one stoplight to spoil the ride on this 469-mile roadway (p376) traversing the southern Appalachian Mountains of Virginia and North Carolina. Along its nearly 217 miles in Virginia, you can watch sublime sunsets, scan for wild-life and lose all sense of the present while gazing at the vast wilderness. Hikes take you deeper into nature, from easy lakeside trails to challenging scrambles to eagles'-nest heights. Camp or spend the night at forest lodges. Don't miss the bluegrass and mountain music scenes of nearby towns such as Floyd and Galax.

NIRMALCHANDRASEKARAN/GETTY IMAGES ©

Delaware Water Gap

7 White-water rafting after a wet spring is a thrilling adventure in this rugged and dramatically beautiful national recreation area just 70 miles east of New York City. Established in 1965, this protected area (p161) along the S-curve in the Delaware River is an unspoiled place to swim, boat, fish, camp, hike and see wildlife. If you're not up for white-water, floating gently past bucolic scenery is a completely satisfying alternative. The current preserved areas cover land in both New Jersey and Pennsylvania.

Appalachian Trail

8 The country's longest footpath (p36) stretches more than 2100 miles, crosses six national parks and slices through 14 states from Georgia to Maine. Deep woods, alpine peaks, cow-dotted farms and foraging bears are part of the landscape. An estimated two to three million people trek a portion annually, inhaling the fresh air and admiring the spectacular scenery. You'll find 544 miles of the trail crossing the western mountains of Virginia, also home to the McAfee Knob. The helpful Appalachian Trail Conservancy (p381) is headquartered near the trail in Harpers Ferry, WV.

Boardwalk Bliss

9 Strolling along the East Coast's beach boardwalks is a rite of passage, be it in Rehoboth Beach (p299), DE; Ocean City (p330), MD; or Virginia Beach (p366; pictured top right), VA. It doesn't matter where. The point is to enjoy the all-star roster of summer indulgence that inevitably lines the walkway – funnel cakes, go-karts, pizza shacks, glow-in-the-dark mini-golf, saltwater taffy shops and amusement park rides. Parents push strollers, tots lick ice-cream cones, and teenagers check each other out. Don't get so caught up you forget to take in the sea views!

Civil War Sites

10 Battlegrounds and museums are scattered across Maryland, West Virginia and Virginia. They include Antietam (p332; pictured right), MD, site of the bloodiest day in American history, with more than 23,000 casualties; Richmond (p350), VA, once the Confederacy capital and now home to several museums delving into the war from various perspectives; and Droop Mountain (p388), WV, where Confederate forces fought with Federal troops in the last significant battle in the Mountain State. In summer, many sites host battle reenactments.

JERRY REGIS/SHUTTERSTOCK ©

Independence National Historic Park

11 Along with Old City, this national historic park (p188), home to the Museum of the American Revolution, Independence Hall (p184; pictured below) and the Liberty Bell, has been dubbed 'America's most historic square mile.' Once the backbone of the United States government, it has become the backbone of Philadelphia's tourist trade. In the park you'll see storied buildings in which the seeds for the Revolutionary War were planted. You'll also find beautiful, shaded urban lawns dotted with squirrels, pigeons and costumed actors.

Mountain Music & Bluegrass

12 Country music traces its roots to the hills and hollers of Appalachia, where the fiddle music of European settlers and the banjo tunes of African slaves mingled with the ballads and songs of Scots-Irish and German pioneers traveling south on the Wilderness Road. Radio shows in the 1920s spread the music far and wide. Today you can catch regular live performances of mountain music and its modern spin-off – bluegrass – along the Crooked Road, a music heritage trail in Virginia. Don't miss the Friday Night Jamboree at the Floyd Country Store (p375; pictured below).

SEAN PAVONE/SHUTTERSTOCK ©

13

14

Catskills

13 Close to New York City, this beautiful mountain region (p132) has been a popular getaway since the 1800s. The state constitution was amended in 1894 so that thousands of acres here were to be 'forever kept as wild forest lands.' In the early 1900s, 'borscht belt' hotels here were summer escapes for middle-class NYC Jews. The majority of these hotels have closed, although orthodox Jewish communities still thrive in many towns – as does a back-to-the-land, hippie ethos on small farms. In the fall, come here for dramatically colorful fall foliage as well as cool inns and delicious eats.

Eastern Shore

14 There's no one quintessential Maryland Eastern Shore (p325) experience. Cracking steamed crabs at a waterfront crab house. Setting sail on an antique yacht. Learning the compelling story of the Underground Railroad. Scanning for wildlife on a reedy salt marsh. Yep, a weekend here is an immersion into a slower way of life, where the past lingers and the landscape is little changed from the days of the first settlers in the 1600s.
Assateague Island (p329)

Jersey Shore

15 The New Jersey coastline (p166) is studded with resort towns from classy to tacky that fulfill the Platonic ideal of how a long summer day should be spent. Super-sized raucous boardwalks where singles more than mingle are a short drive from old-fashioned intergenerational family retreats. When the temperature rises, the entire state tips eastward and rushes to the beach to create memories that they'll view later with nostalgia and perhaps some regret. Below: Atlantic City (p174)

Pittsburgh

16 Well, hello there Pittsburgh (p232). Where have you been hiding? Tucked between the Monongahela and Allegheny Rivers and a mountain ridge, this boom-and-bust city has long been marked by its rumbling freight trains and iconic bridges. Today, this city of stone and steel is enjoying a moment in the spotlight, and rightfully so, impressing locals and visitors alike with wonderful architecture, fantastic nightlife and and an amazing food scene, from humble to haute.

North Fork

17 Unspoiled farmland and wineries (p131) – there are more than 40 vineyards, clustered mainly around the towns of Jamesport, Cutchogue and Southold – offer a mix of fun and scenery on Long Island, not far from hustle of New York City. The Long Island Wine Council provides details of the local wine trail, which runs along Rte 25 north of Peconic Bay. Don't miss Greenport, a charming, laid-back place lined with restaurants and cafes.

Thousand Islands

18 Virtually unknown to downstate New Yorkers, mostly because of its relative inaccessibility, this region (p149) of more than 1800 islands – from tiny outcroppings with space for a towel to larger islands with roads and towns – is a scenic wonderland separating the US from Canada. Once a playground for the very rich, who built Gilded Age dream homes, today it's a watery world for boating, camping, swimming and even shipwreck scuba-diving.

C&O Canal National Historic Park

19 The leafy C&O Canal National Historic Park (p334) is a pleasant time warp. Built in the early 1800s alongside the Potomac River to help boats travel between Cumberland, MD, and Georgetown in DC, the former towpath is reserved today for hikers and cyclists. If you spend any time driving across Maryland, you'll see roadside C&O Canal Byway signs, notifying travelers that the 184.5-mile path is nearby.

Adventuring in West Virginia

20 This wild, wonderful state is an outdoor playground, where adventure starts the moment your car curves around that first mountain road. White-water rafting on the Gauley River, particularly during the fall dam release, ranks among the USA's most epic paddling trips. Rock climbers scale striking Seneca Rocks (p386; pictured above) while newbies enjoy thrills on the nearby *via ferrata* course. Cycling paths track scenic rivers, and the high-plateau hiking atop the Dolly Sods Wilderness (p385) crosses one of the most unique landscapes in the Mid-Atlantic.

Meeting the Founding Fathers in Virginia

21 The accomplishments of America's Founding Fathers are remarkable. How they wrangled 13 fiercely independent states into a cohesive union bound by the Constitution – still revered today – is one of history's miracles. Learning their stories at their homes humanizes their achievements. Visit St John's Church (p351) in Richmond to watch Patrick Henry in action, tour Monticello (p357) to ponder Jefferson's inconsistencies, and enjoy Potomac River views from George Washington's beloved home, Mt Vernon (p345). Top right: Greenhouse on the grounds of Mt Vernon

Pennsylvania Dutch Country

22 The Amish really do drive buggies and plow their fields by hand. In Dutch Country (p219), the pace is slower, and it's no costumed reenactment. For the most evocative Dutch Country experience, go driving along the winding, narrow lanes between the thruways – past rolling green fields of alfalfa, asparagus and corn, past pungent working barnyards and manicured lawns, waving to Amish families in buggies and straw-hatted teens on scooters.

Need to Know

For more information, see Survival Guide (p421)

Currency
US Dollar ($)

Language
English

Visas
Visitors from Canada, the UK, Australia, New Zealand, Japan and many EU countries do not need visas for stays of less than 90 days, with ESTA (Electronic System for Travel Authorization) approval. For other nations, see www.travel.state.gov or www.usa.gov/visas -and-visitors.

Money
ATMs are widely available. Credit cards are accepted at most hotels, restaurants and shops.

Cell Phones
Foreign phones operating on tri- or quad-band frequencies will work in the USA. Or purchase inexpensive cell (mobile) phones with a pay-as-you-go plan here.

Time
Eastern Standard Time (GMT/UTC minus five hours)

When to Go

Warm to hot summers, cold winters
Warm to hot summers, mild winters

Buffalo
GO Jun–Aug

Pittsburgh
GO May–Sep

New York City
GO Sep–Dec

Philadelphia
GO Mar–May & Sep–Nov

Washington, DC
GO Mar–Apr & Sep–Oct

High Season (Jun–Aug)

➡ Warm, sunny days across the region.

➡ Accommodation prices peak (up 30% on average).

➡ Big outdoor music festivals abound, including Firefly Music Festival (Dover, MD) and Floydfest (Floyd, VA).

Shoulder (Apr–May, Sep–Oct)

➡ Milder temperatures; can be rainy.

➡ Wildflowers bloom, especially in May.

➡ Fall foliage areas (ie Blue Ridge Parkway, Catskills) remain busy.

Low Season (Nov–Mar)

➡ Dark, wintry days with moderate snowfall.

➡ Lowest prices for accommodations.

➡ Attractions keep shorter hours or close for the winter.

➡ Winter is high season at ski resorts, with busy ski lifts, accommodations and restaurants.

Useful Websites

Lonely Planet (www.lonely planet.com/usa/eastern-usa) Destination information, hotel bookings, traveler forum and more.

Eater (www.eater.com) Foodie insight into two dozen American cities.

National Park Service (www. nps.gov) Gateway to the USA's greatest natural treasures, its national parks.

New York Times Travel (www. nytimes.com/section/travel) Travel news, practical advice and engaging features.

Roadside America (www. roadsideamerica.com) For all attractions weird and wacky.

Washington Post Travel (www. washingtonpost.com/lifestyle/ travel) Often has features about getaways in cities and towns across the Mid-Atlantic.

Important Numbers

To call a number within the USA, dial 1, followed by the area code and the seven-digit number.

USA country code	1
International access code	011
Emergency	911
Directory assistance	411
International directory assistance	00

Exchange Rates

Australia	A$1	$0.77
Canada	C$1	$0.79
Euro zone	€1	$1.20
Japan	¥100	$0.93
New Zealand	NZ$1	$0.74
UK	UK£1	$1.40

For current exchange rates see www.xe.com.

Daily Costs

Budget: Less than $100

➡ Dorm bed: $30–70

➡ Campsite: $15–30

➡ Room in a budget motel: $60–80

➡ Lunch from a cafe or food truck: $8–15

➡ Travel on public transit: $0–5

Midrange: $150–250

➡ Room in a midrange hotel: $80–200

➡ Dinner in a popular restaurant: $20–40

➡ Car rental per day: from $30

Top end: More than $250

➡ Room in a top hotel/resort: from $250

➡ Dinner in a top restaurant: $60–100

➡ Big night out (plays, concerts, clubs): $60–200

Opening Hours

Typical opening times are as follows:

Banks 8:30am to 4:30pm Monday to Friday (and possibly 9am to noon Saturday)

Bars 5pm to midnight Sunday to Thursday, to 2am Friday and Saturday

Nightclubs 10pm to 3am Thursday to Saturday

Post offices 9am to 5pm Monday to Friday

Shopping malls 9am to 9pm

Stores 9am to 6pm Monday to Saturday, noon-5pm Sunday

Supermarkets 8am to 8pm, some open 24 hours

Arriving in New York & the Mid-Atlantic

John F Kennedy International Airport, NY The AirTrain ($5) links to the subway ($2.75), which makes the one-hour journey into Manhattan. Express bus to Grand Central or Port Authority costs $18. Taxis cost a flat $52 excluding tolls, tip and rush hour surcharge.

Ronald Reagan Washington National Airport, DC Metro trains (around $2.65) depart every 10 minutes or so between 5am (from 7am weekends) and 11:30pm (to 1am Friday and Saturday); they reach the city center in 20 minutes. A taxi is $19 to $26.

Dulles International Airport, DC The Silver Line Express bus runs every 15 to 20 minutes from Dulles to Wiehle-Reston East Metro station between 6am and 10:40pm (from 7:45am weekends). Total time to the city center is 60 to 75 minutes; total cost around $11. A taxi is $62 to $73.

Union Station, DC All trains and many buses arrive at this huge station near the Capitol. There's a Metro stop inside for easy onward transport. Taxis queue outside the main entrance.

Dangers & Annoyances

➡ In New York City, be aware of pickpockets, particularly in mobbed areas like Times Square or Penn Station at rush hour.

➡ The DC Metro stops running at 11:30pm (1am on weekends).

For much more on **getting around**, see p432

see p432

If You Like...

Museums

Smithsonian Institution
The nation's premier treasure chest is a group of 19 (free!) museums. (p293)

Metropolitan Museum of Art
The most incredible encyclo-pedic museum in the Americas comes stocked with its own Egyptian temple. (p72)

Philadelphia Museum of Art
Simply one of the best fine-arts museums to be found in the USA. (p186)

Virginia Museum of Fine Arts
A visual feast, from the tiny details of Faberge eggs to the grand *Chloe* sculpture. (p351)

Walters Art Museum Vast personal, adventurous collection of works from medieval armor to the exotic Chamber of Wonders. (p311)

Newseum This fun, sparkling new museum celebrates free-dom of expression and traces the history of journalism. (p264)

American Revolution Museum at Yorktown Experience the Revolutionary War with a 4D movie, significant artifacts and a mock battlefield encampment. (p364)

Longtime Food Favorites

Every American city has that one place that's been a local favorite for decades.

Barney Greengrass After a century in the business, BG still serves up some of the best smoked fish in NYC. (p96)

Faidley The lump crab cakes are legendarily good at this seafood stall in Baltimore, MD. (p318)

Original Oyster House Operat-ing since 1870, this Pittsburgh fave often has a long lines for its fish sandwiches. (p237)

Texas Tavern Get the cheesy western burger at this Roanoke, VA, hamburger hut, established in 1930. (p374)

Mrs. Robino's This long-running Italian joint in Wilmington, DE, serves up heaping helpings of pasta. (p303)

Thrasher's French Fries These thick fries are a boardwalk tradi-tion in Rehoboth, DE, and Ocean City, MD. (p300)

Jim's Drive-In A carhop takes your order at this hamburger-and-shake place on the outskirts of Lewisburg, WV. (p393)

Outdoor Activities

Appalachian Trail Walk all 2160 miles or experience the sublime scenery on a day hike. (p381)

New River Gorge National River Legendary white water rips through a West Virginian primeval forest gorge that's utterly Eden-like. (p389)

C&O Canal National Historic Park Follow 184.5 miles of cy-cling bliss on this 12ft-wide path tracking the Potomac across Maryland. (p334)

NROCKS Outdoor Adventure Not ready for rock climbing? Try the fixed-anchor *via ferrata* course in Circleville, WV. (p386)

Lake Placid Home to two Winter Olympic games, Lake Placid has some of the best skiing in the state. (p148)

Kayaking Explore the salt marshes of coastal Delaware and Maryland with outfitters such as Quest Fitness Kayak. (p298)

Batsto Village Get into the spirit of the Pines – or Pine Barrens – on a bike or on foot in New Jersey. (p165)

Cherry Springs State Park In Pennsylvania, head into the mountains for some of the best stargazing east of the Mississippi. (p228)

Top: Kayaking the Potomac River, Great Falls (p334), Maryland
Bottom: Historic re-enactment at Colonial Williamsburg (p361), Virginia

PLAN YOUR TRIP IF YOU LIKE...

History

The Mid-Atlantic is home to numerous Revolutionary War and Civll War hot spots.

Washington, DC See where Lincoln was assassinated and Martin Luther King Jr gave his most famous speech. (p245)

Williamsburg Step into the 1700s in this preserved Virginian town, the world's largest living history museum. (p361)

Gettysburg These gentle Pennsylvania hills conceal the legacy of the largest battle fought on American soil. (p226)

Harpers Ferry West Virginia's fascinating open-air museum of 19th-century village life is framed by mountains and rivers. (p380)

Historic Tredegar This Richmond, VA, museum examines the Civil War from the perspective of soldiers, slaves and citizens. (p351)

Historic St Mary's City Recreates a 17th-century port town in Southern Maryland. (p336)

Washington Crossing State Park In New Jersey, track the infantrymen who forded the icy river on Christmas 1776. (p163)

Offbeat America

Mystery Hole Gravity works wonders – or does it? – at this roadside attraction near Fayetteville, WV. (p390)

American Visionary Art Museum Peruse outsider art (including pieces created by the clinically insane) at this Baltimore, MD, gem. (p314)

Dinosaur Kingdom II Union soldiers ride dinosaurs in this zany attraction in the Shenandoah Valley, VA. (p372)

Ellwood Manor The final resting place for General Stonewall Jackson's amputated arm; in Fredericksburg, VA. (p349)

Month By Month

January

The New Year starts chilly, with occasional snowstorms sending folks to the grocery store in a panic for milk and bread. Ski resorts kick into high gear.

✨ Mummers Parade

Something like a mix of Mardi Gras with a marching band competition, the elaborate costumes, music and deep lore of the various mummer divisions and brigades make this Philadelphia parade a must-see. (p201)

☆ Dr Martin Luther King Jr's Birthday

On the third Monday in January and the weekend just prior, Washington, DC, celebrates MLK's legacy with concerts, films and the recitation of his famous 'I Have a Dream' speech on the Lincoln Memorial steps.

February

Despite indulging in wintertime mountain getaways, many Americans dread February for its long, dark nights and frozen days. For foreign visitors, this can be the cheapest time to travel, with ultra-discount flights and hotel rates.

☆ Groundhog Day

It's the holiday so famous that Bill Murray and Andie MacDowell made it the backdrop for one of the best romantic comedies of the '90s. Come to Punxsutawney, PA, and see if 'Phil' checks his shadow, presaging either more winter or an early spring (www.groundhog.org).

✨ Chinese New Year

Bringing fire to the cold winter, the Chinatown parade (www.dcparade.com) in Washington, DC, lights up with dancing dragons and firecrackers. It's scheduled around the lunar calendar, meaning it sometimes falls in late January. Festivities occur along H and I Sts between 6th and 8th Sts.

March

✨ St Patrick's Day

On the 17th, or the closest available Saturday or Sunday, the patron saint of Ireland is honored with brass bands and ever-flowing pints of Guinness. There are parades in Washington, DC, and Baltimore, MD.

✨ National Cherry Blossom Festival

The brilliant blooms of Japanese cherry blossoms around DC's Tidal Basin are celebrated with concerts, parades, *taiko* drumming, kite-flying and other events during the three-week festival (www.nationalcherryblossomfestival.org). More than 1.5 million people go annually, so book ahead.

April

The weather is warming up, but April can still be unpredictable, with chilly weather mixed with a few teasingly warm days.

🏃 White House Easter Egg Roll

More than 20,000 families from around the US descend on the South Lawn on Easter Monday for storytelling, games, music and dance. The big event is the massive egg hunt (www.whitehouse.gov/easteregg-roll), featuring thousands of wooden eggs. It's been a tradition since 1878.

☆ Tribeca Film Festival

A major star of the indie movie circuit in New York City, with loads of celebs walking the red carpet.

May

True spring is here, and May is one of the loveliest times to travel across the Mid-Atlantic, with blooming wildflowers and generally mild sunny weather. Summer crowds and high prices are yet to arrive.

🎆 Dominion Energy Riverrock Festival

Music and outdoor adventure converge on Brown's Island on Richmond, VA's James River for this three-day celebration, the largest sports and music festival (www.riverrockrva.com) in the US.

☆ Delfest

Bluegrass bands take the stage at this family-friendly music festival (www.delfest.com) – named for award-winning bluegrass musician and vocalist Del McCoury – in Cumberland, MD.

June

Hello summer! Americans spend more time at outdoor cafes and restaurants, and head to the shore or to national parks. School is out; vacationers fill the highways and resorts, bringing higher prices.

☆ SummerStage

In New York City, Central Park's SummerStage (June to August), features an incredible lineup of music and dance. Django Django, Femi Kuti, Shuggie Otis and the Martha Graham Dance Company are among recent standouts. Most events are free. There's also a SummerStage Kids program. (p85)

☆ Hudson Valley Shakespeare Festival

Summer theater company near Cold Spring, NY stages impressive outdoor productions of the Bard's classics at the magnificent Boscobel House & Gardens.

🍴 Richmond Greek Festival

From baklava to gyros to spanakopita, it all tastes good at this elbow-to-elbow food festival (www.greek-festival.com) in Richmond, VA, where the music and dancing – and the retsina – keep the vibe convivial.

🎆 HONfest

Revel in the friendliness of Baltimore's working women – they traditionally call folks 'hon' – with art, food and three stages of music and events in Hampden. (p316)

🎆 Capital Pride

Some 250,000 people attend DC's gay pride party (www.capitalpride.org) held in early to mid-June. The parade travels from Dupont Circle to Logan Circle, featuring wild floats and entertainment along the way. There's also a festival and concert with big-name headliners.

☆ Firefly Music Festival

Four days of music and camping in Dover, DE, with big-name favorites and on-the-rise newcomers spanning various genres. Past headliners include Eminem, The Weeknd, Chance the Rapper and Bob Dylan. (p306)

☆ Smithsonian Folklife Festival

For 10 days around Independence Day, this extravaganza celebrates international and US cultures on the Mall. It features folk music, dance, crafts, storytelling and ethnic fare, and highlights a diverse mix of countries. (p274)

July

With summer in full swing, Americans break out the backyard barbecues or head for the beach. The prices are high and the crowds can be fierce, but it's one of the liveliest times to visit.

🎆 Independence Day

On July 4, huge crowds gather on the Mall to watch marching bands parade and to hear the Declaration of Independence read from the steps of the National Archives. Later, the National Symphony Orchestra plays a concert on the Capitol's steps, followed by mega-fireworks.

☆ Battle of Gettysburg Reenactment

In early July, thousands of costumed 'soldiers' and spectators flock to Gettysburg National Military Park for one of the largest regular historical reenactments in the world (www.gettysburgreenactment.com). (p226)

☆ Artscape

Listen to the music, watch the films, admire the sculptures and appreciate the dancers. Yep, art in all its forms grabs the spotlight in Baltimore, MD, during America's largest free arts festival. (p316)

☆ Floydfest

Rain. Mud. Broiling sun. Terrible storms. Whatever the universe throws at the crowd, loyal patrons return year after year to camp, commune and dance in the dirt at this music festival held just off the Blue Ridge Parkway in Virginia (www.floydfest.com).

August

Expect blasting heat in August, with temperatures and humidity less bearable the further south you go. You'll find people-packed beaches, high prices and empty cities on weekends, when residents escape to the nearest waterfront.

☆ Old Fiddlers' Convention

The jamming starts in the parking lot at this annual mountain music competition in Galax, VA, that's been running for more than 80 years. You'll hear fiddles, banjos, mandolins and more, all played with heart and fire (www.oldfiddlersconvention.com).

September

As summer winds down, cooler days arrive, making for pleasant outings region-wide. The kids are back in school, and concert halls, gallery spaces and performing-arts venues kick off a new season.

✖ Asbury Park Oyster Festival

Three days of scrumptious bivalves, crab cakes and other sea-bred snacks alongside Asbury, New jersey's famous boardwalk.

✖ RoadKill Cook-off

Follow the mountain roads to Marlinton, WV, for this tongue-in-cheek food festival featuring exotic foods of the region – like squirrel (http://pccocwv.com).

October

Temperatures drop as fall brings fiery colors to northern climes. It's high season where the leaves are most brilliant; elsewhere expect lower prices and smaller crowds.

✺ Autumn Glory Festival

Admire the colorful leaves on the wooded slopes

around Deep Creek Lake in Western Maryland during this five-day celebration of fall. (p335)

✖ Apple Scrapple Festival

There's a scrapple chunkin' contest at this shindig (www.applescrapple.com) in Bridgeville that pays homage to Delaware's favorite pieces of pork – the offal! Try a scrapple sandwich. We're not sure where the apples come in.

☆ Bridge Day

Watch BASE jumpers leap from the New River Gorge Bridge in Fayetteville, WV, on the third Saturday of October. It's the only day the bridge is open for jumps. (p390)

🏃 Marine Corps Marathon

This popular road race (www.marinemarathon.com) is held on the last Sunday in October. The course winds along the Potomac and takes in Georgetown, the entire length of the Mall, the Tidal Basin and Arlington National Cemetery.

🏃 Halloween

It's not just for kids; adults celebrate Halloween at masquerade parties. In Manhattan, folks don wild costumes for the Village Halloween Parade.

November

This is generally low season across the region, with cold winds discouraging visitors. Prices are lower (although

airfares skyrocket around Thanksgiving). There's much happening culturally in the main cities.

Thanksgiving

On the fourth Thursday of November, Americans gather with family and friends over daylong feasts of roast turkey, sweet potatoes, cranberry sauce, wine, pumpkin pie and loads of other dishes. New York City hosts a huge parade, and there's pro football on TV.

December

Winter arrives, though skiing conditions in the mountains of the Mid-Atlantic usually aren't ideal until January. Christmas lights and holiday fairs make the region come alive during the festive season.

National Christmas Tree & Menorah Lighting

In early December, the president switches on the lights to the National Christmas Tree (www.thenationaltree.org). Then they, or a member of their administration, do the honors for the National Menorah. Live bands and choral groups play holiday music, which adds to the good cheer.

New Year's Eve

Americans are of two minds when it comes to ringing in the New Year. Some join festive crowds to celebrate; others plot a getaway to escape the mayhem. Whichever you choose, plan well in advance. Expect high prices.

Top: Independence Day parade (p274), Washington, DC

Bottom: Pumpkin pie cooked for Thanksgiving

Itineraries

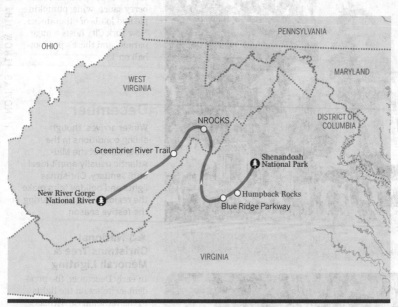

PENNSYLVANIA

OHIO

MARYLAND

WEST
VIRGINIA

DISTRICT OF
COLUMBIA

NROCKS

Greenbrier River Trail

Shenandoah
National Park

New River Gorge
National River

Humpback Rocks

Blue Ridge Parkway

VIRGINIA

Mountain Adventures

This trip is for those who like their nature ancient and wild: timbered mountains, raging rivers and towering rock formations.

In Virginia, kick off with a few days at **Shenandoah National Park**. This sliver of gorgeousness straddles the Blue Ridge Mountains, so named for their color when glimpsed in the hazy cerulean distance. Soak up the beauty driving the scenic Skyline Drive and pull over to hike a few miles, winding past spring wildflowers, summer waterfalls and fiery fall leaves. Drive south of the park to climb the iconic **Humpback Rocks** beside the **Blue Ridge Parkway**.

Cruise a few hours north to the sprawling Monongahela National Forest in wet and wild West Virginia, where you can rock climb Seneca Rocks, tackle a fixed-anchor *via ferrata* trail at **NROCKS** or pedal the **Greenbrier River Trail**. From here, drive over rugged mountains to **New River Gorge National River**. End this trip rafting the wild Gauley River or the scenic New River, which is really very old. Outfitters provide whitewater rafting gear for the Class V rapids.

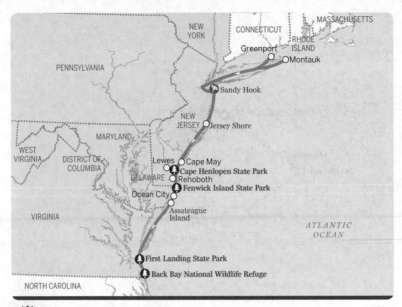

2 WEEKS

Exploring the Coast

This region isn't named the Mid-Atlantic for nothing. New York, New Jersey, Delaware, Maryland and Virginia all border the Atlantic Ocean. Their beaches and beach towns each have something unique to offer.

Escape the urban jungle of New York City with three days at the pretty beaches of **Greenport** and **Montauk** on Long Island. Next up is four days on the wild strands of the infamous **Jersey Shore**, which is dotted with resort towns stretching south from wide-beached **Sandy Hook** to **Cape May**, where bird-watching and whale-watching (May to December) are top-notch. Hop the **Cape May-Lewes Ferry** to continue south for three relaxing days in Delaware.

In **Lewes**, Delaware, explore the historic downtown then bike ride to The Point at **Cape Henlopen State Park**. The next day, drive to **Rehoboth** and take a stroll on the tourist-trappy boardwalk. Don't miss a beer sampling at famous Dogfish Head Brewings & Eats before a fine seafood dinner on Wilmington Ave. Just south, enjoy an ocean swim at **Fenwick Island State Park**. Continue south to spend two days in coastal Maryland. In **Ocean City** things get wild on another festive boardwalk. The scene is more serene on **Assateague Island**. Wild horses run free on the Maryland side of this barrier island, while the Virginia section is home to a wildlife refuge.

Drive south across the Chesapeake Bay Bridge Tunnel – hold tight! – to camp at **First Landing State Park** just steps from the sand. To conclude the trip, take your pick: a convivial boardwalk-and-beach day in Virginia Beach or a quiet hike in the remote **Back Bay National Wildlife Refuge**.

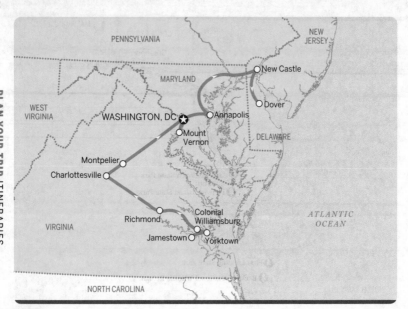

Colonial Days Tour

The roots of the USA's government took hold in riverside Colonial towns and valley villages where the Founding Fathers lived, learned and legislated. Begin with three days in the Tidewater region of Virginia, where you can brush up on Colonial-era history. Start in **Jamestown**, where Pocahontas helped the New World's first English settlement survive, then head to **Yorktown** to learn about the decisive battle that ended the Revolutionary War. From here it's a short drive to **Colonial Williamsburg** where you can wander through an 18th-century village come to life with costumed reenactors.

Your next four days will be spent exploring the low-lying Piedmont region of Virginia. Your first stop is **Richmond**, where Patrick Henry gave his impassioned 'Give Me Liberty, or Give Me Death' speech in St John's Episcopal Church in 1775. Then visit the Virginia State Capitol, designed by Thomas Jefferson. Drive west to **Charlottesville** to explore gorgeous Monticello, Jefferson's revered mountaintop home. Honor the wine-loving third president with a glass at a pretty winery. Spectacular **Montpelier**, home of James Madison, the architect of the Constitution, is also in the region.

Next up is the nation's capital, **Washington, DC**, where you'll spend four days learning about the US government from its earliest days. Don't miss the striking Jefferson Memorial before perusing Colonial artifacts at the National Museum of American History. Explore the first president's beloved home, **Mount Vernon** just outside Alexandria beside the Potomac River. Drive east to spend two days in charming **Annapolis**. Wander the first floor of the Maryland State House, where Washington famously resigned his military commission after the Revolutionary War, ensuring that the country would be led by a civilian, not a military leader, and that power would be shared with Congress. Exhibits at the US Naval Academy Museum trace the development of America's navy.

The final day of this tour is a short romp through Delaware, nicknamed the First State because it was the first of the thirteen original states to ratify the Constitution. Dine in an 18th-century tavern in historic **New Castle** then tour the John Dickinson Plantation – former home of the man nicknamed the 'Penman of the Revolution' – and the Old State House in **Dover**.

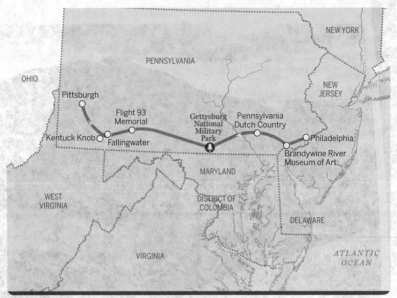

Packed in Pennsylvania

On this trip, we're taking in as much of the Keystone State as possible. By the end of this journey you'll have taken in some of America's most important history and gorgeous art, and been exposed to some iconic Mid-Atlantic architecture.

Start with a couple of days in **Philadelphia**. Explore Independence National Historic Park – make sure to go early to the Independence Visitor Center to secure a timed ticket to visit Independence Hall. Before or after, also drop into the Liberty Bell Center. On the next day, get in some more historical background at the excellent Museum of the American Revolution or learn all about Philly's favorite founding father Benjamin Franklin at Franklin Court. Clop down the cobbles of Elfreth's Alley and explore the boutiques and art galleries of the Old Town. Don't leave the city without browsing Cezannes, Renoirs and Picassos at the Barnes Foundation, and catching live music at live music at Johnny Brenda's or Union Transfer.

On the next day, drive west, making sure to stop in at the **Brandywine River Museum of Art**, situated in the dark-green Brandywine Valley. Continue west to **Pennsylvania Dutch Country**, and consider a tour of the Amish Farm & House. Have a big smorgasbord dinner, and the next day explore local folkways at the Landis Valley Museum.

After two days here, proceed further west and make a detour to **Gettysburg National Military Park**. Here you can easily spend a whole day walking the paths once laid down by the opposing armies of the Civil War. West of here is the elegiac **Flight 93 memorial**. You may want to bunk down in the Laurel Highlands to keep within close proximity to **Fallingwater** and **Kentuck Knob**, two of the most fascinating residences ever dreamed up by Frank Lloyd Wright. When you've finished getting your architectural fix on, proceed north to Pittsburgh.

In **Pittsburgh**, make sure to take a ride on the Duquesne Incline funicular and stop into the Mattress Factory and the Warhol Museum. Have a night out in the East Liberties before tackling the next day: exploring the Carnegie Museums, the Frick and Schenley Park. Have a night out in Pittsburgh's North Side or Polish Hill area, and as you sip that cold beer, be content that you've just taken in a ton of Pennsylvania.

Adirondack Mountains (p144), New York State

Plan Your Trip

Outdoor Activities

Smoky mountains, wave-bashed beaches, reedy marshes, river-cut gorges: New York and the Mid-Atlantic have no shortage of spectacular settings for adventure. No matter your passion – hiking, cycling, kayaking, rafting, surfing or diving – you'll find world-class places to commune with the great outdoors.

Best Outdoors

Best Hiking

Appalachian Trail, Shenandoah National Park (VA); Dolly Sods Wilderness (WV); Adirondack Wilderness (NY)

Best Cycling

C&O Canal National Historic Park (MD); Greenbrier Trail (WV); Great Allegheny Passage (PA & MD)

Best Paddling

New River Gorge National River (WV) for white-water rafting; Upper James River Water Trail (VA) for canoeing; Eastern Shore (VA and MD) for kayaking

Best Rock Climbing

Seneca Rocks (WV)

Best Wildlife-Watching

Shenandoah National Park (VA); Blackwater National Wildlife Refuge (MD)

Hiking & Trekking

Almost anywhere you go, great hiking and backpacking are within easy striking distance. Shenandoah National Park, the Blue Ridge Parkway and the Dolly Sods Wilderness are ideal for short and long hikes. Beyond them, you'll find troves of state-maintained footpaths. There's no limit to the terrain you can explore, from a coastal marsh trail at Assateague Island National Seashore in Maryland to the multistate North Country National Scenic Trail (www.nps.gov/noco) winding across rugged landscapes in New York and Pennsylvania.

Resources

Survive Outdoors (www.surviveoutdoors.com) Dispenses safety and first-aid tips, plus helpful photos of dangerous critters.

Wilderness Survival (Gregory Davenport; 2006) Easily the best book on surviving nearly every contingency.

American Hiking Society (www.americanhiking. org) Links to 'volunteer vacations' building trails.

Backpacker (www.backpacker.com) Premier national magazine for backpackers, from novices to experts.

National Park Service (www.nps.gov) The federal government agency responsible for the management and conservancy of all national park resources, including hiking trails and campsites.

Blue Ridge Outdoors (www.blueridgeoutdoors. com) Magazine and website covering hiking and outdoor activities in the Blue Ridge Mountains.

Cycling

Cycling's popularity increases by the day. New York is constantly adding more cycle lanes, and Washington, DC, rates as among the most bike- (and therefore, eco-) friendly cities in the eastern USA. A growing number greenways have started striping the east's picturesque countryside. The popular and scenic greenways (www. roanokeoutside.com/land/greenways) in Roanoke, VA, used by both commuters and the workout crowd, are an example of how to do it right.

Several abandoned rail lines across the region have been converted into cycling paths, offering gentle rides through quaint villages, over bridges and alongside verdant pastures.The C&O Canal National Historic Park (p334), which runs east–west across Maryland, is a popular one. In Virginia, the leafy Virginia Creeper Trail (p375) rolls into downtown Abingdon from the Blue Ridge Mountains. The Greenbrier River Trail (p392) in West Virginia tracks the pretty Greenbrier River.

Mountain bikers should steer for the forests and mountains flanking Harrisonburg, VA in the Shenandoah Valley.

In summer, rocket down the slopes at Snowshoe Mountain Resort (p387) in West Virginia.

Resources

Bicycling (www.bicycling.com) This magazine has information on city rides, off-road trails and much in between.

Rails-to-Trails Conservancy (www.railstotrails.org) Publishes free trail reviews at www.traillink.com.

Kayaking & Canoeing

Paddlers will find their bliss in the eastern USA. Rentals and instruction are yours for the asking.

Kayaking hot spots include the Eastern Shore, where you can explore tranquil barrier islands like Chincoteague, VA (p365) and Assateague, MD (p329). In Maryland, also consider exploring the marshy water trails along the Chesapeake Bay, particularly near Leonardtown (p337) in southern Maryland. In Delaware there is good paddling along the Atlantic Coast, particularly around Fenwick Island State Park (p301).

Kayakers and canoeists can also explore trails in the Blackwater National Wildlife Refuge (p327) on Maryland's Eastern Shore. For mountain views as you paddle, head to the Shenandoah Valley (p368) of Virginia for an excursion on the Upper James River Water Trail (p372) in the Blue Ridge Mountains.

Resources

American Canoe Association (www.american canoe.org) Has a water-trails database for canoeing and kayaking, as well as information on local

paddling clubs and courses (including stand-up paddleboarding).

White-water Rafting

West Virginia has an arsenal of famous white water. First, there's the New River Gorge National River (p389), which, despite its name, is one of the oldest rivers in the world. Slicing from North Carolina into West Virginia, it cuts a deep gorge, known as the Grand Canyon of the East, producing frothy rapids in its wake.

Then there's the Gauley (p389), arguably among the world's finest white water. Revered for its ultra-steep and turbulent chutes, the venerable Appalachian river is a watery roller coaster, dropping more than 668ft and churning up 100-plus rapids in a mere 28 miles. Six more rivers, all in the same neighborhood, offer training grounds for less-experienced river rats.

Resources

American Whitewater (www.americanwhite water.org) Works to preserve America's wild rivers; has links to local rafting clubs.

Rock Climbing

Scads of climbers head to Seneca Rocks (p386), a striking sliver of sandstone walls in the Monongahela National Forest in West Virginia. Just south. NROCKS Outdoor Adventure (p386) offers guided trips on a one-mile *via ferrata* course, which follows fixed anchors across a towering double-fin formation. You can also find great climbing in New York at the Shawangunk Ridge ('The Gunks') in New Paltz

---

THE APPALACHIAN TRAIL

Completed in 1937, the country's longest footpath is 2180 miles, crossing six national parks, traversing eight national forests and hitting 14 states from Georgia to Maine. Misty mountains, deep woods, flowery pastures and bear sightings are the rewards. Each year roughly 2500 hardy souls attempt to hike the entire trail – only one in four makes it all the way through. But don't let that discourage you. It's estimated that two to three million people trek a portion of the Appalachian Trail annually, thanks to easy-to-access day hikes up and down its length. See www.appalachian trail.org for more information.

New River (p389), West Virginia

(p138), a short drive from the west bank of the Hudson River.

Resources

Climbing (www.climbing.com) Cutting-edge rock climbing news and information since 1970.

SuperTopo (www.supertopo.com) One-stop shop for rock-climbing guidebooks, free topo maps and route descriptions.

Surfing

The Atlantic states harbor some terrific and unexpected surfing spots – especially if you're after more moderate swells. One great spot to hang 10 is Long Island, NY (p123). Here you'll find more than a dozen surfing areas dotting the area, from Montauk's oft-packed Ditch Plains to Nassau County's Long Beach, with its 3-mile stretch of curling waves. Beginners can test their skills on the inviting waves in Virginia Beach (p266).

Resources

Surfer (www.surfermag.com) Has travel reports covering the eastern seaboard and just about every break in the USA.

Surfing America (www.surfingamerica.org) The national governing body for the sport of surfing.

Skiing & Winter Sports

Ski season typically runs from mid-December though early April. In summer, many resorts are great for mountain biking and hiking, courtesy of ski lifts. Ski packages (including airfare, hotel and lift tickets) are easy to find through resorts, travel agencies and online travel booking sites, and can be good deals.

In Lake Placid, NY (p148), you can luge or bobsled at old Olympic facilities. At Snowshoe Mountain Resort, WV (p387) you'll find 59 trails across three ski areas. There are 15 miles of groomed cross-country skiing trails at White Grass (p386) in Canaan Valley, also in West Virginia.

Plan Your Trip

Eat & Drink Like a Local

The best seafood in the country is served on the Eastern Shore and in seafaring places such as Norfolk, VA, and Annapolis and Baltimore, MD. Oysters and crab cakes are a must. The farmlands of Virginia, Maryland, New York and Pennsylvania produce a range of vegetables that make their way to chefs' tables across the region. Ethnic cuisine shines in New York City, Washington, DC, and Northern Virginia, while regional specialties like pierogies in Pennsylvania and pepperoni rolls in West Virginia trace their origins to Europe.

The Year in Food

Food festivals make their annual appearance typically between April and September.

Spring (Mar–May)

One of the best times to hit local markets, with bounty from farm and field – ramps (wild onions), strawberries, rhubarb and spring lamb) – plus Easter treats arrive.

Summer (Jun–Aug)

A great time for seafood feasting by the shore, outdoor barbecues and country fairs. Don't miss fresh berries, peaches and corn on the cob. Food festival season is in full swing.

Fall (Sep–Nov)

Crisp days bring apple picking, pumpkin pies, harvest wine festivals and major food-focused events, including Thanksgiving.

Winter (Dec–Feb)

Hearty stews, roasted late-harvest vegetables, plus decadent holiday treats are the order of the day. Get toasty by the fire with a hot toddy.

Local Specialties

Delaware, Maryland and Virginia share a long coastline; all three are known for their fresh and delicious seafood. Berry farms and apple and pear orchards are found across the Mid-Atlantic.

NYC: Foodie Heaven

They say that you could eat at a different restaurant every night of your life in New York City and not exhaust the possibilities. Considering that there are more than 25,000 restaurants in the five boroughs, with scores of new ones opening each year, it's true. Owing to its huge immigrant population and an influx of more than 60 million tourists annually, New York captures the title of America's greatest restaurant city. Its diverse neighborhoods serve up authentic Italian food and thin-crust pizza, all manner of Asian food, French haute cuisine and classic Jewish deli food, from bagels to piled-high pastrami on rye. More exotic cuisines are found here as well, from Ethiopian to Scandinavian.

Don't let NYC's image as expensive get to you: you can eat well here without breaking the bank, especially if you limit your cocktail intake. There may be no such thing as a free lunch in New York, but compared to other world cities, eating here can be a bargain.

Maryland: Crab Cakes, Oysters & More

Bordering the Chesapeake Bay and the Atlantic, Maryland is famous across the country for its fresh seafood. Spicy steamed blue crabs are a specialty, and folks learn at a young age how to crack quickly through a bushel of 'em and pluck out the biggest chunks of tender meat. Order a bushel at one of the many waterside crab houses, and you'll soon find your picnic table covered with newspapers or cheap white paper to catch the drippings and mess. Chesapeake Bay crabs are harvested in warmer months, so summer is the best time to try them.

Chesapeake Bay oysters have been harvested for centuries and are still enthusiastically slurped down by hungry masses today. At a Maryland raw bar, sample a few from different regions – you will notice a difference in taste. For a roundup of seafood restaurants, check out the listings for Maryland's Crab & Oyster Trail (www.visitmaryland.org/article/maryland-crab-oyster-trail), broken down by region.

Other specialties include pit beef: lean-cut beef cooked over high heat then sliced thinly and piled onto a Kaiser roll; horseradish sauce is the condiment of choice. For dessert, the 12-layer Smith Island cake – a stack of thin yellow cakes and chocolate icing – is a sight to behold...and devour.

Virginia: Oysters, Ham, Peanuts & Produce

Seafood lovers should make their way to the Eastern Shore and Hampton Roads, where fresh oysters and crabs are harvested from the Chesapeake Bay and served up fresh at waterfront seafood restaurants.

Peanuts are a big crop for farms dotting the low-lying fields that stretch west from Hampton Roads. Cured meats are also a specialty, stemming from the days when local Native American tribes taught settlers how to preserve meat. The town of Smithfield is known globally for its namesake hams. These salty country favorites are often a highlight at holiday dinners across the state.

West of the Blue Ridge Mountains, the Shenandoah Valley is an apple-producing powerhouse. The terrain across the valley is also known for its unique microclimates, each conducive to the production of different types of fruit and produce. For this reason you'll find a wide array of vegetables and berries at local farmers markets. During the day, you might even see a local farmer strolling into one of the many farm-to-table restaurants with offerings fresh from the field.

West Virginia: Pepperoni Rolls, Pizza & Fluffy Biscuits

You'll find baskets of wrapped pepperoni rolls on the counters of convenience stores across the Mountain State. Soft rolls stuffed with cured pepperoni, these easy-to-eat snacks trace back to an Italian immigrant who came to West Virginia to work in the coal mines. He later opened a bakery in Fairmont; remembering his mining days, he created a snack that would be easy to eat with one hand. Though they're sold statewide, the many bakeries in Fairmont offer some of the best.

Italian immigrants are also the reason you'll see so many independently owned pasta and pizza joints across the state. Tasty Pies & Pints (p391) is an extraordinarily popular mini-chain offering craft beer and gourmet pizza; it got its start in Fayetteville and now has outposts across the state and region.

Biscuits and gravy is also a favorite dish throughout the state. The biscuits should be buttermilk and the gravy filled with sausage. You won't find anything more satisfying to eat after a night out. If you can't find a diner, swing by a Tudor's Biscuit World (www.tudorsbiscuitworld.com) – there's one in every in town that's worth a damn.

Because the state has so many farms, you'll find that mountain towns, some of them fairly remote, usually have one or two fantastic farm-to-table restaurants that spotlight regional and seasonal bounty.

Pennsylvania: Apple Butter to Shoo-fly Pie

Gastronomically speaking, Pennsylvania sits at the juncture of the North and the South, and draws on both deep rural-farm traditions and waves of immigrant influence. While Pennsylvania isn't particularly well known outside of the Mid-Atlantic for its unique foodstuffs, there are menu items here you'll be hard pressed to find elsewhere – or at least they won't be up to Keystone State snuff. These culinary treats include the following:

Apple Butter A delicious treat from Pennsylvania Dutch country, this is basically extremely concentrated apple sauce, with a dark-brown color and a deep, almost spicy flavor.

Cheesesteak The Philadelphia treat: chopped steak, onions, peppers and gooey melted cheese.

Lebanon bologna The Pennsylvania Dutch twist on this meat product is dried and smoked, giving it a look and flavor more reminiscent of salami.

Pierogies These filled dumplings from Eastern Europe are a staple of many menus in the western part of the state. The most common fillings in Pennsylvania are potatoes and cheese.

Pretzels Sure, you've probably got pretzels where you come from, but the Pennsylvania version – grounded in German and Swiss baking traditions – is big, soft, salty and delicious.

Primanti Brothers sandwich The 'Primanti Bros' sandwich is to Pittsburgh what the cheesesteak is to Philadelphia: a hybrid of meat and carbs that soaks up a late night of drinking like no other. The original sandwich layers meat, tomatoes, coleslaw and a handful of french fries.

Shoofly Pie Basically a molasses pie, often topped with brown sugar, Shoofly Pie is a staple of menus out in Pennsylvania Dutch country (but is found statewide).

Delaware: Scrapple Baby!

Oh Delaware, what's going on with you and scrapple? This, er, delicacy is basically pork fillings (snout, livers and hearts) combined with cornmeal and flour to form a loaf, which is sliced, fried and served at breakfast or between two slices of bread. You'll find a scrapple-flavored vodka – Off the Hoof – at the Painted Stave Distilling (p302) in Smyrna. Seafood is top-notch in the First State too.

Habits & Customs

For breakfast, Americans love their eggs and bacon, waffles, hash browns and big glasses of orange juice. Most of all, they love a steaming cup of coffee. After a midmorning snack break, the lunch hour of most American workers affords just enough time for a sandwich, quick burger or hearty salad. While you may (rarely) spot diners drinking a glass of wine or beer with their noontime meal, the days of the three-martini lunch are long gone.

Early in the evening, people settle in for a more substantial weeknight dinner, which, given the workload of so many two-career families, might be takeout or prepackaged dishes. Americans usually eat dinner between 6pm and 8pm; in smaller towns, it may be hard to find anywhere to eat after 8:30pm or so. Dinner parties usually begin around 6:30pm or 7pm, with cocktails followed by a meal. If invited to dinner, it's polite to be prompt – ideally, you should plan to arrive within 15 minutes of the designated time. Americans are notoriously informal in their dining manners, although they will usually wait until everyone is served before eating.

Food Experiences

Meals of a Lifetime

Woodberry Kitchen (p319) Within a former flour mill, this Baltimore, MD, hot spot embraces regional ingredients.

Henlopen City Oyster House (p300) The seafood dishes and service are standouts at this James Beard–nominated Rehoboth, DE, restaurant.

L'Opossum (p355) Fun with seafood, steaks and decor – check out those *David* statues! – in Richmond, VA.

Smorgasburg (p100) Eat your way into a stupor at this vast open-air NYC market.

Tail Up Goat (p283) Try the luscious lamb ribs and the homemade breads in Adams Morgan, DC.

Blacksmith Bar & Restaurant (p328) This cozy former blacksmith shop in Berlin, MD, offers gourmet comfort food and superb crab cakes.

Thyme Bistro (p389) Try the delicious salmon salad at this classic bistro in Weston, WV.

Plan Your Trip
Travel with Children

In New York and across the Mid-Atlantic, you'll find fun distractions for all ages: bucket-and-spade adventures at the beach, amusement parks, zoos, eye-popping aquariums and natural-history exhibits, hands-on science museums, camping adventures, battlefields, leisurely bike rides through the countryside and plenty of other activities likely to wow young ones.

New York & the Mid-Atlantic for Kids

Accommodations

Motels and hotels typically have rooms with two beds, which are ideal for families. Some also have roll-away beds or cribs that can be brought into the room for an extra charge – but keep in mind these are usually portable cribs, which not all children sleep well in. Some hotels offer 'kids stay free' programs for children up to 12 or sometimes 18 years old. Be wary of B&Bs, as many don't allow children; inquire before reserving.

Babysitting

Resort hotels may have on-call babysitting services; otherwise, ask the front-desk staff or concierge to help you make arrangements. Always ask if babysitters are licensed and insured, what they charge per hour per child, whether there's a minimum fee, and if they charge extra for transportation or meals. Most tourist bureaus list local resources for childcare and recreation facilities, medical services and so on.

Best Regions for Kids

New York, New Jersey & Pennsylvania

NYC offers adventures such as row-boating in Central Park and kid-friendly museums. Head to the Jersey Shore for Boardwalk fun and to Pennsylvania for Amish Country horse-and-buggy rides.

Washington, DC

Washington, DC, has unrivaled allure for families, with free museums, a panda-loving zoo and boundless green spaces.

Virginia

Visit the Historic Triangle for a history-themed trip then hit a regional amusement park. There's hiking and wildlife watching in Shenandoah National Park and along the Blue Ridge Parkway.

Dining

The local restaurant industry seems built on family-style service: children are not just accepted at most places, but are often encouraged by special children's menus with smaller portions and lower prices. In some restaurants children under a certain age even eat for free. Restaurants will usually provide high chairs and booster seats. Some restaurants may also offer children crayons and puzzles, and occasionally you'll see live performances by cartoon-like characters.

Restaurants without children's menus don't necessarily discourage kids, though higher-end restaurants might. Even at the nicer places, however, if you show up early enough (right at dinnertime opening hours, often 5pm or 6pm), you can usually eat without too much stress – and you'll likely be joined by other foodies with kids. You can ask if the kitchen will make a smaller order of a dish, or if they will split a normal-size main dish between two plates for the kids. Chinese, Mexican and Italian restaurants seem to be the best bet for finicky young eaters.

Farmers markets are growing in popularity in the region, and every sizable town has at least one a week. This is a good place to assemble a first-rate picnic, sample local specialties and support independent growers in the process. After getting your stash, head to the nearest park or waterfront.

Driving & Flying

Every car rental agency should be able to provide an appropriate child seat, since these are required in every state, but you need to request when booking and expect to pay around $14 more per day.

Domestic airlines don't charge for children under two years. Those two and up must have a seat and discounts are unlikely. Amtrak, America's national train service, offers free rides for children under two years of age and half-price fares on the lowest available adult fare for most trains for children aged two through 12 years, with an accompanying adult.

Children's Highlights

Outdoor Adventure

Shenandoah National Park, VA (p356) Hike and look for wildlife.

New River Gorge National River, WV (p389) Go white-water rafting.

Cape Henlopen State Park, DE (p297) Cycle trails near the coast.

Upper James River Water Trail, VA (p372) Hop in a tube and float in the shadows of mountains.

Deep Creek Lake, MD (p335) It's all about the water sports in this big mountain lake.

Central Park, NYC (p56) It's urban wilds at their best: 21 playgrounds, rowboats on the lake and 800 green acres.

Pondering the Past

Williamsburg, VA (p361) Don 18th-century garb and mingle with costumed interpreters in the history-rich triangle where America began.

Great Falls Tavern, MD (p334) Take a ride in an 18th-century **canal boat** (www.nps.gov/choh; 11710 MacArthur Blvd, Potomac; 🚹) on the Potomac River.

Harpers Ferry National Historic Park, WV (p380) Wander through the historic buildings to learn the town's role in John Brown's raid.

Mount Vernon, VA (p345) Tour the home of the America's first president and learn about his passions and accomplishments.

Museum of the American Revolution, PA (p188) Hands-on exhibits make for a compelling story about America's beginnings.

Historic St Mary's City, MD (p336) Costumed docents roam a living history museum recreating a 17th-century port community.

Zoos, Aquariums & Theme Parks

Bronx Zoo, NYV (p81) Hop the subway from Manhattan to one of the USA's biggest and best zoos.

National Zoo, DC (p271) Come see the giant pandas, the African lions and and the Asian elephants.

National Aquarium, MD (p310) Roam the seven stories to shudder at blacktip reef sharks and smile at the clownfish.

Virginia Aquarium & Marine Science Center, VA (p367) More than 300 species, from river otters to sand tiger sharks.

Six Flags, DC (www.sixflags.com/america) It's the Washington, DC, outpost of America's stalwart amusement park chain.

Rainy Day Activities

National Air and Space Museum, DC (p250) Inspire budding aviators with rockets, spacecraft, old-fashioned biplanes and ride simulators.

Newseum, DC (p264) Junior journalists report 'live from the White House' via the TV studio – and get the take-home video to prove it.

International Spy Museum, DC (p265) Kids get to become secret agents and identify disguises, find hidden cameras and go on GPS-driven scavenger hunts.

American Museum of Natural History, NYC (p72) Kids of all ages will enjoy a massive planetarium, immense dinosaur skeletons and 30 million other artifacts.

Beckley Exhibition Coal Mine, WV (p392) Take a ride 1500ft into a former coal mine and learn about mining life.

American Revolution Museum at Yorktown, VA (p364) The 4D Movie *The Siege* will jolt you to attention as you learn about the great battle ending the Revolutionary War.

Planning

To find family-oriented accommodations and restaurants among our reviews, just look for the child-friendly icon.

When to Go

➡ Peak travel season is June to August, when schools are out and the weather is warmest. Expect high prices and abundant crowds – meaning long lines at amusement and water parks, fully booked resorts and heavy traffic on the roads; book well in advance for popular destinations.

➡ High season for winter resorts (in Virginia and West Virginia) runs from late December through March.

Need to Know

➡ Many public toilets have a baby-changing table (sometimes in men's toilets, too), and gender-neutral 'family' facilities appear in airports.

➡ Medical services and facilities in America are of a high standard.

➡ Items such as baby food, formula and disposable diapers (nappies) are widely available – including organic options – in supermarkets across the country.

➡ Single parents or guardians traveling with anyone under 18 should carry proof of legal custody or a notarized letter from the non-accompanying parent(s) authorizing the trip. This isn't required, but it can help avoid potential problems entering the USA.

Helpful Resources

For all-round information and advice, check out Lonely Planet's *Travel with Children*. To get the kids excited, check out *Not for Parents: USA* (also by Lonely Planet), filled with cool stories about candy bars, astronauts, heroic animals and more.

Baby's Away (www.babysaway.com) Rents cribs, high chairs, car seats, strollers and even toys at locations across the country.

Family Travel Files (www.thefamilytravelfiles.com) Ready-made vacation ideas, destination profiles and travel tips.

Travel BaBees (www.travelbabees.com) Another reputable baby-gear rental outfit, with locations nationwide.

Regions at a Glance

New York City is the East's hub, a world center for fashion, food, arts and finance. In neighboring New Jersey and Pennsylvania, beaches, mountains and literal horse-and-buggy hamlets join the landscape.

The capital of the United States, Washington, DC, is a great big repository for the history and culture of the nation. It's also home to some of the finest museums and monuments in the world. And darn good restaurants too.

Neighbor Virginia boasts a diverse and beautiful landscape filled with Colonial-era and Civil War historic sites. Maryland is home to the best seafood in the country, harvested along the Eastern Shore, while Baltimore shines with museums. In Delaware, grand homes and gardens impress in Wilmington, while the beaches entertain DC weekenders. The rugged mountains of West Virginia are packed tight with outdoor adventures.

New York City

Arts
Food
Nightlife

Enrich Your Mind

Home to cultural powerhouses like Broadway and the Met, NYC also shines with small galleries and intimate theaters showcasing cutting-edge creativity.

Food Choices

In a single neighborhood you'll find gastropubs, sushi counters, tapas bars, French bistros, barbecue joints, pizza parlors, vegan cafes and good old-fashioned delis whipping up toasted bagels with lox and cream cheese.

Creatures of the Night

All-night lounges; taco shops that double as late-night cabarets; clubs that clang to the thump of DJ-ed beats; and after-after-parties on the roof as the sun rises – an alternate universe lurks between the cracks of everyday life.

p48

New York State

Arts
History
Outdoors

Culture Spot

Buffalo has its share of impressive museums and Beacon is home to world-renowned Dia:Beacon.

A Rich Past

Women's rights grab the spotlight in Seneca Falls, while the stories of Franklin and Eleanor Roosevelt enliven Hyde Park. For Revolutionary War history, head to Sleepy Hollow and Tarrytown.

Get Outside

The outdoors lurks just beyond the city's gaze, with hiking in the Adirondack wilderness and Catskill mountains. Enjoy ocean frolics in the Hamptons and Montauk. Rock climbing in the New Paltz and skiing at Lake Placid round out the fun.

p122

New Jersey

History
Food
Outdoors

Getting Revolutionary

Many sites cover key events in the Revolutionary War. You can also learn about the state's blue-collar dockside roots in Hoboken. For upper-crust distractions, tour Princeton, an Ivy League school dating from the mid-1700s.

Seafood Feast

Over 130 miles of shoreline means one thing: seafood! From chowder to oysters, mussels, scallops and octopus, you'll find it all here. In the summer you might have a wait – but hey, you're not at work!

Going Wild

Of course you're going to hike and bike the Pine Barrens, a swath of eerie cedar bogs that might be the home of the Jersey Devil. Scan for birds at the Cape May Observatory and in the Sandy Hook National Recreation Area.

p157

Philadelphia

History
Art
Food

Founding Fathers

Stand where the Declaration of Independence was signed then check out the Liberty Bell. The Museum of the American Revolution spotlights the country's early journey to unification.

Murals

Street art has been raised to a fine art with professionals collaborating on giant painting projects with at-risk youths, current and ex-prisoners, and others in the community. There are 3000-plus official murals – and countless unofficial ones.

Cheesesteak Central

Want to try the city's most famous sandwich? Take the taste test between the originator Pat's King of Steaks and the upstart Geno's Steaks, who square off across E Passyunk Ave.

p182

Pennsylvania

History
Culture
Food

Religion & Rebellion

Dig deeper into the state's long-running and very traditional religious orders in the Dutch Country. For Civil War history, travel to Gettysburg, the site of the largest battle fought on American soil.

Fine Art to Fallingwater

For fine art displays it's hard to go wrong in Pittsburgh, home to numerous world-class museums. Frank Lloyd Wright's famous house – Fallingwater – perches prettily in the western reaches of the state.

Homegrown to Haute

Savor regional specialties like apple butter and shoo-fly pie in the Dutch Country. Pittsburgh shares an enticing mix of buzz-worthy new restaurants as well as old faves.

p218

Washington, DC

Arts
History
Food

The Nation's Treasure Chest

The capital has a superb and diverse collection of museums and galleries. The grand monuments honoring leaders, veterans and world-changing events can be unexpectedly moving.

Times Past

Themed history museums tell the stories of Native Americans and African Americans. Others share an overview of US history and globally significant events such as the Holocaust. Mount Vernon provides insights into the life of former owner George Washington.

Culinary Delights

An array of international restaurants keeps the DC dining scene vibrant. Chef-driven neighborhood spots are leading the city's current dining boom.

p245

Delaware

History
Beaches
Microbreweries

Mansions & Museums

Mansions in the Brandywine Valley pay homage to great entrepreneurs, while museums in Wilmington and Dover delve deep into specialty topics such as furniture and Victrolas.

Coastal Variety

There's a golden strand for every mood and personality along the coast, where you can explore history, enjoy fine dining, party hard or simply sunbathe on the sand.

Hops & Hospitality

The First State may be small but the brewery scene is strong, led by nationally known Dogfish Head, famous for its uber-hoppy beers. At breweries from the cities to the coast, you can expect good food, welcoming and knowledgable service and interesting seasonal selections.

p295

Maryland

Seafood
Arts
Outdoors

Shore Eats

Blue crabs and oysters have been harvested from Chesapeake Bay for generations. Crab houses – the most scenic places to crack open the crustaceans – dot the numerous inlets. Oysters across the region are made for slurping.

Bohemian Baltimore

Baltimore shines with edgy collections, visionary art, quirky personal treasures and up-to-the-minute temporary shows. The new Sagamore Pendry hotel mixes it up with eye-catching artwork and design details that give a nod to Charm City.

Take it Easy

Outdoor fun is a breeze. Paddle salt marshes along the coast, pedal the level C&O Canal towpath or hike to waterfalls in the western mountains.

p307

Virginia

History
Outdoors
Music

Patriots & Rebels

Colonial sights abound in Hampton Roads. Many of the nation's Founding Fathers had homes in Virginia; most are open for tours. The Civil War was fought across the state; battlefields dot the landscape.

Beaches & Mountains

Beaches work for every mood, from contemplation on Assateague Island to partying at Virginia Beach. Trails in Shenandoah National Park and the Blue Ridge Parkway offer valley views, wooded trails and wildlife.

Mountain Music

The Crooked Road heritage trail twists through the mountains and hollers of southwest Virginia, passing live-music venues jumping with old-time jams and bluegrass shows. A handful of small museums share the history.

p339

West Virginia

Adventure
History
Food

Wild & Wonderful

White-water rafting in this mountainous state is a blast, but there are also calm sections for family fun and wildlife watching. Rock climbing, mountain biking and downhill skiing offer thrills.

Mining & Famous Feuds

Coal mining has been a key state industry for generations. Museums spotlight everything from daily life in mining towns to the famous conflicts between labor and bosses. Learn the story of the feuding Hatfields and McCoys in Tug Valley.

Culinary Fun

Farm-to-table fare is a fine-dining option across the state, but the ubiquitous pepperoni rolls and biscuit-and-gravy joints keep everybody happy. Gourmet pizzas from Pies & Pints are a statewide favorite.

p377

On the Road

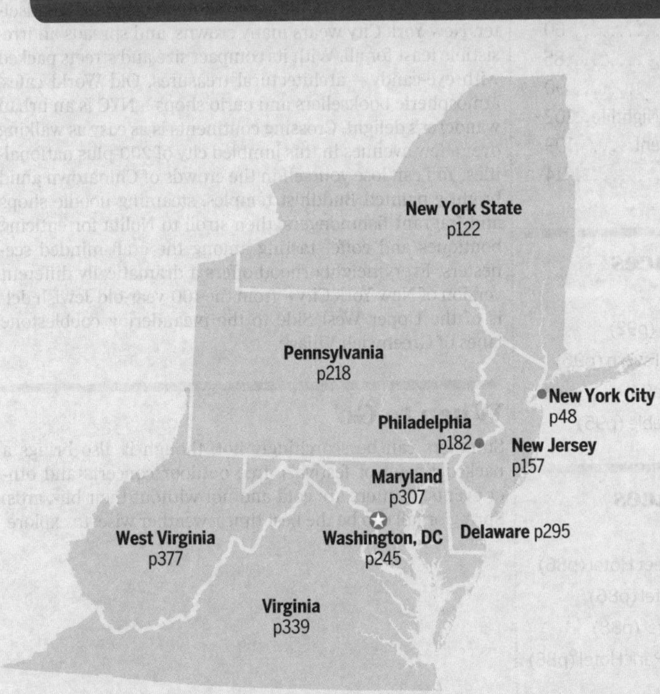

New York State
p122

Pennsylvania
p218

New York City
p48

Philadelphia
p182

New Jersey
p157

Maryland
p307

West Virginia
p377

Washington, DC
p245

Delaware p295

Virginia
p339

New York City

212, 718, 347, 646, 332 / POP 8.6 MILLION

Best Places to Eat

➜ Chefs Club (p92)

➜ Gramercy Tavern (p96)

➜ RedFarm (p94)

➜ Foragers Table (p95)

Best Places to Stay

➜ Crosby Street Hotel (p86)

➜ Bowery Hotel (p86)

➜ NoMad Hotel (p88)

➜ Gramercy Park Hotel (p88)

Why Go?

Epicenter of the arts. Dining and shopping capital. Trendsetter. New York City wears many crowns, and spreads an irresistible feast for all. With its compact size and streets packed with eye-candy – architectural treasures, Old World cafes, atmospheric booksellers and curio shops – NYC is an urban wanderer's delight. Crossing continents is as easy as walking over a few avenues in this jumbled city of 200-plus nationalities. You can lose yourself in the crowds of Chinatown amid brightly painted Buddhist temples, steaming noodle shops and fragrant fishmongers, then stroll to Nolita for enticing boutiques and coffee-tasting among the craft-minded scenesters. Every neighborhood offers a dramatically different version of New York City – from the 100-year-old Jewish delis of the Upper West Side to the meandering cobblestone lanes of Greenwich Village.

When to Go

Summers can be scorchingly hot, though it also brings a packed lineup of festivals, free outdoor concerts and other events. Winters are cold and not without their blizzards. Spring or fall can be the best times, weather wise, to explore.

New York City Highlights

1 **Statue of Liberty** (p52) Enjoying skyline views from the crown of Lady Liberty.

2 **Central Park** (p56) Exploring the park's natural and cultural treasures.

3 **Metropolitan Museum of Art** (p72) Communing with art fans in front of masterpieces.

4 **Markets** Visiting vendor-filled markets like Smorgasburg (p100).

5 **High Line** (p64) Joining the hustle and bustle on an elevated green space.

6 **Brooklyn Bridge** (p60) Soaking up sunset views.

7 **National September 11 Memorial & Museum** (p54)

Reflecting on the stories of the devastating 2001 attack.

8 **Broadway & Times Square** (p111) Watching a play then strutting under the bright lights of Times Square.

9 **Empire State Building** (p69) Starring in your own movie from the observation decks of this cinematic icon.

NEIGHBORHOODS AT A GLANCE

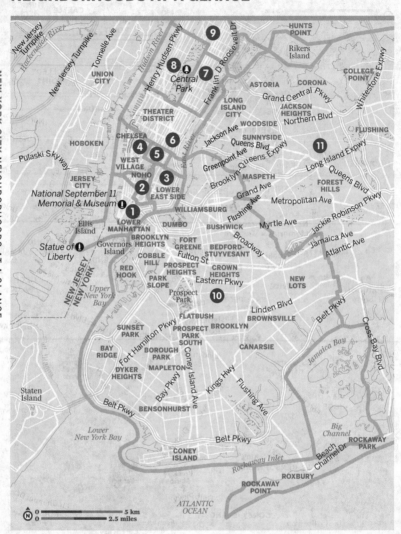

❶ Financial District & Lower Manhattan (p60)

Home to icons such as Wall St, the National September 11 Memorial and the Statue of Liberty, the southern end of Manhattan pulses with business-like energy during the day before settling into quiet nights. Tribeca, however, hums well after dark with its cache of restaurants and lounges.

❷ SoHo & Chinatown (p61)

Sacred temples, hawkers peddling bric-a-brac and steam-filled soup-dumpling parlors line the hurried streets of Chinatown. SoHo next door provides the counterpoint with streamlined thoroughfares and storefronts representing the biggest name brands in the world. Tucked in between is Little Italy (emphasis on the 'little').

❸ East Village & Lower East Side (p63)

Old meets new on every block of this downtown duo – two of the city's hottest 'hoods for nightlife and cheap eats that lure students, bankers and scruffier types alike.

❹ West Village, Chelsea & the Meatpacking District (p64)

Quaint, twisting streets and well-preserved town houses offer endless options for intimate dining and drinking in the West Village. The Meatpacking District next door has trendy nightlife options galore; further up is Chelsea, home to hundreds of art galleries and a vibrant gay scene.

❺ Union Square, Flatiron District & Gramercy (p65)

Though short on sights, there's lots happening on and around Union Square, which bustles with protesters, buskers and businessfolk. North of there is grassy Madison Square Park, an elegant oasis en route to Midtown. The peaceful streets around Gramercy are mostly residential, with a handful of high-end eating and drinking spots.

❻ Midtown (p65)

This is the home of the NYC found on postcards: Times Square, Empire State Building, Broadway theaters, canyons of skyscrapers, and bustling crowds. The Museum of Modern Art (MoMA), Bryant Park, the grand shops along Fifth Ave and the gay bars of Hell's Kitchen are also here.

❼ Upper West Side & Central Park (p70)

New York's antidote to the endless stretches of concrete, Central Park is a verdant escape from honking horns and sunless sidewalks. Lining the park with inspired residential towers, the Upper West Side is home to the Lincoln Center.

❽ Upper East Side (p72)

High-end boutiques line Madison Ave and mansions run parallel along Fifth Ave, which culminates in an architectural flourish called Museum Mile – one of the most cultured strips in the city, if not the world.

❾ Harlem & Upper Manhattan (p73)

Harlem and Hamilton Heights – a bastion of African American culture – offers global cuisine and a buzzing music scene. Head to Inwood for leafy park space, or try Morningside Heights to soak up student life

❿ Brooklyn (p77)

These days Brooklyn is shorthand for 'artsy cool,' but there's far more here than hipster stereotypes. This sprawling borough is home to historic and culturally diverse neighborhoods, with singularly fantastic dining, drinking, shopping and entertainment options – not to mention some of the best river views in the five boroughs.

⓫ Queens (p82)

A patchwork of communities, Queens is trailblazer territory for return visitors and locals alike. Gorge at the ethnic delis of Astoria, ogle contemporary art in Long Island City, devour steamed pork buns in Flushing, and ride the surf in Rockaway Beach.

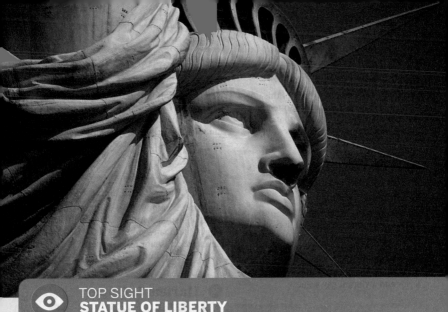

Image credit: FRANK SCHEFELBEIN/EYEEM/GETTY IMAGES ©

TOP SIGHT
STATUE OF LIBERTY

Lady Liberty has been gazing sternly toward 'unenlightened Europe' since 1886. Dubbed the 'Mother of Exiles,' the statue symbolically admonishes the rigid social structures of the old world. 'Give me your tired, your poor, your huddled masses yearning to breathe free, the wretched refuse of your teeming shore,' she declares in Emma Lazarus' famous 1883 poem 'The New Colossus.'

PRACTICALITIES

➡ Map p62

➡ ☎ 212-363-3200, tickets 877-523-9849

➡ www.nps.gov/stli

➡ Liberty Island

➡ adult/child incl Ellis Island $18.50/9, incl crown $21.50/12

➡ ⊙ 8:30am-5:30pm, hours vary by season

➡ 🚢 to Liberty Island, Ⓢ 1 to South Ferry or 4/5 to Bowling Green, then ferry

From the Suez to the City

To the surprise of many, France's jumbo-sized gift to America was not originally conceived with the US in mind. Indeed, when sculptor Frédéric-Auguste Bartholdi began planning the piece, his vision was for a colossal sculpture to guard the entrance to the Suez Canal in Egypt, one of France's greatest 19th-century engineering achievements. Bartholdi's ode to Gallic ingenuity would incorporate elements of two of the Seven Wonders of the Ancient World: the Colossus of Rhodes and the lighthouse of Alexandria. Despite its appeal to human vanity, the ambitious monument failed to attract serious funding from either France or Egypt, and Bartholdi's dream seemed destined for the scrap heap. Salvation would come from Bartholdi's friend, Édouard de Laboulaye. A French jurist, writer and antislavery activist, de Laboulaye proposed a gift to America as a symbol of the triumph of Republicanism and of the democratic values that underpinned both France and the US. Seeing an opportunity too good to miss, Bartholdi quickly set to work, tweaking his vision and turning his Suez flop into 'Liberty Enlightening the World' – an enviable gift to commemorate America's centennial of the Declaration of Independence.

Creating the Lady

The artist spent most of 20 years turning his dream – to create the hollow monument and mount it in the New York Harbor – into reality. Along the way it was hindered by serious financial problems, but was helped in part by the fund-raising efforts of newspaper publisher Joseph Pulitzer. Lending a further hand was poet Emma Lazarus, whose ode to Lady Liberty was part of a fund-raising campaign for the statue's pedestal, designed by American architect Richard Morris Hunt. Bartholdi's work on the statue was also delayed by structural challenges – a problem resolved by the metal framework mastery of railway engineer Gustave Eiffel (yes, of the famous tower). The work of art was finally completed in France in 1884 (a bit off schedule for the centennial). It was shipped to NYC as 350 pieces packed into 214 crates, reassembled over a span of four months and placed on the US-made granite pedestal. Its spectacular October 1886 dedication included New York's first ticker-tape parade and a flotilla of almost 300 vessels. Put under the administration of the National Park Service in 1933, a restoration of the Lady's oxidized copper began in 1984, the same year the monument made it onto the UN's list of World Heritage Sites.

Liberty Today

Folks who reserve their tickets in advance are able to climb the (steep) 393 steps to Lady Liberty's crown, from where the city and harbor views are breathtaking. That said, crown access is extremely limited, and the only way in is to reserve your spot in advance; the further in advance you can do it, the better (a six-month lead time is allowed). Each customer may only reserve a maximum of four crown tickets, and children must be at least 4ft tall to access the crown.

If you miss out on crown tickets, you may have better luck with tickets to the pedestal, which also offers commanding views. Like crown tickets, pedestal tickets are limited and should be reserved in advance, either online or by phone. Only crown and pedestal ticket holders have access to the Statue of Liberty museum in the pedestal.

If you don't have crown or pedestal tickets, don't fret. All ferry tickets to Liberty Island offer basic access to the grounds, including guided ranger tours or self-guided audio tours. The grounds also host a gift shop and cafeteria. (Tip: bring your own nibbles and enjoy them by the water with the Manhattan skyline stretched out before you.)

DID YOU KNOW?

The Statue of Liberty weighs 225 tons and stretches 305ft and 1in from ground to torch-tip.

The book of law in the statue's left hand is inscribed with July IV MDCCLXXVI (4 July 1776), the date of American independence. The rays on her crown represent the seven seas and continents; the 25 windows adorning it symbolize gemstones. At her feet, chains and a broken shackle indicate her status as free from oppression and servitude. The torch is a 1986 replacement of the original, which is now housed at the on-site museum.

TOP TIPS

➡ If you want to see both the Statue of Liberty and Ellis Island, you'll have to get a ferry before 2pm.

➡ Security screening at the ferry terminal is airport-style – leave the pocketknives at home – and can take up to 90 minutes in high season.

➡ Advance ticket purchase is strongly recommended: it guarantees you a specific time to visit, plus allows you to skip the insanely long queues of people who didn't plan ahead.

MATTHEW T CARROLL/GETTY IMAGES ©

TOP SIGHT
NATIONAL SEPTEMBER 11 MEMORIAL & MUSEUM

The National September 11 Memorial and Museum is a dignified tribute to the victims of the worst terrorist attack to occur on American soil. Titled *Reflecting Absence,* the memorial's two massive reflecting pools feature the names of the thousands who lost their lives. Beside them stands the Memorial Museum, a striking, solemn space documenting that fateful fall day in 2001.

Reflecting Pools

Surrounded by a plaza planted with more than 400 swamp white oak trees, the 9/11 Memorial's reflecting pools occupy the original footprints of the ill-fated Twin Towers. From their rim, a steady cascade of water pours 30ft down toward a central void. The flow of the water is richly symbolic, beginning as thousands of smaller streams, merging into a massive torrent of collective confusion, and ending with a slow journey toward an abyss. Bronze panels frame the pools, inscribed with the names of those who died in the terrorist attacks of September 11, 2001, and in the World Trade Center car bombing on February 26, 1993. Designed by Michael Arad and Peter Walker, the pools are both striking and deeply poignant.

Memorial Museum

The contemplative energy of the monument is further enhanced by the National September 11 Memorial Museum (p174). Standing between the reflective pools, the museum's glass entrance pavilion eerily evokes a toppled tower. Inside the entrance, an escalator leads down to the museum's sub-

DON'T MISS

- Reflecting Pools
- Memorial Museum
- Santiago Calatrava's Oculus

PRACTICALITIES

- Map p66
- www.911memorial.org/museum
- 180 Greenwich St
- memorial free, museum adult/child $24/15, 5-8pm Tue free
- 🕘 9am-8pm Sun-Thu, to 9pm Fri & Sat, last entry 2hr before close
- [S] E to World Trade Center; R/W to Cortlandt St; 2/3 to Park Pl

terranean main lobby. On the descent, visitors stand in the shadow of two steel tridents, originally embedded in the bedrock at the base of the North Tower. Each over 80ft tall and 50 tons in weight, they once provided the structural support that allowed the towers to soar over 1360ft into the sky. They remained standing in the subsequent sea of rubble, becoming immediate symbols of resilience.

The tridents are two of over 10,300 objects in the museum's collection. Among these are the Vesey Street Stairs. Dubbed the 'Survivors Stairs,' they allowed hundreds of workers to flee the WTC site on the morning of 9/11. At the bottom of these stairs is the moving In Memoriam gallery, its walls lined with the photographs and names of those who perished. Interactive touch screens and a central reflection room shed light on the victims' lives. Their humanity is further fleshed out by the numerous personal effects on display. Among these is a dust-covered wallet belonging to Robert Joseph Gschaar, an insurance underwriter working on level 92 of the South Tower. The wallet's contents include a photograph of Gschaar's wife, Myrta, and a $2 bill, given to Myrta by Gschaar as a symbol of their second chance at happiness.

Around the corner from the In Memoriam gallery is the New York City Fire Department's Engine Company 21. One of the largest artifacts on display, its burnt-out cab is testament to the inferno faced by those at the scene. The fire engine stands at the entrance to the museum's main Historical Exhibition. Divided into three sections – *Events of the Day, Before 9/11* and *After 9/11* – its collection of videos, real-time audio recordings, images, objects and testimonies provide a rich, meditative exploration of the tragedy, the events that preceded it (including the WTC bombing of 1993), and the stories of grief, resilience and hope that followed.

The *Historical Exhibition* spills into the monumental Foundation Hall, flanked by a massive section of the original slurry wall, built to hold back the waters of the Hudson River during the towers' construction. It's also home to the last steel column removed during the clean-up, adorned with the messages and mementos of recovery workers, first-responders and loved ones of the victims.

TOP TIPS

➡ In the museum, look for the so-called 'Angel of 9/11,' the eerie outline of a woman's face on a twisted girder.

➡ Outside, take a moment to appreciate Santiago Calatrava's huge white Oculus, inspired by a dove's wings.

➡ Last entry is two hours before closing time.

➡ Entry is free from 5pm to 8pm on Tuesdays.

TAKE A BREAK

Escape the swarm of restaurants serving the lunching Wall St crowd and head to Tribeca for a variety of in-demand eateries, such as Locanda Verde (p91). A good alternative for less expensive dining is **Two Hands** (Map p66; www.twohandsnyc.com; 251 Church St, btwn Franklin & Leonard Sts; lunch & brunch mains $14-19; 🕗8am-5pm; 📶; [S]1 to Franklin St; N/Q/R/W, 6 to Canal St).

RABBIT75_IST/GETTY IMAGES ©

TOP SIGHT
CENTRAL PARK

Birth of a Park

In the 1850s, this area of Manhattan was occupied by pig farms, a garbage dump, a bone-boiling operation and an African American village. It took 20,000 laborers two decades to transform this terrain into a park. Today, Central Park has more than 24,000 trees, 136 acres of woodland, 21 playgrounds and seven bodies of water – and more than 38 million visitors a year.

Strawberry Fields

This tear-shaped **garden** (72nd St on the west side) serves as a memorial to former Beatle John Lennon, who lived directly across the street in the **Dakota apartment building** (1 W 72nd St, at Central Park West). The garden, which was underwritten by his widow Yoko Ono, is composed of a grove of stately elms and a tiled mosaic that reads, simply, 'Imagine.'

Bethesda Terrace & the Mall

The arched walkways of **Bethesda Terrace**, crowned by the magnificent **Bethesda Fountain** (at 72nd St), have long been a gathering area for New Yorkers. To the south is the Mall (featured in countless movies), a promenade shrouded in mature North American elms. The southern stretch, known as **Literary Walk**, is flanked by statues of famous authors.

Central Park Zoo

Officially known as Central Park Wildlife Center (but no one calls it that), this small **zoo** (☎ 212-439-6500; www.centralparkzoo.com; 64th St, at Fifth Ave; adult/child $20/15; ⊙ 10am-5pm Mon-Fri, to 5:30 Sat & Sun Apr-Oct, 10am-4:30pm Nov-Mar; 👶; Ⓢ N/Q/R to 5th Ave-59th St) is home to penguins, snow leopards, poison dart frogs and red pandas. Feeding times in the sea-lion and penguin tanks make for a rowdy spectacle. The attached **Tisch Children's Zoo**, a petting

DON'T MISS

➡ The Mall
➡ The Reservoir
➡ Bethesda Fountain
➡ Conservatory Garden

PRACTICALITIES

➡ Map p78
➡ www.centralparknyc. org
➡ 59th to 110th Sts, btwn Central Park West & Fifth Ave
➡ ⊙ 6am-1am

zoo, has alpacas and mini-Nubian goats and is perfect for small children.

Conservatory & Alice in Wonderland

North of the zoo (at 74th St) is Conservatory Water, where model sailboats drift lazily and kids scramble about on a toadstool-studded statue of Alice in Wonderland. There are Saturday story hours (www.hcastorycenter.org) at 11am from June to September at the Hans Christian Andersen statue, to the west of the water.

Great Lawn & the Ramble

The **Great Lawn** (btwn 79th & 86th Sts; ⏲mid-Apr–mid-Nov) is a massive emerald carpet at the center of the park, surrounded by ball fields and London plane trees. (It's where Simon & Garfunkel played their famous 1981 concert.) Immediately to the southeast is Delacorte Theater (p113), home to an annual Shakespeare in the Park festival, as well as **Belvedere Castle** (☎212-772-0288; W 79th St; ⏲10am-4pm; 👪) [FREE], a bird-watching lookout. Further south is the leafy **Ramble** (midpark from 73rd to 79th Sts), a popular birding destination. On the southeastern end is the **Loeb Boathouse** (☎212-517-2233; www.thecentralparkboathouse.com; btwn 74th & 75th Sts; boating per hr $15; ⏲10am-6:45pm Mar or Apr–mid-Nov; 👪), home to a waterside restaurant that offers rowboat rentals and gondola rides.

Jaqueline Kennedy Onassis Resevoir

The reservoir (at 90th St) takes up almost the entire width of the park and serves as a gorgeous reflecting pool for the city skyline. It is surrounded by a 1.58-mile track that draws legions of joggers in the warmer months. Nearby, at Fifth Ave and 90th St, is a statue of New York City Marathon founder Fred Lebow, peering at his watch.

Summer Happenings in Central Park

During the warm months, Central Park is home to countless cultural events, many of which are free. The two most popular are Shakespeare in the Park (p85), which is managed by the Public Theater, and SummerStage (p85), a series of free concerts.

Tickets for Shakespeare in the Park are given out at 1pm on the day of the performance, but if you want to be sure of getting a seat, line up by 8am and make sure you have something to sit on, and your entire group with you. Tickets are free and there's only one per person; no latecomers are allowed in line.

SummerStage concert venues are generally opened to the public 1½ hours prior to the start of the show. But if it's a popular act, start queuing up early or you won't get in.

TOP TIPS

➡ Hit up Bike & Roll (p83), just one block west of the park, for bike rentals and guided tours.

➡ Avoid the carriage rides. They're a rip-off and the horses lead miserable lives.

➡ Lost in the park? Look for the numbers embossed or painted on one of the lampposts – the first two numbers are the street you're nearest to. If the second number is odd, you're on the west side of the park; if it's even, you're on the east side. (Mnemonic: even means east.)

TAKE A BREAK

Pack a picnic from the assortment of gourmet goodies at Zabar's (p96) or **Whole Foods** (Map p78; ☎212-823-9600; Time Warner Center, 10 Columbus Circle; ⏲7am-11pm; [S] A/C, B/D, 1 to 59th St-Columbus Circle), both a short hop away. Inside the park you can dine alfresco at casual **Le Pain Quotidien** (☎646-233-3768; www.lepainquotidien.com; Mineral Springs Pavilion, off West Dr; mains $12-17.50, pastries $4-7; ⏲7am-8pm; 📶 🌱 👪), or class things up at the elegant **Loeb Boathouse** (mains lunch $26-38, dinner $27-45; ⏲noon-3:30pm Mon-Fri, from 9:30am Sat & Sun year-round, 5:30-9:30pm Mon-Fri, from 6pm Sat & Sun Apr-Nov).

Central Park

THE LUNGS OF NEW YORK

The rectangular patch of green that occupies Manhattan's heart began life in the mid-19th century as a swampy piece of land that was carefully bulldozed into the idyllic nature-scape you see today. Since officially becoming Central Park, it has brought New Yorkers of all stripes together in interesting and unexpected ways. The park has served as a place for the rich to show off their fancy carriages (1860s), for the poor to enjoy free Sunday concerts (1880s) and for activists to hold be-ins against the Vietnam War (1960s).

Since then, legions of locals – not to mention travelers from all kinds of faraway places – have poured in to stroll, picnic, sunbathe, play ball and catch free concerts and performances of works by Shakespeare.

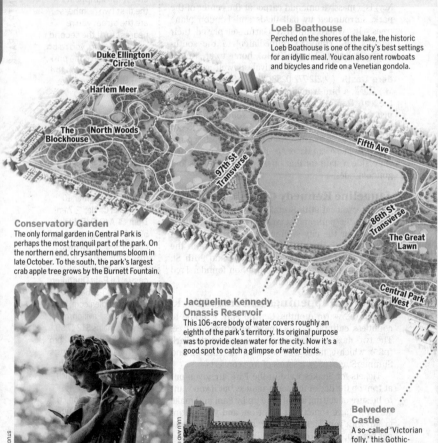

Loeb Boathouse
Perched on the shores of the lake, the historic Loeb Boathouse is one of the city's best settings for an idyllic meal. You can also rent rowboats and bicycles and ride on a Venetian gondola.

Duke Ellington Circle

Harlem Meer

The Blockhouse

North Woods

Fifth Ave

97th St Transverse

86th St Transverse

The Great Lawn

Central Park West

Conservatory Garden
The only formal garden in Central Park is perhaps the most tranquil part of the park. On the northern end, chrysanthemums bloom in late October. To the south, the park's largest crab apple tree grows by the Burnett Fountain.

Jacqueline Kennedy Onassis Reservoir
This 106-acre body of water covers roughly an eighth of the park's territory. Its original purpose was to provide clean water for the city. Now it's a good spot to catch a glimpse of water birds.

Belvedere Castle
A so-called 'Victorian folly,' this Gothic-Romanesque castle serves no other purpose than to be a very dramatic lookout point. It was built by Central Park co-designer Calvert Vaux in 1869.

The park's varied terrain offers a wonderland of experiences. There are quiet, woodsy knolls in the north. To the south is the reservoir, crowded with joggers. There are European gardens, a zoo and various bodies of water. For maximum flamboyance, hit the Sheep Meadow on a sunny day, when all of New York shows up to lounge.

Central Park is more than just a green space. It is New York City's backyard.

Conservatory Water

This pond is popular in the warmer months, when children sail their model boats across its surface. Conservatory Water was inspired by 19th-century Parisian model-boat ponds and figured prominently in EB White's classic book, *Stuart Little*.

CHRISTOPHER PENLER/SHUTTERSTOCK ©

KRIDSADA KAMSOMBAT/SHUTTERSTOCK ©

Bethesda Fountain

This neoclassical fountain is one of New York's largest. It's capped by the *Angel of the Waters*, which is supported by four cherubim. The fountain was created by bohemian-feminist sculptor Emma Stebbins in 1868.

Metropolitan Museum of Art

Alice in Wonderland Statue

79th St Transverse

The Ramble

Fifth Ave

Delacorte Theater

The Lake

Central Park Zoo

65th St Transverse

Sheep Meadow

Strawberry Fields

A simple mosaic memorial pays tribute to musician John Lennon, who was killed across the street outside the Dakota Building. Funded by Yoko Ono, its name is inspired by the Beatles song 'Strawberry Fields Forever.'

The Mall/ Literary Walk

A Parisian-style promenade – the only straight line in the park – is flanked by statues of literati on the southern end, including Robert Burns and Shakespeare. It is lined with rare North American elms.

Columbus Circle

◉ Sights

◉ Financial District & Lower Manhattan

Gleaming with bold, architectural icons, eateries and a booming residential population, Manhattan's southern tip is no longer strictly business. It's in the Financial District that you'll find the National September 11 Memorial and Museum, One World Observatory and Wall Street; historic sites like Fraunces Tavern Museum and Federal Hall; and, just offshore, Ellis Island and Lady Liberty herself. City Hall (and its lovely park) is a central landmark. North of 'FiDi' are the warehouse conversions of Tribeca, a prosperous area with vibrant restaurants and bars, high-end galleries and idiosyncratic retail.

★**Brooklyn Bridge** BRIDGE
(Map p66; ⓢ 4/5/6 to Brooklyn Bridge-City Hall; J/Z to Chambers St; R/W to City Hall) A New York icon, the Brooklyn Bridge, which connects Brooklyn and Manhattan, was the world's first steel suspension bridge. Indeed, when it opened in 1883, the 1596ft span between its two support towers was the longest in history. Although its construction was fraught with disaster, the bridge became a magnificent example of urban design, inspiring poets, writers and painters. Its pedestrian walkway delivers soul-stirring views of lower Manhattan, the East River and the rapidly developing Brooklyn waterfront.

★**One World Observatory** VIEWPOINT
(Map p66; ☑844-696-1776; www.oneworldobservatory.com; cnr West & Vesey Sts; adult/child $34/28; ⊙8am-10pm, last ticket sold at 8:45pm, hours vary by season; ⓢE to World Trade Center; 2/3 to Park Pl; A/C, J/Z, 4/5 to Fulton St; R/W to Cortlandt St) Spanning levels 100 to 102 of the tallest building in the Western Hemisphere, One World Observatory offers dazzling panoramic views from its sky-high perch. On a clear day you'll be able to see all five boroughs and some surrounding states. Not surprisingly, it's a hugely popular attraction. Purchase tickets online in advance; you'll need to choose the date and time of your visit.

★**Ellis Island** LANDMARK
(Map p62; ☑212-363-3200, tickets 877-523-9849; www.nps.gov/elis; ferry incl Statue of Liberty adult/child $18.50/9; ⊙8:30am-6pm, hours vary by season; ⓢ1 to South Ferry or 4/5 to Bowling Green, then ⊕to Ellis Island) Ellis Island is America's most famous and historically important gate-

way. Between 1892 and 1924, over 12 million immigrants passed through this processing station, dreams in tow. Today, its **Immigration Museum** delivers a poignant tribute to the immigrant experience: with narratives from historians, the immigrants themselves and other sources, it brings to life a hefty collection of personal objects, official documents, photographs and film footage. Always purchase your tickets online in advance (at www.statuecruises.com) to avoid soul-crushingly long queues.

★**Museum of Jewish Heritage** MUSEUM
(Map p66; ☑646-437-4202; www.mjhnyc.org; 36 Battery Pl; adult/child $12/free, 4-8pm Wed free; ⊙10am-6pm Sun-Tue, to 8pm Wed & Thu, to 5pm Fri mid-Mar–mid-Nov, to 3pm Fri rest of year, closed Sat; ⊞; ⓢ4/5 to Bowling Green; R/W to Whitehall St) An evocative waterfront museum exploring all aspects of modern Jewish identity and culture, from religious traditions to artistic accomplishments. The museum's core exhibition includes a detailed exploration of the Holocaust, with personal artifacts, photographs and documentary films providing a moving experience. Outdoors is the **Garden of Stones** installation. Created by artist Andy Goldsworthy and dedicated to those who lost loved ones in the Holocaust, its 18 boulders form a narrow pathway for contemplating the fragility of life.

National Museum of the American Indian MUSEUM
(Map p66; ☑212-514-3700; www.nmai.si.edu; 1 Bowling Green; ⊙10am-5pm Fri-Wed, to 8pm Thu; ⓢ4/5 to Bowling Green; R/W to Whitehall St) **FREE** An affiliate of the Smithsonian Institution, this elegant tribute to Native American culture is set in Cass Gilbert's spectacular 1907 **Custom House**, one of NYC's finest beaux-arts buildings. Beyond a vast elliptical rotunda, sleek galleries play host to changing exhibitions documenting Native American art, culture, life and beliefs. The museum's permanent collection includes stunning decorative arts, textiles and ceremonial objects that document the diverse native cultures across the Americas.

Skyscraper Museum MUSEUM
(Map p66; ☑212-968-1961; www.skyscraper.org; 39 Battery Pl; adult/child $5/2.50; ⊙noon-6pm Wed-Sun; ⓢ4/5 to Bowling Green; R/W to Whitehall) Fans of phallic architecture will appreciate this compact, high-gloss gallery, examining skyscrapers as objects of design, engineering and urban renewal. Temporary exhibitions dominate the space, with past exhibitions

exploring everything from New York's new generation of super-slim residential towers to the world's new breed of supertalls. Permanent fixtures include information on the design and construction of the Empire State Building and World Trade Center.

Battery Park PARK
(Map p66; www.nycgovparks.org; Broadway, at Battery Pl; ⊙6am-1am; ⑤4/5 to Bowling Green; R/W to Whitehall St; 1 to South Ferry) Skirting the southern edge of Manhattan, this 12-acre oasis lures with public artworks, meandering walkways and perennial gardens. Its memorials include a Holocaust Memorial and the Irish Hunger Memorial. It was on this very part of the island that the Dutch settled in 1623. And it was right here that the first 'battery' of cannons was erected to defend the fledgling settlement of New Amsterdam. You'll also find historic **Castle Clinton** (🖉212-344-7220; www.nps.gov/cacl; ⊙7:45am-5pm) FREE and the ferry service to Ellis Island and the Statue of Liberty.

Trinity Church CHURCH
(Map p66; 🖉212-602-0800; www.trinitywallstreet.org; 75 Broadway, at Wall St; ⊙7am-6pm, churchyard closes dusk; ⑤1, R/W to Rector St; 2/3, 4/5 to Wall St) New York City's tallest building upon completion in 1846, Trinity Church features a 280ft-high bell tower and a richly colored stained-glass window over the altar. Famous residents of its serene cemetery include Founding Father and first Secretary of the Treasury (and now Broadway superstar) Alexander Hamilton, while its excellent music series includes Concerts at One (1pm Thursdays) and magnificent choir concerts, including an annual December rendition of Handel's *Messiah*.

◉ SoHo & Chinatown

SoHo (South of Houston), NoHo (North of Houston) and Nolita (North of Little Italy) represent three of Manhattan's trendiest neighborhoods, known for boutiques, bars and eateries. To the south, expanding and bustling Chinatown and a nostalgic sliver of Little Italy lure with idiosyncratic street life. Canal St, running from the Manhattan Bridge to the West Side Hwy, and one of the most traffic-clogged arteries in the city, is a world in itself. Taken together, these neighborhoods offer a delicious, contradictory jumble of cast-iron architecture, strutting fashionistas, sacred temples and hook-hung salami.

★**Chinatown** AREA
(Map p66; www.explorechinatown.com; south of Broome St & east of Broadway; ⑤N/Q/R/W, J/Z, 6 to Canal St; B/D to Grand St; F to East Broadway) A walk through Manhattan's most colorful, cramped neighborhood is never the same, no matter how many times you hit the pavement. Peek inside temples and strange storefronts. Catch the whiff of ripe persimmons, hear the clacking of mah-jongg tiles on makeshift tables, eye dangling duck roasts swinging in store windows and shop for anything from rice-paper lanterns and 'faux-lex' watches to tire irons and a pound of pressed nutmeg. America's largest congregation of Chinese immigrants is your oyster.

★**Little Italy** AREA
(Map p66; ⑤N/Q/R/W, J/Z, 6 to Canal St; B/D to Grand St) This once-strong Italian neighborhood (film director Martin Scorsese grew up on Elizabeth St) saw an exodus in the mid-20th century when many of its residents

NEW YORK CITY SIGHTS

---

❶ TOP TIPS FOR EXPLORING THE CITY

➡ MetroCards are valid on subways, buses and the tramway to Roosevelt Island. If staying awhile, buy a 7-Day Unlimited Pass.

➡ If the number on a taxi's top light is lit, it's available. Note that green Boro taxis can't make pick-ups in Manhattan south of W 110th St and E 96th St.

➡ When giving an address, always include the nearest cross street/s (eg 700 Sixth Ave at 22nd St).

➡ The TKTS Booth in **Times Square** (www.tdf.org/tkts; Broadway, at W 47th St; ⊙3-8pm Mon & Fri, 2-8pm Tue, 10am-2pm & 3-8pm Wed & Sat, 10am-2pm Thu, 11am-7pm Sun; ⑤N/Q/R/W, S, 1/2/3, 7 to Times Sq-42nd St) sells half-price, same-day tickets to selected shows and musicals. The **South Street Seaport** (www.tdf.org; cnr Front & John Sts; ⊙11am-6pm Mon-Sat, to 4pm Sun; ⑤A/C, 2/3, 4/5, J/Z to Fulton St; R/W to Cortlandt St) and **Downtown Brooklyn** (www.tdf.org; 1 Metrotech Center, cnr Jay St & Myrtle Ave, Promenade; ⊙11am-6pm Tue-Sat, often closed 3-3:30pm; ⑤A/C, F, R to Jay St-Metrotech) branches also sell next-day matinee tickets.

New York City

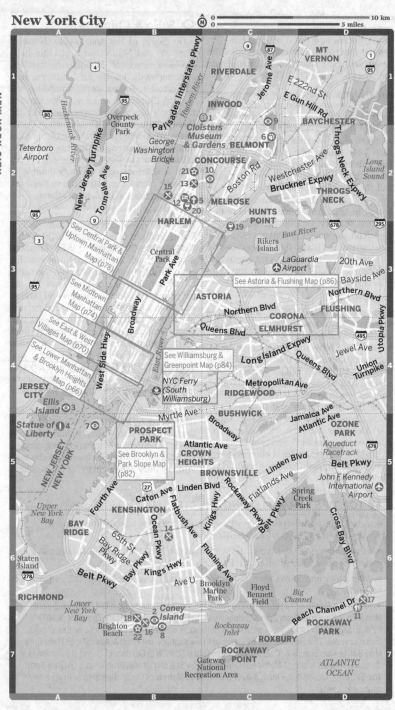

moved to more suburban neighborhoods in Brooklyn and beyond. Today, it's mostly concentrated on Mulberry St between Broome and Canal Sts, a stretch packed with checkerboard tablecloths and (mainly mediocre) Italian fare. If you're visiting in late September, be sure to check out the raucous San Gennaro Festival (www.sangennaro.nyc), which honors the patron saint of Naples.

East Village & Lower East Side

If you need a concise description of this neighborhood duo's ethos, consider its two largest institutions, the New Museum and the Tenement Museum: both continually evolving and simultaneously marked by waves of immigrants. The East Village and the Lower East Side are two of the city's hottest 'hoods for cramming into low-lit lounges; clubs for live music and cheap eats luring students, bankers and scruffier types alike. Luxury high-rise condominiums and hip boutique hotels coexist within blocks of tenement-style buildings. They're inspiring, lively and the perfect place to feel young.

★ Lower East Side Tenement Museum MUSEUM
(Map p70; ☎877-975-3786; www.tenement.org; 103 Orchard St, btwn Broome & Delancey Sts, Lower East Side; tours adult/student & senior $25/20; 🕒visitor center 10am-6:30pm Fri-Wed, to 8:30pm Thu; [S]B/D to Grand St; J/M/Z to Essex St; F to Delancey St) This museum puts the neighborhood's heartbreaking but inspiring heritage on full display in three re-created turn-of-the-20th-century tenement apartments, including the late-19th-century home and garment shop of the Levine family from Poland, and two immigrant dwellings from the Great Depressions of 1873 and 1929. Visits to the tenement building are available only as part of scheduled guided tours, with many departures each day.

★ Merchant's House Museum MUSEUM
(Map p70; ☎212-777-1089; www.merchantshouse.org; 29 E 4th St, btwn Lafayette St & Bowery, NoHo; adult/child $15/free; 🕒noon-5pm Fri-Mon, to 8pm Thu, guided tours 2pm Thu-Mon & 6:30pm Thu; [S]6 to Bleecker St; B/D/F/M to Broadway-Lafayette St) Built in 1832 and purchased by merchant Seabury Tredwell three years later, this red-brick mansion remains the most authentic Federal house in town. It's as much about the city's mercantile past as it is a showcase of 19th-century high-end domestic furnishings. Everything in the house is a testament to what money could buy, from the bronze gasoliers and marble mantelpieces to the elegant parlor chairs, attributed to noted furniture designer Duncan Phyfe. Even the multilevel call bells for the servants work to this day.

★ New Museum of Contemporary Art MUSEUM
(Map p70; ☎212-219-1222; www.newmuseum.org; 235 Bowery, btwn Stanton & Rivington Sts, Lower East Side; adult/child $18/free, 7-9pm Thu by donation; 🕒11am-6pm Tue, Wed & Fri-Sun, to 9pm Thu; [S]R/W to Prince St; F to 2nd Ave; J/Z to Bowery; 6 to Spring St) Rising above the neighborhood, the New Museum of Contemporary Art is a sight to behold: a seven-story stack of off-kilter, white, ethereal boxes designed by Tokyo-based architects Kazuyo Sejima and Ryue Nishizawa

New York City

Top Sights
1 Cloisters Museum & Gardens C1
2 Coney Island B7
3 Ellis Island A4
4 Statue of Liberty A5

Sights
5 Abyssinian Baptist Church B2
6 Bronx Zoo C2
7 Governors Island A5
8 New York Aquarium B7
9 New York Botanical Garden C1
10 Yankee Stadium C2

Activities, Courses & Tours
11 Rockaway Beach D7

Sleeping
12 Easy Living Harlem B2

Eating
13 Charles' Pan-Fried Chicken B2
14 Di Fara Pizza B6
15 Dinosaur Bar-B-Que B2
16 Nathan's Famous B7
17 Rockaway Surf Club D6
18 Totonno's B7

Drinking & Nightlife
19 Bronx Brewery C3
20 Shrine B2

Entertainment
21 Marjorie Eliot's Parlor Jazz B2
22 MCU Park B7

of SANAA and the New York–based firm Gensler. A breath of fresh air along what was a gritty Bowery strip when it arrived back in 2007, it has since been joined by many glossy new constructions.

⊙ West Village, Chelsea & Meatpacking District

Mellow and raucous, quaint and sleekly contemporary, these downtown neighborhoods embody contradictory vibes. The West Village's twisting streets and well-preserved townhouses offer intimate spaces for dining, drinking and being a flaneur. The Meatpacking District has evolved into a modern kind of meat market, with trendy bars and clubs where Manhattan's young professionals go to see and be seen. To the north is Chelsea, home to art galleries and a vibrant gay scene. Tying these neighborhoods together is the High Line, a massive, snake-like park that stretches above them all.

★ High Line   PARK
(Map p70; ✆212-500-6035; www.thehighline.org; Gansevoort St, Meatpacking District; ⊙7am-11pm Jun-Sep, reduced hours Oct-May; 🚇M11 to Washington St; M11, M14 to 9th Ave; M23, M34 to 10th Ave, 🚇A/C/E, L to 8th Ave-14th St; 1, C/E to 23rd St) The High Line, a shining example of brilliant urban renewal, was once a dingy rail line that anchored a district of slaughterhouses. Today, this eye-catching attraction is one of New York's best-loved green spaces, drawing visitors who come to stroll, sit and picnic 30ft above the city – while enjoying fabulous views of Manhattan's ever-changing urban landscape. Its final extension, which loops around the massive construction project at Hudson Yards, ends at 34th St. Perks include stunning vistas of the Hudson River, public art installations, lounge chairs for soaking up some sun, willowy stretches of native-inspired landscaping, food and drink vendors, and a thoroughly unique perspective on the neighborhood streets below.

★ Whitney Museum of
American Art   MUSEUM
(Map p70; ✆212-570-3600; www.whitney.org; 99 Gansevoort St, at Washington St, West Village; adult/child $25/free, pay-what-you-wish 7-10pm Fri; ⊙10:30am-6pm Mon, Wed, Thu & Sun, to 10pm Fri & Sat; 🚇A/C/E, L to 8th Ave-14th St) The Whitney's downtown location opened to much fanfare in 2015. Perched near the foot of the High Line, this architecturally stunning building – designed by Renzo Piano – makes a suitable introduction to the museum's superb collec-

tion. Inside the spacious, light-filled galleries, you'll find works by all the great American artists, including Edward Hopper, Jasper Johns, Georgia O'Keeffe and Mark Rothko.

★ Chelsea Market   MARKET
(Map p70; ✆212-652-2110; www.chelseamarket.com; 75 Ninth Ave, at W 15th St, Chelsea; ⊙7am-2am Mon-Sat, 8am-10pm Sun; 🚇A/C/E, L to 8th Ave-14th St) The Chelsea Market has transformed a former factory into a shopping concourse that caters to foodies. More than two dozen food vendors ply their temptations, including **Mokbar** (ramen with Korean accents), **Takumi Taco** (mixing Japanese and Mexican ingredients), **Tuck Shop** (Aussie-style savory pies), **Bar Suzette** (crepes), **Num Pang** (Cambodian sandwiches), **Ninth St Espresso** (perfect lattes), **Doughnuttery** (piping hot mini-doughnuts) and **L'Arte de Gelato** (rich ice cream).

★ Hudson River Park   PARK
(Map p70; www.hudsonriverpark.org; West Village; ⊙6am-1am; 🚼; 🚇M11 to Washington St; M11, M14 to 9th Ave; M23, M34 to 10th Ave, 🚇1 to Hudson Ave; A/C/E, L to 8th Ave-14th St; 1, C/E to 23rd St) The High Line may be all the rage these days, but one block away from that elevated green space stretches a 5-mile-long ribbon of green that has dramatically transformed the city over the past decade. Covering 550 acres and running from Battery Park at Manhattan's southern tip to 59th St in Midtown, the Hudson River Park is Manhattan's wondrous backyard. The long riverside path is a great spot for cycling, running and strolling.

★ Rubin Museum of Art   GALLERY
(Map p70; ✆212-620-5000; www.rmanyc.org; 150 W 17th St, btwn Sixth & Seventh Aves, Chelsea; adult/child $19/free, 6-10pm Fri free; ⊙11am-5pm Mon & Thu, to 9pm Wed, to 10pm Fri, to 6pm Sat & Sun; 🚇1 to 18th St) The Rubin is the first museum in the Western world to dedicate itself to the art of the Himalayas and surrounding regions. Its collections include textiles from China, metal sculptures from Tibet, Pakistani stone sculptures and intricate Bhutanese paintings, as well as ritual objects and dance masks from various Tibetan regions, spanning from the 2nd to the 19th centuries.

★ Washington Square Park   PARK
(Map p70; Fifth Ave at Washington Sq N, West Village; 🚼; 🚇A/C/E, B/D/F/M to W 4th St-Washington Sq; R/W to 8th St-NYU) What was once a potter's field and a square for public executions is now the unofficial town square of Greenwich Village, and plays host to lounging NYU students, tuba-playing street performers, curi-

ous canines and their owners, speed-chess pros and bare-footed children who splash about in the fountain on warm days.

◉ Union Square, Flatiron District & Gramercy

The bustling, throbbing, frenzied heart of this trio of neighborhoods is Union Square. The triangular Flatiron Building and the verdant respite of Madison Square Park mark the boundary with Midtown's canyons just to the north. **Gramercy Park**, a romantic private oasis, offers a more subdued, stately residential area to roam.

★ Union Square   SQUARE

(Map p70; www.unionsquarenyc.org; 17th St, btwn Broadway & Park Ave S, Union Square; Ⓢ4/5/6, N/Q/R, L to 14th St-Union Sq) Union Square is like the Noah's Ark of New York, rescuing at least two of every kind from the curling seas of concrete. In fact, one would be hard pressed to find a more eclectic cross-section of locals gathered in one public place: suited businessfolk gulping fresh air during their lunch breaks, dreadlocked loiterers tapping beats on their tabla, skateboarders flipping tricks on the southeastern stairs, rowdy college kids guzzling student-priced eats, and throngs of protesting masses chanting fervently for various causes.

★ Flatiron Building   HISTORIC BUILDING

(Map p74; Broadway, cnr Fifth Ave & 23rd St, Flatiron District; Ⓢ N/R, F/M, 6 to 23rd St) Designed by Daniel Burnham and built in 1920, the 20-story Flatiron Building has a narrow triangular footprint that resembles the prow of a massive ship. It also features a traditional beaux-arts limestone and terra-cotta facade, built over a steel frame, that gets more complex and beautiful the longer you stare at it. Best viewed from the traffic island north of 23rd St between Broadway and Fifth Ave, this distinctive structure dominated the plaza back in the dawning skyscraper era of the early 1900s.

Union Square Greenmarket   MARKET

(Map p70; ☎212-788-7476; www.grownyc.org; E 17th St, btwn Broadway & Park Ave S, Union Square; ☺8am-6pm Mon, Wed, Fri & Sat; Ⓢ4/5/6, N/Q/R/W, L to 14th St-Union Sq) 🍴 On most days, Union Square's northern end hosts the most popular of the 53 greenmarkets throughout the five boroughs. Indeed, even celebrity chefs head here for just-picked rarities, including fiddlehead ferns, heirloom tomatoes and fresh curry leaves.

◉ Midtown

The hub of the city, and according to boosters, the crossroads of the world, Midtown *is* the NYC of postcards. More than 300,000 people a day jostle their way through its streets. It's home to icons including Times Square, Broadway theaters, Grand Central Terminal, the Empire State Building and Tiffany & Co Fifth Ave. Cultural knockouts include MoMA, the New York Public Library and the Morgan Library & Museum, with the food-packed streets of Hell's Kitchen nearby.

★ Museum of Modern Art   MUSEUM

(MoMA; Map p74; ☎212-708-9400; www.moma.org; 11 W 53rd St, btwn Fifth & Sixth Aves; adult/child 16yr & under $25/free, 4-8pm Fri free; ☺10:30am-5:30pm Sat-Thu, to 8pm Fri year-round, to 8pm Thu Jul & Aug; ♿; Ⓢ E/M to 5th Ave-53rd St; F to 57th St; E/B/D to 7th Ave-57th St) MoMA's galleries scintillate with heavyweights: Van Gogh, Matisse, Picasso, Warhol, Lichtenstein, Rothko, Pollock and Bourgeois. Since its founding in 1929, the museum has amassed almost 200,000 artworks, documenting the emerging creative ideas and movements of the late 19th century through to those that dominate today. For art buffs, it's Valhalla. For the uninitiated, it's a thrilling crash course in all that is beautiful and addictive about art.

★ Times Square   AREA

(Map p74; www.timessquarenyc.org; Broadway, at Seventh Ave; Ⓢ N/Q/R/W, S, 1/2/3, 7 to Times Sq-42nd St) The intersection of Broadway and Seventh Ave pumps out the NYC of the global imagination – yellow cabs, golden arches, soaring skyscrapers and razzle-dazzle Broadway marquees. It's right here that Al Jolson 'made it' in the 1927 film *The Jazz Singer*, that photojournalist Alfred Eisenstaedt captured a lip-locked sailor and nurse on V-J Day in 1945, and that Alicia Keys and Jay-Z waxed lyrically about the concrete jungle.

Fifth Avenue   AREA

(Map p74; btwn 42nd & 59th Sts; Ⓢ E, M to 5th Ave-53rd St; N/R/W to 5th Ave-59th St) Immortalized in film and song, Fifth Ave first developed its high-class reputation in the early 20th century. The series of mansions called **Millionaire's Row** extended right up to 130th St, though most of those above 59th St faced subsequent demolition or conversion to the cultural institutions now constituting Museum Mile. Despite a proliferation of ubiquitous chains, the avenue's Midtown stretch still glitters with upmarket establishments.

Lower Manhattan & Brooklyn Heights

A map of Lower Manhattan & Brooklyn Heights with the following labeled locations and streets:

SOHO
CHINATOWN
TRIBECA
LOWER MANHATTAN
BATTERY PARK CITY
FINANCIAL DISTRICT

Streets and landmarks:
Desbrosses St, Vestry St, Laight St, Hubert St, Beach St, N Moore St, Franklin St, Hudson St, Varick St, Sixth Ave (Avenue of the Americas), Canal St, Church St, Walker St, White St, Howard St, Baxter St, Little Italy, Cortlandt Al, Lafayette St, Centre St, Mulberry St, Bayard St, Leonard St, Worth St, Thomas St, Duane St, Broadway, Federal Plaza, Thomas Paine Park, Pearl St, Reade St, Chambers St, City Hall, City Hall Park, Elk St, Centre St, Chambers St/Brooklyn Bridge City Hall, Warren St, Murray St, W Broadway, Park Pl, Park Place, NYC Information Center, Police Plaza, Park Row, Spruce St, Beekman St, Gold St, Barclay St, Vesey St, One World Observatory, World Financial Center, World Trade Center, Memorial Plaza, Fulton St, Ann St, John St, Cliff St, Cortlandt St, Liberty St, William St, Maiden La, National September 11 Memorial, National September 11 Memorial Museum, North Cove, Albany St, Carlisle St, Pine St, Broad St, Wall St, Trinity Pl, Rector St, Greenwich St, Washington St, South End Ave, West Side Hwy, Battery Pl, W Thames St, New St, Beaver St, Old Slip, Water St, Front St, Battery Park City Esplanade, Bowling Green, Whitehall St, Vietnam Veterans Plaza, Museum of Jewish Heritage, Robert F Wagner Jr Park, Battery Park, Pier A, Peter Minuit Plaza, South Ferry, Ferry to Governors Island, Ferry to Staten Island, Hudson River, Nelson A Rockefeller Park, River Terr, North End Ave, Hudson River Park, Washington Market Community Park, Ferry to Ellis Island, Ferry to Statue of Liberty, Upper New York Bay, Hugh L Carey Tunnel

Numbered markers: 4, 38, 44, 40, 20, 22, 32, 26, 29, 23, 19, 28, 37, 45, 43, 35, 8, 21, 6, 42, 17, 14, 31, 18, 34, 5, 13, 12, 36, 10, 9, 16

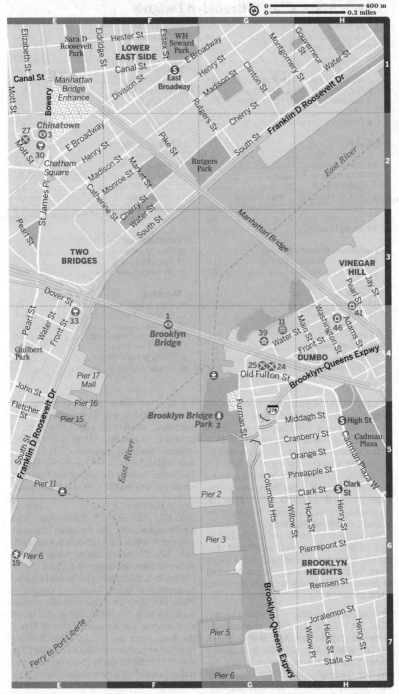

0   400 m
0   0.2 miles

Elizabeth St
Sara D Roosevelt Park
Hester St
Essex St
WH Seward Park
E Broadway

LOWER EAST SIDE

Canal St
Eldridge St
Canal St
Henry St
Madison St
Clinton St
Montgomery St
Gouverneur St
Water St

Canal St
Mott St
Bowery
Manhattan Bridge Entrance
Division St
East Broadway
Rutgers St
Cherry St
South St
Franklin D Roosevelt Dr

Chinatown
27
3
E Broadway
Henry St
Pike St
Rutgers Park

East River

30
Mott St
Chatham Square
Madison St
Market St
Catherine St
Monroe St
Cherry St
Water St
South St

St James Pl
Manhattan Bridge

Pearl St

TWO BRIDGES

VINEGAR HILL
Pearl St
Jay St
41

Dover St
Pearl St
Water St
Front St
33

39
11
Water St
Main St
Washington St
Front St
46
Adams St

Guilbert Park

1
Brooklyn Bridge

DUMBO

John St
Fletcher St
Pier 17 Mall
Pier 16
Pier 15

Brooklyn-Queens Expwy

25 24
Old Fulton St

South St
Franklin D Roosevelt Dr

East River

278

Brooklyn Bridge Park 2
Furman St
Middagh St
High St
Cranberry St
Cadman Plaza
Orange St
Pineapple St
Cadman Plaza W
Clark St
Clark St

Pier 11

Pier 2
Columbia Hts
Willow St
Hicks St
Henry St

Pier 3
Pierrepont St

Pier 6
15

BROOKLYN HEIGHTS
Remsen St

Pier 5
Joralemon St
Hicks St
Henry St
Willow Pl
State St

Ferry to Port Liberte
Pier 6
Brooklyn-Queens Expwy

Lower Manhattan & Brooklyn Heights

Top Sights
1 Brooklyn Bridge F4
2 Brooklyn Bridge Park G5
3 Chinatown E2
4 Little Italy D1
5 Museum of Jewish Heritage B6
6 National September 11 Memorial B4
7 National September 11 Memorial Museum C4
8 One World Observatory B4

Sights
9 Battery Park C6
10 Castle Clinton C6
11 Empire Stores & Tobacco Warehouse G4
12 National Museum of the American Indian C6
13 Skyscraper Museum B6
14 Trinity Church C5

Activities, Courses & Tours
15 Liberty Helicopter Tours E6
16 Staten Island Ferry D7

Sleeping
17 Gild Hall D4
18 Wall Street Inn D5

Eating
19 Arcade Bakery C2
20 Bâtard C1
21 Brookfield Place B4
22 Da Mikele C1
23 Gourmet Garage C2
24 Grimaldi's G4
Hudson Eats .... (see 21)
25 Juliana's G4
Le District .... (see 21)
26 Locanda Verde B2
27 Peking Duck House E2
28 Tiny's & the Bar Upstairs C2
29 Two Hands C2

Drinking & Nightlife
30 Apothéke E2
31 Bluestone Lane C5
32 Brandy Library B1
33 Cowgirl SeaHorse E4
34 Dead Rabbit D6
35 Kaffe 1668 South B3
36 Pier A Harbor House C6

Entertainment
37 Flea Theater C2
38 Soho Rep C1
39 St Ann's Warehouse G4

Shopping
40 Best Made Company C1
41 Brooklyn Flea H4
42 Century 21 .... C4
43 Mysterious Bookshop C3
44 Pearl River Mart C1
45 Philip Williams Posters C3
46 Powerhouse @ the Archway H4

★**Grand Central Terminal** HISTORIC BUILDING
(Map p74; www.grandcentralterminal.com; 89 E 42nd St, at Park Ave; ⌚5:30am-2am; [S]S, 4/5/6, 7 to Grand Central-42nd St) Completed in 1913, Grand Central Terminal – more commonly, if technically incorrectly, called Grand Central Station – is one of New York's beaux-arts beauties. Adorned with Tennessee-marble floors and Italian-marble ticket counters, its glorious main concourse is capped by a **vaulted ceiling** depicting the constellations, designed by French painter Paul César Helleu. When commuters complained that the sky is backwards – painted as if looking down from above, not up – it was asserted as intentional (possibly to avoid having to admit an error).

★**Rockefeller Center** HISTORIC BUILDING
(Map p74; ☎212-332-6868; www.rockefellercenter.com; Fifth to Sixth Aves, btwn W 48th & 51st Sts; [S]B/D/F/M to 47th-50th Sts-Rockefeller Center) This 22-acre 'city within a city' debuted at the height of the Great Depression, with developer John D Rockefeller Jr footing the $100 million price tag. Taking nine years to build, it was America's first multi-use retail, entertainment and office space – a sprawl of 19 buildings (14 of which are the original Moderne structures). The center was declared a National Landmark in 1987. Highlights include the Top of the Rock observation deck and NBC Studio Tours (p84).

Top of the Rock VIEWPOINT
(Map p74; ☎877-692-7625, 212-698-2000; www.topoftherocknyc.com; 30 Rockefeller Plaza, entrance on W 50th St, btwn Fifth & Sixth Aves; adult/child $36/30, sunrise/sunset combo $54/43; ⌚8am-12:30am, last elevator at 11:55pm; [S]B/D/F/M to 47th-50th Sts-Rockefeller Center) Designed in homage to ocean liners and opened in 1933, this 70th-floor open-air observation deck sits atop the **GE Building**, the tallest skyscraper at the Rockefeller Center. Top of the Rock beats the Empire State Building (p69) on several levels: it's less crowded, has wider observation decks (both outdoor and indoor) and offers a view of the Empire State Building itself.

Chrysler Building HISTORIC BUILDING
(Map p74; 405 Lexington Ave, at E 42nd St; ⏲lobby 7am-7pm Mon-Fri; [S]S, 4/5/6, 7 to Grand Central-42nd St) Designed by William Van Alen in 1930, the 77-floor Chrysler Building is primetime architecture: a fusion of Moderne and Gothic aesthetics, adorned with steel eagles and topped by a spire that screams *Bride of Frankenstein*. The building was constructed as the headquarters for Walter P Chrysler and his automobile empire; unable to compete on the production line with bigger rivals Ford and General Motors, Chrysler trumped them on the skyline, and with one of Gotham's most beautiful lobbies.

★**Empire State Building** HISTORIC BUILDING
(Map p74; www.esbnyc.com; 350 Fifth Ave, at W 34th St; 86th-fl observation deck adult/child $37/31, incl 102nd-fl observation deck $57/51; ⏲8am-2am, last elevators up 1:15am; [S]4, 6 to 33rd; Blue and Orange PATH to 33rd St; B/D/F/M, N/Q/R/W to 34th St-Herald Sq) This limestone classic was built in just 410 days – using seven million hours of labor during the Great Depression – and the views from its 86th-floor outdoor deck and 102nd-floor indoor deck are heavenly. Alas, the queues to the top are notorious. Getting here very early or very late will help you avoid delays – as will buying your tickets ahead of time online, where the extra $2 convenience fee is well worth the hassle it will save.

★**Morgan Library & Museum** MUSEUM
(Map p74; ☎212-685-0008; www.themorgan.org; 225 Madison, at E 36th St, Midtown East; adult/child $20/free, 7-9pm Fri free; ⏲10:30am-5pm Tue-Thu, to 9pm Fri, 10am-6pm Sat, 11am-6pm Sun; [S]6 to 33rd St) Incorporating the mansion once owned by steel magnate JP Morgan, this sumptuous cultural center houses a phenomenal array of manuscripts, tapestries and books (with no fewer than three Gutenberg Bibles). Adorned with Italian and Dutch Renaissance artworks, Morgan's personal study is only trumped by his personal library (East Room), an extraordinary, vaulted space adorned with walnut bookcases, a 16th-century Dutch tapestry and zodiac-themed ceiling. The center's rotating exhibitions are often superb, as are its regular cultural events.

New York Public Library HISTORIC BUILDING
(Stephen A Schwarzman Building; Map p74; ☎917-275-6975; www.nypl.org; 476 Fifth Ave, at W 42nd St; ⏲10am-6pm Mon, Thu, Fri & Sat, to 8pm Tue & Wed, 1-5pm Sun, guided tours 11am & 2pm Mon-Sat, 2pm Sun; [S]B/D/F/M to 42nd St-Bryant Park, 7 to 5th Ave) [FREE] Loyally guarded by 'Patience' and 'Fortitude' (the marble lions overlooking Fifth Ave), this beaux-arts show-off is one of NYC's best free attractions. When dedicated in 1911, New York's flagship library ranked as the largest marble structure ever built in the US, and to this day its recently restored **Rose Main Reading Room** steals the breath away with its lavish coffered ceiling. It's only one of several glories inside, among them the **DeWitt Wallace Periodical Room**.

St Patrick's Cathedral CATHEDRAL
(Map p74; ☎212-753-2261; www.saintpatrickscathedral.org; Fifth Ave, btwn E 50th & 51st Sts; ⏲6:30am-8:45pm; [S]B/D/F/M to 47th-50th Sts-Rockefeller Center, E/M to 5th Ave-53rd St) Still shining after a $200 million restoration in 2015, America's largest Catholic cathedral graces Fifth Ave with Gothic Revival splendor. Built at a cost of nearly $2 million during the Civil War, the building did not originally include the two front spires; those were added in 1888. Step inside to appreciate the Louis Tiffany–designed **altar** and Charles Connick's stunning **Rose Window**, the latter gleaming above a 7000-pipe church organ. Walk-in guided tours are available several days a week; check the website for details.

United Nations HISTORIC BUILDING
(Map p74; ☎212-963-4475; http://visit.un.org; visitors gate First Ave at 46th St, Midtown East; guided tour adult/child $22/15, children under 5yr not admitted, grounds access Sat & Sun free; ⏲tours 9am-4:45pm Mon-Fri, visitor center also open 10am-4:45pm Sat & Sun; [S]S, 4/5/6, 7 to Grand Central-42nd St) Welcome to the headquarters of the UN, a worldwide organization overseeing international law, international security and human rights. While the Le Corbusier–designed Secretariat building is off-limits, one-hour guided tours do cover the restored General Assembly Hall, Security Council Chamber, Trusteeship Council Chamber and Economic and Social Council (ECOSOC) Chamber, as well as exhibitions about the UN's work and artworks given by member states. Weekday tours must be booked online and photo ID is required to enter the site.

Museum of Arts & Design MUSEUM
(MAD; Map p74; ☎212-299-7777; www.madmuseum.org; 2 Columbus Circle, btwn Eighth Ave & Broadway; adult/18yr & under $16/free, by donation 6-9pm Thu; ⏲10am-6pm Tue-Sun, to 9pm Thu; 👪; [S]A/C, B/D, 1 to 59th St-Columbus Circle) MAD offers four floors of superlative design and handicrafts, from blown glass and carved wood to elaborate metal jewelry. Its temporary exhibitions are top-notch and

East & West Villages

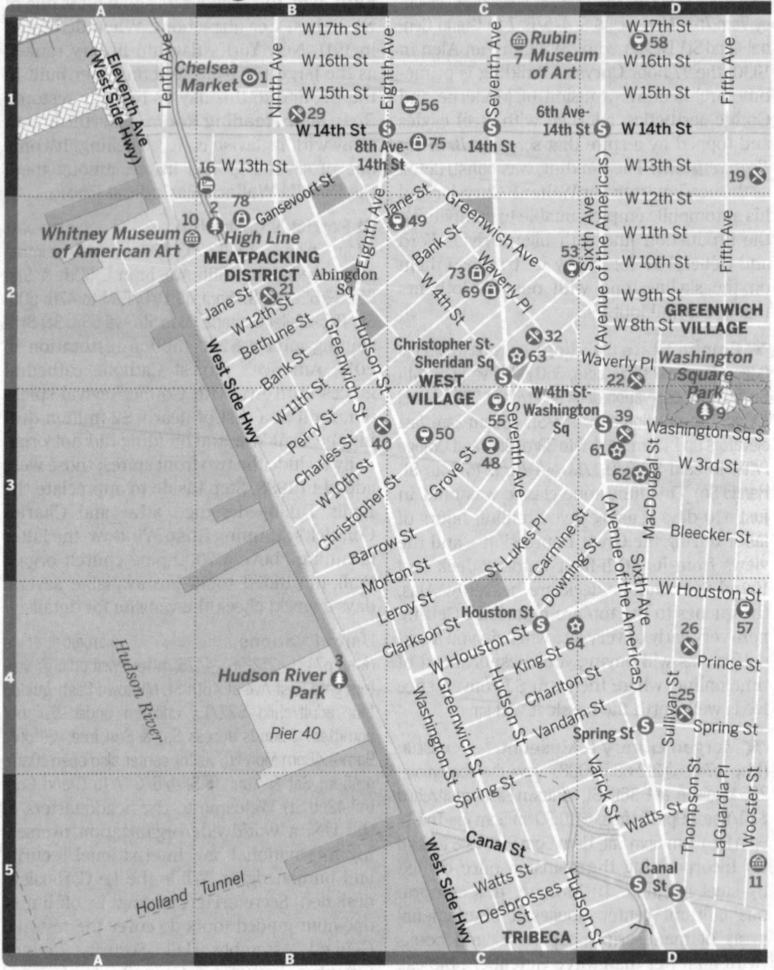

innovative: one past show explored the art of scent. Usually on the first Sunday of the month, artists lead family-friendly explorations of the galleries, followed by hands-on workshops inspired by the current exhibitions. The museum gift shop sells some fantastic contemporary jewelry, while the 9th-floor restaurant/bar Robert (p106) is perfect for panoramic cocktails.

Paley Center for Media CULTURAL CENTER
(Map p74; ☎212-621-6800; www.paleycenter.org; 25 W 52nd St, btwn Fifth & Sixth Aves; suggested donation adult/child $10/5; 🕒noon-6pm Wed & Fri-Sun, to 8pm Thu; [S]E, M to 5th Ave-53rd St) This pop culture repository offers more than 160,000 TV and radio programs from around the world on its computer catalog. Reliving your favorite TV shows on one of the center's consoles is sheer bliss on a rainy day, as are the excellent regular screenings, festivals, speakers and performers.

👁 Upper West Side & Central Park

Since the turn of the century, banks and chain stores have homogenized the Upper West Side's formerly eclectic streetscape, yet walking past rows of brownstones on quiet

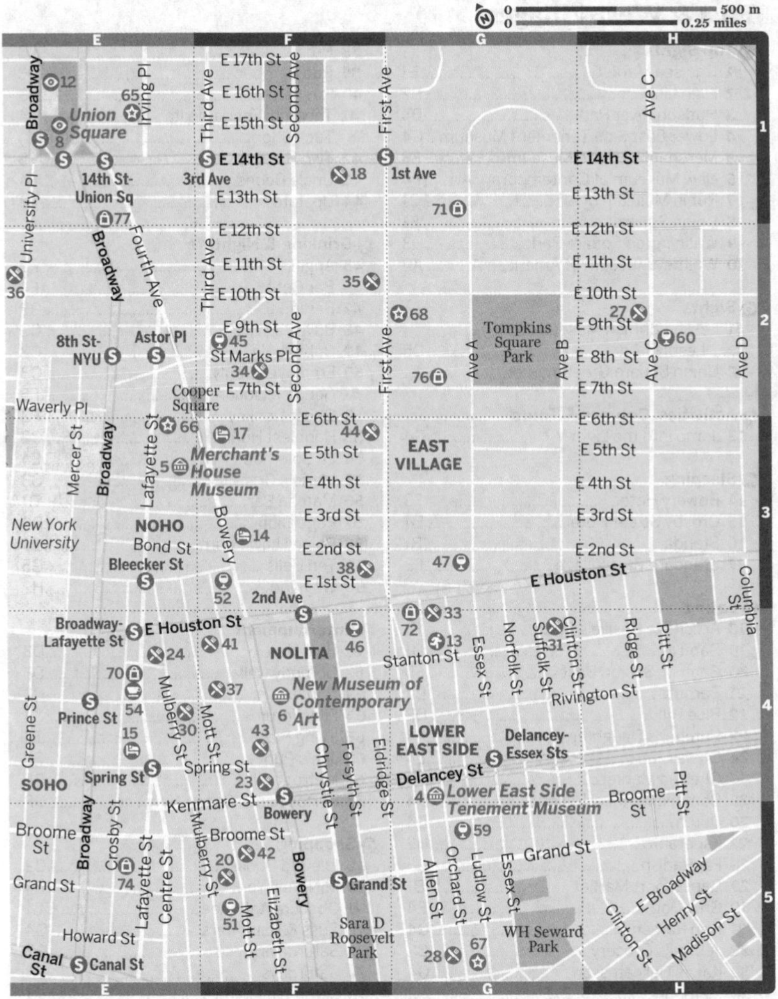

side streets still has the power to make you feel like you've stepped out of a romantic New York movie. Several world-class cultural institutions are located here, and the neighborhood is bordered by two parks: Riverside Park lines the Hudson River, while the verdant expanse of Central Park – the city's best antidote to concrete and honking horns – stretches off to the east.

★Lincoln Center ARTS CENTER

(Map p78; ☎212-875-5456, tours 212-875-5350; www.lincolncenter.org; Columbus Ave, btwn W 62nd & 66th Sts; tours adult/student $25/20; ⏰tours 11:30am & 1:30pm Mon-Sat, 1:30pm & 3pm Sun; 👪; [S]1 to 66th St-Lincoln Center) [FREE] This stark arrangement of gleaming modernist temples houses some of Manhattan's most important performance companies: the New York Philharmonic (p109), the New York City Ballet (p114) and the iconic Metropolitan Opera House (p114), whose lobby's interior walls are dressed with brightly saturated murals by painter Marc Chagall. Various other venues are tucked in and around the 16-acre campus, including a theater, two film-screening centers and the renowned **Juilliard School.**

East & West Villages

Top Sights
1 Chelsea Market B1
2 High Line B2
3 Hudson River Park B4
4 Lower East Side Tenement Museum... G4
5 Merchant's House Museum E3
6 New Museum of Contemporary Art...... F4
7 Rubin Museum of Art C1
8 Union Square E1
9 Washington Square Park D3
10 Whitney Museum of American Art A2

Sights
11 Leslie-Lohman Museum of Gay & Lesbian Art D5
12 Union Square Greenmarket E1

Activities, Courses & Tours
13 Jump into the Light VR G4

Sleeping
14 Bowery Hotel F3
15 Crosby Street Hotel E4
16 Standard B1
17 Standard East Village F3

Eating
18 Artichoke Basille's Pizza F1
19 Babu Ji D1
20 Bánh Mì Saigon Bakery F5
21 Barbuto B2
22 Blue Hill D2
23 Butcher's Daughter F4
24 Chefs Club E4
Chelsea Market .... (see 1)
25 Dominique Ansel Bakery D4
26 Dutch D4
27 Esperanto H2
28 Fat Radish G5
29 Gansevoort Market B1
30 Grey Dog E4
31 Ivan Ramen G4
32 Jeffrey's Grocery C2
33 Katz's Delicatessen G4
34 Mamoun's F2
35 Momofuku Noodle Bar F2
36 Nix E2
37 Prince Street Pizza F4
38 Prune F3
39 Red Bamboo D3
40 RedFarm B3
41 Tacombi Fonda Nolita F4
Tuck Shop .... (see 1)
42 Two Hands F5
43 Uncle Boons F4
44 Upstate F3

Drinking & Nightlife
45 Angel's Share F2
46 Bar Goto F4
47 Berlin G3
48 Buvette C3
49 Cubbyhole C2
50 Employees Only C3
51 Genuine Liquorette F5
52 Ghost Donkey F3
53 Happiest Hour C2
54 La Colombe E4
55 Marie's Crisis C3
56 Matcha Bar C1
57 Pegu Club D4
58 Raines Law Room D1
59 Ten Bells G5
60 Wayland H2

Entertainment
61 Blue Note D3
62 Comedy Cellar D3
63 Duplex C2
64 Film Forum C4
65 Irving Plaza E1
66 Joe's Pub E3
67 Metrograph G5
68 Performance Space New York G2

Shopping
69 Idlewild Books C2
70 MiN New York E4
71 Obscura Antiques G1
72 Russ & Daughters G4
73 Saturdays C2
74 Saturdays E5
75 Screaming Mimi's C1
76 Still House G2
77 Strand Book Store E1
78 Trina Turk B2

★American Museum of Natural History MUSEUM
(Map p78; ☎212-769-5100; www.amnh.org; Central Park West, at W 79th St; suggested admission adult/child $23/13; ⏰10am-5:45pm; 👪; [S]B, C to 81st St-Museum of Natural History; 1 to 79th St) Founded in 1869, this museum contains a veritable wonderland of more than 30 million artifacts – including lots of menacing dinosaur skeletons – as well as the **Rose Center for Earth & Space**, which has a cutting-edge planetarium. From October through May, the museum is home to the **Butterfly Conservatory**, a glasshouse featuring 500-plus butterflies from all over the world.

Upper East Side

★Metropolitan Museum of Art MUSEUM
(Map p78; ☎212-535-7710; www.metmuseum.org; 1000 Fifth Ave, cnr E 82nd St; 3-day pass adult/

senior/child $25/17/free; pay-as-you-wish for residents of NY State & students from CT, NY and NJ; ⏰10am-5:30pm Sun-Thu, to 9pm Fri & Sat; 👪; [S] 4/5/6, Q to 86th St) The vast collection of art contained within this palatial museum (founded in 1870) is one of the world's largest, with more than two million individual objects in its permanent collection: paintings, sculptures, textiles and artifacts from around the globe – even an ancient Egyptian temple straight from the banks of the Nile. 'The Met' has 17 acres of exhibition space to explore, so plan to spend at least several hours here. (Wear comfy shoes.)

★Guggenheim Museum MUSEUM

(Map p78; ☎212-423-3500; www.guggenheim.org; 1071 Fifth Ave, cnr E 89th St; adult/child $25/free, pay-what-you-wish 5-7:45pm Sat; ⏰10am-5:45pm Sun-Wed & Fri, to 7:45pm Sat, closed Thu; 👪; [S] 4/5/6 to 86th St) A New York icon, architect Frank Lloyd Wright's conical white spiral is probably more famous than the artworks inside, which include works by Kandinsky, Picasso and Pollock. Other key additions, often exhibited in the more recent adjoining tower (1992), include paintings by Monet, Van Gogh and Degas, photographs by Mapplethorpe, and important surrealist works. But temporary exhibitions are the real draw – the best of which are stunning site-specific installations by some of the great visionary artists of today.

★Frick Collection GALLERY

(Map p78; ☎212-288-0700; www.frick.org; 1 E 70th St, cnr Fifth Ave; adult/student $22/12, pay-what-you-wish 2-6pm Wed, first Fri of month excl Jan & Sep free; ⏰10am-6pm Tue-Sat, 11am-5pm Sun; [S] 6 to 68th St-Hunter College) This spectacular art collection sits in a mansion built by steel magnate Henry Clay Frick, one of the many such residences lining the section of Fifth Ave that was once called 'Millionaires' Row.' The museum has over a dozen splendid rooms displaying masterpieces by Titian, Vermeer, Gilbert Stuart, El Greco, Joshua Reynolds, Goya and Rembrandt. Sculpture, ceramics, antique furniture and clocks are also on display. Fans of classical music will enjoy the frequent piano and violin **concerts** ($45; ⏰5pm Sun) on Sunday evenings.

Cooper-Hewitt National Design Museum MUSEUM

(Map p78; ☎212-849-8400; www.cooperhewitt.org; 2 E 91st St, cnr Fifth Ave; adult/child $18/free, pay-what-you-wish 6-9pm Sat; ⏰10am-6pm Sun-Fri, to 9pm Sat; [S] 4/5/6 to 86th St) Part of the Smithsonian Institution in Washington, DC, this is the only US museum dedicated to both historic and contemporary design. Housed in the 64-room mansion built by billionaire Andrew Carnegie in 1901, the 210,000-piece collection offers artful displays spanning 3000 years over three floors of the building. The beautiful garden is open to the public and accessible from 90th St or from inside the museum. Mansion tours are at 1:30pm on weekdays, and at 1pm and 3pm on weekends.

Neue Galerie MUSEUM

(Map p78; ☎212-628-6200; www.neuegalerie.org; 1048 Fifth Ave, cnr E 86th St; adult/student $20/10, 6-9pm 1st Fri of the month free; ⏰11am-6pm Thu-Mon; [S] 4/5/6 to 86th St) This restored Carrère and Hastings mansion from 1914 is a resplendent showcase for Austrian and German art, featuring works by Paul Klee, Ernst Ludwig Kirchner and Egon Schiele. In pride of place on the 2nd floor is Gustav Klimt's golden 1907 portrait of Adele Bloch-Bauer – acquired for the museum by cosmetics magnate Ronald Lauder for a whopping $135 million. The fascinating story of the painting's history is told in the 2015 film *Woman in Gold*.

Met Breuer MUSEUM

(Map p78; ☎212-731-1675; www.metmuseum.org/visit/met-breuer; 945 Madison Ave, cnr E 75th St; 3-day pass adult/senior/child $25/17/free; pay-as-you-wish for residents of NY State & students from CT, NY and NJ; ⏰10am-5:30pm Tue-Thu & Sun, to 9pm Fri & Sat; [S] 6 to 77th St; Q to 72nd St) The newest branch of the Metropolitan Museum of Art opened in the landmark former Whitney Museum (p64) building (originally designed by Marcel Breuer) in 2016. Exhibits are dedicated to modern and contemporary art across various media, with sculpture, photographs, video, design and paintings from American and international figures such as Edvard Munch, Yayoi Kusama, Claes Oldenburg, Ettore Sottsass, Dara Birnbaum, Robert Smithson and Mira Schendel. Your ticket gives you three-day admission to the main museum, and medieval exhibits at the Cloisters (p77).

👁 Harlem & Upper Manhattan

★Cathedral Church of St John the Divine CATHEDRAL

(Map p78; ☎tours 212-316-7540; www.stjohndivine.org; 1047 Amsterdam Ave, at W 112th St, Morningside Heights; adult/student $10/8, highlights tour $14, vertical tour $20/18; ⏰7:30am-6pm, Highlights Tour 11am & 2pm Mon, 11am & 1pm Tue-Sat, Vertical

Midtown Manhattan

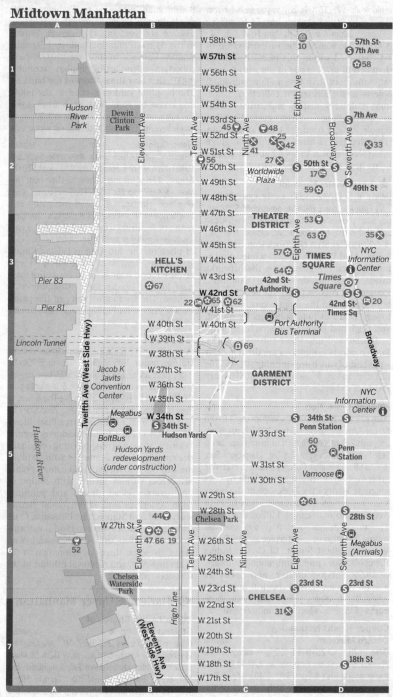

W 58th St
W 57th St
W 56th St
W 55th St
W 54th St
W 53rd St
W 52nd St
W 51st St
W 50th St
W 49th St
W 48th St
W 47th St
W 46th St
W 45th St
W 44th St
W 43rd St
W 42nd St
W 41st St
W 40th St
W 39th St
W 38th St
W 37th St
W 36th St
W 35th St
W 34th St
W 33rd St
W 31st St
W 30th St
W 29th St
W 28th St
W 27th St
W 26th St
W 25th St
W 24th St
W 23rd St
W 22nd St
W 21st St
W 20th St
W 19th St
W 18th St
W 17th St

W 40th St
W 39th St
W 38th St

Hudson River Park
Dewitt Clinton Park
Pier 83
Pier 81
Lincoln Tunnel
Jacob K Javits Convention Center
Hudson River

Eleventh Ave
Tenth Ave
Ninth Ave
Eighth Ave
Broadway
Seventh Ave

Twelfth Ave (West Side Hwy)
Eleventh Ave (West Side Hwy)
High Line

HELL'S KITCHEN
Worldwide Plaza
THEATER DISTRICT
TIMES SQUARE
Times Square
42nd St-Port Authority
Port Authority Bus Terminal
GARMENT DISTRICT

57th St-7th Ave
7th Ave
50th St
49th St
NYC Information Center
42nd St-Times Sq

Megabus
BoltBus
Hudson Yards redevelopment (under construction)
34th St-Hudson Yards
34th St-Penn Station
Penn Station
Vamoose
NYC Information Center

Chelsea Park
Chelsea Waterside Park
28th St
Megabus (Arrivals)
23rd St
23rd St
CHELSEA
18th St

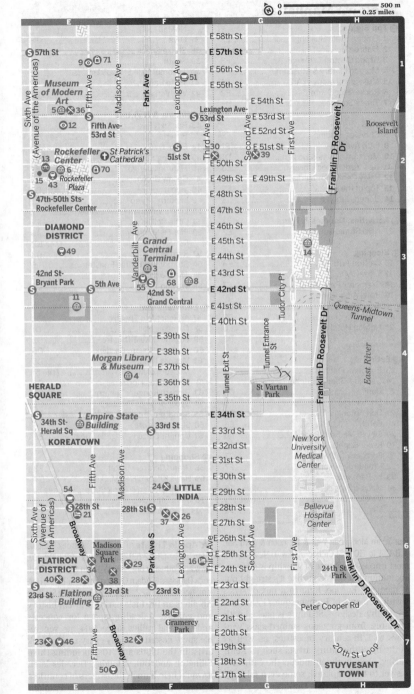

0   500 m
0   0.25 miles

E 58th St

S 57th St

9 71

E 57th St

Museum
of Modern
Art

E 56th St

E 55th St

5 36

Fifth Ave

Madison Ave

Park Ave

Lexington Ave

51

E 54th St

Roosevelt Island

S Fifth Ave-
53rd St

12

S Lexington Ave-
53rd St

E 53rd St

E 52nd St

Second Ave

E 51st St

39

13 Rockefeller
Center

St Patrick's
Cathedral

51st St

30

E 50th St

Third Ave

First Ave

(Franklin D Roosevelt) Dr

6 70

15   43

Rockefeller
Plaza

E 49th St

E 49th St

S 47th-50th Sts-
Rockefeller Center

E 48th St

E 47th St

**DIAMOND
DISTRICT**

E 46th St

E 45th St

14

49

Grand
Central
Terminal

E 44th St

E 43rd St

Vanderbilt Ave

42nd St-
Bryant Park

5th Ave

3

55

68   8

E 42nd St

Tudor City Pl

Queens-Midtown
Tunnel

S   S

42nd St-
Grand Central

E 41st St

11

E 40th St

E 39th St

E 38th St

Tunnel Entrance St

Franklin D Roosevelt Dr

East River

Morgan Library
& Museum

E 37th St

Tunnel Exit St

4

E 36th St

St Vartan
Park

**HERALD
SQUARE**

E 35th St

1 Empire State
Building

E 34th St

S 34th St-
Herald Sq

33rd St

E 33rd St

New York
University
Medical
Center

KOREATOWN

E 32nd St

E 31st St

Madison Ave

E 30th St

54

24

**LITTLE
INDIA**

E 29th St

Bellevue
Hospital
Center

Fifth Ave

S 28th St

28th St

E 28th St

21

37   26

E 27th St

Sixth Ave (Avenue of
the Americas)

E 26th St

E 25th St

Park Ave S

16

Second Ave

First Ave

Broadway

Madison
Square
Park

29

Lexington Ave

E 24th St

24th St
Park

**FLATIRON
DISTRICT**

34

Third Ave

E 23rd St

40   28

38

S 23rd St

23rd St

Peter Cooper Rd

23rd St Flatiron
Building

2

E 22nd St

18

E 21st St

Gramercy
Park

20th St Loop

23   46

32

E 20th St

E 19th St

**STUYVESANT
TOWN**

Franklin D Roosevelt Dr

50

E 18th St

Fifth Ave

Broadway

E 17th St

NEW YORK CITY SIGHTS

Midtown Manhattan

Tour 10am Mon, noon Wed & Fri, noon & 2pm Sat; S B/C, 1 to 110th St-Cathedral Pkwy) New York's most impressive house of worship is a towering monument that looks like it's straight out of medieval Europe. Built in a mix of styles – with elements of Romanesque, Gothic and neo-Gothic design – St John's is packed with treasures, from gorgeous stained-glass windows to 17th-century tapestries, as well as works by 20th-century artists such as Keith Haring. Despite the grandeur, the cathedral has yet to be completed; some even jokingly refer to it as 'St John the Unfinished.'

★ Apollo Theater   HISTORIC BUILDING
(Map p78; ☎ 212-531-5300, tours 212-531-5337; www.apollotheater.org; 253 W 125th St, btwn Frederick Douglass & Adam Clayton Powell Jr Blvds, Harlem; tickets from $22; S A/C, B/D to 125th St) The Apollo is an intrinsic part of Harlem history and culture. A leading space for concerts and political rallies since 1914, its venerable stage hosted virtually every major black artist in the 1930s and '40s, including Duke Ellington and Billie Holiday. Decades later, it would help launch the careers of countless stars, from Diana Ross and Aretha Franklin

to Michael Jackson and Lauryn Hill. Today, its thriving program of music, dance, master classes and special events continues to draw crowds and applause.

★Cloisters Museum & Gardens MUSEUM
(Map p62; ☎212-923-3700; www.metmuseum.org/cloisters; 99 Margaret Corbin Dr, Fort Tryon Park; 3-day pass adult/senior/child $25/17/free; pay-as-you-wish for residents of NY State & students from CT, NY and NJ; 🕐10am-5:15pm Mar-Oct, to 4:45pm Nov-Feb; [S] A to 190th St) On a hilltop overlooking the Hudson River, the Cloisters is a curious architectural jigsaw, its many parts made up of various European monasteries and other historic buildings. Built in the 1930s to house the Metropolitan Museum's medieval treasures, its frescoes, tapestries and paintings are set in galleries that sit around a romantic courtyard, connected by grand archways and topped with Moorish terra-cotta roofs. Among its many rare treasures is the beguiling 16th-century tapestry series *The Hunt of the Unicorn*.

Abyssinian Baptist Church CHURCH
(Map p62; ☎212-862-7474; www.abyssinian.org; 132 Odell Clark Pl, btwn Adam Clayton Powell Jr & Malcolm X Blvds, Harlem; 🕐tourist gospel service 11:30am Sun mid-Sep–Jul; [S] 2/3 to 135th St) A raucous, soulful affair, the superb Sunday gospel services here are the city's most famous. You'll need to arrive at least an hour before the service to queue up, and ensure you adhere to the strict entry rules: no tank tops, flip-flops, shorts, leggings or backpacks. The entry point for tourists is at the southeast corner of West 138th Street and Adam Clayton Powell Jr Blvd.

Brooklyn

★Brooklyn Bridge Park PARK
(Map p66; ☎718-222-9939; www.brooklynbridgepark.org; East River Waterfront, btwn Atlantic Ave & John St, Brooklyn Heights/Dumbo; 🕐6am-1am, some sections to 11pm, playgrounds to dusk; 🐾; 🚌B63 to Pier 6/Brooklyn Bridge Park; B25 to Old Fulton St/Elizabeth Pl, ⛴East River or South Brooklyn routes to Dumbo/Pier 1, [S] A/C to High St; 2/3 to Clark St; F to York St) [FREE] This 85-acre park is one of Brooklyn's best-loved attractions. Wrapping around a bend on the East River, it runs for 1.3 miles from just beyond the far side of the Manhattan Bridge in Dumbo to the west end of Atlantic Ave in Brooklyn Heights. It's revitalized a once-barren stretch of shoreline, turning a series of abandoned piers into beautifully landscaped parkland with jaw-dropping views of Manhattan. There's lots to see and do here, with playgrounds, walkways and lawns galore.

★Coney Island AREA
(Map p62; www.coneyisland.com; Surf Ave & Boardwalk, btwn W 15th & W 8th Sts; [S] D/F, N/Q to Coney Island-Stillwell Ave) About 50 minutes by subway from Midtown, this popular seaside neighborhood makes for a great day trip. The wide sandy beach has retained its nostalgic, kitschy and slightly sleazy charms, wood-plank boardwalk and famous Cyclone roller coaster amid a modern amusement-park area. Nathan's Famous (p100) churns out hot dogs, and the **New York Aquarium** (www.nyaquarium.com; 602 Surf Ave, at W 8th St; $12; 🕐10am-6pm Jun-Aug, to 4:30pm Sep-May, last entry 1hr before closing; 👪) is a big hit with kids, as is taking in an early-evening baseball game at **MCU Park** (☎718-372-5596; www.brooklyncyclones.com; 1904 Surf Ave, at 17th St; tickets $10-20, all tickets on Wed $10), the waterfront stadium for the minor league Brooklyn Cyclones.

★Brooklyn Museum MUSEUM
(Map p82; ☎718-638-5000; www.brooklynmuseum.org; 200 Eastern Pkwy, Prospect Park; suggested admission adult/child $16/free; 🕐11am-6pm Wed & Fri-Sun, to 10pm Thu, to 11pm 1st Sat of month Oct-Aug; 👪; [S] 2/3 to Eastern Pkwy-Brooklyn Museum) This encyclopedic museum is housed in a five-story, 560,000-sq-ft beaux-arts building (designed by McKim, Mead & White), with more than 1.5 million objects, including ancient artifacts, 19th-century period rooms, and sculptures and painting from across several centuries. A great alternative to the packed-to-the-gills institutions in Manhattan, it often features thought-provoking temporary exhibitions. The first Saturday of the month (except September) features special events (live music, performance art) as the museum stays open until 11pm.

★Prospect Park PARK
(Map p82; ☎718-965-8951; www.prospectpark.org; Grand Army Plaza; 🕐5am-1am; [S] 2/3 to Grand Army Plaza; F to 15th St-Prospect Park; B, Q to Prospect Park) The designers of the 585-acre Prospect Park – Frederick Law Olmsted and Calvert Vaux – considered this an improvement on their other New York project, Central Park (p56). Created in 1866, Prospect Park has many of the same features. It's gorgeous, with a long meadow running along the western half, filled with soccer, football, cricket and baseball players (and barbecuers), hilly forests and a lovely lake and boathouse on the east side.

Central Park & Uptown Manhattan

0 — 1 km
0 — 0.5 miles

NEW JERSEY
NEW YORK

Hudson River

Henry Hudson Pkwy

Riverside Dr

Riverside Dr

Broadway

MORNINGSIDE
HEIGHTS

Columbia University

116th St–
Columbia University

W 122nd St

Cathedral Church of
St John the Divine

W 112th St

Cathedral Pkwy
(110th St)

W 110th St
(Cathedral Pkwy)

103rd St

W 102nd St

W 100th St

W 97th St

96th St

Manhattan Ave

Morningside Ave

Morningside Dr

Morningside
Park

116th St

Cathedral
Pkwy
(110th St)

Adam Clayton Powell Jr Blvd
(Eighth Ave)

Apollo
Theater

2

27

28

25th St

Malcolm X Blvd (Lenox Ave)

HARLEM

W 127th St

W 124th St

W 122nd St

W 120th St

W 118th St

W 116th St

W 112th St

St Nicholas Ave

Frederick Douglass Blvd

51

49

43

45

32

125th St

Martin Luther
King Jr Blvd
(W 125th St)

Marcus
Garvey Park

Central Park North

Central Park
North

100

The Pond

The Loch

Great Hill

Harlem
Meer

West Dr

Central Park
West

W 106th St
(Duke Ellington Blvd)

W 104th St

103rd St

Amsterdam Ave

UPPER
WEST SIDE

29

96th St

W 96th St

W 94th St

North
Meadow

East
Meadow

East Dr

12

Fifth Ave

Central Park (110th St)

Madison Ave

Park Ave

La
Marqueta

Lexington Ave

110th St

E 112th St

E 110th St

E 116th St

SPANISH
HARLEM

E 118th St

E 120th St

E 122nd St

125th St

Martin Luther King Jr Blvd
(W 125th St)

E 127th St

Yankee Stadium (1.5mi)

First Ave

Second Ave

Third Ave
(Luis Munoz Marin Blvd)

116th St

E 116th St

Park Ave

Madison Ave

Park Ave North

Central Park North (110th St)

E 106th St

E 104th St

E 102nd St

E 99th St

E 97th St

96th St

E 96th St

E 94th St

103rd St

UPPER
EAST SIDE

Jefferson
Park

Franklin D Roosevelt Dr

East River

Icahn
Stadium

Ward's Island

Robert F Kennedy Bridge
(Triborough Bridge)

Robert F Kennedy Bridge (Triborough Bridge)

Mill Rock
Island

Mill Rock
Light Park

Henry Hudson Pkwy

ASTORIA

Astoria

LONG ISLAND CITY

Vernon Blvd

Rainey Park

East Channel East River

Roosevelt Island Bridge

Roosevelt Island

Main St

Roosevelt Island

Ed Koch Queensboro Bridge

Roosevelt Island

East River

Carl Schurz Park

East End Ave

Franklin D Roosevelt Dr

46

York Ave

E 86th St
E 84th St
E 82nd St

First Ave

Rockefeller University

York Ave

First Ave

E 92nd St
E 90th St
E 88th St

Third Ave

Second Ave

86th St

35

E 80th St
E 79th St
E 78th St
E 76th St
E 74th St
E 72nd St

E 70th St
E 68th St

Second Ave

E 65th St
E 64th St

E 62nd St

Roosevelt Island Tramway

E 59th St
E 57th St

47

Lexington Ave

Park Ave

86th St

77th St

Third Ave

Lexington Ave
63rd St

Lexington Ave-
59th St

E 57th St

Madison Ave

5 Frick Collection

68th St-
Hunter College

Lexington Ave

55

13
6
18

8 Metropolitan Museum of Art

50

17

31

Conservatory Water

30

Madison Ave

25

56

Jacqueline Kennedy Onassis Reservoir

Guggenheim Museum

Fifth Ave

Great Lawn

4 Central Park

15

Turtle Pond

52
22

The Ramble

26 41
19
9
Bethesda Fountain

Naumburg Bandshell

The Mall

11

21

5th Ave-
59th St

57

Fifth Ave

Central Park West

Museum of Natural History

81st St

20

The Lake

42

Sheep Meadow

16

West Dr

The Pond

Central Park West

59th St-
Columbus Circle

24

W 92nd St
W 90th St
W 88th St

86th St

40

Museum of Natural History

1

23

14

74th St

72nd St

Columbus Ave

66th St-
Lincoln Center

38

48
53

Amsterdam Ave

34
39

W 86th St
W 82nd St
W 80th St
W 79th St

American Museum of Natural History

W 74th St

72nd St

W 70th St
St

Ninth Ave

W 62nd St

W 60th St

Broadway

37
44

36
33

Broadway

72nd St

Lincoln Center

54

W 66th St

W 58th St
W 57th St

West End Ave

86th St

58

79th St

W 84th St
W 78th St
W 76th St

West End Ave

W 57th St

Riverside Dr

Henry Hudson Pkwy

Riverside Park

West Side Hwy

Hudson River

Brooklyn Botanic Garden GARDENS
(Map p82; ☎718-623-7200; www.bbg.org; 150 Eastern Pkwy, Prospect Park; adult/student/child $15/8/free, 10am-noon Fri free, Tue-Fri Dec-Feb free; ⏲8am-6pm Tue-Fri, from 10am Sat & Sun Mar-Oct, shorter hours rest of year; 👪; [S] 2/3 to Eastern Pkwy-Brooklyn Museum; B, Q to Prospect Park) One of Brooklyn's most picturesque attractions, this 52-acre garden is home to thousands of plants and trees, as well as a Japanese garden where river turtles swim alongside a Shinto shrine. The best time to visit is late April or early May, when the blooming cherry trees (a gift from Japan) are celebrated in Sakura Matsuri, the Cherry Blossom Festival (www.bbg.org).

👁 The Bronx

Home of hip-hop, known for its gritty South Bronx street culture and its web of highways carrying other New Yorkers further north, the Bronx is actually as green as it is urban: Wave Hill, Van Cortlandt Park, Pelham Bay Park and the New York Botanical Garden are just a few of its leafy areas. Orchard Beach, the 'Bronx Riviera,' draws crowds in summertime and America's oldest and largest

Central Park & Uptown Manhattan

Top Sights
1 American Museum of Natural History C6
2 Apollo Theater C1
3 Cathedral Church of St John the Divine B2
4 Central Park D6
5 Frick Collection D7
6 Guggenheim Museum D5
7 Lincoln Center C8
8 Metropolitan Museum of Art D6

Sights
9 Bethesda Terrace D7
10 Blockhouse C3
11 Central Park Zoo D8
12 Conservatory Garden D3
13 Cooper-Hewitt National Design Museum D5
14 Dakota Building C7
15 Great Lawn D6
16 Literary Walk D7
17 Met Breuer E6
18 Neue Galerie D5
19 Ramble D6
20 Strawberry Fields C7
21 Tisch Children's Zoo D8

Activities, Courses & Tours
22 Belvedere Castle D6
23 Bike & Roll C6
24 Central Park Bike Tours C8
25 Central Park Conservancy D8
26 Loeb Boathouse D6

Sleeping
27 Aloft Harlem C1
28 Harlem Flophouse C1
29 Hostelling International New York B3
30 Loews Regency Hotel E8
31 Mark D6
32 Mount Morris House B&B D1
33 NYLO Hotel B6

Eating
34 Barney Greengrass B5
35 Boqueria E6
36 Burke & Wills B6
37 Cafe Lalo B6
38 Épicerie Boulud C8
39 Jacob's Pickles B5
40 Kefi C5
41 Lakeside Restaurant at Loeb Boathouse D6
42 Le Pain Quotidien C7
43 Maison Harlem C1
44 Peacefood Cafe B6
45 Red Rooster D1
46 Tanoshi F7
47 Two Boots E6
48 Whole Foods C8

Drinking & Nightlife
49 Bier International C2
Caledonia ..... (see 47)
50 Cantor Roof Garden Bar D6
Ginny's Supper Club ..... (see 45)
Manhattan Cricket Club ..... (see 36)
51 Silvana C2

Entertainment
52 Delacorte Theater D6
Elinor Bunin Munroe Film Center ..... (see 7)
Film Society of Lincoln Center ..... (see 7)
Frick Collection Concerts ..... (see 5)
53 Jazz at Lincoln Center C8
Metropolitan Opera House ..... (see 7)
New York City Ballet ..... (see 7)
New York Philharmonic ..... (see 7)
54 Walter Reade Theater C7

Shopping
55 Argosy E8
56 Barneys D8
57 Bergdorf Goodman D8
58 Zabar's B6

WORTH A TRIP

WORTH A TRIP: GOVERNORS ISLAND

Off-limits to the public for 200 years, former military outpost **Governors Island** (Map p62; www.govisland.com; ⌚10am-6pm Mon-Fri, to 7pm Sat & Sun May-Oct, later hours Fri & Sat Jun-Aug; [S] 4/5 to Bowling Green; 1 to South Ferry) [FREE] is now one of New York's most popular seasonal playgrounds. Each summer, free **ferries** (Map p66; www.govisland.com; Battery Maritime Bldg, 10 South St; round-trip adult/child $3/free, 10-11:30am Sat & Sun free; ⌚departures 10am-4:15pm Mon-Fri, to 5:30pm Sat & Sun May-Oct, later hours Fri & Sat Jun-Aug; [S] 1 to South Ferry; R/W to Whitehall St; 4/5 to Bowling Green) make the seven-minute trip from Lower Manhattan to the 172-acre oasis. Thirty acres of island parkland include 6-acre, art-studded Liggett Terrace; 10-acre Hammock Grove (complete with 50 hammocks); and the 14-acre Play Lawn, with natural-turf ball fields for adult softball and Little League baseball. Also check out **The Hills**, an ambitious quartet of constructed hills offering spectacular city and harbor views; one of the hills has four slides built-in, including the longest in NYC (57ft). Inspiring views are also on tap along the Great Promenade: running for 2.2 miles along the island's perimeter, the path takes in everything from Lower Manhattan and Brooklyn to Staten Island and New Jersey. Bike rental is available on the island.

Besides serving as a successful military fort in the Revolutionary War, the Union Army's central recruiting station during the Civil War, and the take-off point for Wilbur Wright's famous 1909 flight around the Statue of Liberty, Governors Island is where the 1988 Reagan–Gorbachev summit signaled the beginning of the end of the Cold War. You can visit the spot where that famous summit took place at the **Admiral's House**, a grand, colonnaded military residence built in 1843. Other historic spots include **Fort Jay**, fortified in 1776 for what became a failed attempt to prevent the British from invading Manhattan; **Colonel's Row**, a collection of lovely 19th-century brick officers' quarters; and the creepy **Castle Williams**, a 19th-century fort that was later converted to a military penitentiary. The best way to explore it all is with the National Park Service (www.nps.gov/gois), whose rangers conduct guided tours of the historic district.

zoo is here. Architectural gems line art-deco Grand Concourse, and Arthur Ave is the place for old-school Italian red-sauce joints.

Yankee Stadium STADIUM

(Map p62; ☎718-293-4300, tours 646-977-8687; www.mlb.com/yankees; E 161st St, at River Ave; tours $20; [S] B/D, 4 to 161st St-Yankee Stadium) The Boston Red Sox like to talk about their record of eight World Series championships in the last 90 years…well, the Yankees have won a mere 27 in that period. The team's magic appeared to have moved with them across 161st St to the new Yankee Stadium, where they played their first season in 2009 – winning the World Series there in a six-game slugfest against the Phillies. The Yankees play from April to October. Hour-long guided tours of the site mainly run every 20 minutes between 11am and 1:40pm, and usually include the on-site museum, dugout, press box, clubhouse, field and Monument Park (home to plaques commemorating greats like Babe Ruth and Joe DiMaggio). You can purchase tickets in advance through Ticketmaster (www.ticketmaster.com).

Bronx Zoo ZOO

(Map p62; ☎718-220-5100; www.bronxzoo.com; 2300 Southern Blvd; full experience tickets adult/child $37/27, suggested donation Wed; ⌚10am-5pm Mon-Fri, to 5:30pm Sat & Sun Apr-Oct, to 4:30pm Nov-Mar; [S] 2, 5 to West Farms Sq-E Tremont Ave) This 265-acre zoo is the country's biggest and oldest, with over 6000 animals and re-created habitats from around the world, from African plains to Asian rainforests. It's deservedly popular, with especially large crowds on discounted Wednesdays and weekends, and any day in July or August (try to go Monday morning). If heading in on the subway, the southwest Asia Gate (a couple blocks north of the West Farms Sq–E Tremont Ave stop, up Boston Rd) is your easiest access point.

New York Botanical Garden GARDENS

(Map p62; ☎718-817-8716; www.nybg.org; 2900 Southern Blvd; all-garden pass weekdays adult/child $23/10, weekends $28/12, grounds only NYC residents $15/4, Wed & 9-10am Sat grounds admission free; ⌚10am-6pm Tue-Sun; 👪; [R] Metro-North to Botanical Garden) First opened in 1891 and incorporating 50 acres of old-growth forest, this

Brooklyn & Park Slope

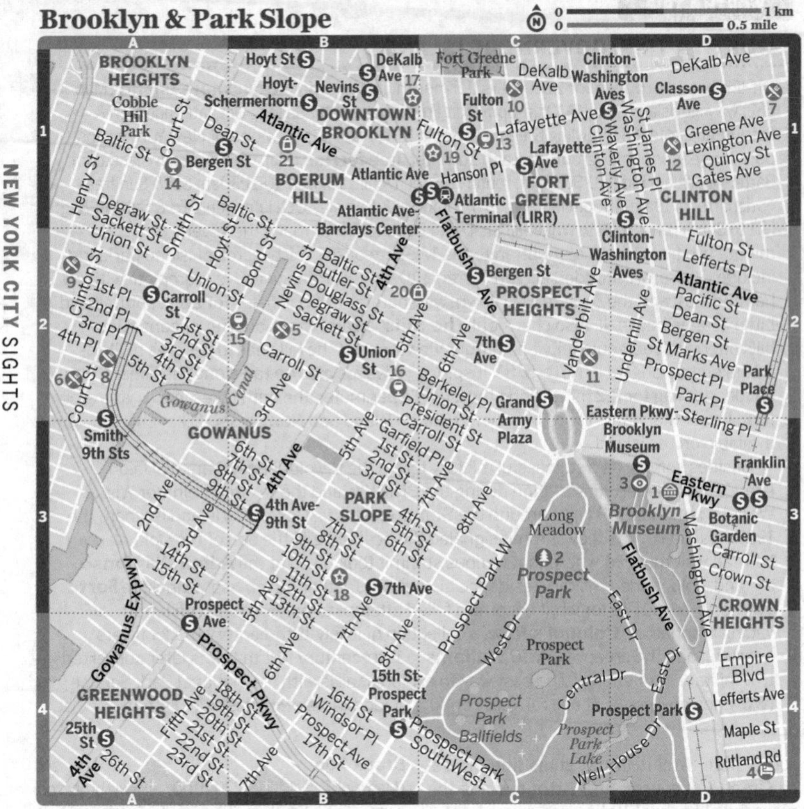

is home to the restored Enid A Haupt Conservatory, a grand, Victorian iron-and-glass edifice that is now a New York landmark. See the website for a list of regular events, which include themed walking tours, children's book readings and film screenings.

Queens

The largest of the city's boroughs and with nearly half of its residents foreign-born, Queens is truly a world apart. But other than downtown Flushing and East River condominiums, it's mostly a suburban, low-rise sprawl and a patchwork of diverse communities. Terra incognita to other New Yorkers and far from the fashionable Brooklyn confines, pockets of Queens are as fascinating as anywhere in the city. Gorge at diners and delis from around the world, ride the surf in hip Rockaway Beach and visit contemporary art centers scattered throughout the borough.

★ Museum of the Moving Image — MUSEUM

(Map p86; ☎718-777-6888; www.movingimage.us; 36-01 35th Ave, Astoria; adult/child $15/9, admission free 4-8pm Fri; 🕐10:30am-5pm Wed & Thu, to 8pm Fri, 10:30am-6pm Sat & Sun; [S]M, R to Steinway St) This super-cool complex is one of the world's top film, television and video museums. Galleries show a collection of 130,000-plus artifacts, including Elizabeth Taylor's wig from *Cleopatra*, nearly everything related to *Seinfeld* and a whole room of vintage arcade games. Interactive displays – such as a DIY flipbook station – show the science behind the art.

★ MoMA PS1 — GALLERY

(Map p86; ☎718-784-2084; www.momaps1.org; 22-25 Jackson Ave, Long Island City; suggested donation adult/child $10/free, NYC residents or with MoMA ticket free, Warm Up party online/at venue $18/22; 🕐noon-6pm Thu-Mon, Warm Up parties noon-9pm Sat Jul-Aug; [S]E, M to Court Sq-23rd St; G, 7 to Court

Brooklyn & Park Slope

Sq) At MoMA's hip contemporary outpost, set in a converted former public school, you'll be peering at videos through floorboards, schmoozing at DJ parties and debating the meaning of nonstatic structures while staring through a hole in the wall. Exhibitions explore everything from Middle Eastern video art to giant mounds of thread, often installed specifically at the space.

Louis Armstrong House NOTABLE BUILDING
(Map p86; ☎718-478-8274; www.louisarmstronghouse.org; 34-56 107th St, Corona; adult/child $12/8; ⏲10am-5pm Tue-Fri, noon-5pm Sat & Sun, last tour 4pm; [S]7 to 103rd St-Corona Plaza) At the peak of his career and with worldwide fame at hand, legendary trumpeter Armstrong settled in this modest Queens home, and lived there until his death in 1971. The place has been immaculately preserved in groovy style, down to the dazzling turquoise kitchen fixtures. Guided tours (40 minutes) tell Armstrong's story through audio clips and insightful commentary.

Activities

★Staten Island Ferry CRUISE
(Map p66; www.siferry.com; Whitehall Terminal, 4 South St, at Whitehall St; ⏲24hr; [S]1 to South Ferry; R/W to Whitehall St; 4/5 to Bowling Green) [FREE] Staten Islanders know these hulking, orange ferryboats as commuter vehicles, while Manhattanites like to think of them as their secret, romantic vessels for a spring-day escape. Yet many tourists (at last count, two million a year) are clued into the charms of the Staten Island Ferry, whose 25-minute, 5.2-mile journey between Lower Manhattan and the Staten Island neighborhood of St George is one of NYC's finest free adventures.

Jump into the Light VR AMUSEMENT PARK
(Map p70; ☎646-590-1172; www.jumpintothelight.com; 180 Orchard St, East Village; $30; ⏲1pm-11pm Mon-Thu, 1pm-midnight Fri, 10am-midnight Sat, 10am-11pm Sun; [S]F to Delancy) Ready to jump off a skyscraper, climb a mountain, parachute from a plane and kill a whole bunch of zombies? Then head to this incredible, first-of-its-kind virtual reality arcade, where you can explore all the different activities and, best of all, start to understand how cool VR is going to be. Interactive artwork and other futuristic tech is also on display.

Bike & Roll CYCLING
(Map p78; ☎212-260-0400; www.bikeandrollnyc.com; 451 Columbus Ave, btwn 81st & 82nd Sts; bike rentals per hr/day adult from $10/45, child $6/30; ⏲9am-6pm; 👪; [S]B, C to 81st St-Museum of Natural History; 1 to 79th St) Located just one block from Central Park, this friendly outfit rents out bicycles for adults and kids, with helmet, U-lock, handlebar bag, rear storage rack and a free cycling map all included. Baby seats are available too. Credit cards only.

Liberty Helicopter Tours SCENIC FLIGHTS
(Map p66; ☎800-542-9933; www.libertyhelicopters.com; Pier 6, East River, Lower Manhattan; per person $224-309; [S]1 to South Ferry; R/W to Whitehall St) Enjoy a bird's-eye view of the skyscrapers as a helicopter whisks you high above New York's concrete jungle. Just get ready to shell out for the privilege – flights run from just 12 to 20 minutes. (Be sure to read the fine print regarding heliport fees and the necessary ID to bring.)

Williamsburg & Greenpoint

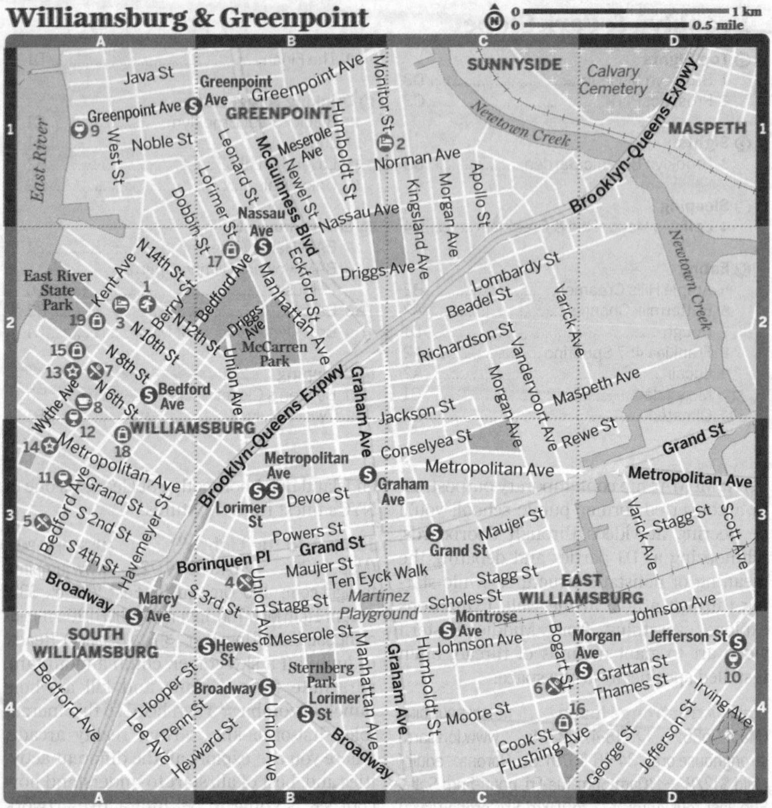

Rockaway Beach SURFING

(Map p126) Surfboards on the subway? A discordant sight no doubt, but it's only a 75-minute ride on the A train from Midtown, or a 57-minute ferry ride from Wall St, to the pier at 108th St to the break for the beach off 90th St in the Rockaways. It's a tight-knit group of wave worshippers who have revitalized this section of the beachfront.

☞ Tours

NBC Studio Tours WALKING

(Map p74; ☎212-664-3700; www.thetouratnbcstudios.com; 30 Rockefeller Plaza, entrance at 1250 Sixth Ave; tours adult/child $33/29, children under 6yr not admitted; ⏰8:20am-2:20pm Mon-Thu, to 5pm Fri, to 6pm Sat & Sun; [S] B/D/F/M to 47th-50th Sts-Rockefeller Center) Peppered with interesting anecdotes, this revamped, one-hour tour takes TV fans through parts of the NBC Studios, home to iconic TV shows *Saturday Night Live* and *The Tonight Show Starring Jimmy Fallon*. Stops usually include the beautifully restored art deco rotunda, two studios and the NBC Broadcast Operations Center. Things get interactive in the Tour Studio, where you can 'star' or 'produce' your own talk show segment. Book online to avoid the queues.

Museum Hack WALKING

(☎347-282-5001; www.museumhack.com; 2hr tour adult/student from $69/59) For a fascinating, alternative perspective of the Met, sign up for a tour with Museum Hack. Knowledgeable but delightfully irreverent guides take on topics like 'Badass Witches' (a look at the dark arts in Egypt and the Middle Ages), paradigm-shifting feminist artists and an 'Unhighlights Tour' that will take you to corners of the museum few visitors know about.

Central Park Bike Tours CYCLING

(Map p78; ☎212-541-8759; www.centralparkbiketours.com; 203 W 58th St, at Seventh Ave; rentals per 2hr/day $20/40, 2hr tours $49; ⏰8am-8pm, tours 9am, 10am, 1pm & 4pm; [S] A/C, B/D, 1

Williamsburg & Greenpoint

to 59th St-Columbus Circle) This place rents out good bikes (helmets, locks and bike map included) and leads two-hour guided tours of Central Park and the Brooklyn Bridge area.

✦ Festivals & Events

Shakespeare in the Park   THEATER
(www.publictheater.org; ⊙ Jun-Aug) The much-loved Shakespeare in the Park pays tribute to the Bard, with free performances in Central Park. It's a magical experience. The catch? You'll have to wait hours in line to score tickets, or win them in the online lottery.

Tribeca Film Festival   FILM
(📞 212-941-2400; www.tribecafilm.com; ⊙ Apr) Founded in 2003 by Robert De Niro and Jane Rosenthal, the Tribeca Film Festival is now a major star of the indie movie circuit. Gaggles of celebs come to walk the red carpets each spring.

Armory Show
(📞 212-645-6440; www.thearmoryshow.com; Piers 92 & 94, West Side Hwy, at 52nd & 54th Sts; ⊙ Mar) New York's biggest contemporary art fair sweeps into the city in March, showcasing the works of thousands of artists from around the world. Join the city's moneyed players, international collectors and young Brooklyn bohemians in wandering the acres of event space spread over two piers that jut into the Hudson River. Bring a flush bank account if you plan on buying.

SummerStage   PERFORMING ARTS
(www.cityparksfoundation.org/summerstage; Rumsey Playfield, Central Park, access via Fifth Ave & 69th St; ⊙ Jun-Sep; 🚇; Ⓢ 6 to 68th St-Hunter College) One of the best-loved events in Central Park is the series of outdoor concerts known as SummerStage. Every summer the park hosts dozens of performances, showcasing a wide mix of cultural fare – indie rock, jazz, modern dance, rockabilly, African, zydeco and more.

🛏 Sleeping

In general, expect high prices and small spaces. Room rates waver by availability, not season. Of course, you'll pay dearly during holidays. Accommodations fill up quickly – especially in summer – and range from boxy cookie-cutter chains to stylish boutiques. No Manhattan neighborhood has a monopoly on one style and you'll find better-value hotels in Brooklyn and Queens. A few B&Bs and hostels are scattered throughout.

🛏 Financial District & Lower Manhattan

Gild Hall   BOUTIQUE HOTEL $$
(Map p66; 📞 212-232-7700; www.thompsonhotels .com/hotels/gild-hall; 15 Gold St, at Platt St; r from $229; ❄🤶; Ⓢ 2/3 to Fulton St) Boutique and brilliant, Gild Hall's entryway leads to a bi-level library and wine bar that exudes hunting-lodge chic. Rooms fuse Euro elegance and American comfort with high tin ceilings, glass-walled balconies, Sferra linens and well-stocked minibars. King-size beds sport leather headboards, which work perfectly in their warmly hued, minimalist surroundings.

Wall Street Inn   HOTEL $$
(Map p66; 📞 212-747-1500; www.thewallstreet inn.com; 9 S William St; r $140-280; ❄🤶; Ⓢ 2/3 to Wall St) The sedate stone exterior of this affordable, intimate inn belies its warm, colonial-style interior. Beds are big and plush, and rooms have glossy wood furnishings and long drapes. The bathrooms are full of appreciated touches, like Jacuzzis in the

Astoria & Flushing

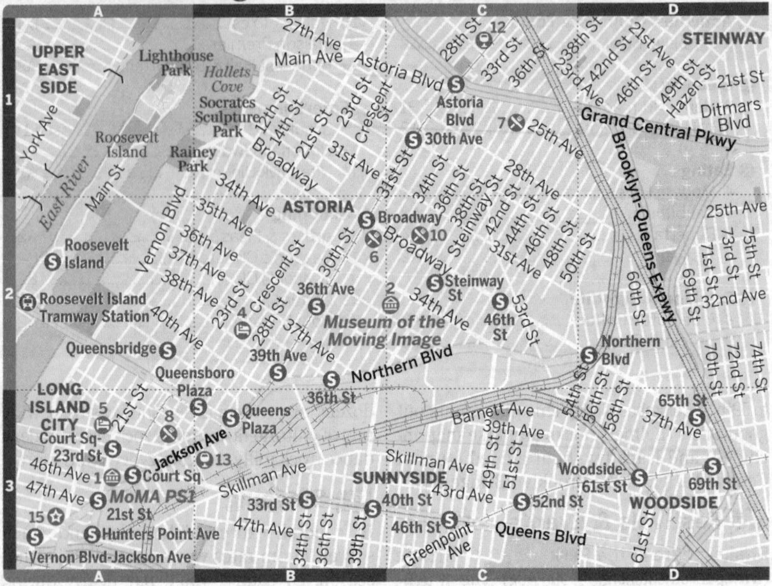

deluxe rooms and tubs in the others. Wi-fi and breakfast are included.

🛏 SoHo & Chinatown

★Crosby Street Hotel BOUTIQUE HOTEL **$$$**

(Map p70; ☎212-226-6400; www.firmdalehotels.com; 79 Crosby St, btwn Spring & Prince Sts, SoHo; r from $725; 🚭❄📶; [S]6 to Spring St; N/R to Prince St) Step into Crosby Street for afternoon tea and you'll never want to leave. It's not just the scones and cream that will grab you, but the eccentric, loft-like lobby, buzzing bar, film screening room and one-of-a-kind rooms. Some are starkly black and white while others are as floral as an English garden, but all are plush, refined and subtly playful.

🛏 East Village & Lower East Side

Bowery Hotel BOUTIQUE HOTEL **$$$**

(Map p70; ☎212-505-9100; www.theboweryhotel.com; 335 Bowery, btwn 2nd & 3rd Sts, East Village; r $295-535; ❄@📶; [S]F/V to Lower East Side-2nd Ave; 6 to Bleecker St) Pick up your old-fashioned gold room key with its red tassel in the dark, hushed lobby filled with antique velvet chairs and faded Persian rugs. Then follow the mosaic-tiled floors to your room with huge factory windows and elegant four-poster beds. Settle in to watch a movie on your 42in plasma TV, or raid the luxury bathroom goodies.

🛏 West Village, Chelsea & Meatpacking District

Standard BOUTIQUE HOTEL **$$$**

(Map p70; ☎212-645-4646; www.standardhotels.com; 848 Washington St, at 13th St, Meatpacking District; d from $500; ❄📶; [S]A/C/E, L to 8th Ave-14th St) Hipster hotelier André Balazs has built a wide, boxy, glass tower that straddles the High Line. Every room has sweeping Meatpacking District views and is filled with cascading sunlight, which makes the Standard's glossy, wood-framed beds and marbled bathrooms glow in a particularly homey way. There's also a hyper-modern **Standard** (Map p70; ☎212-475-5700; 25 Cooper Sq (Third Ave), btwn 5th & 6th Sts; r from $360; ❄📶; [S]R/W to 8th St-NYU; 4/6 to Bleecker St; 4/6 to Astor Pl) in the East Village.

Hôtel Americano HOTEL **$$$**

(Map p74; ☎212-216-0000; www.hotel-americano.com; 518 W 27th St, btwn Tenth & Eleventh Aves, Chelsea; r from $325; ❄📶🏊; [S]1, C/E to 23rd St) Design geeks will go giddy when they walk into one of Hôtel Americano's perfectly polished rooms. It's like sleeping in a bento box,

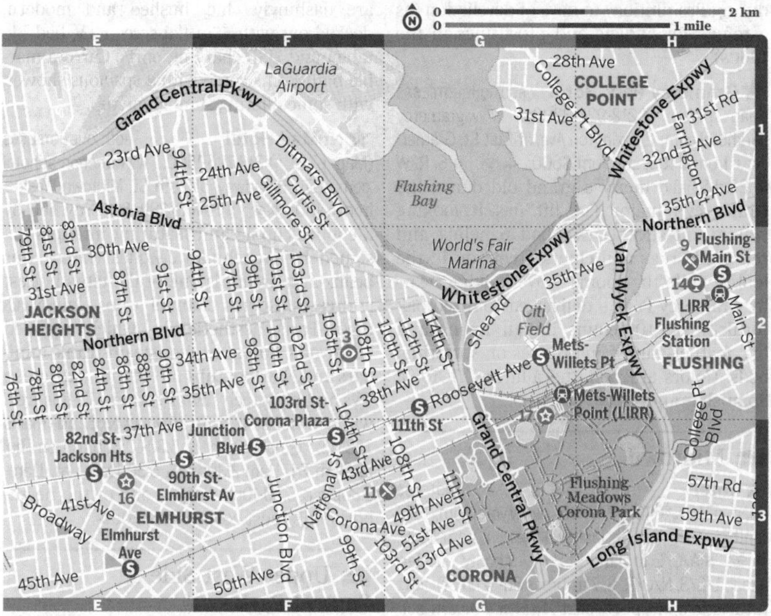

Astoria & Flushing

Top Sights
1 MoMA PS1 .... A3
2 Museum of the Moving Image C2

Sights
3 Louis Armstrong House F2

Sleeping
4 Boro Hotel B2
5 Local NYC A3

Eating
6 Bahari B2
7 Kabab Cafe C1
8 M Wells Steakhouse A3
9 Nan Xiang Xiao Long Bao H2
10 Pye Boat Noodle C2
11 Tortilleria Nixtamal G3

Drinking & Nightlife
12 Bohemian Hall & Beer Garden C1
13 Dutch Kills B3
14 The COOP H2

Entertainment
15 Creek and the Cave A3
16 Terraza 7 .... E3
17 USTA Billie Jean King National Tennis Center G2

but the food's been replaced by a carefully curated selection of minimalist and muted furniture. Oh, and that thing hanging from the ceiling that looks like a robot's head? It's a suspended fireplace, of course.

Union Square, Flatiron District & Gramercy

Carlton Arms HOTEL $
(Map p74; ☎212-679-0680; www.carltonarms.com; 160 E 25th St, at Third Ave, Gramercy; d with shared/private bath $130/160; ❄📶; [S]6 to 23rd St or 28th St) The Carlton Arms channels the downtown edgy art-world scene of yesteryear with the works of artists from all over the world adorning nearly every inch of the interiors. Murals follow the walls up five flights of stairs, and into each of the tiny guest rooms and shared bathrooms (there is a small sink in each guest room). Not surprisingly, it draws an eclectic mix of bohemian travelers, who don't mind the rustic accommodations in exchange for big savings. Prepare to work those legs: there's no elevator. The Carlton Arms has gone through many incarnations during its 100 years as a hotel, from nights of subterfuge (the lobby was a speakeasy

during Prohibition) to days of dereliction (as a refuge for addicts and prostitutes in the 1960s).

★**Gramercy Park Hotel** BOUTIQUE HOTEL **$$$**
(Map p74; ☎212-920-3300; www.gramercyparkhotel.com; 2 Lexington Ave, at 21st St, Gramercy; r from $400, ste from $600; ❄📶; [S]6, R/W to 23rd St) Formerly a grand old dame, the Gramercy's major face-lift has it looking young and sexy. Dark wood paneling and red suede rugs and chairs greet you in the lobby, while the rooms – overlooking nearby Gramercy Park – deliver customized oak furnishings, 400-count Italian linens and big, feather-stuffed mattresses on sprawling beds. Colors are rich and alluring, fit for a Spanish grandee.

Midtown

★**Yotel** HOTEL **$$**
(Map p74; ☎646-449-7700; www.yotel.com; 570 Tenth Ave, at 41st St, Midtown West; r from $190; ❄📶; [S]A/C/E to 42nd St-Port Authority Bus Terminal; 1/2/3, N/Q/R, S, 7 to Times Sq-42nd St) Part futuristic spaceport, part *Austin Powers* set, this cool 669-room option bases its rooms on airplane classes: premium cabin (economy), first cabins (business) and VIP suites (first); some first cabins and VIP suites include a private terrace with hot tub. Small but cleverly configured, premium cabins include automated adjustable beds, while all cabins feature floor-to-ceiling windows with killer views, slick bathrooms and iPod connectivity.

Citizen M HOTEL **$$**
(Map p74; ☎212-461-3638; www.citizenm.com; 218 W 50th St, btwn Broadway & Eighth Ave, Midtown West; r from $300; ❄📶; [S]1, C/E to 50th St) A few steps from Times Square, Citizen M is a true millennial. Speedy self-service counters provide lightning-fast check-in and check-out, communal areas are upbeat, contemporary and buzzing, and rooms are smart and compact. A tablet in each controls lighting, blinds and room temperature, and the plush mattresses, free movies and soothing rain showers keep guests purring. On-site perks include gym, rooftop bar and 24-hour canteen.

★**Knickerbocker** BOUTIQUE HOTEL **$$$**
(Map p74; ☎212-204-4980; http://theknickerbocker.com; 6 Times Sq, at 42nd St; d from $463; ❄📶; [S]A/C/E, N/Q/R/W, S, 1/2/3, 7 to Times Sq-42nd St) Originally opened in 1906 by John Jacob Astor, the 330-room Knickerbocker exudes a restrained, monochromatic elegance (unlike its Times Square location!). Rooms are dashingly chic, hushed and modern, decked out with 55in flat-screen TV, bedside tablet and USB charging ports. Carrara marble bathrooms come with a spacious shower, with some offering standalone tub.

★**NoMad Hotel** BOUTIQUE HOTEL **$$$**
(Map p74; ☎212-796-1500; www.thenomadhotel.com; 1170 Broadway, at 28th St, Midtown West; r from $400; ❄📶; [S]N/R to 28th St) Crowned by a copper cupola and featuring interiors designed by Frenchman Jacques Garcia, this beaux-arts dream is one of the city's hottest addresses. Rooms channel a nostalgic NYC-meets-Paris aesthetic, in which recycled hardwood floors, leather-steam-trunk minibars and clawfoot tubs mix it with flat-screen TVs and high-tech LED lighting. Wi-fi is free, while in-house restaurant/bar **NoMad** (mains $28-45; 🕐noon-2pm & 5:30-10:30pm Mon-Thu, to 11pm Fri, 11am-2:30pm & 5:30-11pm Sat, 11am-2:30pm & 5:30-10pm Sun) is one of the neighborhood's most coveted hangouts.

Upper West Side & Central Park

Hostelling International New York HOSTEL **$**
(HI; Map p78; ☎212-932-2300; www.hinewyork.org; 891 Amsterdam Ave, at 103rd St; dm $40-98; ❄📶; [S]1 to 103rd St) This red-brick mansion from the 1880s houses HI's 672 well-scrubbed and maintained bunks. It's rather 19th-century industrial, but benefits include good public areas, a backyard (that sees barbecue action in the summer), a communal kitchen and a cafe. There are loads of activities on offer, from walking tours to club nights. There are attractive private rooms with private bathrooms, too. The hostel is alcohol-free.

NYLO Hotel BOUTIQUE HOTEL **$$**
(Map p78; ☎212-362-1100; www.nylo-nyc.com; 2178 Broadway, at 77th St; r from $280; ❄📶; [S]1 to 77th St) This modern boutique hotel has 285 casually stylish rooms with warm tones. Niceties include plush bedding, wood floors, elegant lighting, roomy (for New York) bathrooms, coffeemakers and flat-screen TVs. 'NYLO Panoramic' rooms have private terraces and extravagant Manhattan views.

Upper East Side

Loews Regency Hotel HOTEL **$$$**
(Map p78; ☎212-759-4100; www.loewshotels.com/regency-hotel; 540 Park Ave, btwn E 61st & 62nd Sts; d from $400; ❄@📶; [S]N/Q/R, 4/5/6 to 59th St, F, Q to Lexington Ave-63rd St) This fabled luxury hotel is looking smarter than ever. Rooms are

equipped for both leisure and business, with luxury Frette linens, roomy desks with ergonomic chairs, and walk-in showers – some also have balconies. Well-lit bathroom mirrors and pro-style blow-dryers make getting ready in the morning that much easier.

Mark HOTEL $$$
(Map p78; ☑212-744-4300; www.themarkhotel.com; 25 E 77th St, cnr Madison Ave; d/ste from $600/1200; ✳🐾; Ⓢ6 to 77th St) French designer Jacques Grange left his artful mark on the Mark, with bold geometric shapes and rich, playful forms that greet visitors in the lobby (the zebra-striped marble floor is pure eye candy). Upstairs, lavishly renovated rooms and multibedroom suites boast a more subdued aesthetic, though one equally embracing of high style.

🛏 Harlem & Upper Manhattan

Harlem Flophouse GUESTHOUSE $
(Map p78; ☑347-632-1960; www.harlemflophouse.com; 242 W 123rd St, btwn Adam Clayton Powell Jr & Frederick Douglass Blvds, Harlem; d with shared bath $99-150; 🐾; ⓈA/B/C/D, 2/3 to 125th St) Rekindle Harlem's Jazz Age in this atmospheric 1890s town house, its nostalgic rooms decked out with brass beds and vintage radios (set to a local jazz station). It feels like a step back in time, which also means shared bathrooms, no air-con and no TVs. The owner is a great source of local information.

Easy Living Harlem B&B $
(Map p62; www.easylivingharlem.com; 214 W 137th St, btwn Adam Clayton Powell Jr & Frederick Douglass Blvds, Harlem; d $130-150; 🐾; ⓈA/B/C, 2/3 to 135th St) This very welcoming four-bedroom guesthouse offers excellent value for its attractive but simply furnished rooms, each with polished wood floors and ample natural light. Guests are made to feel at home and welcome to use the kitchen, have a cup of tea or coffee, and relax in the small garden.

Mount Morris House B&B GUESTHOUSE $$
(Map p78; ☑917-478-6213; www.mountmorrishousebandb.com; 12 Mt Morris Park W, btwn 121st & 122nd Sts, Harlem; ste/apt from $175/235; ✳🐾; Ⓢ2/3 to 125th St) Set inside a stunning Gilded Age town house from 1888, this cozy inn offers three extravagantly spacious slumber options: a one- and a two-bedroom suite and a studio apartment with a fully equipped kitchen. Each one impresses with lovely original details and period furnishings, including Persian-style rugs and brocaded settees, not to mention fireplaces and vintage bathtubs.

Aloft Harlem HOTEL $$
(Map p78; ☑212-749-4000; www.aloftharlem.com; 2296 Frederick Douglass Blvd, btwn 123rd & 124th Sts, Harlem; r from $206; ✳🐾; ⓈA/C, B/D, 2/3 to 125th St) Designed for younger travelers, Aloft channels a luxury vibe but at accessible prices. Guest rooms are snug (285 sq ft) but chic, with crisp white linens, fluffy comforters and colorful striped bolsters. The modern bathrooms are small (no tubs) but highly functional and feature amenities courtesy of Bliss, the upscale spa chain.

🛏 Brooklyn

A short train ride across the East River and you'll find bigger and (sometimes) brighter rooms – and a lot more bang for your buck. Downtown Brooklyn and Williamsburg are home to a number of brand-new and often quite chic hotels, while small B&Bs in classic houses can be found in residential areas such as Prospect Lefferts Gardens and Ditmas Park. Note: The borough covers more than 70 sq miles and transport between its neighborhoods can be a challenge, so pick an area (ie northern or southern Brooklyn) that offers the best proximity to the sights you're most interested in seeing.

Lefferts Manor Bed & Breakfast B&B $
(Map p82; ☑347-351-9065; www.leffertsmanorbedandbreakfast.com; 80 Rutland Rd, btwn Flatbush & Bedford Aves, Prospect Lefferts Gardens; r with shared bath $109-139, with private bath $149; ⊖@🐾; ⓈB, Q to Prospect Park) Six sunny rooms in this classic Brooklyn brownstone feature tiled closed fireplaces, subtle color palettes and historically styled decor. Five rooms upstairs share two gleaming-white bathrooms, while the Parlor Suite has a private toilet and a clawfoot tub in a curtained niche. Downtown Manhattan is only 30 minutes away by subway. Optional continental breakfast is available; three-night minimum stay.

Williamsburg Hotel BOUTIQUE HOTEL $$
(Map p84; ☑718-362-8100; www.thewilliamsburghotel.com; 96 Wythe Ave, at N 10th St, Williamsburg; d from $265; 🐾; ⓈL to Bedford Ave) Williamsburg's newest boutique hotel, just two blocks from the water, has 110 guest rooms with spectacular river and Manhattan views; it's worth paying extra for one of the 'terrace' rooms on the north side, which give you an unbroken view of the Empire State Building, Chrysler Building and Upper East Side from your artificial-grass-carpeted balcony (some have swing chairs).

Henry Norman Hotel
BOUTIQUE HOTEL $$

(Map p84; ☑646-604-9366; www.henrynorman hotel.com; 251 N Henry St, btwn Norman & Meserole Aves, Greenpoint; lofts from $239; ❈☏; ☐B48 to Nassau Ave/Monitor St, ☒G to Nassau Ave) Set in a former 19th-century warehouse, this striking brick building (once home to artists' lofts) offers bohemian chic in its high-ceilinged rooms, with hardwood floors, muted color schemes (decorated in white and gray), artwork on the walls and iPod docking stations. Pricier rooms have terraces (some with city views) and better-equipped kitchenettes. Discounted rates can be found on the website.

🛏 Queens

Local NYC
HOSTEL $

(Map p86; ☑347-738-5251; www.thelocalny.com; 13-02 44th Ave, Long Island City; dm/d from $45/99; ❈☏; ☒E, M to Court Sq-23rd St) This hostel has clean and small, simply designed rooms, with comfy mattresses and plenty of light. Guests have access to a fully stocked kitchen and the airy cafe-bar is a fine place to meet other travelers, with good coffee by day, and wine and beer by night. Throughout the week, there's a regular lineup of events (movie nights, live music, pub quizzes). Friendly staff are helpful in highlighting some of NYC's lesser-known gems. Don't miss the view from the rooftop.

Boro Hotel
DESIGN HOTEL $

(Map p86; ☑718-433-1375; www.borohotel.com; 38-28 27th St, Long Island City; r from $179; P❈☏❈; ☒N/Q to 39th Ave) The Boro offers minimalist city luxe (Frette linens, plush robes, soaking tubs) for far less than you'd pay in Manhattan – with the benefit of skyline views from the floor-to-ceiling windows. The hyper-minimalist, wood-floor rooms have high ceilings; many have expansive balconies. Continental breakfast is better than average, with flaky croissants and Greek yogurt.

🍴 Eating

From inspired iterations of world cuisine to quintessentially local nibbles, New York City's dining scene is infinite, all-consuming and a proud testament to its kaleidoscope of citizens. An outstanding meal is always only a block away.

🍴 Financial District & Lower Manhattan

Arcade Bakery
BAKERY $

(Map p66; ☑212-227-7895; www.arcadebakery.com; 220 Church St, btwn Worth & Thomas Sts; pastries from $3, sandwiches $10, pizzas $10-14; ☺8am-4pm Mon-Fri; ☒1 to Franklin St) It's easy to miss this little treasure in the vaulted lobby of a 1920s office building, with a counter trading in beautiful, just-baked goods. Edibles include artful sandwiches and (between noon and 4pm) a small selection of puff-crust pizzas with combos like mushroom, caramelized onion and goat's cheese. Top of the lot is one of the city's finest almond croissants.

Brookfield Place
FOOD HALL, MARKET $$

(Map p66; ☑212-978-1698; www.brookfield placeny.com; 230 Vesey St, at West St; ☏; ☒E to World Trade Center; 2/3 to Park Pl; R/W to Cortlandt St; 4/5 to Fulton St; A/C to Chambers St) This polished, high-end office and retail complex offers two fabulous food halls. Francophile foodies should hit Le District (☑212-981-8588; www.ledistrict.com; market mains $12-30, Beaubourg dinner mains $25-37; ☺Beaubourg 7:30am-11pm Mon-Fri, from 8am Sat & Sun, other hours vary), a charming and polished marketplace with several stand-alone restaurants and counters selling everything from stinky cheese to steak *frites*. One floor above is Hudson Eats (☑212-417-2445; dishes from $7; ☺10am-9pm Mon-Sat, noon-7pm Sun), a fashionable enclave of upmarket fast bites, from sushi and tacos to salads and burgers.

Da Mikele
PIZZA $$

(Map p66; ☑212-925-8800; www.luzzosgroup. com/about-us-damikele; 275 Church St, btwn White & Franklin Sts; pizzas $17-21; ☺noon-11pm Sun-Thu, to midnight Fri & Sat; ☒1 to Franklin St; A/C/E, N/Q/R, J/Z, 6 to Canal St) An Italo-Tribeca hybrid where pressed tin and recycled wood meet retro Vespa, Da Mikele channels *la dolce vita* (the sweet life) with its weeknight *aperitivo* (5pm to 7pm), where your drink includes a complimentary spread of lip-smacking bar bites. However, pizzas are the specialty. We're talking light, beautifully charred revelations, simultaneously crisp and chewy, and good enough to make a Neapolitan weep.

★Locanda Verde
ITALIAN $$$

(Map p66; ☑212-925-3797; www.locandaverde nyc.com; 377 Greenwich St, at N Moore St; mains lunch $23-34, dinner $27-50; ☺7am-11pm Mon-Thu, to 11:30pm Fri, 8am-11:30pm Sat, to 11pm Sun; ☒A/C/E to Canal St; 1 to Franklin St) Step through the velvet curtains into a scene of loosened button-downs, black dresses and slick bar staff behind a long, crowded bar. This celebrated brasserie showcases modern, Italo-inspired fare like housemade rigatoni with rabbit *genovese* or grilled swordfish with eggplant caponata. Weekend brunch is no less creative: try scampi and grits or lemon ricotta pancakes with blueberries. Bookings recommended.

Bâtard MODERN AMERICAN **$$$**
(Map p66; ☎212-219-2777; www.batardtribeca.com; 239 W Broadway, btwn Walker & White Sts; 2/3/4 courses $59/79/95; ⏰5:30-10pm Mon-Sat; [S]1 to Franklin St; A/C/E to Canal St) Austrian chef Markus Glocker heads this warm, Michelin-starred hot spot, where a pared-back interior puts the focus squarely on the food. Glocker's dishes are beautifully balanced and textured, whether it's a crispy *branzino* (sea bass) with cherry tomatoes, basil and asparagus; risotto with rabbit sausage, broccoli spigarello and preserved lemon; or scallop crudo with avocado mousse, lime, radish and black sesame.

Tiny's & the Bar Upstairs MODERN AMERICAN **$$$**
(Map p66; ☎212-374-1135; www.tinysnyc.com; 135 W Broadway, btwn Thomas & Duane, Tribeca; mains $24-33; ⏰8am-midnight Mon-Fri, 9am-midnight Sat, 9am-10pm Sun; [S]1 to Franklin; A, C to Chambers) The rustic interiors of this 200-year-old Tribeca townhouse alone make it worth a visit – think antique wallpaper, salvaged wood paneling, original tin ceilings, pressed copper and marble bar tops, and handmade tiles – but you won't regret staying for a meal or a drink. The wood-burning fireplace in the dining room makes it extra cozy on those chilly NYC winter evenings.

🍴 SoHo & Chinatown

★Prince Street Pizza PIZZA **$**
(Map p70; ☎212-966-4100; 27 Prince St, btwn Mott & Elizabeth Sts, Nolita; pizza slices from $2.95; ⏰11:45am-11pm Sun-Thu, to 4am Fri & Sat; [S]N/R to Prince St; 6 to Spring St) It's a miracle the oven door hasn't come off its hinges at this classic slice joint, its brick walls hung with shots of B-list celebrity fans. Ditch the average cheese slice for the exceptional square varieties (the pepperoni will blow your socks off). The sauces, mozzarella and ricotta are made in-house and while the queues can get long, they usually move fast.

Two Hands CAFE **$**
(Map p70; www.twohandsnyc.com; 164 Mott St, btwn Broome & Grand Sts, Nolita; dishes $11-16; ⏰8am-5pm; 🥕; [S]B/D to Grand St; J/Z to Bowery) Named after the crime-com film starring Heath Ledger, Two Hands encapsulates Australia's relaxed, sophisticated cafe culture. Dream of Byron Bay over small-batch specialty coffee and out-of-the-box grub, such as sweet-corn fritters ($14) with spinach, avocado, sour cream, pickled beets and chili, or a healthier-than-thou acai bowl ($12).

Grey Dog AMERICAN **$**
(Map p70; ☎212-966-1060; www.thegreydog.com; 244 Mulberry St, Nolita; mains $11.50-17; ⏰7:30am-10pm Mon-Fri, 8:15am-10pm Sat & Sun; [S]F/M/D/B to Broadway-Lafayette) Whether you're looking to share a plate of cheese with your friends or indulge in a proper New York brunch, the Grey Dog won't disappoint. It does scrumptious takes on American classics that have full-on flavor without overdoing it. The order-at-the-counter system keeps this place bustling all day long. After the kitchen closes it stays open for desserts and cocktails.

Dominique Ansel Bakery BAKERY **$**
(Map p70; ☎212-219-2773; www.dominiqueansel.com; 189 Spring St, btwn Sullivan & Thompson Sts, SoHo; desserts $5.50-6.50; ⏰8am-7pm Mon-Sat, 9am-7pm Sun; [S]C/E to Spring St) One of NYC's best and most well-known patisseries has much more up its sleeve than just cronuts (its world-famous doughnut-croissant hybrid), including buttery *kouign-amman* (a Breton cake), gleaming berry tarts, and the Paris-New York, a chocolate/caramel/peanut twist on the traditional Paris-Brest. If you do insist on scoffing a cronut, head in by 7:30am on weekdays (earlier on weekends) to beat the 'sold out' sign.

Tacombi Fonda Nolita MEXICAN **$**
(Map p70; ☎917-727-0179; www.tacombi.com; 267 Elizabeth St, btwn E Houston & Prince Sts, Nolita; tacos $4-7; ⏰11am-midnight Sun-Wed, to 1am Thu-Sat; [S]F to 2nd Ave; 6 to Bleecker St) Festively strung lights, foldaway chairs and Mexican men flipping tacos in an old VW Kombi: if you can't make it to the Yucatan shore, here's your Plan B. Casual, convivial and ever-popular, Tacombi serves up fine, fresh tacos, including a *barbacoa* (roasted black Angus beef). Wash down the goodness with a pitcher of sangria and start plotting that south-of-the-border getaway.

Bánh Mì Saigon Bakery VIETNAMESE **$**
(Map p70; ☎212-941-1541; www.banhmisaigonnyc.com; 198 Grand St, btwn Mulberry & Mott Sts, Little Italy; sandwiches $7-8; ⏰7am-6pm; [S]N/Q/R, J/Z, 6 to Canal St) This no-frills storefront doles out some of the best banh mi in town – we're talking crisp, toasted baguettes generously stuffed with hot peppers, pickled carrots, daikon, cucumber, cilantro and your choice of meat. Top billing goes to the classic barbecue pork version. Tip: head in by 3pm

as the banh mi sometimes sell out, upon which the place closes early. Cash only.

★**Uncle Boons** THAI $$
(Map p70; ☏646-370-6650; www.uncleboons.com; 7 Spring St, btwn Elizabeth St & Bowery, Nolita; small plates $12-16, large plates $21-29; ⏰5:30-11pm Sun-Thu, to midnight Fri & Sat; ☏; ⓢJ/Z to Bowery; 6 to Spring St) Michelin-star Thai is served up in a fun, tongue-in-cheek combo of retro wood-paneled dining room with Thai film posters and old family snaps. Spanning the old and the new, zesty, tangy dishes include fantastically crunchy *mieng kum* (betel-leaf wrap with ginger, lime, toasted coconut, dried shrimp, peanuts and chili; $13), *kao pat puu* (crab fried rice; $26) and chicken and banana blossom salad ($15).

Butcher's Daughter VEGETARIAN $$
(Map p70; ☏212-219-3434; www.thebutchers daughter.com; 19 Kenmare St, at Elizabeth St, Nolita; salads & sandwiches $13-15, dinner mains $16-19; ⏰8am-10pm; ☑; ⓢJ to Bowery; 6 to Spring St) The butcher's daughter certainly has rebelled, peddling nothing but fresh herbivorous fare in her whitewashed cafe. While healthy it is, boring it's not: everything from the soaked organic muesli to the spicy kale Caesar salad with almond Parmesan or the dinnertime Butcher's burger (vegetable and black-bean patty with cashew cheddar cheese) is devilishly delish.

★**Chefs Club** FUSION $$$
(Map p70; ☏212-941-1100; www.chefsclub.com; 275 Mulberry St, Nolita; mains $19-68; ⏰5:30-10:30pm Mon-Sat) Chefs Club sounds more like a discount warehouse than the spectacular dining spot it really is: visiting chefs prepare a menu for anywhere from three weeks to three months, offering their finest selections in menus that span the flavors of the globe.

★**Dutch** MODERN AMERICAN $$$
(Map p70; ☏212-677-6200; www.thedutchnyc.com; 131 Sullivan St, at Prince St, SoHo; mains lunch $18-66, dinner $27-66; ⏰11:30am-10:30pm Mon-Thu, to 11pm Fri, 10am-11pm Sat, to 10:30pm Sun; ⓢC/E to Spring St; R/W to Prince St; 1 to Houston St) Whether perched at the bar or dining snugly in the back room, you can always expect smart, farm-to-table comfort grub at this see-and-be-seen stalwart. Flavors traverse the globe, from crispy fish tacos with wasabi and yuzu ($18) to veal schnitzel ($35). Reservations are recommended, especially for dinner and all day on weekends. Cocktails delight – try the Macadamia Maitai ($16).

★**Peking Duck House** CHINESE $$$
(Map p66; ☏212-227-1810; www.pekingduck housenyc.com; 28a Mott St, Chinatown; Peking duck per person $45; ⏰11:30am-10:30pm Sun-Thu, 11:45am-11pm Fri & Sat; ⓢJ/Z to Chambers St; 6 to Canal St) Offering arguably the best Peking duck in the region, the eponymous restaurant has a variety of set menus that include the house specialty. The space is fancier than some Chinatown spots, making it great to come with someone special. Do have the duck: perfectly crispy skin and moist meat make the slices ideal for a pancake, scallion strips and sauce.

✖ East Village & Lower East Side

Esperanto BRAZILIAN $$
(Map p70; ☏212-505-6559; www.esperantony. com; 145 Ave C, at E 9th St, East Village; mains $17-27; ⏰4-11pm Mon-Wed, 10am-11pm Thu & Sun, to 2am Fri & Sat; ⓢL to 1st Ave) Esperanto's vibrant green facade and large patio call to mind the glory days of Alphabet City, before the neighborhood began to trend toward gray and glass condos and sleek cocktail bars. Here you can sit outside all night sipping caipirinhas or enjoying strips of brilliantly bloody steak with chimichurri sauce. It's also a great place to get *feijoada* (traditional Brazilian meat stew).

Mamoun's MIDDLE EASTERN $
(Map p70; ☏646-870-5785; www.mamouns.com; 30 St Marks Pl, btwn Second & Third Aves, East Village; sandwiches $4-7, plates $7.50-12.73; ⏰11am-2am Mon-Wed, to 3am Thu, to 5am Fri & Sat, to 1am Sun; ⓢ6 to Astor Pl; L to 3rd Ave) This former grab-and-go outpost of the beloved NYC falafel chain has expanded its iconic St Marks storefront with more seating inside and out. Come late on a weekend to find a line of inebriated bar hoppers ending the night with a juicy shawarma covered in Mamoun's famous hot sauce.

Artichoke Basille's Pizza PIZZA $
(Map p70; ☏212-228-2004; www.artichoke pizza.com; 328 E 14th St, btwn First & Second Aves, East Village; artichoke slice $6; ⏰11am-5am; ⓢL to 1st Ave) This mini-chain run by two Italian guys from Staten Island is legendary among New Yorkers who like their pizza full of toppings. The signature pie is a rich, cheesy treat with artichokes and spinach; the plain Sicilian is thinner, with emphasis solely on the crisp crust and savory sauce. Lines usually form fast.

GET YOUR COFFEE HERE

Stumptown Coffee Roasters (Map p74; ☎855-711-3385; www.stumptowncoffee.com; 18 W 29th St, btwn Broadway & Fifth Ave; 🕒6am-8pm Mon-Fri, from 7am Sat & Sun; [S] N/R to 28th St) Hipster baristas serving Portland's favorite cup o' joe.

Bluestone Lane (Map p66; ☎718-374-6858; www.bluestonelaneny.com; 30 Broad St, Financial District, entrance on New St; 🕒7am-5:30pm Mon-Fri, 8am-5pm Sat & Sun; [S] J/Z to Broad St; 2/3, 4/5 to Wall St) Aussie brewing prowess in the shadow of Wall St.

Blue Bottle Coffee (Map p84; www.bluebottlecoffee.com; Store A, 76 N 4th St, at Wythe Ave, Williamsburg; coffees $3-5; 🕒6:30am-7pm Mon-Fri, 7am-7:30pm Sat & Sun; [S] L to Bedford Ave) Specialty coffee roasted on-site in Brooklyn.

La Colombe (Map p70; ☎212-625-1717; www.lacolombe.com; 270 Lafayette St, btwn Prince & Jersey Sts, Nolita; 🕒7:30am-6:30pm Mon-Fri, from 8:30am Sat & Sun; [S] N/R to Prince St; 6 to Spring St) Sucker-punch roasts for the downtown cognoscenti.

Little Collins (Map p74; ☎212-308-1969; http://littlecollinsnyc.com; 667 Lexington Ave, btwn 55th & 56th Sts, Midtown East; 🕒7am-5pm Mon-Fri, 8am-4pm Sat & Sun; [S] E, M to 53rd St; 4/5/6 to 59th St) A tribute to Melbourne coffee culture in Midtown East.

Kaffe 1668 South (Map p66; ☎212-693-3750; www.kaffe1668.com; 275 Greenwich St, btwn Warren & Murray Sts; 🕒6:30am-9pm Mon-Thu, to 8:30pm Fri, 7am-8pm Sat & Sun; 📶; [S] A/C, 1/2/3 to Chambers St) Caffeinated glory (and room to sit) in Tribeca.

Matcha Bar (Map p70; www.matchabarnyc.com; 256 W 15th St, btwn Seventh & Eighth Aves, Chelsea; drinks from $6; 🕒8am-7pm Mon-Fri, from 9am Sat & Sun; [S] A/C/E, L to 8th Ave-14th St) Skip the traditional espresso and treat yourself to a rich, flavorful matcha latte.

★Momofuku Noodle Bar — NOODLES $$

(Map p70; ☎212-777-7773; http://noodlebar-ny.momofuku.com; 171 First Ave, btwn E 10th & 11th Sts, East Village; mains $14-21; 🕒noon-11pm Sun-Thu, to 1am Fri & Sat; [S] L to 1st Ave; 6 to Astor Pl) With just 30 stools and a no-reservations policy, you'll have to wait to cram into this bustling phenomenon. Queue for the special – homemade ramen noodles in broth, served with poached egg and pork belly – or some interesting combos. The menu changes daily and includes buns (such as brisket and horseradish), snacks (smoked chicken wings) and desserts.

Ivan Ramen — JAPANESE $$

(Map p70; ☎646-678-3859; www.ivanramen.com; 25 Clinton St, btwn Stanton & East Houston Sts, East Village; mains $15-19; 🕒12:30-10pm Sun-Thu, to 11pm Fri & Sat) After creating two ramen hot spots in Tokyo, chef Ivan Orkin brought his concept to the Big Apple. And while the title of best ramen in NYC is hotly contested, this *izakaya*-style spot (a Japanese pub serving tapas-style food) would rank among the finalists. If ramen's not your thing, order some starters including steamed pork buns, fried chicken and miso-roasted cauliflower.

Upstate — SEAFOOD $$

(Map p70; ☎646-791-5400; www.upstatenyc.com; 95 First Ave, btwn E 5th & 6th Sts, East Village; mains $15-18; 🕒5-10:30pm; [S] F to 2nd Ave) Upstate serves outstanding seafood dishes and craft beers. The small, always-changing menu features the likes of beer-steamed mussels, seafood stew, scallops over mushroom risotto, softshell crab and wondrous oyster selections. There's no freezer – seafood comes from the market daily, so you know you'll be getting only the freshest ingredients. Lines can be long, so go early.

Prune — AMERICAN $$$

(Map p70; ☎212-677-6221; www.prunerestaurant.com; 54 E 1st St, btwn First & Second Aves, East Village; dinner $25-36, mains brunch $14-24; 🕒5:30-11pm, also 10am-3:30pm Sat & Sun; [S] F to 2nd Ave) Expect lines around the block on the weekend, when the hungover show up to cure their ills with Prune's brunches and excellent Bloody Marys (in 11 varieties). The small room is always busy as diners pour in for grilled trout with mint and almond salsa, seared duck breast and rich sweetbreads. Reservations available for dinner only.

Fat Radish — MODERN BRITISH $$$

(Map p70; ☎212-300-4053; www.thefatradishnyc.com; 17 Orchard St, btwn Hester & Canal Sts, Lower East Side; mains $20-29; 🕒5:30-10pm Sun-Tue, to midnight Wed-Sat, also 11am-3:30pm Sat & Sun; [S] F to East Broadway; B/D to Grand St) The young and fashionable pack into this dimly lit dining room with exposed white brick and industrial touches. There's a loud buzz and people checking each other out, but the mains – typical of the local, seasonal, haute-pub-food fad – are worth your attention. Start with big briny oysters before moving on to heritage pork chops with glazed squash or brook trout with seaweed aioli.

🍴 West Village, Chelsea & Meatpacking District

★Chelsea Market MARKET $

(Map p70; www.chelseamarket.com; 75 Ninth Ave, btwn 15th & 16th Sts, Chelsea; ⏰7am-2am Mon-Sat, 8am-10pm Sun; [S]A/C/E, L to 8th Ave-14th St) In a shining example of redevelopment and preservation, the Chelsea Market has taken a factory formerly owned by cookie giant Nabisco (creator of Oreo) and turned it into an 800ft-long shopping concourse that caters to foodies. Taking the place of the old factory ovens that churned out massive numbers of biscuits are eclectic eateries that fill the renovated hallways of this food haven.

Gansevoort Market MARKET $

(Map p70; www.gansmarket.com; 353 W 14th St, at Ninth Ave, Meatpacking District; mains $5-20; ⏰7am-9pm; [S]A/C/E, L to 8th Ave-14th St) Inside a brick building in the heart of the Meatpacking District, this sprawling market is the latest and greatest food emporium to land in NYC. A raw, industrial space lit by skylights, it features several dozen gourmet vendors slinging tapas, arepas, tacos, pizzas, meat pies, ice cream, pastries and more.

Red Bamboo VEGAN $

(Map p70; ☎212-260-7049; www.redbamboo-nyc.com; 140 W 4th St, btwn Sixth Ave & MacDougal St; mains $8-14; ⏰12:30-11pm Mon-Thu, to 11:30pm Fri, noon-11:30pm Sat, to 11pm Sun; [S]A/C/E, B/D/F/M to W 4th St-Washington Sq) Flaky, hot bites of popcorn shrimp, gooey chicken Parmesan, chocolate cake so rich you can barely finish – Red Bamboo offers all of that and more soul and Asian food options. The catch? Everything on its menu is vegan (some dishes do offer the option of real cheese). This is a must try for vegans, vegetarians or anyone looking to try something new.

★Barbuto MODERN ITALIAN $$

(Map p70; ☎212-924-9700; www.barbutonyc.com; 775 Washington St, at W 12th St, West Village; mains $24-33; ⏰lunch noon-3:30pm, dinner 5:30-11pm Mon-Thu, to midnight Fri & Sat, to 10pm Sun; [S]A/C/E, L to 8th Ave-14th St; 1 to Christopher St-Sheridan Sq) Occupying a cavernous garage space with sweeping see-through doors that roll up and into the ceiling during the warmer months, Barbuto slaps together a delightful assortment of nouveau Italian dishes, such as duck breast with plum and crème fraîche, and calamari drizzled with squid ink and chili aioli.

Babu Ji INDIAN $$

(Map p70; ☎212-951-1082; www.babujinyc.com; 22 E 13th St, btwn University Pl & Fifth Ave, West Village; mains $18-28; ⏰dinner 5-10:30pm Sun-Thu, to 11:30pm Fri & Sat, brunch 11:30am-3pm Sat & Sun; [S]4/5/6, N/Q/R/W, L to 14th St-Union Sq) A playful spirit marks this excellent Australian-run Indian restaurant, which recently relocated to Union Sq. You can assemble a meal from street food–style dishes such as *papadi chaat* (chickpeas, pomegranate and yogurt chutney) and potato croquettes stuffed with lobster, or feast on heartier dishes like tandoori lamb chops or scallop coconut curry. A $62 tasting menu is also on offer. It all happens beneath the benevolent gaze of *babujis* (respected elders), whose photos adorn the walls.

Nix VEGETARIAN $$

(Map p70; ☎212-498-9393; www.nixny.com; 72 University Pl, btwn 10th & 11th Sts, West Village; mains $20-28; ⏰11:30am-2:30pm & 5:30-11pm Mon-Thu, from 5pm Fri, 10:30am-2:30pm & 5-11pm Sat, 10:30am-2:30pm & 5-10:30pm Sun; [S]4/5/6, N/Q/R/W, L to 14th St-Union Sq) At this understated Michelin-starred eatery, head chefs Nicolas Farias and John Fraser transform vegetables into high art in beautifully executed dishes that delight the senses. Start off with tandoor bread and creative dips like spiced eggplant with pine nuts before moving on to richly complex plates of cauliflower tempura with steamed buns, or spicy tofu with chanterelle mushrooms, kale and Szechuan pepper.

★RedFarm FUSION $$$

(Map p70; ☎212-792-9700; www.redfarmnyc.com; 529 Hudson St, btwn W 10th & Charles Sts, West Village; mains $19-57, dumplings $14-20; ⏰5-11:45pm Mon-Sat, to 11pm Sun, plus 11am-2:30pm Sat & Sun; [S]A/C/E, B/D/F/M to W 4th St-Washington Sq; 1 to Christopher St-Sheridan Sq) RedFarm transforms Chinese cooking into pure, delectable artistry at this small, buzzing space on Hudson St. Fresh crab and eggplant bruschetta, juicy rib steak (marinated overnight in papaya, ginger and soy) and pastrami egg rolls are among the many creative dishes that brilliantly blend cuisines. Other hits include spicy crispy beef, pan-fried lamb dumplings and grilled jumbo-shrimp red curry.

★**Foragers Table** MODERN AMERICAN $$$
(Map p74; ☎212-243-8888; www.foragersmarket.com/restaurant; 300 W 22nd St, at Eighth Ave, Chelsea; mains $22-39; ⏰dinner 5:30-10pm Mon-Sat, brunch 9am-3pm Sat & Sun; ✍; [S]1, C/E to 23rd St) Owners of this outstanding restaurant run a 28-acre farm in the Hudson Valley, from which much of their seasonal menu is sourced. It changes frequently, but recent temptations include Long Island duck breast with roasted acorn squash, apples, chanterelle mushrooms and figs, grilled skate with red quinoa, creamed kale and *cippolini* onion and deviled farm eggs with Dijon mustard.

★**Jeffrey's Grocery** MODERN AMERICAN $$$
(Map p70; ☎646-398-7630; www.jeffreysgrocery.com; 172 Waverly Pl, at Christopher St, West Village; mains $22-35; ⏰8am-11pm Mon-Wed, to 1am Thu-Fri, 9:30am-1am Sat, to 11pm Sun; [S]1 to Christopher St-Sheridan Sq) This West Village classic is a lively eating and drinking spot that hits all the right notes. Seafood is the focus: there's an oyster bar and beautifully executed selections, such as mussels with crème fraîche, tuna steak tartine, and sharing platters. Meat dishes include hanger steak with roasted veggies in a *romesco* (nut and red pepper) sauce.

★**Blue Hill** AMERICAN $$$
(Map p70; ☎212-539-1776; www.bluehillfarm.com; 75 Washington Pl, btwn Sixth Ave & Washington Sq W, West Village; prix-fixe menu $95-108; ⏰5-11pm Mon-Sat, to 10pm Sun; [S]A/C/E, B/D/F/M to W 4th St-Washington Sq) A place for Slow Food junkies with deep pockets, Blue Hill was an early crusader in the 'Local is Better' movement. Chef Dan Barber, who hails from a farm family in the Berkshires, MA, uses harvests from that land and from farms in upstate New York to create his widely praised fare.

🍴 Union Square, Flatiron District & Gramercy

Tacombi Café El Presidente MEXICAN $
(Map p74; ☎212-242-3491; www.tacombi.com; 30 W 24th St, btwn Fifth & Sixth Aves, Flatiron District; tacos $4-7, quesadillas $7-8; ⏰11am-midnight Mon-Sat, to 10:30pm Sun; [S]F/M, R/W to 23rd St) Channeling the cafes of Mexico City, Tacombi covers numerous bases, from juice and liquor bar to taco joint. Score a table, order a margarita and hop your way around a menu of Mexican street-food deliciousness. Top choices include *esquites* (grilled corn with *cotija* cheese and chipotle mayonnaise, served in a paper cup) and succulent *carnitas michoacan* (beer-marinated pork) tacos.

Mad Sq Eats MARKET $
(Map p74; www.madisonsquarepark.org/mad-sq-food/mad-sq-eats; General Worth Sq, Flatiron District; ⏰spring & fall 11am-9pm; [S]R/W, F/M, 6 to 23rd St) A biannual, pop-up culinary market with stalls run by some of the city's coolest eateries and hottest chefs. Bites span a range of street foods, from arancini and empanadas to lobster rolls and ice-cream sandwiches. See the website for dates and vendors.

Shake Shack BURGERS $
(Map p74; ☎646-889-6600; www.shakeshack.com; Madison Square Park, cnr E 23rd St & Madison Ave, Flatiron District; burgers $4.20-9.50; ⏰7:30am-11pm Mon-Fri, from 8:30am Sat & Sun; [S]R/W, F/M, 6 to 23rd St) The flagship of chef Danny Meyer's gourmet burger chain, Shake Shack whips up hyper-fresh burgers, hand-cut fries and a rotating line-up of frozen custards. Veg-heads can dip into the crisp portobello burger. Lines are long – but worth it – and you can digest the filling meal while people-watching at tables and benches in the park.

Eataly FOOD HALL $$
(Map p74; ☎212-229-2560; www.eataly.com; 200 Fifth Ave, at W 23rd St, Flatiron District; ⏰7am-11pm; ✍; [S]R/W, F/M, 6 to 23rd St) Mario Batali's sleek, sprawling temple to Italian gastronomy is a veritable wonderland. Feast on everything from vibrant *crudo* (raw fish) and *fritto misto* (tempura-style vegetables) to steamy pasta and pizza at the emporium's string of sit-down eateries. Alternatively, guzzle espresso at the bar and scour the countless counters and shelves for a DIY picnic hamper *nonna* would approve of.

Boqueria Flatiron TAPAS $$
(Map p74; ☎212-255-4160; www.boquerianyc.com; 53 W 19th St, btwn Fifth & Sixth Aves, Flatiron District; tapas $6-19; ⏰11am-10:30pm Sun-Thu, to 11:30pm Fri & Sat; 📶; [S]1 to 18th St; F/M, R/W to 23rd St) A holy union between Spanish-style tapas and market-fresh fare, Boqueria woos the after-work crowd with a brilliant lineup of small plates and larger *raciones*. Lick lips and fingers over the likes of garlicky shrimp with brandy and *guindilla* pepper, or bacon-wrapped dates stuffed with almonds and Valdeón blue cheese. A smooth selection of Spanish wines tops it all off. *¡Buen provecho!*

★**Maialino** ITALIAN $$$
(Map p74; ☎212-777-2410; www.maialinonyc.com; Gramercy Park Hotel, 2 Lexington Ave, at 21st St; mains lunch $24-36, dinner $24-58; ⏰7:30-10am,

OLD-SCHOOL EATS

Barney Greengrass (Map p78; ☎212-724-4707; www.barneygreengrass.com; 541 Amsterdam Ave, at 86th St; mains $12-23.50; ⏲8:30am-4pm Tue-Fri, to 5pm Sat & Sun; [S]1 to 86th St) Perfect plates of smoked salmon and sturgeon for over 100 years in the Upper West Side.

Katz's Deli (Map p70; ☎212-254-2246; www.katzsdelicatessen.com; 205 E Houston St, at Ludlow St, Lower East Side; sandwiches $15-22; ⏲8am-10:45pm Mon-Wed & Sun, to 2:45am Thu, from 8am Fri, 24hr Sat; [S]F to 2nd Ave) Famous Jewish eatery where Meg Ryan famously faked her orgasm in the 1989 movie *When Harry Met Sally.*

Russ & Daughters (Map p70; ☎212-475-4800; www.russanddaughters.com; 179 E Houston St, btwn Orchard & Allen Sts; ⏲8am-6pm Fri-Wed, to 7pm Thu; [S]F to 2nd Ave) A celebrated Jewish deli in the Lower East Side.

Zabar's (Map p78; ☎212-787-2000; www.zabars.com; 2245 Broadway, at W 80th St; ⏲8am-7:30pm Mon-Fri, to 8pm Sat, 9am-6pm Sun; [S]1 to 79th St) Upper West Side store selling gourmet, kosher foods since the 1930s.

Margon (Map p74; ☎212-354-5013; 136 W 46th St, btwn Sixth & Seventh Aves; sandwiches $10-12, mains from $11; ⏲6am-5pm Mon-Fri, from 7am Sat; [S]B/D/F/M to 47th-50th Sts-Rockefeller Center) Unfussy, unchanged Cuban lunch counter in Midtown. The legendary *cubano* sandwich is obscenely good.

noon-2pm & 5:30-10pm Mon-Wed, to 10:30pm Thu & Fri, 10am-2:30pm & 5:30-10:30pm Sat, to 10pm Sat; [S]6, R/W to 23rd St) Fans reserve tables up to four weeks in advance at this Danny Meyer classic, but the best seats in the house are at the walk-in bar, with sociable, knowledgeable staffers. Wherever you're plonked, take your taste buds on a Roman holiday. Maialino's lip-smacking, rustic Italian fare is created using produce from the nearby Union Square Greenmarket.

★Eleven Madison Park MODERN AMERICAN $$$
(Map p74; ☎212-889-0905; www.elevenmadisonpark.com; 11 Madison Ave, btwn 24th & 25th Sts, Flatiron District; tasting menu $315; ⏲5:30-10pm Mon-Wed, to 10:30pm Thu-Sun, also noon-1pm Fri-Sun; [S]R/W, 6 to 23rd St) Fine-dining Eleven Madison Park came in at number one in the 2017 San Pellegrino World's 50 Best Restaurants list. Frankly, we're not surprised: this revamped poster child of modern, sustainable American cooking is also one of only six NYC restaurants sporting three Michelin stars.

★Gramercy Tavern MODERN AMERICAN $$$
(Map p74; ☎212-477-0777; www.gramercytavern.com; 42 E 20th St, btwn Broadway & Park Ave S, Flatiron District; tavern mains $29-36, dining room 3-course menu $129, tasting menus $159-179; ⏲tavern 11:30am-11pm Sun-Thu, to midnight Fri & Sat, dining room 11:30am-2pm & 5-9:45pm Sun-Thu, to 10:30pm Fri & Sat; 📶✍; [S]R/W, 6 to 23rd St) 🌿 Seasonal, local ingredients drive this perennial favorite, a vibrant, country-chic institution aglow with copper sconces, murals and dramatic floral arrangements. Choose from two spaces: the walk-in-only tavern and its à la carte menu, or the swankier dining room and its fancier prix-fixe and degustation feasts. Tavern highlights include a showstopping duck meatloaf with mushrooms, chestnuts and brussels sprouts.

🍴 Midtown

★Totto Ramen JAPANESE $
(Map p74; ☎212-582-0052; www.tottoramen.com; 366 W 52nd St, btwn Eighth & Ninth Aves; ramen $11-18; ⏲noon-4:30pm & 5:30pm-midnight Mon-Sat, 4-11pm Sun; [S]C/E to 50th St) There might be another two branches in Midtown, but purists know that neither beats the tiny 20-seat original. Write your name and number of guests on the clipboard and wait your turn. Your reward: extraordinary ramen. Go for the pork, which sings in dishes like miso ramen (with fermented soybean paste, egg, scallion, bean sprouts, onion and homemade chili paste).

Ess-a-Bagel DELI $
(Map p74; ☎212-980-1010; www.ess-a-bagel.com; 831 Third Ave, at 51st St, Midtown East; bagel sandwiches $3.30-5.25; ⏲6am-9pm Mon-Fri, to 5pm Sat & Sun; [S]6 to 51st St; E/M to Lexington Ave-53rd St) Fresh, toothsome bagels have made this kosher deli a veritable institution. Tell the bagel monger your preference of bagel, then choose from a sprawling counter of cream cheeses and other sandwich fillings. For a classic, opt for scallion cream cheese with lox (salmon), capers, tomato and red onion ($14.25). If the

weather's fine, turn right into 51st St and lunch in pretty Greenacre Park.

★ Smith

AMERICAN $$

(Map p74; 212-644-2700; http://thesmithres taurant.com; 956 Second Ave, at 51st St, Midtown East; mains $18-33; ⊙7:30am-midnight Mon-Thu, to 1am Fri, 9am-1am Sat, to midnight Sun; 🔊; S6 to 51st St) This chic, bustling brasserie has an industrial-chic interior, sociable bar and well-executed grub. Much of the food is made from scratch, the seasonal menus a mix of nostalgic American and Italian inspiration (we're talking hot potato chips with blue cheese fondue, chicken pot pie with cheddar chive biscuit, and Sicilian baked eggs with artichokes, spinach and spicy tomato sauce).

Don Antonio

PIZZA $$

(Map p74; 646-719-1043; www.donantonio pizza.com; 309 W 50th St, btwn Eighth & Ninth Aves, Midtown West; pizzas $10-26; ⊙11:30am-3:30pm & 4:30-11pm Mon-Thu, 11:30am-11:30pm Fri & Sat, to 10:30pm Sun; SC/E, 1 to 50th St) A top spot for authentic Neapolitan-style pizza, this hopping eatery is the offspring of Naples' historic pizzeria Starita. While New York concessions include a cocktail-shaking, solo-diner-friendly bar, the pies here are pure Napoli: chewy, thin-crust wonders with charred edges and sweet, ripe *sugo* (tomato sauce). All pizzas can be made using a wholewheat base, and there's a plethora of gluten-free pizzas too.

Dhaba

INDIAN $$

(Map p74; 212-679-1284; www.dhabanyc.com; 108 Lexington Ave, btwn 27th & 28th Sts; mains $13-27; ⊙noon-midnight Mon-Thu, to 1am Fri & Sat, to 11pm Sun; 🍴; S6 to 28th St) Murray Hill (aka Curry Hill) has no shortage of subcontinental bites, but funky Dhaba packs one serious flavor punch. Mouthwatering standouts include the crunchy, tangy *lasoni gobi* (fried cauliflower with tomato and spices) and the insanely flavorful *murgh bharta* (minced chicken cooked with smoked eggplant).

Danji

KOREAN $$

(Map p74; 212-586-2880; www.danjinyc.com; 346 W 52nd St, btwn Eighth & Ninth Aves, Midtown West; dishes $13-42; ⊙noon-2:30pm & 5pm-midnight Mon-Thu, to 1am Fri & Sat, 11am-3pm & 5pm-1am Sat, 11am-3pm & 4-11pm Sun; SC/E to 50th St) Young gun Hooni Kim woos palates with his Korean creations, served in a snug, slinky, whitewashed space. The simpler lunch menu includes *bibimbap* (a traditional Korean rice dish), while the more expansive dinner list offers small, medium

and large plates. Thankfully, both lunch and dinner menus offer Danji's cult-status *bulgogi* beef sliders, made with heavenly, butter-grilled buns. Head in early or queue.

★ O-ya

SUSHI $$$

(Map p74; 212-204-0200; https://o-ya.restau rant/o-ya-nyc; 120 E 28th St; nigiri $16-38; ⊙5:30-10pm Mon-Sat, closed Sun; S4/6 to 28th St) With the cheapest nigiri pairs at close to $20 each, this is not a spot you'll come to every day. But if you're looking for a special night out and sushi's in the game plan, come here for exquisite flavors, fish so tender it melts like butter on the tongue, and preparations so artful you almost apologize for eating them.

★ ViceVersa

ITALIAN $$$

(Map p74; 212-399-9291; www.viceversanyc.com; 325 W 51st St, btwn Eighth & Ninth Aves; 2-course lunch $26, dinner mains $25-38; ⊙noon-2:30pm & 4:30-11pm Mon-Fri, 4:30-11pm Sat, 11:30am-3pm & 4:30-10pm Sun; SC/E to 50th St) ViceVersa is quintessential Italian: suave and sophisticated, affable and scrumptious. The menu features refined, cross-regional dishes like arancini with black truffle and fontina cheese. For a celebrated classic, order the *casoncelli alla bergamasca* (ravioli-like pasta filled with minced veal, raisins and amaretto cookies and seasoned with sage, butter, pancetta and Grana Padano), a nod to chef Stefano Terzi's Lombard heritage.

★ Modern

FRENCH $$$

(Map p74; 212-333-1220; www.themodern nyc.com; 9 W 53rd St, btwn Fifth & Sixth Aves; 3-/6-course lunch $138/178, 4-/8-course dinner $168/228; ⊙restaurant noon-2pm & 5-10pm Mon-Wed, noon-2pm & 5-10:30pm Thu-Sat, bar 11:30am-10pm Mon-Wed, to 10:30pm Thu-Sat, to 3pm Sun; SE, M to 5th Ave-53rd St) Shining two (Michelin) stars bright, the Modern delivers confident creations like foie gras tart. Fans of *Sex and the City* may know that it was here that Carrie announced her impending marriage to Mr Big. Cocktails are as tasty as the meals.(Hint: If you're on a writer's wage, you can opt for cheaper grub in the adjacent Bar Room.)

★ Le Bernardin

SEAFOOD $$$

(Map p74; 212-554-1515; www.le-bernardin.com; 155 W 51st St, btwn Sixth & Seventh Aves; prix-fixe lunch/dinner $90/160, tasting menus $170-225; ⊙noon-2:30pm & 5:15-10:30pm Mon-Thu, to 11pm Fri, 5:15-11pm Sat; S1 to 50th St; B/D, E to 7th Ave) The interiors may have been subtly sexed-up for a 'younger clientele' (the stunning storm-themed triptych is by Brooklyn artist Ran Ortner), but triple-Michelin-starred Le

Bernardin remains a luxe, fine-dining holy grail. At the helm is French-born celebrity chef Éric Ripert, whose deceptively simple-looking seafood often borders on the transcendental. Life is short, and you only live (er, eat!) once.

Cannibal Beer & Butcher AMERICAN $$$

(Map p74; ☎212-686-5480; www.cannibalnyc.com; 113 E 29th St, btwn Park Ave S & Lexington Ave, Midtown East; small plates $15-18, mains $32-85; ⏲11am-10pm; [S]6 to 28th St) The stuff of red-blooded dreams, this hip, hybrid eatery/bar/butcher peddles over 200 craft beers and a sharp, seasonal menu of mostly carnivorous sharing plates. Graze on competent, housemade charcuterie and sausages ($14) and creative pâtés (think chicken liver with beer, shallot jam and cocoa nibs), all tempered by beautifully textured sides like smoky kale salad with walnuts, Armenian string cheese and bacon.

🍴 Upper West Side & Central Park

Cafe Lalo DESSERTS $

(Map p78; ☎212-496-6031; www.cafelalo.com; 201 W 83rd St, btwn Amsterdam & Columbus Ave; desserts $5-10; ⏲8am-1am Mon-Thu, to 4am Fri, 9am-4am Sat, to 2am Sun; [S]1 to 79th St; B, C to 81st St-Museum of Natural History) The vintage French posters and marble-topped tables make this longtime Upper West Side date spot feel like a Parisian cafe. But really – you're here for the mind-blowing array of desserts: choose (if you can) from 27 different cakes, 23 flavors of cheesecake, nine types of pie, a dozen kinds of fruit tart, cookies, pastries, zabaglione, chocolate mousse and more.

Épicerie Boulud DELI, FRENCH $

(Map p78; ☎212-595-9606; www.epicerieboulud.com; 1900 Broadway, at W 64th St; sandwiches $8-14.50; ⏲7am-10pm Mon, to 11pm Tue-Sat, 8am-10pm Sun; 🌿; [S]1 to 66th St-Lincoln Center) A deli from star chef Daniel Boulud is no ordinary deli. Forget ham on rye – here you can order suckling pig confit, *jambon de Paris* and Gruyère on pressed ciabatta, or paprika-spiced flank steak with caramelized onions and three-grain mustard. Other options at this fast-gourmet spot include salads, soups, roast vegetables, pastry, gelato, coffee…and in the evening, oysters and wine.

Peacefood Cafe VEGAN $

(Map p78; ☎212-362-2266; www.peacefoodcafe.com; 460 Amsterdam Ave, at 82nd St; mains $11-18; ⏲10am-10pm; 🌿; [S]1 to 79th St) This bright and airy vegan haven dishes up a popular fried seitan panini (served on homemade focaccia and topped with cashew cheese, arugula, tomatoes and pesto), as well as pizzas, roasted-vegetable plates and an excellent quinoa salad. There are daily raw specials, energy-fueling juices and rich desserts. Healthy and good – for you, the animals and the environment.

Jacob's Pickles AMERICAN $$

(Map p78; ☎212-470-5566; www.jacobspickles.com; 509 Amsterdam Ave, btwn 84th & 85th Sts; mains $16-24; ⏲10am-12:30am Mon & Tue, to 1:30am Wed, to 2am Thu & Fri, 9am-2am Sat, to 12:30am Sun; [S]1 to 86th St) Jacob's elevates the humble pickle to exalted status at this inviting and warmly lit eatery. Aside from briny cukes and other preserves, you'll find heaping portions of upscale comfort food, such as catfish tacos, wine-braised turkey-leg dinner, and mushroom mac 'n' cheese. The biscuits are top-notch.

Kefi GREEK $$

(Map p78; ☎212-873-0200; www.michaelpsilakis.com/kefi; 505 Columbus Ave, btwn 84th & 85th Sts; small sharing plates $9-19, mains $20-30; ⏲noon-3pm & 5-10pm Mon-Thu, noon-3pm & 5-11pm Fri, noon-11pm Sat, to 10pm Sun; 🌿👪; [S]B, C to 86th St) This homey, whitewashed eatery run by chef Michael Psilakis channels a sleek taverna vibe while dispensing excellent rustic Greek dishes. Expect favorites such as spicy lamb sausage, sheep-milk dumplings and creamy sun-dried-tomato hummus. You can also assemble a feast of meze (sharing plates), including crispy calamari, meatballs and tzatziki, and grilled octopus and bean salad.

Burke & Wills MODERN AUSTRALIAN $$$

(Map p78; ☎646-823-9251; www.burkeandwillsny.com; 226 W 79th St, btwn Broadway & Amsterdam Ave; mains $19-32; ⏲dinner 5:30-11:30pm Mon-Sun, brunch 11am-3pm Sat & Sun; [S]1 to 79th St) This ruggedly attractive bistro and bar brings a touch of the outback to the Upper West Side. The menu leans toward Modern Australian pub grub: juicy kangaroo burgers with triple-fried chips, rack of Australian lamb, braised pork belly with bacon and duck confit, and seafood platters with oysters, clams and crab claws.

🍴 Upper East Side

★Two Boots PIZZA $

(Map p78; ☎212-734-0317; www.twoboots.com; 1617 Second Ave, cnr E 84th St; pizza slices $3.50-4.25; ⏲11:30am-11pm Sun-Tue, to midnight Wed, to

2am Thu, to 4am Fri & Sat; ✎; [S] Q, 4/5/6 to 86th St) With the two 'boots' of Italy and Louisiana as inspiration, this quirky, pioneering NYC chain has over 40 original, eclectic pizza flavors in all (with plenty of vegetarian and vegan options) – all named after comedians, scientists, musicians, local sports teams and even fictional characters. Our favorite? The Tony Clifton (shiitake mushrooms, Vidalia onions, mozzarella and red-pepper pesto).

★Tanoshi SUSHI **$$$**
(Map p78; ☎917-265-8254; www.tanoshisushinyc.com; 1372 York Ave, btwn E 73rd & 74th Sts; chef's sushi selection $95-100; 🕐seatings 6pm, 7:30pm & 9pm Tue-Sat; [S]Q to 72nd St) It's not easy to snag one of the 20 stools at Tanoshi, a wildly popular, pocket-sized sushi spot. The setting may be humble, but the flavors are simply magnificent. Only sushi is on offer and only *omakase* (chef's selection) – which might include Hokkaido scallops, king salmon or mouthwatering *uni* (sea urchin). BYO beer, sake or whatnot. Reserve well in advance.

Boqueria SPANISH **$$$**
(Map p78; ☎212-343-2227; www.boquerianyc.com; 1460 Second Ave, btwn E 76th & 77th Sts; tapas $6-19, paella for 2 $48-69; 🕐noon-10:30pm Mon-Thu, to 11:30pm Fri, 10:30am-11:30pm Sat, to 10:30pm Sun; ✎; [S] 6 to 77th St; Q to 72nd St) This lively, much-loved tapas place brings a bit of downtown cool to the Upper East Side, with nicely spiced *patatas bravas* (fried potatoes in tomato sauce), tender slices of *jamon ibérico* (cured ham) and rich *pulpo a la plancha* (grilled octopus). Head chef Marc Vidal also creates an exquisite seafood paella. Wash it down with a pitcher of excellent sangria.

🍴 Harlem & Upper Manhattan

Charles' Pan-Fried Chicken AMERICAN **$**
(Map p62; ☎212-281-1800; 2461 Frederick Douglass Blvd, btwn 151st & 152nd Sts, Harlem; fried chicken from $12; 🕐11am-10:30pm Mon-Sat, noon-9:30pm Sun; [S]B/D to 155th St) It's a hole-in-the-wall, but charismatic Charles Gabriel makes some of the best fried chicken in the city. Crisp and beautifully seasoned, it's served with sides including collard greens, yams, mac 'n' cheese and corn bread. Don't expect designer touches: just unadorned tables, food on trays, and proof that a book (or chicken joint) must never be judged by its cover.

Maison Harlem FRENCH **$$**
(Map p78; ☎212-222-9224; www.maisonharlem.com; 341 St Nicholas Ave, at 127th St, Harlem; mains $14-32; 🕐11am-midnight Mon-Thu, to 1am Fri, 10am-midnight Sat & Sun; 📶; [S] A/C, B/D to 125th St) Run by two French *amis*, this swinging little bar-bistro is like a second home for locals, who drop in at all hours to nibble on French toast, slurp onion soup, or loosen their belts over slow-cooked duck-leg confit. For the full effervescent effect, head here on weekends when DJs and wine-fueled merriment may just lead to dancing.

Dinosaur Bar-B-Que BARBECUE **$$**
(Map p62; ☎212-694-1777; www.dinosaurbarbque.com; 700 W 125th St, at Twelfth Ave, Harlem; mains $12-26; 🕐11:30am-11pm Mon-Thu, to midnight Fri & Sat, noon-10pm Sun; [S]1 to 125th St) Jocks, hipsters, moms and pops: everyone dives into this honky-tonk rib bar for a rockin' feed. Get messy with dry-rubbed, slow-pit-smoked ribs, slabs of juicy steak and succulent burgers, or watch your waistline with the lightly seasoned grilled-chicken options. The (very) few vegetarian choices include a fantastic version of Creole-spiced deviled eggs.

★Red Rooster MODERN AMERICAN **$$$**
(Map p78; ☎212-792-9001; www.redroosterharlem.com; 310 Malcolm X Blvd, btwn W 125th & 126th Sts, Harlem; mains lunch $18-24, dinner $22-38; 🕐11:30am-10:30pm Mon-Thu, to 11:30pm Fri, 10am-11:30pm Sat, to 10pm Sun; [S]2/3 to 125th St) Transatlantic superchef Marcus Samuelsson laces upscale comfort food with a world of flavors at his effortlessly cool, vibrant brasserie. Like the work of the New York–based contemporary artists displayed on the walls, dishes are up to date: mac 'n' cheese joins forces with lobster, blackened catfish pairs with pickled mango, and spectacular Swedish meatballs salute Samuelsson's home country.

🍴 Brooklyn

Brooklyn's culinary identity, hard to pin down and argued over with the passion of Talmudic scholars, is nevertheless assured. Why else would Manhattanites trek out to the far reaches of Kings County for a meal these days? Credentialed, ambitious chefs have created their own subspecies of restaurant here – small, retro, bespoke and locavore. Williamsburg and Greenpoint have perhaps the greatest variety, followed by the nexus of Carroll Gardens, Cobble Hill and Park Slope; honorable mention goes to a few gems in the Fort Greene/Clinton Hill area. Concentrations of ethnic foodie wonderlands extend from Sunset Park to Brighton Beach.

★ Smorgasburg MARKET $
(www.smorgasburg.com; ⏰Williamsburg 11am-6pm Sat, Prospect Park 11am-4pm Sun Apr-Oct) The largest foodie event in Brooklyn brings together more than 100 vendors selling an incredible array of goodness: Italian street snacks, duck confit, Indian flatbread tacos, roasted-mushroom burgers, vegan Ethiopian comfort food, sea-salt caramel ice cream, passion-fruit doughnuts, craft beer and much more. Smorgasburg locations tend to change from season to season, so check the website for the latest.

★ Dough BAKERY $
(Map p82; ☎347-533-7544; www.doughdoughnuts.com; 448 Lafayette Ave, cnr Franklin Ave, Bedford-Stuyvesant; doughnuts around $3; ⏰6am-9pm; 📶; [S]G to Classon Ave) Situated on the border of Clinton Hill and Bed-Stuy, this tiny, out-of-the-way spot is a bit of a trek, but worth it if you're a pastry fan. Puffy raised doughnuts are dipped in a changing array of glazes, including pistachio, blood orange and hibiscus. Doughnut divinity for the tongue.

★ Ample Hills Creamery ICE CREAM $
(Map p82; ☎347-725-4061; www.amplehills.com; 305 Nevins St, at Union St, Gowanus; cones $4-7; ⏰noon-11pm Sun-Thu, to midnight Fri & Sat, shorter hours in winter; [S]R to Union St; F, G to Carroll St) Ice-cream lovers: we found the mother ship. All of Ample Hills' magnificently creative flavors – snap mallow pop (a deconstructed Rice Krispies treat), Mexican hot chocolate, salted crack caramel – are whipped up right here in the creamery's Gowanus factory. Grab a cone and watch the goods being made through the kitchen's picture window.

Nathan's Famous HOT DOGS $
(Map p62; ☎718-333-2202; www.nathansfamous.com; 1310 Surf Ave, cnr Stillwell Ave, Coney Island; hot dogs from $4; ⏰10am-11pm Mon-Thu, to midnight Fri, 9am-midnight Sat, 9am-11pm Sun; 📶; [S]D/F to Coney Island-Stillwell Ave) The hot dog was invented in Coney Island in 1867, which means that eating a frankfurter is practically obligatory here. The top choice: Nathan's Famous, which has been around since 1916. The hot dogs are the real deal, but the menu runs the gamut from fried clams to fried chicken fingers – yep, the emphasis is on fried.

★ Miss Ada MEDITERRANEAN, ISRAELI $$
(Map p82; ☎917-909-1023; www.missadanyc.com; 184 DeKalb Ave, at Carlton Ave, Fort Greene; mains $16-28; ⏰5:30-10:30pm Tue-Thu, to 11:30pm Fri & Sat, 11am-2pm & 5:30-10:30pm Sun, closed Mon; 👪; [S]G to Fulton St; B, Q/R to DeKalb Ave) One of the newest stars in Fort Greene's dining constellation is this cozy restaurant from chef-owner Tomer Blechman, formerly of Gramercy Tavern (p96). He presents Mediterranean dishes from his native Israel given a new spin with Latvian influences (a nod to his parents' place of birth) and flavored with herbs grown in the large backyard, which features canopied dining in warmer months.

★ Olmsted MODERN AMERICAN $$
(Map p82; ☎718-552-2610; www.olmstednyc.com; 659 Vanderbilt Ave, btwn Prospect & Park Pls, Prospect Heights; small plates $13-16, large plates $20-24; ⏰dinner 5:30-10pm Mon-Thu, 5-10:30pm Fri & Sat, 5-9:30pm Sun, brunch 11:30am-2:30pm Fri, 11am-3pm Sat & Sun; [S]B, Q to 7th Ave) 🌱 Chef-owner Greg Baxtrom creates seasonally inspired dishes so skillfully that even Manhattanites cross the river for this extremely popular restaurant. Olmsted's locavore credentials are evident: much of the menu comes from the restaurant's own backyard garden – which makes a lovely place for cocktails or dessert (try the DIY s'mores) while you wait. Reservations recommended (Mondays are walk-ins only).

★ Modern Love VEGAN, AMERICAN $$
(Map p84; ☎929-298-0626; www.modernlovebrooklyn.com; 317 Union St, at S 1st St, East Williamsburg; mains brunch $16-18, dinner $16-24; ⏰5:30-10:30pm Tue-Thu, to 11pm Fri, 5-11pm Sat, 10am-3pm & 5-10pm Sun, closed Mon; 🥗; [S]L to Lorimer St; G to Metropolitan Ave) This new restaurant from celebrated chef Isa Chandra Moskowitz serving 'swanky vegan comfort food' is a welcome addition to the scene, with delicious, plant-based versions of classics like mac 'n' shews (with creamy cashew cheese and pecan-cornmeal crusted tofu), Manhattan glam chowder, seitan Philly cheesesteak and truffle poutine. It's always buzzing, so bookings are a good idea (though not required).

★ Zenkichi JAPANESE $$
(Map p84; ☎718-388-8985; www.zenkichi.com; 77 N 6th St, at Wythe Ave, Williamsburg; tasting menus vegetarian/regular $65/75; ⏰6pm-midnight Mon-Sat, 5:30-11:30pm Sun; 🥗; [S]L to Bedford Ave) A temple of refined Japanese cuisine, Zenkichi presents beautifully prepared dishes in an atmospheric setting that has wowed foodies from far and wide. The recommendation here is the *omakase,* a seasonal eight-course tasting menu featuring highlights like salmon marinated and cured with *shiso* and basil and topped with caviar, or roasted Hudson Valley duck breast with seasonal vegetables.

Frankies 457 Spuntino   ITALIAN $$

(Map p82; 718-403-0033; www.frankies457.com; 457 Court St, btwn 4th Pl & Luquer St, Carroll Gardens; mains $14-23; 11am-11pm Sun-Thu, to midnight Fri & Sat; ; F, G to Smith-9th Sts) Frankies is a neighborhood magnet, attracting local couples, families and plenty of Manhattanites with hearty pasta dishes like cavatelli with hot sausage and pappardelle with braised lamb. But as a *spuntino* (snack joint), this place is more about the small plates, with a seasonal menu that boasts excellent fresh salads, cheeses, cured meats and heavenly crostini. No reservations.

Rabbithole   MODERN AMERICAN $$

(Map p84; 718-782-0910; www.rabbitholerestaurant.com; 352 Bedford Ave, btwn S 3rd & S 4th Sts, Williamsburg; mains breakfast & lunch $10-18, dinner $18-24; 9am-11pm; ; B62 to S 4th St, J/Z, M to Marcy Ave) A warm and inviting spot in South Williamsburg, the very charming Rabbithole is a fine spot to disappear into, particularly if you're craving breakfast (served till 5pm). There's casual cafe-seating up front for good coffee and even better housemade pastries. Head to the back or the relaxing rear garden for creamy eggs Benedict or fresh fruit and granola.

Buttermilk Channel   AMERICAN $$

(Map p82; 718-852-8490; www.buttermilkchannelnyc.com; 524 Court St, at Huntington St, Carroll Gardens; mains lunch $12-27, brunch $13-24, dinner $16-28; lunch 11:30am-3pm Mon-Fri, brunch 10am-3pm Sat & Sun, dinner 5-10pm Sun-Thu, to 11:30pm Fri & Sat; F, G to Smith-9th Sts) There's nothing quite like crispy, buttermilk-fried chicken or a savory plate of eggs with lox and green onions. Buttermilk Channel (named for the waterway between Brooklyn and Governors Island) offers a range of simple, perfectly executed dishes. A comprehensive list of specialty cocktails – the brunch Bloody Mary menu alone is worth the visit – rounds out this delicious dining experience.

THE BEST OF BROOKLYN PIZZA

New York is known for a lot of things: screeching subways, towering skyscrapers, bright lights. It is also known for its pizza, which comes in gooey, chewy, sauce-soaked varieties. These are some of the top places in Brooklyn to grab a slice or a whole pie: If you want to try several pizzas in one go, sign up for an outing with **Scott's Pizza Tours** (212-913-9903; www.scottspizzatours.com; tours incl pizza $45-65), which will take you to the most vaunted brick ovens around the city by foot or by bus.

Di Fara Pizza (Map p62; 718-258-1367; www.difarany.com; 1424 Ave J, cnr E 15th St, Midwood; pizza slices $5; noon-8pm Tue-Sat, from 1pm Sun; Q to Ave J) In operation since 1964 in the Midwood section of Brooklyn, this old-school slice joint is still lovingly tended to by proprietor Dom DeMarco, who makes the pies himself. Expect long lines.

Totonno's (Map p62; 718-372-8606; www.totonnosconeyisland.com; 1524 Neptune Ave, near W 16th St, Coney Island; pizzas $18-21, toppings $2.50; noon-8pm Thu-Sun; ; D/F, N/Q to Coney Island-Stillwell Ave) A classic, family-owned Coney Island pizzeria that makes pies till the dough runs out.

Grimaldi's (Map p66; 718-858-4300; www.grimaldis-pizza.com; 1 Front St, cnr of Old Fulton St, Brooklyn Heights; pizzas $14-18; 11:30am-10:45pm Mon-Thu, to 11:45pm Fri, noon-11:45pm Sat, to 10:45pm Sun; A/C to High St) Legendary pizzas (and legendary lines) abound at this tourist magnet in Brooklyn Heights.

Juliana's (Map p66; 718-596-6700; www.julianaspizza.com; 19 Old Fulton St, btwn Water & Front Sts, Brooklyn Heights; pizzas $20-32; 11:30am-10pm, closed 3:15-4pm; ; A/C to High St) The home of pizza legend Patsy Grimaldi's celebrated return to the Brooklyn dining scene in 2013.

Lucali (Map p82; 718-858-4086; www.lucali.com; 575 Henry St, at Carroll St, Carroll Gardens; pizzas $24, toppings $3; 5:45-11pm Wed-Mon, closed Tue; ; B57 to Court & President Sts, F, G to Carroll St) Neapolitan-style pies started as a hobby for this noted Carroll Gardens *pizzaiolo* (pizza maker).

Roberta's (Map p84; 718-417-1118; www.robertaspizza.com; 261 Moore St, near Bogart St, East Williamsburg; pizzas $13-19; 11am-midnight Mon-Fri, from 10am Sat & Sun; ; L to Morgan Ave) Divine pies with cheeky names like 'Beastmaster'; set in the artsy district at the confluence of Bushwick and East Williamsburg.

The Finch MODERN AMERICAN $$$
(Map p82; ☎718-218-4444; www.thefinchnyc.com; 212 Greene Ave, btwn St James & Grand, Clinton Hill; mains $27-38; 🕓6-10pm Mon-Fri, 5:30-10pm Sat, 11am-3pm & 5:30-9pm Sun; ❄; 🚌B52, [S]G or C to Clinton-Washington) It might seem odd to have a Michelin-starred restaurant on a quiet residential block of brownstones, but The Finch is deserving of the accolade, serving Modern American cuisine with a relaxed vibe. The menu is perfect for sharing – though you may want the Japanese yams all to yourself – with cooked-to-perfection mains like Swiss chard lasagna and smoked beef short rib.

🍴 Queens

★ Pye Boat Noodle THAI $
(Map p86; ☎718-685-2329; 35-13 Broadway, Astoria; noodles $10-13; 🕓11:30am-10:30pm, to 11pm Fri & Sat; 🌿; [S]N/W to Broadway; M, R to Steinway) Young Thai waitresses in matching fedoras greet you at this cute place decked out like an old-fashioned country house. The specialty is rich, star-anise-scented boat noodles, topped with crispy pork cracklings. There's also delicate seafood *yen ta fo* (mild seafood soup, tinted pink), a rarity in NYC – good with a side of papaya salad (off-menu request: add funky fermented crab).

★ Tortilleria Nixtamal MEXICAN $
(Map p86; ☎718-699-2434; www.tortillerianixtamal.com; 104-05 47th Ave, Corona; tacos $3-4, mains $10-14; 🕓11am-9pm Thu & Sun, to 11pm Fri & Sat; [S]7 to 103rd St-Corona Plaza) The red-and-yellow picnic benches at this lo-fi gem are never short of a roaming gastronome, here for super-authentic Mexican snacks. The secret weapon is the Rube Goldbergian machine, which transforms additive-free masa into super-tasty tacos and tamales.

Nan Xiang Xiao Long Bao DUMPLINGS $
(Map p86; ☎718-321-3838; 38-12 Prince St, Flushing; mains $6-10; 🕓8am-midnight; [S]7 train to Main St) Juicy, savory soup dumplings; thick, sticky noodles; spicy wontons – everything you'd want from a dumpling house you'll find at Nan Xiang Xiao Long Bao. This place is a no-frills affair and is usually very busy, but tables tend to open up quickly and the dishes come out fast. Bring some friends and order in excess. Cash only.

★ Bahari GREEK $$
(Map p86; ☎718-204-8968; 31-14 Broadway, Astoria; mains $12-29; 🕓noon-midnight; 🌿👪; [S]N/Q to Broadway) Many of Astoria's Greek restaurants are standard grill joints. Bahari branches out with the full range of casseroles and stews: moussaka with crusty-creamy bechamel, velvety slow-cooked beans, spinach-flecked rice. A meal of these rich dishes is a bargain, especially in the elegant surroundings. (Note: fish is pricier.) Excellent staff and plenty of room, compared with most NYC restaurants.

Kabab Cafe EGYPTIAN $$
(Map p86; ☎718-728-9858; 25-12 Steinway St, Astoria; mains $12-26; 🕓1-5pm & 6-10pm Tue-Sun; 🌿; [S]N/Q to Astoria Blvd) Chef Ali is a larger-than-life personality and an anchor on the Steinway strip known as Little Egypt – though his creative, earthy food, often served straight from the pan to your plate, ranges much further than his Alexandrian roots. Start with mixed apps, for fluffy green Egyptian-style falafel, then pick any lamb dish.

Rockaway Surf Club TACOS $$
(Map p126; www.rockawaybeachsurfclub.com; 302 Beach 87th St; per taco $3.50, cocktails $9; 🕓11am-11pm late Apr-Sep, 11am-11pm Sat & Sun only Oct) Down in the Rockaways are some of the best tacos in the five boroughs. The Rockaway Surf Club draws inspiration from beachside California taquerias, with a bar inside, and large outdoor dining area where the food is made to order. Whether you surf or just catch rays on the sand, it's the perfect post-beach hangout.

M Wells Steakhouse STEAK $$$
(Map p86; ☎718-786-9060; www.magasinwells.com; 43-15 Crescent St, Long Island City; mains $24-65; 🕓5-11pm Wed-Sat; [S]E, M to 23rd St-Court Sq; G, 7 to Court Sq) Carnivores with a taste for decadence will appreciate Quebecois chef Hugue Dufour's satisfying take on steak. Try the showstopping New York strip, with its Korean-style maple rub, or opt for the perfectly tender Wagyu flank steak. There's also whole trout and a mussels dish for pescatarians, plus a side of poutine for homesick Canadians. Loud, exuberant ambience. Reserve on weekends.

🍷 Drinking & Nightlife

You'll find all species of thirst-quenching venues here, from terminally hip cocktail lounges and historic dive bars to specialty taprooms and Third Wave coffee shops. Then there's the legendary club scene, spanning everything from celebrity staples to gritty, indie hangouts. Head downtown or to Brooklyn for the parts of the city that, as they say, truly never sleep.

LGBTQ+ NYC

From hand-locked married couples leaving the City Clerk's office wearing matching Bride & Bride hats to a rainbow-hued Empire State Building at Pride, there's no doubt that New York City is one of the world's great gay cities. Indeed, few places come close to matching the breadth and depth of queer offerings here, from cabarets and clubs to festivals and readings.

NYC Pride (www.nycpride.org; ⏰ late Jun) Rainbow-clad pomp and circumstance.

Leslie-Lohman Museum of Gay & Lesbian Art (Map p70; ☎ 212-431-2609; www.leslielohman.org; 26 Wooster St, btwn Grand & Canal Sts, Little Italy; suggested donation $9; ⏰ noon-6pm Wed & Fri-Sun, to 8pm Thu; [S] A/C/E, N/Q/R, 1 to Canal St) [FREE] The world's first LGBT art museum.

Industry (Map p74; ☎ 646-476-2747; www.industry-bar.com; 355 W 52nd St, btwn Eighth & Ninth Aves; ⏰ 5pm-4am; [S] C/E, 1 to 50th St) One of the best-loved bar-clubs in kicking Hell's Kitchen.

Marie's Crisis (Map p70; www.mariescrisis.us; 59 Grove St, btwn Seventh Ave & Bleecker St, West Village; ⏰ 4pm-3am Mon-Thu, to 4am Fri & Sat, to midnight Sun; [S] 1 to Christopher St-Sheridan Sq; A/C/E, B/D/F/M to W 4th St-Washington Sq) Sing your heart out at this deliriously fun showtunes bar in the West Village.

Duplex (Map p70; ☎ 212-255-5438; www.theduplex.com; 61 Christopher St, at Seventh Ave S, West Village; cover $10-25; ⏰ 4pm-4am; [S] 1 to Christopher St-Sheridan Sq; A/C/E, B/D/F/M to W 4th St-Washington Sq) Camp quips, smooth crooners and a riotously fun piano bar define this Village veteran.

Eagle NYC (Map p74; ☎ 646-473-1866; www.eagle-ny.com; 554 W 28th St, btwn Tenth & Eleventh Aves, Chelsea; ⏰ 4pm-4am Mon-Sat, from 5pm Sun; [S] 1, C/E to 23rd St) Love-it-or-loathe-it debauchery and plenty of leather.

Financial District & Lower Manhattan

★Dead Rabbit COCKTAIL BAR

(Map p66; ☎ 646-422-7906; www.deadrabbitnyc.com; 30 Water St, btwn Broad St & Coenties Slip; ⏰ Taproom 11am-4am daily, Parlor 5pm-2am Mon-Wed, to 3am Thu-Sat; [S] R/W to Whitehall St; 1 to South Ferry) Named in honor of a dreaded Irish-American gang, this is regularly voted one of the world's best bars. Hit the sawdust-sprinkled Taproom for specialty beers, historic punches and pop-inns (lightly soured ale spiked with different flavors). Come evening, scurry upstairs to the cozy Parlor for meticulously researched cocktails. The Wall St crowd packs the place after work.

Brandy Library COCKTAIL BAR

(Map p66; ☎ 212-226-5545; www.brandylibrary.com; 25 N Moore St, near Varick St; ⏰ 5pm-1am Sun-Wed, 4pm-2am Thu, 4pm-4am Fri & Sat; [S] 1 to Franklin St) When sipping means serious business, settle in at this uber-luxe 'library,' its handsome club chairs facing floor-to-ceiling, bottle-lined shelves. Go for top-shelf cognac, malt whisky or vintage brandies, expertly paired with nibbles such as Gruyère-cheese puffs and a wonderful tartare made to order. Saturday nights are generally quieter than weeknights, making it a civilized spot for a weekend tête-à-tête.

Cowgirl SeaHorse BAR

(Map p66; ☎ 212-608-7873; www.cowgirlseahorse.com; 259 Front St, at Dover St; ⏰ 11am-11pm Mon-Thu, 11am-late Fri, 10am-late Sat, 10am-11pm Sun; [S] A/C, J/Z, 2/3, 4/5 to Fulton St) In a sea of very serious bars and restaurants, Cowgirl SeaHorse is a party ship. Its nautical theme and perfect bar fare – giant plates of nachos piled with steaming meat, and frozen margaritas so sweet and tangy you won't be able to say no to a second round – make this dive a can't-miss for those looking to let loose.

Pier A Harbor House BAR

(Map p66; ☎ 212-785-0153; www.piera.com; 22 Battery Pl, Battery Park; ⏰ 11am-midnight Sun-Wed, to 2am Thu-Sat; 📶; [S] 4/5 to Bowling Green; R/W to Whitehall St; 1 to South Ferry) Looking dashing after a major restoration, Pier A is a super-spacious, casual eating and drinking house right on New York Harbor. If the weather's fine, try for a seat on the waterside deck – picnic benches, sun umbrellas and an eyeful of New York skyline offer a brilliant spot for sipping craft beers or one of the house cocktails on tap.

Asianesque, among them duck wontons and Mandalay coconut shrimp.

SoHo & Chinatown

★Ghost Donkey BAR

(Map p70; ☎212-254-0350; www.ghostdonkey.com; 4 Bleecker St, NoHo; 🕐5pm-2am; [S]6 to Bleecker St; B/D/F/M to Broadway-Lafayette St) Laid-back meets trippy meets craft at this one-of-a-kind, classy mezcal house that gives vibes of Mexico, the Middle East and the Wild West. If the moon had a saloon, this place would fit right in. Dark and dim, yet pink, with low-cushioned couches encircling lower coffee tables, this bar also serves excellent craft cocktails. (Try the frozen house margarita! Tasty, right?)

★Genuine Liquorette COCKTAIL BAR

(Map p70; ☎646-726-4633; www.genuineliquorette.com; 191 Grand St, at Mulberry St, Little Italy; 🕐6pm-midnight Tue-Thu, 5pm-2am Fri, 6pm-2am Sat, closed Sun & Mon; [S]J/Z, N/Q/R/W, 6 to Canal St; B/D to Grand St) What's not to love about a basement bar with canned cocktails and a Farrah Fawcett–themed restroom? You're even free to grab bottles and mixers and make your own drinks. At the helm is Ashlee, the beverage director, who regularly invites New York's finest barkeeps to create cocktails using less celebrated hooch.

★Apothéke COCKTAIL BAR

(Map p66; ☎212-406-0400; www.apothekenyc.com; 9 Doyers St, Chinatown; 🕐6:30pm-2am Mon-Sat, from 8pm Sun; [S]J/Z to Chambers St; 4/5/6 to Brooklyn Bridge-City Hall) It takes a little effort to track down this former opium-den-turned-apothecary bar on Doyers St. Inside, skilled barkeeps work like careful chemists, using local, seasonal produce from Greenmarkets to produce intense, flavorful 'prescriptions.' Their cocktail ingredient ratio is always on point, such as the pineapple-cilantro blend in the Sitting Buddha, one of the best drinks on the menu.

Pegu Club COCKTAIL BAR

(Map p70; ☎212-473-7348; www.peguclub.com; 77 W Houston St, btwn W Broadway & Wooster St, SoHo; 🕐5pm-2am Sun-Thu, to 4am Fri & Sat; [S]B/D/F/M to Broadway-Lafayette St; C/E to Spring St) Dark, elegant Pegu Club (named after a legendary gentleman's club in colonial-era Rangoon) is an obligatory stop for cocktail connoisseurs. Sink into a velvet lounge and savor seamless libations such as the silky-smooth Earl Grey MarTEAni (tea-infused gin, lemon juice and raw egg white). Grazing options are suitably

East Village & Lower East Side

Bar Goto BAR

(Map p70; ☎212-475-4411; www.bargoto.com; 245 Eldridge St, btwn E Houston & Stanton Sts, Lower East Side; 🕐5pm-midnight Tue-Thu & Sun, to 2am Fri & Sat; [S]F to 2nd Ave) Maverick mixologist Kenta Goto has cocktail connoisseurs spellbound at his eponymous hot spot. Expect meticulous, elegant drinks that revel in Koto's Japanese heritage (the sake-spiked Sakura Martini is utterly smashing), paired with authentic, Japanese comfort bites, such as *okonomiyaki* (savory pancakes).

Berlin CLUB

(Map p70; ☎reservations 347-586-7247; 25 Ave A, btwn First & Second Aves, East Village; 🕐8pm-4am; [S]F to 2nd Ave) Like a secret bunker hidden beneath the ever-gentrifying streets of the East Village, Berlin is a throwback to the neighborhood's more riotous days of wildness and dancing. Once you find the unmarked entrance, head downstairs to the grotto-like space with vaulted brick ceilings, a long bar and tiny dancefloor, with funk and rare grooves spilling all around.

Angel's Share BAR

(Map p70; ☎212-777-5415; 8 Stuyvesant St, 2nd fl, near Third Ave & E 9th St; 🕐6pm-1:30am Sun-Wed, to 2am Thu, to 2:30am Fri & Sat; [S]6 to Astor Pl) Show up early and snag a seat at this hidden gem, behind a Japanese restaurant on the same floor. It's quiet and elegant, with seriously talented mixologists serving up creative cocktails, plus a top-flight collection of whiskeys. You can't stay if you don't have a table or a seat at the bar, and they tend to go fast.

Ten Bells BAR

(Map p70; ☎212-228-4450; www.tenbellsnyc.com; 247 Broome St, btwn Ludlow & Orchard Sts, Lower East Side; 🕐5pm-2am Mon-Fri, from 3pm Sat & Sun; [S]F to Delancey St; J/M/Z to Essex St) This charmingly tucked-away tapas bar has a grotto-like design, with flickering candles, dark tin ceilings, brick walls and a U-shaped bar that's an ideal setting for a conversation with a new friend.

Wayland BAR

(Map p70; ☎212-777-7022; www.thewaylandnyc.com; 700 E 9th St, cnr Ave C, East Village; 🕐4pm-4am Mon-Fri, from 11am Sat & Sun; [S]L to 1st Ave) Whitewashed walls, weathered floorboards and salvaged lamps give this urban outpost a Mississippi flair, which goes well with the live music (bluegrass, jazz, folk) featured Monday to Wednesday nights. The drinks, though, are the real draw – try the 'I Hear Banjos-Encore,' made of apple-pie moonshine, rye whiskey and applewood smoke, which tastes like a campfire (but slightly less burning).

West Village, Chelsea & Meatpacking District

Employees Only
BAR

(Map p70; ☎212-242-3021; www.employeesonly nyc.com; 510 Hudson St, btwn W 10th & Christopher Sts, West Village; ⊗6pm-4am; ⒮1 to Christopher St-Sheridan Sq) Duck behind the neon 'Psychic' sign to find this hidden hangout. Bartenders are ace mixologists, fizzing up crazy, addictive libations like the Ginger Smash and an upscale Bellini. Great for late-night drinking and eating, courtesy of the on-site restaurant that serves till 3:30am – housemade chicken soup is ladled out to stragglers. The bar gets busier as the night wears on.

Happiest Hour
COCKTAIL BAR

(Map p70; ☎212-243-2827; www.happiest hournyc.com; 121 W 10th St, btwn Greenwich St & Sixth Ave, West Village; ⊗5pm-late Mon-Fri, from 2pm Sat & Sun; ⒮A/C/E, B/D/F/M to W 4th St-Washington Sq; 1 to Christopher St-Sheridan Sq) A super-cool, tiki-licious cocktail bar splashed with palm prints, '60s pop and playful mixed drinks that provide a chic take on the fruity beach cocktail. The crowd tends to be button-down after-work types and online daters. Beneath sits its serious sibling, **Slowly Shirley**, an art-deco-style subterranean temple to beautifully crafted, thoroughly researched libations.

Gallow Green
BAR

(Map p74; ☎212-564-1662; www.mckittrickhotel .com/gallow-green; 542 W 27th St, btwn Tenth & Eleventh Aves, Chelsea; ⊗5pm-midnight Mon-Wed, to 1am Thu & Fri, 11a-1am Sat, to midnight Sun; ⒮1, C/E to 23rd St; 1 to 28th St) Run by the creative team behind Sleep No More theater (p112), Gallow Green is a rooftop bar festooned with vines, potted plants and fairy lights. It's a great add-on before or after experiencing the show, with waitstaff in period costume, a live band most nights and tasty rum-filled cocktails. You'll want to make a reservation.

Buvette
WINE BAR

(Map p70; ☎212-255-3590; www.ilovebuvette.com; 42 Grove St, btwn Bedford & Bleecker Sts, West Village; ⊗7am-2am; ⒮1 to Christopher St-Sheridan Sq; A/C/E, B/D/F/M to W 4th St-Washington Sq) The rustic-chic decor here (think delicate tin tiles and a swooshing marble counter) makes it the perfect place for a glass of wine – no matter the time of day. For the full experience at this self-proclaimed *gastrothèque,* grab a seat at one of the surrounding tables and nibble on small plates while enjoying Old World wines (mostly from France and Italy).

Pier 66 Maritime
BAR

(Map p74; ☎212-989-6363; www.pier66mari time.com; Pier 66, at W 26th St, Chelsea; ⊗weather permitting noon-midnight May-Sep, noon-midnight warm days Apr & Oct, closed Nov-Mar; ⒮1, C/E to 23rd St) Salvaged from the bottom of the sea (or at least the Chesapeake Bay), the lightship *Frying Pan* and the two-tiered dockside bar where it's moored are fine go-to spots for a sundowner. On warm days, the rustic open-air space brings in the crowds, who laze on deck chairs and drink ice-cold beers ($7/25 for a microbrew/pitcher).

Cubbyhole
LGBT

(Map p70; ☎212-243-9041; www.cubbyholebar. com; 281 W 12th St, at W 4th St, West Village; ⊗4pm-4am Mon-Fri, from 2pm Sat & Sun; ⒮A/C/E, L to 8th Ave-14th St) This West Village dive bills itself as 'lesbian, gay and straight friendly since 1994.' While the crowd is mostly ladies, as its motto suggests it's a welcoming place for anyone looking for a cheap drink. It's got a great jukebox, friendly bartenders and plenty of regulars who prefer to hang and chat rather than hook up and leave.

Union Square, Flatiron District & Gramercy

★Flatiron Lounge
COCKTAIL BAR

(Map p74; ☎212-727-7741; www.flatironlounge. com; 37 W 19th St, btwn Fifth & Sixth Aves, Flatiron District; ⊗4pm-2am Mon-Wed, to 3am Thu, to 4am Fri, 5pm-4am Sat, to 1am Sun; ☏; ⒮F/M, R/W, 6 to 23rd St) Head through a dramatic archway and into a dark, swinging, art deco–inspired fantasy of lipstick-red booths, racy jazz tunes and sassy grown-ups downing seasonal drinks. Cocktails run $15 a pop, but happy-hour cocktails are only $10 (4pm to 7pm weekdays).

Birreria
BEER HALL

(Map p74; ☎212-937-8910; www.eataly.com; 200 Fifth Ave, at W 23rd St, Flatiron District; ⊗11:30am-11pm; ⒮F/M, R/W, 6 to 23rd St) The crown jewel of Italian food emporium Eataly (p95) is this rooftop beer garden tucked betwixt the Flatiron's corporate towers. An encyclopedic beer menu offers drinkers some of the best suds on the planet. If you're hungry, the signature beer-braised pork shoulder will pair nicely, or check out the seasonally changing menu of the on-site pop-up restaurant (mains $17 to $37).

Raines Law Room COCKTAIL BAR
(Map p70; www.raineslawroom.com; 48 W 17th St, btwn Fifth & Sixth Aves, Flatiron District; 🕐5pm-2am Mon-Thu, to 3am Fri & Sat, 5pm-1am Sun; [S]F/M to 14th St, L to 6th Ave, 1 to 18th St) A sea of velvet drapes and overstuffed leather lounge chairs, the perfect amount of exposed brick, expertly crafted cocktails using meticulously aged spirits – these folks are as serious as a mortgage payment when it comes to amplified atmosphere. Reservations (recommended) are only accepted Sunday to Tuesday. Whatever the night, style up for a taste of a far more sumptuous era.

Lillie's Victorian Establishment BAR
(Map p74; ☎212-337-1970; www.lilliesnyc.com; 13 E 17th St, btwn Broadway & Fifth Ave, Union Square; 🕐11am-4am; [S]4/5/6, L, N/Q/R/W to 14th St-Union Sq) This is one of those places where the name says it all. Step in and be taken to the era of petticoats and watch fobs with high, stamped-tin ceilings, red-velvet love seats and walls covered in vintage photographs in extravagant gilded frames. The food and cocktail list is decidedly modern, but the ambience is enough to fulfill the fantasy.

🍷 Midtown

★The Campbell COCKTAIL BAR
(Map p74; ☎212-297-1781; www.thecampbellnyc.com; Grand Central Terminal; 🕐noon-2am) As swanky as swank can be, the only thing missing at the Campbell is elevation – you don't get the sweeping skyline view that some NYC bars have. Instead, you can sip top-shelf signature cocktails beneath a stunning hand-painted ceiling, restored along with the room with touches that make it seem Rockefeller or Carnegie might just join you.

★Bar SixtyFive COCKTAIL BAR
(Map p74; ☎212-632-5000; www.rainbowroom.com/bar-sixty-five; 30 Rockefeller Plaza, entrance on W 49th St; 🕐5pm-midnight Mon-Fri, 4-9pm Sun, closed Sat; [S]B/D/F/M to 47th-50th Sts-Rockefeller Center) Not to be missed, sophisticated SixtyFive sits on level 65 of the GE Building at Rockefeller Center (p68). Dress well (no sportswear or guests under 21) and arrive by 5pm for a seat with a multimillion-dollar view. Even if you don't score a table on the balcony or by the window, head outside to soak up that sweeping New York panorama.

Waylon BAR
(Map p74; ☎212-265-0010; www.thewaylon.com; 736 Tenth Ave, at W 50th St; 🕐4pm-4am Mon-Thu, noon-4am Fri-Sun; [S]C/E to 50th St) Slip on your spurs, partner, there's a honky-tonk in Hell's! Celebrate Dixie at this saloon-style watering hole, where the jukebox keeps good folks dancing to Tim McGraw's broken heart, where the barkeeps pour American whiskeys and tequila, and where the grub includes Texan-style Frito pie and pulled pork sandwiches. For live country-and-western sounds, stop by some Thursdays between 8pm and 11pm.

Robert COCKTAIL BAR
(Map p74; ☎212-299-7730; www.robertnyc.com; Museum of Arts & Design, 2 Columbus Circle, btwn Eighth Ave & Broadway; 🕐11:30am-10pm Mon & Tue, to 11pm Wed-Fri, 10:30am-11pm Sat, to 10pm Sun; [S]A/C, B/D, 1 to 59th St-Columbus Circle) Perched on the 9th floor of the Museum of Arts & Design (p69), '60s-inspired Robert is technically a high-end, Modern American restaurant. While the food is satisfactory, we say visit late afternoon or post-dinner, find a sofa and gaze out over Central Park with a MAD Manhattan (bourbon, blood orange vermouth and liqueured cherries). Check the website for live jazz sessions.

Rum House COCKTAIL BAR
(Map p74; ☎646-490-6924; www.therumhousenyc.com; 228 W 47th St, btwn Broadway & Eighth Ave; 🕐noon-4am; [S]N/R/W to 49th St) This sultry slice of old New York is revered for its rums and whiskeys. Savor them straight up or mixed in impeccable cocktails like 'The Escape,' a potent piña-colada for adults. Adding to the magic is nightly live music, spanning solo piano tunes to jaunty jazz trios and sentimental divas. Bartenders here are careful with their craft; don't expect them to rush.

Lantern's Keep COCKTAIL BAR
(Map p74; ☎212-453-4287; www.iroquoisny.com; Iroquois Hotel, 49 W 44th St, btwn Fifth & Sixth Aves, Midtown West; 🕐5-11pm Mon, to midnight Tue-Fri, 7pm-1am Sat; [S]B/D/F/M to 42nd St-Bryant Park)

Cross the lobby of the Iroquois Hotel to slip into this dark, intimate cocktail salon. Its specialty is classic drinks, shaken and stirred by passionate, personable mixologists. If you're feeling spicy, request a Gordon's Breakfast (not on the menu!), a fiery melange of gin, Worcestershire sauce, hot sauce, muddled lime and cucumber, salt and pepper. Reservations are recommended.

Flaming Saddles   GAY
(Map p74; ☎212-713-0481; www.flamingsaddles.com/nyc; 793 Ninth Ave, btwn 52nd & 53rd Sts, Midtown West; ⊙3pm-4am Mon-Fri, noon-4am Sat & Sun; ⓈC/E to 50th St) A country-and-western gay bar in Midtown! *Coyote Ugly* meets *Calamity Jane* at this Hell's Kitchen hangout, complete with studly bar-dancing barmen in skintight jeans, aspiring urban cowboys and a rough 'n' ready vibe. Slip on them Wranglers or chaps and hit the Saddle: you're in for a fun and boozy ride. There's Tex Mex bar food if you get hungry.

⬤ Upper West Side & Central Park

★Manhattan Cricket Club   LOUNGE
(Map p78; ☎646-823-9252; www.mccnewyork.com; 226 W 79th St, btwn Amsterdam Ave & Broadway; ⊙6pm-late Mon-Sat; Ⓢ1 to 79th St) Above an Australian bistro (p98; ask its host for access), this elegant drinking lounge is modeled on the classy Anglo-Aussie cricket clubs of the early 1900s. Sepia-toned photos of batsmen adorn the gold brocaded walls, while mahogany bookshelves and Chesterfield sofas create a fine setting for quaffing well-made (but pricey) cocktails. It's a guaranteed date-pleaser.

⬤ Upper East Side

Caledonia   BAR
(Map p78; ☎212-734-4300; www.caledoniabar.com; 1609 Second Ave, btwn E 83rd & 84th Sts; ⊙5pm-4am Mon-Thu, 4pm-4am Fri-Sun; ⓈQ, 4/5/6 to 86th St) The name of this dimly lit, dark-wood bar is a dead giveaway: it's devoted to Scottish whisky, with over a hundred single malts to choose from (be they Highlands, Islands, Islay, Lowlands or Speyside), as well as some blends and even a few from the US, Ireland and Japan. The bartenders know their stuff and will be happy to make recommendations.

⬤ Harlem & Upper Manhattan

Shrine   BAR
(Map p62; www.shrinenyc.com; 2271 Adam Clayton Powell Jr Blvd, btwn 133rd & 134th Sts, Harlem; ⊙4pm-4am; Ⓢ2/3 to 135th St) To see what's happening on the global music scene, friendly, unpretentious Shrine – run by the talented team behind **Silvana** (Map p78; www.silvana-nyc.com; 300 W 116th St; ⊙8am-4am; Ⓢ2/3 to 116th St) – is a great place to start. Here you'll find live bands taking the small stage every day of the week. Blues, reggae, Afro-beat, funk, soca, Ethiopian grooves and indie rock are among the sounds you'll hear, with no cover charge.

Ginny's Supper Club   COCKTAIL BAR
(Map p78; ☎212-421-3821; www.ginnyssupperclub.com; 310 Lenox Ave, btwn W 125th & 126th Sts, Harlem; ⊙6pm-midnight Thu, to 3am Fri & Sat, brunch 10:30am-12:30pm Sun; Ⓢ2/3 to 125th St) Looking straight out of the TV series *Boardwalk Empire,* this roaring basement supper club is rarely short of styled-up regulars sipping cocktails, nibbling on soul and global bites – from the Red Rooster (p99) kitchen upstairs – and grooving to live jazz from 7:30pm Thursday to Saturday and DJ-spun beats from 11pm Friday and Saturday. Don't miss the weekly Sunday gospel brunch (reservations recommended).

Bier International   BEER HALL
(Map p78; ☎212-280-0944; www.bierinternational.com; 2099 Frederick Douglass Blvd, at 113th St, Harlem; ⊙4pm-midnight Mon-Wed, to 1am Thu & Fri, noon-1am Sat, noon-midnight Sun; ⓈB, C, 1 to 110th St-Cathedral Pkwy; 2/3 to 110th St-Central Park North) A fun, buzzing beer garden that peddles some 18 different drafts from Germany, Belgium and the UK, plus local brews from the Bronx Brewery and Brooklyn's Sixpoint. The extensive menu makes it worthwhile to stick around. Think catfish tacos, truffle fries with shaved Parmesan and Vienna-style schnitzel. Cash only.

⬤ Brooklyn

★House of Yes   CLUB
(Map p84; www.houseofyes.org; 2 Wyckoff Ave, at Jefferson St, Bushwick; tickets free-$40; ⊙hours vary by event, Tue-Sat; ⓈL to Jefferson St) Anything goes at this highly regarded warehouse venue, with two stages, three bars and a covered outdoor area, which offers some of the most creative themed performance

and dance nights in Brooklyn. You might see aerial-silk acrobats, punk bands, burlesque shows, drag queens or performance artists, with DJs spinning house and other deep beats for an artsy, inclusive crowd.

★Maison Premiere COCKTAIL BAR

(Map p84; ☎347-335-0446; www.maisonpremiere.com; 298 Bedford Ave, btwn S 1st & Grand Sts, Williamsburg; 🕑2pm-2am Mon-Wed, to 4am Thu & Fri, 11am-4am Sat, to 2am Sun; [S]L to Bedford Ave) We kept expecting to see Dorothy Parker stagger into this old-timey place, which features an elegant bar full of syrups and essences, suspender-wearing bartenders and a jazzy soundtrack to further channel the French Quarter New Orleans vibe. The cocktails are serious business: the epic list includes more than a dozen absinthe drinks, various juleps and an array of specialty cocktails.

June WINE BAR

(Map p82; ☎917-909-0434; www.junebk.com; 231 Court St, btwn Warren & Baltic, Cobble Hill; happy hour 5-7pm Mon-Fri, brunch 11am-4pm Sat & Sun, dinner 5:30pm-midnight Sun-Thu, to 1am Fri & Sat; [S]F or G to Bergen Street) Natural wines might not be everyone's thing, but there's a good chance you'll be converted at this gem of a bar in Cobble Hill. The French-inspired decor adds a glamorous air, while the outdoor terrace is pure romance in summer. True to June's natural ethos, the food menu is seasonal (mains $23 to $30); the brussels sprouts are a standout in winter.

Black Forest Brooklyn BEER HALL

(Map p82; ☎718-935-0300; www.blackforestbrooklyn.com; 733 Fulton St, btwn S Elliot Pl & S Portland Ave, Fort Greene; 🕑10am-midnight Mon-Thu, to 2am Fri, 9am-2am Sat, to 10pm Sun; [S]G to Fulton St; C to Lafayette Ave) Two German Brooklynites opened this hip take on a traditional beer hall, with dark ceiling timbers, exposed brick and handsome waiters in red-checked shirts serving up liters of imported Bavarian lagers, pilsners, wheat beers and more on draft. (Can't pick? Try the 13-beer flight.) A full menu of German food features numerous veggie options along with wursts and schnitzels.

Lavender Lake PUB

(Map p82; ☎347-799-2154; www.lavenderlake.com; 383 Carroll St, btwn Bond Sts & Gowanus Canal, Gowanus; 🕑4pm-midnight Mon-Thu, to 2am Fri, noon-2am Sat, to 10pm Sun; [S]F, G to Carroll St; R to Union St) This little gem of a bar – named after the old local nickname for the colorfully polluted Gowanus Canal – is set in a former horse stable and serves carefully selected craft beers and a few seasonal cocktails, which include ingredients such as jalapeño-infused tequila. The light-strewn garden is a brilliant summery spot. There's good food, too (mains $11 to $23).

Union Hall BAR

(Map p82; ☎718-638-4400; www.unionhallny.com; 702 Union St, near Fifth Ave, Park Slope; 🕑4pm-4am Mon-Fri, 1pm-4am Sat & Sun; [S]R to Union St) Anyone seeking an authentically Brooklyn night out should look no further than Union Hall. This bar and event space is located in a converted warehouse and boasts a double-sided fireplace, towering bookshelves, leather couches and two full-size indoor bocce courts. Head to the basement for live music and comedy.

Brooklyn Barge BEER GARDEN

(Map p84; ☎929-337-7212; www.thebrooklynbarge.com; 3 Milton St, off West St, Greenpoint; 🕑4pm-1am Mon & Tue, 11am-1am Wed-Sun May-Oct; 🐾; [S]G to Greenpoint Ave) Greenpoint's newest summer drinking spot isn't just on the waterfront – it's on the *water*. A floating barge moored to land via a wooden bridge is home to an alfresco bar serving local beers on draft, summery bespoke cocktails and some wines and cider, as well as a menu of plates for sharing, nachos, tacos and sandwiches from the repurposed-shipping-container kitchen.

Radegast Hall & Biergarten BEER HALL

(Map p84; ☎718-963-3973; www.radegasthall.com; 113 N 3rd St, at Berry St, Williamsburg; 🕑noon-3am Mon-Fri, from 11am Sat & Sun; [S]L to Bedford Ave) This Austro-Hungarian beer hall in Williamsburg offers up a huge selection of Bavarian brews, and a kitchen full of munchable meats. You can hover in the dark, woody bar area or sit in the adjacent hall, which has a retractable roof and communal tables to feast at – perfect for pretzels, sausages and burgers. Live music every night; no cover.

Queens

★Bohemian Hall & Beer Garden BEER GARDEN

(Map p86; ☎718-274-4925; www.bohemianhall.com; 29-19 24th Ave, Astoria; 🕑5pm-1am Mon-Thu, 3pm-3am Fri, noon-3am Sat, to midnight Sun; [S]N/Q to Astoria Blvd) This Czech community center kicked off NYC's beer-garden craze, and nothing quite matches it for space and heaving drinking crowds, which pack every picnic table under the towering trees in summer. There's obligatory food (dumplings, sausages); the focus is on the cold and foamy Czech beers. Some nights folk bands set up, with the occasional cover charge of $5.

The COOP   BAR
(Map p86; ☏718-358-9333; www.thecoopnyc.com; 133-42 39th Ave #103, Flushing; ⏰noon-2am Sun-Wed, noon-3am Thu-Sat; ⒮7 to Main St) Crisp cocktail culture meets Korean fusion food at the COOP, located in the middle of Flushing's bustling main drag. Enjoy a full meal of Korean delicacies, or just order a round of small plates such as pork belly sliders or kimchi egg rolls (mains $12 to $25). The chic vibe makes it a perfect place to start a night out.

Dutch Kills   BAR
(Map p86; ☏718-383-2724; www.dutchkillsbar. com; 27-24 Jackson Ave, Long Island City; ⏰5pm-2am; ⒮E, M or R to Queens Plaza; G to Court Sq) When you step into Dutch Kills – through an unassuming door on an old industrial building in Long Island City – you are stepping back in time. This speakeasy-style bar is all about atmosphere and amazing craft cocktails. Its menu of specialty drinks is extensive, but if you're looking for an old standard, you can trust the expert bartenders to deliver.

🍸 The Bronx

Bronx Brewery   BREWERY
(Map p62; ☏718-402-1000; www.thebronx brewery.com; 856 E 136th St, btwn Willow & Walnut Aves; ⏰3-7pm Mon-Wed, 3-8pm Thu & Fri, noon-8pm Sat, noon-7pm Sun; ⒮6 to Cypress Ave) This buzzing South Bronx microbrewery comes with a small taproom, where you can pony up to the bar and choose from a changing line-up of eight or so quality brews on draft. There's also a backyard (open weekends in the summer) that beckons long, lazy drinking sessions.

☆ Entertainment

Actors, musicians, dancers and artists flock to the bright lights of the Big Apple, hoping to finally get that big break. The result? Audiences are spoiled by the continual influx of supremely talented, dedicated, boundary-pushing performers. Like the song goes: if you can make it here, you can make it anywhere.

Live Music

★Jazz at Lincoln Center   JAZZ
(Map p78; ☏reservations for Dizzy's Club Coca-Cola 212-258-9595, tickets to Rose Theater & Appel Room 212-721-6500; www.jazz.org; Time Warner Center, 10 Columbus Circle, Broadway at W 59th St; ⒮A/C, B/D, 1 to 59th St-Columbus Circle) Perched atop the Time Warner Center, Jazz at Lincoln Center consists of three state-of-the-art venues: the mid-sized Rose Theater; the panoramic, glass-backed Appel Room; and the intimate, atmospheric Dizzy's Club Coca-Cola. It's the last of these that you're most likely to visit, given its nightly shows. The talent is often exceptional, as are the dazzling Central Park views.

★Carnegie Hall   LIVE MUSIC
(Map p74; ☏212-247-7800; www.carnegiehall.org; 881 Seventh Ave, at W 57th St; tours adult/child $17/12; ⏰tours 11:30am, 12:30pm, 2pm & 3pm Mon-Fri, 11:30am & 12:30pm Sat Oct-Jun; ⒮N/R/W to 57th St-7th Ave) Few venues are as famous as Carnegie Hall. This legendary music hall may not be the world's biggest, nor its grandest, but it's definitely one of the most acoustically blessed venues around. Opera, jazz and folk greats feature in the Isaac Stern Auditorium, with edgier jazz, pop, classical and world music in the popular Zankel Hall. The intimate Weill Recital Hall hosts chamber-music concerts, debut performances and panel discussions.

New York Philharmonic   CLASSICAL MUSIC
(Map p78; ☏212-875-5656; www.nyphil.org; Lincoln Center, Columbus Ave at W 65th St; 🎵; ⒮1 to 66 St-Lincoln Center) The oldest professional orchestra in the US (dating back to 1842) holds its season every year at David Geffen Hall (known as Avery Fisher Hall until 2015); music director Jaap van Zweden took over from Alan Gilbert in 2017. The orchestra plays a mix of classics (Tchaikovsky, Mahler, Haydn) and contemporary works, as well as concerts geared toward children.

Blue Note   JAZZ
(Map p70; ☏212-475-8592; www.bluenote.net; 131 W 3rd St, btwn Sixth Ave & MacDougal St, West Village; ⒮A/C/E, B/D/F/M to W 4th St-Washington Sq) This is by far the most famous (and expensive) of the city's jazz clubs. Most shows are $15 to $30 at the bar or $25 to $45 at a table, but can rise for the biggest stars. There's also jazz brunch on Sundays at 11:30am. Go on an off night, and don't talk – all attention is on the stage!

★**Terraza 7** LIVE MUSIC
(Map p86; ☎ 347-808-0518; www.terraza7.com; 40-19 Gleane St, Elmhurst; 🕓 4pm-4am; [S] 7 to 82nd St-Jackson Hts) Come to Queens for multicultural eats, then stay for equally diverse sounds at this cool bi-level performance space. It makes creative use of the tiny room, setting the live band in a loft above the bar. Latin jazz is the mainstay, but performers can hail from as far away as Morocco.

★**Barbès** LIVE MUSIC, JAZZ
(Map p82; ☎ 347-422-0248; www.barbesbrooklyn.com; 376 9th St, at Sixth Ave, Park Slope; requested donation for live music $10; 🕓 5pm-2am Mon-Thu, to 4am Fri, 2pm-4am Sat, to 2am Sun; [S] F, G to 7th Ave; R to 4th Ave-9th St) This compact bar and performance space, named after a North African neighborhood in Paris, is owned by French musician (and longtime Brooklyn resident) Olivier Conan, who sometimes plays here with his Latin-themed band Las Rubias del Norte. There's live music all night, every night: the impressively eclectic lineup includes Afro-Peruvian grooves, West African funk and gypsy swing, among other sounds.

★**Marjorie Eliot's Parlor Jazz** JAZZ
(Map p62; ☎ 212-781-6595; 555 Edgecombe Ave, Apartment 3F, at 160th St, Washington Heights; donations appreciated; 🕓 3:30pm Sun; [S] A/C to 163rd St-Amsterdam Ave; 1 to 157th St) Each Sunday the charming Ms Eliot provides one of New York's most magical experiences: free, intimate jazz jams in her own apartment. Dedicated to her two deceased sons, the informal concerts feature a revolving lineup of talented musicians, enchanting guests from all over the globe. Go early, as this event is popular (there's usually a line by 2:30pm).

Brooklyn Bowl LIVE MUSIC
(Map p84; ☎ 718-963-3369; www.brooklynbowl.com; 61 Wythe Ave, btwn N 11th & N 12th Sts, Williamsburg; 🕓 6pm-close Mon-Fri, from noon Sat & Sun; [S] L to Bedford Ave; G to Nassau Ave) A 23,000-sq-ft venue inside the former Hecla Iron Works Company combines **bowling** (Map p84; ☎ 718-963-3369; www.brooklynbowl.com; 61 Wythe Ave, btwn N 11th & N 12th Sts, Williamsburg; lane rentals per 30min $25, shoe rentals $5; 🕓 6pm-late Mon-Fri, from noon Sat & Sun; 👪; [S] L to Bedford Ave; G to Nassau Ave), microbrews, food and top-notch music. In addition to the live bands (and occasional DJs) that regularly tear up the stage, there are NFL game days, karaoke and DJ nights. It's age 21 and up, except for 'family bowl' time on weekends (noon to 5pm Saturday, to 6pm Sunday).

Joe's Pub LIVE MUSIC
(Map p70; ☎ 212-539-8778, tickets 212-967-7555; www.joespub.com; Public Theater, 425 Lafayette St, btwn Astor Pl & 4th St, NoHo; [S] 6 to Astor Pl; R/W to 8th St-NYU) Part bar, part cabaret and performance venue, intimate Joe's serves up both emerging acts and top-shelf performers. Past entertainers have included Patti LuPone, Amy Schumer, the late Leonard Cohen and British songstress Adele (in fact, it was right here that Adele gave her very first American performance, back in 2008).

Irving Plaza LIVE MUSIC
(Map p70; ☎ 212-777-6817; www.irvingplaza.com; 17 Irving Pl, at 15th St, Union Square; [S] 4/5/6, N/Q/R, L to 14th St-Union Sq) Rocking since 1978, Irving Plaza has seen them all: the Ramones, Bob Dylan, U2, Pearl Jam, you name it. These days it's a great in-between stage for quirkier rock and pop acts, from indie chicks Sleater-Kinney to hard rockers Disturbed. There's a cozy floor around the stage, and good views from the mezzanine.

Sports

Madison Square Garden SPECTATOR SPORTS, CONCERT VENUE
(MSG, 'the Garden'; Map p74; www.thegarden.com; 4 Pennsylvania Plaza, Seventh Ave, btwn 31st & 33rd Sts; [S] A/C/E, 1/2/3 to 34th St-Penn Station) NYC's major performance venue – part of the massive complex housing Penn Station (p120) – hosts big-arena performers, from Kanye West to Madonna. It's also a sports arena, with New York Knicks (www.nba.com/knicks.com) and New York Liberty (www.liberty.wnba.com) basketball games and New York Rangers (www.nhl.com/rangers) hockey games, as well as boxing and events like the Annual Westminster Kennel Club Dog Show.

★**Gotham Girls Roller Derby** SPECTATOR SPORT
(www.gothamgirlsrollerderby.com; tickets from $30; 🕓 Mar-Aug; 👪) NYC's only all-female and skater-operated roller derby league has four borough-inspired home teams: the Bronx Gridlock, Brooklyn Bombshells, Manhattan Mayhem and Queens of Pain. These are some of the highest-level players of the sport you're likely to see: their top travel team, the All-Stars, are five-time world champions –

including a recent undefeated stretch for four years running.

USTA Billie Jean King National Tennis Center

SPECTATOR SPORT

(Map p86; ☎718-760-6200; www.usta.com; Flushing Meadows Corona Park, Corona; §7 to Mets-Willets Pt) The US Open, one of the city's premier sporting events, takes place in late August. As of 2016, the Arthur Ashe Stadium (capacity 23,771) now has a retractable roof, there's a new stadium (the Grandstand, which replaced the Old Grandstand), and outer courts have been renovated. Tickets usually go on sale at Ticketmaster in April or May, but are hard to get for marquee games. General admission to early rounds is easier.

Theater

★ **Eugene O'Neill Theatre**

THEATER

(Book of Mormon; Map p74; ☎tickets 212-239-6200; www.bookofmormonbroadway.com; 230 W 49th St, btwn Broadway & Eighth Ave; §N/R/W to 49th St, 1 to 50th St, C/E to 50th St) The Eugene O'Neill Theatre's shows have ranged from family-friendly *Annie* all the way to uproarious *The Best Little Whorehouse in Texas*, with nearly as wild an ownership ride as well – bought and sold numerous times over its nearly a century lifetime. It was originally the Forrest Theatre, then the Coronet Theatre, and was finally christened the Eugene O'Neill Theatre in 1959. Among the factoids, playwright Neil Simon owned it before selling in 1982 to its current owners.

★ **Richard Rodgers Theatre**

THEATER

(Hamilton; Map p74; ☎tickets 877-250-2929; www.hamiltonmusical.com; 226 W 46th St, btwn Seventh & Eighth Aves; §N/R/W to 49th St) This theater opened in 1926 and is unique for several reasons. One, it was the first to allow all patrons to enter through the same set of doors (generally there were separate entrances for the less expensive ticket-holders, aka riff-raff, to come through). It also has the honor of being the venue for the highest number of Best Play and Best Musical Tony Awards.

★ **Flea Theater**

THEATER

(Map p66; ☎tickets 212-226-0051; www.theflea.org; 20 Thomas St, btwn Church St & Broadway; 🖥; §A/C, 1/2/3 to Chambers St; R/W to City Hall) One of NYC's top off-off-Broadway companies, Flea is famous for staging innovative and timely new works. A brand-new location offers three performance spaces, including one named for devoted alum Sigourney

ON BROADWAY

In the early 20th century, clusters of theaters settled into the area around Times Square and began producing popular plays and suggestive comedies – a movement that had its roots in early vaudeville. By the 1920s, these messy works had evolved into on-stage spectacles like *Show Boat*, an all-out Oscar Hammerstein production about the lives of performers on a Mississippi steamboat. In 1943, Broadway had its first runaway hit – *Oklahoma!* – that remained on stage for a record 2212 performances.

Today, Broadway musicals are shown in one of 40 official Broadway theaters: lavish early-20th-century jewels that surround Times Square and are a major component of cultural life in New York. If you're on a budget, look for off-Broadway productions. These tend to be more intimate, inexpensive and often just as good.

For information about last-minute and discount tickets, see p61.

Weaver. The year-round program also includes music and dance productions, as well as shows for young audiences (aged five and up) and a rollicking late-night competition series of 10-minute plays.

Playwrights Horizons

THEATER

(Map p74; ☎212-564-1235; www.playwrightshorizons.org; 416 W 42nd St, btwn Ninth & Tenth Aves, Midtown West; §A/C/E to 42nd St-Port Authority Bus Terminal) An excellent place to catch what could be the next big thing, this veteran 'writers' theater' is dedicated to fostering contemporary American works. Notable past productions include Kenneth Lonergan's *Lobby Hero*, Bruce Norris' Tony Award–winning *Clybourne Park*, as well as Doug Wright's *I Am My Own Wife* and *Grey Gardens*.

★ **Al Hirschfeld Theatre**

THEATER

(Kinky Boots; Map p74; ☎tickets 877-250-2929; www.kinkybootsthemusical.com; 302 W 45th St, btwn Eighth & Ninth Aves; ⊙box office 10am-8pm Mon-Sat, noon-6pm Sun; §A/C/E to 42nd St-Port Authority Bus Terminal) Originally the Martin Beck Theatre, this spectacular building was renamed in 2003 when it was purchased from the Beck family. When it opened in 1924 to great acclaim, it proceeded to be the venue for some of Broadway's best-loved shows for decades, including *Pirates of Penzance, Romeo and Juliet, The Crucible, Guys and Dolls, Hair* and many more. Vast and opulent, it has seating for over 1400 for performances, with as many as 200 dressing rooms for actors backstage.

★ **St Ann's Warehouse** THEATER
(Map p66; ☎718-254-8779; www.stannsware house.org; 45 Water St, at Old Dock St, Dumbo; ☒B25 to Water/Main Sts, ⒮A/C to High St; F to York St) This avant-garde performance company hosts innovative theater, music and dance happenings – everything from genre-defying music by new composers to strange and wondrous puppet theater. In 2015, St Ann's moved from its old home several blocks away to this location in the historic Tobacco Warehouse in Brooklyn Bridge Park.

Signature Theatre THEATER
(Map p74; ☎tickets 212-244-7529; www.signa| turetheatre.org; 480 W 42nd St, btwn Ninth & Tenth Aves, Midtown West; ⒮A/C/E to 42nd St-Port Authority Bus Terminal) Looking good in its Frank Gehry–designed home - complete with three theaters, bookstore and cafe – Signature Theatre is devoted to the work of its playwrights-in-residence, both past and present. To date, featured dramatists have included Tony Kushner, Edward Albee, Athol Fugard and Kenneth Lonergan. Shows aside, the theater also runs talks with playwrights, directors, designers and actors. Aim to book performances one month in advance.

Second Stage Theater THEATER
(Tony Kiser Theater; Map p74; ☎tickets 212-246-4422; www.2st.com; 305 W 43rd St, at Eighth Ave, Midtown West; ⊙box office noon-6pm Sun-Fri, to 7pm Sat; ⒮A/C/E to 42nd St-Port Authority Bus Terminal) This is the main venue run by Second Stage Theater, a nonprofit theater company famed for debuting the work of talented emerging writers as well as that of the country's more established names. If you're after well-crafted contemporary American theater, this is a good place to find it.

Sleep No More THEATER
(Map p74; ☎box office 212-904-1880; www.sleep nomorenyc.com; 530 W 27th St, btwn Tenth & Eleventh Aves, Chelsea; tickets from $135; ⊙7pm-midnight Mon-Sat; ⒮1, C/E to 23rd St) One of the most immersive theater experiences ever conceived, *Sleep No More* is a loosely based retelling of *Macbeth* set inside a series of Chelsea warehouses that have been redesigned to look like the 1930s-era McKittrick Hotel and its hopping jazz bar.

BAM Harvey Theater THEATER
(Harvey Lichtenstein Theater; Map p82; ☎718-636-4100; www.bam.org; 651 Fulton St, near Rockwell Pl, Fort Greene; ⒮B, Q/R to DeKalb Ave; 2/3, 4/5 to Nevins St) This theater, one of NYC's most important cultural institutions, has hosted long runs by important artists like Tony Kushner, Peter Brook and Laurie Anderson. The building itself is a striking combination of ornate and elegant with gritty and industrial – so very Brooklyn. (The balcony seats, narrow and elevated, aren't the most comfortable, though, and some have obstructed sight lines.)

Performance Space New York THEATER
(Map p70; ☎212-477-5829; www.performance spacenewyork.org; 150 First Ave, at E 9th St, East Village; ⒮L to 1st Ave; 6 to Astor Pl) Formerly PS 122, this cutting-edge theater reopened in January 2018 with an entirely new facade, state-of-the-art performance spaces, artist studios, a new lobby and roof deck. The bones of the former schoolhouse remain, as does its experimental theater bona fides: Eric Bogosian, Meredith Monk, the late Spalding Gray and Elevator Repair Service have all performed here.

Soho Rep THEATER
(Soho Repertory Theatre; Map p66; ☎212-941-8632; www.sohorep.org; 46 Walker St, btwn Church St & Broadway; ⒮A/C/E, 1 to Canal St) This is one of New York's finest off-Broadway companies, wowing theater fans and critics with its annual trio of sharp, innovative new works. Allison Janney, Ed O'Neill and John C Reilly all made their professional debuts here, and the company's productions have garnered more than a dozen Obie (Off-Broadway Theater) Awards. Check the website for current or upcoming shows.

Delacorte Theater THEATER
(Map p78; www.publictheater.org; Central Park, enter at W 81st St; ⒮B, C to 81st St) Every summer the Joseph Papp Public Theater presents its fabulous free productions of Shakespeare in the Park (p85) at Delacorte Theater, which Papp began back in 1954, before the lovely, leafy, open-air theater was even built. Productions are usually superb, but regardless of their quality, it's a

magical experience and waiting in line for tickets is a rite of passage for newcomers to the city.

Comedy

★Upright Citizens Brigade Theatre COMEDY

(UCB; Map p74; ☎212-366-9176; www.ucbtheatre.com; 555 W 42nd St, btwn Tenth & Eleventh Aves, Hell's Kitchen; free-$10; ⏰7pm-midnight; [S]A/C/E to 42nd St-Port Authority) Comedy sketch shows and improv reign at the new location of the legendary venue, which receives drop-ins from casting directors and often features well-known figures from TV. Entry is cheap, and so are the beer and wine. You'll find quality shows happening nightly, from about 7:30pm, though the Sunday-night Assscat Improv session is always a riot.

Magnet Theater COMEDY

(Map p74; ☎tickets 212-244-8824; www.magnettheater.com; 254 W 29th St, btwn Seventh & Eighth Aves, Midtown West; [S]1/2 to 28th St; A/C/E to 23rd St; 1/2/3 to 34th St-Penn Station) Tons of comedy in several incarnations (mostly improv) lures the crowds at this theater-cum-training-ground for comics. Performances vary weekly, though regular favorites include Megawatt (featuring the theater's resident ensembles) and the Friday Night Sh*w, the latter using the audience's written rants and confessions to drive the evening's shenanigans.

Creek and the Cave COMEDY

(Map p86; ☎646-944-9255; www.creeklic.com; 10-93 Jackson Ave, Long Island City; ⏰11am-2am Sun-Thu, to 4am Fri & Sat; [S]7 to Vernon Blvd-Jackson Ave) The biggest and best known of a handful of fringy comedy clubs in the neighborhood, the Creek and the Cave has two stages, a Mexican restaurant, a chilled-out backyard and a bar with well-maintained pinball machines. With so much fun in one place, it's no surprise this venue is a kind of clubhouse for young comedy scenesters.

Comedy Cellar COMEDY

(Map p70; ☎212-254-3480; www.comedycellar.com; 117 MacDougal St, btwn W 3rd St & Minetta Lane, West Village; cover $12-24; [S]A/C/E, B/D/F/M to W 4th St-Washington Sq) This long-established basement comedy club in Greenwich Village features mainstream material and a good list of regulars (Colin Quinn, Judah Friedlander, Wanda Sykes), plus occasional high-profile drop-ins like Dave Chappelle, Jerry Seinfeld and Amy Schumer. Its success continues: Comedy Cellar now boasts another location at the Village Underground around the corner on W 3rd St.

In addition to the cover there is a two-item (food or drinks) minimum per show.

Cinemas

★Museum of Modern Art CINEMA

(MoMA; Map p74; ☎212-708-9400; www.moma.org; 11 W 53rd St, btwn Fifth & Sixth Aves; adult/child $25/free, 4-9pm Fri free for all; ⏰10:30am-5:30pm Sat-Thu, to 8pm Fri year-round, to 8pm Thu Jul & Aug; [S]B/D/F/M to 47th-50th Sts-Rockefeller Center) Not only a palace of visual art, MoMA hosts an incredibly well-rounded selection of celluloid gems, from documentary shorts and Hollywood classics to experimental works and international retrospectives.

Film Society of Lincoln Center CINEMA

(Map p78; ☎212-875-5367; www.filmlinc.com; Lincoln Center; [S]1 to 66th St-Lincoln Center) The Film Society is one of New York's cinematic gems, providing an invaluable platform for a wide gamut of documentary, feature, independent, foreign and avant-garde art pictures. Films screen in one of two facilities at Lincoln Center: the **Elinor Bunin Munroe Film Center** (☎212-875-5232), a more intimate, experimental venue, or the Walter Reade Theater (p114), with wonderfully wide, screening-room-style seats.

Metrograph CINEMA

(Map p70; ☎212-660-0312; www.metrograph.com; 7 Ludlow St, btwn Canal & Hester Sts, Lower East Side; tickets $15; [S]F to East Broadway; B/D to Grand St) The newest movie mecca for downtown cinephiles, this two-screen theater with red velvet seats shows curated arthouse flicks. Most you'll never find at any multiplex, though the odd mainstream pic like *Magic Mike* is occasionally screened. In addition to movie geeks browsing the bookstore, you'll find a stylish and glamorous set at the bar or in the upstairs restaurant.

Film Forum CINEMA

(Map p70; ☎212-727-8110; www.filmforum.com; 209 W Houston St, btwn Varick St & Sixth Ave, SoHo; tickets $15; ⏰noon-midnight; [S]1 to Houston St) Plans are in the works to expand to four screens, but for now Film Forum is still a three-screen nonprofit cinema with an astounding array of independent films, revivals and career retrospectives from greats such as Orson Welles. Theaters are small, so get there early for a good viewing spot. Showings often include director talks or other film-themed discussions for hardcore cinephiles.

Walter Reade Theater CINEMA
(Map p78; ☎212-875-5601; www.filmlinc.com; Lincoln Center, 165 W 65th St, btwn Broadway & Amsterdam Ave; [S]1 to 66th St-Lincoln Center) The Walter Reade boasts some wonderfully wide, screening-room-style seats. Every September it hosts the New York Film Festival, featuring plenty of New York and world premieres. At other times of the year you can catch independent films, career retrospectives and themed series.

Nitehawk Cinema CINEMA
(Map p84; ☎718-782-8370; www.nitehawkcinema.com; 136 Metropolitan Ave, btwn Berry & Wythe Sts, Williamsburg; tickets adult/child $12/9; 👪; [S]L to Bedford Ave) This indie triplex has a fine lineup of first-run and repertory films, a good sound system and comfy seats…but the best part is that you can dine and drink all during the movie. Munch on hummus plates, sweet-potato risotto balls or short-rib empanadas, matched by a Blue Point toasted lager, a negroni or a movie-themed cocktail invention.

Performing Arts

★Brooklyn Academy of Music PERFORMING ARTS
(BAM; Map p82; ☎718-636-4100; www.bam.org; 30 Lafayette Ave, at Ashland Pl, Fort Greene; 📶; [S]B/D, N/Q/R, 2/3, 4/5 to Atlantic Ave-Barclays Ctr) Founded in 1861, BAM is the country's oldest performing-arts center. With several neighboring venues located in the Fort Greene area, the complex offers innovative and edgier works of opera, modern dance, music, cinema and theater – everything from Merce Cunningham retrospectives and multimedia shows by Laurie Anderson to avant-garde interpretations of Shakespeare and other classics.

★National Sawdust LIVE PERFORMANCE
(Map p84; ☎646-779-8455; www.nationalsawdust.org; 80 N 6th St, at Wythe Ave, Williamsburg; 👪; [S]L to Bedford Ave) Covered in wildly hued murals, this arts space dedicated to cutting-edge multidisciplinary programming opened to much fanfare in 2015. You can see daring works like contemporary opera with multimedia projections, electro-acoustic big-band jazz and concerts by experimental composers, along with more globally infused performances – Inuit throat singing, African tribal funk, and the singing of Icelandic sagas, among other things.

Metropolitan Opera House OPERA
(Map p78; ☎tickets 212-362-6000, tours 212-769-7028; www.metopera.org; Lincoln Center, Columbus Ave at W 64th St; [S]1 to 66th St-Lincoln Center) New York's premier opera company is the place to see classics such as *Carmen, Madame Butterfly* and *Macbeth,* not to mention Wagner's Ring Cycle. It also hosts premieres and revivals of more contemporary works, such as John Adams' *The Death of Klinghoffer*. The season runs from September to April.

New York City Ballet DANCE
(Map p78; ☎212-496-0600; www.nycballet.com; Lincoln Center, Columbus Ave at W 63rd St; 👪; [S]1 to 66th St-Lincoln Center) This prestigious ballet company was first directed by renowned Russian-born choreographer George Balanchine back in the 1940s. Today, the company has 90 dancers and is the largest ballet organization in the US, performing 23 weeks a year at Lincoln Center's David H Koch Theater. During the holidays the troupe is best known for its annual production of *The Nutcracker*.

BAM Howard Gilman Opera House OPERA
(Map p82; ☎718-636-4100; www.bam.org; 30 Lafayette Ave, at Ashland Pl, Fort Greene; [S]B/D, N/Q/R, 2/3, 4/5 to Atlantic Ave-Barclays Ctr) The Peter Jay Sharp Building, a turn-of-the-20th-century beaux-arts masterpiece that is the main building of the Brooklyn Academy of Music, houses this venue that stages film, dance, music and theater. BAM regularly presents a small program of operas, as well as live HD simulcasts of the Metropolitan Opera.

🛍 Shopping

Not surprisingly for a capital of commercialism, creativity and fashion, New York City is quite simply one of the best shopping destinations on the planet. Every niche is filled. From indie designer-driven boutiques to landmark department stores, thrift shops to haute couture, record stores to the Apple store, street-eats to gourmet groceries, it's quite easy to blow one's budget.

Financial District & Lower Manhattan

★Century 21 FASHION & ACCESSORIES

(Map p66; ☎212-227-9092; www.c21stores.com; 22 Cortlandt St, btwn Church St & Broadway; ⏲7:45am-9pm Mon-Wed, to 9:30pm Thu & Fri, 10am-9pm Sat, 11am-8pm Sun; [S]A/C, J/Z, 2/3, 4/5 to Fulton St; R/W to Cortlandt St) For penny-pinching fashionistas, this giant cut-price department store is dangerously addictive. Physically dangerous as well, considering the elbows you might have to throw to ward off the competition beelining for the same rack. Not everything is a knockout or a bargain, but persistence pays off. You'll also find accessories, shoes, cosmetics, homewares and toys.

★Philip Williams Posters VINTAGE

(Map p66; ☎212-513-0313; www.postermuseum.com; 122 Chambers St, btwn Church St & W Broadway; ⏲10am-7pm Mon-Sat; [S]A/C, 1/2/3 to Chambers St) You'll find nearly half a million posters in this cavernous treasure trove, from oversized French advertisements for perfume and cognac to Eastern European film posters and retro-fab promos for TWA. Prices range from $15 for small reproductions to thousands of dollars for rare, showpiece originals like an AM Cassandre. There's a second entrance at 52 Warren St.

★Pearl River Mart DEPARTMENT STORE

(Map p66; ☎212-431-4770; www.pearlriver.com; 395 Broadway, at Walker St; ⏲10am-7:20pm; [S]N/Q/R/W, J/M/Z, 6 to Canal St) Pearl River has been a downtown shopping staple for 40 years, chock-full of a dizzying array of Asian gifts, housewares, clothing and accessories: silk men's pajamas, cheongsam dresses, blue-and-white Japanese ceramic tableware, clever kitchen gadgets, paper lanterns, origami and calligraphy kits, bamboo plants and more lucky-cat figurines than you can wave a paw at. A great place for gifts.

Mysterious Bookshop BOOKS

(Map p66; ☎212-587-1011; www.mysteriousbookshop.com; 58 Warren St, btwn W Broadway & Church St; ⏲11am-7pm Mon-Sat; [S]1/2/3, A/C to Chambers St) With more crime per square inch than any other corner of the city, this mystery-themed bookstore peddles everything from classic espionage and thrillers to contemporary Nordic crime fiction and literary criticism. You'll find both new and secondhand titles, including rare first editions, signed copies, obscure magazines and picture books for budding sleuths. Check the website for in-store events.

Best Made Company FASHION & ACCESSORIES

(Map p66; ☎646-478-7092; www.bestmadeco.com; 36 White St, at Church St; ⏲noon-7pm Mon-Fri, 11am-7pm Sat, to 6pm Sun; [S]A/C/E to Canal St; 1 to Franklin St) Give your next camping trip a Manhattan makeover at this store/design-studio hybrid. Pick up cool handcrafted axes, leather duffel bags, sunglasses, enamel camping mugs and even designer dartboards and first-aid kits, many emblazoned with their signature 'X' logo. A small, smart collection of men's threads includes designer flannel shirts and pullovers, sweatshirts and rugged knitwear from Portland's Dehen Knitting Mills.

SoHo & Chinatown

★Saturdays FASHION & ACCESSORIES

(Map p70; ☎212-966-7875; www.saturdaysnyc.com; 31 Crosby St, btwn Broome & Grand Sts, SoHo; ⏲store 10am-7pm, coffee bar 8am-7pm Mon-Fri, from 10am Sat & Sun; 📶; [S]N/Q/R/W, J/Z to Canal St; 6 to Spring St) SoHo's version of a surf shop sees boards and wax paired up with designer grooming products, graphic art and surf tomes, and Saturdays' own line of high-quality, fashion-literate threads for dudes. Styled-up, grab a coffee from the in-house espresso bar, hang in the back garden and fish for some crazy, shark-dodging tales. There's a second branch in the **West Village** (Map p70; ☎347-246-5830; 17 Perry St, at Waverly St; ⏲10am-7pm; [S]A/C/E, L to 8th Ave-14th St; 1/2/3 to 14th St).

★MiN New York COSMETICS

(Map p70; ☎212-206-6366; www.min.com; 117 Crosby St, btwn Jersey & Prince Sts, SoHo; ⏲11am-7pm Tue-Sat, noon-6pm Mon & Sun; [S]B/D/F/M to Broadway-Lafayette St; N/R to Prince St) This super-friendly, chic, library-like fragrance apothecary has exclusive perfumes, bath and grooming products, and scented candles. Look out for artisanal fragrance 'stories' from MiN's own line. Prices span affordable to astronomical, and the scents are divine. Unlike many places, here there's no pressure to buy.

East Village

Still House HOMEWARES

(Map p70; ☎212-539-0200; www.stillhousenyc.com; 117 E 7th St, btwn First Ave & Ave A, East Village; ⏰noon-8pm Mon-Fri, 11am-8pm Sat, to 7pm Sun; [S]6 to Astor Pl) Step into this petite, peaceful boutique to browse sculptural glassware and pottery: handblown vases, geometric tabletop objects, ceramic bowls and cups, and other finery for the home. You'll also find minimalistic jewelry, delicately bound notebooks and small framed artworks for the wall.

Obscura Antiques ANTIQUES

(Map p70; ☎212-505-9251; www.obscuraantiques.com; 207 Ave A, btwn E 12th & 13th Sts, East Village; ⏰noon-8pm Mon-Sat, to 7pm Sun; [S]L to 1st Ave) This small cabinet of curiosities pleases both lovers of the macabre and inveterate antique hunters. Here you'll find taxidermied animal heads, tiny rodent skulls and skeletons, butterfly displays in glass boxes, Victorian-era post-mortem photography, disturbing little (dental?) instruments, German landmine flags (stackable so tanks could see them), old poison bottles and glass eyes.

West Village, Chelsea & Meatpacking District

Trina Turk CLOTHING

(Map p70; ☎212-206-7383; www.trinaturk.com; 67 Gansevoort St, btwn Greenwich & Washington Sts, West Village; ⏰11am-7pm Mon-Sat, noon-6pm Sun; [S]A/C/E, L to 8th Ave-14th St) Anyone with a yen for '70s-inspired prints should take themselves to the Trina Turk boutique. The wife and husband team behind the unisex brand have cultivated a range that harkens back to the vibrant heyday of California cool with shift dresses, floral blazers, statement pants, and swimsuits that range from board shorts to ultra-skimpy briefs.

Screaming Mimi's VINTAGE

(Map p70; ☎212-677-6464; www.screamingmimis.com; 240 W 14th St, btwn Seventh & Eighth Aves, Chelsea; ⏰noon-8pm Mon-Sat, 1-7pm Sun; [S]A/C/E, L to 8th Ave-14th St) If you dig vintage threads, you may just scream, too. This fun-tastic shop carries an excellent selection of yesteryear pieces, organized – ingeniously – by decade, from the '50s to the '90s. (Ask to see the small, stashed-away collection of clothing from the 1920s through '40s.)

Idlewild Books BOOKS

(Map p70; ☎212-414-8888; www.idlewildbooks.com; 170 Seventh Ave S, at Perry St, West Village; ⏰noon-8pm Mon-Thu, to 6pm Fri-Sun; [S]1 to Christopher St-Sheridan Sq; 1/2/3 to 14th St; A/C/E, L to 8th Ave-14th St) Named after JFK airport's original moniker, this indie travel bookstore gets feet seriously itchy. Books are divided by region and cover guidebooks as well as fiction, travelogues, history, cookbooks and other stimulating fare for delving into different corners of the world. The store also runs popular language classes in French, Italian, Spanish and German; see the website for details.

Union Square, Flatiron District & Gramercy

★**Strand Book Store** BOOKS

(Map p70; ☎212-473-1452; www.strandbooks.com; 828 Broadway, at E 12th St, West Village; ⏰9:30am-10:30pm Mon-Sat, from 11am Sun; [S]L, N/Q/R/W, 4/5/6 to 14th St-Union Sq) Beloved and legendary, the iconic Strand embodies downtown NYC's intellectual *bona fides* – a bibliophile's Oz, where generations of book lovers carrying the store's trademark tote bags happily lose themselves for hours. In operation since 1927, the Strand sells new, used and rare titles, spreading an incredible 18 miles of books (over 2.5 million of them) among three labyrinthine floors.

Midtown

★**MoMA Design & Book Store** GIFTS, BOOKS

(Map p74; ☎212-708-9700; www.momastore.org; 11 W 53rd St, btwn Fifth & Sixth Aves; ⏰9:30am-6:30pm Sat-Thu, to 9pm Fri; [S]E, M to 5th Ave-53rd St) The flagship store at the Museum of Modern Art (p65) is a fab spot for souvenir shopping. Besides gorgeous books (from art and architecture tomes to pop-culture readers and kids' picture books), you'll find art prints and posters and one-of-a-kind knickknacks. For furniture, lighting, homewares, jewelry, bags and MUJI merchandise, head to the MoMA Design Store across the street.

Tiffany & Co JEWELRY, HOMEWARES

(Map p74; ☎212-755-8000; www.tiffany.com; 727 Fifth Ave, at E 57th St; ⏰10am-7pm Mon-Sat, noon-6pm Sun; [S]F to 57th St; N/R/W to 5th Ave-59th St) Ever since Audrey Hepburn gazed longingly through its windows, Tiffany & Co has won countless hearts with its glittering diamond rings, watches, silver Elsa Peretti heart necklaces, crystal vases and glassware. But wait, there's more, including handbags and travel-friendly gifts like letter openers. Swoon, drool, but whatever you do, don't harass the elevator attendants with tired 'Where's the breakfast?' jokes.

Saks Fifth Ave DEPARTMENT STORE
(Map p74; ☎212-753-4000; www.saksfifthavenue.com; 611 Fifth Ave, at E 50th St; 🕙10am-8:30pm Mon-Sat, 11am-7pm Sun; [S] B/D/F/M to 47th-50th Sts-Rockefeller Center, E, M to 5th Ave-53rd St) Graced with vintage elevators, Saks' 10-floor flagship store is home to the 'Shoe Salon,' NYC's biggest women's shoe department (complete with express elevator and zip code). Other fortes include the cosmetics and men's departments, the latter home to destination grooming salon John Allan's and a sharply edited offering of fashion-forward labels. The store's January sale is legendary.

Argosy BOOKS, MAPS
(Map p78; ☎212-753-4455; www.argosybooks.com; 116 E 59th St, btwn Park & Lexington Aves, Midtown East; 🕙10am-6pm Mon-Fri, to 5pm Sat Sep-late May; [S] 4/5/6 to 59th St; N/Q/R to Lexington Ave-59th St) Bookstores like this are becoming as rare as the books they contain, but since 1925 this landmark has stocked fine antiquarian items such as books, old maps, art monographs and more. There's also an interesting booty of Hollywood memorabilia, from personal letters and signed books to contracts and autographed publicity stills. Prices range from costly to clearance.

Barneys DEPARTMENT STORE
(Map p78; ☎212-826-8900; www.barneys.com; 660 Madison Ave, at E 61st St; 🕙10am-8pm Mon-Wed & Sat, to 9pm Thu & Fri, 11am-7pm Sun; [S] N/R/W to 5th Ave-59th St) Serious fashionistas swipe their plastic at Barneys, respected for its collections of top-tier labels like Isabel Marant Étoile, Mr & Mrs Italy and Lanvin. For (slightly) less expensive deals geared to a younger market, shop street-chic brands on the 8th floor. Other highlights include a basement cosmetics department and Genes, a futuristic cafe with touch-screen communal tables for online shopping.

Bergdorf Goodman DEPARTMENT STORE
(Map p78; ☎212-753-7300, 888-774-2424; www.bergdorfgoodman.com; 754 Fifth Ave, btwn W 57th & 58th Sts; 🕙10am-8pm Mon-Sat, 11am-7pm Sun; [S] N/Q/R/W to 5th Ave-59th St, F to 57th St) Not merely loved for its Christmas windows (the city's best), plush BG, at this location since 1928, leads the fashion race, led by its industry-leading fashion director Linda Fargo. A mainstay of ladies who lunch, its draws include exclusive collections of Tom Ford and Chanel shoes and a coveted women's shoe department. The men's store is across the street.

Hell's Kitchen Flea Market MARKET
(Map p74; ☎212-220-0239; www.annexmarkets.com/hells-kitchen-foundation; W 39th St, btwn Ninth & Tenth Aves; 🕙9am-5pm Sat & Sun; [S] A/C/E to 42nd St-Port Authority Bus Terminal) This weekend flea market lures both collectors and the common curious with its wonderful booty of vintage furnishings, accessories, clothing and unidentifiable objects from past eras.

Grand Central Market MARKET
(Map p74; www.grandcentralterminal.com/market; Grand Central Terminal, Lexington Ave, at 42nd St, Midtown East; 🕙7am-9pm Mon-Fri, 10am-7pm Sat, 11am-6pm Sun; [S] S, 4/5/6, 7 to Grand Central-42nd St) It's not all arrivals and departures at Grand Central. The station also harbors a 240ft corridor lined with perfectly coiffed fresh produce and artisanal treats. Stock up on anything from crusty bread and fruit tarts to lobsters, chicken pot pies, Spanish quince paste, fruit and vegetables, and roasted coffee beans. There's even a Murray's Cheese stall, peddling milky wonders like cave-aged Gruyère.

🛍 Brooklyn

★Artists & Fleas MARKET
(Map p84; ☎917-488-4203; www.artistsandfleas.com; 70 N 7th St, btwn Wythe & Kent Aves, Williamsburg; 🕙10am-7pm Sat & Sun; [S] L to Bedford Ave) In operation for over a decade, this popular Williamsburg flea market has an excellent selection of crafty goodness. Over a hundred artists, designers and vintage vendors sell their wares: clothing, records, paintings, photographs, hats, handmade jewelry, one-of-a-kind T-shirts, canvas bags and more. Two locations in Manhattan are smaller but open daily: one in SoHo, the other inside the Chelsea Market (p64).

Brooklyn Flea MARKET
(Map p66; www.brooklynflea.com; 80 Pearl St, Manhattan Bridge Archway, Anchorage Pl at Water St, Dumbo; 🕙10am-6pm Sun Apr-Oct; 👪; 🚌B67 to York/Jay Sts, [S] F to York St) Every Sunday

from spring through early fall, several dozen vendors sell their wares inside a giant archway under the Manhattan Bridge, ranging from antiques, records and vintage clothes to craft items, housewares and furniture. A slightly smaller indoor version, with around 60 vendors, runs every Saturday and Sunday (10am to 6pm) in SoHo (Sixth Ave at Watt St).

Twisted Lily PERFUME, COSMETICS
(Map p82; ☎347-529-4681; www.twistedlily.com; 360 Atlantic Ave, btwn Bond & Hoyt Sts, Boerum Hill; 🕐12:30-7:30pm Tue-Sun; [S] F, G to Hoyt-Schermerhorn) Come out smelling like a rose from this boutique specializing in indie scents from around the world. Shop for perfumes and scented candles by fragrance notes (bergamot, clary sage, honeysuckle and many others); attentive staff will help you pick whatever your nose desires. The shop also carries niche skincare, hair and men's grooming products.

Powerhouse @ the Archway BOOKS
(Map p66; ☎718-666-3049; www.powerhousebooks.com; 28 Adams St, cnr Water St, Dumbo; 🕐10am-7pm; 📶; [S] A/C to High St; F to York St) An important part of Dumbo's cultural scene, Powerhouse Books hosts changing art exhibitions, book-launch parties and weird and creative events in its large, airy new digs just under the Manhattan Bridge. You'll also find intriguing books on urban art, photography and pop culture – all products of its namesake publishing house.

Rough Trade MUSIC
(Map p84; ☎718-388-4111; www.roughtradenyc.com; 64 N 9th St, btwn Kent & Wythe Aves, Williamsburg; 🕐11am-11pm Mon-Sat, to 10pm Sun; 📶; [S] L to Bedford Ave) This sprawling, 10,000-sq-ft record store – a London import – stocks thousands of titles on vinyl and CD, plus some music-themed indie books and magazines. It also has in-store DJs, listening stations, art exhibitions, and coffee and doughnuts from the on-site Brompton Bike Cafe. A small concert hall onsite hosts live music regularly (admission generally $10 to $20). Free table tennis upstairs.

Beacon's Closet VINTAGE
(Map p84; ☎718-486-0816; www.beaconscloset.com; 74 Guernsey St, btwn Nassau & Norman Aves, Greenpoint; 🕐11am-8pm; [S] L to Bedford Ave; G to Nassau Ave) Twenty-something groovers find this massive 5500-sq-ft warehouse of vintage clothing part goldmine, part grit. Lots of coats, polyester tops and '90s-era T-shirts are displayed by color, but the sheer mass can take time to conquer. You'll also find shoes of all sorts, flannels, hats, handbags, chunky jewelry and brightly hued sunglasses. There are other branches in **Bushwick** (Map p84; ☎718-417-5683; 23 Bogart St, btwn Varet & Cook Sts, Bushwick; 🕐11am-8pm; [S] L to Morgan Ave) and **Park Slope** (Map p82; ☎718-230-1630; 92 Fifth Ave, cnr Warren St, Park Slope; 🕐noon-9pm Mon-Fri, 11am-8pm Sat & Sun; [S] 2/3 to Bergen St; B, Q to 7th Ave).

Catbird JEWELRY
(Map p84; ☎718-599-3457; www.catbirdnyc.com; 219 Bedford Ave, btwn N 4th & 5th Sts, Williamsburg; 🕐noon-8pm Mon-Fri, 11am-7pm Sat, noon-6pm Sun; [S] L to Bedford Ave) 🌿 Still going strong in Williamsburg after 14 years, this jewelry shop stocks both its own pieces – made in a studio a few blocks away – and jewelry from independent makers around the world. Everything is either sterling silver or gold, and uses conflict-free, authentic gems. Catbird specializes in rings, especially stacking sets and engagement rings (hey, no pressure).

[i] Information

MEDICAL SERVICES

Emergency services can be stress-inducing and slow (unless your medical condition is absolutely dire); a visit should be avoided if other medical services can be accessed to mitigate the situation.

Bellevue Hospital Center (☎212-562-4141; www.nychealthandhospitals.org/bellevue; 462 First Ave, at 27th St, Midtown East; [S] 6 to 28th St) Major public hospital with emergency room and trauma center.

Callen-Lorde Community Health Center (☎212-271-7200; www.callen-lorde.org; 356 W 18th St, btwn Eighth & Ninth Aves; 🕐8:15am-8:15pm Mon-Thu, 9:45am-4:45pm Fri, 8:30am-3:15pm Sat; [S] A/C/E, L to 8th Ave-14th St) This medical center, dedicated to the LGBT community and people living with HIV/AIDS, serves people regardless of their ability to pay.

Lenox Hill Hospital (☎212-434-2000; www.northwell.edu/find-care/locations/lenox-hill-hospital; 100 E 77th St, at Lexington Ave; 🕐24hr; [S] 6 to 77th St) A good hospital with a 24-hour emergency room and multilingual translators in the Upper East Side.

Mount Sinai Hospital (☎212-241-6500; www.mountsinai.org/locations/mount-sinai; 1468 Madison Ave, at E 101st St; 🕐24hr; [S] 6 to 103rd St) An excellent hospital in the Upper East Side.

New York County Medical Society (📞212-684-4670; www.nycms.org) Provides doctor referrals over the phone, based on type of problem and language spoken.

New York-Presbyterian Hospital (📞212-305-2500; www.nyp.org/locations/newyork-pres byterian-columbia-university-medical-center; 630 W 168th St, at Ft Washington Ave; S A/C, 1 to 168th St) Reputable hospital.

Planned Parenthood (Margaret Sanger Center; 📞212-965-7000; www.plannedparenthood. org; 26 Bleecker St, btwn Mott & Elizabeth Sts, NoHo; ⊗8am-6:30pm Mon, Tue, Thu & Fri, to 8:30pm Wed, to 4:30pm Sat; S B/D/F/V to Broadway-Lafayette St; 6 to Bleecker St) Provides birth control, STD screenings and gynecological care.

Tisch Hospital (New York University Langone Medical Center; 📞212-263-5800; www.nyulan gone.org/locations/tisch-hospital; 550 First Ave; ⊗24hr) Large, state-of-the-art facility with highly regarded departments in every critical care specialty.

TOURIST INFORMATION

NYC Information Center (Map p74; 📞212-484-1222; www.nycgo.com; Broadway Plaza, btwn W 43rd & 44th Sts; ⊗8am-8pm; S N/Q/R/W, S, 1/2/3, 7, A/C/E to Times Sq-42nd St) There are official NYC Visitor Information Centers throughout the city. The main office is in Midtown. In this web-based world you'll find infinite online resources to get up-to-the-minute information about New York. In person, try one of the official branches of NYC Information Center: **Macy's Herald Square** (Map p74; 📞212-484-1222; Macy's, 151 W 34th St, at Broadway; ⊗10am-10pm Mon-Sat, to 9pm Sun; S B/D/F/M, N/Q/R/W to 34th St-Herald Sq), **City Hall** (Map p66; 📞212-484-1222; City Hall Park, at Broadway; ⊗9am-6pm; S 4/5/6 to Brooklyn Bridge-City Hall; R/W to City Hall; J/Z to Chambers St) and South Street Seaport.

Explore Brooklyn (www.explorebk.com) has up-to-date event listings and lots of of other info on this much-loved borough.

❶ Getting There & Away

With its three bustling airports, two main train stations and a monolithic bus terminal, New York City rolls out the welcome mat for millions of visitors who come to take a bite out of the Big Apple each year.

Direct flights are possible from most major American and international cities. Figure six hours from Los Angeles, seven hours from London and Amsterdam, and 14 hours from Tokyo. Consider getting here by train instead of car or plane to enjoy a mix of bucolic and urban scenery en route, without unnecessary traffic hassles, security checks and excess carbon emissions.

BROOKLYN TRANSPORT

Boat

The **NYC Ferry** (Map p62; www.ferry.nyc; S 10th St, off Kent Ave, Williamsburg; one-way trip $2.75; 🚌B32, Q59 to Kent Ave, S J/M/Z to Marcy Ave) runs from Manhattan's Wall St to E 34th St, with Brooklyn stops in Dumbo, Williamsburg, Greenpoint, Cobble Hill, Red Hook and Sunset Park.

Bus

Take the B61 or B57 for Red Hook. The B62 runs from downtown to Williamsburg/Greenpoint.

Subway

Seventeen lines travel to/from Brooklyn; all run through downtown. Key routes from Manhattan include the A/C, 2/3, 4/5, D/F, N/R/Q and L trains. The G runs only between Queens and Brooklyn, from Long Island City to south of Prospect Park.

Taxi

Apple-green Boro Taxis can pick up passengers only in Upper Manhattan and the four outer boroughs (but can drop off anywhere in NYC). Hail them on the street or request one through the Curb smartphone app.

Flights, tours and rail tickets can be booked online at www.lonelyplanet.com/bookings.

AIR

John F Kennedy Airport

Fifteen miles from Midtown in southeastern Queens, **John F Kennedy International Airport** (JFK; Map p126; 📞718-244-4444; www.kennedyairport.com; S A to Howard Beach or E, J/Z to Sutphin Blvd-Archer Ave then Airtrain to JFK) has six working terminals, serves nearly 50 million passengers annually and hosts flights coming and going from all corners of the globe. You can use the AirTrain (free within the airport) to move from one terminal to another.

The timeline is uncertain, but a massive $10 billion overhaul of the airport was recently approved. Architectural and structural changes are the focus, but plans also call for a substantial upgrade of amenities and transportation alternatives.

LaGuardia Airport

Used mainly for domestic flights, **LaGuardia** (LGA; 📞718-533-3400; www.laguardiaairport. com; 🚌M60, Q70) is smaller than JFK but only

8 miles from midtown Manhattan; it sees nearly 30 million passengers per year.

Much maligned by politicians and ordinary travelers alike, the airport is set to receive a much-needed $4 billion overhaul of its terminal facilities. Scheduled in phases from 2018 to 2021, plans call for a single, unified terminal to replace the four existing stand-alone ones, as well as an upgrade in amenities and transportation alternatives.

Newark Liberty International Airport

Don't write off New Jersey when looking for airfares to New York. About the same distance from Midtown as JFK (16 miles), **Newark** (EWR; ✆973-961-6000; www.newarkairport.com) brings many New Yorkers out for flights (there's some 40 million passengers annually). It's a hub for United Airlines and offers the only nonstop flight to Havana, Cuba, in the New York City area. A $2.4 billion redevelopment of Terminal A is scheduled to be completed in 2022.

BOAT

Seastreak (www.seastreak.com) has daily commuter services between Atlantic Highlands and Highlands, New Jersey and Pier 11 near Wall St and E 35th St; there's also summer services to Sandy Hook (return $46) in New Jersey. Martha's Vineyard (one way/round trip $165/240, five hours) in Massachusetts is accessible on summer weekends from E 35th St.

Cruise ships dock at the Manhattan Cruise Terminal in Hell's Kitchen on the west side of Manhattan at several piers from W 46th to 54th Sts.

If you're arriving in NYC by yacht, there are ports at an exclusive boat slip at the World Financial Center, and at a long-term slip at the 79th St Boathouse on the Upper West Side.

BUS

For long-distance bus trips, you'll arrive and depart from the world's busiest bus station, the **Port Authority Bus Terminal** (Map p74; ✆212-502-2200, bus information 212-564-8484; www.panynj.gov/bus-terminals; 625 Eighth Ave, at W 42nd St; ⊗9am-10pm; ⓈA/C/E to 42nd St-Port Authority Bus Terminal), which sees more than 65 million passengers each year. Efforts to replace the aging and less-than-salubrious station are always on the agenda. Bus companies leaving from here include the following:

Greyhound (www.greyhound.com) Connects New York with major cities across the country.

Peter Pan Trailways (www.peterpanbus.com) Daily express services to Boston, Washington, DC, and Philadelphia.

Short Line Bus (www.shortlinebus.com) Serves northern New Jersey and upstate New York, focusing on college towns such as Ithaca and New Paltz; part of Coach USA.

Trailways (www.trailwaysny.com) Bus service to upstate New York, including Albany, Ithaca and Syracuse, as well as Montreal, Canada.

Budget Buses

A number of budget bus lines operate from locations on the west side of Midtown:

BoltBus (Map p74; ✆877-265-8287; www.boltbus.com; W 33rd St, btwn Eleventh & Twelfth Aves; 🛜) Services from New York to Philadelphia, Boston, Baltimore and Washington, DC. The earlier you purchase tickets, the better the deal. Notable for its free wi-fi, which occasionally actually works.

Megabus (Map p74; ✆877-462-6342; https://us.megabus.com; 34th St, btwn 11th & 12th Aves; 🛜; Ⓢ7 to 34th St-Hudson Yards) Travels from New York to Boston, Washington, DC, and Toronto, among other destinations. Free (sometimes functioning) wi-fi. Departures leave from 34th St near the Jacob K Javits Convention Center and **arrivals** (Map p74; 7th Ave & 27th St) come to 27th and 7th.

Vamoose (Map p74; ✆212-695-6766; www.vamoosebus.com; cnr Seventh Ave & 30th St; from $20; Ⓢ1 to 28th St; A/C/E, 1/2/3 to 34th St-Penn Station) Buses head to Arlington, VA and Bethesda, MD, both not far outside Washington, DC.

TRAIN

Penn Station (W 33rd St, btwn Seventh & Eighth Aves; Ⓢ1/2/3, A/C/E to 34th St-Penn Station) The oft-maligned departure point for all Amtrak (www.amtrak.com) trains, including the Acela Express services to Princeton, NJ, and Washington, DC (note that this express service costs twice as much as a normal fare). All fares vary, based on the day of the week and the time you want to travel. There's no baggage-storage facility at Penn Station. Renewal work and maintenance issues affected Amtrak and LIRR lines out of Penn Station in the summer of 2018, which may be continued; be aware that some services may be compromised.

Long Island Rail Road (www.mta.info/lirr) Serves more than 300,000 commuters each day, with services from Penn Station to points in Brooklyn and Queens, and on Long Island. Prices are broken down by zones. A peak-hour ride from Penn Station to Jamaica Station (en route to JFK via AirTrain) costs $10.25 if you buy it at the station (or a whopping $16 onboard!).

NJ Transit (www.njtransit.com) Also operates trains from Penn Station, with services to the suburbs and the Jersey Shore.

New Jersey PATH (www.panynj.gov/path) An option for getting into NJ's northern points, such as Hoboken and Newark. Trains ($2.75) run from Penn Station along the length of Sixth

Ave, with stops at 33rd, 23rd, 14th, 9th and Christopher Sts, as well as at the reopened World Trade Center site.

Metro-North Railroad (www.mta.info/mnr) The last line departing from the magnificent Grand Central Terminal, it serves Connecticut, Westchester County and the Hudson Valley.

ⓘ Getting Around

Check the Metropolitan Transportation Authority website (www.mta.info) for public transportation information (buses and subway). Delays have increased as ridership has expanded.

Subway Inexpensive, somewhat efficient and operates around the clock, though navigating lines can be confusing. Single ride is $2.75 with a MetroCard.

Buses Convenient during off hours – especially when transferring between the city's eastern and western sides. Uses the MetroCard; same price as the subway.

Taxi Meters start at $2.50 and increase roughly $5 for every 20 blocks. See www.nyc.gov/taxi.

Bicycle The city's popular bike-share program Citi Bike provides excellent access to most parts of Manhattan.

Inter-borough ferries The New York City Ferry (www.ferry.nyc) provides handy transport between waterside stops in Manhattan, Brooklyn and Queens.

NEW YORK CITY GETTING AROUND

TO/FROM THE AIRPORT

John F Kennedy International Airport The AirTrain ($5) links to the subway ($2.75), which makes the one-hour journey into Manhattan. Express buses to Grand Central or Port Authority cost $18. Taxis cost a flat $52, excluding tolls, tip and rush-hour surcharge.

LaGuardia Airport The closest airport to Manhattan but the least accessible by public transit: take the Q70 express bus from the airport to the 74th St–Broadway subway station. Express buses to Midtown cost $15. Taxis range from $34 to $53, excluding tolls and tip.

Newark Liberty International Airport Take the AirTrain ($5.50) to Newark Airport train station, and board any train bound for New York's Penn Station ($13). Taxis range from $60 to $80 (plus $15 toll and tip). Allow 45 minutes to one hour of travel time.

BICYCLE

Hundreds of miles of designated bike lanes have been added over the past decade. Add to this the excellent bike-sharing network Citi Bike (www.citibikenyc.com), and you have the makings for a surprisingly bike-friendly city. Hundreds of Citi Bike kiosks in Manhattan and parts of Brooklyn house the iconic bright blue and very sturdy bicycles, which have reasonable rates for short-term users. Nearly 14 million City Bike 'trips' were taken in 2016 and there are there are an estimated 12,000 bikes in the system.

To use a Citi Bike, purchase a 24-hour or three-day access pass ($12 or $24 including tax) at any Citi Bike kiosk. You will then be given a five-digit code to unlock a bike. Return the bike to any station within 30 minutes to avoid incurring extra fees. Reinsert your credit card (you won't be charged) and follow the prompts to check out a bike again. You can make an unlimited number of 30-minute checkouts during those 24 hours or three days.

Helmets aren't required by law, but strongly recommended. You'll need to bring your own. City parks like Central Park, the Brooklyn Waterfront Greenway and Prospect Park in Brooklyn are good places to test out your comfort level on wheels in less stressful environments than the chaotic city streets. And most importantly, for your safety and that of others, obey traffic laws.

You'll find routes and bike lanes for every borough on NYC Bike Maps (www.nycbikemaps.com). For downloadable maps and point-to-point route generator, visit NYC DOT (www.nyc.gov/html/dot/html/bicyclists/bikemaps.shtml). Free bike maps are also available at most bike shops.

PUBLIC TRANSPORTATION

Tickets & Passes

➤ The yellow-and-blue MetroCards (www.mta.info/metrocard) are the swipe cards used for all of NYC's public transportation. You can purchase or add value at one of several easy-to-use automated machines at any station. Each ride on the subway or bus (except for express buses) deducts $2.75 from the card.

➤ Purchase the MetroCard itself for $1 at kiosks in subway stations, and load it with credit ($21, which will give you eight rides, is a good start). If you plan to ride a lot, buy a 7-Day Unlimited Pass ($32). These cards are handy for visitors – particularly if you're jumping around town to a few different places in one day.

➤ The subway kiosks take credit or ATM cards (larger machines also take cash). When you need to add more credit, just insert your card and follow the prompts (tip: when it asks for your ZIP, input '99999' if you're not from the USA).

➤ Transfers from subway to bus, or bus to subway, are free. Just swipe/insert your card, and no extra charge will be deducted.

New York State

POP 19.8 MILLION

Best Places to Eat

➜ Dockside Bar and Grill (p129)

➜ Black Sheep (p154)

➜ Clam Bar at Napeague (p130)

➜ Phoenicia Diner (p133)

Best Places to Stay

➜ Scribner's Catskill Lodge (p140)

➜ Inns of Aurora (p143)

➜ Adirondack Loj (p148)

➜ InnBuffalo off Elmwood (p153)

Why Go?

Long Island and upstate New York – generally accepted as anywhere north of the NYC metro area – shouldn't be missed. Long Island has cozy beach towns, while upstate is a dream destination for those who cherish the great outdoors. The Hudson River valley acts as an escape route from the city, leading eager sojourners north. From Albany, the 524-mile Erie Canal cuts due west to Lake Erie, passing spectacular Niagara Falls, Buffalo and Rochester. In the east you'll find the St Lawrence River and its thousands of islands, as well as the magnificent Adirondack and Catskills mountains. Head to the middle of the state and you'll be ensconced in the serene Finger Lakes.

When to Go
New York City

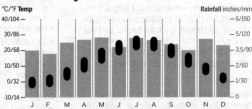

°C/°F Temp — 40/104 — 30/86 — 20/68 — 10/50 — 0/32 — -10/14 —
Rainfall inches/mm — 6/150 — 5/120 — 3.5/90 — 2/60 — 1/30 — 0
J F M A M J J A S O N D

Jan–Mar Ski resorts of the Catskills and Adirondacks in full swing.

late May– early Sep Memorial Day through to Labor Day is for beaches and lakeside resorts.

Oct–Nov Peak leaf-peeping times across the state with crowds in Catskills and Hudson Valley.

History

The lands of New York state have been inhabited for thousands of years and its history includes the rise and fall of civilizations, marvels of statecraft, engineering and architecture, and the lives of dynamic activists and artists.

ℹ️ Information

New York State Office of Parks, Recreation and Historic Preservation (☑️ 518-474-0456; www.parks.ny.gov) Camping, lodging and general info on all state parks. Reservations can be made up to nine months in advance.

ℹ️ Getting There & Away

Three major airports – JFK International Airport (p431), LaGuardia Airport (p431) and Newark Liberty International Airport (p431) – serve New York City and its surrounds with international arrivals. Major regional airports include Buffalo Niagara International Airport (p154), Greater Rochester International Airport (p151) and Albany International Airport (p147).

Amtrak (www.amtrak.com) has train services across the state and into Canada, crossing the border at Niagara Falls.

Greyhound (www.greyhound.com) and Trailways (www.trailways.com) provide bus service all over the state, including many destinations that aren't accessible by train.

ℹ️ Getting Around

Amtrak trains make it relatively easy to reach destinations north of NYC along the east side of the Hudson River and all the way across to Buffalo and Niagara Falls in the west of the state. There are also relatively frequent buses between major population centers, as well as fairly ubiquitous taxi service, especially with the recent expansion of Uber and Lyft into northern New York state. However, to access all of New York's great outdoors, and particularly areas such as the Catskills, Adirondacks and Finger Lakes, a car is necessary.

LONG ISLAND

Technically, the 118 miles of Long Island includes the boroughs of Brooklyn and Queens on the west edge, but in the popular imagination, 'Long Island' begins only where the city ends, in a mass of traffic-clogged expressways and suburbs that every teenager aspires to leave. (Levittown, the first planned 1950s subdivision, is in central Nassau County.) But there's plenty more out on 'Lawn-guy-land' (per the local accent). Push

past the central belt of 'burbs to windswept dunes, proud stands of pine, glitzy summer resorts, fresh farms and wineries, and whaling and fishing ports established in the 17th century. Then you'll see why loyalists prefer the nickname 'Strong Island.'

ℹ️ Information

Long Island Convention & Visitors Bureau (www.discoverlongisland.com) Detailed listings on museums, activities and other attractions all over Long Island.

ℹ️ Getting There & Away

Thanks to Long Island Rail Road (LIRR; www.mta.info/lirr), which runs three lines from NYC's Penn Station to the furthest east ends of the island, it's possible to visit without a car. Additionally, the Hampton Jitney (www.hamptonjitney.com) and Hampton Luxury Liner (www.hamptonluxuryliner.com) buses connect Manhattan to various Hamptons villages and Montauk; the former also picks up in Brooklyn, and runs to the North Fork. With a car, however, it is easier to visit several spots on the island in one go. I-495, aka the Long Island Expwy (LIE), runs down the middle of the island – but avoid rush hour, when it's commuter hell.

South Shore

Easily accessible by public transit, South Shore beaches can get crowded, but they're a fun day out. Not nearly as much of a schlep as the Hamptons, and far more egalitarian, the beach towns along these barrier islands each have their own vibe and audience – you can get lost in the crowds or go solo on the dunes. Long Beach is just over the border from Queens, and its main town strip is busy with ice-cream shops, bars and eateries.

👁️ Sights

Fire Island National Seashore ISLAND (☑️ 631-687-4750; www.nps.gov/fiis; FREE) Federally protected, this island offers sand dunes, forests, clean beaches, camping (dune-camping permits $20), hiking trails, inns, restaurants, 15 hamlets and two villages. The scenery ranges from car-free areas of summer mansions and packed nightclubs to stretches of sand where you'll find nothing but pitched tents and deer.

Most of the island is accessible only by ferry (☑️ 631-665-3600; www.fireislandferries.com; 99 Maple Ave, Bay Shore; one way adult/child $10/5) and is free of cars – regulars haul their belongings on little wagons instead.

New York State Highlights

1 Catskills (p132) Escaping to verdant wilderness on NYC's doorstep, with cool inns and delicious eats.

2 Adirondacks (p144) Exploring dense forests and beguiling lakes, plus mountain sports galore.

3 Buffalo (p151) Taking in post-industrial Buffalo on Lake Erie, packed with incredible architecture and art.

4 Niagara Falls (p154) Walking or sailing to within yards of this soaking natural wonder.

5 Long Island (p123) Visiting magnificent dunes and beaches, important historic sites and renowned vineyards.

6 Beacon (p137) Marvelling at the epic scale sculptures and installations at Dia: Beacon in this revived Hudson River town.

7 Ithaca (p141) Chilling in this laid-back college town, gateway to the scenic Finger Lakes region.

8 Albany (p145) Admiring the state capital's excellent museums and the stunning architectural ensemble at its heart.

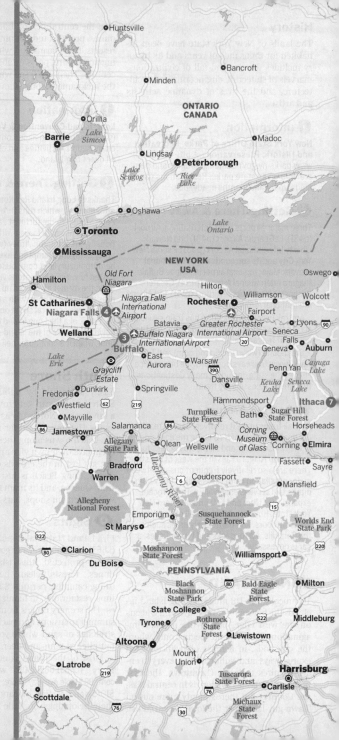

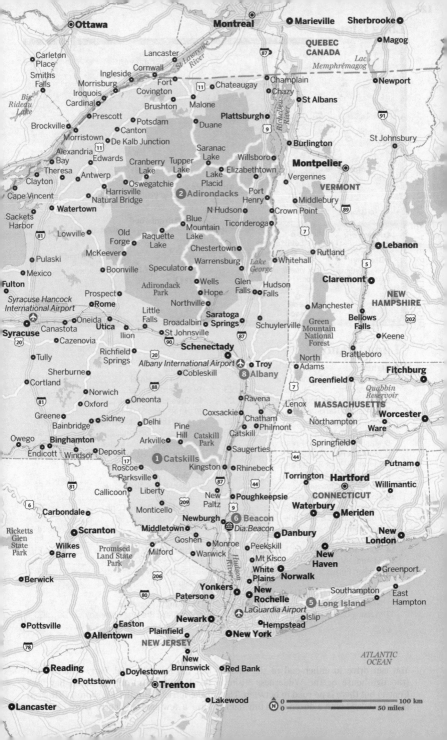

Long Island

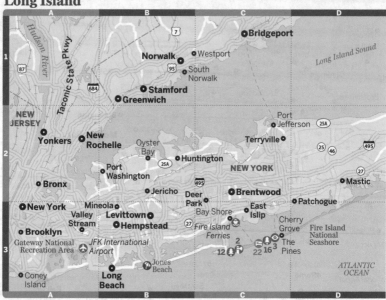

Long Island

You can drive to either end of the island (the lighthouse or the Wilderness Visitor Center) but there is no road in between. The island is edged with a dozen or so tiny hamlets, mostly residential. Party-center Ocean Beach Village and quieter Ocean Bay Park (take ferries from the Bayshore LIRR stop) have a few hotels; Cherry Grove and the

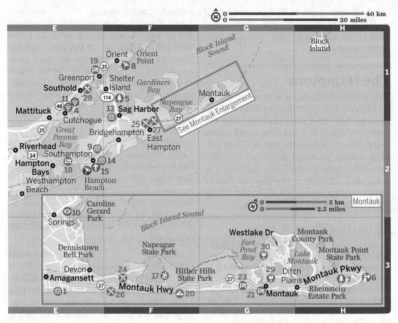

Pines (ferries from Sayville) are gay enclaves, also with hotels.

Robert Moses State Park
STATE PARK

(☑ 631-669-0449; www.parks.ny.gov; 600 Robert Moses State Pkwy, Babylon, Fire Island; per car $10, lounge chairs $10, golf $11, surfing $25; ⊙ dawn-dusk) Robert Moses State Park, one small part of Fire Island accessible by car, lies at the westernmost end and features wide, soft-sand beaches with mellower crowds than those at Jones Beach. It's also adjacent to the **Fire Island Lighthouse** (Fire Island National Seashore; ☑ 631-661-4876; www.fireisland-dlighthouse.com; adult/child $8/4; ⊙ 9:30am-6pm Jul & Aug, shorter hours rest of year), which you can walk to from here.

Sunken Forest
FOREST

(☑ 631-597-6183; www.nps.gov/fiis; Fire Island; ⊙ visitor center mid-May–mid-Oct) **FREE** This 300-year-old forest, a surprisingly dense stretch of trees behind the dunes, is easily accessible via a 1.5-mile boardwalk trail looping through it. It's pleasantly shady in summer, and vividly colored when the leaves change in fall. It's accessible by its own ferry stop (Sailors Haven, where there's also a visitor center), or a long walk in the winter season, after the ferry shuts down. Ranger-guided tours available.

🛌 Sleeping & Eating

From rustic old-school motels to campgrounds, and comfy B&Bs to unique boutique hotels that might set you back a month's rent, you can find something in your comfort zone, especially if you go at the edge of the seasons – try spring and fall for some quality time alone with the surf and sand.

Seashore Condo Motel
HOTEL $$

(☑ 631-583-5860; www.seashorecondomotel.com; Bayview Ave, Ocean Bay Park, Fire Island; r from $240; ❄ 🐾) Small, wood-paneled rooms without many frills, despite the price.

Madison Fire Island Pines
BOUTIQUE HOTEL $$$

(☑ 631-597-6061; www.themadisonfi.com; 22 Atlantic Walk, Fire Island Pines, Fire Island; r from $250; ❄ 🐾 🏊) Fire Island's first 'boutique' hotel, which rivals anything Manhattan has to offer in terms of amenities, but also has killer views from a rooftop deck, and a gorgeous pool.

Sand Castle
SEAFOOD $$

(☑ 631-597-4174; www.fireislandsandcastle.com; 106 Lewis Walk, Cherry Grove, Fire Island; mains $15-30; ⊙ 11am-11pm Mon, Tue & Thu-Sat, 9:30am-11pm Sun May-Sep) One of Fire Island's only oceanfront (rather than bayfront) options, Sand Castle serves up satisfying appetizers (fried calamari, portobello fries) and lots of seafood temptations (mussels, crab cakes, seared sea scallops). Nice cocktails and people-watching.

The Hamptons

This string of villages is a summer escape for Manhattan's wealthiest, who zip to mansions by helicopter. Mere mortals take the Hampton Jitney bus and chip in on rowdy rental houses. Behind the glitz is a long cultural history, as noted artists and writers have lived here. Beneath the glamour, the gritty and life-risking tradition of fishing continues. The area is small, connected by often traffic-clogged Montauk Hwy.

ⓘ Getting There & Away

Driving the Montauk Hwy (Rte 27) to and from New York involves careful planning to avoid major congestion, and it's often at a standstill within the Hamptons itself on busy weekends. Better to take the ever-popular Hampton Jitney out here from Manhattan or Brooklyn – it serves the entire Hamptons with frequent comfortable buses. The LIRR is a second but often more time-consuming option.

ⓘ Getting Around

The app-driven, converted turquoise school buses offered by Hampton Hopper (www.hamptonhopper.com) are an economical, hassle-free way around the towns and run into the bar hours.

East Hampton

📞 631 / POP 21,457

Don't be fooled by the oh-so-casual-looking summer attire, heavy on pastels and sweaters tied around the neck – the sunglasses alone are probably equal to a month's rent. Some of the highest-profile celebrities have homes here.

◉ Sights

East Hampton Town Marine Museum　　　MUSEUM
(📞 631-324-6850; www.easthamptonhistory.org; 301 Bluff Rd, Amagansett; $5; ⏰10am-4:30pm Sat, Jul & Aug) One of your last outposts before you drive on to Montauk, this small museum dedicated to the fishing and whaling industries is as interesting as its counterpart (p128) in Sag Harbor, full of old harpoons, boats half the size of their prey, and a beautiful black-and-white photographic tribute to the local fishers and their families.

Pollock-Krasner House　　　ARTS CENTER
(📞 631-324-4929; www.stonybrook.edu/pkhouse; 830 Springs Fireplace Rd; admission $5, guided tours $10; ⏰1-5pm Thu-Sat May-Oct) Tour the home of husband-and-wife art stars Jackson Pollock and Lee Krasner – worth it just to see the paint-spattered floor of Pollock's studio. Reservations required for the guided tour at noon.

✗ Eating

John Papas　　　DINER $$
(📞 631-324-5400; www.johnpapascafe.com; 18 Park Pl; omelettes $7-13, mains $15-25; ⏰6am-3pm Wed, to 9pm Thu-Tue) As unpretentious as you can get in East Hampton – it's a diner, folks! Breakfast, including hearty omelettes, is served all day in the family-oriented dining room. A few of the owner's Greek specialties (moussaka, gyros) plump up the menu.

Nick & Toni's　　　MEDITERRANEAN $$$
(📞 631-324-3550; www.nickandtonis.com; 136 N Main St, East Hampton; pizzas $17, mains $32-48; ⏰5:30-9:30pm Mon, Wed & Thu, to 10:30pm Fri & Sat, 11:30am-2:30pm & 6-10pm Sun) Serves finely prepared Italian specialties using locally sourced ingredients; wood-fired pizzas are available on Monday, Thursday and Sunday. Despite attracting celebrity regulars, it treats nonfamous customers well.

Sag Harbor

📞 631 / POP 2274

The old whaling town of Sag Harbor, on Peconic Bay, is edged with historic homes, and its main street has a number of fine restaurants and shops. You can pick up a walking-tour map at the Sag Harbor Chamber of Commerce.

◉ Sights

Sag Harbor Whaling & Historical Museum　　　MUSEUM
(📞 631-725-0770; www.sagharborwhalingmuseum.org; 200 Main St; adult/child $6/2; ⏰10am-5pm May-Nov) The cool collection here includes actual artifacts from 19th-century whaling ships: sharp flensing knives, battered pots for rendering blubber, delicate scrimshaw and more. It's a bit surreal to see photos of the giant mammals in a village that's now a cute resort town.

🛏 Sleeping & Eating

American Hotel　　　HOTEL $$$
(📞 631-725-3535; www.theamericanhotel.com; 49 Main St; r $345-465; 🅿❋❅) An old-world ho-

tel that's still excellent and modern, with a popular downstairs restaurant and bar that continues to be a center of the social scene. An ideal choice for any lover of European elegance and efficiency. If you can get it, there's a split-level attic apartment on the top floor.

★ **Dockside Bar and Grill** SEAFOOD $$$
(📞631-725-7100; www.docksidesagharbor.com; 26 Bay St; mains $26-32; ⏰11:30am-10pm) A local favorite inside the American Legion Hall (the original bar's still there); the seafood-heavy menu features a prize-winning, stick-to-the-spoon chowder and luscious avocado-lobster spring rolls, among other mouthwatering delights. The outdoor patio can be nice in the summer.

Southampton

📍631 / POP 56,790

Compared with some of its neighbors, Southampton is an old-money, rather conservative spot. It's home to sprawling old mansions, awe-inspiring churches, a main street with no 'beachwear' allowed, and some lovely beaches. Pick up maps and brochures about the town at the Southampton Chamber of Commerce, squeezed among a group of high-priced, artsy-crafty shops and decent restaurants. There's a local edge there, somewhere, but you'll have to dig to find it.

◉ Sights

Parrish Art Museum MUSEUM
(📞631-283-2118; www.parrishart.org; 279 Montauk Hwy, Water Mill; adult/child $12/free; ⏰10am-5pm Wed-Mon, to 8pm Fri) In a sleek, long barn designed by Herzog & de Meuron, this institution spotlights local artists such as Jackson Pollock, Willem de Kooning and Chuck Close. For more Pollock, make reservations to see his nearby paint-drizzled studio and home.

Southampton Historical Museum MUSEUM
(📞631-283-2494; www.southamptonhistoricalmuseum.org; 17 Meeting House Lane; adult/child $4/free; ⏰11am-4pm Wed-Sat Mar-Dec) Before the Hamptons was the Hamptons, there was this clutch of buildings, now nicely maintained and spread around Southampton. The main museum is Rogers Mansion, once owned by a whaling captain. You can also visit a former dry-goods store, now occupied by a local jeweler, around the corner on Main St; and a 17th-century homestead, the Halsey House (Saturday only July to October).

St Andrew's Dune Church CHURCH
(www.standrewsdunechurch.com; 12 Gin Lane; ◉service 11am Sun Jun-Sep) The triple spires of this 19th-century red wooden church glow beautifully in the afternoon light. You can come to Sunday service if so inclined, admiring the stained glass and quaint wooden pews, or simply enjoy a stroll along the placid waterway across the street from the curious iron pot donated by an early congregant. The building was the earliest life-saving station in New York, and is well worth the short drive or walk from downtown.

🛏 Sleeping & Eating

Easterner Motel MOTEL $$$
(📞631-283-9292; www.easternermotel.com; 639 E Montauk Hwy; d from $395; ❋ 🛜 🏊) Five miles west of Southampton, the Easterner has eight comfortable rooms in an old-fashioned property along the highway. Includes an outdoor pool, barbecue grill and aging basketball court, so though you're a bit removed from town, you'll never have to leave.

Sip 'n Soda ICE CREAM $
(📞631-283-9752; www.sipnsoda.com; 40 Hampton Rd; ice cream $3-6, mains $8-11; ⏰7:30am-6pm Tue-Thu, to 10pm Fri-Mon May-Sep, 7:30am-5pm Oct-Apr) Founded by the Parash family in 1958, Sip 'n Soda seemingly has the original paneled walls and pew-like booths, but more importantly, the lime rickey recipe remains intact. Your sweet tooth will thank you, and you can also grab burgers and typical diner fare.

La Parmigiana ITALIAN $$
(📞631-283-8030; www.laparmigianaitalianrestaurant.com; 48 Hampton Rd; pizzas $10-25, sandwiches $11-14, pasta $19-25; ⏰11:30am-10pm Tue-Sat, from 12:30 Sun) A local, low-key hangout since 1974 – folks come and go with their take-out orders or sometimes linger at the bar. The bar menu is diverse, from meatballs to oysters, along with very affordable pies and $25 bottles of wine – what's the hurry? The fried ravioli is to die for.

Montauk

📍631 / POP 3326

Towards the east-pointing tip of Long Island's South Fork, you'll find the mellow town of Montauk, aka 'The End,' and the famous surfing beach Ditch Plains. With the surfers have come affluent hipsters and boho-chic hotels, but the area is still far less of a scene than the Hamptons, with proudly blue-collar residents and casual seafood restaurants.

Route 27, the Montauk Hwy, divides east of Napeague State Park, with the Montauk Hwy continuing down the center of the peninsula while Old Montauk Hwy hugs the water. The roads converge at the edge of central Montauk and Fort Pond, a small lake. Two miles east is a large inlet called Lake Montauk, with marinas strung along its shore.

◉ Sights

Lost at Sea Memorial   MEMORIAL
(2000 Montauk Hwy, Montauk Lighthouse; Montauk State Park parking fee $8; ⊙ 10:30am-5:30pm Sun-Fri, to 7pm Sat mid-Jun–Aug, reduced hours mid-Apr–mid-Jun & Sep-Nov) Visitors to the Montauk Lighthouse may not immediately notice a smaller 15ft structure at the eastern end of the park, where the 60ft cliffs fall off into the sea, but for local fishers it's a daily reminder of their struggle against the power of the sea. The 8ft, 2600lb bronze statue set on a 7ft slab of granite is inscribed with the names of those lost to the waves, from the colonial days of New York to the present.

Montauk Point State Park   STATE PARK
(☑ 631-668-3781; www.parks.ny.gov; 2000 Montauk Hwy/Rte 27; per car $8; ⊙ dawn-dusk) Covering the eastern tip of the South Fork is Montauk Point State Park, with its impressive **lighthouse** (☑ 631-668-2544; www.montauklighthouse.com; adult/child $11/4; ⊙ 10:30am-5:30pm Sun-Fri, to 7pm Sat mid-Jun–Aug, reduced hours mid-Apr–mid-Jun & Sep-Nov). A good place for windswept walks, surfing, surf fishing (with permit), and seal-spotting – call the park for the schedule; rangers will set up spotting scopes to better view the frisky pinnipeds.

🛏 Sleeping

Hither Hills State Park   CAMPGROUND $
(☑ 631-668-2554; www.parks.ny.gov; 164 Old Montauk Hwy; campsites state residents/nonresidents $31/70) These wooded dunes form a natural barrier between Montauk and the Hamptons. The 189-site campground caters for tents and RVs, and there are spots for fishing (permit required) and hiking through the dunes; online reservations ($9 fee) are a must. The park's western border is the stunning **Walking Dunes** (Napeague Harbor Rd).

★ Sunrise Guesthouse   GUESTHOUSE $$$
(☑ 631-668-7286; www.sunrisebnb.com; 681 Old Montauk Hwy; r/ste $395/495; P ❋ 🛜) A tasteful yet homey four-room B&B a mile from town, and just across the road from the beach. The breakfast is ample and delicious, served in a comfy dining area with a million-dollar view. Low-season rates are a significant saving. Summer weekends require a two-night minimum stay.

Ocean Resort Inn   HOTEL $$$
(☑ 631-668-2300; www.oceanresortinn.com; 95 S Emerson Ave; r & ste from $399; ❋ @ 🛜) All rooms at this small, L-shaped hotel open onto a large porch or balcony. It's walking distance to the beach and the main town. Rates drop significantly in the low season.

🍴 Eating & Drinking

★ Clam Bar at Napeague   SEAFOOD $$
(☑ 631-267-6348; www.clambarhamptons.com; 2025 Montauk Hwy, Amagansett; mains $15-30; ⊙ 11:30am-6pm Apr-Oct, 11:30am-6pm Sat & Sun Nov & Dec) You won't get fresher seafood or a saltier waitstaff, and holy mackerel, those lobster rolls are good, even if you choke a bit on the price. Three decades in business – the public has spoken – with cash only, of course. Locals favor this one. Find it on the road between Amagansett and Montauk.

Lobster Roll   SEAFOOD $$
(☑ 631-267-3740; www.lobsterroll.com; 1980 Montauk Hwy, Amagansett; mains $14-28; ⊙ 11:30am-9:30pm Jun-Sep, 11:30am-8pm Fri-Sun May) 'Lunch' is the sign to look for on the roadside west of Montauk, marking this clam-and-lobster shack that has been in operation since 1965. It's now infamous as the liaison site in the Showtime television series *The Affair*.

Montauk Brewing Company   MICROBREWERY
(☑ 631-668-8471; www.montaukbrewingco.com; 62 S Erie Ave; ⊙ 2-7pm Mon-Fri, noon-7pm Sat & Sun) 'Come as you are,' preaches the small tasting room, and Cobain's family hasn't asked for their lyrics back yet. There's a more-than-palatable rotating range of cervezas, from lagers to stouts, and an outdoor patio on which to enjoy them in the right weather. Take a mixed six-pack to go.

Montauket   BAR
(☑ 631-668-5992; 88 Firestone Rd; ⊙ noon-10pm) Experts agree: this is the best place to watch the sun go down on Long Island. An unassuming slate-blue-shingled building, full of local flavor (and people).

ℹ Getting There & Away

Montauk is the last stop on the eastbound Jitney bus (www.hamptonjitney.com; $29) as well as the Long Island Railroad. Suffolk County bus 10C runs to Montauk from East Hampton – transfer to bus 94 to cover the rest of the distance to the lighthouse.

North Fork & Shelter Island

The North Fork is known for its bucolic farmland and vineyards (though weekends can draw rowdy limo-loads on winery crawls). Rte 25, the main road through **Jamesport**, **Cutchogue** and **Southold**, is pretty and edged with farm stands; the less-traveled Rte 48 also has many wineries.

The largest town on the North Fork is laid-back **Greenport**, with working fishing boats, a history in whaling and a **vintage carousel** (www.villageofgreenport.org; $2; ⊙10am-9pm) in Mitchell Park. It's compact and easily walkable from the LIRR station.

Like a pearl in Long Island's claw, Shelter Island rests between the North and South Forks. The island is a smaller, more low-key version of the Hamptons, with a touch of maritime New England. Parking is limited; long Crescent Beach, for instance, has spots only by permit. If you don't mind a few hills, it's a nice place to visit by bike, and Mashomack Nature Preserve is a wildlife lover's dream.

◉ Sights

Pugliese Vineyards   WINERY
(☑631-734-4057;   www.pugliesevineyards.com; 34515 Main Rd, Cutchogue; tastings from $12; ⊙11am-5pm Sun-Fri, to 6pm Sat Jun-Sep) Producing wine since 1980, Pugliese does especially nice sparkling varieties. The winery is family run (with some vintages named after favorite aunts) and small scale, unlike some of its more corporate-feeling neighbors. Enjoy a sip next to the koi pond outside.

Lenz Winery   WINERY
(☑631-734-6010; www.lenzwine.com; 38355 Main Rd, Peconic; ⊙10am-6pm Jun-Sep, to 5pm Oct-May) Established in 1978, this is one of the oldest North Fork wineries, and still one of the more eclectic, focusing on European-style wines. The sparkling wines and Gewürztraminer are especially good. Flights from $12.

Mashomack Nature Preserve   NATURE RESERVE
(☑631-749-1001;   www.shelter-island.org/ mashomack.html; Rte 114, Shelter Island; donation adult/child $3/2; ⊙9am-5pm Mar-Sep, to 4pm Oct-Feb, closed Tue Sep-Jun) The 2000 acres of this

Shelter Island reserve, shot through with creeks and marshes, are great for kayaking, birding and hiking (no cycling allowed). Take precautions against ticks, an ever-present problem on the island.

Orient Beach State Park   BEACH
(☑631-323-2440; www.parks.ny.gov/parks/106; 40000 Main Rd, Orient; weekends per car $10, kayaks per hr $25; ⊙8am-dusk, swimming only Jul & Aug) A sandy slip of land at the end of the North Fork where you can swim in the calm ocean water (July and August) or rent kayaks to paddle in the small bay. True believers can view four different lighthouses, including the Orient Point Lighthouse, known as 'the coffee pot' for its stout bearing.

To best see the lighthouse, go up the road to Orient Point County Park, which has a half-mile trail to a white-rock beach.

⌱ Sleeping & Eating

Greenporter Hotel   BOUTIQUE HOTEL $$$
(☑631-477-0066; www.greenporterhotel.com; 326 Front St, Greenport; r from $344; ✳︎🛜🐾) An older motel redone with white walls and Ikea furniture, this place is decent value for the area, and they make improvements each year. Its on-site restaurant, Cuvée, is very good.

North Fork Table & Inn   AMERICAN $$$
(☑631-765-0177; www.nofoti.com; 57225 Main Rd, Southold; 3-course set menu $75, 6-course tasting menu $125; ⊙5:30-8pm Mon, Thu & Sun, to 10pm Fri & Sat) A favorite foodies' escape, this four-room inn (rooms from $250) has an excellent farm-to-table restaurant, run by alums of the esteemed Manhattan restaurant Gramercy Tavern. Dinner is served Thursday to Monday, but if you're hankering for a gourmand-to-go lunch ($11 to $15), the inn's food truck is parked outside Friday to Sunday from 11:30am to 3:30pm.

Claudio's   SEAFOOD $$$
(☑631-477-0627; www.claudios.com; 111 Main St, Greenport; mains $25-36; ⊙11:30am-9pm Sun-Thu, to 10pm Fri & Sat May-Oct) A Greenport legend, owned by the Portuguese Claudio family since 1870. For a more casual meal, hit Claudio's Clam Bar on the nearby pier.

❶ Getting There & Away

The Hampton Jitney (www.hamptonjitney.com) bus picks up passengers on Manhattan's East Side on 96th, 83rd, 77th, 69th, 59th and 40th Sts. It makes stops in 10 North Fork villages.

If you're driving, take the Midtown Tunnel out of Manhattan, which will take you onto I-495/

Long Island Expwy. Take this until it ends at Riverhead and follow signs onto Rte 25. You can stay on Rte 25 for all points east, but note that the North Rd (Rte 48) is faster as it does not go through the town centers.

The Long Island Rail Road's line is the Ronkonkoma Branch, with trips leaving from Penn Station and Brooklyn and running out to Greenport.

To get from the North Fork to the South Fork (or vice versa), take the North Ferry (www.northferry.com; $11) and the South Ferry (www.southferry.com; $14) services, crossing Shelter Island in between. There is no direct ferry – you must take one and then the other.

CATSKILLS

This beautiful mountainous region west of the Hudson Valley has been a popular getaway since the 19th century. The romantic image of mossy gorges and rounded peaks, as popularized by Hudson Valley School painters, encouraged a preservation movement: in 1894 the state constitution was amended so that thousands of acres are 'forever kept as wild forest lands.' In the early 20th century, the Catskills became synonymous with so-called 'borscht belt' hotels, summer escapes for middle-class NYC Jews. The vast majority of these hotels have closed, although orthodox Jewish communities still

thrive in many towns – as does a back-to-the-land, hippie ethos on numerous small farms. In the fall, this is the closest place to NYC with really dramatic colors in the trees.

ⓘ Getting There & Away

There is some bus service, the most useful being Trailways (www.trailwaysny.com) from NYC to Woodstock (from $30, three hours) and Phoenicia (from $26, 2½ hours). However, if you really want to tour the area, having a car is essential.

Phoenicia & Mt Tremper

This quirky pair of hamlets (just down the highway from one another) are the perfect jumping off point to explore the Catskills. Phoenecia is the bigger of the two, while Mt Tremper boasts a few impressive hotels. Outdoor activities are easily arranged and include hiking, cycling, floating down the creek on an inner tube or swimming in mountain pools in summer and skiing at nearby **Belleayre Mountain** (☑845-254-5600; www.belleayre.com; 181 Galli Curci Rd, Highmount; 1-day lift pass weekday/weekend $56/68; ⊙9am-4pm Dec-Mar) in winter. Fall is prime time to visit and also the best season for a jaunt in an open-air carriage on the Delaware & Ulster Railroad between nearby Arkville and Roxbury.

Catskills Region

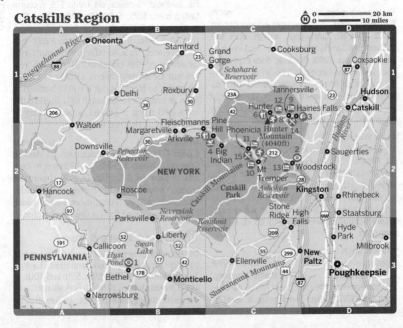

⊙ Sights & Activities

Belleayre Beach SWIMMING
(☑845-254-5202; www.belleayre.com/summer/
belleayre-beach; 33 Friendship Manor Rd, Pine Hill;
per person/car $5/14; ☺10am-6pm Mon-Fri, to
7pm Sat & Sun mid-Jun–Aug) Near the base of
Belleayre Mountain ski resort, this lake is
a popular and refreshing swimming spot.
Boats, kayaks and paddle boards can be
rented, and there's also volleyball and basketball courts and a climbing wall.

Town Tinker Tube Rental WATER SPORTS
(☑845-688-5553; www.towntinker.com; 10 Bridge
St, Phoenicia; tubes per day $20, package incl trans-
port $30; ☺9am-6pm, last rental 4pm Jun-Sep)
Visit this outfitter for everything you need to
ride an inner tube down wet and wild (and
cold!) Esopus Creek.

🛏 Sleeping & Eating

★**Graham & Co** MOTEL $$
(☑845-688-7871; www.thegrahamandco.com; 80
Rte 214, Phoenicia; r $175-275; ✳🔊🐾) There's a
lot going for this hipster motel an easy walk
from the center of town. Rooms are white-
washed and minimalist with the cheapest
ones in a 'bunkhouse' where bathrooms are
shared. There's a comfy den with a fireplace, a
provisions store, an outdoor pool in summer,
a wigwam and lawn games!

Foxfire Mountain House BOUTIQUE HOTEL $$
(www.foxfiremountainhouse.com; 72 Andrew Lane,
Mt Tremper; r $175-450; ☺restaurant dinner Fri-
Sun; P🐾✳🔊) Hidden in the forest, this
chic hotel channels modern '70s rugged cool
in its 11 individually decorated rooms (the
cheapest of which share a bathroom) and
one three-bedroom cottage. The cozy restaurant (offering dinner Friday to Sunday)
and bar, open to nonguests, serves French-
inspired cuisine such as *steak au poivre*
(peppercorn steak) and *coq au cidre* (chick-
en cooked in cider).

★**Phoenicia Diner** AMERICAN $
(☑845-688-9957; www.phoeniciadiner.com; 5681
Rte 28, Phoenicia; mains $10-14; ☺7am-5pm Thu-
Mon; 🐾) New York hipsters and local families
rub shoulders at this elevated roadside diner.
The appealing menu offers all-day breakfast,
skillets, sandwiches and burgers – all farm-
fresh and fabulous. There's also a bar.

★**Tavern 214** GASTROPUB $$
(☑845-688-7383; www.tavern214.com; 76 State
Rte 214; mains $24-38, small plates $17-19; ☺4-
10pm Sun, Mon & Thu, to 11pm Fri & Sat; 🔊) Tav-
ern 214 has a great menu of classic Ameri-
can comfort-food-inspired entrees, but it's in
the small plates that this lodge style tavern
shines. Duck breast quesadillas, decon-
structed poke bowls, and sausage and pep-
per sliders have all recently made appear-
ances on the menu. Of course, because it's
the Catskills, there is a preference for locally
sourced produce and meat.

🛈 Getting There & Away

Trailways (www.trailwaysny.com) runs buses to
Phoenicia from NYC (from $26, 2½ hours) and
Mt Tremper is a short drive once you're there.

Tannersville
☑518, 838 / POP 510
The small town of Tannersville, which pri-
marily services the nearby ski resort of
Hunter Mountain, also offers access to the
gorgeous Kaaterskill Falls. There are su-
perb hikes and drives in the area, as well as
rustically charming hotels in which to stay
and enjoy the beautiful mountain scenery.
Tannersville itself sports a main street lined
with brightly painted shops and houses.
Continued on p140

NEW YORK STATE TANNERSVILLE

ROAD TRIP >
HUDSON VALLEY

• •

Immediately north of New York City, green becomes the dominant color and the vistas of the Hudson River and the mountains breathe life into your urban-weary body. The history of the region, home to the Hudson River School of painting in the 19th century and a retreat for Gilded Age industrialists, is preserved in the many grand estates, flowering gardens and picturesque villages.

❶ The Cloisters

This trip along the Hudson begins at one of New York City's most magnificent riverside locations. Gaze at medieval tapestries, frescoes, carvings and gold treasures, including a St John the Evangelist plaque dating from the 9th century, inside the Cloisters Museum & Gardens (p77). This magnificent Metropolitan Museum annex, built to look like an old castle, is set in Fort Tryon Park overlooking the Hudson River, near the northern tip of Manhattan and not far from the George Washington Bridge. Works such as an ivory sculpture of the Virgin Mary (1290), ancient stained-glass windows, and oil on wood religious paintings are displayed in galleries connected by grand archways and topped by Moorish terracotta roofs, all facing an airy courtyard. The extensive grounds – with rolling hills blanketed in lush green grass – contain more than 250 varieties of medieval herbs and flowers. In summer months, concerts and performances are held regularly.

The Drive > Rte 9A north crosses a bridge over the Spuyten Duyvil Creek, marking the boundary between Manhattan and the Bronx with some nice river views. Taking Rte 9 north is a slow option compared to hopping on I-87, the New York Thruway, and you pass through some rundown parts of Yonkers, but you do get a feel for several nice residential communities. The whole drive is about 18.5 miles long.

❷ Tarrytown

Washington Irving's home, **Sunnyside** (☑ 914-591-8763, Mon-Fri 914-631-8200; www.

hudsonvalley.org; 3 W Sunnyside Lane, Tarrytown; adult/child $12/6; ◷ tours 10:30am-3:30pm Wed-Sun May–mid-Nov), a quaint, cozy Dutch cottage – which Irving said had more nooks and crannies than a cocked hat – has been left pretty much the way it was when the author who dreamed up the Headless Horseman and Ichabod Crane lived there. The wisteria he planted 100 years ago still climbs the walls, and the spindly piano inside still carries a tune.

Not far north on Rte 9 is **Philipsburg Manor** (☑ Mon-Fri 914-631-8200, Sat & Sun 914-631-3992; www.hudsonvalley.org; 381 N Broadway, Sleepy Hollow; adult/child $12/6; ◷ tours 10:30am-3:30pm Wed-Sun May–mid-Nov), a working farm in 17th-century Dutch style. Wealthy Dutchman Frederick Philips brought his family here around 1680 and meticulously built his new farm. Inside the rough-hewn clapboard barns and three-story, whitewashed fieldstone manor, it's all sighs and clanks as old fireplaces and strained beams do their work.

From Philipsburg Manor, grab a shuttle to the sprawling splendor of **Kykuit** (☑ 914-366-6900; www.hudsonvalley.org; 200 Lake Rd, Pocantico Hills; tour adult/child from $28/26; ◷ tours Thu-Sun May-Sep & early Nov, Wed-Mon Oct), the Rockefeller family's old European-style estate perched on a bluff high atop the Hudson River. The exterior is stately neoclassical revival, while inside it's more fine-art gallery than summer home. Outside, the carefully sculpted gardens, dotted with modern art installations from the likes of Giacometti and Picasso, are a delight to wander through.

Length 5 days; 115 miles/185km

Great for... Food; History; Outdoors

Best Time to Go Grounds of historic estates open mid-May to September

The Drive > Start this 32-mile drive by crossing over the Hudson River at one of its widest points on the New NY Bridge (technically, the Governor Mario M. Cuomo Bridge) to South Nyack. This new eight-lane span started to replace the decommissioned Tappan Zee Bridge in late 2017. Take the Palisades Pkwy north from here.

③ Bear Mountain & Harriman State Parks

Surprisingly, only 40 miles north of New York City is a pristine forest with miles of hiking trails, along with swimming and wilderness camping. The 72 sq miles of **Harriman State Park** (☎ 845-947-2444; www.parks.ny.gov; Seven Lakes Dr, Bear Mountain Circle, Ramapo; per car late May-Sep $10; ☉ dawn-dusk) were donated to the state in 1910 by the widow of railroad magnate Edward Henry Harriman, director of the transcontinental Union Pacific Railroad and frequent target of Teddy Roosevelt's trustbusters. Adjacent **Bear Mountain State Park** (☎ 845-786-2701; www.parks.ny.gov; Palisades Pkwy/Rte 6, Bear Mountain; per car $10; ☉ 8am-dusk) offers great views from its 1305ft peak, with the Manhattan skyline looming beyond the river and surrounding greenery, and there's a restaurant and lodging at the inn on Hessian Lake. In both parks there are several scenic roads snaking their way past mountain-fed streams and secluded lakes with gorgeous vistas; you'll spot shy, white-tailed deer, stately blue herons and – in the remotest regions – even a big cat or two.

Head to **Fort Montgomery State Historic Site** (☎ 845-446-2134; www.parks.ny.gov; 690 Rte 9W, Fort Montgomery; museum $3; ☉ 9am-5pm Wed-Sun Apr-Oct) in Bear Mountain for picture-perfect views from its cliffside perch overlooking the Hudson. The pastoral site was host to a fierce skirmish with the British on October 6, 1777. American soldiers hunkered behind fortresses while they tried to hold off the enemy; the ruins are still visible in the red earth. A museum at the entrance has artifacts and more details on the bloody battle.

DETOUR: SAUGERTIES

Two great sights near the small attractive town of Saugerties, 27 miles north of Rhinebeck on the west side for the Hudson River, justify this detour; cross the Kingston-Rhinecliff Bridge and take Rte 9W north to get here. Near the town is **Opus 40 Sculpture Park & Museum** (☎845-246-3400; www.opus40.org; 50 Fite Rd, Saugerties; adult/child $10/3; 🕒11am-5:30pm Thu-Sun Jun-Sep), where artist Harvey Fite worked for nearly four decades to coax an abandoned quarry into an immense work of land art, all sinuous walls, canyons and pools. You can also hike along a half-mile nature trail to the picturesque 1869 **Saugerties Lighthouse** (☎845-247-0656; www.saugertieslighthouse.com; 168 Lighthouse Dr, Saugerties; tour suggested donation adult/child $5/3; 🕒trail dawn-dusk) on the point where Esopus Creek joins the Hudson. Book well in advance if you wish to stay in one of the two charming guestrooms here. Classic rock lovers may also want to search out **Big Pink** (www.bigpinkbasement.com; Parnassus Lane, West Saugerties; house $497; ❄📶), the house made famous by Bob Dylan and the Band, although note it's on a private road. It's possible to stay at both the lighthouse and Big Pink, but you'll need to book well ahead.

The Drive > It's only 14 miles to West Point – take Rte 9W to the town of Highland Falls and continue on Main St until you reach the parking entrance for West Point Visitors Center on the right.

4 West Point

Occupying one of the most breathtaking bends in the river is West Point US Military Academy. Prior to 1802, it was a strategic fort with a commanding position over a narrow stretch of the Hudson. **West Point Guided Tours** (☎845-446-4724; www.westpointtours.com; 2107 N South Post Rd, West Point; adult/child $16.50/13.50; 🕒tours 9am-4:45pm) offers one- and two-hour combo walking and bus tours of the stately campus; try to go when school is in session since the cadets' presence livens things up. Guides move swiftly through the academy's history, noting illustrious graduates (too many to mention… Robert E Lee, Ulysses S Grant, Buzz Aldrin and Norman Schwarzkopf are on the list) as well as famous drop-outs (Edgar Allen Poe for one). Guides will also explain the rigorous admissions criteria for parents hoping to land a spot for their kids. At least as interesting is the highly regimented daily collegiate life they lead.

Next to the visitor center is the fascinating – even for the pacifists among us – **West Point Museum** (☎845-938-2638; www.usma.edu/museum; 2107 N South Post Rd, West Point; 🕒10:30am-4:15pm) [FREE], which traces the role of war and the military throughout human history. Displays of weapons from Stone Age clubs to artillery pieces highlight technology's role in the evolution of warfare, and elaborate miniature dioramas of important moments such as the siege of Avaricum (52 BC) and the Battle of Austerlitz (1805) will mesmerize anyone who played with toy soldiers as a kid. Give yourself enough time to take in the substantial exhibits and when you've had enough of fighting check out the paintings, prints and drawings by Hudson River School artists scattered around the museum.

Note that non-US citizens may have to travel in bus tour groups and certainly need a passport to be allowed onto the grounds of West Point, an active military base.

The Drive > On this 11.5-mile drive, take Rte 218 north leaving Highland Falls and connect to Rte 9W (not Storm King Hwy which Rte 218 becomes). Exit on Quaker Ave, right on Rte 32 and left on Orrs Mills Rd. You can see Storm King from the New York State Thruway (and vice versa) but there's no convenient exit.

5 Storm King Art Center

Part sculpture garden and part sculpture landscape, **Storm King Art Center** (☎845-534-3115; www.stormking.org; 1 Museum Rd, off Old Pleasant Hill Rd, New Windsor; adult/child $18/8; 🕒10am-5:30pm Wed-Sun Apr-Oct, to 4:30pm Nov & Dec) in Mountainville, on the west side of the Hudson River, is a giant open-air museum on 500 acres. The spot was founded in 1960 as a museum for painters, but it soon began to acquire larger installations and monumental works that were placed outside in natural 'rooms' created by the land's indigenous breaks and curves. There's a small museum on-site, formerly a 1935 residence designed like a Norman chateau, and plenty of picnic sites that visitors are encouraged to use (there is also a cafe).

Across the expanse of meadow is the *Storm King Wall,* artist Andy Goldsworthy's famously sinuous structure that starts with rocks, crescendos up and across some hills, encompasses a tree, then dips down into a pond, slithering out the other side and eventually disappearing into the woods. Other permanent pieces were created by Alexander Calder, Henry Moore, Richard Serra and Alice Aycock, to name a few.

The Drive > Rte 32 takes you past the rundown riverside town of Newburgh. If you have time, turn right on Washington St; near the river is Washington's Headquarters State Historic Site where the small stone house that served as General George Washington's longest-lasting Revolutionary War base is preserved as a museum. Otherwise, head over the Newburgh-Beacon bridge ($1.50 toll).

❻ Beacon

This formerly scruffy town is now on the map of art world cognoscenti because of the **Dia: Beacon** (☏845-440-0100; www.diaart.org; 3 Beekman St; adult/child $15/free; ⊙11am-6pm Thu-Mon Apr-Oct, 11am-4pm Thu-Mon Nov & Dec, 11am-4pm Fri-Mon Jan-Mar), a former factory, now a major museum. Inside its industrial walls are big names on a big scale, including an entire room of light sculptures by Dan Flavin, and a hangar-sized space to house Richard Serra's mammoth steel *Torqued Ellipses*.

Beacon's Main St offers many small galleries and craft shops, including **Hudson Beach Glass** (☏845-440-0068; www.hudson beachglass.com; 162 Main St, Beacon; ⊙10am-6pm Mon-Sat, 11am-6pm Sun), a boutique gallery where you can buy artfully designed, handcrafted pieces and watch glassblowers at work. If you have time, stroll down to the mini-rapids of Fishkill Creek or strike out on the trail up to the summit of **Mount Beacon** (www.scenichudson.org/parks/mountbeacon; Route 9D at Howland Ave) for spectacular views of the area.

The Drive > Strip-mall-lined Rte 9 north passes through Poughkeepsie (puh-kip-see), the largest city on the east bank and home to Vassar and Marist colleges. During this 22-mile drive, stop (exit on Marist Dr/Rte 9G north and then left on Parker Ave) for a stroll and incomparable river views on a converted railroad bridge, now a state park known as the Walkway Over the Hudson.

❼ Hyde Park

Hyde Park, just north of Poughkeepsie, has long been associated with the Roosevelts, a prominent family since the 19th century. The **Franklin D Roosevelt Home** (☏845-486-7770; www.nps.gov/hofr; 4097 Albany Post Rd; adult/child $20/free, museum only adult/child $10/

Cloisters Museum & Gardens (p77)

WALLKILL VALLEY RAIL TRAIL

Start Ulster

End Gardiner

Duration two days

Distance 21 miles

Difficulty Easy

Explore the beautiful Wallkill Valley, nestled within the larger Hudson Valley, by walking this 22-mile stretch of trail that was once a major railway. Although it's quite long, this is a fairly easy hike to tackle as it's mostly flat and weaves in and out of towns along the way.

Start at the northern end in **Ulster**, near Kingston, and begin walking south along the trail. On this first half you'll pass several small lakes, and cross the Roundout Creek over the **Rosendale Trestle**, a well-preserved 100-year-old railway bridge. Continue south, where part of the road is asphalt, until you come to the town of **New Paltz**, which is about 11 miles from where you started. You can walk to the **New Paltz Hostel** (☑845-255-6676; www.newpaltzhostel.com; 145 Main St; dm/r from $40/70; ☀🛜) from the trail to crash for the night.

The second half of the walk continues on a mostly gravel road and will take you away from the Wallkill River and into the fertile Hudson Valley farmlands. Just past New Paltz you'll find yourself along the **Wallkill River**, which makes for a great swimming hole if you're hiking on a hot day. Past that you'll mostly find yourself meandering through farmland. The views here tend to be blocked by tall hedges, but you'll find a few places where the folliage lessens and you can take in the breadth of your surroundings. After crossing a few bucolic bridges and walking through a number of quaint towns, the trail ends in the town of **Gardiner**. For now, that is. There is talk of expanding the trail even further south.

There are hiking opportunities galore in the Hudson Valley, Hike the Hudson Valley (www.hikethehudsonvalley.com) is a great resource for trail information.

free; ⊙9am-4pm), an estate of 1520 acres and formerly a working farm, includes a library, which details important achievements in FDR's presidency; a visit usually includes a guided tour of Springwood, FDR's lifelong home where he delivered his fireside chats.

Two miles to the east is **Val-Kill** (☑845-229-9422; www.nps.gov/elro; 54 Valkill Park Rd/Rte 9G; adult/child $10/free; ⊙9am-5pm daily May-Oct, 12:30pm-4pm Thu-Mon Nov-Apr). This 181-acre estate includes Val-Kill Cottage, a two-story building that was originally a furniture factory started by Eleanor Roosevelt to teach young men a trade during the Depression; and Stone Cottage, the former first lady's home after the death of her husband, now a small museum.

Just north of here is the 54-room **Vanderbilt Mansion** (☑845-229-7770; www.nps.gov/vama; 119 Vanderbilt Park Rd; grounds free, tours adult/child $10/free; ⊙9am-4:30pm), a Gilded Age spectacle of lavish beaux arts design built by the fabulously wealthy Frederick Vanderbilt, grandson of Cornelius, a Staten Island farmer who made millions buying up railroads. Nearly all of the original furnishings imported from European castles and villas remain in this country house – the smallest of any of the Vanderbilt family's! Hudson River

views are best from the gardens and the Bard Rock trail on the property.

Further north is Staatsburg, a hot spot for antiquing. If you prefer to look rather than buy, duck into the 100-year-old **Staatsburg State Historic Site** (☑845-889-8851; www.parks.ny.gov; Old Post Rd, Staatsburg; adult/child $8/free; ⊙tours 11am-4pm Thu-Sun mid-Apr–Oct, noon-3pm Thu-Sun late Nov-Dec) FREE, a beaux arts mansion boasting 79 luxurious rooms filled with Flemish tapestries, gilded plasterwork, period paintings and Oriental art.

The Drive > It's only 10 miles north on Rte 9 to Rhinebeck; it's a fairly ordinary stretch but at least it's less congested and less heavily trafficked compared to further south.

⑧ Rhinebeck

Just 3 miles north of the charming small town of Rhinebeck is the **Old Rhinebeck Aerodrome** (☑845-752-3200; www.oldrhinebeck.org; 9 Norton Rd, Red Hook; museum adult/child $12/8, airshows adult/child $25/12, flights $100; ⊙10am-5pm May-Oct, airshows from 2pm Sat & Sun), with a collection of pre-1930s planes and automobiles. There are air shows on weekends in the summer; the vintage aircraft that take off at 2pm on Saturdays and Sundays are reserved for a highly choreographed period dog-fight. If vicarious thrills aren't enough you can don helmets and goggles and take an open-cockpit 15-minute flight ($100 per person) in a 1929 New Standard D-25 four-passenger biplane.

In a large red barn out the back of the **Beekman Arms** (☎845-876-7077; www.beek mandelamaterinn.com; 6387 Mill St; r $289-569; P✳🏠), widely considered the longest continually operating hotel in the US, is the **Beekman Arms Antique Market** (☎845-876-3477; www.beekmandelamaterinn.com/antique-market; ☉11am-5pm), where some 30 local antiques dealers offer up their best Americana.

The Drive > Go with Rte 9G north rather than Rte 9 for this 25-mile drive; it's more rural and every once in a while opens up to views of the Catskill Mountains on the other side of the river in the distance.

❾ Hudson

Gentrification has upgraded parts of the historic port of Hudson into a facsimile of tony areas of Brooklyn or Manhattan. Warren St, the main commercial strip, is lined with antiques and interior-design stores, galleries, and stylish restaurants and cafes, all patronized by a well-heeled, taste-conscious crowd.

There's still some rough edges to the town, though, which in the early 19th century prospered as a busy river port, and was later adopted by the LGBT community as an affordable bolthole. Stroll the riverfront and side streets to spot fine heritage architecture, including the recently restored **Hudson Opera House** (☎518-822-1438; www.hudsonoperahouse.org; 327 Warren St; ☉gallery 9am-5pm Mon-Fri, noon-5pm Sat & Sun; ♿).

Just a few miles south of town is **Olana** (☎518-828-0135; www.olana.org; 5720 Rte 9G; house tours adult/child $9/free; ☉grounds 8am-sunset daily, house tours 10am-4pm Tue-Sun Jun-Oct, 11am-3pm Fri-Sun Apr & May, 11am-3pm Sat & Sun Jan-Mar), the splendid-looking 'Persian fantasy' home of Frederic Church, one of the primary artists of the Hudson River School of painting. Church designed the 250-acre property, creating a lake and planting trees and orchards, with his idealized version of a landscape in mind, so that the grounds became a complementary part of the natural views across the valley, with the eastern escarpment of the Catskills looming overhead. On a house tour you can appreciate the totality of Church's aesthetic vision, as well as view paintings from his own collection.

OLEGALBINSKY/GETTY IMAGES ©

Philipsburg Manor (p134)

Continued from p133

⊙ Sights & Activities

Kaaterskill Falls   WATERFALL
For the best view of New York State's highest falls – 260ft, compared to Niagara's 167ft – without a strenuous hike, head to the **viewing platform** (Laurel House Rd, Palenville). Popular paintings by the Hudson River Valley School of painters in the mid-1800s elevated this two-tier cascade to iconic status, making it a major draw for hikers, artists and nature lovers. There's parking just above on Rte 23A; be sure to stick to the shoulder and keep your eyes on cars coming around the bend on your walk down to the trailhead.

Hunter Mountain   SKIING
(☑ 518-263-4223; www.huntermtn.com; 64 Klein Ave, Hunter; day lift pass weekday/weekend $75/85; ☺ 9am-4pm Dec-Mar) Spectacular views from the 56 trails (including some challenging black runs that are a minefield of moguls) draw crowds of snowhounds to Hunter; avoid weekends and holidays if you don't relish lines at the lifts. Snowmaking ensures that skiing continues through the season, whatever the weather.

Zipline New York   ADVENTURE SPORTS
(☑ 518-263-4388; www.ziplinenewyork.com; Hunter Mountain, Rte 23A; zip-line tours $89-119) Throughout the year Hunter Mountain is also the location of this zip-line course that's not for the faint hearted. The longest of the six zip lines is 650ft and 60ft above the ground.

🛏 Sleeping & Eating

★**Scribner's Catskill Lodge**   LODGE $$
(☑ 518-628-5130; www.scribnerslodge.com; 13 Scribner Hollow Rd; r $165-395; 🅿️☺❄🛜⛷🐾) Run by a super-cool staff, this 1960s motor lodge has been given a stylish contemporary makeover. Snow-white painted rooms, some of which feature gas-fired stoves, contrast with the warm tones of the long library lounge with pool table and comfy nooks.

The attached **Prospect** (☑ 518-628-5150; www.scribnersprospect.com; 13 Scribner Hollow Rd; mains $21-36; ☺ 8-11am Mon & Tue, 6-9pm Wed, Thu & Sun, 6-10pm Fri, 11am-2pm & 6-10pm Sat; 🛜) restaurant and bar is also excellent, and in summer there's an outdoor pool to lounge by and take in the splendid views.

Deer Mountain Inn   BOUTIQUE HOTEL $$$
(☑ 518-589-6268; www.deermountaininn.com; 790 Rte 25; r/cottage from $250/800; ☺ restaurant 5-10pm Thu-Sun; 🅿️☺❄🛜) There are only six

rooms and two cottages (sleeping up to nine guests) at this gorgeous arts-and-crafts-style property within a vast mountainside estate. It's all been interior designed to the max.

**Last Chance Cheese
Antiques Cafe**   AMERICAN $$
(☑ 518-589-6424; www.lastchanceonline.com; 6009 Main St; mains $10-27; ☺ 11am-9:30pm Fri & Sat, to 8pm Sun) A fixture on Main St since 1970, this is part roadhouse with live bands, part candy store and cheese shop, and part restaurant, serving hearty meals. Many of the antiques and whatnots that decorate the place are for sale, too.

❶ Getting There & Away

The drive along Rte 23A to and from Tannersville is one of the most scenic in the Catskills, but take it slowly as there are several hairpin bends. It's possible to reach Tannersville from NYC by bus with Trailways (www.trailwaysny.com), but you'll have to change services in Kingston.

Woodstock

📞 845 / POP 5820

A minor technicality: the 1969 music festival was actually held in Bethel, an hour's drive west. Nonetheless, the town of Woodstock still attracts an arty, music-loving crowd and cultivates the free spirit of that era, with rainbow tie-dye style and local grassroots everything, from radio to a respected indie film festival and a farmers market (fittingly billed as a farm festival).

⊙ Sights

**Center for Photography at
Woodstock**   ARTS CENTER
(☑ 845-679-9957; www.cpw.org; 59 Tinker St; ☺ noon-5pm Thu-Sun) 𝗙𝗥𝗘𝗘 Founded in 1977, this creative space gives classes, hosts lectures and mounts exhibitions that expand the strict definition of the art form, thanks to a lively artist-in-residence program.

This was formerly the Café Espresso, and Bob Dylan once had a writing studio above it – that's where he typed up the liner notes for *Another Side of Bob Dylan* in 1964 – and Janis Joplin was a regular performer.

🛏 Sleeping & Eating

White Dove Rockotel   INN $$
(☑ 845-306-5419; www.thewhitedoverockotel. com; 148 Tinker St; ste $170-275; 🛜🐾) This purple-painted Victorian certainly stands out from the crowd – but it's nothing compared

to the rooms! The six units, split over two properties, are decorated with psychedelic colors, posters, record players and vintage vinyl. The suites feature kitchens. It's one of the few places in town that doesn't require guests to book two or more nights. There are two designated pet-friendly suites.

Woodstock Inn on the Millstream INN $$
(☑ 845-679-8211; www.woodstock-inn-ny.com; 48 Tannery Brook Rd; r/cottage from $169/375; ❄ ✆) Pleasantly decorated in quiet pastels, some of the rooms at this inn surrounded by serene, flower-filled grounds, come with kitchenettes, electric fireplaces and large tubs.

★**Garden Cafe** VEGAN $
(☑ 845-679-3600; www.thegardencafewoodstock.com; 6 Old Forge Rd; mains $9-20; ⊗ 11:30am-9pm Mon, Wed & Thu, to 9:30pm Fri, 10am-9:30pm Sat, to 9pm Sun; ✆) All the ingredients used at this relaxed, charming cafe are organic. The food served is appealing, tasty and fresh, and includes salads, sandwiches, rice bowls and veggie lasagna. It also serves freshly made juices, smoothies, organic wines, craft beers, and coffee with a variety of nondairy milks.

FINGER LAKES

In west-central New York, the rolling hills are cut through by 11 long narrow bodies of water appropriately named the Finger Lakes. The region is an outdoor paradise, as well as the state's premier wine-growing region, with more than 120 vineyards.

At the south of Cayuga Lake, Ithaca, home to Ivy League Cornell University, is the region's gateway. At the northern tip of Seneca Lake, Geneva is a pretty and lively town, thanks to the student population at Hobart and William Smith Colleges. Here the restored 1894 Smith Opera House is a vibrant center for performing arts.

To the west, Y-shaped Keuka Lake is edged by two small state parks that keep it relatively pristine; it's a favorite for trout fishing. Base yourself at sweet little Hammondsport, on the southwest end. Arts and crafts lovers should also schedule a stop in Corning to see the brilliant glass museum there.

❶ Getting There & Away

Ithaca is the region's major hub with several daily bus connections to NYC (from $36, five hours, daily). **Ithaca Tompkins Regional Airport** (ITH; ☑ 607-257-0456; www.flyithaca.com; 1 Culligan Dr) has direct flights to Detroit, Newark and Philadelphia.

WAIT, WHERE'S WOODSTOCK?

The site of the 1969 Woodstock Music & Art Fair, on Max Yasgur's farm outside Bethel, the **Bethel Woods Center for the Arts** (☑ 866-781-2922; www.bethelwoodscenter.org; 200 Hurd Rd, Bethel; museum adult/child $15/6; ⊗ museum 10am-7pm daily May-Sep, to 5pm Thu-Sun Oct-Dec) is 70 miles southwest of the town of Woodstock. It's now home to an outdoor amphitheater with great summer concerts and an evocative museum with exhibits that burst with the music and images that made Woodstock such a cultural force.

Ithaca

☑ 607 / POP 30,760

An idyllic home for college students and first-wave hippies, Ithaca, on the southern tip of Cayuga Lake, is the largest town around the Finger Lakes. With an art-house cinema, good eats and great hiking ('Ithaca is gorges' goes the slogan, for all the surrounding canyons and waterfalls), it's both a destination in itself and a convenient halfway point between NYC and Niagara Falls.

The center of Ithaca is a pedestrian street called the Commons. On a steep hill above is Ivy League Cornell University, founded in 1865, with a small business strip at the campus' front gates, called Collegetown. The drive from Ithaca up scenic Rte 89 (west side) or Rte 90 (east side) to Seneca Falls, at the north end of Cayuga Lake, takes about an hour.

◉ Sights

★**Herbert F Johnson Museum of Art** MUSEUM
(☑ 607-255-6464; www.museum.cornell.edu; 114 Central Ave; ⊗ 10am-5pm Fri-Wed, to 7:30pm Thu) FREE IM Pei's brutalist building looms like a giant concrete robot above the ornate neo-Gothic surrounds of Cornell's campus. Inside you'll find an eclectic collection ranging from medieval wood carvings to modern masters and an extensive collection of Asian art. It's worth a visit if only for the panoramic views of Ithaca and Cayuga Lake from the top floor galleries.

Just down the hill behind the museum is Fall Creek, with a scenic bridge across it.

Finger Lakes

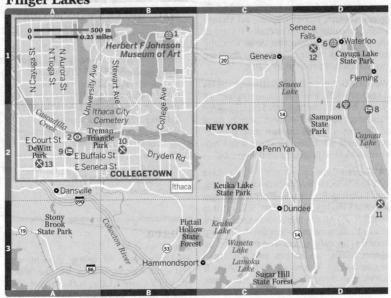

Finger Lakes

Cornell Botanic Gardens GARDENS
(📞 607-255-2400; www.cornellbotanicgardens.
org; 124 Comstock Knoll Dr; ⏰ 9am-5pm Sun-Thu,
to 6pm Fri & Sat) FREE The verdant spaces in
and around campus includes a 100-acre arboretum, a botanical garden and numerous
trails. Stop at the Nevin Welcome Center for
maps and to find out about tours. A great
way to reach here is by hiking up the dramatic **Cascadilla Gorge** (College Ave Bridge),
which starts near the center of town.

Robert H Treman State Park STATE PARK
(📞 607-273-3440; www.parks.ny.gov; 105 Enfield
Falls Rd; per car mid-Apr–mid-Oct $8) Five and
a half miles southwest of Ithaca, the biggest state park in the area offers extensive
trails and a very popular swimming hole

(late June to early September). Treman's
gorge trail passes a stunning 12 waterfalls:
don't miss Devil's Kitchen and Lucifer Falls,
a multi-tiered wonder that spills Enfield
Creek over rocks for about 100ft. There's
also camping here from $18 per night per
site and a few cabins (from $60).

🛏 Sleeping

⭐ **William Henry Miller Inn** B&B $$
(📞 877-256-4553; www.millerinn.com; 303 N Auro-
ra St; r $195-290; ❄ @ 📶) Gracious and grand,
and only a few steps from the Commons,
this is a historic home with luxurious rooms
(two with whirlpool tubs and two in a sepa-
rate carriage house), gourmet breakfast and
a dessert buffet.

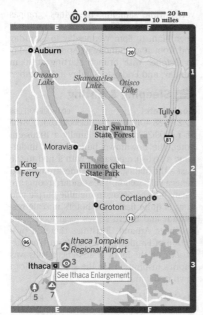

★**Inns of Aurora**   HISTORIC HOTEL **$$$**
(☎315-364-8888; www.innsofaurora.com; 391 Main St, Aurora; r $200-400; P❋❄) This beautiful historic hotel is composed of four properties: the main Aurora Inn, built in 1833 and little changed on the outside since, with 10 lovely rooms and a splendid dining room; Rowland House with 10 more rooms; EB Morgan House with seven rooms; and Wallcourt Hall, the most modern of the designs, but with no lake views. Pick up the hotel's excellent self-guided walking tour of the town.

Firelight Camps   TENTED CAMP **$$$**
(☎607-229-1644; www.firelightcamps.com; 1150 Danby Rd; tents $239-349; ☺mid-May–Oct; ❄) Glamping comes to Ithaca at this attractive site attached to the La Tourelle Hotel and with quick access to the trails of nearby Buttermilk Falls State Park. The safari-style canvas tents rise over hardwood platforms and comfy beds. The bathhouse is separate. There's a campfire in the evenings and yoga on Saturday mornings.

✖️ **Eating**

Carriage House   BREAKFAST **$**
(☎607-645-0152; www.carriagehousecafe.com; 305 Stewart Ave; mains $8-14; ☺9am-2pm Tue-Fri, to 3pm Sat & Sun) Carriage House (which is located in a renovated carriage house, natch)

serves brunch throughout the week. The menu is full of delicious sandwiches (including an incredible BLT), egg dishes, pancakes and salads, as well as fun cocktails. The Loft Bar (4:30pm to 11pm Wednesday and Thursday, to midnight Friday and Saturday) is located in the upstairs of the Carriage House.

★**Hazelnut Kitchen**   AMERICAN **$$**
(☎607-387-4433; www.hazelnutkitchen.com; 53 East Main St, Trumansburg; mains $23-28; ☺5-9:30pm Thu-Mon) The chefs at this cozy place, 11 miles northwest of Ithaca, source quality produce from local farmers to create dishes that have made this arguably the finest restaurant in the region. It's well worth opting for the four-course tasting menu (price varies), where the chefs will personally present each seasonally inspired dish.

★**Moosewood Restaurant**   VEGETARIAN **$$**
(☎607-273-9610; www.moosewoodcooks.com; 215 N Cayuga St; mains $10-20; ☺10:30am-8:30pm Sun-Thu, to 9pm Fri & Sat; ☑) Established in 1973, this near-legendary veggie restaurant is run by a collective. It has a slightly upscale feel, with a full bar and global menu. It is very popular so reservations are recommended, especially during Cornell events.

ℹ️ **Getting There & Away**

Ithaca is the region's major hub with several daily bus connections to NYC (from $36, five hours, daily). **Ithaca Tompkins Regional Airport** (ITH; ☑607-257-0456; www.flyithaca.com; 1 Culligan Dr) has direct flights to Detroit, Newark and Philadelphia.

> **WORTH A TRIP**
>
> ## WORTH A TRIP: AURORA
>
> Around 28 miles north of Ithaca on the east side of Cayuga Lake is the picturesque village of Aurora. Established in 1795, the village has over 50 buildings on the National Register of Historic Places, including parts of the campus of Wells College, founded in 1868 for the higher education of women (it's now co-ed). The Inns of Aurora, which is composed of four grand properties – the Aurora Inn (1833), EB Morgan House (1858), Rowland House (1903) and Wallcourt Hall (1909) – is a wonderful place to stay. Alternatively stop by the Aurora Inn's lovely dining room for a meal with lakeside views and pick up a copy of the self-guided walking tour of the village.

DON'T MISS

CORNING MUSEUM OF GLASS

On the banks of the Chemung River, the attractive town of Corning owes its fortunes to Corning Glass Works, a company most Americans associate with sturdy Corningware plates, but which now excels in industrial materials of all kinds. The massive **Corning Museum of Glass** (800-732-6845; www.cmog.org; 1 Museum Way; adult/child $19.50/free; 9am-8pm Jun-Aug, to 5pm Sep-May) is home to fascinating exhibits on glassmaking, both as an art since ancient Egyptian days, and in the name of science. The contemporary art and design wing is the highlight, with a stunning exhibition of glass art and sculpture from the last 25 years. There are also live demonstrations of glassblowing, and you can sign up to make your own glass trinkets (additional cost).

Seneca Falls

315, 680 / POP 8850

The quiet, post-industrial town of Seneca Falls is said to have inspired visiting director Frank Capra to create Bedford Falls, the fictional small American town in his classic movie *It's a Wonderful Life*. Indeed, you can stand on a bridge crossing the town's river and just picture Jimmy Stewart doing the same. The town also has a special place in the history of women's suffrage.

Sights

Women's Rights National Historical Park　　　MUSEUM
(315-568-0024; www.nps.gov/wori; 136 Fall St; 9am-5pm Fri-Sun Jan, 9am-5pm Feb-Dec) FREE
Visit the chapel where Elizabeth Cady Stanton and friends declared in 1848 that 'all men and women are created equal,' the first step towards women's suffrage. The adjacent museum tells the story, including the complicated relationship with abolition.

Knapp Winery & Restaurant　　　WINERY
(607-930-3495; www.knappwine.com; 2770 Ernsberger Rd, Romulus; tastings $5; 10am-5:30pm Apr-Nov, 10:30am-5pm Mon-Sat, 11:30am-5pm Sun Dec-Mar) This winery, 12 miles south of Seneca Falls, has a wide lawn surrounded by gnarly roots and rioting wildflowers; you can look out over the trellis-covered vine-

yards while sampling the wines, grappas and limoncellos. The winery restaurant is open 11am to 5pm Wednesday to Saturday and from 10am Sunday in April; daily May to October with brunch starting at 10am Sunday; and Friday to Sunday in November.

Sleeping & Eating

Gould Hotel　　　BOUTIQUE HOTEL $$
(877-788-4010; www.thegouldhotel.com; 108 Fall St; r $209-259;) Originally a 1920s-era hotel, the downtown building has undergone a stylish renovation with a nod to the past – the mahogany bar comes from an old Seneca Falls saloon. The standard rooms are small, but the decor, in metallic purple and gray, is quite flash. The hotel's upscale restaurant and tavern serves local food, wine and beer. Around Christmas there's a projection of Frank Capra's film *It's a Wonderful Life* on the lobby wall; Seneca Falls was Capra's inspiration for the small American town in the movie.

Mac's Drive In　　　BURGERS $
(315-539-3064; www.macsdrivein.net; 1166 US-20/Rte 5, Waterloo; mains $4-8; 10:30am-10pm Fri-Sun Apr-Oct) Midway between Seneca Falls and Geneva, this classic drive-in restaurant established in 1961 (and little changed since) serves up burgers, fried chicken and fish dinners at bargain prices.

THE ADIRONDACKS

The Adirondack Mountains (www.visitadirondacks.com) may not compare in drama and height with mountains in the western US, but they more than make up for it in area: the range covers 9375 sq miles, from the center of New York just north of the state capital Albany, up to the Canadian border. And with 46 peaks over 4000ft high, the Adirondacks provide some of the most wild-feeling terrain in the east. Like the Catskills to the south, much of the Adirondacks' dense forest and lake lands are protected by the state constitution, and it's a fabulous location to see the color show of autumn leaves. Hiking, canoeing and backcountry camping are popular activities, and there's good fishing, along with powerboating on the bigger lakes.

Sights

Adirondack Museum　　　MUSEUM
(518-352-7311; www.adkmuseum.org; Rte 28N-30, Blue Mountain Lake; adult/child $20/12;

⊙10am-5pm Jun-Sep; 🚻) Set on 30 acres, this museum has creative exhibits on the mountains' human-centered stories, from the mining and logging industries to quirky hermits and Victorian tourists. There are lots of hands-on exhibits and activities for kids, including a bouldering wall and snow-shoeing, even in summertime. You can easily spend half a day here. Consider having lunch in the attached cafe overlooking Blue Mountain Lake.

❶ Getting There & Away

The area's main airport is in Albany (p147), although Adirondack Regional Airport (p143) in Saranac Lake has connections via Cape Air (www.capeair.com) to Boston.

Both Greyhound (www.greyhound.com) and Trailways (www.trailwaysny.com) serve Albany and various towns in the Adirondacks, though a car is essential for exploring widely.

Amtrak (www.amtrak.com) runs from NYC to Albany (from $44, 2½ hours) and on to Ticon-deroga ($69, five hours) and Westport ($69, six hours), both on Lake Champlain, with a bus connection to Lake Placid ($94, seven hours).

Albany

📞 518, 838 / POP 98,110

Built between 1965 and 1976, the architectural ensemble of government buildings in Albany's central Empire State Plaza is a sight to behold and includes the excellent New York State Museum, as well as a fine collection of modern public art. In downtown and leafy Washington Park, stately buildings and gracious brownstones speak to the state capital's wealthy past.

Albany became state capital in 1797 because of its geographic centrality to local col-onies and its strategic importance in the fur trade. These days it's as much synonymous with legislative dysfunction as with political power. Its struggling economy is reflected in the number of derelict and abandoned buildings (the ones with white cross signs on a red background). Even so, the locals' friendliness and the city's usefulness as a gateway to the Adirondacks and Hudson Valley make it worth more than a casual look.

⊙ Sights

★**Empire State Plaza** PUBLIC ART
(📞518-473-7521; www.empirestateplaza.org) **FREE** While the plaza's ensemble of architecture surrounding a central pool is hugely impressive, it's the splendid collection of modern American art liberally sprinkled outside, inside and underground the complex that is the true highlight here. The collection includes sculptures and massive paintings by Mark Rothko, Jackson Pollock, Alexander Calder and many other star artists.

★**New York State Museum** MUSEUM
(📞518-474 5877; www.nysm.nysed.gov; 222 Madison Ave; 9:30am-5pm Tue-Sun) **FREE** There are exhibits on everything from New York's original Native Amerian residents, the state's history of activism, its architectural and engineering marvels and more in this top class museum. A large chunk is dedicated to the history and development of New York City. The section on 9/11, including a damaged fire truck and debris from the site, is very moving. Don't miss a ride on the gorgeous antique carousel on the 4th floor.

New York State Capitol HISTORIC BUILDING
(📞518-474-2418; www.hallofgovernors.ny.gov; Washington Ave; ⊙guided tours 10am, noon, 2pm

---

GREAT CAMPS

The Adirondacks' 'great camps' were typically lake and mountainside compounds of grandiose log cabins built in the latter half of the 19th century, as rustic retreats for the wealthy. A prime example is **Great Camp Sagamore** (Sagamore Institute; 📞315-354-5311; www.greatcampsagamore.org; Sagamore Rd, Raquette Lake; tours adult/student $18/10; ⊙hours vary May–mid-Oct), a former Vanderbilt vacation estate on the west side of the Adirondacks, now open to the public for tours, workshops and overnight stays on occasional history-oriented weekends. Less ostentatious is **White Pine Camp** (📞518-327-3030; www.whitepinecamp.com; 432 White Pine Rd, Paul Smiths; r/cabin from $165/315; 📶), 12 miles northwest of Saranac Lake. This collection of cozy cabins is set amid pine forests, wetlands and scenic Osgood Pond – a boardwalk leads out to an island on which sits a Japanese-style teahouse and an antique all-wood bowling alley. The camp's charm comes through in its modest luxuries such as claw-foot tubs and wood-burning fireplaces. Naturalist walking tours are open to nonguests on select days from mid-June to September.

The Adirondacks

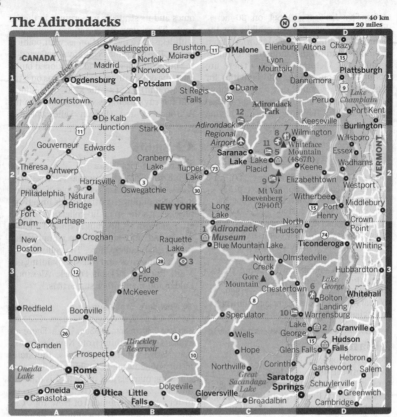

& 3pm Mon-Fri) **FREE** Completed in 1899, this grand building is the heart of the state government. The interior features detailed stone carving, carpentry, and tile and mosaic work, with highlights being the Great Western Staircase, the Governor's Reception Room and the HH Richardson–designed Senate Chamber.

🛏 Sleeping & Eating

⭐ **Washington Park Inn**   BOUTIQUE HOTEL **$$**
(☏ 518-225-4567; www.washingtonparkinn.com; 643 Madison Ave; r $139-169; P ❋ @ 🛜) Rocking chairs on the covered porch and tennis rackets for guests to use on the courts in the park across the road set the relaxed tone for this appealing hotel in one of Albany's heritage buildings. Rooms are big and with simple and clean decoration, and food and drink is available on a serve-yourself basis around the clock from the well-stocked kitchen.

⭐ **Cafe Madison**   BREAKFAST **$**
(☏ 518-935-1094; www.cafemadisonalbany.com; 1108 Madison Ave; mains $12-14; ⊙ 7:30am-2pm Mon-Thu, to 3pm Fri-Sun; 🍽) Highly popular breakfast spot, especially on the weekend, when 30-minute waits for one of the cozy booths or tables is not uncommon (you might have more luck sitting at the bar). The staff know all the regulars and the menu includes inventive omelets, crepes, vegan options and a wide variety of specialty cocktails, such as cajun Bloody Marys.

Hollow   PUB FOOD **$$**
(☏ 518-426-8550; www.thehollowalbany.com; 79 N Pearl St; mains $11-28; ⊙ 11:30am-late Mon-Fri, from noon Sat; 🍽) Vegetarians who crave pub food will be in heaven at the Hollow, which has an extensive menu of meatless takes on old favorites such as seitan hot wings, vegan Philly cheesesteak and a tempeh Reuben. There are meat options as well. Live music

The Adirondacks

◎ Top Sights
1 Adirondack Museum C3

◎ Sights
2 Fort William Henry Museum............... D4
3 Great Camp Sagamore.......................B3
4 Hyde Collection Art Museum............. D4
5 Lake Placid Olympic Museum.............C2
Olympic Center ....(see 5)

◎ Activities, Courses & Tours
Lake George Steamboat
Cruises ....(see 2)
6 Pinnacle Trail View............................D3
7 Whiteface Mountain C2
8 Whiteface Veteran's Memorial
Highway.......................................C2

◎ Sleeping
9 Adirondack Loj C2
10 Cornerstone Victorian........................C3
11 Lake Placid Lodge..............................C2
12 White Pine Camp C1

◎ Eating
Liquids & Solids at the
Handlebar ....(see 5)
Morgan & Co.................................(see 4)

◎ Drinking & Nightlife
Top of the Park..............................(see 5)

and a cool brick-and-glass interior round out the dining experience.

Drinking & Nightlife

A strip of bars on North Pearl St downtown gets hopping when workers spill out of the nearby government buildings. For local craft-beer options, check out the Albany Craft Beverage Trail (www.albanycraftbeverages.org).

Information

Albany Heritage Area Visitors Center (☑ 518-434-0405; www.albany.org; 25 Quackenbush Sq; 9am-4pm Mon-Fri, 10am-3pm Sat, from 11am Sun) As well as tourist information, the center has an exhibit about Albany's history, the Henry Hudson Planetarium and a gift shop. Check the website for special events.

Getting There & Away

As state capital, Albany has the full range of transport connections. **Albany International Airport** (☑ 518-242-2200; www.albanyairport.com; Albany Shaker Rd, Colonie) is 10 miles north of downtown. The Amtrak **Albany-Rensselaer Station** (☑ 800-872 7245; www.

amtrak.com; 525 East St, Rensselaer), on the east bank of the Hudson River, has connections with NYC (from $44, 2½ hours), upstate New York and beyond. Greyhound (www.greyhound.com) and Trailways (www.trailwaysny.com) bus services use the centrally located **bus terminal** (☑ 518-427-7060; 34 Hamilton St).

Lake George

Lake George covers 45 square miles of the Adirondacks and attracts thousands of visitors to its shores every summer for swimming, boating, and just staring at its shimmering waters in admiration. The town of Lake George is a major tourist center with arcades, fireworks every Thursday in July and August, and paddleboat rides. It's a chaotic good time for those looking to dive into summer-by-the-lake culture. Anyone looking for a more mellow experience will find nearby towns that offer a less hectic atmosphere, such as upscale Bolton Landing, cozy Glens Falls and bucolic Warrensburg. In the winter, Lake George freezes over and most of the towns surrounding it go into hibernation. Other than skiing up in North Creek you won't find many winter activities and most restaurants and hotels stay closed until early summer.

◎ Sights & Activities

Fort William Henry Museum   MUSEUM
(☑ 518-668-5471; www.fwhmuseum.com; 48 Canada St, Lake George; adult/child $17/8, ghost tours $18/8; ⊙ 9:30am-6pm May-Oct; ◉) Guides dressed as 18th-century British soldiers muster visitors along, with stops for battle reenactments that include firing period muskets and cannons, at this replica of the 1755 wooden fort. Check online for details of the evening ghost tours.

Hyde Collection Art Museum   MUSEUM
(☑ 518-792-1761; www.hydecollection.org; 161 Warren St, Glens Falls; adult/child $12/free; ⊙ 10am-5pm Tue-Sat, noon-5pm Sun) This remarkable gathering of art was amassed by local newspaper heiress Charlotte Pryun Hyde. In her rambling Florentine renaissance mansion in Glens Falls, you'll stumble across Rembrandts, Rubens, Matisses and Eakins, as well as tapestries, sculptures and turn-of-the-century furnishings.

Pinnacle Trail View   HIKING
(Edgecomb Pond Rd, Bolton Landing) At the end of this steep 1.5-mile hike are incredible views of Lake George and the surrounding area. The parking area and trailhead are just west of Bolton Landing.

Lake George Steamboat Cruises CRUISE
(☑ 518-668-5777; www.lakegeorgesteamboat.com; 57 Beach Rd, Lake George; adult/child from $16/7.50; ☺ May-Oct) This company has been running cruise boats on Lake George since 1917. In season take your pick from a variety of cruise options on its three vessels: the authentic steamboat *Minnie-Ha-Ha*, the 1907-vintage *Mohican* and the flagship *Lac du Saint Sacrement*.

🍴 Sleeping & Eating

★ **Cornerstone Victorian** B&B $$
(☑ 518-623-3308; www.cornerstonevictorian.com; 3921 Main St, Warrensburg; r $119-199; P ✳ 🛜) There are many Victorian themed B&Bs in New York state, but few offer a gourmet, five-course breakfast each morning. The menu changes daily and alone is worth the price of a stay, although you'll also find that the rooms are comfortable and the hospitality of the hosts, Doug and Louise, extends well beyond the breakfast table.

★ **Morgan & Co** AMERICAN $$$
(☑ 518-409-8060; www.morganrestaurant.com; 65 Ridge St, Glens Falls; mains $27-44; ☺ 4-10pm Tue & Wed, to 11pm Thu-Sat, 10am-8pm Sun) Morgan & Co is the offspring of husband and wife Steve Butters and Rebecca Newell-Butters (who is a *Chopped* winner) and specializes in modern American cuisine with more than a few hints of international flair. Many of the dishes have a twist – ginger caesar salad, beef brisket bolognese – but the real draw here is that everything is exquisitely prepared. The three-course *prix fixe* dinner ($43.95) is a great deal.

❶ Getting There & Away

Albany International Airport (p147) is 50 miles south of Lake George. Amtrak stops in Fort Edwards, about 20 minutes by car from Lake George. Greyhound (www.greyhound.com) and Trailways (www.trailwaysny.com) also have long-distance buses to the region. A rental car is the best way of getting around the lake area.

Lake Placid

☑ 518, 838 / POP 2440
The resort town of Lake Placid is synonymous with snow sports – it hosted the Winter Olympics in 1932 and 1980. Elite athletes continue to train here; the rest of us can ride real bobsleds, speed-skate and more. Mirror Lake, which is right downtown, freezes thick enough for ice-skating, tobogganing and dogsledding. The town is also pleasant in summer, as the unofficial center of the High Peaks region of the Adirondacks and a great base for striking out on a hike or going canoeing or kayaking on one of the area's many lakes.

◉ Sights & Activities

Olympic Center STADIUM
(☑ 518-523-3330; www.whiteface.com; 2634 Main St; tours $10, adult/child skating $8/5, skating shows $10/8; ☺ 10am-5pm daily, skating shows 4:30pm Fri; ♿) This is the location of the 1980 'Miracle on Ice,' when the upstart US hockey team trumped the unstoppable Soviets. In winter you can skate on the outside oval rink and year-round take a one-hour tour of the stadium. Also here is a small **museum** (www.lpom.org; adult/child $7/5; ☺ 10am-5pm). There are usually figure-skating shows on Fridays, with an additional show Saturdays at 7:30pm in July and August.

Whiteface Mountain SKIING
(☑ 518-946-2223; www.whiteface.com; 5021 Rte 86, Wilmington; full-day lift ticket adult/child from $68/44, gondola only $20/16; ☺ 8:30am-4pm Dec–Apr) This top-class Olympic ski area, 10 miles northeast of Lake Placid, has a 3430ft vertical drop, 98% snowmaking coverage and over 80 trails suitable for all skill levels.

The Cloudsplitter Gondola also runs through the summer and fall (9:30am to 5pm Saturday and Sunday June, daily July and August, and Friday to Sunday September and October), providing spectacular views of the Adirondacks.

Whiteface Veteran's Memorial Highway SCENIC DRIVE
(www.whiteface.com; Rte 431; driver & vehicle $12, additional passengers $8; ☺ 8:45am-5:30pm mid-Jun–mid-Oct) Whiteface, the state's 5th highest peak at 4867ft, is the only summit in the Adirondacks accessible by car, with a neat castle-style lookout and cafe at the top. It can be socked in with clouds, making for an unnerving drive up, but when the fog clears, the 360-degree view is awe-inspiring. Tolls are paid at Lake Steven.

🍴 Sleeping & Eating

★ **Adirondack Loj** LODGE $
(☑ 518-523-3441; www.adk.org; 1002 Adirondack Loj Rd; dm/r from $60/169, lean-tos winter/summer from $22.50/40; P 🛜) The Adirondack Mountain Club runs this rustic retreat on the shore of pretty Heart Lake. All rooms in the lodge share communal bathrooms. Rates for rooms in the lodge include breakfast, and since it's 8 miles south of Lake Placid,

you'll want to arrange a trail lunch and dinner here, too. Camping sites, lean-tos and cabins are also available. From here hiking trails take off in all directions, including to nearby Mt Jo.

★ **Lake Placid Lodge** HERITAGE HOTEL $$$
(☑518-523-2700; www.lakeplacidlodge.com; 144 Lodge Way; r $800-1800; ⊙May-Mar; P☺☀ @☎) Overlooking Lake Placid and channeling the rustic glamor of classic Gilded Age Adirondack lodges, this luxury hotel offers 13 gorgeously decorated rooms and cabins. The cabins are 19th-century originals, but the main hotel is a remarkable reconstruction following a devastating 2008 fire.

Liquids & Solids at the Handlebar AMERICAN $$
(☑518-837-5012; www.liquidsandsolids.com; 6115 Sentinel Rd; mains $15-24; ⊙4-10pm Tue-Sat, 5-9pm Sun) It's all about craft beers, creative cocktails and fresh, inventive dishes at this rustic bar and restaurant where the kielbasa sausages and other charcuterie are made in-house. Mains may include dishes such as cauliflower stroganoff or crispy confit pork.

🍸 Drinking & Nightlife

★ **Top of the Park** COCKTAIL BAR
(☑518-523-3632; www.topofthepark.bar; 2407 Main St; ⊙3pm-midnight) Top of the Park bucks the trend of other lakeside options in Lake Placid, which tend to be chintzy and uninspired. This small bar has fantastic mixologists who specialize in inventive, well balanced cocktails. There is also a tasty menu of small plates. Try to get a seat on the patio overlooking the lake.

❶ Getting There & Away

Trailways (www.trailwaysny.com) serves Lake Placid. Amtrak (www.amtrak.com) runs once a day to Westport, with a bus connection to Lake Placid ($94, seven hours). **Adirondack Regional Airport** (☑518-891-4600; www.adirondackairport.com; 96 Airport Rd), 17 miles northwest near Saranac Lake, has connections via Cape Air (www.capeair.com) to Boston.

LAKE ONTARIO & THOUSAND ISLANDS

To downstate New Yorkers, this region is the source of the Thousand Islands salad dressing made of ketchup, mayonnaise and relish. In fact, it's a scenic wonderland along Lake Ontario and the St Lawrence River with 1864 islands of all shapes and sizes either side of the US–Canada maritime border. The area was a Gilded Age playground for the rich; now it's more populist. Pros: beautiful sunsets, good-value lodging and Canada across the water. Cons: dead in winter and large mosquitoes in summer (bring repellent).

The historic port of Oswego is the region's southern gateway and makes a good base for exploring places like Sackets Harbor, where reenactors stage an annual War of 1812 Weekend. On the north side, Clayton and Alexandria Bay both offer boat tours to the islands in the St Lawrence River, or you could camp amid glorious nature in the Wellesley Island State Park.

❶ Getting There & Away

The main airport for the region is **Syracuse Hancock International Airport** (☑315-454-4330; www.syrairport.org; 1000 Colonel Eileen Collins Blvd, Syracuse); connections here include NYC on JetBlue and Delta; Newark, Washington, DC, and Chicago on United; and Toronto on Air Canada. Cars can be rented at the airport or in downtown Syracuse, which is connected to other parts of the state by bus and train.

St Lawrence River Shore

Summer on the western shores of the Lawrence River, which separate New York state from Canada, sees thousands flock to the smattering of small waterfront towns that cater to all kinds of fun in the water. Alexandria Bay (A-Bay or Alex Bay), Clayton and Cape Vincent are the best places to hunker down to experience some of the sunny frivolity. They are all a bit rundown and tacky, but fun, nonetheless, and if you need a break you can always explore the region's wineries and distilleries, or some of the many islands from which the region gets its name. There is incredible nature and unique sights like a castle to discover. Be aware that in winter things more or less close down.

⊙ Sights & Activities

★ **Antique Boat Museum** MUSEUM
(☑315-686-4104; www.abm.org; 750 Mary St, Clayton; adult/child $14/8; ⊙9am-5pm May–mid-Oct) There are some gorgeous examples of boat-making craft on display at this waterside museum, where you can view the still-working antique boats and try your hand at rowing traditional wooden skiffs.

★ **Boldt Castle** CASTLE
(☑800-847-5263; www.boldtcastle.com; Heart Island; adult/child $9.50/6.50; ⊙10am-6:30pm May-

Sep, 11am-5pm Oct) This Gothic gem, a replica of a German castle, was (partly) built by hotelier George C Boldt in the late 19th century. In 1904, midway through construction, Boldt's wife died, and the project was abandoned. Since 1977 the Thousand Islands Bridge Authority has spent millions restoring the place to something of its planned grandeur.

Singer Castle   CASTLE
(☑877-327-5475; www.singercastle.com; Dark Island; adult/child $14.50/7.50; ☺10am-4pm mid-

May–mid-Oct) This stone castle, on Dark Island in the middle of the St Lawrence River, was built in 1905 by American entrepreneur Frederick Bourne. It's full of secret passages and hidden doors and has a dungeon – all of which you'll see on a tour. Uncle Sam runs boats from Alex Bay; **Schermerhorn Harbor** (☑315-324-5966; www.schermerhornharbor. com; 71 Schermerhorn Landing, Hammond; shuttle to Singer Castle $31.25; ☺10:30am-2:30pm late May-Aug) also visits.

Thousand Islands & St Lawrence River Shore

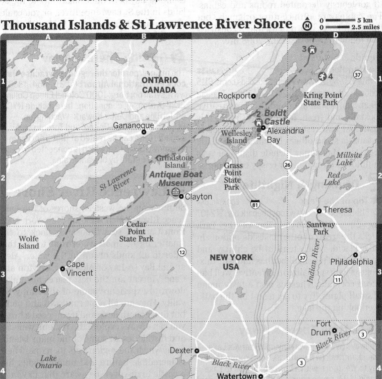

Thousand Islands & St Lawrence River Shore

Uncle Sam Boat Tour
BOATING

(☑ 315-482-2611; www.usboattours.com; 45 James St, Alexandria Bay; adult/child $23/11.75) The main offering from the largest boat-tour operator in the area is a two-hour ride that visits both the US and Canada sides of the river (no passport required) and stops at Boldt Castle.

🛏 Sleeping & Eating

★ Wooden Boat Inn
MOTEL $

(☑ 315-686-5004; www.woodenboatinn.com; 606 Alexandria St, Clayton; r/boat from $99/275; ☺ May-Oct; ✴ 🏵) This efficient inn is known for its clean rooms and friendly owners. The six motel rooms are great value, but anyone with a nautical bent should book the 36ft trawler moored on the riverfront.

★ HI Tibbetts Point Lighthouse
HOSTEL $

(☑ 315-654-3450; www.hihostels.com; 33439 County Hwy 6, Cape Vincent; dm from $30; ☺ mid-Jun–early Sep; 🅿 🏵) A 27-mile scenic seaside drive west of Clayton will bring you to the 1827 lighthouse complex at Cape Vincent. The lighthouse keepers' house is now a well-kept hostel. Book ahead – there are only 18 beds – and bring all you'll need to eat as there's nothing else around here.

Dockside Pub
AMERICAN $$

(☑ 315-482-9849; www.thedocksidepub.com; 17 Market St, Alexandria Bay; mains $8-18; ☺ 11am-midnight Sun-Thu, to 2am Fri & Sat; 🚼) Unpretentious pub fare – burgers, fries, pizza and some specials. Despite the name its location is inland, with no dock view.

WESTERN NEW YORK

Tourism in this region revolves around Buffalo, New York State's second-largest city. After being the largest and most prosperous metropolis along the Great Lakes at the turn of the 19th century, Buffalo fell on hard times in the 20th, but is bouncing back in the 21st. Its amazing stock of heritage architecture is being restored and reinvented into hotels, museums and other businesses.

The area first developed thanks to the hydroelectric power of Niagara Falls and the Erie Canal, which linked the Great Lakes to the Atlantic Ocean. The falls are now better known as a tourist destination, with millions of visitors flocking here annually.

Rochester, about an hour northeast, shares a similar economic trajectory but has long been buoyed by its rich history of activism. The city was home to the famed suffragette Susan B Anthony and civil rights pioneer Frederick Douglass, among other 19th and 20th century iconoclasts.

❶ Getting There & Away

Buffalo Niagara International Airport (p154) is a regional hub with the widest range of flights, but you can also fly into and out of Niagara Falls International Airport (p156) and the **Greater Rochester International Airport** (☑ 585-753-7000; www2.monroecounty.gov; 1200 Brooks Ave). Amtrak runs trains to Buffalo, Rochester and Niagra, with connections to and from NYC, Albany, Toronto, and from Buffalo to/from Chicago. Greyhound (www.greyhound.com) has bus services to all three locations. For other places in the region you are best getting there by rental car.

Buffalo

☑ 716 / POP 256,900

The winters may be long and cold, but Buffalo stays warm with a vibrant creative community and strong local pride. Settled by the French in 1758, the city is believed to derive its name from *beau fleuve* (beautiful river). With power from nearby Niagara Falls, it boomed in the early 1900s; Pierce-Arrow cars were made here, and it was the first American city to have electric streetlights. One of its nicknames – Queen City – was because it was the largest city along the Great Lakes.

Those rosy economic times are long over, leaving many abandoned buildings in their wake. But revival is in Buffalo's air. Masterpieces of late 19th- and early 20th-century architecture, including designs by Frank Lloyd Wright and HH Richardson, have been magnificently restored. There's a park system laid out by Frederick Law Olmsted, of NYC's Central Park fame, great museums, and a positive vibe that's impossible to ignore.

◎ Sights & Activities

★ Buffalo City Hall
ARCHITECTURE

(☑ 716-852-3300; www.preservationbuffaloniagara.org; 65 Niagara Sq; ☺ tours noon Mon-Fri) FREE This 32-story art deco masterpiece, beautifully detailed inside and out and opened in 1931, towers over downtown. It's worth joining the free tour at noon that includes access to the mayor's office, the council chamber and the open-air observation deck.

★ Martin House Complex
ARCHITECTURE

(☑ 716-856-3858; www.darwinmartinhouse.org; 125 Jewett Pkwy; tour basic/extended $19/37;

Buffalo

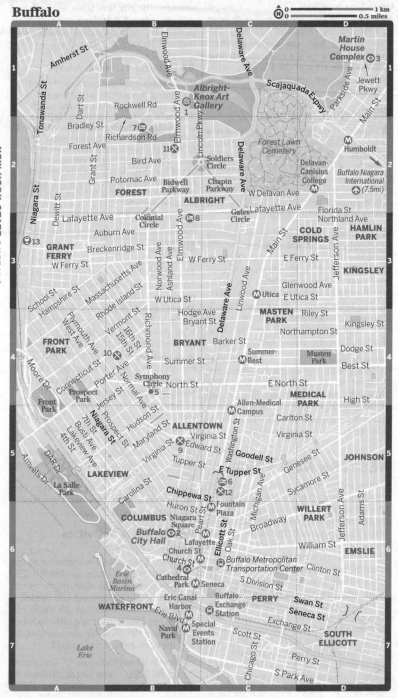

⊙tours hourly 10am-3pm Wed-Mon) This 15,000-sq-ft house, completed in 1905, was designed by Frank Lloyd Wright for his friend and patron Darwin D Martin. Representing Wright's Prairie House ideal, it consists of six interconnected buildings, each meticulously restored inside and out. Two tour options (book online) offer different levels of detail on this elaborate project.

★**Albright-Knox Art Gallery** MUSEUM
(☑716-882-8700; www.albrightknox.org; 1285 Elmwood Ave; adult/child $12/6; ⊙10am-5pm Tue-Sun) The gallery's superb collection, which ranges from Degas and Picasso to Ruscha, Rauschenberg and other abstract expressionists, occupies a neoclassical building planned for Buffalo's 1905 Pan American Expo. Its temporary exhibits are particularly creative and compelling.

Graycliff Estate ARCHITECTURE
(☑716-947-9217; www.graycliffestate.org; 6472 Old Lake Shore Rd, Derby; tours 1/2hr $18/34) Occupying a dramatic clifftop location on Lake Erie, 16 miles south of downtown Buffalo, this 1920s vacation home was designed by Frank Lloyd Wright for the wealthy Martin family. A lengthy restoration was completed in 2018, and you can learn a lot about Wright's overall plan on interesting tours (book in advance).

Guaranty Building ARCHITECTURE
(Prudential Building; www.hodgsonruss.com/Louis-Sullivans-Guaranty-Building.html; 140 Pearl

Buffalo

St; ⊙interpretive center 7:15am-9pm) FREE Completed in 1896 for the Guaranty Construction company, this gorgeous piece of architecture has a facade covered in detailed terra-cotta tiles and a superb stained-glass ceiling in its lobby. The interpretative center provides details of how groundbreaking this Adler & Sullivan–designed building was when it was built, when it was the tallest building in Buffalo.

Explore Buffalo TOURS
(☑716-245-3032; www.explorebuffalo.org; 1 Symphony Circle) Architectural and history tours around the Buffalo area by bus, on foot and by bicycle and kayak.

🛏 Sleeping

★**Hostel Buffalo Niagara** HOSTEL $
(☑716-852-5222; www.hostelbuffalo.com; 667 Main St; dm/r $31/85; ❄@🞉) Conveniently located in Buffalo's downtown Theater District, this hostel occupies three floors of a former school, with a basement rec room, plenty of kitchen and lounge space, a small art gallery, and spotless if institutional bathrooms. Services include laundry facilities, free bikes, and lots of info on local music, food and arts happenings.

★**InnBuffalo off Elmwood** GUESTHOUSE $$
(☑716-867-7777; www.innbuffalo.com; 619 Lafayette Ave; ste $179-299; ❄🞉) Ellen and Joe Lettieri have done a splendid job restoring this 1898 mansion, originally built for local brass and rubber magnate HH Hewitt. Ellen and Joe are happy to share how much of the buildings original grandeur was uncovered in their restorations, which is evident in the nine superbly decorated suites, some with original features such as Victorian needle-spray showers.

Hotel Henry HERITAGE HOTEL $$
(☑716-882-1970; www.hotelhenry.com; cnr Rockwell Rd & Cleveland Circle; r $189-279; ℗❄🞉) Occupying a grand late-19th-century 'lunatic asylum,' Hotel Henry preserves much of the stately architecture of Henry Richardson's original building. Its 88 rooms, reached off super-broad corridors, have tall ceilings and contemporary decor.

🍴 Eating & Drinking

EXPO Market FOOD HALL $
(☑716-218-8989; www.expobuffalo.com; 617 Main St; mains $8-12; ⊙10am-9pm Mon-Fri, 11am-8pm Sat; 🞉) Modeled after Chelsea Market in NYC, this modern food hall attached to the

classy Market Arcade in the Theater District is super popular with locals. Take your pick from Mexican wraps, salads, sushi, gourmet hot dogs and more, as well as a full bar.

★ **Cole's** AMERICAN $$
(☎716-886-1449; www.colesonelmwood.com; 1104 Elmwood Ave; mains $12-15; ⊙11am-11pm Mon-Thu, to midnight Fri & Sat, to 10pm Sun; ☎) Since 1934 this atmospheric restaurant and bar has been dishing up local favorites such as beef on weck (roast beef on a caraway-seed roll) – try it with a side of spicy Buffalo chicken wings, or go for one of the juicy burgers. It's handy for lunch if you are visiting the Delaware Park area and its museums.

★ **Betty's** AMERICAN $$
(☎716-362-0633; www.bettysbuffalo.com; 370 Virginia St; mains $16-24; ⊙8am-9pm Tue-Sat, 9am-10pm Sat, to 2pm Sun; ☎) On a quiet Allentown corner, bohemian Betty's does flavorful, fresh interpretations of American comfort food such as meatloaf. Brunch is deservedly popular and there's a pleasant bar.

Plenty of vegetarian, as well as gluten- and dairy-free, options are on the menu.

★ **Black Sheep** INTERNATIONAL $$$
(☎716-884-1100; www.blacksheepbuffalo.com; 367 Connecticut St; mains $25-30; ⊙5-10pm Wed-Sat, 11am-2pm Sun) Black Sheep likes to describe its style of western New York farm-to-table cuisine as 'global nomad,' which means you might find exciting, unique takes on chimichangas, pierogies and vegetable lasagna on the menu. You can also eat at the bar, which serves creative cocktails and local craft ales.

★ **Resurgence Brewing Company** MICROBREWERY
(☎716-381-9868; www.resurgencebrewing.com; 1250 Niagara St; ⊙4-10pm Tue-Thu, to 11:30pm Fri, noon-11:30pm Sat, to 5pm Sun) Housed in a former engine factory that was later to became a dog pound, Resurgence typifies Buffalo's skill at adaptive reuse of its infrastructure. The beers ($8 for a tasting flight) are excellent, with some 20 different ales on tap from fruity sweet Loganberry Wit to a porter with an amazing peanut-butter flavor The food menu includes artisanal pizza, sandwiches and meat and cheese boards ($4 to $12).

❶ Getting There & Away

Buffalo Niagara International Airport (BUF; ☎716-630-6000; www.buffaloairport.com; 4200 Genesee St), about 10 miles east of downtown, is a regional hub. JetBlue Airways offers affordable round-trip fares from NYC.

NFTA (www.nfta.com), the local transit service, runs express bus 204 to the **Buffalo Metropolitan Transportation Center** (☎716-855-7300; www.nfta.com; 181 Ellicott St) downtown. Greyhound buses also pull in here. NFTA local bus 40 goes to the American side of Niagara Falls ($2, one hour); express bus 60 also goes to the area, but requires a transfer.

From Amtrak's downtown **Exchange Street Station** (☎716-856-2075; www.amtrak.com; 75 Exchange St), you can catch trains to NYC (from $66, eight hours), Niagara Falls (from $14, one hour), Albany (from $52, five hours) and Toronto (from $33, three hours). All services also stop at **Buffalo-Depew Station** (55 Dick Rd), 8 miles east, where you can also board trains to Chicago (from $75, 11 hours).

❶ Getting Around

In downtown Buffalo, Metro Rail (www.metro.nfta.com) trains are free for stops between Theater District and Harborcenter along Main St.

Niagara Falls

☑716 / POP 48,630

It's a tale of two cities: Niagara Falls, New York (USA), and Niagara Falls, Ontario (Canada). Both overlook a natural wonder – 150,000 gallons of water per second, plunging more than 1000ft – and both provide a load of tourist kitsch around it. The Canadian side offers somewhat better views and a much larger town. However, the view from the New York side is still impressive and the falls surroundings are far more pleasant as they are preserved within a beautifully landscaped state park. The town itself is also largely devoid of the commercial razzmatazz you'll find on the Canadian side; if that's what you want, it's easy to walk across the Rainbow Bridge between the two – just be sure to bring your passport.

◉ Sights & Activities

The area around the falls is New York's first state park, pleasantly landscaped by Frederick Law Olmsted in the 1880s. From the walking paths, you can see the American Falls and their western portion, the Bridal Veil Falls. Walk out onto the deck of the Prospect Point Observation Tower (☎716-278-1796; www.niagarafallsstatepark.com; $1.25; ⊙hours vary) for a better view, or midway across the windy Rainbow Bridge, where you can also see the Horseshoe Falls on the Canadian side.

Upstream from the main falls, cross the small bridge to Goat Island, which forms

Niagara Falls

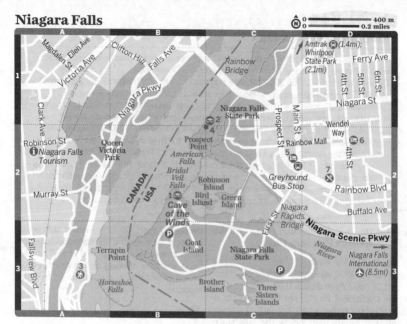

the barrier between the American Falls and Horseshoe Falls. From Terrapin Point, on the southwest corner, there's a fine view of Horseshoe Falls. Additional pedestrian bridges lead further to the **Three Sisters Islands** in the upper rapids.

⭐**Cave of the Winds** VIEWPOINT
(☑716-278-1730; www.niagarafallsstatepark. com; Goat Island Rd; adult/child $19/16; ☺from 9am May-Oct, closing times vary) On the north corner of Goat Island, don a souvenir rain poncho and sandals (provided) and take an elevator down to walkways just 25ft from the crashing water at the base of Bridal Veil Falls. (Despite the name, the platforms run in front of the falls, not into a cave.)

Old Fort Niagara MUSEUM
(☑716-745-7611; www.oldfortniagara.org; Youngstown; adult/child $12/8; ☺9am-7pm Jul & Aug, to 5pm Sep-Jun) This 1726 French-built fortress, restored in the 1930s, defends the once very strategic point where the Niagara River flows into Lake Ontario. It has engaging displays of Native American artifacts, small weapons, furniture and clothing, as well as breathtaking views from its windblown ramparts. In summer months there are tours and demonstrations by costumed guides of what life was like here in the past.

Niagara Falls

◎ **Top Sights**
 1 Cave of the Winds.............................B2

◎ **Sights**
 2 Prospect Point Observation Tower.... C1

◆ **Activities, Courses & Tours**
 3 Journey Behind the Falls A3
 4 Maid of the Mist C2

🛏 **Sleeping**
 5 Giacomo...C2
 6 Seneca Niagara Resort & Casino D2

🍴 **Eating**
 7 Third Street Retreat Eatery & Pub D2

Surrounding the fort are hiking trails in **Fort Niagara State Park**.

Whirlpool State Park PARK
(☑716-284-4691; www.parks.ny.gov; Robert Moses State Pkwy) This park, 3 miles north of the falls, sits just above a sharp bend in the Niagara River – a bend that creates a giant whirlpool easily visible from your vantage point. Steps take you 300ft to the gorge below and mind you don't tumble into the vortex. There's also the option of following the Devil's Hole Trail (1.5 miles) downstream

DON'T MISS

NIAGARA FALLS, CANADA

The Canadian side of the falls is blessed with superior views. **Horseshoe Falls**, on the west half of the river, are especially photogenic from Queen Victoria Park. **Journey Behind the Falls** (905-356-2241; www.niagaraparks.com; 6650 Niagara Pkwy; adult/child $11.50/7.50; 9am-8pm, vary by season) gives access to a spray-soaked viewing area.

The Canadian town is also livelier, in a touristy way. Chain hotels dominate, but there is an HI hostel, and some older motels have honeymooners' heart-shaped tubs. For more local info, visit **Niagara Falls Tourism office** (905-356-6061; www.niagarafallstourism.com; 5400 Robinson St; 9am-5pm), near the base of the Skylon Tower observation deck.

Crossing the Rainbow Bridge and returning costs US$3.75/50¢ per car/pedestrian. Walking takes about 10 minutes; car traffic can grind to a standstill in summer or if there's a major event on in Toronto. US citizens and overseas visitors must show a passport or an enhanced driver's license at immigration at either end. Driving a rental car from the US over the border should not be a problem, but check with your rental company.

to the Devil's Hole staircase at the top of the gorge at Devil's Hole State Park.

★ Maid of the Mist
BOATING

(716-284-8897; www.maidofthemist.com; 1 Prospect St; adult/child $19.25/11.20; hours vary) The traditional way to see Niagara Falls is on this boat cruise, which has ferried visitors into the rapids right below the falls since 1846. Make sure you wear the blue poncho they give you, as the torrential spray from the falls will soak you.

🛏 Sleeping & Eating

Seneca Niagara Resort & Casino RESORT $$
(877-873-6322; www.senecaniagaracasino.com; 310 4th St; r $215-400; P⊛❋@📶🏊) With some 600 spacious rooms and suites, and a lively casino, this purple-and-glass-covered tower is the American town's answer to the tourist glitz across on the Canadian side of the falls. A variety of music and comedy shows are staged here, too, headlined by relatively big names.

Giacomo BOUTIQUE HOTEL $$$
(716-299-0200; www.thegiacomo.com; 222 1st St; r from $247; P❋@📶) A rare bit of style among the bland chain hotels and motels of Niagara, the luxe Giacomo occupies part of a gorgeous art-deco office tower, with spacious, ornately decorated rooms. Even if you're not staying here, have a drink in the 19th-floor lounge (bar open from 5pm) for spectacular views, and music on Saturday.

Third Street Retreat Eatery & Pub AMERICAN $
(716-371-0760; www.thirdstreetretreat.com; 250 Rainbow Blvd; mains $7-12; 9am-3pm Tue-Thu, to 9pm Fri & Sat, 10am-3pm Sun) The walls are decorated with old LP covers at this popular local spot serving all-day breakfasts and other comforting pub-grub dishes. There's a good selection of beers on tap or in bottles, plus a pool table and darts in an upstairs section.

❶ Getting There & Away

NFTA (www.nfta.com) bus 40 connects downtown Buffalo and Niagara Falls ($2, one hour); the stop in Niagara Falls is at 1st St and Rainbow Blvd. Express bus 60 goes to a terminal east of the town center; you'll have to transfer to bus 55 to reach the river. The **Amtrak train station** (716-285-4224; www.amtrak.com; 825 Depot Ave) is about 2 miles north of downtown; the station on the Canadian side is more central, but coming from NYC, you have to wait for Canadian customs. From Niagara Falls, daily trains go to Buffalo ($14, 35 minutes), Toronto (from $47, three hours) and NYC (from $66, nine hours). **Greyhound** (www.greyhound.com; 240 1st St) buses stop at the Quality Inn.

Flights from Florida and South Carolina are offered by Allegiant Air and Spirit Airlines to **Niagara Falls International Airport** (716-297-4494; www.niagarafallsairport.com; 2035 Niagara Falls Blvd).

❶ Getting Around

In summer, the **Niagara Scenic Trolley** (www.niagarafallsstatepark.com; adult/child $3/2; hours vary) runs a 3-mile loop around the American-side attractions.

Parking costs $10 to $20 a day on either side of the falls. Most midrange hotels offer complimentary parking to guests, while upscale hotels on the Canadian side tend to charge $15 to $20 a day. To avoid traffic mayhem in summer, you can park along Niagara Falls Blvd and ride the NFTA bus 55 west to the river.

New Jersey

POP 9 MILLION

Why Go?

Everything you've seen on TV, from the McMansions of *Real Housewives of New Jersey* to the thick accents of *The Sopranos*, is at least partially true. But Jersey (natives lose the 'New') is at least as well defined by its high-tech and banking headquarters, and a quarter of it is lush farmland (hence the Garden State nickname) and pine forests. And on the 127 miles of beautiful beaches, you'll find, yes, the guidos and guidettes of *Jersey Shore*, but also many other oceanfront towns, each with a distinct character.

Best Places to Eat

→ Mompou (p160)

→ Mediterra Restaurant & Taverna (p163)

→ Kelsey & Kim's Café (p176)

→ Porta (p169)

Best Places to Stay

→ Lambertville House (p164)

→ Asbury Hotel (p169)

→ Quaker Inn (p171)

→ Congress Hall (p180)

When to Go
Newark

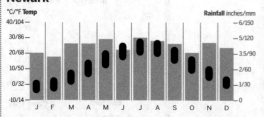

Apr–May Canoeing and kayaking on the Delaware; birdwatching and biking in Cape May.

Jun–Aug Full-on funnel-cake and Ferris-wheel madness: the definitive Shore experience.

Sep–Oct Harvest celebrations at the 50-plus wineries, apple and pumpkin picking, and fall Shore stays.

New Jersey Highlights

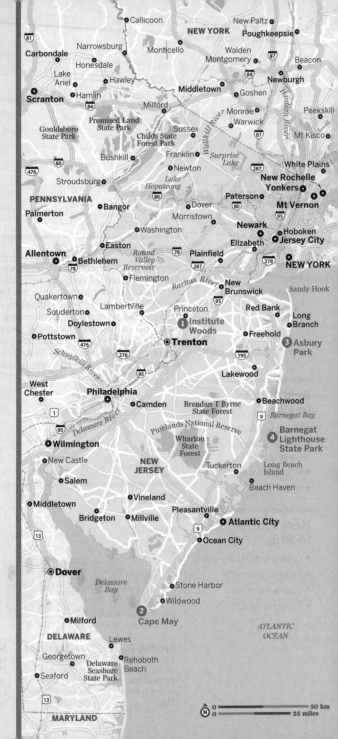

1 Institute Woods (p161) Exploring nearly 600 acres of woodland within spitting distance of the Princeton campus.

2 Willow Creek Winery (p181) Kicking back with a glass of white or red at Cape May's latest entry in the winery sweepstakes.

3 Asbury Festhalle and Biergarten (p169) Knocking back liters of beer German-style and noshing on a few wursts in up-and-coming Asbury Park.

4 Barnegat Lighthouse State Park (p173) Scampering up the 200-plus steps to a view of the roaring ocean below and meandering through the adjacent nature center ripe with berry bushes and birdsong.

Callicoon
NEW YORK
New Paltz
Poughkeepsie
Carbondale
Narrowsburg
Monticello
Walden
Montgomery
Beacon
Honesdale
Lake Ariel
Hawley
Newburgh
Scranton
Hamlin
Middletown
Goshen
Milford
Monroe
Mt Kisco
Peekskill
Promised Land State Park
Sussex
Warwick
Gouldsboro State Park
Childs State Forest Park
Surprise Lake
White Plains
Bushkill
Franklin
New Rochelle
Stroudsburg
Newton
Lake Hopatcong
Paterson
Yonkers
PENNSYLVANIA
Bangor
Dover
Mt Vernon
Palmerton
Morristown
Newark
Hoboken
Washington
Elizabeth
Jersey City
Allentown
Easton
Plainfield
NEW YORK
Bethlehem
Round Valley Reservoir
Flemington
Raritan River
New Brunswick
Sandy Hook
Quakertown
Lambertville
Princeton
Red Bank
Long Branch
Souderton
Doylestown
Institute Woods
Freehold
Asbury Park
Pottstown
Trenton
Lakewood
West Chester
Philadelphia
Camden
Brendan T Byrne State Forest
Beachwood
Barnegat Bay
Pinelands National Reserve
Wilmington
Wharton State Forest
Barnegat Lighthouse State Park
New Castle
NEW JERSEY
Tuckerton
Long Beach Island
Salem
Beach Haven
Middletown
Vineland
Pleasantville
Bridgeton
Millville
Atlantic City
Dover
Ocean City
Delaware Bay
Stone Harbor
Milford
Wildwood
DELAWARE
Cape May
Lewes
ATLANTIC OCEAN
Georgetown
Rehoboth Beach
Seaford
Delaware Seashore State Park
MARYLAND

0   50 km
0   25 miles

History

New Jersey has been an important crossroads since before it was a state, and its location between the major cities of the Northeast, its lengthy coastline and rivers, as well as the location of one of the country's biggest ports, Newark, ensure that it will have an ongoing role in the United States' story.

❶ Getting There & Away

Though many NJ folks love their cars, there are other transportation options.

PATH Train (www.panynj.gov/path) Connects lower Manhattan to Hoboken, Jersey City and Newark.

NJ Transit (www.njtransit.com) Operates buses and trains around the state, including bus service to NYC's Port Authority and downtown Philadelphia, and trains to Penn Station, NYC. Train service has declined severely in the past decade – fair warning.

New York Waterway (www.nywaterway.com) New York Waterway ferries run up the Hudson River and from the NJ Transit train station in Hoboken to the World Financial Center in Lower Manhattan.

NORTHERN NEW JERSEY

Stay east and you'll experience the Jersey (sub)urban jungle. Go west to find its opposite: the peaceful, refreshing landscape of the Delaware Water Gap.

❶ Getting There & Away

Northern New Jersey is served by NJ Transit buses and trains, and by the underground PATH system, which connect lower Manhattan with Hoboken and Newark Penn Station. Hoboken even has ferry service to Manhattan's West Side. Further south, Princeton and Lambertville have less frequent bus service to NYC. Parking in crowded cities such as Hoboken and Newark is nigh impossible.

Hoboken

📞 201 / POP 54,379

The Square Mile City is among the trendiest of zip codes, with real-estate prices to match. On weekends the bars come alive, and loads of restaurants line Washington St. If you can step over the designer dogs, and navigate the mega-strollers, trolling black Uber cars with NY plates, and lines for Carlo the Cake Boss, it's a good walking town with amazing views of NYC. Get here before the chain stores do.

◉ Sights & Activities

Liberty State Park   PARK
(📞201-915-3403; www.libertystatepark.org; 200 Morris Pesin Dr; ⊙6am-10pm) This attractive park hosts outdoor concerts with the Manhattan skyline as a backdrop. It also has a great bike trail, and the historic railroad terminal where immigrants embarked after being processed at Ellis Island. There's ferry service to Ellis Island and the Statue of Liberty. The 'Empty Sky' memorial inside the park is a touching tribute to the 749 New Jersey residents who died on September 11, 2001.

Hoboken Historical Museum   MUSEUM
(📞201-656-2240; www.hobokenmuseum.org; 1301 Hudson St; adult/child $4/free; ⊙2-7pm Tue-Thu, 1-5pm Fri, noon-5pm Sat & Sun) This small museum conveys a sense of Hoboken that's hard to imagine today – a city of blue-collar Irish and Italian Catholic immigrants, toiling in the shipyards and docks. It offers self-guided walking tours of Frank Sinatra's Hoboken haunts, and *On the Waterfront* film locales.

★**Hackensack Riverkeeper**   CANOEING
(📞201-920-4746; www.hackensackriverkeeper. org; Laurel Hill County Park, Secaucus; per paddler/passenger $25/15) From April until October, join this environmental organization on canoe, kayak and pontoon trips through the Meadowlands, a huge wetlands slowly being restored after decades of abuse. Moonlight paddles twice a month past the old insane asylum are sure to be hair-raising. Accessible by public transit as a short walk from the Secaucus Junction Rail Station.

⌂ Sleeping & Eating

W Hotel   BOUTIQUE HOTEL $$$
(📞201-253-2400; www.whoboken.com; 225 River St; r from $283; 🅿❋🛜🏊🐾) If you stay on this side of the river you can look *at* Manhattan, and these riverfront rooms have stunning vistas, as well as all the trappings of the swanky Starwood chain, like a fitness center and spa, and even special treatment for your pup ($100).

M & P Biancamano   ITALIAN $
(📞201-795-0274; 1116 Washington St; ⊙8:30am-6pm Mon-Fri, until 5pm Sat) We only have three words for the melt-in-your-mouth 'mutz' (mozzerella) that Peter Biancamano prepares fresh every morning at 6am: Oh. My. God.

For a taste of the competition, we also recommend trying Vito's (📞201-792-4944; www.vitosdeli.com; 806 Washington St; heros from $5.50; ⊙8am-6pm Tue-Fri, to 5pm Sat, 9am-3pm Sun).

Carlo's Bake Shop BAKERY $
(Cake Boss; ☑201-659-3671; www.carlosbakery.com; 95 Washington St; pastries & cookies $6-10, cakes $25-35; ⊙7am-9pm Sun-Thu, to 10pm Fri & Sat) Oh yes, the Cake Boss can get crowded since Carlo's TV fame, and you have to take a number to get service. But if you can sweat it out, the cookies and cakes from the original location are still worth the wait. Tip: if you have a friend from Hoboken with a verifiable ID, you can skip the line!

La Isla CUBAN $
(☑201-659-8197; www.laislarestaurant.com; 104 Washington St; breakfast $8-11, sandwiches $8-10, mains $18-21; ⊙7am-10pm Mon-Sat, 10am-9pm Sun) The most authentic Cuban choice in town since 1970, the Formica counters ring with plates spilling over with grilled Cuban sandwiches, *maduros* (fried plantains) and rice with pigeon peas – all to the soundtrack of staccato Spanish chatter and salsa, under the watchful eye of Celia Cruz portraits. Forget the fancier 'uptown' branch – this is the real thing.

Amanda's GASTRONOMY $$$
(☑201-798-0101; www.amandasrestaurant.com; 908 Washington St; mains $24-36; ⊙5-10pm Mon-Fri, 11am-3pm & 5-11pm Sat, 11am-3pm & 5-9pm Sun) For three decades the Flynn family has served first-rate fare in these conjoined, converted brownstones, each room with a different theme. An extensive wine list and monthly wine evenings make this a classy option. The bar dinner special (Sunday to Thursday) is great value.

🍸 Drinking & Nightlife

Pilsener Haus & Biergarden BEER GARDEN
(☑201-683-5465; www.pilsenerhaus.com; 1422 Grand St; ⊙5pm-1am Mon-Thu, from 4pm Fri, noon-midnight Sat & Sun) An old-school European beer hall in the fashion of Asbury Park's Festhalle (p169), this place also features huge wooden tables and towering ceilings. Plates of Austro-Hungarian faves like spätzle and sauerbraten are surefire accompaniments to the dozens of beer on tap. You could do wurst.

ℹ Getting There & Away

NY Waterway (www.nywaterway.com) runs the ferry between 39th St on Manhattan's West Side and Hoboken ($9, eight minutes). There is frequent, if crowded, NJ PATH train service from lower Manhattan to Hoboken terminal. Parking is atrocious – don't even think about driving here.

Newark

☑973 / POP 281,764

An economic engine of Jersey during the Industrial Age, Newark has been long mired in images of the 1960s race riots. Crime, poverty and dwindling finances continue to mar the city's reputation, though downtown streets bustle with shoppers and office workers during warmer months.

A day trip to the Portuguese–Spanish Ironbound district, blocks from Newark Penn Station, is worthwhile – Ferry St comes alive on soccer-match days at **Red Bull Arena** (www.newyorkredbulls.com; 600 Cape May St, Harrison) – as is a trip to Newark's surprisingly fabulous museum. Pulitzer Prize–winning writer Philip Roth set much of his fiction in Newark, where he was born and raised.

◉ Sights

Newark Museum MUSEUM
(☑973-596-6544; www.newarkmuseum.org; 49 Washington St; adult/child $15/8, planetarium $12/6; ⊙noon-5pm Wed-Sun) This brick-and-limestone mansion, a legacy of the Ballantine beer family, is now part of an impressive museum with the biggest Tibetan art collection in the western hemisphere. In fact, the 14th Dalai Lama consecrated its Buddhist altar. There's also impressive Asian and American modern collections, as well as a planetarium – allow a couple of hours to soak it all up. It's a long walk across from Penn Station, so you may wish to consider a taxi.

🛏 Sleeping & Eating

Hotel Indigo
Newark Downtown BOUTIQUE HOTEL $$
(☑973-242-0065; www.ihg.com; 810 Broad St; r from $150; ❋ᴥ) This sleek hotel down the alley from the Prudential Center might be jumping the gun on gentrification in Newark, but our only complaint was its location, set in the middle of some uncomfortable urban malaise. It's a convenient place to stay after a show or game at the arena.

★ **Mompou** TAPAS $$
(☑973-578-8114; www.mompoutapas.com; 77 Ferry St; tapas $8-12, mains $22-26; ⊙11:30-10pm Mon-Thu, to 11pm Fri & Sat) With a zinc bar and a snappy cocktail list, this bar-lounge hums with convivial conversation. Tapas include *bacaloa* (salted-cod croquettes), *patatas bravas*, *txistorra* (basque sausage) and, our fave, calamari in chocolate sauce. There's a patio out back, and live flamenco on weekends.

DELAWARE WATER GAP

With one foot in Pennsylvania and the other in New Jersey, the place where the Delaware River makes a tight S-curve through the ridge of the Kittatinny Mountains was, in the days before air-conditioning, a popular resort destination. In the modern era it remains an area of surpassing dramatic beauty, a slice of rugged wilderness within a day's trip of the largest urban conurbations on the North American eastern seaboard. The current preserved areas dates from 1965, when the **Delaware Water Gap National Recreation Area** (✷570-426-2452; www.nps.gov/dewa; 1978 River Rd, Bushkill) was established, covering land in both NJ and Pennsylvania. Unsurprisingly, the main activities in the area include hiking and boating. Dozens of trails crisscross the park, while a 25-mile stretch of the Appalachian Trail runs along the Kittatinny Ridge.

The Delaware River is very popular with boaters. Tubing is a big summertime activity – but bear in mind your peaceful idyll on the river may be broken by beer-chugging weekend tubers. Tubing outfits can be found up and down the river; their usual package is to charge around $50 to drive you out to a river access point in a rusty school bus, provide a tube, and pick you up further downstream. Plenty of outfitters either lead padding tours up the river or rent out canoes and kayaks. Paddlers can camp alongside the river.

Note that entrance to the park is free, but there is a $10 fee for cars and a $2 fee for bicycles. The **park headquarters** (✷570-426-2452; www.nps.gov/dewa; 1978 River Rd, Bushkill; ☉8:30am-4:30pm Jun-Aug, Mon-Fri only Sep-May) has maps, camping info, hiking trails and can alert you to any hazards in the park.

Casa Vasca   BASQUE $$
(✷973-465-1350; 141 Elm St; mains $15-25; ☉11am-10pm Mon-Fri, noon-10pm Sat & Sun) A Spanish hideout a few blocks off Ferry St, Casa Vasca's white-tablecloth look belies its down-home Basque cooking, featuring delights such as *pulpo a la gallega* (Galician octopus) and garlic shrimp.

Iberia Peninsula   PORTUGUESE $$$
(✷973-344-5611; www.iberiarestaurants.com; 63-69 Ferry St; mains $26-44; ☉noon-midnight) The granddaddy of all Portuguese–Spanish restaurants seems to sprawl forever: the outdoor bar and stage are the center of the action on match days at Red Bull Arena and Portugal Day festivities. If you're pre-gaming, appetizers at the bar will satisfy, but if you're sticking around, the *rodizio* – endless skewers of 10 different meats – may be in order.

❶ Getting There & Away

New Jersey PATH trains service both Newark and neighboring Harrison. The AirTrain connects Newark Liberty International Airport to PATH, NJ Transit and Amtrak at Newark Penn Station. NJ Transit connects to points south.

Princeton

✷609 / POP 12,307

Settled by an English Quaker missionary, this tiny town is filled with lovely architecture and several noteworthy sites, number

one of which is its Ivy League university. Princeton is more upper-crust than collegiate, with preppie boutiques edging central Palmer Sq. Just over a mile from campus and town, however, you can escape to the idyllic Institute Woods, a 600-acre forested retreat.

Like any good seat of learning, Princeton has a bookstore, record store, brew pub and indie cinema, all within blocks of the rabbit's warren of streets and alleys that crisscross Palmer Sq, as well as innumerable sweet shops, cafes and ice-cream specialty stores.

◉ Sights

★ Institute Woods   FOREST
(www.ias.edu; 1 Einstein Dr; ☉dawn-dusk) Walk 1½ miles down Mercer St to a bucolic slice of countryside seemingly completely removed from the jammed-up campus-area thoroughfares. Nearly 600 acres have been set aside here, and birders, joggers and dog-walkers luxuriate on the soft, loamy pathways. It's an avian paradise during the spring warbler migration.

It's sited adjacent to the Institute for Advanced Study, and connects with the Delaware and Raritan Canal (p163).

Princeton University   UNIVERSITY
(✷609-258-3000; www.princeton.edu) Built in the mid-1700s, this institution soon became one of the largest structures in the early

colonies. Now it's in the top-tier Ivy League. You can stroll around on your own, or take a student-led tour.

★ Princeton University

Art Museum MUSEUM

([📱]609-258-3788; www.princetonartmuseum.org; McCormick Hall; ⏱10am-5pm Tue-Sat, to 9pm Thu, noon-5pm Sun) **FREE** This wide-ranging collection is particularly strong on antiquities, Asian art and photography.

🛏 Sleeping & Eating

Inn at Glencairn B&B $$

([📱]609-497-1737; www.innatglencairn.com; 3301 Lawrenceville Rd/Rte 206; r from $209; [📶]) The best value in the Princeton area: five serene rooms in a renovated Georgian manor, 10 minutes' drive from campus. The property is visited by flocks of goldfinches and also, legend has it, by the unquiet spirit of a British soldier from the Revolutionary War era: listen for Lord Ralston's footsteps at night.

Nassau Inn INN $$$

([📱]609-921-7500; www.nassauinn.com; 10 Palmer Sq; r from $299; [❄][📶]) It's pricey, because of its prime location, and the history-soaked rooms can feel a little frumpy (some may prefer the new wing). Visit the classic Yankee Doodle Tap Room to admire the photos of famous alumni, even if you don't stay the night.

Chuck's Spring Street Cafe CHICKEN $

([📱]609-921-0027; www.chucksspringstreetcafe. com; 16 Spring St; 14/21 wings $12.50/18.50; ⏱11am-9:30pm) Locals rave and students crave the twice-cooked splendor of Chuck's crispy, tangy buffalo wings. Yes, there are tasty sandwiches and fried fish choices, too, but the wing is the thing at Chuck's, and you can order up to 100 at a time.

★ Mistral MEDITERRANEAN $$

([📱]609-688-8808; www.mistralprinceton.com; 66 Witherspoon St; sharing plates $11-17, mains $17-27; ⏱5-9pm Mon & Tue, 11:30am-3pm & 5-10pm Wed-Sat, 10:30am-3pm & 4-9pm Sun) Princeton's

Princeton

most creative restaurant offers plates made to share, with flavors ranging from the Caribbean to Scandinavia. Sit at the chef's counter for a bird's-eye view of the controlled chaos in the open-plan kitchen. The boisterous bar next door is a convenient waiting place or next stop for the night.

★ **Mediterra Restaurant & Taverna** MEDITERRANEAN $$
(☑609-252-9680; www.mediterrarestaurant.com; 29 Hulfish St; mains $16-24; ⊙11:30am-10pm Mon-Thu, to 11pm Fri & Sat, to 9pm Sun) Centrally located in Palmer Sq, Mediterra is the sort of upscale, contemporary place designed for a college town. Visiting parents, flush students and locals all crave the dishes here, which highlight locally sourced and organic ingredients, and reflect the owners' mixed Chilean–Italian heritage. The fish and small plates, such as bruschetta, are particularly good. The daily happy hour (4pm to 6:30pm) features half-price tapas and, sometimes, live music.

🔒 Shopping

Princeton Record Exchange MUSIC
(☑609-921-0881; www.prex.com; 20 S Tulane St; ⊙10am-9pm Mon-Sat, 11am-6pm Sun) For those who still have a CD player, and maybe a turntable too. Over 140,000 slabs of non-digitized, fossil-fuel-produced musical selections (but who's counting?) – many for under $5.

Labyrinth Books BOOKS
(☑609-497-1600; www.labyrinthbooks.com; 122 Nassau St; ⊙9am-8pm Mon-Fri, 11am-6pm Sat & Sun) Aptly named – you can wander over two floors of eclectic new and used books.

Princeton

Thomas Sweet Chocolate CHOCOLATE
(☑609-924-7222; www.thomassweet.com; 29 Palmer Sq West; ⊙10am-9pm Mon-Sat, 11am-6pm Sun) In a town rich with sweet choices, this shop has been pleasing Princetonian palates for four decades. In addition to the chocolate bonanza, they have nice accompaniments like Mexican hot-chocolate disks. Their famed Thomas Sweet Ice Cream shop is further down Nassau Street.

ℹ Getting There & Around

Coach USA (www.coachusa.com) express buses 100 and 600 run frequently between Manhattan and Princeton ($15, 1½ hours). NJ Transit (www.njtransit.com) trains run frequently from New York Penn Station to Princeton Junction railway station ($16, one to 1½ hours). The 'Dinky' shuttle will then run you to Princeton campus ($3, five minutes).

The free Princeton freeB bus (www.princeton nj.gov/resources/free-jitney-shuttle), servicing the entire town, can also take you to the Dinky station.

Lambertville

☑609 / POP 3812
On the banks of the Delaware River is Lambertville and its sister town across the water, New Hope, PA. Lambertville is the preppier of the two. Stroll or cycle along the peaceful canal towpaths that edge the river; a few miles south is where George Washington crossed the Delaware in December 1776 (as depicted in Emanuel Leutze's iconic painting). Expect antiques, chummy restaurants and a low-key vibe.

◉ Sights & Activities

Lambertville is right on the 60-mile **D&R Canal Towpath** (Delaware and Raritan Canal Towpath; www.njhiking.com; Riverfront), great for walking, jogging or cycling. Nearby parks like Washington's Crossing offer history along with your hike. The canal and river are relaxing fishing spots, while 18 miles north you can rent a canoe, kayak or tube in Milford.

Washington Crossing State Park STATE PARK
(☑609-737-0623; www.state.nj.us; 355 Washington Crossing-Pennington Rd, Titusville; per car Jun-Aug $7; ⊙8am-7pm) Ten days before the battle at Princeton on Christmas night 1776, George Washington led his army across the ice-packed Delaware River from the Pennsylvania side to the New Jersey side in a raging snowstorm. He took the risk knowing that if he didn't win something before winter closed

CYCLING THE D&R TOWPATH

For history and cycling buffs, this is a can't-miss two-wheel tour of some pivotal points in American history. You'll pass sites where Washington and his troops turned the tide against the British Army, and immerse yourself in the museums and student smorgasbord of eateries in Ivy League Princeton. You might get back in time for some antiquing in Lambertville, but don't rush it.

South of Lambertville on the D&R towpath, you'll hit Washington Crossing State Park (p163) after 7 miles. Soak up the history and stumble around the grounds, recouping with a snack before heading further south along the river and past the capital of Trenton. Turn north here towards Princeton; you'll reach it about 20 miles after Washington Crossing, at the Millstone Aqueduct and Footbridge. Enjoy the Institute Woods (p161) and troll the town for sweets, microbrews and falafel. If you're ambitious, head back toward Lambertville on the towpath or Rte 518; otherwise crash for the night and head back in the morning.

in, his army might desert him entirely come spring. Washington Crossing State Park, seven miles southwest of Lambertville, offers an overstuffed exhibit in the visitor center, historic buildings and nice trails through pretty woods. A Lambertville theater troupe puts on plays here in the summer.

Sleeping

Bridge Street House GUESTHOUSE $$
(☑ 609-397-5900; www.bridgestreethouse.com; 75 Bridge St; r $155-225; P ❋ 🛜) Proprietor Carol is a local artist who includes a small gallery in this 1850s-era guesthouse, which includes a comfy common coffee room, a shared courtyard and upstairs rooms with exposed, original beams and clawfoot tubs. A blend of modern and post-colonial, the rooms can feel a bit small, or perhaps just cozy.

★ **Lambertville House** HISTORIC HOTEL $$$
(☑ 609-397-0200; www.lambertvillehouse.com; 32 Bridge St; r $315-400; P ❋ 🛜) The rooms, named for historic figures, may creak a bit with age, but the four-poster beds, immaculate wooden furniture and Jacuzzi tubs more than make up for it, as does the convivial bar

in the lobby. The heart-of-town location on Bridge St is another plus. Ask for a room with a balcony.

Eating & Drinking

Sneddon's Luncehnette DINER $
(☑ 609-397-3053; 47 Bridge St; mains $6-10; ⊙ 6am-2pm) From the laminated baby-blue menus to the counter swivel-stools, Sneddon's is old-school style and, by Lambertville standards, pretty reasonable for stacks of pancakes, omelets and other eggy delights. It's cheap, charming and cash only.

★ **Swan** AMERICAN $$
(☑ 609-397-1960; www.antons-at-the-swan.com; 43 S Main St; burgers & pizzas $11, mains $15-30; ⊙ 5-10pm Tue-Fri, 1-10pm Sat, 1-9pm Sun) This late 19th-century building – once the village hotel – is a local hang-out that charms with historical bric-a-brac and warm service, and wins you over with favorites such as the mashed-potato-and-onion pizza. Seriously. The bar menu is cheaper and more fun than Anton's at the Swan, the adjoining white-tablecloth option.

Lambertville Station AMERICAN $$
(☑ 609-397-8300; www.lambertvillestation.com; 11 Bridge St; mains $19-29, tapas $7-16; ⊙ 11am-10pm Sun-Thu, to 11pm Fri & Sat) Join the denizens of the wine cellar for late-night tasty tapas, cheese plates and bites from the raw bar. Ingredients are sourced from more than a dozen local farms and suppliers. Alternatively, head upstairs for a more traditional lunch and dinner.

❶ Getting There & Away

Trans-Bridge Lines (www.transbridgelines.com) runs buses from New York's Port Authority to Lambertville ($26, two hours).

PINE BARRENS

New Jersey is America's most densely populated state, but you'd never know it in the million or so acres of state parks and wildlife refuges that make up Pinelands National Reserve (☑ 609-894-7300; www.nj.gov/pinelands). That's the official name, but to Jersey natives the area will always be the Pine Barrens, an apt adjective for the flat, sandy-soil forest and eerie cedar bogs. And never mind its rare conifers and orchids – this is foremost the home of the sinister Jersey Devil. Ask any local you meet about it – or read John McPhee's 1968 classic, *The Pine Barrens*.

The 50-mile Batona Trail cuts through east–west, rewarding hikers with wild blueberries in midsummer. The route passes the Apple Pie Hill Fire Tower, giving a view over a veritable sea of forest from Atlantic City to Philadelphia. Call ahead to ensure the tower is open.

◉ Sights

St Vladimir Russian Orthodox Church   CHURCH
(☑732-928-1248; https://stvladnj.org; 134 Perrineville Rd/Rte 571, Jackson) Driving through the Pines, this majestic structure seems to pop up out of nowhere. It's a functioning parish, so not for sightseers, but worth a gander from the parking lot. It's just blocks away from Pushkin Rd.

Whitesbog Village   FARM
(☑609-893-4646; www.whitesbog.org; 120 W Whites Bogs Rd, Browns Mills; ☺dawn-dusk) FREE Visit one of New Jersey's first cranberry bogs, and the place where the highbush blueberry was cultivated. Nature trails wind through the property.

Batsto Village   HISTORIC SITE
(☑609-561-0024; www.batstovillage.org; 31 Batsto Rd, Hammonton; ☺9am-4pm) FREE This 18th-century village is an open-air museum that introduces the bog-iron industry, and also has a nature center. Guided tours ($3) of the central Batsto Mansion take place Wednesday to Sunday only. There's a handy smartphone tour of the grounds: scan the barcode and no human contact required! To get here, take Rte 542 8 miles east from Hammonton. There are miles of hiking and biking trails that wind around Batsto Lake and connect with longer trails going to Atsion, Brendan Byrne State Forest and beyond. Two canoe launches are located a quarter-mile west on Rte 542.

🏃 Activities

The Pine Barrens are a nature lover's delight, full of opportunities to hike, observe nature, canoe, swim, bike and fish.

For the true hiker, the Batona (for BAck TO NAture) Trail snakes through 50 miles of the Pines from Ong in the north to Quaker Bridge, Batsto, finally terminating in the southeast of the Pines in the Bass River Reserve. It passes landmarks like the Carranza Memorial and Apple Pie Hill, whose summit is worth climbing if the fire tower is open (views of the surrounding area are spectacular).

Wharton State Forest   HIKING
(www.state.nj.us; Hammonton) New Jersey's largest single tract of parkland forest, Wharton comprises Batsto Village and many other sites. The main entrance is at Batsto Village and there is no fee. You can hike for miles, fish, canoe, swim and observe nature to your heart's content. You can camp or spend the night in a cabin.

Apple Pie Hill Fire Tower   HIKING
(☑609-726-9010; www.njhiking.com/nj-hikes-apple-pie-hill; Wharton State Forest, Tabernacle) The out-and-back 8.2-mile hike from the Carranza Memorial (www.post11.org/carranza.html; Carranza Rd) to this fire tower can lead to the most spectacular view in the Pines, but only if the tower is staffed. Call the Forest Service to ensure that it is, and, as always, protect yourself from ticks.

Micks Pine Barrens Canoe Rental   CANOEING
(☑609-726-1380; www.mickscanoerental.com; 3107 County Rd 563, Chatsworth; rental per day kayak/canoe $45/60; ☺9am-5pm mid-Apr–mid-Oct, from 8:30 Sat & Sun) This outfitter has maps and other details for water trips in the area.

🛏 Sleeping & Eating

Atsion Campground   CAMPGROUND $
(☑609-268-0444; www.camping.nj.gov; 744 Hwy 206, Shamong; tent & RV sites $25; ☺Apr-Oct) Try to reserve a lakeside spot at this pleasant campground. Note that campsites are 'dry' (no running water) in winter. The park office can give you a complete list of campsites in the state forest, some of which are designated

> **TICKS**
>
> Ticks are common in the woods of New Jersey and can transmit Lyme disease, which is hard to diagnose and has long-term debilitating effects. The first step in prevention is deterrence: wear long pants, a long shirt and high socks (no matter how nerdy they look), and cover your head with a bandanna or hat. After you leave the woods, it's recommended to check your body everywhere, and carefully check your hair – that small bump might be a tick. To remove a tick, do not grasp between your fingers and squeeze – that will release its toxins. Use a pair of tick tweezers instead. If you remove it within 24 hours of its attachment to your person, doctors say that you should avoid transmission of the disease.

as primitive and can be reached only on foot or by canoe. Reserve campsites online.

The neighboring 1826 **Atsion Mansion** (☏609-268-0444; Atsion Village, Rte 206 & Washington Rd; ⊗tours 1pm & 2pm Sat Jun-Sep) FREE of Philadelphia ironmaster Samuel Richards, restored to former glory, is an added bonus.

Penza's Pies at the Red Barn Cafe CAFE $
(☏609-567-3412; www.penzaspies.com; cnr Rte 206 & Myrtle St, Hammonton; pie slice $5, mains $9-12; ⊗8am-5pm) This rather grandmotherly place sells more than 20 pies and quiches ($20 to $28) and an assortment of local produce, and serves a breakfast menu focused on variations on the egg family. Folks come from Atlantic City and beyond to bring whole pies back home. Cash only. The road sign just says 'Red Barn.'

Lucille's Luncheonette DINER $
(Country Cooking; ☏609-698-4474; 1480 Main St, Barnegat; $5-10; ⊗7am-3pm) A solid Jersey favorite, patron saint and chef Lucille passed in 2016, but her heirs keep up the tradition of delicious, heaping bowls of chili and home-baked pies.

Drinking & Entertainment

Valenzano Winery WINERY
(☏609-268-6731; www.valenzanowine.com; 109 Rte 206, Shamong; ⊗11am-5pm Mon-Fri, to 4pm Sat & Sun) Estate wines and Jersey blends are served in a pleasant tasting room. For $10 you get eight samples. We found the hearty Chambourcin quite nice. It's 9 miles north of Penza's Pies on Rte 206.

Albert Music Hall LIVE MUSIC
(Pinelands Cultural Society; ☏609-971-1593; www.alberthall.org; 131 Wells Mill Rd, Waretown; Sat/Sun $5/10) Not to be confused with the Royal Albert Hall of London, this venue packs a punch with smokin' live bluegrass and warmed-up hot dogs. American folk legend Pete Seeger played two benefits here to raise money for the new venue in the 1970s. Shows every Saturday at 6:30pm and a Sunday bluegrass jam at noon. It's 2 miles east of Rte 69 and a quarter-mile west of Rte 9.

❶ Getting There & Away

Rte 206 is the main thoroughfare connecting most everything in this remote region. If you head off into the Pine Barrens, be sure to bring a GPS, although service can be spotty. Amtrak has a sparsely attended station (no waiting area or ticket office) in Atco, near Rte 30.

JERSEY SHORE

Perhaps the most famous and revered feature of New Jersey is its sparkling shore – and heading 'down the shore' (in local parlance – never 'to the beach') is an essential summer ritual. Stretching from Sandy Hook to Cape May, the coastline is dotted with resort towns both tacky and tony. It's mobbed on summer weekends (traffic is especially bad on the bridges to the barrier islands), and finding good-value accommodations is nearly as difficult as locating untattooed skin. By early fall, however, you could find yourself blissfully alone on the sand.

❶ Getting There & Away

Driving early in the day to summer destinations is a must.

New Jersey Transit (www.njtransit.com) runs twice-daily special Shore Express trains from June to September, stopping in Asbury Park, Bradley Beach, Belmar, Spring Lake, Manasquan, Point Pleasant Beach and Bay Head. You can buy a beach tag along with your train ticket, and there are two northbound express trains returning in the evening.

NJ Transit buses from New York's Port Authority service Seaside Heights/Seaside Park, Island Beach State Park, Atlantic City, Wildwood and Cape May. Greyhound (www.greyhound.com) runs special buses to Atlantic City.

Sandy Hook

The northernmost tip of the Jersey Shore is the Sandy Hook Gateway National Recreation Area, a 7-mile barrier island at the entrance to New York Harbor. From your beach blanket, you can see the NYC skyline. The wide beaches, including NJ's only legal nude beach (Gunnison), are edged by a system of bike trails, while the bay side is great for fishing, kayaking or bird-watching. Historic Fort Hancock and the nation's oldest operational lighthouse give a glimpse of

BEACH FEES

Many communities on the Jersey Shore charge $5 to $9 for access, issuing a badge (also called a tag) for the day. From Long Beach Island north to near Sandy Hook, all beaches have a fee; the southern Shore is mostly, but not entirely, free. If you're staying a few days, it's worthwhile investing in a weekly badge, although some hotels provide them.

Jersey Shore

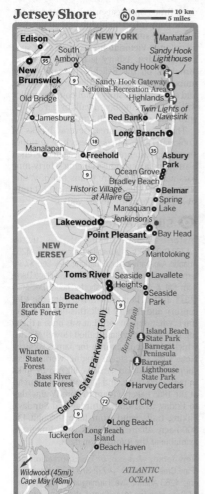

birding in a holly forest; outstanding views of Manhattan's skyline on clear days; beautiful white dunes; and even a nude beach alongside a gay beach (area G).

Best of all, you can get here via a ferry from Lower Manhattan in a cool and salty 45 minutes. Bring your bike along for the ride, and you can enjoy the paved bike paths through the dunes and pedal on to the nearby towns of Atlantic Highlands and Highlands.

Twin Lights of Navesink LIGHTHOUSE
(☏732-872-1814; www.twinlightslighthouse.com; Lighthouse Rd, off Rte 36, Highlands; ☺10am-noon & 1-4pm Wed-Sun) FREE If you can't get enough of Jersey lighthouses, the medieval-like brownstone double towers of Navesink offer an awesome – and free – view of Sandy Hook Bay. Trivia: it's the highest point on the Atlantic seaboard at 260ft, and a lung-busting climb from town.

Henry Hudson Trail HIKING
(☏732-495-2115; www.monmouthcountyparks.com; 369 Shore Dr & Lighthouse Point Rd, Popmora Point, Highlands; ☺dawn-dusk) For 12 miles north of Highlands, this former railway right-of-way – flat and mostly paved – winds up to Aberdeen, with views of wetlands, streams, and some high-end ocean-front homes. Bikers, hikers and dog-walkers can pick up the trail in Highlands or towns along the way.

Kranky Cycles CYCLING
(☏732-921-1166; www.krankycycles.com; 321 Bay Ave, Highlands; per 2hr/day $20/50; ☺10am-6pm) More than 25 miles of bike paths and trails surround the Highlands, and Garrett will get you crankin' on either a standard or electric bike (remember those headwinds!) for a fair price. You can drop your ride off as late as midnight. The cafe next door doesn't have good coffee, but it does have lots of live music.

Sandy Hook Kayaks KAYAKING
(☏732-708-4004; www.sandyhookkayaks.com; 100 Hartshorne Dr, Parking Lot C; ☺10:30am-5:30pm Mon-Fri, to 6:30pm Sat & Sun) Rent or take lessons on kayaks, stand-up paddle-boards (SUPs) and paddle boats and explore the gentle waters of the Hook's Spermaceti Cove on guided group tours. The co-owner, Patrick, is actually the Guinness World Record Holder at one-armed push-ups with a 40lb weight, if that inspires confidence.

🛏 Sleeping & Eating

Camp Gateway CAMPGROUND $
(☏347-630-1124; www.recreation.gov; 26 Hudson Rd; sites $30; ☺May-Oct) A basic camping

Sandy Hook's prior importance as a military and navigational site.

👁 Sights & Activities

Bug spray is recommended as biting flies can be a nuisance at dusk.

Sandy Hook Gateway
National Recreation Area NATURE RESERVE
(☏718-354-4606; www.nps.gov/gate; 128 S Hartshorne Dr, Highlands; parking May-Sep $15; ☺5am-9pm Apr-Oct) FREE Here you'll find the nation's oldest lighthouse (☏732-872-5970; 85 Mercer Rd, Highlands; ☺visitor center 9am-5pm, tours half-hourly 1-4:30pm) FREE; excellent

JERSEY SHORE: BEST BEACHES

Avalon and Stone Harbor (p179) Small, beautiful white sand beaches near Cape May, and rarely crowded.

Holgate and Loveladies (Long Beach Island; p173) Often have some great sand bars to wade and relax in during low tide.

Sandy Hook (p166) Peace, quiet, and Verrazano views from the northernmost tip of the Shore.

facility with the great advantage of being smack-dab in the middle of the Sandy Point Peninsula. Reservations can be made up to six months in advance. You'll be conveniently near hiking trails and surf fishing, among other things, but don't forget that bug repellent. Tent camping only.

Et Al Fine Food SANDWICHES $

(☏848-300-2076; www.etalfinefood.com; 71 Waterwitch Ave; sandwiches & salads $9-14; ☺10am-8pm Mon-Fri, 9am-5pm Sat & Sun) Former Manhattan executive chef Kim Ramin got it in her noodle to come back home to Jersey and set up on the Shore, where she whips up yummy hot sandwiches like Cubans and BLTs and a range of healthier salads and wraps. Juices are pricey but delicious.

Bahr's Landing SEAFOOD $$

(☏732-872-1247; www.bahrslanding.com; 2 Bay Ave, Highlands; sandwiches $10-19, mains $17-28; ☺Sun-Thu 11:30am-9pm, Fri & Sat to midnight; ℗) A century of seafood tradition on the docks, with views facing the Hook. You can hardly go wrong, but we found the cups of chowder, Maine mussels and lobster roll particularly delish. Long waits in the summer, but if you're lucky you'll get a table with a view.

❶ Getting There & Away

A fast ferry service, **Seastreak** (☏800-262-8743; www.seastreak.com; 35 Hartshorne Dr, Sandy Hook; one way/return $27/46, bicycle $5), runs between Sandy Hook (and the Highlands) and Pier 11 in lower Manhattan.

Asbury Park

☏732 / POP 15,767

During decades of economic stagnation, the town of Asbury Park had nothing more to its name than the fact that state trouba-

dour Bruce Springsteen got his start at the Stone Pony (p170) nightclub here in the mid-1970s. But since 2000, blocks of previously abandoned Victorian homes have seen such a revival that Asbury is sometimes called 'Brooklyn on the Beach.' Thousands more units are projected over the next few years, and a looming 16-story hotel/condo complex will dominate the boardwalk by early 2019, with units starting at $1.2 million.

The downtown area, several blocks of Cookman and Bangs Aves, has antiques shops, hip restaurants (from vegan to French bistro) and an art-house cinema. Thirty-nine bars and counting lure trains full of young NY-based revelers to the convenient NJ transit depot, like moths to the vodka.

◉ Sights & Activities

Historic Village at Allaire MUSEUM

(☏732-919-3500; www.allairevillage.org; 4263 Atlantic Ave, Farmingdale; parking May-Sep $7, interpretive program adult/child $3/2; ☺village 11am-4pm Sat & Sun Apr-Nov, shorter hours Dec-Mar) FREE Just a 15-minute-drive from the 21st century and Asbury Park, this quirky museum is what remains of what was once a thriving 19th-century village called Howell Works, which produced bog iron for James Allaire's New York City steam engine works. Visit shops and historic gardens, all run by folks in period costume, and bake your own bread at the 1835 bakery (10am to 4pm Wednesday to Friday, to 4:30pm Saturday and Sunday). Hiking trails wind from here through the 3000-acre Allaire State Park. A birding list is available at the information desk.

New Jersey Museum of Transportation RAIL

(Pine Creek Railroad; ☏732-870-1520; www.njmt. org; 4263 Atlantic Ave, Farmingdale; $4; ☺noon-4:00pm Mon-Fri, to 4:30pm Sat & Sun Jun-Aug, shorter hours rest of year) Kids absolutely love the 15-minute circuit around the old tracks at Farmingdale on a historic narrow-gauge railroad. It's conveniently located next to Historic Allaire Village – and those who may not find Allaire alluring will like the trains a bit more than the iron-bog saga.

Cheesequake State Park HIKING

(☏732-566-3208; www.state.nj.us; 300 Gordon Rd, Matawan; park entrance weekday/weekend $10/20, kayak nature tours $20) A unique blend of pine barrens, salt-and-fresh-water swamps, hardwood forest and white cedar, Cheesequake (from the Lenape *cheseh-oh-ke* or 'upland') is just 30 minutes north of Asbury Park by car and is also accessible by train (3 miles from Aberdeen-Matawan Station). There are four easy-to-moderate trails for family treks, swimming and eco-tours by kayak (reserve from June through August).

Deal Lake Dock Company
KAYAKING

(📞732-403-0730; www.deallakedock.com; Deal Lake Boat Ramp, 799 7th Ave; per hour $20-30, per half-day $50-55; ⊙10am-6pm Apr-Sep) Canoes, kayaks and paddleboards can be rented here, and there's a bait shop too, if it's angling you're after. If you just want to float and check out the ample avian and amphibian life, the folks here can tell you the best places to find that.

🛏 Sleeping

⭐ Asbury Hotel
BOUTIQUE HOTEL $$$

(📞732-774-7100; www.theasburyhotel.com; 210 5th Ave; d $375-425; P❄🐾🛋) Wow. From the performance space and lobby stocked with LP records, old books and a solarium to the rooftop bar, this hotel oozes style. Two blocks from Convention Hall and the boardwalk, you could stay inside all day, playing pool or lounging by the rooftop one. Weeknights are a better deal. On the flip side: you'll get charged for coffee in a paper cup. But it does have an ice-skating rink in winter: very cool.

Breakers on the Ocean
HOTEL $$$

(📞732-449-7700; www.breakershotel.com; 1507 Ocean Ave, Spring Lake; s/ste $255/435; ❄🛋) Steps from 'the breakers,' this upscale 19th-century hotel offers rooms with ocean views, and some have gas fireplaces and whirlpools. It's a nice place for a weekend couples getaway, and there's even an outdoor swimming pool if the Atlantic's not your cup of tea. The Seashell Dining Room is a bit pricey, but oh so good.

🍴 Eating

⭐ Porta
ITALIAN $

(📞732-776-7661; www.pizzaporta.com; 911 Kingsley St; pizzas $14, mains $10-22; ⊙noon-midnight Mon-Fri, 11am-midnight Sat & Sun) A high-ceilinged, hardwood-picnic-table heaven, with customized ovens from Naples and thin-crust pizzas vetted by the Associazione Verace Pizza Napoletana. A glass of red and a side of meatballs at the lively happy hour will fill your belly without emptying your wallet, but if the octopus salad is on the menu, order it – you'll think you've died and gone to heaven.

America's Cup
CAFE $

(📞732-988-2000; www.americascupcoffee.com; 633 Cookman Ave; breakfast $5-10; ⊙7:30am-6pm)

Nautical theme, coffee-bag-covered chairbacks, subtle music and a long list of 'bad-ass' waffles. And nice, fresh coffee. Lovely.

Sunset Landing
CAFE $

(📞732-776-9732; www.sunsetlandingap.com; 1215 Sunset Ave; mains $5-8; ⊙7am-2pm Tue-Sun) On Deal Lake, about 10 blocks from the beach, Sunset Landing is like a Hawaiian surf shack transported to a suburban Asbury lakeside. Vintage longboards crowd the wooden rafters, cheesy omelets are super-fresh, and delicious specialty pancakes come with cranberries, cinnamon, coconut, macadamia nuts and other island flavors. Cash only.

Ask for the owners' tangy homemade avocado-mango salsa, and the fire-breathing local brand on sale by the bottle.

Tides
SEAFOOD $$$

(📞732-897-7744; www.hoteltides.com; 408 7th Ave; mains $28-40; ⊙5:30-9pm Wed, Thu & Sun, to 10pm Fri & Sat) Catering to AP's expanding tastes (what's a cherry *gastrique,* anyway?), Tides does seafood and Italian to perfection, though you may also find comfort and lower prices via its bar menu and the burgers, fish and chips, and crab cakes.

Moonstruck
ITALIAN $$$

(📞732-988-0123; www.moonstrucknj.com; 517 Lake Ave; mains $22-40; ⊙5-10pm Wed-Sun, to 11pm Sat) With views of Wesley Lake dividing Asbury and Ocean Grove and an extensive martini menu, it's hard to find fault. The menu is eclectic, though it leans towards Italian with a good selection of pastas; the meat and fish dishes have varied ethnic influences.

🍷 Drinking & Nightlife

Asbury Festhalle and Biergarten
BEER GARDEN

(📞732-997-8767; www.asburybiergarten.com; 527 Lake Ave; ⊙4pm-1am Mon-Fri, 11am-1am Sat & Sun) Deutschland by the Sea: quaff from 41 draft ales on the rooftop beer garden or check out live music in a space as big as two barns, with classic long beer-hall tables. Snack on pretzels bigger than your face, fill up on plates of wurst (mains $13 to $20) or work your way through the 12 different schnapps on offer.

Asbury Park Distilling
DISTILLERY

(📞732-455-3934; www.asburyparkdistilling.com; 527 Lake Ave; ⊙Thu & Fri from 5pm, Sat & Sun from 3pm) A distilling revolution has taken the Garden State by storm since a bill that allows craft distillers was passed in

Asbury Park & Ocean Grove

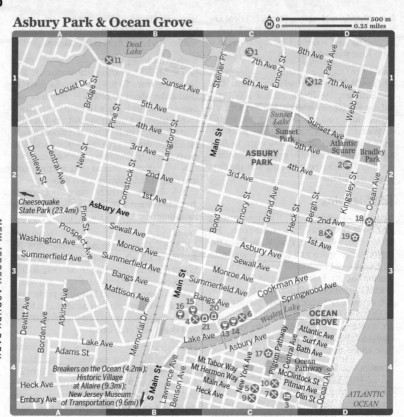

2013. This newcomer to the scene serves up craft whisky and gin and is connected by a glass door to the Asbury Festhalle and Biergarten (p169).

Bond Street Bar BAR
(☎732-774-1575; 208 Bond St; ⊙10am-2am) If you've had enough of the fancy side of AP, come here: burgers, corn dogs and beer are all five bucks, and sometimes less. No frills, cash only and the bar staff sell shirts that say 'Bond Street Bar: Go F*** Yourself.'

Johnny Mac House of Spirits BAR
(☎732-776-6666; www.johnnymacbar.com; 208 Main St; ⊙11am-2am) How can you beat a free slice of pizza with every drink? Themed nights such as Wednesday's Speed Dating night, three levels of different activities such as Skee-Ball, and subterranean tunnels to other bars. God doesn't protect drunks, but he may send them here.

☆ Entertainment

Silver Ball Museum Arcade ARCADE
(Pinball Hall of Fame; ☎732-774-4994; www.silverballmuseum.com; 1000 Ocean Ave; per hour/half-day $10/15; ⊙11am-midnight Mon-Thu, to 1am Fri & Sat, 10am-10pm Sun) Dozens of pinball machines in mint condition, from mechanical 1950s games to modern classics such as Addams Family. Play all you like, for a single price.

Stone Pony LIVE MUSIC
(☎732-502-0600; www.stoneponyonline.com; 913 Ocean Ave; ⊙box office noon-5pm Wed-Mon & during shows) Best known as the bar where Bruce Springsteen launched his career, the Pony has continued to be a respectable rock venue – a genuine, sweaty, feet-stick-to-the-floor club – and hosts a big outdoor festival at the beginning of summer.

Tickets are also on sale here for shows at the Paramount Theater and Convention Hall on the boardwalk.

Asbury Park & Ocean Grove

Shopping

Words! BOOKS

(📞732-455-5549; 623 Cookman Ave; ⊙11am-5pm) Amiable proprietor Jan has a nice collection of new and used titles, including a few Lonely Planet guides. For those who still like the feel of the printed page, this is the indie antidote to the iPad and Kindle.

Hold Fast Records MUSIC

(📞732-988-0066; www.holdfastasburypark.net; 611 Cookman Ave; ⊙11am-7pm Mon-Sat, to 6pm Sun) Vinyl, CDs, vintage posters and a slightly cranky owner straight out of *High Fidelity*: the perfect recipe for an eclectic shopping experience. And if you're driving down the Shore, you need music for your car!

ⓘ Getting There & Away

New Jersey Transit's Asbury Park Station is at the intersection of Cookman and Main Sts and is about 45 minutes from NYC. Some late-night trains run during the summer.

Ocean Grove

📞732 / POP 3342

Just south of Asbury Park, Ocean Grove is a kind of time and culture warp. 'God's Square Mile at the Jersey Shore,' as it's known, was founded by Methodists in the 19th century as a revival camp, and it's still a dry town (no liquor) and the beach is closed on Sunday mornings. The Victorian architecture is so covered in gingerbread trim that you may want to eat it. At the center, around a 6500-seat wooden auditorium with a huge pipe organ, the former revival camp is now Tent City – a historic site with more than a hundred quaint canvas tents used as summer homes.

🛏 Sleeping & Eating

★**Quaker Inn** INN $$

(📞732-775-7525; www.quakerinn.com; 39 Main Ave; r $103-206; ❄🐾) A great old creaky Victorian with 28 rooms, some of which open onto wraparound porches or balconies. There's a nice common area and library to linger over your coffee, and the managers, Liz and Mark, reflect the town's charm and hospitality. Light sleepers take note: the walls are a bit thin.

Nagle's Fountain ICE CREAM $

(📞732-776-9797; 43 Main Ave; ice cream $3, mains $6-10; ⊙8:30am-9pm Wed-Mon) This lovingly tended old soda fountain and cafe has been operating since the 1880s. Check out real estate prices from days of yore on the bathroom walls, and try New Jersey's ubiquitous classic – the pork roll – with your egg cream.

Starving Artist CAFE $

(📞732-988-1007; 47 Olin St; mains $3-9; ⊙8am-3pm Mon, Tue & Thu-Sat, to 2pm Sun; 🐾) The menu at this adorable eatery with a large outdoor patio highlights breakfast, the grill, and fried seafood; tasty ice cream is served at the adjacent shop. Stuffed French toast and 'loaded' potatoes are a morning must; bust out the crayons while you wait for your meal.

Bürbelmaiers BRITISH $

(📞732-774-3674; www.burbelmaiers.com; 69 Main Ave; pies $8; ⊙9am-6pm Fri-Tue) Chomp down on a savory pie – think meaty, not sweet – from this husband-and-wife team (Pete Burbela and Courtney Maier Burbela) who also make their own pickles, sauerkraut and chutneys. Elbow your way onto the communal table in front of the faux fire or just nosh on the flaky crusted wonders while meandering Main Ave.

Seagrass SEAFOOD $$

(☑732-869-0770; www.seagrassnj.com; 68 Main Ave; mains $21-29; ⊙11:30am-9pm Wed & Thu, to 10pm Fri & Sat, noon-8pm Sun) Seagrass is dominated by a large fish tank that suffuses the entire restaurant in a purplish glow, with paintings of tropical fish that complete the vibe. Asbury Park powerbrokers may be at the next table munching on the amazing scallops, or the '3 for $30' special with soup or salad, main and dessert. BYOB.

☆ Entertainment

Great Auditorium LIVE PERFORMANCE

(☑732-775-0035, tickets 800-965-9324; www. oceangrove.org; 21 Pilgrim Pathway; recitals free, concerts $13; ⊙organ recitals 7:30pm Wed & noon Sat Jul & Aug) Towering over the tents, the 1894 mustard-yellow Great Auditorium shouldn't be missed: its vaulted interior, amazing acoustics and historic 11,000-pipe organ recall Utah's Mormon Tabernacle. Make sure to catch a recital or concert (Wednesday or Saturday during the summer) or one of the open-air services held in the boardwalk pavilion (May to September).

❶ Getting There & Away

Driving along the S Main St (Rte 71) from the north or south, you'll see the impressive gates that mark the entranceway to Ocean Grove's Main Ave. If you're taking the NJ Transit's Shore Express, disembark at neighboring Asbury Park and walk or taxi over to Ocean Grove. Academy buses from New York's Port Authority (www. academybus.com) go directly to Ocean Grove ($19, 1½ hours).

Barnegat Peninsula

Locals call this 22-mile stretch 'the barrier island,' though it's technically a peninsula, connected to the mainland at Point Pleasant Beach. Surfers should seek out Inlet Beach in Manasquan, immediately north (not on the peninsula), for the Shore's most reliable year-round waves.

South of Mantoloking and Lavallette, midway down the island, a bridge from the mainland (at Toms River) deposits the hordes in Seaside Heights, location of the MTV reality show *Jersey Shore,* and epitome of the deliciously tacky Shore culture. It's still a sticky pleasure to lick a Kohr's orange-vanilla twist cone and stroll through the boardwalk's raucous, deeply tanned, scantily clad crowds, refueling at an above-average number of bars. Look out for the 1910 Dentzel-Looff carousel, and the 310ft Ferris wheel and German-built roller coaster added in 2017.

For a bit of quiet, escape south to residential Seaside Park and the wilderness of Island Beach State Park beyond.

◉ Sights

Island Beach State Park PARK

(☑732-793-0506; www.islandbeachnj.org; Seaside Park; per car weekday/weekend $12/20 May-Sep, $5/10 Oct-Apr; ⊙8am-8pm Mon-Fri, 7am-8pm Sat & Sun May-Sep, 8am-dusk Oct-Apr) This beautiful tidal island offers fishing, wildlife (from foxes to ospreys and other shorebirds), more than 40 trees and shrubs, including pepperbush and prickly pear cactus, and a killer view of Barnegat Lighthouse. Of the 10 miles of relatively untouched beach, one is open for swimming; the rest makes a nice bike ride. On the bay side, the lush tidal marshes are good for kayaking.

Jenkinson's AMUSEMENT PARK

(☑732-295-4334; www.jenkinsons.com; 300 Ocean Ave, Point Pleasant Beach; aquarium adult/child $14/8, beach $10/3; ⊙rides noon-11pm, aquarium 10am-10pm Jul & Aug, hours vary Sep-Jun) The focus is on kids at this boardwalk in Point Pleasant Beach: small-scale rides, mini-golf, an aquarium and plenty of candy.

🛏 Sleeping

Luna-Mar Motel MOTEL $

(☑732-793-7955; www.lunamarmotel.com; 1201 N Ocean Ave, Seaside Park; r from $129; ❋🛜❄) Directly across the road from the beach, this tidy motel has tile floors (no sandy carpets). Rates include beach badges.

🍴 Eating & Drinking

Music Man ICE CREAM $

(☑732-854-2779; www.themusicman.com; 2305 Grand Central Ave, Lavallette; ice cream $3-8; ⊙11am-midnight) Have a little razzle-dazzle with your ice-cream sundae – the waitstaff belt out Broadway show tunes all night (from 5:30pm Friday to Sunday in June and daily in July and August). Cash only.

Martell's Tiki Bar BAR

(☑732-892-0131; www.tikibar.com; 308 Boardwalk, Point Pleasant Beach; ⊙11am-11pm Sun-Thu, to 12:30am Fri & Sat) A place margarita pitchers go to die. Look for the neon-orange palm trees and listen for the live bands. The Lobster House next door has every form of crustacean imaginable.

ℹ Getting There & Away

NJ Transit (www.njtransit.com) has a special Shore Express train (no transfer required) to Shore towns between Asbury Park and Bay Head; in the summer months it includes a beach pass. It also offers direct bus service to Seaside Heights from New York's Port Authority (bus 137; $27, 1½ hours) and Newark's Penn Station (bus 67; $17, one hour) from the end of June to Labor Day.

Long Beach Island

Accessible only by a bridge (Rte 72) across Manahawkin Bay, Long Beach Island is an 18-mile-long barrier island at the dead center of the Jersey Shore. LBI, as it's known, is a string of townships, all with beautiful beaches and strong surf culture (Ron Jon started here). South of the bridge, Long Beach and Beach Haven are where the action is, while quieter, more affluent Surf City, Harvey Cedars and Barnegat Light – punctuated by a beautiful lighthouse – are to the north.

There are seven – count 'em, *seven* – mini-golf courses on the island, with a 36-hole, split-level course coming to Barnegat Light.

⊙ Sights & Activities

Edwin B Forsythe National
Wildlife Refuge   HIKING
(Brigantine Unit; ☎ 609-652-1665; www.fws.gov; 800 Great Creek Rd, Oceanville; $4) This smaller section of the massive 47,000 acre Forsythe NWR stretches north 50 miles to Brick Township. There's an 8-mile driving circuit, but it's well worth getting out on the hiking trails and meandering through the forests and marshes, which are home to abundant wildlife. Friends of Forsythe offers a free two-hour tram tour with a wildlife expert on Saturdays at 1:30.

Barnegat Lighthouse State Park   STATE PARK
(☎ 609-494-2016; www.state.nj.us; off Long Beach Blvd; lighthouse adult/child $3/1; ⊙ state park 8am-6pm, lighthouse 10am-4:30pm) 'Old Barney,' the 1859 lighthouse at the north tip of LBI, receives half a million visitors each year. The adjoining state park, filled with berry and holly bushes, bustles with bird life. If you can clamber up 217 steps, it's worth the view.

South End Surf 'n' Paddle   SURFING
(☎ 609-492-8823; www.southendsurfnpaddle. com; 220 S Bay Ave, Beach Haven; surfboards per half-day $20, SUPs per 2hr $35, boogie board/kayak per day $10/50) Like a slice of Maui mys-teriously transported 6000 miles east, Ken and company rent and sell boards, stand-up paddleboards, kayaks and even ukuleles. All come with instruction. There are even yoga classes if the waves beat you down.

Shore Brake Cyclery   CYCLING
(☎ 609-342-0480; www.shorebrakecyclery.com; 3801 Long Beach Blvd, Brant Beach; per hour $10-12, per day $22-30; ⊙ 9am-5pm) Charley Kulp and his adorable chocolate-brown Lab will set you up with wheels, but call in advance to book a ride in July and August, when the island's full and bikes can be scarce.

⊨ Sleeping & Eating

Jolly Roger Motel   MOTEL $$
(☎ 609-492-6931; www.jollyrogerlbi.com; 5416 S Long Beach Blvd, Holgate; r $150-200; ⊙ Apr-Oct; ❋ 🛜) At the southern end of Long Beach Island, the Jolly Roger is unpretentious, comfortable and quiet – while still reasonably close to Beach Haven's main activities. Only 44 steps to the beach. You heard it here first.

Chicken or the Egg   BREAKFAST $
(☎ 609-492-3695; www.492fowl.com; 207 N Bay Ave, Beach Haven; breakfasts $6-10, wings $8-14; ⊙ 7am-9pm Sun-Thu, to 10pm Fri & Sat) An LBI classic for a quarter-century, you can get breakfast all day – the six-egg omelet is a true challenge – but many come for the 'cheggs,' or delicious wings, with 17 choices of sauce. If you come early for breakfast, you'll beat the inevitable line. And if you get that 4am hot-sauce fever, there's 24-hour service all summer long.

Mud City Crab House   SEAFOOD $$
(Seafood Grill & Market; ☎ 609-978-3660; www. mudcitycrabhouse.com; 1185 E Bay Ave, Manahawkin; mains $22-28; ⊙ 11am-10pm Thu-Tue) At first you might ask: a three-hour wait for crab cakes? And then you taste them – lumps of crab, hardly any filler, and so good that they're the most popular takeout item (save some time and order them that way). Serving the maritime favorite Narragansett ales, the only drawback is the wait – thankfully, the airstream trailer outside is a bar.

ℹ Getting There & Away

The TAZ10 bus (www.transportazumah.com) runs from outside NYC's Port Authority and from Newark Airport ($40) to most of LBI's towns on weekends. Other train and bus service requires you to get off at Manahawkin and take a taxi across to the island.

NEW JERSEY LONG BEACH ISLAND

Atlantic City

♪ 609 / POP 38,735

Atlantic City (AC) may be the largest city on the Shore, but the vision of 'Vegas on the East Coast' has foundered and casinos gone bankrupt. But the hotels can be a bargain and the lovely beach is free and often empty because visitors are indoors playing the slots. And in contrast with many homogeneous beach enclaves, the population here is more diverse.

As for the Prohibition-era glamour depicted in the HBO series *Boardwalk Empire*, there's little trace – though you can still ride

Atlantic City

along the boardwalk on a wicker rolling chair. The first boardwalk was built here, and if Baltic Ave rings a bell, it's because the game Monopoly uses AC's street names. A later contribution: the Miss America pageant, though it's now held in Vegas; the Miss'd America drag pageant fills the gap.

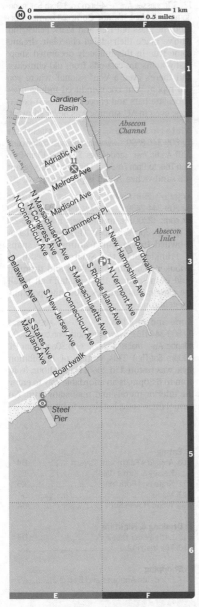

◉ Sights

Historic Pipe Organ THEATRE
(Boardwalk Hall; www.boardwalkorgans.org; 2301 Boardwalk; ⏰organ recital noon Mon-Fri Jun-Aug, noon Wed Sep-May, tours 10am Wed) **FREE** A non-profit institute runs tours, recitals and silent films to maintain the Boardwalk Hall's two historic – and impressive – pipe organs: the 'sonic Mount Rushmore.'

Absecon Lighthouse LIGHTHOUSE
(☑609-449-1360; www.abseconlighthouse.org; 31 S Rhode Island Ave; adult/child $7/4; ⏰10am-8pm Thu, to 5pm Fri-Wed Jul & Aug, 11am-4pm Thu-Mon Sep-Jun) New Jersey's tallest lighthouse at 171ft (228 steps), Absecom (Ab-see-cum) gives you a bird's-eye view of AC. Moonlight climbs are offered monthly during summer and fall.

Steel Pier AMUSEMENT PARK
(☑866-386-6659; www.steelpier.com; 1000 Boardwalk; ⏰1pm-midnight Mon-Fri, noon-midnight Sat & Sun Jul & Aug, shorter hours Apr-Jun) The Steel Pier, directly in front of the Taj Mahal casino, was the site of the famous high-diving horses that plunged into the Atlantic before crowds of spectators from the 1920s to the '70s. Today it's a collection of amusement rides, games of chance, candy stands and a Go-Kart track.

African American Heritage Museum of Southern New Jersey MUSEUM
(☑609-350-6662; www.aahmsnj.org; Noyes Arts Garage, 2200 Fairmount Ave; ⏰11am-6pm) **FREE** At this worthwhile endeavor by Ralph E Hunter showcasing the history of African Americans in Atlantic City and the USA, there's nice artwork from both sides of the Atlantic, as well as historical exhibits that shine a light on the ugly stereotyping and racism blacks have faced in America. Donations requested.

Ripley's Believe it or Not! MUSEUM
(Odditorium; ☑609-347-2001; www.ripleys.com; 1441 Boardwalk; adult/child $18/12; ⏰10am-10pm) Robert Ripley spent a lifetime collecting bizarre stuff, and a lot of it's here. Two-headed goat fetuses, a baling-wire Jimi Hendrix head, the world's smallest car, and a roulette wheel made of 14,000 jellybeans – you'll have fun for about the cost of a movie.

Atlantic City Historical Museum MUSEUM
(☑609-347-5839; www.atlanticcityexperience.org; 1 N Tennessee Ave, Atlantic City Free Public Library; ⏰9:30am-5pm Mon, Fri & Sat, to 6:30pm Tue-Thu) **FREE** Small but informative – you'll learn all about AC's quirkiest details, such as the high-diving horses that once leapt off a 40ft tower at Steel Pier.

NEW JERSEY ATLANTIC CITY

🛏 Sleeping

Fanta Sea Resorts   HOTEL $

(Atlantic Palace; ☑609-344-8800; www.fanta-searesorts.com; 1507 Boardwalk; ste $79-99) We found these suites quite accommodating. Used frequently by couples and families as time-shares or long-term rentals, they're open to other guests, and with fully equipped kitchens you can make yourself right at home. In their other property on N Maine Ave, request rooms ending in 16 through 19 for killer balcony vistas of Brigantine and the briny deep.

Tropicana Casino and Resort   HOTEL $

(☑609-340-4000; www.tropicana.net; 2831 Boardwalk; r from $89; 🅿❄🛜🏊) The Trop is a sprawling city-within-a-city, including a casino, the Boogie Nights disco, a spa and high-end restaurants. We recommend the newer 'Havana' wing, and try to get up above the 40th floor for spectacular views. Weekday rates can be incredibly cheap.

Borgata   HOTEL $$$

(☑855-408-1729; www.theborgata.com; 1 Borgata Way; r $249-279; 🅿❄🛜🏊) A few steps up from the Boardwalk hotels and casino (metaphorically), and across town (literally), the Borgata offers a classy experience – for a price. The choice of spas, salons, indoor/outdoor pools, and concert venues (two) make this a luxurious option if you win big or already have the dosh.

🍴 Eating

★ Kelsey & Kim's Café   SOUTHERN US $

(Kelsey's Soul Food; ☑609-350-6800; www.kelseysac.com; 201 Melrose Ave; mains $9-12; ⊙8am-9pm Sun-Thu, to 10pm Fri & Sat) In the pretty residential Uptown area, this friendly cafe does excellent Southern comfort food, from morning grits and waffles to fried whiting and barbecue brisket. BYOB makes it a deal.

There's also a newer downtown location at 1545 Pacific Ave that offers live music and is open evenings only.

Made   SWEETS $

(Atlantic City Chocolate; www.madeacchocolate.com; 121 S Tennessee Ave; ⊙4-9pm Fri, 1-9pm Sat, noon-8pm Sun & Mon) It's not Oompa Loompas behind the glass but Deb and Mark Pellegrino, who've made their global chocolate dreams come true in this uniquely decorated shop: many items are cast-offs from old churches, and there's even a 'confessional' where you can repent your cocoa-induced indulgences. Chocolate bars and chocolate-infused beverages: even in AC, sinning was never so sweet.

White House Subs   SANDWICHES $

(☑609-345-8599; www.whitehousesubshop.com; 2301 Arctic Ave; sandwiches $7-16; ⊙10am-8pm Mon-Thu, to 9pm Fri-Sun) The legendary giant sub sandwiches. A half is plenty for two.

Angelo's Fairmount Tavern   ITALIAN $$

(☑609-344-2439; www.angelosfairmounttavern.com; 2300 Fairmount Ave; mains $15-25; ⊙11:30am-3pm & 5-10pm) This beloved family-owned Italian joint features more snaps of Frankie than the Sinatra Museum in Hoboken. The tunes, trinkets and tiramisu (and even some of the waitstaff) all recall the classic '50s Ratpack vibe, and portions are generous.

Knife and Fork Inn   AMERICAN $$$

(☑609-344-1133; www.knifeandforkinn.com; 3600 Atlantic Ave; mains $28-54; ⊙11:30am-10pm Fri, 4-10pm Sat-Thu) This vestige of Prohibition style was restored in 2005. Happy hour, from 4pm to 6:30pm, is an affordable way to enjoy the interior murals and mahogany trim. No formal dress code, but dress to impress.

Atlantic City

🍷 Drinking & Nightlife

Iron Room
BAR

(🌐 609-348-6400; www.ironroomac.com; 648 N Albany Ave; ⊙3-11pm Tue-Sat, 11am-3pm Sun) This high-end rectangular room away from the Boardwalk mixes spirits with unobtrusive classic rock while you melt into the seat cushions along the wall, helped by the $14 specialty drinks and a chalkboard full of craft beers. The bar menu is a relative bargain with items like foie gras fries. Chartreuse? Gin? Rye? It's got it all.

The Irish Pub
BAR

(🌐 609-344-9063; www.theirishpub.com; 164 St James Place; ⊙24hr) The name says it all. Dark paneling lined with memorabilia from the golden age of drinking (Jack Dempsey boxing posters), this pub gets you going up or coming down: it's open 24 hours. Save some room for the St James potatoes, a gooey casserole of french fried potatoes, gravy and melted cheese.

Little Water Distillery
DISTILLERY

(🌐 609-344-7867; www.littlewaterdistillery.com; 807 Baltic Ave; ⊙5-9pm Fri, 1-8pm Sat, to 6pm Sun) AC's first legal hooch house since the days of Prohibition, these crafty brothers plan on turning out 20,000 gallons of the hard stuff – specifically whisky and rum – per year. A cigar lounge outside completes the scene; the specialty cocktail nights might be your thing if you don't like it straight up. Entrance on Lexington Ave.

🛍 Shopping

Princeton Antiques and Books
BOOKS

(🌐 609-344-1943; www.princetonantiques.com; 2917 Atlantic Ave; ⊙8:30am-5pm Mon-Fri, to 1pm Sat) Maybe you didn't come to Sin City to shop for books, but this musty maze of literary castoffs, off the beaten casino track, is kind of irresistible. 'We Buy the Old' on the awning speaks volumes. If you can't find what you want among the quarter-million titles, the book-finding librarians promise to do so.

ℹ Information

Atlantic City Visitor Center (DO AC; 🌐 609-348-7100; www.atlanticcitynj.com; Boardwalk at Mississippi Ave; ⊙9:30am-5pm) Main tourist office branch.

Atlantic City Visitor Welcome Center (DO AC; 🌐 609-449-7130; www.atlanticcitynj.com; Atlantic City Expwy, Mile 3.5; ⊙9am-5pm Wed-Sun) Under the giant tepee in the middle of the Atlantic City Expwy.

OFF THE BEATEN TRACK

LUCY THE ELEPHANT

This six-story wooden **pachyderm** (🌐 609-823-6473; www.lucytheelephant. org; 9200 Atlantic Ave, Margate; adult/child $8/4; ⊙10am-8pm Mon-Sat, to 5pm Sun Jun-Aug, reduced hours Sep-May) was constructed in 1881 as a land developer's weird scheme to attract customers. It's in Margate (just south of AC), and you can climb up inside on a guided tour (on the half-hour). Factoid: Lucy makes a brief appearance in the Jack Nicholson cult classic *The King of Marvin Gardens*. Like the movie's other characters, she is in great disrepair.

ℹ Getting There & Away

The small **Atlantic City International Airport** (ACY; 🌐 609-573-4700; www.acairport.com; 101 Atlantic City International Airport, Egg Harbor Township) is a 20-minute drive from the town center. If you happen to be coming from Florida (where most of the flights come from), it's a great option for South Jersey or Philadelphia.

The only train service is NJ Transit (www. njtransit.com) from Philadelphia (one way $11, 1½ hours), arriving at the **train station** (🌐 973-491-9400; www.njtransit.com; 1 Atlantic City Expwy) next to the convention center. AC's **bus station** (🌐 609-345-5403; www.njtransit. com; 1901 Atlantic Ave) receives NJ Transit and Greyhound service from NYC ($25 to $36, 2½ hours) and Philadelphia ($11 to $23, 1½ hours). A casino will often refund much of the fare (in chips, coins or coupons) if you get a bus, such as Greyhound's Lucky Streak service, directly to its door. When leaving AC, buses first stop at various casinos and only stop at the bus station if not already full.

Wildwood

🌐 609 / POP 5230

Wildwood, and its neighboring towns of North Wildwood and Wildwood Crest, is a virtual outdoor museum of 1950s motel architecture and neon signs. The community has a relaxed atmosphere, somewhere between clean-cut fun and wild party. The beach is the widest in NJ (a proposal to ferry beach-goers across the sands on camel was recently floated) and there's no admission fee. Along the 2-mile boardwalk, several massive piers have roller coasters and rides best suited to aspiring astronauts.

Wildwood

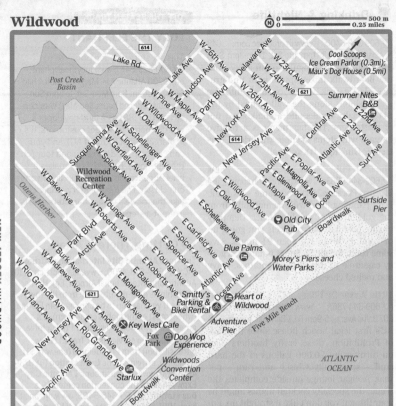

Sights & Activities

Doo Wop Experience　　　　MUSEUM
(☑609-523-1958; www.doowopusa.org; 4500 Ocean
Ave; ⊙noon-9pm, trolley tours 8pm Tue & Thu Jun-
Aug) FREE The Doo Wop Preservation League
runs this small museum that tells the story of
Wildwood's 1950s heyday. Its 'neon-sign garden' shows off relics from no-longer-standing
buildings. Some summer nights, a trolley
tour (adult/child $12/6) departs from here,
passing the most colorful landmarks.

Smitty's Parking & Bike Rental　　CYCLING
(☑609-523-9113; cnr Young & Ocean Aves; ⊙6am-
dusk) A convenient block from the boardwalk, you can rent single bikes, tandems and
surreys (bikes with benches).

Sleeping

Summer Nites B&B　　　　B&B $$
(☑609-846-1955; www.summernites.com; 2110 At-
lantic Ave, North Wildwood; r $175-315; P❄) North

of the noise and lights, in an unassuming
white house, is a coolest vintage experience:
real jukeboxes play 45s, the breakfast room is
a perfectly re-created diner, and the themed
rooms are dominated by wall-size murals and
framed, signed memorabilia. Treat yourself
like a King: stay in the Elvis Suite.

Starlux　　　　BOUTIQUE HOTEL $$
(☑609-522-7412; www.thestarlux.com; 305 E
Rio Grande Ave; r/ste from $259/362; P❄@❄)
The sea-green-and-white Starlux has the
soaring profile, the boomerang-decorated
bedspreads, the lava lamps and the sail-
boat-shaped mirrors, plus it's clean as a
whistle. Even more authentically retro are its
two chrome-sided Airstream trailers (sleeping three comfortably). Rooms in a separate
house behind the hotel are discounted.

Blue Palms　　　　BOUTIQUE HOTEL $$
(☑609-522-0606; www.bluepalmsresort.com;
3601 Atlantic Ave; d $175-355; P❄❄) A block

from the boardwalk, this property offers convenient family suites with microwaves, kitchenettes and multiple beds and televisions, as well as discounts at the pier. Free bikes and friendly staff make this property a winner. Standard rooms available, too.

Heart of Wildwood
HOTEL $$

(609-522-4090; www.heartofwildwood.com; cnr Ocean & E Spencer Aves; r $150-250; P❄❈🐾) If you're here for water slides and roller coasters, book a room at Heart of Wildwood, facing the amusement piers. It's not fancy, but gets high marks for cleanliness (the tile floors help), and from the heated rooftop pool you can watch the big wheel go round and round. Smallish suites are handy for families, with stoves, sinks and fridges.

✗ Eating

Maui's Dog House
HOT DOGS $

(609-846-0444; www.mauisdoghouse.com; 806 New Jersey Ave, North Wildwood; hot dogs $4-8; ☺11am-8pm) Since 1999 Maui and Liz have served up quality dogs, more than 20 varieties in all. The fave remains Forget About It and *don't* forget the Cardiac Fries with that. It's high-quality fast food, and weekly specials like pulled pork keep 'em comin' back. Served in dog bowls, but no pets allowed.

Cool Scoops Ice Cream Parlor
ICE CREAM $

(609-729-2665; www.coolscoops.com; cnr 12th & New Jersey Aves, North Wildwood; $4-8) Trading heavily on Wildwood's nostalgia for the '50s, this old-school ice cream joint hits just the right notes, with Elvis statues, booths made of old Ford Fairlane autos, and classic TV shows broadcast on period TV sets (no streaming!). There's even an old barber chair in the men's room. And the ice cream? You can't go wrong.

Key West Cafe
BREAKFAST $

(609-522-5006; www.keywestcafe.us; 4701 Pacific Ave; mains $8-10; ☺7am-2pm) Basically every permutation of pancakes and eggs imaginable, all freshly prepared – oh, and lunch too. Bonus: it's open year-round. The eggs Benedict is a fave among frequent diners.

🍷 Drinking & Nightlife

Old City Pub
PUB

(609-846-1110; www.oldcitypub.com; 3301 Atlantic Ave; ☺3pm-2am Tue-Thu, noon-2am Fri-Sun) The owners of the old Tucker's exposed this joint for what it is: a lovely old Victorian with vaulted windows and high ceilings, and walls tastefully painted in muted two-

tone green against an exposed-brick backdrop. Hearty pub fare is the order of the day (mains $8 to $12). Live music at night.

Try the Angels on Horseback (scallops wrapped in bacon) – a mouthwatering delight best washed down with a can of PBR.

ℹ️ Getting There & Around

New Jersey Transit (www.njtransit.com) runs bus service to Wildwood from NYC ($46, 4½ hours, possible transfer in Atlantic City) and express bus service from Philadelphia's 30th St Station during summer ($30, 2½ hours). Driving from the Garden State Pkwy, take Rte 47 into Wildwood; from the south a more scenic route from Cape May is Rte 109, then Ocean Dr.

Since 1949 a miniature rubber-tired tram has run the length of the boardwalk, intermittently chirping, 'Watch the tram car, please.' It runs from 11am to 1am and costs $3 one way. Cycling around can be fun too, and some hotels let you use their wheels for free.

Cape May
609 / POP 3500

Established in 1620, Cape May is a town with deep history and some 600 gorgeous Victorian buildings. Its sweeping beaches are a draw in summer, but its year-round population of about 3500 makes it a lively off-season destination, unlike most of the Jersey Shore. Whales can be spotted off the coast May to December, and migratory birds are plentiful in spring and fall: just check in at the Cape May Bird Observatory. The state's booming wine industry is represented by six different sites here, among them trendy Willow Creek (p181). And thanks to the location on New Jersey's southern tip (it's Exit 0 from the turnpike), you can watch the sun rise or set over the water.

🔘 Sights & Activities

Cape May Point State Park
STATE PARK

(www.state.nj.us; ☺8am-4pm) The 190-acre Cape May Point State Park, just off Lighthouse Ave, has 2 miles of trails, plus the famous 1859 Cape May Lighthouse (609-884-5404; www.capemaymac.org; 215 Lighthouse Ave; adult/child $8/5; ☺10am-5pm May-Sep, shorter hours rest of year). You can climb the 199 stairs to the top for the view. Short, easy trails (0.5 to 2 miles) are great for birding and a breath of salty ocean air.

Cape May Bird Observatory
BIRD SANCTUARY

(609-884-2736; www.njaudubon.org; ☺9am-4:30pm Apr-Oct, closed Tue Nov-Mar) FREE Cape

Cape May

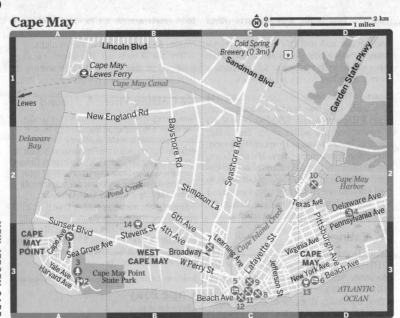

May is one of the country's top birding spots, with more than 400 species during the spring and fall migration seasons, when neotropical birds are heading south for the winter or north to breed for the summer. The mile-long loop trail here is a good introduction, and there are plenty of books, binoculars and birding bric-a-brac in the bookstore.

Aqua Trails　KAYAKING
(☑609-884-5600; www.aquatrails.com; 1600 Delaware Ave; rental per hour s/double $25/35, tours from $45/75) Based at Cape May's nature center, this outfitter rents gear and leads tours through the wetlands at sundown and during the full moon.

🛌 Sleeping

⭐ **Congress Hall**　HOTEL $$$
(☑609-884-8421; www.caperesorts.com; 200 Congress Pl; r from $459; ❄🎧🏊) Opened in 1816, the enormous Congress Hall is a local landmark, now suitably modernized without wringing out all the history. It's got everything you could ask for, including a spa and bicycle rentals, but can come off as a bit highfalutin. Just before and after the high season you'll find good deals.

Icona　HOTEL $$$
(☑609-898-8100; www.iconacapemay.com; 1101 Beach Ave; r from $410; 🅿❄🎧🏊) A 2016 vin-

tage property run by the up-and-coming Achristavest developers, which have three other Shore sites. You'll feel a bit pampered here: clean rooms, kind staff and a mellow atmosphere, just steps from the beach. A small pool was added in 2018.

🍴 Eating

Mad Batter　AMERICAN $
(☑609-884-5970; www.madbatter.com; 19 Jackson St, Carroll Villa Hotel; brunch $8-13; ⊙8am-10pm) Tucked away in a white Victorian B&B, this restaurant is locally beloved for brunch – including fluffy oat pancakes and rich clam chowder. Dinner is fine but pricier, with mains around $30. The Chesapeake Bay Benedict, stuffed with crab, is to die for.

Kohr Brothers Frozen Custard　ICE CREAM $
(☑609-884-8610; www.kohrbros.com; 512 Washington St, Washington Mall; ⊙11am-10pm) Nothing says summer like the traditional orange-and-vanilla swirl cone, a Shore favorite for 100 years.

Cabanas　BURGERS $
(☑609-884-4800; www.cabanasonthebeach.com; 429 Beach Ave; burgers $12-15; ⊙3-10pm Wed & Thu, noon-10pm Fri-Sun) The surfboard marks the entrance, and vintage surf-themed bric-a-brac lines the walls. It's a huge sports bar with more TVs than Howard Hughes' bed-

Cape May

room, but it's fun and the staff are friendly. Local acoustic artists can sometimes be heard above the din.

Uncle Bill's Pancake House
AMERICAN $

(☑609-884-7199; www.unclebillspancakehouse.com; 261 Beach Ave; mains $7; ⊘6:30am-2pm Mar-Jan) The size (and decor) of a high-school cafeteria from the 1950s, Uncle Bill's has been drawing in crowds for its butter-drenched flapjacks for 50 years. If you miss this locale, there are seven other Uncles up and down the Shore.

Bella Vida Cafe
COSTA RICAN $$

(☑609-884-6332; www.bellavidacafe.com; 406 N Broadway, West Cape May; mains lunch $8-12, dinner $17-25; ⊘8am-3pm Sun-Thu, to 9pm Fri & Sat; ☑) The Bella Vida offers a *Tico*-themed healthy but delicious alternative to the Shore diet of pancakes and funnel cakes, and the Costa Rican coffee is superb. There's a lot of veggie and gluten-free items, and smoothies and fresh-pressed carrot juice feature on the morning breakfast menu.

Lobster House
SEAFOOD $$$

(☑609-884-8296; www.thelobsterhouse.com; 906 Schellengers Landing Rd; mains $14-30; ⊘11:30am-3pm & 4:30-10pm Apr-Dec, to 9pm Jan-Mar; ☑) This clubby-feeling classic on the wharf serves local oysters and scallops. No reservations means very long waits – go early or late, or have a drink on the boat-bar, the *Schooner American*, docked next to the restaurant.

🍷 Drinking & Nightlife

★ Willow Creek Winery
WINERY

(☑609-770-8782; www.willowcreekwinerycapemay.com; 168 Stevens St; tasting $20; ⊘11am-5pm Mon-Thu, to 9:30pm Fri, to 7pm Sat, to 6pm Sun) The 'baby' of Cape May's six wineries, this former lima bean and dairy farm christened its first bottles in 2011, and produces a solid combo of reds and whites. The weekend tapas menu and sangria bar is pretty mind-blowing, and a tour around the 50 acres on an electric tram is a kick. The 'educational tasting' will smarten up your palate.

You can pick up fresh Jersey produce like sweet corn and peaches at their nearby Legates Farm.

Hemingway's Restaurant
COCKTAIL BAR

(☑609-884-5611; www.hemingwayscapemay.com; Grand Hotel, 1045 Beach Ave; ⊘8am-9pm Sun-Thu, to 10pm Fri & Sat) It's hard to imagine the *Old Man and the Sea* author shaking his thing to the hits of the '70s and '80s, but it's fun to try. We're certain he at least would've enjoyed sitting at the bar and watching. The live DJ sets up weekends at 9pm. Sailfish *and* swordfish on the walls.

Cold Spring Brewery
MICROBREWERY

(☑609-898-2300; www.hcsv.org/cold-spring-brewery; 733 Seashore Rd, Historic Cold Spring Village; ⊘noon-8pm Tue-Sat, until 6pm Sun) Sip a red, wheat, porter or pale ale while soaking in the vibe of the 1804 restored Cape May barn. It's nice to know your drinking leads to something – profits from the beer sales fund the adjoining Historic Cold Spring Village.

It's $12 to tour the old village, but no cost to visit the brew-barn.

❶ Getting There & Around

NJ Transit (www.njtransit.com) buses serve Cape May from NYC ($48, three to five hours; may involve a transfer at Atlantic City) and a discounted round-trip express bus from Philadelphia during the summer months ($33, three hours). For onward car travel, the **Cape May-Lewes Ferry** (☑800-643-3779; www.cmlf.com; 1200 Lincoln Blvd; car/passenger $47/10; ⊘7am-6pm Apr-Oct) crosses the bay in 1½ hours to Lewes, Delaware, near Rehoboth Beach.

On the cape itself, the Great American Trolley Company (www.gatrolley.com) will whisk you around from the park-and-ride lot to the gazebo and beach locations ($1, noon to 11pm, late June to early September). Look for the purple-and-white signs on any corner.

Philadelphia

☎ 215, 267 / POP 1.57 MILLION

Why Go?

Blessed with the glamour and culture of a big city, 'Philly' as it's affectionately known, also delights visitors with its rich history and small-town charm. Because the city's oldest buildings are so well-preserved, America's oldest history and role in building democracy are sometimes more accessible here than in the nation's capital. Moreover, it's a beautiful place that's easy and rewarding to explore, its streets dotted with gracious squares and linked by cobbled alleys. Eating is also a highlight here, with two of the city's most loved attractions – Reading Terminal Market and the South 9th Street Italian Market – placing food front and center.

Best Places to Eat

➡ Reading Terminal Market (p193)

➡ Zahav (p205)

➡ Valley Green Inn (p210)

➡ Vetri Cucina (p206)

➡ CHeU Noodle Bar (p206)

Best Places to Stay

➡ AKA University City (p204)

➡ Apple Hostels (p201)

➡ Thomas Bond House B&B (p202)

When to Go
Philadelphia

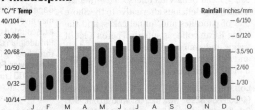

Apr & May Spring offers sunshine without the heat and crowds of high summer.

Sep A great time to visit, especially during the Fringe Festival.

Dec & Jan Perfect for museum-hopping; there's also the Mummer's parade.

stitutional Convention. Following his assassination, President Abraham Lincoln lay in state here for two days from April 22, 1865.

Second Floor & West Wing

On the main hall's 2nd floor are the **Governor's Council Chamber**, where royal governors conducted affairs of state; the **Long Gallery**, a reception area that during the 19th-century was a museum for the paintings of Charles Willson Peale – now on display at the **Second Bank of the US** (☑215-965-2305; 420 Chestnut St; ⊘11am-5pm Sat & Sun Mar-Nov, extended hours May-Sep) – and the **Committee of the Assembly's Chamber**, originally a storeroom for military goods and later housing the US Marshal's Office in the 19th century.

Leaving the main hall, the separate West Wing houses the Great Essentials Exhibit, where you can see original printed copies of the Declaration of Independence, the Articles of Confederation and the US Constitution. No ticket is necessary to visit here.

Congress Hall

You don't need a ticket to visit **Congress Hall** (☑215-965-2305; cnr S 6th & Chestnut Sts; ⊘9am-5pm, tours every 20-30min), on the far west side of the Independence Hall compound This is where the first legislators met when Philly was the nation's capital. The nation's first two presidents were inaugurated here. Entrance is by tour (20 minutes) only, March through December. The building is self-guided in January and February.

American Philosophical Society

The oldest learned society in the US was founded in 1743 by Benjamin Franklin with the aim of 'promoting useful knowledge.' It continues on its mission by mounting a different themed exhibition each year on American history and science in its **museum** (☑215-440-3440; www.amphilsoc.org/visit-museum; 104 S 5th St; adult/child $5/2; ⊘10am-4pm Thu-Sun, mid-Apr–Dec) on the east side of the Independence Hall, the only section of the complex not run by the National Park.

TOP TIPS

➡ Between March and December Independence Hall generally requires a timed ticket; reserve online (fee $1.50) or go in the morning to the Independence Visitor Center (p216) where a limited number of timed daily tickets are available for free.

➡ You don't need a ticket for the hall if you visit after 5pm during the longer summer opening hours.

➡ Arrive at the security screening area in the east wing of Independence Hall approximately 30 minutes prior to the time on your timed entry ticket.

➡ Take a toilet break in the Independence Visitor Center before your tour as there are no facilities inside Independence Hall.

TAKE A BREAK

For coffee and lights bites you can't go wrong with Frieda (p204). Or stay in the revolutionary mood with a meal at City Tavern (p205) on the location where the Founding Fathers supped.

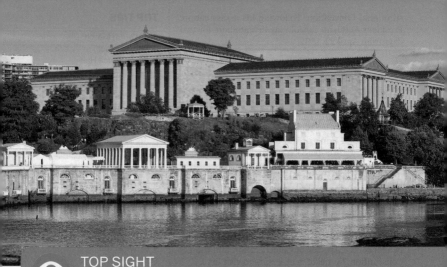

TOP SIGHT
PHILADELPHIA MUSEUM OF ART

The city's premier cultural institution occupies a Grecian temple–like building housing a superb collection of Asian art, Renaissance masterpieces, post-impressionist works and modern pieces by Picasso, Duchamp and Matisse among others. Especially notable are galleries filled with complete architectural ensembles, including a medieval cloister, Chinese and Indian temples and a Japanese teahouse.

Main Building

There's an enormous amount to see in the museum's main building, however your ticket does cover two days' admission here and at other locations. Many start by climbing the broad stone steps to the east entrance (some holding fists aloft like Rocky) from where they first see the impressive Great Stair Hall, above which spins Alexander Calder's mobile *Ghost*, and around which hang the 17th-century Constantine Tapestries. This entrance provides access to the 1st- and 2nd-floor galleries, while the west entrance comes in on the ground floor where there are cloakrooms and other amenities.

In the 1st floor's south wing, the American art galleries are notable for superb works by Charles Willson Peale, Thomas Eakins, William Merritt Chase and Henry Ossawa Tanner. The north wing includes European art of the mid-19th century (this is where you'll see Van Gogh's Sunflowers) moving through to the modern and contemporary galleries with works by the likes of Picasso, Jasper Johns, Andy Warhol and Cy Twombly. Here too is the world's largest collection of pieces by the conceptual artist Marcel Duchamp, including *Fountain,* a 1950 replica of the porcelain urinal that created such a furor in the art world when first displayed in 1917.

DON'T MISS

➡ Grand Stairs and *Ghost* mobile

➡ Marcel Duchamp's works

➡ *Sunkaraku* Japanese teahouse

➡ *Sunflowers,* by Vincent van Gogh

➡ *The Agnew Clinic,* by Thomas Eakins

PRACTICALITIES

➡ Map p194

➡ ☑ 215-763-8100

➡ www.philamuseum. org

➡ 2600 Benjamin Franklin Pkwy, East Fairmount Park

➡ adult/student/child $20/14/free

➡ ⊘10am-5pm Tue, Thu, Sat & Sun, to 8:45pm Wed & Fri

➡ 🚌32, 38, 43

On the 2nd floor, the south wing's Asian Art collection should not be skipped. Highlights include *Sunkaraku,* a ceremonial teahouse from Japan, and a Ming-dynasty reception hall from the Palace of Zhao, as well as many stunning oriental paintings, ceramics and carpets. Room 204 contains a medieval fountain and cloisters from the Abbey of Saint-Génis-des-Fontaines. Room 297 houses a complete Robert Adam–designed drawing room from Lansdowne House, while in Room 292 hangs William Turner's vivid *Burning of the Houses of Parliament.* All these recommendations barely scratch the surface of a museum that can keep you engrossed for days.

Upgrading the Museum

A $196-million program is underway to rejuvenate the museum and prepare it for the coming decades. In what is called the Core Project, architect Frank Gehry is creating new galleries and common areas, adding 67,000 sq ft of public space to the museum and helping to improve navigation and circulation for visitors.

The new central Forum will provide a connecting space and clear views between Lenfest Hall at the western entrance and the Great Stairs Hall at the eastern entrance. The north entrance, closed since 1975, will be reopened and connected to the Forum. A north–south Vaulted Walkway, long closed off, will also be publicly accessible. Other less obvious but necessary tweaks to the building include replacing windows with energy efficient ones, upgrading the building's air-conditioning and improving lighting. All this work should be completed by 2020.

If extra funding can be secured, the post-2020 stage of the plan will see an even bigger expansion, also designed by Frank Gehry. New galleries will be excavated beneath the famous steps leading to the east entrance. Visitors will be able to see straight through the museum, from its west entrance to the Benjamin Franklin Pkwy. Plans and a scale model for this upgrade can be seen in Room 154 of the main building.

Other Locations

Your ticket also includes entry to the Perelman Building (2525 Pennsylvania Ave), which hosts good rotating exhibits devoted to photography, fashion, art and design; and the Rodin Museum (2151 Benjamin Franklin Pkwy; www.rodinmuseum.org), housing a superb collection of works by the French sculptor Auguste Rodin. The museum also administers the historic mansions Cedar Grove (1 Cedar Grove Dr, West Fairmount Park; www.philamuseum.org/historichouses; 🚌 38) and Mount Pleasant (3800 Mt Pleasant Dr, East Fairmount Park). The former is open seasonally and only by guided tour. The latter is currently closed for renovations but is worth visiting to view its elegant Georgian architecture.

TOP TIPS

➡ On the first Sunday of the month and every Wednesday after 5pm, the museum has a pay-what-you-want policy.

TAKE A BREAK

There are several places to eat and drink in the museum, including a couple of cafes and a restaurant that's part of the Frank Gehry upgrade. Alternatively, get a breath of fresh air on the short walk from the western entrance to Cosmic Cafe at Lloyd Hall (Map p190; 📞 215-978-0900; http://cosmic foods.com; 1 Boathouse Row, East Fairmount Park; sandwiches $8-14; ⊗ 8am-8pm; 📶; 🚌 32), next to Boathouse Row.

History

Philadelphia's prominence in US history is a source of great civic pride. The 17th-century creation of idealistic English Quaker William Penn, the city's name comes from ancient Greek and means 'brotherly love.' A past state and national capital, Philly was where the colonies declared their independence; it later developed into the leading industrial city in the US. The most recent century has seen it weather a roller-coaster of economic boom, bust and recovery.

Sights

Most visitors will spend time in central Philadelphia, in the Old City (location of the Independence National Historical Park), Society Hill, Center City and Benjamin Franklin Pkwy areas located between the Delaware and Schuylkill (*skoo*-kill) Rivers. The original William Penn–dictated grid pattern of the streets means it's easy to navigate, with distances between sights walkable or just a short ride away on public transport. West of the Schuylkill is the area known as University City, home to several campuses as well as a large chunk of Fairmount Park.

In the north of the city, Manayunk is worth visiting for its shopping and riverside location, while Germantown is a great place to view heritage architecture. South Philadelphia includes the gourmet destinations of the Italian Market and East Passyunk Ave, lined with top restaurants, as well as the city's major sports stadiums.

PHILADELPHIA: TOP TIPS

- Invest in a rechargeable Key Card as soon as you arrive at the airport or 30th St Station. It can be used on all SEPTA public transport services including the subway, trolleys and buses.
- A good way to get around the major sights is on the PHLASH downtown loop bus (day pass $5).
- In the summer book your visit Independence Hall online (entry is by timed ticket) or arrive early at the Independence Visitor Center to receive one of the limited number of free tickets to the historic hall.
- Make dinner reservations for midrange and top-end restaurants. Arrive early for hot spots that don't take reservations.

Old City & Society Hill

★Independence National Historical Park — PARK

(Map p198; ☎215-965-2305; www.nps.gov/inde; Old City; 🕑visitor center & most sites 9am-5pm; [S]5th St) This L-shaped park, between 6th, 2nd, Walnut and Arch Sts, protects and honors the history and institutions that formed the foundation of the United States government. You'll see storied buildings in which the seeds for the Revolutionary War were planted and the US government came into bloom. You'll also find beautiful, shaded urban lawns dotted with plenty of squirrels, pigeons and, in warmer months, costumed actors. Rangers can provide information about it all at the Independence Visitor Center (p216).

★Museum of the American Revolution — MUSEUM

(Map p198; ☎215-253-6731; www.amrevmuseum.org; 101 S 3rd St; adult/student/child $19/17/12; 🕑10am-5pm Sep-late May, 9:30am-6pm late May-Aug; [S]2nd St) This impressive, multimedia-rich museum will have you virtually participating in the American Revolution; interactive dioramas and 3D experiences take you all the way from contentment with British rule to the eventual rejection of it. Learn about the events, people, cultures and religions that participated in one of the world's most important revolutions. Lots of hands-on displays and video stories mean kids will have as much fun as adults. Note that all tickets are timed: reserve them early online.

★Benjamin Franklin Museum — MUSEUM

(Map p198; ☎215-965-2305; www.nps.gov/inde; Market St, btwn 3rd & 4th Sts, Old City; adult/child $5/2; 🕑9am-5pm, to 7pm late May-early Sep; [S]2nd St) This underground museum is dedicated to Franklin's storied life as a printer (he started the nation's first newspaper), inventor (Bifocals! Lightning rods!) and political figure who signed the Declaration of Independence. The exhibition, divided into five areas, with each focusing on a particular trait of the man, is inventively laid out with interactive elements and plenty of famous Franklin quotations. In the same courtyard, don't miss the **printing office** (Franklin Court; 🕑10am-5pm) [FREE], where park rangers demonstrate an 18th-century printing press similar to that used by Franklin.

Liberty Bell Center — HISTORIC SITE

(Map p198; ☎215-965-2305; www.nps.gov/inde; 526 Market St, Old City; 🕑9am-5pm, to 7pm late May-early Sep; [S]5th St) [FREE] A glass-walled building protects this icon of Philadelphia history from the elements. You can peek from outside, or join the line to file past, reading about the history and significance of the 2080lb object along the way. The line – and it can be a long one in peak summer months – starts on the building's north end.

The gist of the story: originally called the State House Bell, it was made in 1751, to commemorate the 50th anniversary of Pennsylvania's constitution. Mounted in Independence Hall (p184), it tolled on the first public reading of the Declaration of Independence. The crack developed in the 19th century, and the bell was retired in 1846.

National Museum of American Jewish History   MUSEUM

(Map p198; ☎215-923-3811; www.nmajh.org; 101 S Independence Mall E; adult/student/child $15/13/ free; ☺10am-5pm Tue-Fri, to 5:30pm Sat & Sun; ⓢ5th St) Covering four floors, with lots of multimedia displays and intriguing items such as Iriving Berlin's piano and a Yiddish typewriter, this excellent museum is a solid introduction to the history and role of Jewish culture in the US, covering everything from entertainment to the Civil Rights movement.

Mother Bethel AME Church   CHURCH

(Map p194; ☎215-925-0616; www.motherbethel.org; 419 St 6th St, Society Hill; ☺10am-3pm Tue-Sat, services 8am & 10:45am Sun; ⓠ12, 40, 57) FREE This major historical building is the birthplace of the African Methodist Episcopal (AME) church and is the oldest piece of real estate continually owned by African Americans in the US. The present church, the fourth on the site, dates from 1889 and features gargoyles on its bell tower. The main chapel on the 2nd floor has beautiful stained-glass windows and magnificent woodwork.

Franklin Square   SQUARE

(Map p198; www.historicphiladelphia.org; Chinatown; ⓢ5th St) Ringed by busy roads, this square – one of the originals from William Penn's masterplan for his new city – feels somewhat cut off from the other sights of the Old City. Nonetheless, you will find a pretty fountain, a carousel ($3) and a mini-golf course (adult/child $9/7), as well as a seasonal burger shack.

Benjamin Franklin Bridge   BRIDGE

(Map p198; www.drpa.org/bridges/ben-franklin -bridge.html; pedestrian entrance 5th St, Old City; ☺walkway 6am-8pm Oct-Apr, until 9pm May-Sep; ⓠ47, ⓢ5th St or Chinatown) For breathtaking views of the city and Delaware River it's possible to walk or cycle across this 1.8-mile,

800,000-ton suspension bride, which was the longest of its type when it was completed in 1926. Designed by Paul Cret, the bridge connects Philadelphia with Camden, New Jersey, and carries both cars and trains. It is most striking when illuminated at night.

While the southern walk and cycleway undergoes an $8-million upgrade during 2018 and much of 2019, the north walkway will be open.

Betsy Ross House   MUSEUM

(Map p198; ☎215-686-1252; http://historicphil adelphia.org; 239 Arch St, Old City; guided tour adult/child $7/6, self-guided tour adult/child $5/4; ☺10am-4pm, closed Mon Jan & Feb; ⓢ2nd St) Legend has it that this is where America's first flag was made, although most historians doubt it – and it's pretty certain that the actual house Ross lived in was next to this one. Even so, it's a highly popular tourist stop. You get to meet 'Betsy Ross' herself: ask her questions and watch her at work on a flag. The tour has a fun 'history mystery' game for kids, as well.

Science History Institute   MUSEUM

(Map p198; ☎215-925-2222; www.sciencehistory. org; 315 Chestnut St, Old City; ☺10am-5pm Tue-Sat; ⓢ5th St) FREE A must-stop for scientists and young explorers, this museum offers not just a look back at the history of chemicals and the materials made from them, but a view into how these products affect our modern lives. Learn about everything from how crayons get their colors to measuring the chemical composition of things in space. The museum is open until 8pm on the first Friday of each month between March and December.

Elfreth's Alley   STREET

(Map p198; ☎215-574-0560; www.elfrethsalley. org; off 2nd St, btwn Arch & Quarry Sts, Old City; tour $5; ☺museum house noon-5pm Fri-Sun Apr-Nov; ⓢ2nd St) FREE This picturesque, cobblestone lane has been occupied since the 1720s, making it America's oldest residential street. The 32 well-preserved Federal and Georgian row houses are inhabited by regular Philadelphians, so be considerate in the narrow space.

Dream Garden   PUBLIC ART

(Map p198; ☎215-238-6450; 601 Walnut St, Old City; ☺8am-6pm Mon-Fri, 10am-1pm Sat; ⓢ5th St) FREE In the east lobby of the Curtis Center is a masterpiece of American craft: a luminous, wall-size Tiffany mosaic of more than 100,000 pieces of glass depicting a lush landscape designed by Maxfield Parrish in 1916.

Greater Philadelphia

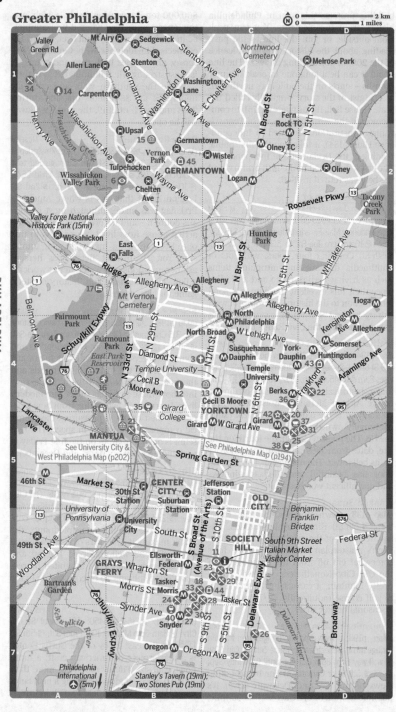

Valley
Green Rd

Mt Airy

Sedgewick

Allen Lane

Stenton

Carpenter

Stenton Ave

Washington
Lane

E Chelten Ave

Chew Ave

Northwood
Cemetery

Melrose Park

Upsal

15

Vernon
Park

Germantown

Wister

45

GERMANTOWN

Fern
Rock TC

Olney TC

Olney

Tulpehocken

Chelten
Ave

6

Wayne Ave

Logan

Roosevelt Pkwy

13

Tacony
Creek
Park

Wissahickon
Valley Park

39

Valley Forge National
Historic Park (15mi)

Wissahickon

East
Falls

1

13

Hunting
Park

Ridge Ave

Allegheny Ave

Allegheny

Allegheny

Allegheny

Allegheny Ave

Tioga

Allegheny

76

17

Mt Vernon
Cemetery

Fairmount
Park

North
Philadelphia

North Broad

W Lehigh Ave

Somerset

Kensington Ave

1

4

Schuylkill Expwy

Fairmount
Park

13

East
Park
Reservoir

Diamond St

3

Susquehanna-
Dauphin

York-
Dauphin

Huntingdon

Aramingo Ave

43

10

76

7

16

Temple University

Cecil B
Moore Ave

12

13

Temple
University

Berks

36

Frankford Ave

22

95

9

2

35

Girard
College

YORKTOWN

Cecil B Moore

42

20

8

1

21

Girard

W Girard Ave

Girard

37

MANTUA

5

41

25

31

38

See University City &
West Philadelphia Map (p202)

See Philadelphia Map (p194)

Spring Garden St

46th St

Market St

30th St
Station

CENTER
CITY

Suburban
Station

Jefferson
Station

OLD
CITY

Benjamin
Franklin
Bridge

676

13

University of
Pennsylvania

University
City

South St

SOCIETY
HILL

Federal St

49th St

Woodland Ave

Ellsworth-
Federal

11

23

South 9th Street
Italian Market
Visitor Center

GRAYS
FERRY

Wharton St

Tasker-
Morris

18

33

44

19

29

Delaware Expwy

Broadway

Bartram's
Garden

76

Morris St

24

Morris

30

28

Tasker St

40

27

Synder Ave

Snyder

Oregon

Oregon Ave

32

95

Schuylkill River

Delaware River

Philadelphia
International
(5mi)

Stanley's Tavern (19mi);
Two Stones Pub (19mi)

Greater Philadelphia

Sights

1 Boathouse Row B5
2 Cedar Grove A4
3 Church of the Advocate B4
4 Fairmount Park A4
5 Fairmount Waterworks B5
6 Historic Rittenhouse Town B2
7 Mount Pleasant A4
8 Philadelphia Zoo A4
9 Please Touch Museum A4
10 Shofuso Japanese House & Garden A4
11 South 9th Street Italian Market C6
12 Staircases & Mountaintops: Ascending Beyond the Dream B4
13 Wagner Free Institute of Science C4
14 Wissahickon Valley Park A1
15 Wyck B2

Activities, Courses & Tours

16 Smith Memorial Playground A4

Sleeping

17 Chamounix Mansion Hostel A3

Eating

18 Brigantessa B6
19 Center City Pretzel Co C6
20 CHeU Fishtown C5
21 Cosmic Cafe at Lloyd Hall B5
22 Furfari's Soft Pretzels D4
23 Geno's Steaks C6
24 Hardena/Waroeng Surabaya B6
25 Joe's Steaks & Soda Shop C5
26 John's Roast Pork C7
27 Le Virtù B7
28 Noord C6
29 Pat's King of Steaks C6
30 Saté Kampar B7
31 Stock D5
32 Tony Luke's C7
33 Townsend B6
34 Valley Green Inn A1

Drinking & Nightlife

35 Crime & Punishment Brewing Co B4
36 Evil Genius Beer Company C4
37 La Colombe Fishtown C5
38 Philadelphia Distilling C5
39 Pilgrim Roasters A2
40 Second District Brewing B7

Entertainment

41 Johnny Brenda's C5
42 Pig Iron Theatre Company C5

Shopping

43 Amalgum Comics & Coffeehouse D4
Fante's Kitchen Shop .... (see 11)
44 Philly Typewriter C6
45 Uncle Bobbie's Coffee & Books B2

Tamanend PUBLIC ART

(Map p198; Front & Market Sts, Old City; [S] 2nd St) Rare are the public artworks dedicated to Native Americans in US cities. This majestic 20ft sculpture by Raymond Sandoval commemorates the chief of the Lenni-Lenape tribe, who welcomed William Penn upon his arrival to Pennsylvania in 1682. Tamanend was considered the patron saint of America prior to Independence and on May 1, Tamanend Day, bells were rung in his honor.

National Constitution Center MUSEUM

(Map p198; ☎215-409-6600; www.constitutioncenter.org; 525 Arch St, Old City; adult/child $14.50/11; ⏰9:30am-5pm Mon-Sat, from noon Sun; [S] 5th St) This whiz-bang museum makes the US Constitution jump off the page, starting with a dramatic theater-in-the-round presentation by a single actor relating the evolution of the American project. This is followed by a dizzying array of interactive exhibits, from voting booths to trivia games. You can also see an original version of the Bill of Rights and be sworn in as president. Go early, both for lighter crowds and a fresher brain – this place is hard to skim through.

Logan Square & Fairmount

★Barnes Foundation MUSEUM

(Map p194; ☎215-278-7200; www.barnesfoundation.org; 2025 Benjamin Franklin Pkwy, Spring Garden; adult/student/child $25/5/free; ⏰10am-5pm Wed-Mon; 🚌7, 32, 33, 38, 48) In the first half of the 20th century, collector and educator Albert C Barnes amassed a remarkable trove of artwork by Cézanne, Degas, Matisse, Renoir, Van Gogh and other European stars. Alongside, he set beautiful pieces of folk art from Africa and the Americas – an artistic desegregation that was shocking at the time. Today's Barnes Foundation is a contemporary shell, inside which is a faithful reproduction of the galleries of Barnes' original mansion (still in the Philadelphia suburbs).

The art is hung according to Barnes' vision, a careful juxtaposition of colors, themes and materials. In one room, all the portraits appear to be staring at a central point. Even more remarkable: you've likely never seen any of these works before, because Barnes' will limits reproduction and lending.

The first Sunday of the month admission is free. Tickets are limited to four per person and there's a focus on family activities.

Parkway Central Library LIBRARY

(Map p194; ☎215-686-5322; www.freelibrary.org; 1901 Vine St, Spring Garden; ⏰9am-9pm Mon-Thu, to 6pm Fri, to 5pm Sat, 1-5pm Sun; ☐27, 32, 33, 38) FREE Worth visiting for its splendid architecture, this main branch of the Free Library of Philadelphia has free tours at 10am on Tuesday, Thursday, Saturday and the first Sunday of the month, and at 2pm on Monday, Wednesday, Friday and Saturday. From Monday to Saturday there's a tour at 11am of the Rare Book Department, with its collection of works and manuscripts relating to Charles Dickens, Edgar Allan Poe and Americana. Also based in the library is the Culinary Literacy Center (www.facebook.com/freelibrarycook), which offers a wide range of programs for those interested in learning about cooking and nutrition.

Fairmount Waterworks MUSEUM

(Map p190; ☎215-685-0723; http://fairmount waterworks.org; 640 Waterworks Dr, East Fairmount Park; admission by donation, tours $10; ⏰10am-5pm Tue-Sat, 1-5pm Sun; ☐32, 38) FREE A National Historic Engineering Landmark, this beautiful Greek Revival complex was built in 1815 and pumped water from the Schuylkill River for the city's consumption until 1909. It was one of Philadelphia's biggest tourist attractions in its day and is still well worth a visit for its excellent interpretative center, where you can learn about the pumping station's history, the area's natural history, and conservation of water resources and the environment. See the website for various guided tours of the center and around the park.

Please Touch Museum MUSEUM

(Map p190; ☎215-581-3181; www.pleasetouchmuseum.org; 4231 Ave of the Republic, West Fairmount Park; $19; ⏰9am-5pm Mon-Sat, 11am-5pm Sun; ☐38) Parents will have a lot of fun at what's definitely a kiddo goldmine: splash around learning about bubbles, race toy cars, wander through a 'wonderland' of trick mirrors and illusions, ride a beautiful antique fairground carousel. Note the arm of the Statue of Liberty…made out of toys!

Memorial Hall is where the 1876 Centennial Exposition was held and is one of the few remaining buildings in the park from that event. Its basement houses a scale-model of the Exposition (costs extra).

Eastern State Penitentiary MUSEUM

(Map p194; ☎215-236-3300; www.easternstate.org; 2027 Fairmount Ave, Fairmount; adult/child $14/10; ⏰10am-5pm; ☐48, 43, 33, 32, 7) The modern prison didn't just happen – it was invented, and Eastern State Penitentiary was the first, opened in 1829 and finally closed in 1971. A self-guided audio tour leads you through the eerie, echoing halls; one stop is Al Capone's famously luxurious cell. There's also info on America's current prison system, and art installations throughout. It's a popular stop, so expect crowds at peak times. From mid-September through Halloween, it hosts a truly terrifying haunted house.

Fairmount Park PARK

(Map p190; https://myphillypark.org; ☐32, 38) FREE The snaking Schuylkill River bisects this 2050-acre green space, the largest city park in the US, splitting it into east and west sections. On either side of the river are cycling and jogging paths, playing fields, lawns, public art and several historic mansions.

In East Fairmount Park you can admire the Victorian-era rowing clubs at Boathouse Row (www.boathouserow.org; 1 Boathouse Row); there's a fine view from the terraces of the Fairmount Waterworks.

West Fairmount Park was the site of the Centennial Exposition in 1876. Memorial Hall, built for the expo, now houses the Please Touch Museum. Nearby is beautiful Shofuso Japanese House & Garden (www.japanesehouse.org; Horticultural Dr; adult/child $12/8; ⏰10am-4pm Wed-Fri, 11am-7pm Sat & Sun Apr-Oct), which is a particular treat in cherry-blossom season. This section of the park also includes the 42-acre Philadelphia Zoo (☎215-243-1100; www.philadelphiazoo.org; 3400 W Girard Ave; adult/child $25/20; ⏰9:30am-5pm Mar-Oct, to 4pm Nov-Feb), the first zoo in the US.

Franklin Institute MUSEUM

(Map p194; ☎215-448-1200; www.fi.edu; 222 N 20th St, Logan Sq; adult/child $23/19, special exhibits extra; ⏰9:30am-5pm; ☐33, 38, 48) You could easily spend the better part of the day touring this world-class science museum. As well as being the venue for temporary blockbuster science exhibitions, there's a planetarium, IMAX cinema and great permanent features such as a giant two-story replica of a beating heart where kids can crawl through the arteries. The institute was founded in 1824 by Benjamin Franklin; a memorial to him in the lobby includes a stunning 20ft-high

WORTH A TRIP

WISSAHICKON VALLEY PARK

Covering 2042 acres, this beautiful, wooded **park** (Map p190; www.fow.org; Valley Green Rd, Wissahickon; 🚆Wissahickon or Tulpehocken) follows the Wissahickon Creek from its confluence with the Schuylkill River up to the city's northwest boundary. With vehicle access to the park mostly banned it's a wonderful spot for hiking, mountain biking or horseback riding. A detailed map of the park is produced by Friends of the Wissahickon.

If you're coming by train, Wissahickon is the station closest to the southern end of the park while Tulpehocken is not far east of the location of the **Historic Rittenhouse Town** (Map p190; ☎215-438-5711; https://rittenhousetown.org; 208 Lincoln Dr, Wissahickon Valley Park; adult/child $5/2.50; 🕒1-5pm Sat & Sun early Jun-end Sep; 🚆Tulpehocken) where the first paper mill in North America was established in the late 17th century. Alternatively, drive into the park along Valley Green Rd and park next to the Valley Green Inn (p210).

marble statue in a rotunda modeled after the Pantheon in Rome. The museum hosts much of the Philadelphia Science Festival (www.philasciencefestival.org) each April.

Rocky STATUE

(Map p194; www.associationforpublicart.org/artwork/rocky; 2600 Benjamin Franklin Pkwy, Fairmount; 🚌32, 38, 43) A major Philly selfie spot is this 1980 work by A Thomas Schomberg of the fictional boxer Rocky Balboa from the 1976 Oscar-winner *Rocky*. The statue was created for a scene in *Rocky III* and had various locations around town before ending up back in its spiritual home here next to the Museum of Art steps in 2006.

👁 Chinatown & Center City East

★Reading Terminal Market MARKET

(Map p194; ☎215-922-2317; www.readingterminalmarket.org; 51 N 12th St; 🕒8am-6pm; [S]11th or 13th St, 🚆Jefferson) Keeping the balance right between food market and dining destination, Reading Terminal Market dates back to 1893 and is a city institution. The 75 local stalls crammed into 75,000 sq ft provide a strong flavor of Philly's cultural melting pot, embracing everything from Pennsylvania Dutch to Thai cuisine and attracting everyone from billionaires to blue-collar workers. Among the many highlights are Bassetts ice cream, Miller's Twist buttery pretzels, DiNic's roast pork sandwiches, and Amish meals at **Dutch Eating Place** (🕒8am-3pm Tue-Wed, to 5pm Thu-Sat). On weekends and around lunch it's very busy; think twice about visiting with small children or large groups (at least with the latter, you can fan out to join different lines).

Join the Taste of Philly Food Tour (p201) for an in-depth look around the market, including tastings.

★Masonic Temple HISTORIC BUILDING

(Map p194; ☎215-988-1917; https://pamasonictemple.org; 1 N Broad St, Center City; adult/child $15/5; 🕒tours 10am, 11pm, 1pm, 2pm & 3pm Tue-Sat; [S]13th, 15th or City Hall) Although the fortress-like exterior of this 1873 building is pretty impressive, it's the spectacular interiors – which took a further 15 years to complete – that really blow visitors away. Fans of secret societies and theatrical design will be in raptures as each meeting room sports an astonishingly detailed theme – Moorish, Egyptian, Renaissance and more. Freemasonry's roots in the city stretch back to colonial times – in the library, where tours of the building start and finish, you can view George Washington's masonic apron. Most of the mural paintings and primary designs are by German immigrant George Herzog. This was also one of the first buildings in the city to be lighted by electricity.

Fabric Workshop & Museum MUSEUM

(Map p194; ☎215-561-8888; http://fabricworkshopandmuseum.org; 1214 Arch St, Center City; suggested donation $5; 🕒10am-6pm Mon-Fri, noon-6pm Sat & Sun; [S]11th or 13th St, 🚆Jefferson) The only such organization of its kind in the US is a wonderful place to discover how creative artists and craftspeople can be with textiles and fabrics. Founded in 1977, it has hosted an artist-in-residence program that has attracted figures of the caliber of Louise Bourgeois, Dale Chihuly and Roy Lichtenstein. Many of the astonishing works can be viewed in the museum as well as bought in the shop.

👁 South Philadelphia

Philadelphia's Magic Gardens GARDENS

(Map p194; ☎215-733-0390; www.phillymagicgardens.org; 1020 South St, Bella Vista; adult/

student/child $10/8/5; 11am-6pm Wed-Mon, to 8pm Fri & Sat Apr-Oct; 23, 40) The ongoing life's work of mosaic mural artist Isaiah Zagar, this is a folk-art wonderland of mirror mosaics, bottle walls and quirky sculpture. Zagar's mosaic murals can be seen around the city – visit here first, and you'll know what to look for. It also hosts small exhibitions of other artists' work with a focus on those who are self-taught and making mosaics or folk-art works.

Between November and March site tours (adult/student/child $15/12/8) are held at 3pm on Saturday and Sunday. Between April

Philadelphia

and October there are walking tours around the area at 3pm Friday through Sunday.

South 9th Street Italian Market MARKET
(Map p190; ☎215-278-2903; http://italianmarketphilly.org; 9th St btwn Fitzwater & Wharton Sts, Bella Vista; ⊗8am-5pm Tue-Sat, to 3pm Sun; ☐47, ⑤Ellsworth-Federal) One of the most vibrant parts of South Philadelphia, this several-blocks-long commercial strip is lined with produce stalls that sell their wares under awnings on the street. Stores include traditional butchers, fishmongers and delis. The northern end is still predominantly Italian;

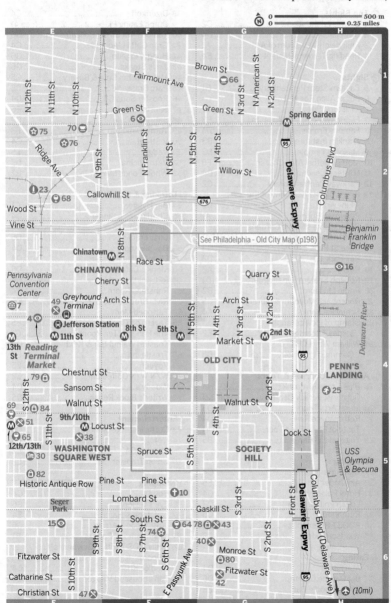

See Philadelphia - Old City Map (p198)

PHILADELPHIA SIGHTS

south of Washington St skews Mexican, so you can pick up tortillas and tortellini in the same trip. Mondays are traditionally a rest day for some vendors, but the market is still open, as are several of the shops. Stop by the **Visitor Center** (919 S 9th St; ☉10am-5pm Mon-Fri, 9am-5pm Sat, 10am-4pm Sun) to pick up a map and discount coupons before shopping.

Philadelphia

Rittenhouse Square & Center City West

★City Hall NOTABLE BUILDING

(Map p194; ☎215-686-2840; www.phlvisitorcenter.com; cnr Broad & Market Sts; tower adult/student $8/4, interior & tower adult/student $15/8; 🕐tower tours every 15min 9:30am-4:15pm, interior tour 12:30pm Mon-Fri; [S]City Hall & 15th St) Completed in 1901 following 30 years of construction, City Hall takes up a whole block, and at 548ft is the world's tallest structure without a steel frame. The view from the observation area immediately beneath the 27-ton bronze statue of William Penn that crowns the tower takes in most of the city (reserve tickets as space is limited). The daily interior tour is a treat, too, and will give you a greater appreciation of this grand building. In winter, there's **ice-skating** (www.rothmaninstitute.com; 1 S 15th St, Center City; adult/child $5/3, skate rental $10; 🕐noon-9pm Mon-Thu, to 11pm Fri, 11am-11pm Sat, 11am-8pm Sun mid-Nov–late Feb) in Dilworth Park on the west side of the plaza.

Mütter Museum MUSEUM

(Map p194; ☎215-560-8564; www.muttermuseum.org; 19 S 22nd St, Rittenhouse; adult/child $18/13; 🕐10am-5pm; 🚌22nd St) Maintained by the College of Physicians, this unique, only-in-Philadelphia attraction is a museum dedicated to rare, odd or disturbing medical conditions. Not for the squeamish, its nonetheless fascinating exhibits include a saponified body, a conjoined female fetus, incredibly realistic wax models of medical conditions, and skulls by the dozen. The College of Physicians also hosts many events in the building, including classical music concerts and lectures – check the website. Note there's $2 off admission on Monday and Tuesday.

Schuylkill Banks PARK

(Map p194; www.schuylkillbanks.org; entrances off Walnut St & 25th St, Schuylkill River; 🚌9, 12, 21, 42, 🚌22nd St) This wonderful outdoor recreation area covers around 8 miles of Schuylkill River, mostly on the east bank from below the Fairmount Dam through the heart of Philadelphia. Dedicated cycling and jogging trails have been created, and various other activities happen throughout the year, including outdoor movie screenings, yoga, and kayak and boat tours – check the website.

Pennsylvania Academy of the Fine Arts MUSEUM

(Map p194; ☎215-972-7600; www.pafa.org; 118-128 N Broad St, Center City; adult/student/child $15/8/free; 🕐10am-5pm Tue-Fri, 11am-5pm Sat & Sun; [S]Race-Vine, City Hall & 15th) This prestigious arts school, founded in 1805, occupies two buildings including a masterwork of Victorian Gothic architecture designed by Frank Furness and George Hewitt. Start your tour of the museum's collection in that building, where the interior design nearly – but not quite – overshadows the works on display. The key piece is *The Gross Clinic* by Thomas Eakins, a former student and later teacher at the academy.

Ownership of this canvas is shared with the Philadelphia Museum of Art (p186), where it will return for five years from 2022. The collection continues in the neighboring contemporary building where you can see temporary exhibitions. Guided tours are held at 1pm and 2pm Thursday to Saturday and are included in the admission fee.

Rosenbach Museum & Library MUSEUM

(Map p194; ☎215-732-1600; https://rosenbach.org; 2008-2010 Delancy Pl, Rittenhouse; adult/child $10/5; 🕐noon-5pm Tue & Fri, to 8pm Wed & Thu, to 6pm Sat & Sun; 🚌17) The list of famous authors in the collection here could fill a book itself: Edgar Allan Poe, James Joyce, Maurice Sendak, George Washington, Lewis Carroll, Bram Stoker…to name a few. If you fancy a peek at *Ulysses*, this is the place. Admission includes a guided tour through the museum and library. Hands-on tours, which allow access to rare and important items not usually on view to the public, are offered at 3pm most Fridays and Sundays (registration two weeks in advance is necessary).

MURAL ARTS PROGRAM

When Philadelphia hired artist Jane Golden in 1984 to assist with tackling a graffiti problem, no one could have realized quite how successful her Mural Arts Program (p201) would eventually become. Today, with some 3000-plus official murals – and countless other unofficial ones – Philadelphia can justifiably lay claim to being the world's largest outdoor art gallery. Street art has been raised to a fine art with professional creatives collaborating on giant painting projects with at-risk youths, current and former prisoners, and just about anyone in the community. Visit the website for a round-up of the murals, with addresses and descriptions of the work.

◉ University City & West Philadelphia

Penn Museum
MUSEUM

(Map p202; ☎215-898-4000; www.penn.museum; 3260 South St, University City; adult/child $15/10; ⊙10am-5pm Tue-Sun, to 8pm first Wed; ▣21, 30, 40, Ⓜ36th St Station) U Penn's magical museum, the largest of its type in the US, contains archaeological treasures from ancient Egypt, Mesopotamia, the Mayan world and more. In April 2018 its new Middle East galleries opened, part of an ongoing transformation of the institution that will see various parts of it under wraps until around 2020. Take a moment or two to admire the building's eclectic 19th-century architecture and design, which includes a Japanese gate, arts-and-crafts brickwork, a rotunda, public gardens, sculptures by Alexander Stirling Calder and a koi pond. The Stoner Courtyard is the location for a series of outdoor summer concerts ($10; ⊙5-8pm Wed mid-Jun–early Sep).

30th St Station
HISTORIC BUILDING

(Map p202; 30th & Market Sts, University City; ⊙24hr; Ⓢ30th St, Ⓡ30th St) FREE The grandness of Graham, Anderson, Probst and White's 1930s design for this station makes

Philadelphia – Old City

N   0 _____ 200 m
     0 _____ 0.1 miles

it worth a visit even if you're not catching a train. The enormous neoclassical station's main concourse, with its coffer 95ft ceiling painted in red, gold and cream, and marble-faced walls, is one of Philadelphia's most impressive spaces. Corinthian columns support *port cochere* (coach gate) on the station's east and west sides.

The east end of the concourse is overlooked by a giant bronze statue: the *Pennsylvania Railroad WWII Memorial* (aka *Angel of Resurrection*) was designed by Walter Hancock, who served in the US army as one of the 'Monuments Men' who recovered art looted by the Nazis. In a room off the concourse's north side look for Karl Bitter's *Spirit of Transportation,* an 1895 sculptural frieze originally commissioned for long-gone Broad St Station.

Philadelphia

Wyck HISTORIC BUILDING

(Map p190; ☎215-848-1690; http://wyck.org; 6026 Germantown Ave, Germantown; garden free, house suggested donation $8; 🕒noon-4pm Thu-Sat Apr-Nov; 🚌23, 🚆Tulpehocken) Set in lovely gardens, which are open year-round, Wyck was the ancestral home of a Germantown family between 1690 and 1973. The house was renovated by William Strickland (architect of the Second Bank of the US and the Merchants' Exchange) in 1824 and is furnished with many original family belongings. Its rose garden, the oldest such garden in its original plan in the US, is planted with 50-plus cultivars of heritage roses.

Fishtown & Northern Liberties

★**Rail Park** PARK

(Map p194; https://therailpark.org; Broad & Noble Sts, Callowhill; [S]Spring Garden: Broad St Line) The old Reading Viaduct is the location of the first phase of this ambitious project to reuse 3 miles of decommissioned rail lines between Fairmount Park and Center City. A bridge over N 13th St has been rebuilt, old rail girders have been incorporated into planters and quotes in different languages are carved into paving stones.

Swing seats on the viaduct section of the park provide great views of Shepard Fairey's mural **The Stamp of Incarceration: James Anderson** (Map p194; www.muralarts.org/artworks/open-source/the-stamp-of-incarceration/; 1131 Callowhill St). Look also for an old train dining car parked at the Broad St end of the park, which is set to be turned into a visitors' center.

Philadelphia – Old City

Top Sights

1 Benjamin Franklin Museum C3
2 Independence Hall B4
3 Independence National Historical Park B2
4 Museum of the American Revolution C4

Sights

5 American Philosophical Society B4
6 Benjamin Franklin Bridge B1
7 Betsy Ross House C2
8 Congress Hall A4
9 Dream Garden A4
10 Elfreth's Alley D2
11 Franklin Court Printing Museum C3
12 Franklin Square A1
13 Liberty Bell Center A3
14 National Constitution Center B2
15 National Museum of American Jewish History B3
16 Science History Institute C3
17 Second Bank of the US B4
18 Tamanend D3

Sleeping

19 Apple Hostels C3
20 Lokal Hotel C2
21 Thomas Bond House B&B D4

Eating

22 City Tavern C4
23 Cuba Libre C3
24 Fork C3
25 Franklin Fountain D3
26 Frieda C4
27 High Street on Market C3
28 Morimoto A3
29 Talula's Daily A4
30 The Bourse B3
31 Zahav C4

Drinking & Nightlife

32 Khyber Pass Pub C3
33 Menagerie Coffee C3

Entertainment

34 Ritz 5 C4
35 Ritz At The Bourse B3
36 Ritz East D4

Shopping

37 Art in the Age C2
38 Shane Confectionery D3

NORTH CENTRAL PHILADELPHIA

Home to the campus of Temple University (www.temple.edu), North Central Philadelphia is a largely African American neighborhood that has a couple of outstanding sights.

The **Wagner Free Institute of Science** (Map p190; ☑ 215-763-6529; www.wagner freeinstitute.org; 1700 W Montgomery Ave, North Central Philadelphia; suggested donation adult/ child \$10/5; ☻9am-4pm Tue-Fri; ⓢCecil B Moore) FREE is home to over 100,000 natural-history specimens, from dinosaur bones and a stuffed saber-toothed cat to starfish and mounted butterflies. All have been preserved just as they were presented in the 1890s by this extraordinary museum's founder William Wagner. No photos are allowed but drawing is encouraged and there's a packed schedule of evening lectures and family-friendly weekend programs – all free.

Three blocks north of the museum it's recommended you call ahead to arrange a visit to the extraordinary **Church of the Advocate** (Map p190; ☑ 215-978-8008; www. churchoftheadvocate.org; 1801 W Diamond St, North Central Philadelphia; ☻visits by appointment, services 10am Sun; ⓢSusquehanna-Dauphin) FREE. A fine example of Gothic Revival architecture, this 1897 Episcopal church was a center of activism during the Civil Rights movement and the site of the National Conference of Black Power in 1968. However, it's for its series of protest art murals by Walter Edmonds and Richard Watson, created in the early 1970s, that the church is most notable. These amazing, occasionally violently in-your-face images place African American experiences and faces at the forefront.

While in the area swing by the Martin Luther King Jr Recreation Center to view the mural **Staircases & Mountaintops: Ascending Beyond the Dream** (Map p190; www.muralarts.org/artworks/staircases-and-mountaintops-ascending-beyond-the-dream/; 2101 Cecil B Moore Ave, North Philadelphia West; ⓢCecil B Moore). This huge black-and-white image is based on a photograph by William Lovelace, showing MLK and his wife, Coretta Scott King, leading a voting rights march from Selma to Montgomery, AL, in March 1965.

Edgar Allan Poe National Historic Site
HISTORIC SITE

(Map p194; ☑ 215-597-8780; www.nps.gov/edal; 532 N 7th St, Poplar; ☻9am-5pm Fri-Sun; ⓢSpring Garden: Market-Frankford Line) FREE Often called the creator of the horror story, Edgar Allan Poe lived for six years in Philadelphia, in five different houses. This historic site, his only Philly home still remaining, is now a small but interesting museum, with a lot of original items and restored rooms. Don't miss the creepy brick cellar (complete with cobwebs) thought to have inspired Poe's masterwork 'The Black Cat.' A statue of a raven stands outside.

Rodeph Shalom Synagogue
SYNAGOGUE

(Map p194; ☑ 215-627-6747; https://rodephsha lom.org; 615 N Broad St, Poplar; donation \$5; ☻by appointment; ⓢSpring Garden: Broad Street Line) Home to the oldest Jewish Ashkenazi congregation in the US, Rodeph Shalom is one of the most beautiful pieces of religious architecture in Philadelphia. The 1927 building, designed by Simon & Simon, features Babylonian and Assyrian patterns on its exterior, while the spectacular domed interior is a riot of stenciled mosaics, gilt and stained glass with Byzantine and Moorish allusions.

Historians bemoan the fact that a Frank Furness–designed synagogue was torn down in the 1920s to create this building. Photos of the Furness building hang in the synagogue's contemporary main entrance, added in 2015, which also includes an interesting Museum of Jewish Art.

🏃 Activities

Philadelphia offers fantastic options for cyclists and joggers, especially once you escape traffic-clogged Center City. There are several places in which you can learn skills, such as cooking, pottery or a new language. Or you can relax with activities such as outdoor yoga at lovely spots including **Race Street Pier** (Map p194; www.delawareriverwaterfront.com; Race St & Delaware Ave, Penn's Landing; ☻7am-11pm; ⓢ2nd St) and **Schuylkill Banks Park** (Map p194; https://yogaonthebanks.com; 25th & Locust St entrance, Schuylkill Banks; suggested donation \$5; ☻11am Sat & Sun, 6:30pm Tue May-Nov).

Blue Cross Riverrink
SKATING

(Map p194; ☑ 215-925-7465; www.riverrink.com; 101 S Columbus Blvd, Penn's Landing; admission free, skating \$3, skate rental \$10; ☻1-11pm Mon-Thu, to 1am Fri, 11am-1pm Sat, 11am-11pm Sun;

S 2nd St) From December to March, Winterfest sees this dual-purpose rink covered with ice for skating, activities, food stalls, performances and other events, while from Memorial Day to Labor Day, Summerfest takes place here with rollerskating.

Smith Memorial Playground PLAYGROUND
(Map p190; 215-765-4325; http://smithplay ground.org; 3500 Reservoir Dr, East Fairmount Park; ⊙10am-4pm Tue-Sun Oct-Mar; 10am-6pm Tue-Fri, to 7pm Sat & Sun Apr-Sep; 32) A boon to parents seeking to entertain kids of 10 years or younger, this playground and playhouse has been serving the community since 1899. The 6.5-acre playground includes a giant wooden slide, swings, a giant net climber and many other pieces of play equipment.

In the Playhouse, children aged five and younger can take part in activities such as riding a train, messing around in a room full of kid-sized cars and tricycles with real traffic lights, and playing with puppets. Check the website for details of programs and events throughout the year.

☞ Tours

Mural Arts Tours TOURS
(Map p194; 215-925-3633; www.muralarts.org/ tours; 118-128 N Broad St, Center City; tours $23-32; S Race-Vine or City Hall & 15th St) The best way to appreciate the transformative nature of the Mural Arts Program across Philadelphia is to join one of its guided tours of the city's numerous outdoor murals. Walking and trolley tours are held between April and Thanksgiving, while in the colder months you can join the excellent Love Letters tour, which use the subway.

The Mural Mile, a free self-guided tour and map, is available online.

Taste of Philly Food Tour FOOD & DRINK
(Map p194; 800-838-3006, 215-545-8007; www. tasteofphillyfoodtour.com; Reading Terminal Market, 51 N 12th St, Center City; adult/child $17/10; ⊙10am Wed & Sat; S 11th or 13th) Snack and learn Philly food lore during this 75-minute tour around Reading Terminal Market with food writer Carolyn Wyman. Reservations are recommended, particularly in busy holiday periods, but you can also just turn up at the meeting point at the market's Welcome Desk, by the entrance on 12th and Filbert.

Philly Brew Tours FOOD & DRINK
(215-866-2337; www.citybrewtours.com; tours $70-99) Around a dozen city microbreweries are on the itineraries offered by this craft-

beer tour company. Their tours last between three and five hours and include three to four stops, depending on the option you go for.

Liberty Brew Tours FOOD & DRINK
(267-606-7403; www.libertybrewtours.com; tours $90) Three local craft-beer enthusiasts are behind these tours, which take in a selection of microbreweries in and around the city, as well as further afield in Bucks County.

✷ Festivals & Events

★ Mummers Parade CARNIVAL
(http://phillymummers.com; ⊙Jan 1) Uniquely Philly: a cross between Mardi Gras and a marching band competition, the elaborate costumes, music and deep lore of the various mummer divisions and brigades make this a must-see in the bracing cold of winter. The parade starts by City Hall and moves down Broad St to finish at Washington Ave.

Wawa Welcome America! CULTURAL
(https://welcomeamerica.com; ⊙Jun & Jul) Philadelphia pulls out all the stops for this week-long festival celebrating the country's Independence. It culminates in giant fireworks displays on July 4 over Penn's Landing and the Philadelphia Museum of Art.

Fringe Festival PERFORMING ARTS
(www.fringearts.com; ⊙mid-Sep) Running since 1996, the Fringe Festival sees 17 days in mid-September packed with performance art, events, productions and creative craziness.

🛌 Sleeping

Because central Philadelphia is so compact, choosing the area to be based in is generally not much of an issue. Most hotels, including plenty of national chains, are in busy, business district Center City; competition keeps a cap on rates, but do book ahead for busy times of the year such as holidays and graduations. A smattering of B&Bs can be found across the Schuylkill River near University City.

🛌 Old City & Society Hill

★ Apple Hostels HOSTEL $
(Map p198; 215-922-0222; www.applehos tels.com; 33 Bank St, Old St; dm/d with shared bathroom from $26/80; ✱@❀; S 2nd St) The Old City's best hostel is hidden down an alley and spans both sides of the street. The apple-green color scheme fits the name, but this Hosteling International–affiliated place

is also strong on details: two spotless kitchens, lounges and a library, plus power outlets in lockers, USB ports and reading lights at every bed, free coffee and earplugs.

There are male, female and coed dorms, plus eight private rooms. The friendly staff run nightly activities such as walking tours, pasta nights and a Thursday bar crawl.

★Thomas Bond House B&B B&B **$$**
(Map p198; ☎215-923-8523; www.thomasbondhousebandb.com; 129 S 2nd St, Old City; r from $135; 🚭❄📶; [S]2nd St) Though this charming four-story brick building does not have an elevator, you have to accept certain things to stay in a house built in 1769 by celebrated Philadelphia physician Dr Thomas

University City & West Philadelphia

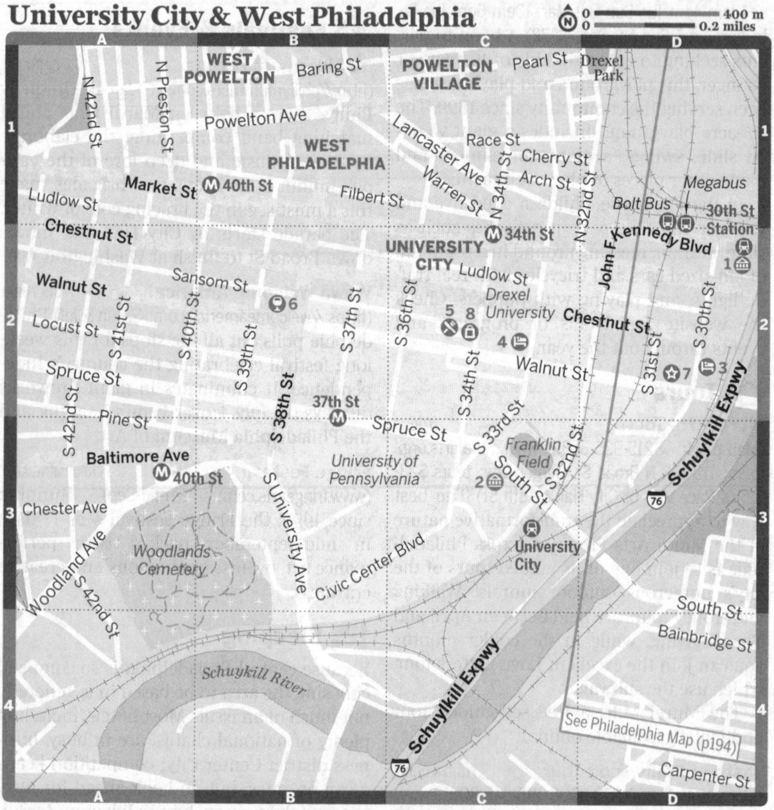

University City & West Philadelphia

Sights
1 30th St Station....D2
2 Penn Museum....C3

Sleeping
3 AKA University City....D2
4 Study at University City....C2

Eating
5 White Dog Cafe....C2

Drinking & Nightlife
6 City Tap House....B2

Entertainment
Summer Nights Concert Series....(see 2)
7 World Cafe Live....D2

Shopping
8 Penn Book Center....C2

Bond. The 12 rooms are all different, some with fireplaces and some with four-post beds, all with period furniture.

Lokal Hotel
BOUTIQUE HOTEL **$$**

(Map p198; [📞]267-702-4345; https://staylokal. com; 139 N 3rd St, Old City; 1-/2-bedroom apts from $195/240; [§]2nd St) A boutique hotel for the Airbnb generation. There's no front desk for the six self-catering units stacked above a trendy barbershop. Everything is managed remotely with apps and devices, but staff are happy to show up in person at your super-chic design pad should you need them.

🛏 Logan Square & Fairmount

Chamounix Mansion Hostel
HOSTEL **$**

(Map p190; [📞]215-878-3676; www.philahostel.org; 3250 Chamounix Dr, West Fairmount Park; dm$22, r with kitchen $55; [⊘]closed Dec 15-Jan 15; [P][@][🛜]; [🚌]38 & 40) In a lovely wooded area of Fairmount Park, this handsome Hosteling International hostel is best for guests with their own transport. In its public areas, set with antiques, harp, oriental rugs and paintings, the place is more like a B&B than a hostel; the dorms themselves are basic. There's also a great communal kitchen and free bicycles for getting around. A downside is that the building is closed (and all guests have to leave) between 11am and 4:30pm and there's a 2am curfew, not that you'd want to be wandering around this isolated part of the park at that hour. The hostel is also closed from December 15 for a month. From the bus stop on the corner of Ford and Cranston Rds it's around a 1-mile walk to the hostel, which is at the end of Chamounix Dr.

Logan Philadelphia
HOTEL **$$$**

(Map p194; [📞]215-963-1500; http://curiocollec tion3.hilton.com; 1 Logan Sq, Logan Sq; r from $300; [⊖][@][🛜][🏊][🐾]; [🚌]) Custom art installations and a courtyard with fountain greet you on arrival at this comfortable and supremely well-placed hotel that is literally steps from some of the city's top tourist attractions. It's part of the Hilton Hotel group, so you can expect a certain level of comfort and amenities, which include a good-sized gym and small swimming pool.

🛏 Rittenhouse Square & Center City West

AKA Rittenhouse
APARTMENT **$$**

(Map p194; [📞]215-825-7000; www.stayaka.com/ aka-rittenhouse-square; 135 S 18th St, Rittenhouse;

apt from $200; [⊖][✳][@][🛜]; [🚌]9, 12, 21, 42, [🚇]19th St) Reopened following a building renovation in 2018, this branch of the upscale rental apartment operation offers studios through to penthouses in a lovely beaux-arts building steps from Rittenhouse Sq. Its chic minimalist style has bags of appeal and there's the well-regarded a.kitchen+bar on the ground floor, should you need a meal or drink. Rates include complimentary access to a nearby gym with a pool.

Windsor Suites
HOTEL **$$**

(Map p194; [📞]215-981-5678; www.thewindsor suites.com; 1700 Benjamin Franklin Pkwy, Center City; ste from $125; [P][⊖][✳][@][🛜][🏊][🐾]; [§]City Hall & 15th St, [🚇]Suburban) The comfortable and roomy suites here come with full kitchens; some also have balconies. There are options for extended stays or monthly rentals, as well as good facilities, including a rooftop pool (May to mid-September). Staff are friendly and the hotel allows pets to stay free (they even get their own amenities).

ROOST Rittenhouse
APARTMENT **$$**

(Map p194; [📞]267-469-0349; http://myroost. com/rittenhouse; 1831 Chestnut St, Rittenhouse; apt from $245; [P][⊖][✳][🛜][🐾]; [🚌]9, 17, 21, 42, trolley 19th St) These ROOST luxe apartments have a great location on Chestnut St and are available in generous sizes from studios to two bedrooms. They are usually rented for a minimum of seven to 10 days and come with full kitchens, washer/dryers, 24-hour services, amenities and access to a local gym.

★Rittenhouse Hotel
HOTEL **$$$**

(Map p194; [📞]215-546-9000; www.rittenhouse hotel.com; 210 W Rittenhouse Sq, Rittenhouse; d from $400; [P][⊖][✳][@][🛜][🏊][🐾]; [🚌]9, 12, 17, 21, 42) Rooms at this five-star – excuse us, make that five-*diamond* – hotel on Rittenhouse Sq have marble baths. Of the downtown options with a half-Olympic–sized pool, this is one of the nicest. It serves a top-notch brunch and a soothing afternoon tea service with music. Thursdays through Saturdays a live jazz band plays in the library bar.

★Hotel Palomar
DESIGN HOTEL **$$$**

(Map p194; [📞]215-563-5006; www.hotelpalo mar-philadelphia.com; 117 S 17th St, Rittenhouse; r from $260; [P][✳][🛜][🐾]; [§]City Hall & 15th St, [🚇]Suburban) One of Philadelphia's two hotels in the excellent Kimpton chain, the Palomar offers stylish rooms with a jokey elegance that includes leopard-spot bathrobes. Nice touches include yoga mats in all rooms and free bicycles (on a first-come, first-served basis).

🛏 Chinatown & Center City East

★ Alexander Inn
BOUTIQUE HOTEL $$

(Map p194; ☎215-923-3535; www.alexanderinn. com; 301 S 12th St, Midtown Village; s/tw/d from $125/139/139; ❄❇@🛜; 🚇23, 40) Online photos undersell this place. The impeccably kept rooms have a subdued, slightly vintage style; some have old-fashioned half-size tubs. Original architectural details – including stained-glass windows, oak moldings, marble-tiled floors – add to the atmosphere.

The included continental breakfast is convenient, and free snacks are available throughout the day.

🛏 University City & West Philadelphia

★ AKA University City
APARTMENT $$

(Map p202; ☎215-372-9000; www.stayaka.com; 2929 Walnut St, University City; 1-bed apt from $208; 🅿❇@🛜♿; 🚇21, 42, 🚆30th St) All of the rental units on the upper 18 floors of Cira Centre South have spectacular views. However it's the sophisticated looks inside that will capture your attention. Rooms are spacious, contemporary and equipped with full kitchens. With facilities including an Olympic-length pool, gym, yoga studio (with free classes) and lovely lounge, you might never want to leave.

Study at University City
BOUTIQUE HOTEL $$

(Map p202; ☎215-387-1400; www.thestudyatuni versitycity.com; 20 S 33rd St, University City; d from $210; ❄❇@🛜; 🚇21, 30, 42) This snazzy hotel is right smack in the middle of everything University City has to offer. Rooms sport contemporary design and are spacious, as is the lobby, which functions as a common area where people meet, read, chat and work. You can grab breakfast at the attached stylish restaurant and lounge.

The brass spectacles outside fit the 'study' theme. Parts of the lobby have museum-quality works of art on display.

🍴 Eating

Reflecting its tradition of welcoming folks from far and wide, Philadelphia has an incredibly diverse, vibrant food scene. German and Italian heritages are predominant, but these days they're part of a brilliant mix that runs the gamut from Burmese noodles to vegan delights. Whether you're in search of the ideal cheesesteak or a James Beard Award winner, Philly delivers.

Foodies should zone in on the hot restaurant strips of E Passyunk Ave, between Dickinson and McKean Sts in South Philadelphia, and Frankford Ave in Fishtown. You'll also find plenty of choice and many top spots in Center City, particularly in Midtown Village and the Gayborhood, and Chinatown.

For cheap eats, including the legendary Philly cheesesteak, South St is a go-to spot. Bargain eats are also a feature of University City, as are food trucks. In fact food trucks are a common sight across the city; Food Truck Nation (www.foodtrucknation.us) has found Philadelphia to be among the top five friendliest cities in the US for these mobile meal outlets.

🍴 Old City & Society Hill

Frieda
CAFE $

(Map p198; ☎215-600-1291; http://friedaforgen erations.com; 320 Walnut St, Old City; mains $7.50-13.50; ⊙8am-5pm Tue-Fri, 9am-4:30pm Sat & Sun; 🛜; 🚆5th St) This awesome place aims to connect people of all ages to eat, drink, share and learn something new. It doesn't like to be labeled as one thing or another, but we can assure you it's a great spot for anything from an artisanal tea served with freshly baked cakes and pastries, to a healthy lunch or brunch. Check online for their monthly schedule of drop-in classes including those dedicated to drawing, learning a language or learning how to play games such as mahjongg. They screen films with discussions afterwards and host good-value set dinners a couple of times a month. Not to be missed.

Franklin Fountain
ICE CREAM $

(Map p198; ☎215-627-1899; www.franklinfoun tain.com; 116 Market St, Old City; sundaes $10-12; ⊙noon-midnight Mon-Thu, from 11am Fri-Sun; 🚆2nd St) It's cash only at this fantastic yet kitsch-free throwback, from the phosphates and vintage ice-cream flavors (try the teaberry) right down to the ancient telephone and the carton cups. In a nod to modern sensibilities there are vegan ices and treats, too. Also check out the same company's equally old-school Shane Confectionery (p215) down the block.

The Bourse
FOOD HALL $

(Map p198; ☎215-625-0300; http://thebourse philly.com; 111 S Independence Mall E, Old City;

🍴 University City & West Philadelphia

★White Dog Cafe AMERICAN $$
(Map p202; ☎215-386-9224; www.whitedog.com; 3420 Sansom St, University City; dinner mains $18-29; ⏰11:30am-9:30pm Mon-Fri, 10am-10pm Sat, 10am-9pm Sun; 🚌30, 42, [S]34th St) If the dozen Boston terriers on the wall seem incongruous with the food, don't worry: this place has been serving farm-to-table since 1983. Come here for your truffles and artisanal cheeses, peak summer tomatoes and plenty more. Yes, the Greyhound is the signature drink. Need you have asked?

🍴 Rittenhouse Square & Center City West

Rooster Soup Co AMERICAN $
(Map p194; ☎215-454-6939; www.roostersoupcompany.com; 1526 Sansom St, Center City; mains $6-13; ⏰11am-8pm Mon-Fri, 10am-8pm Sat & Sun; [S]City Hall & 15th St, 🚆Suburban) Its chicken soup with smoked matzo balls is legendary, and it's great that you can rock up anytime for the all-day brunch items. But the best part of this basement-level classic-styled diner is that 100% of its profits support vulnerable locals through the volunteer kitchen charity Broad Street Ministry.

Mark your calendar for their karaoke parties held on the last Saturday of the month from 8pm to 1am. On weekends they also offer bottomless Bloody Marys or mimosas for $15.

Metropolitan Cafe & Bakery CAFE $
(Map p194; ☎215-545-6655; www.metropolitanbakery.com; 262 S 19th St, Rittenhouse; sandwiches from $9.50, pizza $15-17; ⏰7:30am-7pm Mon-Fri, 8am-6pm Sat & Sun; 🚌9, 12, 17, 21, 42) Great breads, tender pastries and good coffee make for a perfect breakfast or lunch at this flagship location of Metropolitan. It's also famous for its granola. The cafe here is closed on Monday.

There are several other locations around town including a branch in Reading Terminal Market (p193).

★V Street VEGAN $$
(Map p194; ☎215-278-7943; http://vstreetfood.com; 126 S 19th St, Rittenhouse; mains $13-14; ⏰5-10pm Mon-Thu, 11am-3pm & 5-10pm Fri-Sun; 🌱; 🚌9, 17 21, 42, 🚋19th St) Street food from around the world is the influence for the fab vegan menu here. Make sure you sample the delicious *dan dan* noodles, in which the spices are not dialed down; you will break out in a sweat in a good way. There are plenty of counter seats for single diners.

V Street is managed by the same team behind Vedge; they also operate the **Wiz Kid** cafe next door, serving vegan versions of cheesesteak sandwiches.

Abe Fisher JEWISH $$
(Map p194; ☎215-867-0088; http://abefisherphilly.com; 1623 Sansom St, Rittenhouse; small plates $13-18, 3-course prix-fixe $39; ⏰5-10pm Mon-Thu, to 11pm Fri & Sat, to 9pm Sun; [S]City Hall & 15th St, 🚆Suburban) Chef Yehuda Sichel's menu riffs on the foods of the Jewish diaspora, offering quirky, punchy takes on staples such as cholent (a beef stew) served as a potpie, and veal schnitzel in tacos. It's all small plates, shareable and with free-flowing sparkling water.

Next door, under the same ownership, is equally hot snack bar **Dizengoff** (☎215-867-8181; http://dizengoffhummus.com; 1625 Sansom St, Rittenhouse; hummus from $10; ⏰10:30am-7pm; 🌱), for hummus straight out of Tel Aviv.

★Gran Caffè L'Aquila ITALIAN $$$
(Map p194; ☎215-568-5600; http://grancaffelaquila.com; 1716 Chestnut St, Rittenhouse; mains $18-30; ⏰7am-10pm Mon-Thu, to 11pm Fri, 8am-11pm Sat, to 10pm Sun, bar open 1hr later; 🚌9, 21, 42, 🚋19th St) Mamma mia, this is impressive Italian food. Not only are the flavors everything you could ask for, one of the owners is an award-winning gelato maker and the 2nd floor has its own gelato factory. Some of the main courses even have savory gelato as a garnish. Coffee is house-roasted and the dapper waitstaff are eager to please.

The three co-owners came here after their village in Italy was destroyed by a 2014 earthquake. Reservations are highly recommended.

Parc Brasserie FRENCH $$$
(Map p194; ☎215-545-2262; www.parc-restaurant.com; 227 S 18th St, Rittenhouse; mains from $23; ⏰7:30am-11pm, to midnight Fri, 10am-midnight Sat, to 10pm Sun; 🚌9, 12, 17, 21, 42) Soak up the elegant Rittenhouse Sq vibe at this enormous, polished bistro right on the park. Dinner is a little steep, but brunch and lunch are good value, and prime people-watching time. For dessert, try the beer float (lambic, to get technical). Yum!

CLASSIC PHILLY FLAVOR: CHEESESTEAKS & SANDWICHES

If there's one thing you must eat while in town its a cheesesteak. Philadelphians argue over the nuances of these hot sandwiches comprised of thin-sliced, griddle-cooked beef on a chewy roll: there are pork, chicken and even vegan versions available, but die-hard fans will tell you that only the classic beef really qualifies. And don't get people started on where the best one is to be found – there's as many opinions on this as there are areas of the city.

What a visitor most needs to know is how to order. First say the kind of cheese you want – prov (provolone), American (melty yellow) or whiz (molten orange Cheez Whiz). Then 'wit' (with) or 'widdout' (without), referring to fried onions: 'Prov wit,' for example, or 'whiz widdout. And if it's a take-out place, have your money ready – cheesesteak vendors are famously in a hurry.

Pat's King of Steaks (Map p190; 215-468-1546; www.patskingofsteaks.com; 1237 E Passyunk Ave, Passyunk Sq; cheesesteak $11; 24hr; 45, 47, Ellsworth-Central) Invented the cheesesteak, way back in 1930.

Jim's Steaks (Map p194; 215-928-1911; www.jimssouthstreet.com; 400 South St, Queen Village; sandwiches $10; 10am-1am Mon-Thu, to 3am Fri & Sat, from 11am Sun; 40, 47, 57) 'Pizza steak' – topped with tomato sauce – is an option, as are hoagies (cold-cut sandwiches on long rolls).

Tony Luke's (Map p190; 215-551-5725; www.tonylukes.com; 39 E Oregon Ave, South Philadelphia; sandwiches $7.50-11; 8am-midnight Mon-Thu, 6am-2am Fri & Sat, 11am-8pm Sun; 57) Famous for its roast pork sandwich, it also does a great veggie-only version.

John's Roast Pork (Map p190; 215-463-1951; www.johnsroastpork.com; 14 E Snyder Ave, Pennsport; sandwiches $6-12; 9am-7pm Tue-Sat; 25, 79) Classic, cash-only joint in business since 1930.

Joe's Steaks & Soda Shop (Map p190; 215-423-5637; http://joessteaks.com; 1 W Girard Ave, Fishtown; cheesesteak from $6.75; 11am-10pm Sun-Wed, to midnight Thu, to 3am Fri & Sat; Girard: Market-Frankford Line) Eat in or take-away at this Fishtown joint that offers a vegan cheesesteak.

Geno's Steaks (Map p190; 215-389-0659; www.genosteaks.com; 1219 S 9th St, Passyunk Sq; cheesesteak from $10; 24hr; 45, 47, Ellsworth-Federal) With a dazzling sign on a triangular street corner, it's hard to miss.

South Philadelphia

Hardena/ Waroeng Surabaya
INDONESIAN $
(Map p190; 215-271-9442; www.facebook.com/pg/hardena.waroengsurabaya; 1754 S Hicks St, Newbold; mains from $8; 11:30am-8:30pm Wed-Mon; Tasker-Morris) Short of a trip to Jakarta you are unlikely to find better authentic Indonesian food than that served at James Beard–nominated Hardena. Order at the counter the superb-value rice plates with a choice of two dishes, or go the whole hog with a *rijsttafel* platter ($25) that includes eight dishes plus crackers and satay.

Chairs on casters and plastic cutlery are quirks that add to the charm.

Saté Kampar
MALAYSIAN $
(Map p190; 267-324-3860; www.facebook.com/satekampar; 1837 E Passyunk Ave, East Passyunk; mains $12-15; 11:30am-2:30pm & 5-10pm; Snyder) You will not find more authentic or delicious Malaysian food in Philadelphia than that served here. Skewers of meat or tofu are grilled to order and come with a classic Malay peanut sauce or a Hainanese sauce sweetened with pineapple.

Sabrina's Cafe
BREAKFAST $
(Map p194; 215-574-1599; www.sabrinascafe.com; 910 Christian St, Bella Vista; breakfast $10-14; 8am-5pm; 47, Ellsworth-Federal) Sabrina's made its name here in the Italian Market area with its brunch: stuffed French toast, gooey pork sandwiches or, for the daring, the 'Barking Chihuahua' – in short, what you need to ease into the day, in a pret-

ty atmosphere. But do be prepared for a long wait (anything up to an hour) for a table at weekends.

There's also a **Fairmount branch** (Map p194; 📋 215-636-9061; 1804 Callowhill St, Spring Garden; breakfast $10-14; ⏰ 8am-10pm Tue-Sat, to 4pm Sun & Mon), near Benjamin Franklin Parkway.

Big Gay Ice Cream   ICE CREAM $
(Map p194; 📋 267-886-8024; www.biggayice cream.com; 1351 South St, Center City; ice cream from $4; ⏰ noon-10pm Sun-Thu, to 11pm Fri & Sat; ⓢ Lombard-South Station) Ranked one of the best ice creams in the world, Big Gay Ice Cream is not a Philly original (it's NYC-based), but who can resist the lure of its signature 'Salty Pimp' cone: vanilla, dulce de leche and a chocolate shell. The descriptions are as double-entendre-filled as the cones are good, so prepare for chuckles as you peruse the menu.

★ **Noord**   EUROPEAN $$
(Map p190; 📋 267-909-9704; www.noordphilly. com; 1046 Tasker St, East Passyunk; mains $19-28; ⏰ 5-10pm Wed & Thu, to 10:30pm Fri & Sat, 11am-2pm & 5-9pm Sun; 🚌 45, 47, ⓢ Tasker-Morris) Think Dutch comfort food rather than new-Scandi cuisine at this welcoming BYOB just off the main E Passyunk drag. Jovial Netherlands-born chef Joncarl Lachman offers dishes such as *gehaktballen* (sirloin meatballs) and herring sliders, and makes a very generous and delicious seafood stew.

There are many tempting and out-of-the-ordinary options on the Sunday brunch menu, too, such as vinegar-braised beef with Gouda.

Hungry Pigeon   AMERICAN $$
(Map p194; 📋 215-278-2736; www.hungrypigeon. com; 743 S 4th St, Queen Village; mains $16-28, 4-course dinner $45; ⏰ 7am-11pm Mon-Thu, to midnight Fri, 9am-midnight Sat & Sun; 🚌 40, 57) Although it's a pleasant spot for breakfast or a drink at its bar, Hungry Pigeon comes into its own for dinner, when chefs Scott Schroeder and Pat O'Malley flex their culinary talents. You can let them choose what to serve or pick from dishes that may include roasted beet salad, pasta fagioli or a pot roast.

Famous 4th Street Delicatessen   DELI $$
(Map p194; 📋 215-922-3274; www.famous4th streetdelicatessen.com; 700 S 4th St, Queen Village; sandwiches $18-24; ⏰ 8am-9pm; 🚌 40, 57) In business since 1923, this corner Jewish deli

is famous for its monster-sized sandwiches, big enough for two to share. The menu is a roll-call of Jewish soul food, from chopped liver to hot corned beef and even matzoh brei (an omelet made with matzoh).

★ **Le Virtù**   ITALIAN $$$
(Map p190; 📋 215-271-5626; http://levirtu.com; 1927 E Passyunk Ave, East Passyunk; mains $23-36, degustation menu from $45; ⏰ 5-10pm Mon-Thu, to 10:30pm Fri & Sat, 4-9:30pm Sun; ⓢ Snyder) Chef Joe Cicala is dedicated, obsessively so, to the cuisine of Abruzzo, the region east of Rome, where he long studied with home cooks. Old-school ways are married wherever possible with the cream of local produce. Tuesdays are BYOB.

Cicala also runs more casual **Brigantessa** (Map p190; 📋 267-318-7341; www.brigantes samenu.com; 1520 E Passyunk Ave, East Passyunk; pizzas $16, mains $26; ⏰ 5pm-midnight Mon-Fri, noon-midnight Sat & Sun; 🚌 45, 47, ⓢ Tasker-Morris) up the street, with a broader menu that includes pizzas.

Townsend   FRENCH $$$
(Map p190; 📋 267-639-3203; www.townsend restaurant.com; 1623 E Passyunk Ave, East Passyunk; mains $28-34; ⏰ 5pm-2am Wed-Sun; 🚌 47, ⓢ Tasker-Morris) Townsend Wentz's elegant, white-tablecloth restaurant is a dream date spot. Service is excellent and the food is delicious if sometimes a little skimpy on the portions. If you're hankering for dishes such as a melt-in-the-mouth seared foie gras or a perfectly roasted barramundi, then you won't be disappointed.

🍴 Fishtown & Northern Liberties

★ **Stock**   SOUTHEAST ASIAN $$
(Map p190; 📋 302-559-4872; www.stockphilly. com; 308 E Girard Ave, Fishtown; 🥢; ⓢ Girard: Market-Frankford Line) At this no-frills BYOB it's all about the taste of the food – which is delicious and authentic. Piquant salads, such as the Burmese gin thoke or Vietnamese-style green papaya, come piled high, while steaming large bowls of noodles are lovingly made and packed with flavor.

★ **CHeU Fishtown**   ASIAN $$
(Map p190; 📋 267-758-2269; www.cheufishtown. com; 1416 Frankford Ave, Fishtown; noodles $12-14; ⏰ noon-3pm & 5-10pm Mon-Thu, to 11pm Fri, noon-11pm Sat, noon-10pm Sun; ⓢ Girard: Market-Frankford Line) Asian buns, dumplings and noodles

DON'T MISS

SOFT PRETZELS

You can thank the early German settlers of Pennsylvania for the city's soft pretzels, a beloved breakfast snack served from food trucks and in cafes and takeaways across the city. Get them fresh from the factory at **Center City Pretzel Co** (Map p190; ☎215-463-5664; www.centercitypretzel.com; 816 Washington Ave, Passyunk Sq; pretzel 40¢; ⏰4am-noon Mon-Sat, 6:30-10:30am Sun; 🚌47, [S]Ellsworth-Federal) and **Furfari's Soft Pretzels** (Map p190; ☎267-884-4204; 2025 Frankford Ave, Kensington; pretzel 40¢; ⏰1am-noon Mon-Sat; [M]Berks).

with a Jewish mama's twist (smoked matzo balls and brisket in the ramen, for example) have made CHeU a hit. The fusion dishes taste great and the funky diner-meets-punk-street-art feel of the place is appealing.

🍴 Philadelphia

★Valley Green Inn AMERICAN $$
(Map p190; ☎215-247-1730; www.valleygreeninn.com; Valley Green Rd, Wissahickon Valley Park; mains $14-29; ⏰noon-3pm & 4-8pm Nov-Apr, noon-4pm & 5-10pm May-Oct; 🚆St Martins) The welcome couldn't be warmer at this idyllic creekside inn that dates back to the 1850s and appears little changed since then. The menu is stacked with classic American comfort food such as grilled-cheese sandwiches, crab cakes and bacon-wrapped meatloaf, all done supremely well. Call ahead to make a booking as it's a popular wedding venue and can be very busy on weekends.

🍷 Drinking & Nightlife

In this city with strong working-class pride, dive bars and pubs are well-represented, but so are slick cocktail lounges, wine bars, craft breweries and gastropubs. Philly's Old City boasts the highest concentration of liquor licenses in the US after New Orleans. For LGBT nightspots, head to the 'Gayborhood'; look for the rainbow-trimmed street signs between Chestnut, Pine, Juniper and 11th Sts.

🍷 Old City & Society Hill

★Khyber Pass Pub CRAFT BEER
(Map p198; ☎215-238-5888; www.khyberpasspub.com; 56 S 2nd St, Old City; ⏰10am-2am; 📶; [S]2nd St) A wide range of craft beers from across the US are sold at this friendly all-day bar. Happy hour runs 4pm to 6pm and the beer menu includes handy tasting notes.

This is also a good-value place to eat. Despite the pub's name, the food is Southern American, featuring dishes such as a beignet (small doughnuts), shrimp, tasso and grits.

🍷 Logan Square & Fairmount

Bar Hygge MICROBREWERY
(Map p194; ☎215-765-2274; www.barhygge.com; 1720 Fairmount Ave, Fairmount; craft cocktails $10; ⏰4-11pm Mon-Fri, from 10:30am Sat & Sun; [S]Fairmount) Pronounced 'Hug-uh,' Hygge has a weekend brunch that can't be beat, but the real gems are its housemade Techne draft beers, which include English-style ales, IPAs and porters: all are excellent. The walls are made of cut-up pieces of wine barrels, making for interesting, artsy ambience.

Don't like beer? Sample the cocktails: fresh ingredients, such as lavender or shiso-infused simple syrup, make these creations delicate and delicious.

Crime & Punishment Brewing Co MICROBREWERY
(Map p190; ☎215-235-2739; http://crimeandpunishmentbrewingco.com; 2711 W Girard Ave, Brewerytown; ⏰4pm-midnight Mon-Wed, to 1am Fri, 11-1am Sat, 11am-midnight Sun; 📶; 🚆W Girard Ave & 27th St) It's rare to come across a craft-beer brewery that celebrates Russian literature, but such is Crime & Punishment, where the ales are anything but hard labor. There are some unique and tasty beers to sample including their flagship IPA Space Race and the Polish sour-style Grod Inquisitor.

Keeping with the Eastern European theme are snacks such as pierogi and Kielbasa sausage sandwiches. The bar also acts as a gallery space with new exhibitions opening on the first Friday of each month.

🍷 Chinatown & Center City East

★Dirty Franks BAR
(Map p194; ☎215-732-5010; www.dirtyfranksbar.com; 347 S 13th St, Washington Sq West; ⏰11am-2am; 🚌23, 40) In business since 1933, Franks' regulars call this bar an 'institution' with some irony, but it does have grunge style as well as housing the Off The Wall gallery. Like many Philly dives, it offers the 'citywide special': a shot of Jim Beam and a can of PBR

for $2.50. Need cheaper? Try the 'DF Shelf of Shame' beer for just two bucks!

The bar's exterior is decorated with the mural **Famous Franks** (www.muralarts.org/artworks/famous-franks).

★ **Charlie was a Sinner**   COCKTAIL BAR
(Map p194; ☑ 267-758-5372; http://charliewasasinner.com; 131 S 13th St, Midtown Village; ⊙ 4pm-2am; Ⓢ Walnut-Locust or 13th St) Charlie, apparently, sinned during the building's sketchy past as a brothel. Never mind, it's a catchy name for what is now a sophisticated cocktail bar and restaurant where food and booze are both vegan. Watch the mixologist blowtorch wood chips to create the smoke that perfumes some of the bar's creations.

Double Knot   BAR
(Map p194; ☑ 215-631-3868; www.doubleknotphilly.com; 120 S 13th St, Midtown Village; ⊙ 7am-midnight; Ⓢ 13th St or Walnut-Locust) This is one of the few places in Philly that serves sake properly (poured into an overflowing cup inside a wooden *masu* container). They also makes great craft cocktails and have a delicious food menu. It can get crowded, but the stylish decor and friendly service make it a fun spot to grab a bite and late-night drink.

From 5pm they open up the basement, which hides an impressive Japanese restaurant with a sushi bar and *robatayaki* (flame-grilled cooked items).

Writer's Block Rehab   COCKTAIL BAR
(Map p194; ☑ 267-603-6960; www.facebook.com/writersblockrehab/; 1342 Cypress St, Midtown Village; ⊙ 8am-noon & 4-10pm Mon-Thu, 8am-noon & 3pm-1am Fri, noon-1am Sat, noon-11pm Sun; Ⓢ Walnut-Locust) Cafe by day, cocktail bar by night, this quirky bar, just south of the Gayborhood, is a bit of a gem. Wordsmiths will love its trompe l'oeil library wallpaper, chandeliers made of vintage globes and menus in hardcover books – all showing a dedication to the literary theme. It's a cool spot for a quiet drink whether you're blocked or not.

🍴 University City & West Philadelphia

★ **City Tap House**   CRAFT BEER
(Map p202; ☑ 215-662-0105; www.ucity.citytap.com; The Radian, 3925 Walnut St, University City; ⊙ 11:30am-midnight Mon-Fri, from 11am Sat & Sun; 🚍 40, 🚊 37th St) You can get very merry working your way through the 60 beers on tap here. This, plus the outdoor terrace on two

levels and decent food, make City Tap House the area's best bar by far.

🍴 Rittenhouse Square & Center City West

★ **Elixir Coffee Roasters**   CAFE
(Map p194; ☑ 239-404-1730; www.elixrcoffee.com; 207 S Sydenham St, Rittenhouse; ⊙ 7am-8pm Mon-Fri, 8am-7pm Sat & Sun; 🛜; Ⓢ Walnut-Locust) Tucked in an alley, this hopping coffee spot has a warehouse theme, complete with meat-locker doors for the bathrooms. Funky miniature terrariums, murals on the walls, good wi-fi and quality hand-dripped coffees make it a fun stop for that cup of joe.

★ **Monk's Cafe**   BAR
(Map p194; ☑ 215-545-7005; www.monkscafe.com; 264 S 16th St, Rittenhouse; ⊙ 11:30am-2am, kitchen to 1am; Ⓢ Walnut-Locust) Hop fans crowd this mellow wood-paneled place for Belgian and American craft beers on tap – it has one of the best selections in the city. For those needing assistance, a 'Beer Bible' is available.

There's also a reasonably priced food menu, with typical mussels-and-fries as well as a daily vegan special.

R2L Restaurant   LOUNGE
(Map p194; ☑ 215-564-5337; https://r2lrestaurant.com; 50 S 16th St, Center City; ⊙ lounge 4pm-1am Mon-Thu, 4pm-2am Fri & Sat, 4-11pm Sun; Ⓢ City Hall & 15th St, Ⓡ Suburban) The view, the view, the view. And did we mention the

CRAFT BREWING & DISTILLING

America's oldest still-active brewery is Pennsylvania's Yuengling (www.yuengling.com), first brewed in Pottsville in 1829. The beer – which is a good one – is commonly available across the city, where it competes with a fast-growing number of craft beers.

Philly is also going back to its roots as a US center for alcohol production with new microbreweries such as Second District Brewing and Crime & Punishment Brewing Co joining established players Yards and Manayunk Brewing Company. Craft distilling of gin, rum, whiskey and vodka is also on the rise, with several distilleries open for tours and tastings on the weekends.

view? This upscale spot serves up the nightscape of Philly along with whatever is on the menu. Craft cocktails are smooth and balanced, but even tap water would seem ritzy when you're looking out at the cosmos of lights below you.

Happy hour (4:30pm to 6:30pm Monday to Friday) offers $3 beers, $7 wines, $8 cocktails and snacks from $2.

Dandelion
PUB

(Map p194; ☑ 215-558-2500; http://thedandelionpub.com; 124 S 18th St, Rittenhouse; beers $4; ⊙ 11:30am-2am Mon-Fri, 10am-2am Sat & Sun; ☐ 9, 12, 17, 21, 42, ☐ 19th St) The bustling atmosphere of an English country inn and great food set this gastropub apart, and the bar is open until 2am. Craft cocktails, such as the Pimm's Deluxe, are fun, and the plethora of beer options (draft and bottled) means there's something for everyone.

If you plan on dining, reservations are highly recommended. It even does afternoon tea (from $20) from 3pm to 5pm.

Ranstead Room
LOUNGE

(Map p194; ☑ 215-563-3330; 2013 Ranstead St, Rittenhouse; ⊙ 6pm-2am; ☐ 9, 17, 21, 42, ☐ 19th St) This popular speakeasy stays on the down low with no website and no clear sign – look for the double R on the door. Inside it's all dim lights, red-and-black wallpaper, and great craft cocktails, making it a good choice for those seeking somewhere cozy and intimate. The menu is great, but bartender's choice is better.

South Philadelphia

★ Second District Brewing
MICROBREWERY

(Map p190; ☑ 215-575-5900; http://seconddistrictbrewing.com; 1939 S Bancroft St, Newbold; ⊙ 11am-midnight; ☐ 2, Ⓢ Snyder) A converted auto workshop is the location for this South Philly microbrewery that's one to watch. They like to experiment with their brewing here, so there's bound to be something interesting and unique on the menu of 10 draft beers, such as the Entwife, an English-style

---

LGBTQ+ PHILADELPHIA

Wherever you fall on the gender-sexuality spectrum, Philly will open its arms to you. In 1965, four years before the Stonewall riots, Independence Hall was the site of one of the first gay-rights protests in US history. The area affectionately nicknamed the 'Gayborhood' may have been rebranded Midtown Village, but you'll still see plenty of rainbow flags and LGBT-friendly bars and businesses here.

A focal point of the Gayborhood is the **William Way LGBT Community Center** (Map p194; ☑ 215-732-2220; www.waygay.org; 1315 Spruce St, Midtown Village; ⊙ 11am-10pm Mon-Fri, noon-5pm Sat & Sun; Ⓢ Walnut-Locust), on the side of which is painted the LGBT history mural **Pride and Progress** (www.muralarts.org/artworks/pride-progress-2). Art shows, regular meet ups and support groups are held here.

Another place to plug into the local LGBT scene is the secondhand bookstore Philly AIDS Thrift @ Giovanni's Room (p215), which often holds author talks on the weekends.

For a drinking and nightlife, consider:

Woody's (Map p194; ☑ 215-545-1893; http://woodysbar.com; 202 S 13th St, Midtown Village; ⊙ 7pm-2am; Ⓢ 13th St or Walnut-Locust) Philly's most famous LGBT bar is the anchor of the Gayborhood.

Tavern on Camac (TOC; Map p194; ☑ 215-545-0900; www.tavernoncamac.com; 243 S Camac St, Midtown Village; ⊙ piano bar 4pm-2am, restaurant 6pm-1am Wed-Mon, club 9pm-2am Tue-Sun; Ⓢ Walnut-Locust) Stalwart of the Gayborhood, with a piano bar downstairs and DJs upstairs.

Toasted Walnut Bar & Kitchen (Map p194; ☑ 215-546-8888; www.facebook.com/toasted-walnutphiladelphia; 1316 Walnut St, Midtown Village; ⊙ 4pm-2am Tue-Sat, from 3pm Sun.; Ⓢ 13th St or Walnut-Locust) Newer venue catering primarily to women who are into women.

Voyeur (Map p194; ☑ 215-735-5772; www.voyeurnightclub.com; 1221 St James St, Midtown Village; cover charge $10-20; ⊙ midnight-3:30am Tue-Sun; Ⓢ Walnut-Locust) For dancing until near dawn, this after-hours club is your option.

dark mild beer, or the cave-aged (and potent) barleywine.

In an inspired move they use the spent grain from the brewing to make a burger, and also have some vegan options on the menu.

★Tattooed Mom BAR
(Map p194; ☎215-238-9880; www.tattooedmomphilly.com; 530 South St, Queen Village; 🕒noon-2am; 🚌40, 47) It feels a little disrespectful to call such a fun and fabulously decorated place a 'dive bar', but the friendly staff and patrons of Tatttooed Mom likely wouldn't mind and that label just easily sums up the bar's casual, welcome-to-all nature.

Check online for details of the great lineup of events here, including a monthly comedy show, craft-making party and local political forum.

🍷 Fishtown & Northern Liberties

★Trestle Inn BAR
(Map p194; ☎267-239-0290; www.thetrestleinn.com; 339 N 11th St, Callowhill; 🕒5pm-1am Wed-Thu, to 2am Fri & Sat; [S]Spring Garden: Broad Street Line) On a dark corner this classed-up old dive is notable for its friendliness and craft cocktails, which can be enjoyed in a happy hour that lasts from 5pm until 8pm. From 9pm on Thursday and 10pm on Friday and Saturday go-go dancers get their groove on under the disco ball as DJs play hits from the 1960s onward.

There's a cover charge of $5 after 10pm at the weekends.

★La Colombe Fishtown COFFEE
(Map p190; ☎267-479-1600; www.lacolombe.com; 1335 Frankford Ave, Fishtown; 🕒7am-7pm Sun-Thu, to 9pm Fri & Sat; 📶; [S]Girard: Market-Frankford Line) All the stops have been pulled out for the Philadelphia gourmet-coffee giant's flagship store in a converted Fishtown warehouse. Here you'll find a self-serve cafe, bakery and distillery producing Different Drum, a coffee-infused rum which you can sample in a variety of cocktails. The kitchen serves food until 3pm.

Philadelphia Distilling DISTILLERY
(Map p190; ☎215-671-0346; http://philadelphiadistilling.com; 25 E Allen St, Fishtown; tours $15; 🕒4-11pm Thu & Fri, 1-11pm Sat & Sun; [S]Girard: Market-Frankford Line) The old Ajax Metal warehouse near the Delaware riverfront has been revamped into this impressive craft spirits operation, with a sophisticated bar and inventive cocktail list. The award-winning Bluecoast American Dry gins are flavored with citrus, cilantro and angelica root.

One-hour informative tours start with a punch cocktail and finish with a tasting of the spirits range, including their 120 proof Vieux Carré absinthe.

The Random Tea Room TEAHOUSE
(Map p194; ☎267-639-2442; http://therandomtearoom.com; 713 N 4th St, Northern Liberties; 🕒10am-8pm; [S]Spring Garden: Market-Frankford Line) This charming antique-style cafe dedicated to teas and infusions is practically unique in Philly. The 40-plus artisanal blends can be enjoyed by cup or pot, there's art on the walls by local artists and a tempting selection of bakes and savory nibbles, as well as chai oats.

Evil Genius Beer Company MICROBREWERY
(Map p190; ☎215-425-6820; http://evilgeniusbeer.com; 1727 N Front St, Fishtown; 🕒4-10pm Wed & Thu, to midnight Fri, noon-midnight Sat, to 9pm Sun; [S]Berks) Silly names – Purple Monkey Dishwater (a chocolate peanut porter) and Ma! The Meatloaf (a Belgium white ale) – for serious beer is the stock in trade of Evil Genius, which operates out of this barn-like space. Sample a flight of five for $12 with 5oz tasters going for $2.50.

Tours of the brewery ($8; 1pm and 1:30pm Saturday) include a pint and are on a first-come, first-served basis.

🍷 Philadelphia

★Pilgrim Roasters COFFEE
(Map p190; ☎267-331-5213; www.pilgrimroasters.com; 4120 Main St, Manayunk; 🕒6am-6pm Mon-Fri, 7am-7pm Sat, 8am-5pm Sun; 📶; 🚆Manayunk) Dan Faehl and Ryan Connelly are the passionate and friendly duo behind this coffee roaster and cafe. Take your pick from four daily featured coffees, all single origin and with different flavor profiles. A Scandinavian light roasting technique means there's no bitter taste from the beans and the drinks are reasonably priced.

☆ Entertainment

Curtis Institute of Music CLASSICAL MUSIC
(Map p194; ☎215-893-7902; www.curtis.edu; 1726 Locust St, Rittenhouse; student recitals admission free; 🕒8pm most Mon, Wed & Fri; 🚌9, 12, 17, 21,

42, Ⓢ Walnut-Locust) One of the finest music conservatories in the world, the Curtis only accepts exceptionally gifted students into its tuition-free programs. If you attend one of the free student recitals (highly recommended!), mainly of solo and chamber works, you'll witness some extraordinary performances in the institute's elegant wood-paneled Field Concert Hall.

Performances by the Curtis' opera students, symphony orchestra and alumni are generally ticketed from around $25.

Ritz At The Bourse   CINEMA
(Map p198; ☑ 215-440-1181; www.landmarktheatres.com/philadelphia/ritz-at-the-bourse; 400 Ranstead St, Old City; tickets $8-10.25; Ⓢ 5th St) The place to come to see independent and art-house movies as well as special-event screenings such as those offered by National Theatre Live and the Royal Opera House from the UK. Every Friday at midnight they also screen cult movies such as *The Rocky Horror Picture Show*.

Landmark runs a couple more cinemas in the area that show highbrow movies: **Ritz 5** (Map p198; ☑ 215-440-1184; www.landmarktheatres.com/philadelphia/ritz-five; 214 Walnut St, Old City; tickets $8-10.25; Ⓢ 2nd St) and **Ritz East** (Map p198; ☑ 215-925-4535; www.landmarktheatres.com/philadelphia/ritz-east; 125 S 2nd St, Old City; tickets $8-10.25; Ⓢ 2nd St).

L'etage   CABARET
(Map p194; ☑ 215-592-0656; http://creperie-beaumonde.com; 624 S 6th St, Queen Village; ⊙ 7:30pm-1am Tue-Thu & Sun, 7pm-2am Fri & Sat; 🚌 40, 47) Great cabaret, club nights and other events all happen here. Shows could be a tryout of a new musical, male queer 'boylesque', or, on rare occasions, Martha Graham Cracker, alter ego of Dito Van Reigersberg and one of Philly's top drag talents. The downstairs crêperie (noon to 9pm Tuesday to Thursday, until 10pm Friday, 10am to 10pm Saturday, 10am to 9pm Sunday) serves authentic savory and sweet crêpes in a cozy space with a fireplace.

World Cafe Live   LIVE MUSIC
(Map p202; ☑ 215-222-1400; www.worldcafelive.com; 3025 Walnut St, University City; cover $10-40; ⊙ from 11am Fri, from 5pm Sat-Thu; 🚌 21, 42, Ⓢ 30th St) Home to U Penn's radio station, WXPN, this former factory is one of Philly's premier live-music venues. There are upstairs and downstairs performance spaces for jazz, folk and global acts, plus good food.

Pig Iron Theatre Company   THEATER
(Map p190; ☑ 215-425-1100; www.pigiron.org; 1417 N 2nd St, Fishtown; Ⓢ Girard: Market-Frankford Line) One of Philly's most exciting and original contemporary theater companies, Pig Iron shows can be bizarre combinations of vaudeville, clowning and silence, by turns hilarious and surreal. This is the company's studio space, which very occasionally is open for performances.

PhilaMOCA   PERFORMING ARTS
(Philadelphia Mausoleum of Contemporary Art; Map p194; ☑ 267-519-9651; www.philamoca.org; 531 N 12th St, Poplar; Ⓢ Spring Garden: Broad Street Line) A former tombstone store, then producer Diplo's studios, this eclectic space now has an equally eclectic program of cult movie nights, live-music shows, art, comedy and more.

Johnny Brenda's   LIVE MUSIC
(Map p190; ☑ 215-739-9684; www.johnnybrendas.com; 1201 N Frankford Ave, Fishtown; tickets $10-15; ⊙ kitchen 11am-1am, showtimes vary; Ⓢ Girard: Market-Frankford Line) One of the hubs of Philly's indie-rock scene, this is a great small venue with a balcony, plus a solid restaurant and bar with equally indie-minded beers.

Union Transfer   CONCERT VENUE
(Map p194; ☑ 215-232-2100; www.utphilly.com; 1026 Spring Garden St, Poplar; tickets $15-40; Ⓢ Spring Garden: Broad Street Line) Opened in 2011, this music hall is one of the best spaces in Philly for bigger-name bands, with eclectic bookings and good bar service.

🛍 Shopping

🛍 Old City & Society Hill

★ Art in the Age   FOOD & DRINKS
(Map p198; ☑ 215-922-2600; www.artintheage.com; 116 N 3rd St, Old City; ⊙ 11am-7pm Mon-Sat, noon-6pm Sun; Ⓢ 2nd St) Designed as a boutique homage to the cocktail, this spot is both a home-bar supply store and tasting room. Settle down at its bar for a tasting ($7 or $10 depending on your poison) or buy hand-crafted spirits, artisanal bitters and cordials, pickles, long-handled stir spoons, strainers, shakers, recipe books and other cocktail necessities.

They partner with local distillers New Liberty to create spirits inspired by Philly's history.

★**Shane Confectionery** FOOD & DRINKS
(Map p198; ☑215-922-1048; http://shanecan
dies.com; 110 Market St, Old City; ⊙9am-9pm
Mon & Tue, 11am-8pm Wed & Thu, 11am-10pm Fri &
Sat, 11am-9pm Sun; S2nd St) Since 1863 this
wonderfully old-school candy shop has
been making sweet treats, including butter-
creams and slabs, from antique molds. With
the shop assistants dressed in Victorian garb
it's like stepping back in time. Settle down
in the historic hot-chocolate kitchen in the
back where you can indulge in a flight of luscious drinks for $12.

Tours ($10) of the operation are held on
Fridays at 6:30pm.

🔒 Fishtown & Northern Liberties

★**Amalgum Comics & Coffeehouse** BOOKS
(Map p190; ☑215-427-3300; www.amalgamphil
ly.com; 2578 Frankford Ave, Kensington; ⊙7am-
8pm Tue-Fri, 8am-8pm Sat, 10am-6pm Sun; SHu-
ntingdon) Reveling in geek culture is this
mashup of a comic book store and cafe,
the passion project of owner Ariell Johnson. Check its Facebook page for details of
the many events held here including anime
screenings, monthly book clubs and author
signings.

🔒 Chinatown & Center City East

★**Ten Thousand Villages** ARTS & CRAFTS
(Map p194; ☑215-574-2008; www.tenthou
sandvillages.com; 1122 Walnut St, Midtown Village;
⊙10am-7pm Mon-Sat, noon-5pm Sun; S11th
St, 🚇Jefferson) 🍃 Browse a globe-trotting
selection of goods at this ethically focused
handicrafts store supporting fair-trade initiatives around the world. Pick up anything
from Peruvian woolly hats to singing bowls
from Nepal.

The business's roots go back to the late
1940s, when Edna Ruth Byler, a woman
from Akron, Pennsylvania, started to trade
in the unique textiles she'd found on a visit
to Puerto Rico.

★**Lapstone & Hammer** FASHION & ACCESSORIES
(Map p194; ☑215-592-9166; www.lapstoneand
hammer.com; 1106 Chestnut St, Midtown Village;
⊙10am-7pm Mon-Sat, noon-5pm Sun; S11th St,
🚇Jefferson) Occupying the former home of
Pauline's, an old art-deco bridal store, Lap-

stone & Hammer's range of male streetwear
and high fashion is artfully displayed.
Among the international labels, such as
Comme des Garçon and Adidas, are local
brands including Divine Lorraine (named
after a storied city hotel) and L&H's own
sweatshirts, T-shirts and utility pants.

★**Philly AIDS Thrift @ Giovanni's Room** BOOKS
(Map p194; ☑215-923-2960; www.queerbooks.
com; 345 S 12th St, Washington Sq West; ⊙11am-
8pm Mon-Thu, to 9pm Fri & Sat, to 7pm Sun; 🚌23,
40) Every shape and shade of LGBTQI book
and magazine appears to be on sale at this
long-running secondhand bookstore. It carries many other book genres, too, as well as
some recorded music, clothing and other
bits and bobs. Check its website for details
of author readings and other events (usually
held on weekend evenings).

🔒 Rittenhouse Square & Center City West

★**Boyd's** FASHION & ACCESSORIES
(Map p194; ☑215-564-9000; www.boydsphila.
com; 1818 Chestnut St, Rittenhouse; ⊙9:30am-
6pm Mon-Sat, to 8pm Wed; 🚇19th St) Boyd's has
been in business since 1938, initially specializing in men's clothing, but branching out
into womenswear in 1990 when they moved
into the original Pennsylvania Academy of
Fine Arts building. It's a grand space, especially following 2018 renovations, in which
to browse and buy top designer labels.

★**Stadler-Khan** GIFTS & SOUVENIRS
(Map p194; ☑267-242-7154; www.stadler-kahn.
com; 1724 Sansom St, Rittenhouse; ⊙11am-6pm
Mon & Wed-Fri; SCity Hall & 15th St, 🚇19th St)
Easily missed is this quirky store by designer
Alex Stadler, who sells his textile and cloth-
ing designs alongside a colorful mishmash
of arty gifts, crafts and vintage products.
You'll find everything from felt doughnuts
to Lucite table lamps.

🔒 Logan Square & Fairmount

★**Neighborhood Potters** ARTS & CRAFTS
(Map p194; ☑215-236-1617; www.sandiandneil.
com; 2034 Fairmount Ave, Fairmount; ⊙noon-
4pm Sat; 🚌48, 43, 33, 32, 7) Sandi and Neil
are the couple behind this creative pottery
studio and gallery, which opens its doors
to shoppers for a few hours each weekend
if it doesn't have an exhibition on (when it

keeps longer hours). You can also take pottery classes here.

South Philadelphia

Fante's Kitchen Shop   HOMEWARES
(Map p190; ☑215-922-5557; www.fantes.com; 1006 S 9th St, Bella Vista; ☺9am-5pm Tue-Sat, 9:30am-1:30pm Sun; 🚌47, ⓈEllsworth-Federal) If you need a device of any kind for your kitchen Fante's is sure to have it. This family-run business started as a furniture store but switched over to kitchenware in the 1980s and has never looked back. Unique items that you might not find elsewhere include stove-top toasters, pizzelle irons and cavarola boards for printing designs into pasta.

Eye's Gallery   ARTS & CRAFTS
(Map p194; ☑215-925-0193; www.eyesgallery.com; 402 South St, Queen Village; ☺11am-7pm Mon-Thu, to 8pm Fri & Sat, noon-7pm Sun; 🚌40, 57) Julia and Isaiah Zagar set up this gallery specializing in folk art, fashion and jewelry in 1968 as a place to sell Isaiah's work along with that of fellow traveler-artists. The products on sale here, many of which are created by artisans in places such as Peru, Mexico and India, add a brilliant burst of color and creativity to South St.

Little Moon + Arrow   TOYS
(Map p194; ☑267-457-5403; www.littlemoonandarrow.com; 729 S 4th St, Queen Village; ☺11am-7pm Tue-Sat, to 5pm Sun; 🚌40, 57) We doubt you'll find a more adorable selection of handmade toys and kids' clothing – all made from organic materials – in Philadelphia. Choose between wooden toys by Grimms from Germany, the colorful animal creations of So Heart Felt and calming tinctures of Mothercraft, among other items.

Philly Typewriter   VINTAGE
(Map p190; ☑267-992-3230; www.phillytypewriter.com; 1439 E Passyunk Ave, Passyunk Sq; ☺10am-6pm Tue-Thu & Sat, to 7pm Fri; 🚌45, 47, ⓈEllsworth-Federal) Are you suffering digital burnout? The solution lies at this store that stocks refurbished vintage typewriters, manual and electric. Genial co-owner Bryan Kravitz and his staff will happily extol the virtues of these analog keyboards, which are displayed like museum pieces and start at around $275.

University City & West Philadelphia

★ Penn Book Center   BOOKS
(Map p202; ☑215-222-7600; www.pennbookcenter.com; 130 S 34th St, University City; ☺10am-6pm Mon-Sat; 🚌21, 30, 42, Ⓢ34th St) In its fifth decade, this friendly indie bookstore is not just a store, but a community worth seeking out and supporting. There's a good selection of local authors and knowledgeable staff.

Philadelphia

★ Uncle Bobbie's Coffee & Books   BOOKS
(Map p190; ☑215-403-7058; www.unclebobbies.com; 5445 Germantown Ave, Germantown; ☺7am-9pm Mon-Thu, to 11pm Fri, 8am-11pm Sat, 8am-7pm Sun; 🛜; 🚌23, 🚇Germantown) Temple University professor Marc Lamont Hill is the owner and passionate force behind this ace cafe and bookstore specializing in black writers and literature. The shelves that line the several rooms of the cozy cafe are piled with a wonderful range of tomes and own-brand goods, including T-shirts and totes.

Bobbie's hosts readings, movie screenings and other events. The coffee and snacks are also pretty tasty.

ℹ Information

MEDICAL SERVICES

Hospital of the University of Pennsylvania (☑800-789-7366; www.pennmedicine.org; 3400 Spruce St, University City; ☺24hr; 🚌30, 40, 42, 🚇University City) Philadelphia's largest medical facility.

Mazzoni Center (☑215-563-0652; www.mazzonicenter.org; 1348 Bainbridge St, Hawthorne; ☺9am-5pm Mon-Fri; ⓈLombard-South) Clinic and support center focusing on the health and wellness of Philly's LGBT community.

TOURIST INFORMATION

Run by the city and the National Park Service, the **Independence Visitor Center** (Map p198; ☑800-537-7676; www.phlvisitorcenter.com; 599 Market St, Old City; ☺8:30am-6pm Sep-May, 8:30am-7pm Jun-Aug; Ⓢ5th St) covers the Independence National Historical Park and all of the sights in Philadelphia.

The city tourism service has convenient branches at **City Hall** (Map p194; ☑267-514-4757; www.phlvisitorcenter.com/attraction/city-hall-visitor-center; City Hall, Center City; ☺9am-5pm Mon-Fri, 11am-4pm occasional Sat;

Ⓢ City Hall & 15th St), **Logan Sq** (Map p194; ⊘ 267-514-4760; www.phlvisitorcenter.com; 200 N 18th St; ⊘ 9:30am-5:30pm Mon-Sat, to 5pm Sun May-Sep; ▣ 27, 32, 33) and **JFK Plaza** (Map p194; ⊘ 215-683-0246; www.phlvisitor-center.com; 1599 John F Kennedy Blvd, Center City; ⊘ 10am-5pm Mon-Sat; Ⓢ City Hall & 15th St).

❶ Getting There & Away

Most international visitors arrive by air.

It's easy to reach Philadelphia by bus or train from major East Coast cities. The fast, commuter-oriented Acela train links Boston, New York and Washington, DC, to Philly's 30th St Station.

Flights, cars and tours can be booked online at lonelyplanet.com/bookings.

AIR

Philadelphia International Airport (PHL; ⊘ 215-937-6937; www.phl.org; 8000 Essington Ave, Southwest Philadelphia; ▣ Airport Line), 10 miles southwest of Center City, is a hub for American Airlines, and is served by direct international flights. There are five terminals so check which one you are arriving at and departing from before you set off.

SEPTA's Regional Rail service connects the airport to the city. Trains run regularly between 5am and midnight, take around 30 minutes and cost $6.75 to Center City stations ($9.25 to other stations). From the airport to Center City taxis charge a fixed flat rate of $28.50 for the first person, plus $1 for each additional person. SEPTA buses 37 and 108 serve the airport.

BUS

Greyhound (www.greyhound.com), Peter Pan Bus Lines (www.peterpanbus.com), NJ Transit (www.njtransit.com) and the no-frills Chinatown Bus (www.chinatown-bus.org) all depart from the **Greyhound Terminal** (Map p194; ⊘ 215-931-4075; www.greyhound.com; 1001 Filbert St, Chinatown; Ⓢ 11th St, ▣ Jefferson) downtown, near the convention center; Greyhound goes nationwide, Peter Pan focuses on the northeast, NJ Transit gets you to New Jersey and the Chinatown bus connects to NYC.

From just west of 30th St Station, **Megabus** (Map p202; http://us.megabus.com; JFK Blvd & N 30th St, University City; Ⓢ 30th St, ▣ 30th St) serves major US cities in the northeast and Toronto. For NYC and Boston, **Bolt Bus** (Map p202; ⊘ 877-265-8287; www.boltbus.com; JFK Blvd &

N 30th St, University City; Ⓢ 30th St, ▣ 30th St) has the roomiest buses.

Fares to NYC (2½ hours) can be as low as $9 when booked online.

CAR & MOTORCYCLE

From the north and south, I-95 (Delaware Expwy) follows the east edge of the city along the Delaware River, with several exits for Center City. In the north of the city, I-276 (Pennsylvania Turnpike) runs east over the river to connect with the New Jersey Turnpike.

TRAIN

Just west of downtown across the Schuylkill, beautiful neoclassical **30th St Station** (⊘ 1800-872-7245; www.amtrak.com; 2955 Market St, University City; Ⓢ 30th St) is a major hub. From here, Amtrak provides service on its Northeast Corridor line to New York City ($58 to $115, one to 1½ hours), Boston ($102 to $200, five to 5¾ hours), and Washington, DC ($58 to $114, two hours), as well as to Lancaster ($19 to $37, one hour) and Pittsburgh ($67 to $131, 7½ hours).

A slower but cheaper way to get to NYC is on regional SEPTA (www.septa.org) to Trenton ($9, 50 minutes), then NJ Transit (www.njtransit.com) to NYC's Penn Station ($16.75, 1½ hours). NJ Transit's Atlantic City Rail Line also connects 30th St Station with the seaside resort ($10, 90 minutes).

❶ Getting Around

For timetables and further information check with **SEPTA** (⊘ 215-580-7800; www.septa.org), which operates Philadelphia's transit system.

Walking Downtown, it's barely 2 miles between the Delaware and Schuylkill Rivers, so you can walk most places.

Subway & Trolley Philly has two subways and a trolley line (fare $2.50). Purchase the stored-value key card for discounted fares.

Buses Convenient for quick hops across Center City and further afield.

Taxi Easy to hail Downtown. Flag fall is $2.70, then $2.30 per mile or portion thereof. All licensed taxis have GPS and most accept credit cards. Uber and Lyft are also commonly used.

Bicycle Walk-up rates for Philly's bike-share system Indego are $4 for 30 minutes.

Ferries From late May to early September the RiverLink ferry connects Penn's Landing and Camden's waterfront.

Pennsylvania

POP 12.8 MILLION

Best Places to Eat

➡ Paris 66 (p238)
➡ Legume (p238)
➡ Butcher & the Rye (p237)
➡ Horse Inn (p223)

Best Places to Stay

➡ Cork Factory (p222)
➡ Priory Hotel (p235)
➡ Nemacolin Woodlands Resort & Spa (p240)
➡ Susquehannock Lodge (p229)

Why Go?

A horse and buggy trundles through the Lancaster fog before it is overtaken by a Philadelphia-bound sports car driven by a young tech entrepreneur. In Pittsburgh, children of immigrants who work as nurses in the city's burgeoning hospitals break into experimental contemporary art. In Gettysburg, descendants of Union soldiers proudly fly Confederate flags. This is Pennsylvania, which contains within its 46,000 sq miles some of the eastern seaboard's most striking landscapes, culture clashes and contradictions.

Massive elk herds lope across forested ravines in the Pennsylvania Wilds; former steel towns embrace wine-fueled arts walks; cities populated by the descendants of America's founders live side by side with immigrants; Mennonites who eschew modern tech run agribusiness empires. This state never fails to fascinate, and while it's wowing you with its culture, it's also feeding you great food and awesome landscapes.

When to Go
Pittsburgh

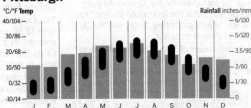

Jan Catch the craziness of the Mummer's Parade, Philadelphia's most famous festival.

Apr–May Nothing is prettier than a road trip through rolling pastureland when the flowers are in bloom.

Oct Autumn's festive chill brings apple pies, pumpkin spice and haunted Halloween hay rides.

History

Pennsylvania was the second state admitted to the nascent United States (Delaware beat it by five days) and, as such, lays claim to a long and storied history, at least by American standards. Many of the milestones in Pennsylvania history have been, in turn, milestones for the entire USA.

❶ Getting There & Away

Pennsylvania is home to a number of airports, several of them with international connections; the eastern end is near the giant hub of New Jersey's Newark International, with connections across the world. Trains serve many of its major cities, while buses service most towns. That said, with so much of this state's beauty lying off the beaten path, renting a car and driving around on your own is highly recommended.

The main air access points are Philadelphia International Airport (p431) and Pittsburgh International Airport (p239). Both of these cities are also major hubs for Amtrak trains and Greyhound buses.

PENNSYLVANIA DUTCH COUNTRY

Lancaster County and the broader space between Reading and the Susquehanna River is the center of the so-called Pennsylvania Dutch community (see p224). Small settlements in the area include train-mad Strasburg and pretty, red-brick Lititz. Ephrata is headquarters of Ten Thousand Villages, a massive Mennonite-run fair-trade imports store with branches all over the country.

❶ Information

Discover Lancaster Visitors Center (📞717-299-8901, 800-723-8824; www.discoverlancaster.com; 501 Greenfield Rd, Lancaster; ⊗9am-5pm Mon-Sat, 10am-4pm Sun Jun-Oct, 10am-4pm Nov-May) Just off Rte 30, with info on all of Pennsylvania, as well as good area maps and free coffee.

Zimmerman Center for Heritage (📞717-252-0229; www.susquehannaheritage.org/explore-2/zimmerman-center/; 1706 Long Level Rd, Wrightsville; ⊗10am-4pm Tue-Sun) Offers guided hikes, lectures and general info on outdoor activities in the region.

❶ Getting There & Away

A car is the most practical way to get here; get a good map (cell service is poor) and take smaller

roads. Amtrak serves the **Lancaster Train Station** (📞800-872-7245; www.amtrak.com; 53 McGovern Ave) with frequent trains from Philadelphia ($19 to $26, 1¼ hours), and once-daily service from Pittsburgh ($58, 6¼ hours).

Lancaster

📞717 / POP 59,218

Lancaster lies within the heart of Pennsylvania Dutch Country, and is a natural base for many tourists looking to explore the region. It's an odd town, home of secular higher education institutions (Pennsylvania College of Art and Design and Franklin & Marshall College); religious schools (Lancaster Theological Seminary and Lancaster Bible College); and a burgeoning tourism industry that showcases both traditional Amish simplicity and more contemporary farm-to-table branding – which happens to jibe well with the area's rural charms.

The area is essentially farmland interrupted by strip malls and kitschy attractions. Modern Lancaster is, if anything, a balance between kitsch and the granular charm of authentic Pennsylvania countryside. For all that, the town feels refreshingly urban, especially after a night or day trip to Amish country.

◉ Sights

Landis Valley Museum　　　MUSEUM

(📞717-569-0401; www.landisvalleymuseum.org; 2451 Kissel Hill Rd; adult/child $12/8; ⊗9am-5pm Wed-Sat, noon-5pm Sun year-round, plus 9am-5pm Tue Mar-Dec; 🅿) Based on an 18th-century village, this open-air museum is the best way to get an overview of early Pennsylvania Dutch culture, and Mennonite culture in particular. Costumed staff are on hand to demonstrate tin-smithing, among other things, and there's a tavern, gun shop and several beautiful crafts exhibits.

Phillips Museum of Art　　　MUSEUM

(📞717-358-3879; www.fandm.edu/phillips-museum; 600 College Ave; ⊗noon-4pm Tue, Wed & Fri-Sun, 2-6pm Thu) FREE At this art museum you'll find art and *objets d'art* sourced from across different eras of American history, plus Soviet recruitment posters and Arabic comics, as well as the thesis work of the talented artists at Franklin & Marshall College. The museum, with its tall glass windows, is inside the Steinman College Center

Pennsylvania Highlights

1 Pittsburgh (p232)
Exploring a steel jungle filled with wonderful architecture, fantastic nightlife and great food.

2 Fallingwater (p239)
Touring Frank Lloyd Wright's masterpiece of organic design in the lovely Laurel Highlands.

3 Kinzua Bridge Skywalk (p229) Marveling above the twisted wreckage of a train bridge struck by an F1 tornado.

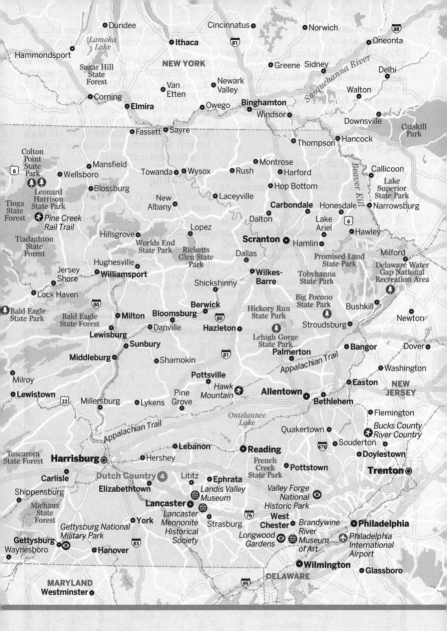

NEW YORK

Dundee • Cincinnatus • Norwich • Oneonta •

Lamoka Lake

Hammondsport • **Ithaca** • Greene • Sidney • Delhi •

Sugar Hill State Forest

Corning • Van Etten • Newark Valley • Walton •

Elmira • Owego • **Binghamton**

Windsor • Downsville •

Fassett • Sayre • Thompson • Hancock • *Catskill Park*

Colton Point State Park • Mansfield • Towanda • Wysox • Rush • Montrose • Harford • Callicoon •

Wellsboro • *Beaver Kill* • *Lake Superior State Park*

Blossburg • New Albany • Laceyville • Hop Bottom • Honesdale • Narrowsburg •

Tioga State Forest • Leonard Harrison State Park • **Carbondale**

Pine Creek Rail Trail • Hillsgrove • Lopez • Dalton • Lake Ariel • Hawley •

Tiadaghton State Forest • Worlds End State Park • Ricketts Glen State Park • **Scranton** • Hamlin • Milford •

Hughesville • Dallas • Promised Land State Park • Delaware Water Gap National Recreation Area

Jersey Shore • **Williamsport** • **Wilkes-Barre** • Tobyhanna State Park •

Lock Haven • Shickshinny • Bushkill •

Bald Eagle State Park • **Berwick** • Big Pocono State Park • Newton •

Bald Eagle State Forest • **Milton** • **Bloomsburg** • Hickory Run State Park • Stroudsburg •

Lewisburg • Danville • **Hazleton** • Lehigh Gorge State Park • **Bangor** • Dover •

Sunbury • Shamokin • **Palmerton** • Washington •

Middleburg • *Appalachian Trail* • **Easton** • **NEW JERSEY**

Milroy • **Pottsville** • Hawk Mountain • **Allentown** • Flemington •

Lewistown • Millersburg • Lykens • Pine Grove • **Bethlehem** • Bucks County River Country •

Ontelaunee Lake • Quakertown • Souderton • **Doylestown** •

Appalachian Trail • **Lebanon** • **Reading** • **Trenton** •

Tuscarora State Forest • Hershey • French Creek State Park • **Pottstown** •

Harrisburg • **Dutch Country** ④ • Lititz • **Ephrata** •

Carlisle • **Elizabethtown** • Landis Valley Museum • Valley Forge National Historic Park • **Philadelphia** •

Shippensburg • **Lancaster** • **West Chester** • Brandywine River Museum of Art • Philadelphia International Airport

Michaux State Forest • York • Lancaster Mennonite Historical Society • Strasburg • Longwood Gardens •

Gettysburg • Gettysburg National Military Park • **Hanover** • **Wilmington** • **Glassboro** •

Waynesboro • **DELAWARE**

MARYLAND • **Westminster**

④ **Dutch Country** (p219)
Discovering a slower pace of life.

Lancaster Mennonite
Historical Society   MUSEUM

(📞 717-393-9745; www.lmhs.org; 2215 Millstream Rd; $5; ⏱ 8:30am-4:30pm Tue-Sat) The small museum here displays beautiful glass and woodwork, along with the story of how Mennonites established themselves in this area. There's a well-stocked shop with local craft items and folk art, as well as a bookstore.

🛏 Sleeping

Some very upscale hotels have opened up here, allowing for truly top-notch accommodations as well as the usual chains and B&Bs.

★ Cork Factory   BOUTIQUE HOTEL $$

(📞 717-735-2075; www.corkfactoryhotel.com; 480 New Holland Ave, Suite 3000; r from $160; P⊖❖🐾) An abandoned brick behemoth of a factory now houses this hotel, one of the more stylish properties in the area. The posh rooms are outfitted with exposed brick, un-

derstated decor and a general sense of casual cool. It's a short drive from downtown.

Lancaster Arts Hotel   HOTEL $$

(📞 717-299-3000; www.lancasterartshotel.com; 300 Harrisburg Ave; d $180-220, ste $270-370; P❖🐾) For a refreshingly hip and urban experience, make a beeline to the snazzy Lancaster Arts Hotel, a member of the Historic Hotels of America, housed in an old brick tobacco warehouse and featuring a groovy designer-hotel ambience.

🍴 Eating

When you tire of bellying up to the buffet line, Lancaster has excellent farm-to-table options. Tomato Pie Cafe is in Lititz, a cute-as-a-kitten town 8 miles north of Lancaster.

★ Tomato Pie Cafe   CAFE $

(📞 717-627-1762; www.tomatopiecafe.net; 23 N Broad St, Lititz; mains $7-11; ⏱ 7am-9pm Mon-Sat, 8am-5pm Sun; 🐾) The creative fresh food

Lancaster

0 ——— 400 m
0 ——— 0.2 miles

and the complex coffee drinks wouldn't be out of place in a city, but the atmosphere is pure 'friendly small town.' Tomato pie is their signature dish: a rich, soft, cheesy mix that's unique and worth a try. The espresso here is excellent, as is the intriguing curry naan grilled cheese.

Central Market MARKET $
(☎717-735-6890; www.centralmarketlancaster.com; 23 N Market St; snacks from $2; ☉6am-4pm Tue & Fri, to 2pm Sat) This market has all the regional gastronomic delicacies – fresh horseradish, whoopie pies, soft pretzels and sub sandwiches stuffed with cured meats and dripping with oil. You'll find Spanish and Middle Eastern food as well, which makes for a nice break. The market's also stuffed with handicraft booths staffed by plain-dressed, bonneted Amish women (who drive a good bargain).

★ Horse Inn AMERICAN $$
(☎717-392-5528; www.horseinnlancaster.com; 540 E Fulton St; mains $11-28; ☉5pm-midnight Tue-Thu, to 1am Fri & Sat) This is easily one of our favorite spots in Lancaster, a gastropub located on top of a random staircase stuffed with shuffleboard tables and random bits of Pennsylvania paraphernalia, complemented by dark lighting and great shifting menu – one night you might nosh on Korean fried cauliflower, or chicken cooked in coconut milk and ginger. Eclectic, fun and delicious to boot.

★ John J Jeffries Restaurant AMERICAN $$
(☎717-431-3307; www.johnjjeffries.com; 300 Harrisburg Ave; small plates $8-16, mains $20-29;

Lancaster

A FARM STAY

If you like your vacations to be working ones, check out A Farm Stay (www.afarmstay.com), which represents several dozen farm stays that range from stereotypical B&Bs to Amish farms. Most include breakfast, private bathrooms and some activity such as milking cows, gathering eggs or simply petting a goat.

☉5:30-10pm Mon-Sat, to 9pm Sun; ⏺) ✈ The entire Lancaster area is known for its deep agricultural heritage, and no other restaurant seems to encapsulate the farm-to-table ethos like John J Jeffries. A shifting menu sourced from small local farms keeps diners happy with dishes like grass-fed steak and pork-belly gorditas.

Lancaster Brewing Co PUB FOOD $$
(☎717-391-6258; www.lancasterbrewing.com; 302 N Plum St; mains $11-23; ☉11:30am-10pm; ⏺) This brewery, established in 1995, is a local favorite. The restaurant serves hearty but sophisticated food – lamb chops with tzatziki, hummus tacos or pretzel-crusted chicken, say – and housemade sausages at tables with copper-clad tops and great views of the brewing tanks.

★ Maison EUROPEAN $$$
(☎717-293-5060; www.maisonlancaster.com; 230 N Prince St; mains $26-32; ☉5-10pm Wed-Sat; ⏺) A husband-and-wife team run this homey but meticulous place downtown, giving local farm products a rustic Italian-French treatment: pork braised in milk, housemade rabbit sausage, fried squash blossoms or handmade gnocchi, depending on the season.

🍷 Drinking & Nightlife

Nightlife here tends to be quiet, but bars and breweries can be busy on weekends. Several watering holes are just outside Lancaster.

Hildy's BAR
(☎717-397-2495; 448 W Frederick St; ☉2pm-2am Mon-Fri, 1pm-2am Sat, 1pm-midnight Sun) Lots of Lancaster seems to be getting fancy these days – farm-to-table and craft cocktails and all that – but not Hildy's. This still feels like a bar's bar, all smoky and dive-y and full of salty-and-sweet locals.

ROAD TRIP > PENNSYLVANIA DUTCH COUNTRY

• •

The Amish really do drive buggies and plow their fields by hand. In Dutch Country, the pace is slower, and it's no costumed reenactment. For the most evocative experience, go driving along the winding, narrow lanes between the thruways – past rolling green fields of alfalfa, asparagus and corn, past pungent working barnyards and manicured lawns, waving to Amish families in buggies and straw-hatted teens on scooters.

❶ Lancaster

A good place to start is the walkable, red-brick historic district of Lancaster (LANK-uh-stir), just off Penn Sq. The Romanesque-

revival-style Central Market (p222), which is like a smaller version of Philadelphia's Reading Terminal Market, has all the regional gastronomic delicacies – fresh horseradish, whoopie pies, soft pretzels and sub

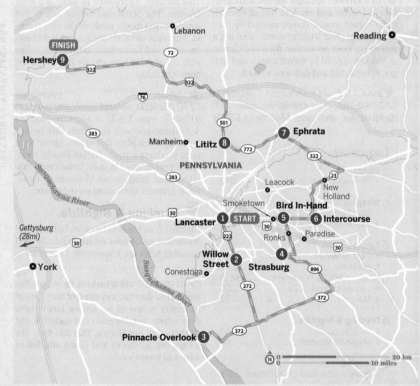

Length 3–4 Days; 102 miles/164km

Great for... Families; Food & Drink; History & Culture

Best Time to Go Less crowded early spring or September

sandwiches stuffed with cured meats and dripping with oil. You'll find surprises too, such as Spanish and Middle Eastern food. Plus, of course, the market is crowded with handicraft booths staffed by plain-dressed, bonneted Amish women.

In the 18th century, German immigrants flooded southeastern Pennsylvania, and only some were Amish. Most lived like the costumed docents at the Landis Valley Museum (p219), a re-creation of Pennsylvania German village life that includes a working smithy, stables and more. It's a few miles north of Lancaster off Rte 272/Oregon Pike.

The Drive > From downtown Lancaster head south on Prince St, which turns into Rte 222 and then Rte 272 all the way to Willow Street.

❷ Willow Street

Before the arrival of European émigrés, Coney, Lenape, Mohawk, Seneca and other Native Americans lived in the area. However, Pennsylvania remains one of the few states with no officially recognized tribal reserves – or, for that matter, tribes. In something of a gesture to rectify their erasure from history, a replica longhouse now stands on the property of the 1719 Hans Herr House (☎717-464-4438; www.hansherr.org; 1849 Hans Herr Dr; combined guided tour adult/child $15/7; ☉9am-4pm Mon-Sat Apr-Nov), regarded as the oldest original Mennonite meeting house in the western hemisphere. Today, it displays colonial-era artifacts in period furnished rooms; there's also a blacksmith shop and a barn. 'Living history interpreters' provide an idea of how life was lived in the 18th century.

The Drive > The simplest route is Rte 272 south to Rte 372 west. If you have time, however, head west on W Penn Grant Rd and then left on New Danville Pike, which turns into Main St in Conestoga. From there, follow Main St to a T-junction and turn left on River Rd, passing Tucquan Glen Nature Preserve on the way.

❸ Pinnacle Overlook

High over Lake Aldred, a wide portion of the Susquehanna River just up from a large dam, is this overlook (8am to 9pm) with beautiful views and eagles and other raptors soaring overhead. This and the adjoining Holtwood Environmental Preserve are parts of a large swath of riverfront property maintained by the Pennsylvania Power & Light Co (PPL). But electrical plant infrastructure and accompanying truck traffic is largely kept at bay, making this a popular spot for locals (non-Amish that is, as it's too far to travel by horse and buggy). The 4-mile-long Fire Line Trail to the adjoining Kelly's Run Natural Area is challenging and steep in parts, and the rugged Conestoga Trail follows the east side of the lake for 15 miles. It's worth coming out this way if only to see more rough-hewn landscape and the rural byways that reveal another facet to Lancaster County's character, which most visitors bypass.

The Drive > You could retrace your route back to Willow Street and then head on to Strasburg, but to make a scenic loop, take Rte 372 east passing some agrarian scenes as well as suburban housing to the small hamlet of Georgetown. Make a left onto Rte 896 – vistas open up on either side of the road.

❹ Strasburg

The main attraction in Strasburg is trains – the old-fashioned, steam-driven kind. Since 1832, the Strasburg Railroad (☎866-725-9666; www.strasburgrailroad.com; 301 Gap Rd, Ronks; coach class adult/child $15/8; ☷) has run the same route (and speed) to Paradise and back that it does today, and wooden train cars are gorgeously restored with stained glass, shiny brass lamps and plush burgundy seats. Several classes of seats are offered including the private President's Car; there's also a wine-and-cheese option.

The Railroad Museum of Pennsylvania (☎717-687-8628; www.rrmuseumpa.org; 300 Gap Rd, Ronks; adult/child $10/8; ☉9am-5pm Tue-Sat, noon-5pm Sun year-round, plus 9am-5pm Mon Apr-Oct) has 100 mechanical marvels to climb around and admire; even more delightful is the HO-scale National Toy Train Museum (☎717-687-8976; www.nttmuseum.org; 300 Paradise Lane, Ronks; adult/child $7/4; ☉10am-5pm May-Oct, hours vary Nov-Apr; ☷). The push-button

DETOUR: GETTYSBURG

From Lancaster (p224), take Hwy 30 west (also referred to as Lincoln Hwy) for 55 miles right into downtown Gettysburg. This tranquil, compact and memorial-laden town saw one of the Civil War's most decisive and bloody battles for three days in July 1863. It's also where, four months later, Lincoln delivered his Gettysburg Address consecrating, eulogizing and declaring the mission unfinished. Much of the ground where Robert E Lee's Army of Northern Virginia and Major General Joseph Hooker's Union Army of the Potomac skirmished and fought can be explored – either on your own, on a bus tour or on a two-hour guide-led tour in your own car. The latter is most recommended, but if you're short on time it's still worth driving the narrow lanes past fields with dozens of monuments marking significant sites and moments in the battle.

The massive **Gettysburg National Military Park Museum & Visitor Center** (☎717-334-1124; www.nps.gov/gett; 1195 Baltimore Pike; museum adult/child $15/10, bus tour $35/21, licensed guide per vehicle $75; 🕒museum 8am-6pm Apr-Oct, 9am-5pm Nov-Mar, grounds 6am-10pm Apr-Oct, to 7pm Nov-Mar) several miles south of town houses an incredible museum filled with artifacts and displays exploring every nuance of the battle; a film explaining Gettysburg's context and why it's considered a turning point in the war; and Paul Philippoteaux's 377ft cyclorama painting of Pickett's Charge. The aforementioned bus tours and ranger-led tours are booked here.

The annual **Civil War Heritage Days Festival**, taking place from the last weekend of June through the first weekend of July, features living history encampments, battle reenactments, a lecture series and book fair that draws war reenactment aficionados from near and wide. You can find reenactments at other times throughout the year.

interactive dioramas are so up-to-date and clever (such as a 'drive-in movie' that's a live video of kids working the trains), and the walls are packed with so many railcars, that you can't help but feel a bit of Christmas-morning wonder. Stop at the **Red Caboose Motel** next to the museum – you can climb the silo in back for wonderful views ($0.50), and kids can enjoy a small petting zoo.

The Drive > Continue north on S Ronks Rd past Ronks' bucolic farmland scenery, cross busy Rte 30 (Miller's Smorgasbord restaurant is at this intersection) and carry on for another 2 miles to Bird-in-Hand. Still hungry? Smoketown's Good 'N Plenty Restaurant is a mile west of Bird-in-Hand on Rte 340/Old Philadelphia Pike at the intersection with Rte 896.

5 Bird-in-Hand

The primary reason to make your way to this delightfully named Amish town is the **Bird-in-Hand Farmers Market** (☎717-393-9674; www.birdinhandfarmersmarket.com; 2710 Old Philadelphia Pike; lunches $6-11; 🕒8:30am-5:30pm Fri & Sat year-round, plus Wed Apr-Nov & Thu Jul-Oct; [P]), which is pretty much a one-stop shop of Dutch Country highlights. There's fudge, quilts and crafts, and you can buy scrapple (pork scraps mixed with cornmeal and wheat flour, shaped into a loaf and fried), homemade jam and shoofly pie (a pie made of molasses or brown sugar sprinkled with a crumbly mix of brown sugar, flour and butter). Two lunch counters sell cheap sandwiches, homemade pretzels and healthy juices and smoothies. It's worth bringing a cooler to stock up for the onward drive.

The Drive > It's less than 4 miles east on Old Philadelphia Pike/Rte 340 to Intercourse, but traffic can back up, in part because it's a popular route for tourist horse-and-buggy rides.

6 Intercourse

Named for the crossroads, not the act, Intercourse is a little more amenable to walking than Bird-in-Hand. The **horse-drawn buggy rides** (☎717-768-8828; www.amishbuggyrides.com; 3121 Old Philadelphia Pike, Bird-in-Hand; tours adult/child from $10/6; 🕒9am-6pm Mon-Sat Apr-Oct, 10am-4:30pm Mon-Sat Nov-Mar; 👪) on offer can also be fun. How much fun depends largely on your driver: some Amish are strict, some liberal, and Mennonites are different again. All drivers strive to present Amish culture to the 'English' (the Amish term for non-Amish, whether English or not), but some are more openly personal than others.

Kitchen Kettle Village, essentially an open-air mall for tourists with stores selling smoked meats, jams, pretzels and tchotchkes, feels like a Disneyfied version of the Bird-in-the-Hand Farmers Market. It's a one-stop shop for the commercialized 'PA Dutch Country experience,' which means your perception of it will depend on your attitude toward a parking lot jammed with tour buses.

The Drive > Head north on Rte 772 and make your first right onto Centerville Rd, which becomes S Shirk Rd, a country lane that takes you to Rte 23. Turn right here and it's a few miles to Blue Ball (try not to giggle that you're so close to Intercourse) – and then left on the busier Rte 322 all the way to Ephrata.

⑦ Ephrata

One of the country's earliest religious communities was founded in 1732 by Conrad Beissel, an émigré escaping religious persecution in his native Germany. Beissel sought a mystical, personal relationship with God. At its peak there were close to 300 members, including two celibate orders of brothers and sisters, known collectively as 'the Solitary,' who patterned their dress after Roman Catholic monks (the last of these passed away in 1813), as well as married 'households' who were less all-in, if you will.

Today, the collection of austere, almost medieval-style buildings of the **Ephrata Cloister** (☑717-733-6600; www.ephratacloister. org; 632 W Main St; adult/child $10/6; ☺9am-5pm Tue-Sat, noon-5pm Sun Mar-Dec, reduced hours Jan & Feb; ℗) have been preserved and are open to visitors; guided tours are offered or you can take a self-guided audio cell phone tour. There's a small museum and a short film in the visitor center that earnestly and efficiently tells the story of Ephrata's founding and demise – if the narrator's tone and rather somber mise-en-scène are any indication, it was a demanding existence.

The impressive **Green Dragon Farmers Market** (☑717-738-1117; www.greendragonmarket.com; 955 N State St; ☺9am-9pm Fri) has everything from the usual produce, crafts and prepared foods to live chickens and pigs being sold to the highest bidder. For a locally brewed beer, try **St Boniface Craft Brewing Co** (☑717-466-6900; www.stbonifacebrewing.com; 1701 W Main St; ☺4-9pm Tue-Thu, 11am-10:30pm Fri & Sat), offering over a dozen beers.

The Drive > This is a simple 8.5-mile drive; for the most part, Rte 772/Rothsville Rd between Ephrata and Lititz is an ordinary commercial strip.

⑧ Lititz

Like other towns in Pennsylvania Dutch Country, Lititz was founded by a religious community from Europe, in this case Moravians who settled here in the 1740s. However, unlike Ephrata, Lititz was more outward looking and integrated with the world be-

yond its historic center. Many of its original handsome stone and wood buildings still line its streets today. Take a stroll down E Main from the **Sturgis Pretzel House** (☑717-626-4354; www.juliussturgis.com; 219 E Main St; adult/child $3.75/2.75; ☺9am-5pm Mon-Sat, tours to 4:30pm mid-Mar–Dec, 10am-4pm Mon-Sat, tours to 3:30pm mid-Jan–mid-Mar), the first pretzel factory in the country – you can try your hand at rolling and twisting the dough. Across the street is the Moravian Church (c 1787); then head to the intersection with S Broad. Rather than feeling sealed in amber, the small shops, which do seem to relish their small-town quality, are nonetheless the type that sophisticated urbanites cherish. There's an unusual effortlessness to this vibe, from the **Bulls Head Public House** (☑717-626-2115; www.bullsheadpublichouse.com; 14 E Main St; mains $15-25; ☺11:30am-11pm Mon-Fri, 8am-midnight Sat, 11am-11pm Sun), a traditional English-style pub with an expertly curated beer menu, to Greco's Italian Ices, a little ground-floor hole-in-the-wall where local teenagers and families head on weekend nights for delicious homemade ice cream.

The Drive > It's an easy 27 miles on Rte 501 to Hwy 322 and on to Hershey. Both roads pass through a combination of farmland and suburban areas, though the latter is generally a fast-moving highway.

⑨ Hershey

Hershey is home to a collection of attractions that detail, hype and, of course, hawk the many trappings of Milton Hershey's chocolate empire. The pièce de résistance is **Hersheypark** (☑717-534-3900; www.hersheypark.com; 100 W Hersheypark Dr; adult/child $65/42; ☺10am-10pm Jun-Aug, reduced hours Sep-May; ℗), an amusement park with more than 60 thrill rides, a zoo and a water park, plus various performances and frequent fireworks displays. Don a hairnet and apron and punch in a few choices on a computer screen and then voilà, watch your very own chocolate bar roll down a conveyor belt at the Create Your Own Candy Bar attraction ($15), part of Hershey's Chocolate World, a mock factory and massive candy store with over-stimulating features such as singing characters and free chocolate galore. For a more low-key informative visit, try the Hershey Story, The Museum on Chocolate Avenue, which explores the life and fascinating legacy of Mr Hershey through interactive history exhibits; try molding your own candy in the hands-on Chocolate Lab.

THE AMISH

The Amish (ah-mish), Mennonite and Brethren religious communities are collectively known as the 'Plain People.' All are Anabaptist sects (only those who choose the faith are baptized) who were persecuted in their native Switzerland, and from the early 1700s settled in tolerant Pennsylvania. Speaking German dialects, they became known as 'Dutch' (from 'Deutsch'). Most Pennsylvania Dutch live on farms and their beliefs vary from sect to sect. Many do not use electricity, and most opt for horse-drawn buggies – a delightful sight, and sound, in the area. The strictest believers, the Old Order Amish who make up nearly 90% of Lancaster County's Amish, wear dark, plain clothing (no zippers, only buttons, snaps and safety pins), and live a simple, Bible-centered life – but have, ironically, become a major tourist attraction, thus bringing busloads of gawkers and the requisite strip malls, chain restaurants and hotels that lend this entire area an oxymoronic quality, to say the least. Because there is so much commercial development – fast-food restaurants, mini-malls, big-box chain stores, tract housing – continually encroaching on multigenerational family farms, it takes some doing to appreciate the unique nature of the area.

Meduseld Meadery BREWERY
(☑717-208-6144; www.meduseldmeadery.com; 252 Harrisburg Ave; ☺6-11pm Wed-Fri, 3-11pm Sat, 2-5pm Sun) There's no shortage of beer breweries in Pennsylvania, but this was one of the few meaderies we hunted down. Mead, if you didn't know, is a drink made from fermented honey, and it's quite delicious – sweet, but not too much so, and with a light boozy punch. There are over a dozen varieties on tap here, so go wild.

Wanna get really medieval? In spring, Meduseld hosts a local axe-throwing league. Yarr!

Bube's Brewery BREWERY
(☑717-653-2056; www.bubesbrewery.com; 102 N Market St, Mt Joy; ☺11am-2am) This well-preserved 19th-century German brewery-cum-restaurant complex contains several atmospheric bars and four separate dining rooms (one underground); it also hosts costumed 'feasts' and, naturally, brews its own beer. There are murder-mystery-themed dining events and an outdoor *biergarten*.

The brewery is a 15-minute drive from Lancaster in nearby Mt Joy.

🛍 Shopping

★**Pennsylvania Guild of Craftsmen** ARTS & CRAFTS
(☑717-431-8706; www.pacrafts.org; 335 N Queen St; ☺10am-5pm Tue-Sat) Everyone and their quaint grandmother is selling Pennsylvania Dutch artisanal goods in Lancaster, but at the Guild of Craftsmen store, you know you're getting the well-curated real deal. Furniture, home decor, fabrics, kitchen goods and other items make for a perfect souvenir from your trip to Pennsylvania.

ℹ Information

While located in Lancaster, Discover Lancaster Visitors Center (p219) is especially in the know on what's happening across all of Pennsylvania Dutch Country. Just off Rte 30.

PENNSYLVANIA WILDS

North-central Pennsylvania, known as 'the Wilds,' is largely deep forest with an occasional regal building or grand mansion – remnants of the late 19th century, when lumber, coal and oil brought wealth to this now little-visited patch of the state. The cash cow of resource extraction was eventually milked dry by the turn of the 20th century, and the land fell on hard times. Since the bust, this swath of 12 counties has reverted to its wild state; much of the area is national forest or state park land.

👁 Sights & Activities

★**Cherry Springs State Park** STATE PARK
(☑814-435-1037; www.dcnr.pa.gov; 4639 Cherry Springs Rd, Coudersport; one-time fee $5; ☺24hr) Considered one of the best places for stargazing east of the Mississippi, this mountaintop state park seems to have plenty of space, but be sure to book well ahead in July and August, when the Milky Way is almost directly overhead. First-timers will need to pay a one-time $5 fee (not per day).

★**Kinzua Bridge Skywalk**   BRIDGE
(☎814-778-5467; www.visitpaparks.com; 1721
Lindholm Rd, Mt Jewett; ⊙skywalk 8am-dusk, visitor center to 6pm) **FREE** The world's tallest
viaduct when it was built in 1882, this 301ft-
high bridge was rebuilt in steel in 1900 – but
then partially collapsed in 2003, when it was
hit by an F1-grade tornado. The remaining
piece, jutting out into the air, is now an observation deck, with an impressive and perhaps unnerving view over the ruined steel
piers and the valley below.

Leonard Harrison State Park   STATE PARK
(☎570-724-3061; www.dcnr.pa.gov; 4797 Rte 660,
Wellsboro; ⊙park dawn-dusk, visitor center 10am-
4:30pm Mon-Thu, to 6:30pm Fri-Sun; **P**) **FREE**
This park has full views of the Pine Creek
Gorge, aka the Grand Canyon of PA, with
trails that descend 800ft down to the creek
below. A visitor center has modest displays
of local fauna; there are toilets here; and a
viewing deck makes this side more accessible for people not planning to hike. For the
undeveloped side go to Colton Point State
Park instead.

Pine Creek Rail Trail   CYCLING, HIKING
(Wellsboro Junction or Jersey Shore) **FREE** Popular for both hiking and cycling, the Pine
Creek Rail Trail encompasses some 62 miles
of converted railway-run that traverses the
floor of Pine Creek Gorge. There's barely any
grade to the hard-packed trail, which makes
for easy biking or a pleasant walk. The trail
begins (or ends) at Wellsboro Junction and
ends (or begins) in Jersey Shore, Pennsylvania. There are numerous access points to the
trail; we prefer to enter via Leonard Harrison State Park (p229).

🛏 Sleeping & Eating

★**Susquehannock Lodge**   INN $
(☎814-435-2163; www.susquehannock-lodge.com;
5039 Rte 6, Ulysses; r $97-140; **P**❄🐾) A homey
and comfortable place halfway between
Coudersport and Galeton and 15 miles from
Cherry Springs State Park. The owners, a
couple who relocated from Philadelphia decades ago, are happy to help sort out activities in the area. A gorgeous restored sleigh
decorates the porch in the winter months.

Lodge at Glendorn   LODGE $$$
(☎814-362-6511; www.glendorn.com; 1000 Glen-
dorn Dr, Bradford; ste $525-1100; **P**❄🐾🐕)
A legacy of the Wilds' former industrial
wealth, this 1200-acre estate was developed
by an early-20th-century oil baron. Its 'big

house' and log cabins (all with wood-burning
fireplaces) now constitute one of the finest
resorts in the region, catering to the money-
to-burn crowd. The restaurant is excellent,
and the resort fee includes activities from
skeet shooting to curling.

Note that rates can be dramatically dis-
counted in the off-season.

★**Night & Day Coffee Cafe**   CAFE $
(☎570-662-1143;   http://nightanddaycoffee.wix
site.com/cafe; 2 N Main St, Mansfield; sandwiches
$7-10; ⊙7am-7pm Mon-Fri, to 5pm Sat, 8am-5pm
Sun; 🐾) Well worth detouring for, the Night
& Day Coffee Cafe proudly claims to be en-
riching the neighborhood one latte at a time,
and it's doing a good job of it. Boutique
coffees, great chai and a wide selection of
specialty salads and sandwiches make for a
perfect breakfast or a great lunch.

Yorkholo Brewing   AMERICAN $
(☎570-662-0241; www.yorkholobrewing.com; 19
N Main St, Mansfield; mains $11-17; ⊙4-10pm Mon
& Tue, 11am-10pm Wed-Sat, 11am-9pm Sun May-
Oct, reduced hours Nov-Apr) A welcome alter-
native to standard diner food in this area,
this brick-walled brewpub has fresh salads,
bacon-wrapped scallops, creative pizzas and
some excellent Belgian-style beers.

❶ Getting There & Away

Driving is your only option to reach the Pennsyl-
vania Wilds. Allegheny National Forest is about
100 miles northwest of Pittsburgh and 90 miles
southwest of Erie, NY. Route 6 makes for a sce-
nic route that traverses much of the region, with
the tiny college town of Mansfield acting as an
eastern gateway.

WESTERN PENNSYLVANIA

The Alleghenies form the forested, stony
spine of Pennsylvania, and amid the hol-
lows and rushing streams are sylvan glades
so ideally beautiful that Frank Lloyd Wright
once built his most famous house here (not
that he ever lived in it). For all that natu-
ral beauty, this is largely rust-belt country, a
land peppered with steel towns that have
fallen on hard times. But the biggest town
of them all – Pittsburgh – has managed to
reverse the rot of economic depression and
synthesize the area's scrappy mountain spir-
it with an embrace of diversity and oddball
aesthetics.

SEAN PAVONE/SHUTTERSTOCK ©

1. Philly Cheesesteak (p208)
Try Philadelphia's famous beef sandwich (it even comes in a veggie version).

2. City Hall (p197)
Philadelphia's City Hall takes up a whole block and offers views of the city.

3. Pennsylvania Dutch Country (p219)
Amish residents drive horses and buggies along narrow lanes and plow their fields by hand.

4. Fallingwater (p239)
Tour Frank Lloyd Wright's architectural masterpiece in Pennsylvania's Laurel Highlands.

GABOR KOVACS PHOTOGRAPHY/SHUTTERSTOCK ©

ALLEGHENY NATIONAL FOREST

Northwestern Pennsylvania is dominated, even defined, by the Allegheny National Forest (ANF), which blankets this corner of the state with a half million acres of managed woodlands. Once this was a land of native old-growth hemlock and maple, packs of wolves and prowling mountain lions. But extensive logging, black cherry tree cultivation and wildlife hunting has dramatically changed the ecological makeup of the forest.

Since 1923, the area has been managed by the US Forest Service, making it the only national forest in the state, although many private concessions still lay claim to sub-surface mineral rights. The forest is part of the Appalachian foothills; topographically, this is a land of endless ridges, plateaus, hollows and intermittent valleys.

The 7647-acre **Allegheny Reservoir** (www.fs.usda.gov; off SR 346; P) looks as if it were always a deep-blue compliment to the landscape, but in fact it dates only from the 1960s, when the lake was created as a byproduct of the Kinzua Dam. Today this body of water, some 27 miles long, is a popular spot for camping, boating and just soaking in some quiet beauty. In 8500-acre **Cook Forest State Park** (814-744-8407; www.dcnr. pa.gov; 113 River Road, Cooksburg; sunrise-sunset; P) FREE be on the lookout for the 'Forest Cathedral,' which contains the Ancients – a serene grove of 350–450-year-old white pine and hemlock. The rugged **North Country National Scenic Trail** (www. northcountrytrail.org/trail/pennsylvania; 24hr) traverses the park.

Getting There & Away

Pittsburgh and its airport (p239) serves as the major point of entry to the region. Major highways in the region include I-79 and the Pennsylvania Turnpike.

Pittsburgh

412 / POP 303,600

There may be more beautiful cities than Pittsburgh, but few mix the seemingly contradictory aesthetics of filigreed beaux-arts elegance with muscular art-deco swagger. This a city of stone and steel, with old public libraries and brick row houses beside wide bridges and towering skyscrapers. There's an old-school class to Pittsburgh's good looks, underlined by an attitude towards dining, drinking and the arts that is genuinely innovative.

Architecture and attitude set Pittsburgh apart, as does its surroundings. Set between the Monongahela and Allegheny Rivers and the upland ridge of Mt Washington, this city has a distinctive geography; physically, it is very much defined by its mountains and rivers. While this is the main urban center for western Pennsylvania, it has avoided the economic depression of the surrounding region by investing in 'meds and eds' – hospitals and universities – buttressing its economy with expansive intellectual energy.

Sights

Points of interest in Pittsburgh are scattered in every neighborhood, but because of the hills it's difficult to walk between them. Bike, taxi or bus (or light rail in some areas) are the best ways to span suburbs. The usual ride-sharing services are well represented in Pittsburgh.

★ Andy Warhol Museum   MUSEUM
(412-237-8300; www.warhol.org; 117 Sandusky St; adult/child $20/10, 5-10pm Fri $10/5; 10am-5pm Tue-Thu, Sat & Sun, to 10pm Fri) This six-story museum celebrates Pittsburgh's coolest native son, Andy Warhol, who moved to NYC, got a nose job and made himself famous with pop art. The exhibits start with Warhol's earliest drawings and commercial illustrations and include a simulated Velvet Underground happening, a DIY 'screen test' and pieces of Warhol's extensive knickknack collection. Cans of inflatable Campbell's soup are for sale.

★ Duquesne Incline   FUNICULAR
(412-381-1665; www.duquesneincline.org; 1197 W Carson St; one way adult/child $2.50/1.25; 5:30am-12:30am Mon-Sat, 7am-12:30am Sun) This nifty funicular and its **Monongahela Incline** (412-381-1665; www.duquesneincline .org; 5 Grandview Ave; one way adult/child $2.50/1.25; 5:30am-12:30am Mon-Sat, 7am-12:30am Sun) twin down the road, both built in the late 19th century, are Pittsburgh icons, zipping up the steep slope of Mt Washington

every five to 10 minutes. They provide commuters a quick connection, and give visitors great city views, especially at night. You can make a loop, going up one, walking along aptly named Grandview Ave (about 1 mile, or take bus 40) and coming down the other.

If you ride just one, make it the Duquesne (du-*kane*). At the top, you can pay 50¢ to see the gears and cables at work.

★Mattress Factory   ARTS CENTER
(☑ 412-231-3169; www.mattress.org; 500 Sampsonia Way; adult/student $20/15; ☺10am-5pm Tue-Sat, 1-5pm Sun) Since 1977, this art space has hosted the absolute avant-garde. It now occupies several neighborhood buildings, and always has something surprising on, from pitch-black sensory deprivation rooms to surreal caricature galleries to oddly angled experiments in room layout. The spring **Urban Garden Party** ($95; ☺Jun) event is always popular.

Phipps Conservatory   GARDENS
(☑ 412-622-6914; www.phipps.conservatory.org; 1 Schenley Park; adult/child $18/12; ☺9:30am-5pm Sat-Thu, to 10pm Fri; 🚻) 🖉 An impressive steel-and-glass greenhouse with beautifully designed and curated gardens, at the northwest corner of Schenley Park.

Carnegie Museums   MUSEUM
(☑ 412-622-3131; www.carnegiemuseums.org; 4400 Forbes Ave; adult/child both museums $20/12; ☺10am-5pm Mon, Wed, Fri & Sat, to 8pm Thu, noon-5pm Sun; 🚻) Founded in 1895, these neighboring institutions are both tremendous troves of knowledge. The Carnegie Museum of Art has European treasures and an excellent architectural collection, while the Carnegie Museum of Natural History features a complete *Tyrannosaurus rex* skeleton and beautiful old dioramas. The

art museum is open until 11pm on the third Thursday of the month.

Frick Art & Historical Center   MUSEUM
(☑ 412-371-0600; www.thefrickpittsburgh.org; 7227 Reynolds St; ☺10am-5pm Tue-Thu & Sun, to 9pm Fri) **FREE** Henry Clay Frick, of New York City's Frick Collection (p73) fame, built his steel fortune in Pittsburgh. This Frick shows a small art collection (including beautiful medieval icons), plus his cars. For more art and general splendor, join a **tour** (adult/child $12/6) of Clayton, the family mansion.

Center for PostNatural History   MUSEUM
(☑ 412-223-7698; www.postnatural.org; 4913 Penn Ave; by donation; ☺noon-4pm Sun) **FREE** 'Postnatural history,' according to the artist-founder of this quirky museum, is the field of plants and animals designed by humankind. Learn all about spider-silk–making goats, selective breeding and more. Probably not your best first-date spot, but definitely a fun and unconventional place to learn about all things *human*-ipulated.

Cathedral of Learning   TOWER
(☑ 412-624-6001; www.tour.pitt.edu; 4200 Fifth Ave; ☺9am-4pm Mon-Sat, 11am-4pm Sun) **FREE** Soaring 42 stories, this Gothic tower at the center of the University of Pittsburgh is a city landmark. Visit to see the delightful Nationality Rooms, 30 themed classrooms ranging from Russian to Syrian to African. Audio tours are available on Saturdays and Sundays (adult/child $4/2). New rooms may be added in the future.

👉 Tours & Courses

Pittsburgh Glass Center   ART
(☑ 412-365-2145; www.pittsburghglasscenter. org; 5472 Penn Ave; ☺10am-7pm Mon-Thu, to 4pm Fri-Sun) See a variety of glass-making

WORTH A TRIP

FLIGHT 93 NATIONAL MEMORIAL

You can pay your respects to the passengers and crew who struggled to retake control of their plane from hijackers on September 11, 2001, at the **Flight 93 National Memorial** (☑ 814-893-6322; www.nps.gov/flni; 6424 Lincoln Hwy, Stoystown; ☺grounds sunrise-sunset, visitor center 9am-5pm; 🅿). It's at the crash site, in a rural Somerset Country field, only 18 minutes (flying time) from the terrorists' intended target, Washington, DC. It's a solemn place: the names of the dead are carved on a marble wall aligned in the direction of the flight path leading to a fence, beyond which is their final resting place.

By the time you read this, construction should be completed on a 'Tower of Voices,' a 93ft-tall musical instrument that consists of 40 wind chimes representing the flight's passengers and crew.

techniques and even try your hand at making something yourself in a demo. Or take an actual class; the PGC offers everything from newbie level to advanced (prices vary).

Wigle Whiskey
DISTILLERY

(☎412-224-2827; www.wiglewhiskey.com; 2401 Smallman St; tours $20-25; ⊙11am-6pm Mon, 10am-6pm Tue-Sat, to 4pm Sun) This family-owned craft distillery in a brick warehouse in the Strip gives tours on Saturdays (and some Fridays) and has inexpensive sample flights ($10) of the many libations. Whiskey is a top choice, but there's also gin, vodka, bitters and even a housemade absinthe.

'Burgh Bits & Bites
FOOD & DRINK

(☎412-901-7150; www.burghfoodtour.com; tours $43) These two-hour food tours through various neighborhoods are a fun way to discover the city's unique ethnic eats. The Strip District tour is the most popular, but Bits & Bites also visits Bloomfield, Brookline, Lawrenceville, the South Side and more.

Pittsburgh History & Landmarks Foundation
WALKING

(☎412-471-5808; www.phlf.org) This group runs a free walking tour from Market Sq on Fridays at noon, among other excursions. Paid, docent-led tours ($20) are also available.

Pittsburgh

PENNSYLVANIA PITTSBURGH

🛏 Sleeping

★ Priory Hotel INN $$
(☎ 412-231-3338; www.thepriory.com; 614 Pressley St; s $99-129, d $155-229, ste $180-295; P🅿✴🛜) The monks had it good when this was still a Catholic monastery: spacious rooms, high ceilings, a fireplace in the parlor. Breakfast, with its pastries and cold cuts, is reminiscent of a European hostel. It's on the North Side, in the historic-but-scruffy Deutschtown area. The tiny Monk's Bar just off the lobby is open 5pm to 11pm daily – perfect for an evening tipple.

★ Omni William Penn Hotel HOTEL $$
(☎ 412-281-7100; www.omnihotels.com; 530 William Penn Pl; d $159-189, ste $209-540; P🅿⊖✴🛜) Pittsburgh's stateliest old hotel, built by Henry Frick, has a cavernous lobby, with luxury suites that were remodeled in 2016. The great public spaces give it a sense of grandeur that some luxury hotels lack. Worth booking if you have the money…or can find it at a discount, which is often the case in the off-season.

Distrikt Hotel HOTEL $$$
(☎ 412-339-1870; www.distrikthotel.com; 453 Blvd of the Allies; r $229-299; P🅿⊖✴🛜🏊) Some 185

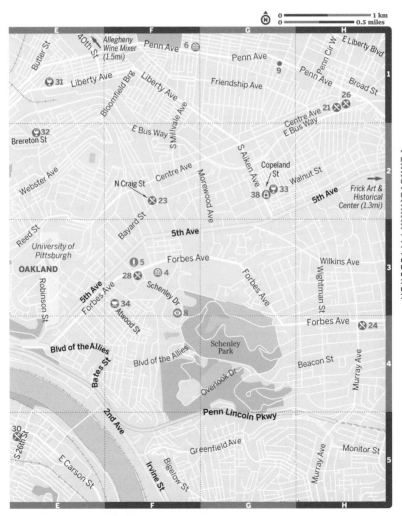

Pittsburgh

bedrooms sprawl across ten floors of the renovated 1924 Salvation Army Building, sitting above a lobby that hums with cool kids working business junkets. Within, the Distrikt makes a concerted effort to provide guests with slick, neutral-colored rooms that straddle the line between design consciousness and comfort. Room rates plunge by $100 or more in the off-season.

Monaco   DESIGN HOTEL $$$
(☑ 412-471-1170;   www.monaco-pittsburgh. com; 620 William Penn Pl; d/ste from $239/404; ⓟ☺❄☂☎☺) The cool Kimpton chain opened this place, done up in eye-popping colors, in 2015. Enthusiastic staff and a good restaurant make it the most chic accommodation downtown. Be sure to check out the chandelier, like a giant dangling peacock's tail of illumination, when you check in.

✖ Eating

★ **Nu Modern Jewish Bistro**   JEWISH $
(☑ 412-422-0220; www.nujewishbistro.com; 1711 Murray Ave; buffet $16; ⊙ 10am-4pm Sat & Sun) One of the 'Burgh's more innovative restaurants, Nu basically takes the classic Jewish deli menu and brunches it up on weekends.

Pick one main (ranging from stacked Reuben sandwiches to brisket and eggs), then nosh on a buffet table of mini bagels, Israeli salads, chicken soup, couscous and other favorites sourced from across the Jewish diaspora.

Carson Street Deli   SANDWICHES $
(☑ 412-381-5335; www.carsonstreetdeliandcraft beer.com; 1507 E Carson St; sandwiches $10; ⊙ 10am-10pm Mon-Thu, to 11pm Fri, 11am-11pm Sat, 11am-8pm Sun) Sandwiches done simply is the name of the game at the Carson Street Deli, where a lovable band of tattooed misfits fix up some of the best meat and cheese between bread in the 'Burgh. There's a nice selection of craft beer available (they even have beer tastings on Wednesdays). Great for a quick Southside lunch.

Pittsburgh Public Market   MARKET $
(☑ 412-281-4505; www.pittsburghpublicmarket. org; 2401 Penn Ave; ⊙ 10am-4pm Wed-Fri & Sun, 9am-5pm Sat) This giant indoor market caters to the need for downtown to have easy access to fresh produce, meats, cheeses and other local products. Note that many vendors are also open on Monday and Tuesday as well.

La Prima
CAFE $

(☑ 412-281-1922; www.laprima.com; 205 21st St; pastries $2-4; ⊙6am-4pm Mon-Wed, to 5pm Thu-Sat, 7am-4pm Sun) Great Italian coffee and pastries have people lined up out the door at peak times. The 'Almond Mele' is the scrumptious signature sweet, but it has a range of other yummy treats (*sfogliatelle,* tarts, cookies etc). If you speak Italian you can enjoy the daily quote, written on the green chalkboard each morning.

Zenith
VEGAN $

(☑ 412-481-4833; www.zenithpgh.com; 86 S 26th St; mains $7-11; ⊙11:30am-8:30pm Thu-Sat, 11am-2:30pm Sun; ☑) All meals are vegan here, though cheese is optional. A visit here is like eating in an antique shop, as everything, including the Formica tables, is for sale. The Sunday buffet brunch ($11.50) draws a great community of regulars.

Breakfast at Shelly's
BREAKFAST $

(☑ 412-245-6785; www.facebook.com/pg/eat atshellys; 740 E Warrington Ave; mains $4.50-11; ⊙8am-2pm Tue-Sun; ☑) Start the day right at this Allentown establishment, which resembles a diner plucked from the 1950s. Dig into a kielbasa sausage breakfast sandwich, enormous breakfast burritos or to-die-for homemade French toast, then face the day, sated and satisfied. Actually, can we get another coffee?

Original Oyster House
SEAFOOD $

(☑ 412-566-7925; www.originaloysterhousepitts burgh.com; 20 Market Sq; mains $11-13; ⊙10am-10pm Mon-Sat, 11am-7pm Sun) Operating since 1870, this place often has a line out the door for its fish sandwiches; just as in olden times, you can still order a glass of buttermilk to drink. With tile floors and lots of photos and memorabilia, it's a historical gem. Food is average, though the ribbon-cut fries are unique. Cash only.

Primanti Bros
SANDWICHES $

(☑ 412-263-2142; www.primantibros.com; 46 18th St; sandwiches $7-10; ⊙24hr) The original location serves up the signature sandwiches Pittsburghers miss when they move away: hot, greasy delights stuffed with grilled meat, french fries and coleslaw. With branches located all around Pittsburgh, you're never too far away from a Primanti Bros fix.

★Dinette
PIZZA $$

(☑ 412-362-0202; www.dinette-pgh.com; 5996 Centre Ave; small plates $6-14, pizza $21; ⊙5-10pm Tue-Thu, to 11pm Fri & Sat; ☑☑) *ℐ* Out in East Liberty, Dinette doesn't just serve awesome pizza, although it does indeed serve awesome pizza (try the salt-cured anchovy pizza with jalapeños, capers, mozzarella and tomatoes – amazing). The owners are committed to sustainably sourced ingredients and paying their workers a living wage – no tipping here. Plus: did we mention the pizza is *really* good?

DiAnoia's Eatery
ITALIAN $$

(☑ 412-918-1875; www.dianoiaseatery.com; 2549 Penn Ave; mains $15-22; ⊙8am-9pm Mon-Thu, to 10pm Fri & Sat, 10am-2:30pm Sun; ☑) There's no shortage of Italian restaurants in Pittsburgh, but DiAnoia has been praised for raising the bar on the genre. Clean, deceptively simple dishes like beef-cheek ravioli and whole roasted fish are served in an inviting dining room that aims to create a grandmother's kitchen – with a bit of contemporary flash.

Porch at Schenley
CAFE $$

(☑ 412-687-6724; www.dineattheporch.com; 221 Schenley Dr; mains $9-24; ⊙11am-11pm Mon-Fri, 10am-11pm Sat, to 9pm Sun; ☑) Cheap and casual doesn't often unite with fresh and farm-to-table, but at the Porch it does. Get great local ingredients served up with flair in a casual yet chic environment; the clientele is a mix of students, professors, locals and out-of-towners. Specials change daily. Takeout only in the morning.

Bar Marco
ITALIAN $$

(☑ 412-471-1900; www.barmarcopgh.com; 2216 Penn Ave; mains $15-28; ⊙5-11pm Tue-Fri, 10am-3pm & 5-11pm Sat & Sun) A Strip District favorite, this is one of the city's more sophisticated kitchens, with an excellent brunch too. Cocktails are creative; you can also try the bartender's suggestion based on what types of drinks you enjoy. The refreshing no-tipping policy means the staff are appropriately compensated in a fair and equitable way.

★Butcher & the Rye
AMERICAN $$$

(☑ 412-391-2752; www.butcherandtherye.com; 212 6th St; mains $20-34; ⊙5-11pm Tue-Thu, to midnight Fri & Sat) Good meat? Good whiskey? Good times. Butcher & the Rye is new-school hip, but its focus on excellent carnivorous fare and brown liquor feels classic. Not so the interior – all clean lines, lounge music and sexy lighting. To be fair, even the meat is presented flash and sexy: try ground-duck dirty pasta or caramelized pork-belly 'pig candy.'

★ **Paris 66** FRENCH $$$

(☑412-404-8166; www.paris66bistro.com; 6018 Centre Ave; dinner mains $20-39; ⊗11am-10pm Mon-Thu, to 11pm Fri & Sat, 10am-3pm Sun) This is top-end French at its best, in a cozy, bistro-style setting. Blink and you'll think you're in France. That said, this isn't *haute cuisine*, but rather solid food of rural France: *coq au vin,* rabbit in mustard sauce, *steak frites* and the rest.

★ **Legume** FUSION $$$

(☑412-621-2700; www.legumebistro.com; 214 N Craig St; mains $23-36, 3-course tasting menu $38; ⊗5-9pm Mon-Thu, to 10pm Fri & Sat) Excellent meats and fish here, with a farm-to-table mindset and a menu that changes daily. If it's available, try the stinging-nettle soup – partly because where else can you try stinging nettles, but mostly because it's out of this world.

🍷 Drinking & Entertainment

★ **Le Mardi Gras** BAR

(☑412-683-0912; www.lemardigras.com; 731 Copeland St; ⊗4pm-2am Mon-Thu, from 2pm Fri & Sat, from 3pm Sun) This excellent dive bar has been open since 1954, and they've probably cleaned the carpets at least once since then. You can still smoke inside, the service is friendly and the bar tries to live up to its namesake by displaying purple, yellow and green (the colors of New Orleans Mardi Gras) and providing general good times.

★ **Allegheny Wine Mixer** WINE BAR

(☑412-252-2337; www.alleghenywinemixer.com; 5326 Butler St; ⊗5pm-midnight Tue-Thu, to 1am Fri-Sun) All the perks of a high-end wine bar – great list, smart staff, tasty nibbles – in the comfort of a neighborhood dive.

★ **Gooski's** BAR

(☑412-681-1658; 3117 Brereton St; ⊗3pm-2am) Pierogis, punk rock, cheap brickhouse-strong drinks and a near-legendary bartender have made this a consistently great dive bar in Polish Hill for decades.

Church Brew Works MICROBREWERY

(☑412-688-8200; www.churchbrew.com; 3525 Liberty Ave; ⊗4-11pm Mon, 11:30am-11pm Tue-Thu & Sun, to midnight Fri & Sat) There are some who put drunkenness next to godliness, and they probably invented Church Brew Works. Gleaming and shining, giant brewery vats sit in what was once the pulpit. If you think this is sacrilegious, you'll want to skip this place – although of course many a great Belgian beer was proudly brewed by highly religious monks.

Butter Joint COCKTAIL BAR

(☑412-621-2700; www.butterjoint.com; 214 N Craig St; ⊗4:30pm-midnight Mon-Sat) If you're looking for a snazzy spot to chat after hours, look no further than Butter Joint, one of the few places to have its own housemade grenadine. Ask the bartender for something special or choose one of the delicious potions on the menu (cocktails $10 to $15).

Spice Island Tea House TEAHOUSE

(☑412-687-8821; www.spiceislandteahouse.com; 253 Atwood St; ⊗11:30am-8:45pm Mon-Thu, to 9:45pm Fri & Sat) If you fancy sipping a quiet cuppa (tea infusions $3.50 to $5.50) while your friend has a cocktail, this is the spot to visit. Alongside a number of delectable teas it also serves Southeast Asian fusion food.

★ **Elks Lodge** LIVE MUSIC

(☑412-321-1834; www.elks.org; 400 Cedar Ave; cover $5; ⊗bluegrass 7pm Wed, big band 7:15pm 1st, 3rd & 5th Thu) Find out why Pittsburgh is known as the Paris of Appalachia at the Elks' Banjo Night, when the stage is packed with players and the audience sings along to all the bluegrass classics. Also hosts a big-band night on the first, third and fifth Thursdays of the month. On the North Side in Deutschtown.

Rex Theater LIVE MUSIC

(☑412-381-6811; www.rextheatre.com; 1602 E Carson St) A converted movie theater, this South Side favorite hosts touring jazz, rock and indie bands.

🛍 Shopping

Kawaii Gifts GIFTS & SOUVENIRS

(☑412-687-2480; www.shopkawaii.com; 5413 Walnut St; ⊗10am-7pm Mon-Fri, to 8pm Sat, 11am-6pm Sun) *Kawaii* means, roughly, 'cute' in Japanese, and Kawaii Gifts is basically an emporium of cuteness with a Japanese twist. You know where we're going with this: Hello Kitty stuff, graphic art, acrylic pins, big chunky toys, manga posters and all the other anime aesthetics you could ever deck out an apartment with.

Pennsylvania Macaroni Co FOOD

(☑412-227-1982; www.pennmac.com; 2010-12 Penn Ave; ⊗6:30am-4:30pm Mon-Sat, 9am-2:30pm Sun) Way beyond just macaroni, this warehouse has bulk products ranging from olive oil by the barrel and dried beans to spices and cheeses by the round. The air inside has the aroma of a Mediterranean market; sometimes they even have tasting platters.

City Books   BOOKS

(🖉412-321-7323; www.citybookspgh.com; 908 Galveston Ave; ☺11am-6pm Tue-Fri, noon-5pm Sat & Sun) The oldest used bookstore in Pittsburgh is a pleasant pile of manuscripts, comfy chairs, jazz music and the musty smell of many words crammed together under one roof. The owners are committed to the Pittsburgh literary scene and frequently host readings and similar events.

ⓘ Information

VisitPITTSBURGH (🖉412-281-7711; www.
visitpittsburgh.com; 120 Fifth Ave, Ste 2800; ☺10am-6pm Mon-Fri, to 5pm Sat, hours vary Sun) Publishes the *Official Visitors Guide* and provides maps and tourist advice.

ⓘ Getting There & Away

Pittsburgh International Airport (PIT; 🖉412-472-3525; www.flypittsburgh.com; 1000 Airport Blvd), 18 miles west of downtown, has direct connections to Europe, Canada and major US cities via a slew of airlines.

The **Greyhound bus station** (Grant Street Transportation Center; 🖉412-392-6514; www.greyhound.com; 55 11th St), at the far edge of the Strip District, has frequent buses to Philadelphia (from $20, six to seven hours), NYC (from $30, 8½ to 11 hours) and Chicago, IL (from $62, 11 to 14 hours).

Pittsburgh is accessible via I-76 or I-79 from the west and I-70 from the east. It's about a six-hour drive from NYC and about three hours from Buffalo.

Pittsburgh has a magnificent old train station – and **Amtrak** (🖉800-872-7245; www.amtrak.com; 1100 Liberty Ave) drops you off in a dismal modern building behind it. Services run daily to Philadelphia (from $67, 7½ hours), NYC (from $79, 9½ hours), Chicago ($91, 10 hours) and Washington, DC ($52, eight hours).

ⓘ Getting Around

Port Authority (www.portauthority.org) provides public transport around Pittsburgh, including the 28X Airport Flyer ($2.75, 40 minutes, every 30 minutes 4:30am to midnight) from the airport to downtown and Oakland. A taxi from the airport costs about $40 (not including tip) to downtown. Various shuttles also make downtown runs for around $25 per person.

Driving in Pittsburgh can be frustrating – roads end with no warning or deposit you suddenly on bridges. Parking is scarce downtown. Where possible, use the extensive bus network, which includes a fast express busway (routes beginning with P). There is also a limited light-rail system, the T, useful for the South Side. Rides on the T downtown are free; other in-city fares are $2.50, plus $1 for a transfer.

Laurel Highlands

Where the Allegheny mountains disperse into the emerald pastureland of lowland Pennsylvania, a hybrid landscape emerges, characterized by a quilt of small townships on the one hand and rolling, wooded hills on the other. This is the Laurel Highlands, a pretty slice of the state that shifts between fine stretches of both pastoral loveliness and wild mountain ruggedness.

As pretty as the natural setting is, it's a human-built structure that constitutes the biggest draw: Fallingwater is the area's most popular tourism destination, and makes for a fascinating (if hurried) day trip from the urban jungle of Pittsburgh.

◉ Sights & Activities

★**Fallingwater**   HOUSE

(🖉724-329-8501; www.fallingwater.org; 1491 Mill Run Rd, Mill Run; adult/child $30/18, grounds only $10; ☺10am-4pm Thu-Tue; 🅿) This Frank Lloyd Wright masterpiece is simply one of the architectural wonders of the world. Completed in 1938 as a weekend retreat for the Kaufmanns, owners of a Pittsburgh department store, Fallingwater blends seamlessly with its natural setting, echoing and simultaneously threading its surroundings through its interior via terraces, ledges, cantilevering, circles and semi-circles. It's accessible only by guided tour, and reservations are recommended. The property also features 2000 acres of attractive forested grounds.

At a total of $155,000, Lloyd Wright's project was extremely over budget, although his commission was only $8000 (to give a sense of building costs at the time, master masons working on the home earned around 85¢ an hour). One of the home's most inventive features, which operates as a natural air conditioner, is the open stairway leading directly down to Bear Run stream. Photos can't do it justice – nor can they transmit the sounds of Fallingwater – and you'll likely need a return visit or two to really appreciate Wright's ingenuity and aesthetic vision.

Kentuck Knob
HOUSE

(🖱 724-329-1901; www.kentuckknob.com; 723 Kentuck Rd, Chalk Hill; adult/child $25/18; ⊗ tours 9am-5pm Mar-Oct, 10am-3pm Nov, 10am-3pm Sat & Sun only Dec) This home, designed in 1953 by Frank Lloyd Wright and completed in 1956, is built into the side of a rolling hill with stunning panoramic views. It's noted for its natural materials and obsessively designed interior – note the hexagonal design and honeycomb skylights. House tours (reservations recommended) last about 45 minutes and include a jaunt through the on-site sculpture garden, with works by Andy Goldsworthy, Ray Smith and others.

Fort Ligonier
FORT

(🖱 724-238-9701; www.fortligonier.org; 200 S Market St, Ligonier; adult/child $10/6; ⊗ 9:30am-5pm Mon-Sat, noon-5pm Sun mid-Apr–mid-Nov, store open Sat & Sun year-round, to 7pm Thu & Fri Jun-Aug) Compared to the Revolutionary War and the Civil War, the French and Indian War, often considered the 'first world war' and known as the Seven Years War in Europe, is less indelibly stamped as a turning point in America's national narrative. The excellent Fort Ligonier, both a museum and a reconstructed fort with enthusiastic and knowledgeable historical interpreters, helps correct this oversight, providing an overview of this war over territory and its significance, both in America and elsewhere.

Cucumber Falls
WATERFALL

(🖱 724-329-8591; www.dcnr.state.pa.us; off Ohiopyle Rd, Ohiopyle State Park, Stewart; ⊗ dawn-dusk; 🅿) Inside Ohiopyle State Park is Cucumber Falls, a small but still impressive waterfall that turns to a beautiful ice sculpture in winter. Nearby is a stretch of riverbed so smooth it's become a series of natural waterslides. Note that both these areas are self-use and care should be taken on the slippery rocks to avoid injury.

Laurel Highlands River Tours
ADVENTURE SPORTS

(🖱 800-472-3846; www.laurelhighlands.com; 4 Sherman St, Ohiopyle; rafting $25-170, ziplining $20-45, mountain-biking trips $75-85; ⊗ 8am-8pm May-Oct, to 5pm Nov-Apr) If you've come to run the rapids on the Youghiogheny River, try this well-equipped operator that offers activities ranging from rafting (prices vary depending on when and how far you you

want to raft) to mountain-biking trips to a zip-line adventure park spaced between 25ft-tall trees.

🍴 Sleeping & Eating

Laurel Guesthouses
GUESTHOUSE $

(🖱 724-329-8531; www.laurelhighlands.com/ guest-houses; 134 Grant St, Ohiopyle; d/tr $95/118; 🅿 ❄ 🛜) This small place has three bedrooms, two shared bathrooms and a kitchen and living room furnished like a comfortable suburban-style home. It's especially good for groups, although this and two other similar setups, the Ferncliff and MacKenzie Guesthouses (which have the same pricing and contact info), get filled in advance during summer months.

★ Nemacolin Woodlands Resort & Spa
RESORT $$$

(🖱 724-329-8555; www.nemacolin.com; 1001 Lafayette Dr, Farmington; r Oct-Apr from $200, May-Sep from $500; 🅿 ❄ ✿ @ 🛜 ❄ 🐾) With a grand, French-chateau-style hotel as the centerpiece of 2000 acres 8 miles south of Ohiopyle, Nemacolin offers a variety of accommodations and restaurants catering to every taste. Rooms in the chateau are large and have high ceilings and chandeliers. (It even has its own airport.)

Polymath Park
BOUTIQUE HOTEL $$$

(🖱 877-833-7829; www.franklloydwrightovernight. net; 187 Evergreen Lane, Acme; houses $390-450; 🅿 ❄ ✿ 🛜) This wooded property has one Frank Lloyd Wright home – Duncan House – and three others designed by Wright apprentices, all available for rent overnight. Don't expect too much Wright flair; the house is one of his modest Usonia-style designs, and the furniture is standard mid-century modern. Only the Duncan house has air-conditioning.

★ Bittersweet
CAFE $

(🖱 724-329-4411; www.bittersweetfresh.com; 205 Farmington-Ohiopyle Road, Farmington; sandwiches $6-9; ⊗ 8am-6pm Mon & Thu-Sat, noon-6pm Sun) A clean, farm-to-table cafe so chic and modern it's almost out of place. Offers good coffee, a selection of pies and pastries, and excellent salads and sandwiches.

Ligonier Tavern
AMERICAN $$

(🖱 724-238-7788; www.ligoniertavern.com; 139 W Main St, Ligonier; mains $10-25; ⊗ 11am-9pm Mon-Thu, to 10pm Fri & Sat, to 8pm Sun) This friendly restaurant is housed in a thoroughly renovated Victorian home just off the central square. There's a variety of salads and sandwiches at lunch, as well as interesting appetizers such as lobster wontons, while the dinner menu includes shepherd's pie, fried zucchini, and cranberry-walnut chicken. Note that despite the official hours, the kitchen closes early if business is slow.

❶ Getting There & Away

Public transportation out this way is sporadic – and sometimes nonexistent – so this area is best visited by car. The drive from the highlands to Pittsburgh via PA-51 is a pretty alternative to the Turnpike. Either way, the area is roughly 60 or so miles southeast of Pittsburgh.

CENTRAL PENNSYLVANIA

Mountainous, forested Central Pennsylvania is most famous for Pennsylvania State University (PSU) in the town of State College, but the region has been experiencing something of a cultural renaissance, particularly in the arenas of food and drink, with urban-quality food and coffee near the university. Elsewhere in the region, great state parks offer great hikes and general outdoors immersion.

❶ Getting There & Away

University Park Airport in State College flies to big hub cities, such as Detroit, Philadelphia, Washington Dulles and Chicago. Buses connect to Philly and Pittsburgh and from there to the rest of the country. You'll be most independent with your own vehicle, however, as many of the places worth visiting aren't within walking distance of each other. Access for most is via I-80.

State College

📱 814 / POP 42,000

A town that wears its *raison d'etre* on its sleeve, State College is home to Penn State University, one of the 10 largest colleges in the country. Time and life seem to revolve around the football season of the Penn State Nittany Lions, at least at first blush. But there's more to this town than beer and ball, even though we'd be remiss to pretend beer and ball aren't pretty important. You can find decent museums and mountain biking trails here in the cup of 'Happy Valley,' a nickname for greater State College, plus the sophisticated **Central Pennsylvania Festival of the Arts** come summer.

◉ Sights & Activities

Matson Museum of Anthropology MUSEUM
(📞814-865-3853; http://anth.la.psu.edu/matson-museum; 409 Carpenter Bldg, Curtin Rd; ⊙11am-4pm Tue-Fri) **FREE** This small museum is packed with ethnographic artifacts from around the world (mainly Africa, the Middle East and the Americas), and is open to self-guided tours, but you should call in advance to make sure they're open. It's small, but the collection is rich and fascinating.

Arboretum GARDENS
(📞814-865-9118; https://arboretum.psu.edu; cnr Park Ave & Bigler Rd; ⊙sunrise-sunset; 🅿) 🚲 **FREE** This outdoor facility, which includes the HO Smith Botanic Gardens, is probably the most peaceful spot for a breath of fresh air in greater State College. Landscapes range from marsh meadows and lotus pools to preserved ancient plants that seemingly stand outside of time.

Palmer Museum of Art MUSEUM
(📞814-865-7672; https://palmermuseum.psu.edu; Curtin Rd; ⊙10am-4:30pm Tue-Sat, noon-4pm Sun) **FREE** This eye-catching building houses 11 galleries and a contemporary sculpture garden, making for a fun, free diversionary day trip into the arts. The main collection includes Japanese woodblocks prints, Hudson River School landscapes, and the works of some Florentine Renaissance masters.

Mt Nittany HIKING
(https://mtnittany.org; 500 Mount Nittany Rd) **FREE** Two steep trails ascend around 650ft up the wooded slopes of Mt Nittany, which dominates the horizon of Happy Valley. You have the choice of a 3.5 mile or 4.6 mile round trip from the trail head, and either way, it's a rocky huff that you'll want to be in good shape for.

🛏 Sleeping

Nittany Lion Inn INN $$
(📞814-865-8500; www.nittanylioninn.psu.edu; 200 W Park Ave; d $140-190, ste $237; 🅿😊❄🛜) This stately inn has served the area since 1936. Rooms, decked out in Penn State blue and white, are spacious for the price, and the location, at the western edge of Penn State's campus, can't be beat.

✗ Eating & Drinking

⭐**Herwig's Austrian Bistro** AUSTRIAN $$
(📞814-272-0738; www.herwigsaustrianbistro.com; 132 W College Ave; mains $14-18; ⊙11am-8pm

DON'T MISS

CENTRAL PENNSYLVANIA STATE PARKS

State parks are scattered all over Central Pennsylvania, itself a part of the mountainous spine that cuts across the state. These parks reflect the landscape: they tend towards forested mountains, rivers and reservoirs. Hiking and hunting are popular throughout. **Black Moshannon State Park** (☑814-342-5960; www.dcnr.pa.gov/stateparks; 4216 Beaver Road, Philipsburg; ☺sunrise-sunset) offers the most landscape diversity, while **Bald Eagle State Park** (☑814-625-2775; www.dcnr.pa.gov/stateparks/findapark/baldeaglestatepark; 149 Main Park Rd, Howard; ☺sunrise-sunset; P) **FREE** is great for highland scenery. **Trough Creek** (☑814-658-3847; www.dcnr.pa.gov/stateparks; 16362 Little Valley Road, James Creek; ☺sunrise-sunset; P) **FREE**, while small, wows visitors with its impressive gorge.

Mon-Wed, to 9pm Thu-Sat) Herwigs has trademarked the phrase 'Where Bacon is an Herb' for good reason: your veggie choices here are pretty slim. But if you're channeling your inner carnivore you're in for a treat. Austrian dishes couldn't be more authentic and meals are reasonably priced. The casual, counter-style spot is hopping with students during the winter, but empties out in summer after graduation.

Note that staff do not expect to see anything left on the plate. While you may be tempted to giggle at their placard admonishing those who can't finish (several options are laid out: paying $35 for a take-home box or working in the kitchen are among the choices), they do not. So come here hungry and prepare to leave absolutely stuffed.

Zola   WINE BAR
(☑814-237-8474; www.zolakitchen.com; 324 W College Ave; ☺11:30am-9pm Tue-Thu, to 10pm Fri & Sat) A classy spot to have an after-dinner beverage, Zola often features live music (Thursday to Saturday).

ℹ Getting There & Away

State College is 160 miles east of Pittsburgh via I-80, and 220 miles northwest of Philadelphia via Hwy 322. University Park Airport connects to major domestic hubs like New York and Philadelphia.

Megabus (p217) runs to Pittsburgh ($10, three hours), Philadelphia ($15, 4½ hours) and NYC ($39, 5½ hours).

SOUTHEASTERN PENNSYLVANIA

Back in the day, the countryside around Philadelphia blended rolling farmland and acres of forested wilderness that, taken together, were considered a prime sylvan retreat on the early eastern seaboard. Today, Southeastern Pennsylvania is still studded with farms, but you'll also find subdivisions filled with the palatial villas of wealthy Philadelphians, as well as some beautiful parks and the sort of arts scene that has clearly benefited from extensive patronage.

This may not be the wildest corner of Pennsylvania, but it feels exceedingly well tended and groomed, and is supremely pleasant for a weekend drive (assuming you don't get caught in traffic on the Baltimore Pike).

☆ Activities

Hawk Mountain   BIRDWATCHING
(☑601-756-6961; www.hawkmountain.org; 1700 Hawk Mountain Rd, Kempton; adult/child $10/5; ☺9am-5pm Dec-Aug, 8am-5pm Sep-Nov) During September, October and November some 18,000 hawks, eagles, osprey, kestrels and vultures pass this particular windy updraft along the Kittatinny Ridge. From Hawk Mountain's North Lookout, more than 17 species fly by, and observers may count a thousand birds in a day. Broad-winged hawks – the rare raptor that flies in a group – have been known to arrive 7000 at a time.

Note that for visitor safety, all trails are closed during the first two days of Pennsylvania's deer-hunting season. (It can't hurt to avoid looking like a deer at other times of the year, too.)

ℹ Getting There & Away

While much of the area deemed 'Southeastern Pennsylvania' lies within a 30-mile radius of Philadelphia – heck, some of it is 'Greater Philadelphia' – exhausting traffic conditions can make a drive out here quite painful during rush hour. That said, driving is still the easiest means of accessing a region ill-served by public transportation.

SEPTA (p217) does provide a bus service ($2.50) out to Chadds Ford multiple times daily from the 69th Street Transportation Center. It's about a 40- to 50-minute ride one way.

Brandywine Valley

Running north from the Pennsylvania–Delaware border southwest of Philadelphia (p303), the Brandywine Valley is a patchwork of rolling, wooded countryside, historic villages, gardens, mansions and museums. It's an odd place – on the one hand, this has traditionally been a rural escape and tony bedroom suburb for the citizens of Philadelphia, and to this day it has the air of an ivy-cloaked, aristocratic enclave. On the other hand, the traffic in the region can be horrendous, which quickly dispels some of the more bucolic charms. Get here on a lazy day outside of rush hour and you'll begin to appreciate the Arcadian aesthetics that attracted such artists as Andrew Wyeth.

◉ Sights

Longwood Gardens   GARDENS
(☑610-388-1000; www.longwoodgardens.org; 1001 Longwood Rd, Kennett Square; adult/child peak $30/16, off-peak $23/12; ⊙9am-6pm Sun-Wed, to 10pm Thu-Sat May-Aug, 9am-6pm daily Sep-Apr) Pierre du Pont, the great-grandson of the DuPont chemical company founder, began designing this property in 1906 with the grand gardens of Europe in mind – especially French and Italian ones. Virtually every inch of the 1050 acres has been carefully sculpted into a display of horticultural magnificence. Whatever your mood, it can't help but be buoyed by the colors of the tulips, which seem too vivid to be real, and the overwhelming variety of species showcasing nature's creativity.

Brandywine River Museum of Art   MUSEUM
(☑610-388-2700; www.brandywine.org/museum; 1 Hoffman's Mill Rd, Chadds Ford; adult/child $18/6; ⊙9:30am-5pm) This showcase of American artwork includes the work of the Brandywine School: Howard Pyle, Maxfield Parrish and the Wyeths (NC, Andrew and Jamie). NC Wyeth's illustrations for popular books such as *The Last of the Mohicans* and *Treasure Island* are displayed along with rough sketches and finished paintings. The facility is a treat in and of itself, all tall glass windows with pleasant views onto the pretty countryside of the Brandywine River Valley.

One of our favorite paintings by Andrew Wyeth that's not among his iconic works is

Snow Hill, a large canvas that despite the snowy, playful scene somehow manages to evoke menace and a haunted quality.

Valley Forge National
Historic Park   HISTORIC SITE, NATIONAL PARK
(☑610-783-1000; www.nps.gov/vafo; 1400 North Outer Line Dr, King of Prussia; ⊙grounds 7am-dusk, welcome center 9am-5pm Sep–mid-Jun, to 6pm mid-Jun–Aug; P♿) FREE After defeat at the Battle of Brandywine Creek and the British occupation of Philadelphia in 1777, General Washington and 12,000 continental troops retreated to Valley Forge. Today, this scad of misty woods – site of a major American military withdrawal, where 2000 continental soldiers died of exposure – symbolizes Washington's endurance and leadership. The Valley Forge National Historic Park contains 5.5 sq miles of preserved rural beauty, located some 20 miles northwest of downtown Philadelphia.

A 30-mile cycling path along the Schuylkill River connects Valley Forge to Philadelphia.

🛏 Sleeping & Eating

Hotel Warner   HOTEL $$
(☑610-692-6920; www.hotelwarner.com; 120 N High St, West Chester; r from $160; P✳@🛜🐾) The art-deco facade and entryway of this 'downtown' West Chester hotel was fashioned out of a 1930s movie theater, lending it a dash of old-time elegance when it opened in 2012. It's modern and fairly generic inside, however, with plush, king-sized beds and large bathrooms. Parking costs $20. The Marquee Bar & Lounge adjoins the lobby.

Millstone Cafe   CAFE
(☑610-388-2700; www.brandywine.org/museum/visit/dining; 1 Hoffman's Mill Rd, Chadds Ford; ⊙10am-3pm; 🍴) The on-site restaurant at the Brandywine River Museum of Art is a great find, and not just as museum restaurants go. The menu trucks in sun-kissed, farm-fresh light breakfast and lunch fare, ranging from crispy brussels sprouts to grilled cheese and green tomato sandwiches. Don't forget a coffee on the way out.

Gables at Chadds Ford   AMERICAN $$$
(☑610-388-7700; www.thegablesatchaddsford.com; 423 Baltimore Pike, Chadds Ford; dinner mains $19-38; ⊙11am-9pm Tue-Thu, to 10pm Fri & Sat, 10:30am-9pm Sun; P) This popular events venue also hosts an excellent on-site New American restaurant that serves locally

sourced cheese plates, crab cakes and filet mignon, all in a setting that evokes both the bucolic beauty and ritzy aristocracy of Chadds Ford. It's romantic of an evening, although it can get crowded too.

ℹ️ Information

The **Brandywine Valley Tourism Information Center** (📞 484-770-8550; www.brandywine valley.com; 302 Greenwood Rd, Kennett Square; 🕒 9am-5pm), just outside of Longwood Gardens, is a good repository of traveler advice.

ℹ️ Getting There & Away

You'll definitely need a car to explore this area fully and with the flexibility it requires, though bus service can bring you to Valley Forge from Philly ($2.50, 90 minutes). Taxis ($75, 30 minutes) and ride-sharing services are also available.

UPSTATE & THE POCONOS

The Poconos mountains – the fun-to-pronounce name comes from the Lenape for 'creek between two hills' – rise in rocky crusts and folds across the northeast corner of Pennsylvania, and contain some 2400 sq miles of mountains, streams, waterfalls, lakes and forests. The mountains are bordered on the east by the Delaware Water Gap, to the west by coal country, and to the south by the Lehigh Valley. The Poconos escarpment lays within mere hours of major urban areas, and for decades this was an easily accessible honeymoon retreat (if you grew up in the area, you might remember lodges advertising heart-shaped beds and martini-glass-shaped bathtubs. Classy!). Today, the region's considerable outdoor charms are the main draw for tourists seeking a wilderness (as opposed to wildly passionate) escape.

🎯 Sights & Activities

Lehigh Gorge State Park   STATE PARK
(📞 570-443-0400; www.dcnr.pa.gov; 3613 State Route 534, White Haven; 🕒 sunrise-sunset; 🅿️) **FREE** The Lehigh River cuts a steep, dramat-

ically arresting gorge through the uplands of Northeast Pennsylvania. The main attraction is the 20-mile Lehigh Gorge Trail, which follows the river and an old railway cut. If you want a real challenge – with a beautiful payoff – attempt the steep climbs and rocky scrambles on the 3-mile Glen Onoko Falls Trail.

Big Pocono State Park   STATE PARK
(📞 570-894-8336; www.dcnr.pa.gov; Camelback Rd, Tannersville; 🕒 sunrise-sunset) **FREE** While there is good hiking in Big Pocono, the main attraction at this 1306-acre park is the drivable summit of Camelback Mountain, which affords views across Pennsylvania, New Jersey and New York. The summit viewpoint is accessible to those in wheelchairs, and the drive up is one of the best in the Poconos.

Bucks County River Country   BOATING
(📞 215-297-5000; www.rivercountry.net; 2 Walters Lane, Point Pleasant; rental per day tube $19-29, kayak $48-58, canoe $35; 🕒 rental 9am-3pm, return by 5pm) North of New Hope on the Pennsylvania side, this outfitter rents rafts, tubes and canoes for floating down the serene Delaware River, and offers transport back to base.

🛏️ Sleeping

⭐ **Black Bass Hotel**   INN $$$
(📞 215-297-9260; www.blackbasshotel.com; 3774 River Rd, Lumberville; d Mon-Fri from $240, Sat & Sun from $395; 🅿️ ❄️ ✳️ 🛜) Originally a small tavern popular with Tory loyalists – that's right, 1740s Tories – this elegant and comfortable nine-room inn is steeped in history. After extensive renovations in 2009, its antique furnishings, memorabilia and artwork were restored and mixed with contemporary amenities. The restaurant and bar are worth having on your radar, even if you don't plan on staying here.

Being only 6 miles north of New Hope, most of the rooms have views of the Delaware Canal and River, which runs behind the property.

ℹ️ Getting There & Away

This area is best visited by car via I-84 or I-80, or Rte 6 if you like stopping to smell the flowers.

Washington, DC

🖋️202 / POP 693,970

Best Places to Eat

➡ Tail Up Goat (p283)

➡ ChiKo (p278)

➡ Dabney (p282)

➡ Ben's Chili Bowl (p280)

➡ Equinox (p279)

Best Places to Stay

➡ Sofitel Lafayette Square (p274)

➡ Kimpton George Hotel (p275)

➡ Chester Arthur House (p276)

➡ Hotel Hive (p274)

➡ Henley Park Hotel (p276)

Why Go?

It's hard not to fall for the nation's capital. Iconic monuments, vast (and free) museums, and restaurants serving global cuisines are just the beginning of the great DC experience. It's also the home to the nation's corridors of power, where you can actually observe the action up close. History lives here too. In a single day, you could gawp at the actual Declaration of Independence at the National Archives; stand where Martin Luther King Jr gave his 'I Have a Dream' speech on the Lincoln Memorial's steps; prowl around the Watergate building; see the flag that inspired the 'Star Spangled Banner' at the National Museum of American History; and be an arm's length from where Lincoln was assassinated in Ford's Theatre. After immersing yourself in politics and history, there's still much to enjoy: leafy cobblestone neighborhoods, sprawling markets, heady multicultural nightspots and verdant parks.

When to Go
Washington, DC

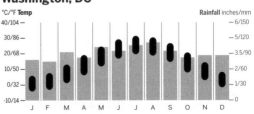

Mar-Apr Cherry blossoms bring crowds during DC's most popular festival.

Jun-Aug School is out for the summer, and tourist numbers surge. Prices are high.

Sep-Oct Smaller crowds, pleasant temperatures. Hotel rates still high.

Washington, DC Highlights

1 **National Air and Space Museum** (p250) Checking out legendary flying machines.

2 **Lincoln Memorial** (p247) Watching the sun set over the monument.

3 **National Museum of African American History & Culture** (p252) Learning about the African American experience in the US.

4 **National Gallery of Art** (p247) Appreciating the masterpiece for free.

5 **Ben's Chili Bowl** (p280) Digging into food in digs appreciated by presidents.

6 **Capitol Hill** (p259) Learning how laws are made in the country's legislative chambers and courts.

7 **Green Spaces** Stretching your legs in pretty spots like Rock Creek Park (p271).

8 **Global Cuisine** Sampling delicious global bites in Adams Morgan (p283).

9 **White House** (p262) Looking around for America's CEO on a tour of his home.

History

A compromise in a fragile new nation, Washington, DC, was built from scratch on a strategically chosen site between north and south. Following the Civil War, tiny Washington grew quickly, and became a vital job creator during the Great Depression and WWII. The 20th century brought turmoil: civil-rights struggles, political scandals and urban blight. By the 21st century, however, Washington's stricken neighborhoods have seen revitalization, even as DC remains the focal point for America's increasingly divided political views.

⊙ Sights

⊙ National Mall

When it comes to top-drawer tourist attractions, the Mall has most other places in the US beat. DC's big-hitters are all here, many of them part of the Smithsonian's portfolio of world-class museums. The icing on the cake is that they can all be visited free of charge.

★Lincoln Memorial   MONUMENT
(Map p254; www.nps.gov/linc; 2 Lincoln Memorial Circle NW; ⊙24hr; 🚌Circulator, Ⓜ Orange, Silver, Blue Line to Foggy Bottom-GWU) Anchoring the Mall's west end is the shrine to Abraham Lincoln, who gazes across the Reflecting Pool beneath his neoclassical, Doric-columned abode. The words of his Gettysburg Address and Second Inaugural speech flank the huge marble statue on the north and south walls. On the steps, Martin Luther King Jr delivered his famed 'I Have a Dream' speech; look for the engraving that marks the spot (it's on the landing 18 stairs from the top). Be sure to visit the lower level museum, featuring interesting displays about Lincoln's life and times, and a video history of the many protests that have taken place here.

★Vietnam Veterans Memorial   MONUMENT
(Map p254; www.nps.gov/vive; 5 Henry Bacon Dr NW; ⊙24hr; 🚌Circulator, Ⓜ Orange, Silver, Blue Line to Foggy Bottom-GWU) Maya Lin's design for this hugely evocative memorial takes the form of a black, low-lying 'V' – an expression of the psychic scar wrought by the Vietnam War. The monument descends into the earth, with the names of the war's 58,000-plus casualties – listed in the order they died – chiseled into the dark, reflective wall. It's a subtle but profound monument – and all the more surprising as Lin was only 21 when she designed it.

ⓘ WASHINGTON, DC: TOP TIPS

➡ Buy a rechargeable Metro SmarTrip card as soon as you arrive at the airport or Union Station. The Metro is the easiest way to get around. The card works on buses, too.

➡ Stock up on snacks before visiting the Mall as it has few good dining options. Typically museums allow you to bring in food, though you can't eat it in the galleries. The Capitol is an exception; no food is allowed inside.

➡ Prioritize your top museum or monument each day, and go there first to beat the crowds. Queues can be lengthy as everyone has to go through security (sometimes a metal detector, sometimes staff checking bags by hand).

➡ Make dinner reservations for restaurants in the midrange and upper price bracket. For hot spots that don't take reservations, arrive an hour before opening time to get in line.

To find a specific name, use the Directory of Names, located at both ends of the wall and arranged alphabetically. Alternatively, download 'The Wall' app from the Apple Store or Google Play. You can also search online at www.vvmf.org/wall-of-faces. There are two other, far more traditional, parts to the memorial, both of which are cast in bronze and neither of which was designed by Lin: the **Three Servicemen Memorial** and the **Vietnam Women's Memorial**.

★National Gallery of Art   MUSEUM
(Map p254; 📞202-737-4215; www.nga.gov; Constitution Ave NW, btwn 3rd & 7th Sts; ⊙10am-5pm Mon-Sat, 11am-6pm Sun; 👶; 🚌Circulator, Ⓜ Green, Yellow Line to Archives) **FREE** Two buildings. Hundreds of masterpieces. Infinite enjoyment. The neoclassical West Building showcases European art through to the early 1900s; highlights include works by da Vinci, Manet, Monet and Van Gogh. The IM Pei–designed East Building displays modern and contemporary art – don't miss Pollock's *Number 1, 1950 (Lavender Mist)*, Picasso's *Family of Saltimbanques* and the massive Calder mobile specially commissioned for the entrance lobby. An underground walkway connects the buildings and is made extraordinary by Leo Villareal's light sculpture, *Multiverse*.

Continued on p255

NEIGHBORHOODS AT A GLANCE

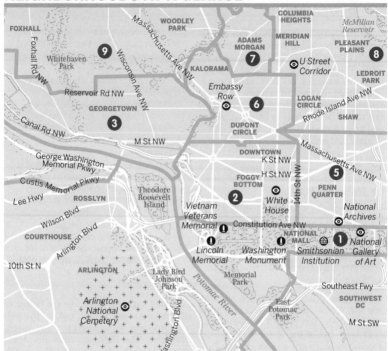

❶ National Mall (p247)

The National Mall is a monument-studded park edged by the magnificent Smithsonian museums. It's a must-visit destination that provides days – if not weeks – of enjoyment and edification for visitors.

❷ Capitol Hill & South DC (p259)

The city's geographic and legislative heart surprises by being mostly a row-house–lined residential neighborhood. The vast area holds top sights such as the Capitol and Library of Congress, but creaky bookshops and cozy pubs also thrive. The areas around Eastern Market and H St NE are locals' hubs, with buzzy restaurants and nightlife.

❸ White House Area & Foggy Bottom (p262)

The White House, aka the president's pad, is likely to take your breath away the first time you see it. The surrounding streets are equally impressive, with a bustle that comes courtesy of this neighborhood's role as America's center of bureaucratic and political business.

❹ Downtown & Penn Quarter (p263)

Penn Quarter forms around Pennsylvania Ave as it runs between the White House and the Capitol. Downtown extends north beyond it. Major sights include the National Archives, the Reynolds Center for American

.

.

Here.

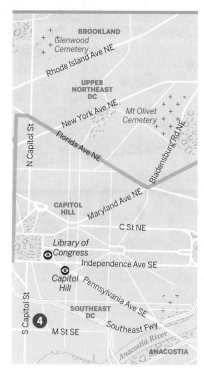

ous residential blocks holding some great far-flung sights.

❻ Dupont Circle & Kalorama (p268)

Dupont offers flashy new restaurants, hip bars, cafe society and cool bookstores. It's also the heart of the city's LGBT community. It used to be where turn-of-the-20th-century millionaires lived; today those mansions hold DC's greatest concentration of embassies. Kalorama sits in the northwest corner and ups the regal quotient.

❼ Adams Morgan (p283)

Adams Morgan has long been Washington's fun, nightlife-driven party zone. It's also a global village of sorts. The result today is a raucous mash-up centered on 18th St NW. Vintage boutiques, record stores and ethnic eats poke up between thumping bars and a growing number of stylish spots for gastronomes.

❽ Georgetown (p269)

Georgetown is DC's most aristocratic neighborhood, home to elite university students, ivory-tower academics and diplomats. Chi-chi brand-name shops, dark-wood pubs and upscale restaurants line the streets. Lovely parks and gardens color the edges.

Art & Portraiture and Ford's Theatre. This is also DC's entertainment district and convention hub, so it stays busy.

❺ Logan Circle, U Street & Columbia Heights (p265)

This neighborhood covers a lot of ground. Logan Circle stars with hot restaurants and stylish bars amid stately old manors. Historic U St has been reborn as a jazzy arts and entertainment district. Columbia Heights booms with Latino immigrants and hipsters. Northeast DC is a stretch of prosper-

❾ Upper Northwest DC (p269)

The leafy lanes and winding boulevards of Upper Northwest DC have long been the place for well-to-do Washingtonians to settle their families. Three popular parks offer plenty of opportunities for hiking, cycling and horseback riding. Two impressive museums – the Kreeger and Hillwood Estate – are among DC's most underrated sights.

◉ TOP SIGHT

NATIONAL AIR & SPACE MUSEUM

The Air and Space Museum is among the Smithsonian's biggest crowd-pullers. Families flock here to view the mind-blowing array of planes, rockets and other contraptions – and all of it is as rousing for adults as kids. Name the historic aircraft or spacecraft – the Wright Brothers' flyer, Lindbergh's *Spirit of St Louis*, Skylab – and it's bound to be on one of museum's two chock-a-block floors.

Milestones of Flight Hall

The museum's entrance hall makes a grand impression. Walk in the Mall-side entrance and look up: Chuck Yeager's sound-barrier-breaking Bell X-1 and Charles Lindbergh's transatlantic-crossing *Spirit of St Louis* hang from the ceiling. Nuclear missiles and rockets rise up from the floor.

1903 Wright Flyers

The Wright Brothers get their own gallery (2nd floor), and its centerpiece is the 1903 biplane they built and flew at Kitty Hawk, North Carolina in 1903. That's right: the world's first airplane is here. Also on display is a bicycle the brothers designed (they started with two-wheelers before moving on to flying machines).

Amelia Earhart's Plane

Amelia Earhart's natty red Lockheed 5B Vega shines in the Pioneers of Flight gallery (2nd floor). She dubbed it her 'Little Red Bus' and in 1932 flew it solo across the Atlantic Ocean – a first for a woman. A few months later she flew it nonstop across the US, a 19-hour journey from Los Angeles to Newark, NJ, for another female first.

DON'T MISS

➜ Lindbergh's *Spirit of St Louis*

➜ Wright Brothers' original airplane

➜ Amelia Earhart's plane

➜ Skylab Orbital Workshop

➜ Chuck Yeager's Bell X-1

PRACTICALITIES

➜ Map p254

➜ ☎ 202-633-2214

➜ www.airandspace. si.edu

➜ cnr 6th St & Independence Ave SW

➜ ⏱ 10am-5:30pm

➜ 🚌 Circulator, Ⓜ Orange, Silver, Blue, Green, Yellow Line to L'Enfant Plaza

Apollo Lunar Module

It looks like it's made of tinfoil, but the Apollo Lunar Module was designed to carry astronauts to the moon. The unit on display was only used for ground testing, and was subsequently modified to resemble the module that Neil Armstrong and Buzz Aldrin stepped out of as the first men on the moon. Find it in the Milestones of Flight Hall.

Skylab Orbital Workshop

Skylab was America's first space station, launched in 1973. The orbital workshop was its largest component, and was where the astronauts lived. Crews of three stayed aboard for up to three months. Walk through to see the shower, exercise bicycle and other cramped quarters. It's part of the Space Race exhibition (1st floor).

How Things Fly Gallery

On the 1st floor near the welcome center, How Things Fly whooshes with interactive gadgets for young ones. Kids can find out their weight on the moon, see a wind tunnel in action and make awesome paper airplanes.

Flight Simulators

Thrill-seekers should head to the Flight Simulator Zone on the 1st floor. You can take a badass VR Transporter experience where you will fly a combat sortie in a simulator that lets you control the action and perform 360-degree barrel rolls ($10 to $12 per person), or hop aboard a more sedate ride simulator ($8 per person).

IMAX Theater & Planetarium

The Lockheed Martin Imax Theater screens a rotating list of films throughout the day. Shows at the Albert Einstein Planetarium send viewers hurtling through space on tours of the universe. Buy your tickets as soon as you arrive, or on the museum website before you visit. Tickets cost $9 for adults, $7.50 for children aged 2-12; there's a surcharge for online orders.

Museum Annex

Only a fraction of the museum's planes and spacecraft fit into the building on the Mall. The leftovers fill two enormous hangars at the **Steven F Udvar-Hazy Center** (☑ 703-572-4118; 14390 Air & Space Museum Pkwy, Chantilly; ⏱ 10am-5:30pm; ♿; Ⓜ Silver Line to Wiehle-Reston East for bus 983) FREE near Dulles Airport. Highlights include the *Enola Gay* (the B-29 that dropped the atomic bomb on Hiroshima) and Space Shuttle *Discovery*. The annex is 2½ miles (about a $12 taxi ride) from Dulles.

TOP TIPS

➡ Stop by the information desk and pick up a map, which shows where all the highlights are located.

➡ Download the museum's free GO FLIGHT app, either before you arrive or on-site using the free wi-fi. It provides extra content (videos, stories etc) about popular items in the collection.

➡ Free 90-minute tours depart from the welcome center daily at 10:30am and 1pm. More tours are often added if docents are available.

TAKE A BREAK

The foyer cafe at the neighboring Hirshhorn Museum (p257) serves coffee, pastries and delectable handmade gelato. For something more substantial, try the Mitsitam Native Foods Cafe (p258) in the adjacent American Indian Museum.

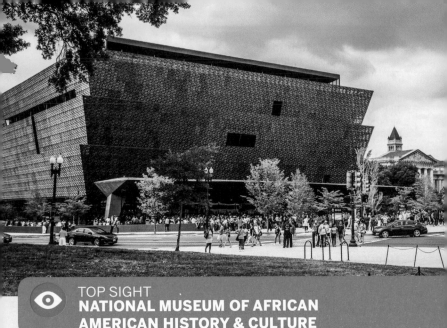

Museums don't get much better than this. Opened in 2016, this magnificently curated and presented museum explores African American life, culture and history through artifacts, interactive exhibitions, installations and shared experiences.

The Building

Architect Philip Freelon and designer David Adjaye were inspired by the three-tiered crowns used in Yoruban art from West Africa when designing the building. Its exterior is wrapped in a bronze-colored metal lattice that pays homage to the intricate ironwork once crafted by enslaved African Americans.

Defending and Defining Freedom

Focusing on the era of Segregation (1876-1968), a fascinating exhibit on the C2 level looks at brave and inspirational African American figures including Ida B Wells, a newspaper editor and anti-lynching activist in Georgia ('The way to right wrongs is to turn the light of truth upon them'); and Madam CJ Walker, America's first self-made female millionaire (she developed a line of beauty products for African American women and built a company with more than 20,000 employees).

Segregation Exhibits

On the C2 level are a handful of exhibits that enable visitors to gain an inkling of what daily life was like for African Americans in the first half of the 20th century, including stools from a segregated Wool-

DON'T MISS

➡ Slavery and Freedom gallery

➡ Musical Crossroads gallery

➡ Segregation exhibits

➡ A Changing America exhibit

➡ Leveling the Playing Field exhibit

PRACTICALITIES

➡ Map p254

➡ ☎ 844-750-3012

➡ www.nmaahc.si.edu

➡ 1400 Constitution Ave NW

➡ ⊙ 10am-5:30pm

➡ 🚊 Circulator, Ⓜ Orange, Silver, Blue Line to Smithsonian or Federal Triangle

worth's lunch counter at Greensboro North Carolina, site of a 1960 sit-in that led to the company removing its policy of racial segregation. Also here is a segregated Pullman Palace passenger car.

A Changing America

The narrative of oppression really starts to recalibrate in the exhibit A Changing America. Tracing the creation and growth of the modern civil rights movement in America, the artifact-rich C1 floor highlights developments since 1968, including the Black Arts Movement, the Black Panthers and the election of Barak Obama as president.

Leveling the Playing Field

African American athletes have long excelled in sports, both in the so-called 'Negro Leagues' formed in the era of segregation and in the subsequent decades, when sport becomes synonymous with power and big business. Baseball, football, basketball, boxing and tennis take center court (and field) in this 3rd-floor exhibit, with loads of audiovisual presentations and artifacts on show.

Musical Crossroads

This fabulous exhibition in the culture galleries on the fourth floor celebrates the contribution that African Americans have made to the global musical scene. See Chuck Berry's 1973 fine-engine-red Cadillac Eldorado, Dinah Washington's fur stole, Louis Armstrong's Selmer trumpet, Little Richard's sequinned jacket, Cab Calloway's tuxedo and much, much more.

TOP TIPS

➜ This museum is very popular, and daily visitor numbers are capped. It's best to book online months in advance or try for one of the same-day tickets released online at 6:30am daily. If you have no luck sourcing a ticket online, ask one of the guards at the front entrance – they sometimes have spare tickets.

➜ Start your tour on the subterranean C3 level.

TAKE A BREAK

The museum's **Sweet Home Café** (☎202-633-6174; www.nmaahc.si.edu/visit/sweet-home-cafe; mains $14-19; ⊙10am-5pm) is a popular lunch stop for museum visitors. It's divided into four stations based on the compass: think buttermilk fried chicken from the South, oyster pan roast from the north, pan-fried trout from the west and catfish po'boys from Louisiana.

National Mall

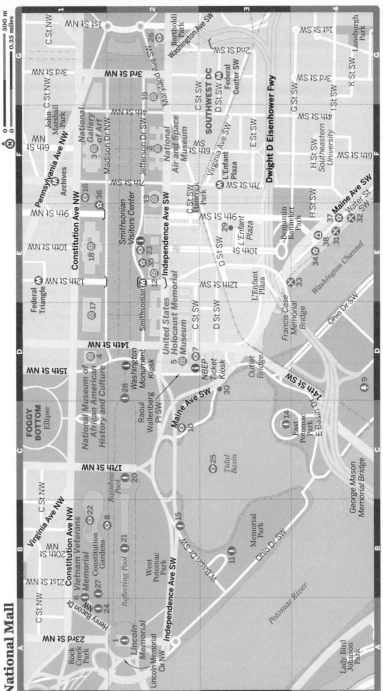

500 m
0.25 miles

Continued from p247

You could spend a full day here easily; consider joining one of the volunteer-led tours or taking advantage of the free, multilanguage 'Director's Tour' audio guide, which introduces the gallery's highlights. There's also a dedicated audio guide for kids. The National Gallery's documentary and avant-garde film program takes place several times a month in the East Building auditorium. Free classical concerts fill the air on Sundays in the West Building's West Garden Court. Check www.nga.gov/calendar for details of all events.

★**United States**
Holocaust Memorial Museum   MUSEUM
(Map p254; ☑202-488-0400; www.ushmm.org; 100 Raoul Wallenberg Pl SW; ⏰10am-5:20pm, extended hours Apr–mid-Jun; ☐Circulator, Ⓜ Orange, Silver, Blue Line to Smithsonian) FREE For a deep understanding of the Holocaust – its victims, perpetrators and bystanders – this harrowing museum is a must-see. The main exhibit gives visitors the identity card of a single Holocaust victim, whose story is revealed as you take a winding route into a hellish past marked by ghettos, rail cars and death camps. It also shows the flip side of human nature, documenting the risks many citizens took to help the persecuted.

To view the permanent exhibit, same-day passes, available at the desk on the 1st floor, are required March through August. The passes allow entrance at a designated time. Arrive early because they do run out. Better yet, reserve tickets in advance via the museum's website for a $1 surcharge. If you have children under 11 years, a gentler installation – 'Remember the Children: Daniel's Story' – is on the 1st floor.

Washington Monument   MONUMENT
(Map p254; www.nps.gov/wamo; 2 15th St NW; ☐Circulator, Ⓜ Orange, Silver, Blue Line to Smithsonian) FREE Peaking at 555ft (and 5in) and comprised of 36,000 blocks of stone, the Washington Monument is the tallest building in the district. It took so long to build that the original quarry ran out; note the delineation in color where the old and new marble meet about a third of the way up. Alas, the

National Mall

monument is closed until spring 2019 for repairs, so you'll have to wait until then for stellar views from the observation deck. When it reopens, you'll need a ticket to get in. Same-day passes for a timed entrance are available at the kiosk by the monument. During peak season it's a good idea to reserve tickets in advance by phone (☏877-444-6777) or online (www.recreation.gov) for a small fee.

Martin Luther King Jr Memorial   MONUMENT
(Map p254; www.nps.gov/mlkm; 1850 W Basin Dr SW; ⊗24hr; 🚍Circulator, Ⓜ Orange, Silver, Blue Line to Smithsonian) Opened in 2011, this was the first Mall memorial to honor an African American. Sculptor Lei Yixin carved the piece, which is reminiscent in concept and style to the Mount Rushmore memorial. Besides Dr King's striking, 30ft-tall image, known as the Stone of Hope, there are two blocks of granite behind him that represent the Mountain of Despair. A wall inscribed with King's powerful quotes about democracy, justice and peace flanks the piece. King's statue, incidentally, is 11ft taller than those of Lincoln and Jefferson in their nearby memorials.

**National Museum
of Natural History**   MUSEUM
(Map p254; ☏202-663-1000; www.naturalhistory.si.edu; cnr 10th St & Constitution Ave NW; ⊗10am-5:30pm, to 7:30pm some days; 👶; 🚍Circulator, Ⓜ Orange, Silver, Blue Line to Smithsonian or Federal Triangle) FREE Arguably the most popular of the Smithsonian museums, so crowds are pretty much guaranteed. Wave to Henry, the elephant who guards the rotunda, then zip to the 2nd floor's Hope Diamond, a 45.52-karat bauble that is said to have cursed its owners, which included Marie Antoinette. The beloved dinosaur hall is under renovation until 2019, but the giant squid (1st floor, Ocean Hall), live butterfly pavilion and tarantula feedings provide the thrills at this kid-packed venue. Adults will find lots to love here too: Easter Island heads (lobby at the Constitution Ave entrance), mummies (2nd floor), ground-floor halls devoted to mammals and oceans, and a vibrant temporary exhibition program.

The butterfly pavilion has a separate admission fee (adult/child two to 12 years $7.50/6.50); it's free on Tuesday. On select days, usually in spring and summer, the museum stays open until 7:30pm.

**National Museum of
American History**   MUSEUM
(Map p254; ☏202-663-1000; www.americanhistory.si.edu; cnr 14th St & Constitution Ave NW; ⊗10am-5:30pm, to 7:30pm some days; 👶; 🚍Circulator, Ⓜ Orange, Silver, Blue Line to Smithsonian or Federal Triangle) FREE Containing all kinds of artifacts of the American experience, this museum has as its centerpiece the flag that flew over Baltimore's Fort McHenry during the War of 1812 – the same flag that inspired Francis Scott Key to pen 'The Star-Spangled Banner' (it's on the entry level). Other highlights include Julia Child's kitchen (1st floor, east wing) and 'The First Ladies' costume exhibit on the 3rd floor. New exhibits include 'American Culture' and 'On with the Show' on the 3rd floor.

East Potomac Park   PARK
(Map p254; Ohio Dr SW; Ⓜ Orange, Silver, Blue Line to Smithsonian) Although only a stone's throw from the National Mall, for tourists, East Potomac Park may as well be in Siberia. The pleasant, green, cherry-blossom-lined expanse is a lovely spot for walking, fishing and general gamboling. Cyclists flock to the scenic 5-mile loop that Ohio Dr makes as it zips around the park's circumference. The East Potomac Park golf course lies at the center. The park sits on a finger of land that extends southward from the Tidal Basin into the Potomac River. On foot, you can access it by following trails that lead from the Thomas Jefferson Memorial under the bridges. If you drive out this way, you can park on the shoulder of Ohio Dr.

Bureau of Engraving & Printing   LANDMARK
(Map p254; ☏202-874-2330; www.moneyfactory.gov; cnr 14th & C Sts SW; ⊗9-10:45am, 12:30-3:45pm & 5-6pm Mon-Fri Mar-Aug, reduced hours Sep-Feb; 🚍Circulator, Ⓜ Orange, Silver, Blue Line to Smithsonian) FREE Cha-ching! The nation's paper currency is designed and printed here. Guides lead 40-minute tours during which you peer down onto the work floor where millions of dollars roll off the presses and get cut (by guillotine!). It's actually a pretty dry jaunt; don't expect exciting visuals or snappy dialogue. In peak season (March to August), timed entry tickets are required. Get in line early at the **ticket kiosk** (Raoul Wallenberg Pl/15th St; ⊗from 8am Mar-Aug). It opens at 8am. Tickets are often gone by 10am.

**Freer-Sackler Museums
of Asian Art**   MUSEUM
(Map p254; ☏202-633-1000; www.asia.si.edu; 1050 Independence Ave SW; ⊗10am-5:30pm; 🚍Circulator, Ⓜ Orange, Silver, Blue Line to Smithsonian) FREE This is a lovely spot in which to while away a Washington afternoon. Japanese silk scrolls, smiling Buddhas, rare

Islamic manuscripts and Chinese jades are exhibited in cool, quiet galleries in two galleries connected by an underground tunnel. The Freer also houses works by American painter James Whistler, including five *Nocturnes*. Don't miss the extraordinarily beautiful blue-and-gold Peacock Room on its ground floor, designed by Whistler in 1876–77 as an exotic showcase for a shipping magnate's collection of Chinese porcelain.

United States Botanic Garden   GARDENS

(Map p254; ☎202-225-8333; www.usbg.gov; 100 Maryland Ave SW; ⊙10am-5pm; 🛋; 🚋Circulator, 🅼Orange, Silver, Blue Line to Federal Center SW) FREE Built to resemble London's Crystal Palace, this garden's iron-and-glass greenhouse provides a beautiful setting to view orchids, ferns and cacti. When you're done with those, seek out the so-called 'Corpse Flower,' *Amorphophallus titanum,* whose name translates to 'giant misshapen penis' and whose erratic blooms smell like rotting flesh. Mmm! Alas, it only blooms every three to five years and it's not on show during its hibernation.

Jefferson Memorial   MONUMENT

(Map p254; www.nps.gov/thje; 900 Ohio Dr SW; ⊙24hr; 🚋Circulator, 🅼Orange, Silver, Blue Line to Smithsonian) Set on the south bank of the Tidal Basin amid the cherry trees, this memorial honors the third US president, political philosopher, drafter of the Declaration of Independence and founder of the University of Virginia. Designed by John Russell Pope to resemble Jefferson's library at the university, the rounded monument was initially derided by critics as 'the Jefferson Muffin.' Inside is a 19ft bronze likeness, and excerpts from Jefferson's writings are etched into the walls.

Hirshhorn Museum   MUSEUM

(Map p254; ☎202-633-1000; www.hirshhorn.si.edu; cnr 7th St & Independence Ave SW; ⊙10am-5:30pm; 🛋; 🚋Circulator, 🅼Orange, Silver, Blue, Green, Yellow Line to L'Enfant Plaza) FREE The Smithsonian's cylindrical art museum shows works from modernism's early days to today's most cutting-edge practitioners. Exhibitions of works drawn from the museum's extensive collection are offered alongside curated shows of work by prominent contemporary artists. Visitors can relax in the 3rd-floor sitting area, which has couches, floor-to-ceiling windows and a balcony offering Mall views. A lobby redesign by Japanese artist Hiroshi Sugimoto opened in 2018, and includes **Dolcezza at Hirshhorn** (www.dolcezzagelato.com; gelato $4, pastries $2-7; ⊙8am-5pm Mon-Fri, from 10am Sat & Sun; 🖥), a gelato and coffee bar. There are free 45-minute guided tours at 12:30pm and 3:30pm daily.

Tidal Basin   WATERFRONT

(Map p254; www.nps.gov/articles/dctidalbasin.htm; 🚋Circulator, 🅼Orange, Silver, Blue Line to Smithsonian) The 2-mile stroll around this constructed inlet incorporates the Franklin Delano Roosevelt and Thomas Jefferson memorials as well as the Floral Library. It's a lovely way to spend a couple of hours – just watch out for low-hanging tree branches near the FDR memorial. During the National Cherry Blossom Festival, the city's annual spring rejuvenation, the basin bursts into a pink-and-white floral collage. Rent a paddleboat from the boathouse (p273) to get out on the water.

Constitution Gardens   GARDENS

(Map p254; www.nps.gov/coga; Constitution Ave NW; ⊙24hr; 🚋Circulator, 🅼Orange, Silver, Blue Line to Foggy Bottom-GWU) FREE Constitution Gardens is a bit of a locals' secret. Quiet, shady and serene, it's a reminder of the size of the Mall – how can such isolation exist amid so many tourists? A copse of trees is set off by a small kidney-shaped pool, punctuated by a tiny island holding the Signers' Memorial, a stone platform honoring those who signed the Declaration of Independence.

National Gallery of Art
Sculpture Garden   GARDENS

(Map p254; www.nga.gov; cnr Constitution Ave NW & 7th St NW; ⊙10am-5pm Mon-Sat, 11am-6pm Sun, extended hours summer & mid-Nov–mid-Mar; 🛋; 🚋Circulator, 🅼Green, Yellow Line to Archives) FREE The gallery's 6-acre garden is studded with whimsical sculptures such as Roy Lichtenstein's *House* (1974), a giant Claes Oldenburg typewriter eraser (1998) and Roxy Paine's *Graft* (2008–09), a stainless steel tree. They are scattered around a fountain – a great place to dip your feet in summer. From mid-November to mid-March the fountain is transformed into an **ice rink** (www.nga.gov/visit/ice-rink.html; adult/child 12yr & under $9/8, skate rental $3.50; ⊙10am-9pm Mon-Thu, to 11pm Fri, 11am-11pm Sat, 11am-9pm Sun mid-Nov–mid-Mar), and the garden stays open a bit later. The **Pavilion Cafe** (☎202-289-3361; www.pavilioncafe.com; sandwiches $10-12, salads $11-13; ⊙10am-4pm Mon-Sat, 11am-5pm Sun, with seasonal late openings) is a popular breakfast and lunch stop.

Franklin Delano Roosevelt
Memorial   MONUMENT

(Map p254; www.nps.gov/frde; 400 W Basin Dr SW; ⊙24hr; 🚋Circulator, 🅼Orange, Silver, Blue Line

WASHINGTON, DC SIGHTS

to Smithsonian) The 7.5-acre memorial pays tribute to the longest-serving president in US history. Visitors are taken through four red-granite areas that narrate FDR's time in office, from the Depression to the New Deal to WWII. The story is told through statuary and inscriptions, punctuated with fountains and peaceful alcoves. It's especially pretty at night, when the marble shimmers in the glossy stillness of the Tidal Basin. The irony is that FDR didn't want a grand memorial. Instead, he requested a modest **stone slab** (Map p262; cnr 9th St & Pennsylvania Ave NW, Penn Quarter; MGreen, Yellow Line to Archives) by the Archives building. DC honored that request too.

National WWII Memorial   MONUMENT
(Map p254; www.nps.gov/wwii; 17th St SW; ⊙24hr; ⊡Circulator, MOrange, Silver, Blue Line to Smithsonian) Dedicated in 2004, this grandiose memorial honors the 16 million US soldiers who served in WWII. Veterans regularly come to pay their respects to the 400,000 Americans who died as a result of the conflict. The plaza's dual arches symbolize victory in the Atlantic and Pacific theaters, and the 56 pillars represent each US state and territory.

National Museum of
the American Indian   MUSEUM
(Map p254; ⌨202-663-1000; www.americanindian.si.edu; cnr 4th St & Independence Ave SW; ⊙10am-

5:30pm; ⌨; ⊡Circulator, MOrange, Silver, Blue, Green, Yellow Line to L'Enfant Plaza) **FREE** Ensconced in an architecturally notable building clad in honey-colored limestone, this museum offers cultural artifacts, video and audio recordings related to the indigenous people of the Americas. Sadly, navigation of the exhibits is confusing on both a curatorial and physical level. The focus on didactic panels at the expense of interpretative labels for artifacts is also problematic. The 'Our Universes' gallery (on Level 4) about Native American beliefs and creation stories is one of the more interesting exhibits. The museum offers storytelling, percussion workshops and lots of other family programming. The ground-floor **Mitsitam Native Foods Cafe** (www.mitsitamcafe.com; mains $12-22; ⊙11am-5pm, reduced hours in winter) is one of the Mall's most popular dining options.

Smithsonian Castle   NOTABLE BUILDING
(Map p254; ⌨202-633-1000; www.si.edu; 1000 Jefferson Dr SW; ⊙8:30am-5:30pm; ⊡Circulator, MOrange, Silver, Blue Line to Smithsonian) James Renwick designed this turreted, red-sandstone fairy-tale in 1855. Today the castle houses the **Smithsonian Visitors Center**, which makes a good first stop on the Mall. Inside you'll find history exhibits, multilingual touch-screen displays, a staffed information desk, free maps, a cafe and the tomb

THE WHARF

The Southwest Waterfront has long been home to the **Maine Avenue Fish Market** (Map p254; 1100 Maine Ave SW; mains $7-13; ⊙8am-9pm; MOrange, Silver, Blue, Yellow, Green Line to L'Enfant Plaza), but the area was otherwise unremarkable – until the Wharf shot up. The huge complex of restaurants, hotels, entertainment venues, parks and piers officially opened in late 2017, and now it buzzes. The public piers are the niftiest bits. The Transit Pier has a winter ice rink, summer mini-golf course and small outdoor stage for free concerts. The Georgetown water taxi departs from here, hence the name. The District Pier is the longest dock, jutting well out into the Washington Channel and hosting a big stage for festivals. The Recreation Pier makes for a fine stroll with its benches, swinging seats and boathouse for kayak and paddleboard rentals.

Loads of eateries sit waterside, including branches of **Shake Shack** (Map p262; ⌨202-800-9930; www.shakeshack.com; 800 F St NW, Penn Quarter; mains $5-10; ⊙11am-11pm Sun-Thu, to midnight Fri & Sat; MRed, Yellow, Green Line to Gallery Pl-Chinatown), **Taylor Gourmet** (Map p260; ⌨202-684-7001; www.taylorgourmet.com; 1116 H St NE; sandwiches $8-13; ⊙11am-9pm Sun-Thu, to 3:30am Fri & Sat; MRed Line to Union Station then streetcar), **Hank's Oyster Bar** (Map p266; ⌨202-462-4265; www.hanksoysterbar.com; 1624 Q St NW; mains $22-30; ⊙11:30am-1am Mon-Thu, 11:30am-2am Fri, 11am-2am Sat, 11am-1am Sun; MRed Line to Dupont Circle) and Dolcezza (p282). Swanky new spots seem to open weekly. The Anthem (p288) and Pearl Street Warehouse (p288) are fab venues for live music. **Politics and Prose** (Map p254; ⌨202-488-3867; www.politics-prose.com/wharf; 70 District Sq SW; ⊙10am-10pm; MOrange, Silver, Blue, Yellow, Green Line to L'Enfant Plaza or Green Line to Waterfront) brings the books. And more is on the way, as you'll see from the ongoing construction that will add to the Wharf for the next several years.

of James Smithson, the institution's founder. His crypt lies inside a little room by the main entrance off the Mall.

◉ Capitol Hill & South DC

The US Capitol, Library of Congress, Supreme Court, Folger Shakespeare Library and Belmont-Paul Women's Equality Monument cluster within a few blocks on Capitol Hill. The US Holocaust Memorial Museum and Bureau of Engraving & Printing are near each other (and the Mall) in Southwest DC. Other sights are further afield in Southeast DC, including those at the Navy Yard and across the river in Anacostia. Almost everything is free.

★ US Capitol LANDMARK
(Map p260; ☎202-226-8000; www.visitthecapitol.gov; 1st St NE & E Capitol St; ⊗8:30am-4:30pm Mon-Sat; Ⓜ Orange, Silver, Blue Line to Capitol South) **FREE** Since 1800, this is where the legislative branch of American government – ie Congress – has met to write the country's laws. The lower House of Representatives (435 members) and upper Senate (100) meet respectively in the south and north wings of the building. Enter via the underground visitor center below the East Plaza. Guided tours of the building are free, but tickets are limited and there's often a long wait. It's best to reserve online in advance (there's no fee).

The hour-long jaunt showcases the exhaustive background of a building that fairly sweats history. You'll watch a cheesy film first, then staff members lead you into the ornate halls and whispery chambers cluttered with the busts, statues and personal mementos of generations of Congress members.

To watch Congress in session, you need a separate pass. US citizens must get one from their representative or senator; foreign visitors should take their passports to the House and Senate Appointment Desks on the upper level. Congressional committee hearings are more interesting (and substantive) if you care about what's being debated; check for a schedule, locations and to see if they're open to the public (they often are) at www.house.gov and www.senate.gov.

Security measures here are strict; no food, liquid or bags larger than 18in.

★ Library of Congress LIBRARY
(Map p260; ☎202-707-8000; www.loc.gov; 101 Independence Ave SE; ⊗8:30am-4:30pm Mon-Sat; Ⓜ Orange, Silver, Blue Line to Capitol South) **FREE** The world's largest library – with 164 million books, manuscripts, maps, photos, films and other items – awes in both scope and

design. The centerpiece is the 1897 Jefferson Building. Gawk at the Great Hall, done up in stained glass, marble and mosaics of mythical characters, then seek out the Gutenberg Bible (c 1455), Thomas Jefferson's round library and the reading room viewing area. Free tours of the building take place between 10:30am and 3:30pm on the half-hour.

Supreme Court LANDMARK
(Map p260; ☎202-479-3030; www.supremecourt.gov; 1 1st St NE; ⊗9am-4:30pm Mon-Fri; Ⓜ Orange, Silver, Blue Line to Capitol South) **FREE** The highest court in the USA sits in a pseudo-Greek temple protected by 13,000lb bronze doors. Arrive early to watch arguments (periodic Monday through Wednesday from October to April). You can visit the permanent exhibits and the building's five-story, marble-and-bronze spiral staircase year-round. On days when court is not in session you can also hear lectures (every hour on the half-hour) in the courtroom. When departing, be sure to exit via the doors that lead to the regal front steps.

If you wish to attend arguments, lines form out front by the court steps starting at 8am. There are usually two queues: one for people who wish to sit through the entire argument, and another for people who want to observe the court in session for 10 to 15 minutes. Bring quarters to use for lockers; you're not allowed to take anything into the courtroom.

When the building was erected in 1935, some justices felt it was too large and didn't properly reflect the subdued influence of the nine justices within. The neoclassical design was meant to evoke a Greek temple. The seated figures in front of the building represent the female Contemplation of Justice and the male Guardian of Law; panels on the front doors depict the history of jurisprudence. The interior grand corridor and Great Hall are no less impressive. Downstairs is an exhibit on the history of the court. Friezes within the courtroom also depict legal history and heroes.

National Postal Museum MUSEUM
(Map p260; ☎202-633-5555; www.postalmuseum.si.edu; 2 Massachusetts Ave NE; ⊗10am-5:30pm; 🚼; Ⓜ Red Line to Union Station) **FREE** The Smithsonian-run Postal Museum is way cooler than you might think. Level 1 has exhibits on postal history from the Pony Express to modern times, where you'll see antique mail planes and touching old letters from soldiers and pioneers. Level 2 holds the world's largest stamp collection. Join the stamp geeks pulling out drawers and snapping photos of

Capitol Hill & South DC

WASHINGTON, DC

0 —— 500 m
0 —— 0.25 miles

M St NW · M St NE · M St NE

Pierce St NE

Fenton Pl NE

Union Market (0.2mi);
Masseria (0.3mi);
Primrose (2mi)

5

Ivy City (0.75mi);
Atlas Brew Works (0.8mi);
United States National Arboretum (1.5mi)

L St NW · L St NE

29

K St NW

I St NW

H St NW

G St NW

N Capitol St

1st St NE

2nd St NE

3rd St NE

4th St NE

6th St NE

West Virginia Ave NE

Florida Ave NE

K St NE

I St NE

H St NE

G St NE

20

18 21

Kenilworth Aquatic Gardens (3.5mi)

BoltBus; Greyhound; Megabus; Peter Pan Bus Lines

Union Station

6

8

14 23

3rd St NE

4th St NE

5th St NE

6th St NE

F St NE

8th St NE

9th St NE

10th St NE

Massachusetts Ave NW

10

Union Station

Columbus Circle

E St NW

E St NE

Maryland Ave NE

11th St NE

12th St NE

13th St NE

New Jersey Ave NW

Louisiana Ave NW

Delaware Ave NE

Massachusetts Ave NE

D St NE

Stanton Park

C St NE

C St NE

Constitution Ave NE

3

7th St NE

Maryland Ave NE

Massachusetts Ave NE

Constitution Ave NE

Tennessee Ave NE

Capitol Plaza

CAPITOL HILL

National Mall

2

US Capitol

7

1st St NE

2nd St NE

5th St NE

A St NE

E Capitol St

E Capitol St NE

Lincoln Park

E Capitol St SE

Library of Congress

1

4

3rd St SE

5th St SE

11

A St SE

Independence Ave SE

Independence Ave SE

North Carolina Ave NE

Kentucky Ave SE

Washington Ave SW

S Capitol St

C St SE

Capitol South

15 24

Seward Square

27

26 28 22

C St SE

North Carolina Ave SE

D St SE

D St SE

South Carolina Ave SE

D St SE

13th St SE

1st St NE

2nd St SE

E St SE

Folger Park

Eastern Market

Pennsylvania Ave SE

E St SE

E St SE

F St SE

Marion Park

13

Garfield Park

17
12

4th St SE

5th St SE

6th St SE

G St SE

9th St SE

10th St SE

H St SW

H St SE

16

8th St SE

I St SE

11th St SE

12th St SE

New Jersey Ave SE

Southeast Fwy

Virginia Ave SE

I St SW

I St SE

K St SW

K St SE

K St SE

5th St SE

SOUTHEAST DC

K St SE

L St SW

L St SE

L St SE

M St SW

Half St SE

1st St SE

Navy Yard

M St SE

M St SE

M St SE

Van St SE

19

Tingey St SE

Patterson Ave SE

Paulding St SE

Dahlgren Ave SE

Parsons Ave SE

10th St SE

11th St SE

Water St SE

N St SW

N St SE

1st St SW

S Capitol St

25

O St SW

O St SE

N Pl SE

Yards Park

9

Anacostia River

Washington Navy Yard

Frederick Douglass National Historic Site (0.8mi)

11th St Bridge

P St SW

the world's rarest stamps (the Ben Franklin Z Grill!), or start your own collection, choosing from among thousands of free international stamps (Guyana, Congo, Cambodia...).The museum is kid-friendly and hosts story times and workshops. It also has a stamp shop where you can browse the catalog of odd-ball US Postal Service stamps and have the 'philatelic clerk' (excellent job title) fetch your selection. Many of the stamps are hot off the press and aren't available elsewhere.

Folger Shakespeare Library   LIBRARY
(Map p260; ☑202-544-4600; www.folger.edu; 201 E Capitol St; ⊙10am-5pm Mon-Sat, noon-5pm Sun; Ⓜ Orange, Silver, Blue Line to Capitol South) **FREE** Bard-o-philes will be all aflutter here, as the library holds the largest collection of old Billy's works in the world. Stroll through the Great Hall to see Elizabethan artifacts, paintings, etchings and manuscripts. The highlight is a rare First Folio that you can peek at. Pop into the evocative on-site theater (p289), a replica of the Elizabethan Globe Theatre; it's worth returning in the evening to catch a show.

Union Station   LANDMARK
(Map p260; ☑202-289-1908; www.unionstationdc.com; 50 Massachusetts Ave NE; ⊙24hr; Ⓜ Red Line to Union Station) DC's main rail and bus hub, a 1907 beaux-arts beauty designed by Daniel Burnham, is an eye popper. The Grand Con-course is patterned after the Roman Baths of Diocletian and is awash in marble and gold filigree. Besides being an architectural gem, the station features an arcade of beyond-the-norm shops and fast-food restaurants. At the time of research, scaffolding covered various parts of the interior. Renovations to expand and modernize the facility are due for completion in late 2020.

Frederick Douglass National Historic Site   HISTORIC SITE
(☑202-426-5961; www.nps.gov/frdo; 1411 W St SE; ⊙9am-5pm Apr-Oct, to 4:30pm Nov-Mar; Ⓜ Green Line to Anacostia then B2 bus) **FREE** Escaped slave, abolitionist, author and statesman Frederick Douglass occupied this beautifully sited hilltop house from 1878 until his death in 1895. Original furnishings, books, photographs and other personal belongings paint a compelling portrait of both the private and public life of this great man. Keep an eye out for his wire-rim eyeglasses on his roll-top desk. Visits into the home – aka Cedar Hill – are by guided tour only.

Belmont-Paul Women's Equality National Monument   HISTORIC SITE
(Map p260; ☑202-546-1210; www.nps.gov/bepa; 144 Constitution Ave NE; ⊙9am-5pm Wed-Sun; Ⓜ Red Line to Union Station) **FREE** This brick house, only steps from the US Capitol, may not look like much, but throughout the

WASHINGTON, DC SIGHTS

Capitol Hill & South DC

20th century it was ground zero for women fighting for their rights. Multimillionaire socialite and suffragist Alva Belmont helped purchase the house in 1929 for the National Woman's Party. Activist Alice Paul lived here for 43 years, spearheading rallies and demonstrations. Designated a national monument in 2016 – the only one dedicated to women's history – it's now a house museum filled with fascinating artifacts celebrating women's historical achievements.

⊙ White House Area & Foggy Bottom

Government buildings are the main draw here. It's difficult to score a ticket to visit the White House, but you should have few problems arranging tickets to tour the Interior and State Departments. These and other notable attractions (White House Visitor Center, Daughters of the American Revolution Museum, Decatur House, Renwick Gallery, Art Museum of the Americas) are all located within a few blocks of each other and so can easily be visited in one day.

★ **White House**   LANDMARK
(Map p262; ☑202-456-2322; www.whitehouse.gov; 1600 Pennsylvania Ave NW; ☉tours 7:30-11:30am Tue-Thu, to 1:30pm Fri & Sat; Ⓜ Orange, Silver, Blue Line to Federal Triangle or McPherson Sq) FREE The

'President's House,' built in stages between 1792 and 1829, is an iconic, imposing building that's thrilling to see but difficult to access. Tours must be pre-arranged: Americans must apply via one of their state's members of Congress; non-Americans must ask their country's embassy in DC for assistance – in reality, there's only a slim chance that the embassy will be able to help source tickets. If you're lucky enough to visit on a tour, you'll see several rooms in the main residence.

Applications are taken from 21 days to three months in advance; the earlier you request during this time frame the better. If this all sounds like too much work, pop into the impressive White House Visitor Center a block away. It's not the real deal, but it does a good job in recounting the property's history and evoking life in the presidential residence. Cars aren't allowed to pass the building on Pennsylvania Ave, so it's possible to take good photos across the North Lawn from this vantage point. Or move to E St NW and take pictures across the South Lawn.

White House Visitor Center   MUSEUM
(Map p262; ☑202-208-1631; www.nps.gov/whho; 1450 Pennsylvania Ave NW; ☉7:30am-4pm; Ⓜ Orange, Silver, Blue Lines to Federal Triangle) FREE Getting inside the White House can be difficult, so here is your back-up plan. Housed in the splendiferous 1932 Patent Search Room

White House Area & Downtown

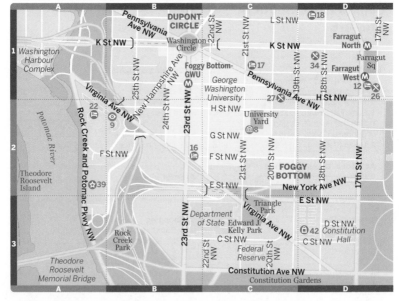

of the Department of Commerce Building, this center has plenty of artifacts, anecdote-packed information panels and informative multimedia exhibits, including a presentation on the history and lives of the presidential families and an interactive touchscreen tour of the White House. It's obviously not the same as seeing the real deal firsthand, but is well worth visiting regardless.

Textile Museum   MUSEUM
(Map p262; ☎202-994-5200; www.museum.gwu.edu; 701 21st St NW; suggested donation $8, children free; ⊙11am-5pm Mon & Fri, to 7pm Wed & Thu, 10am-5pm Sat, 1-5pm Sun; Ⓜ Orange, Silver, Blue Line to Foggy Bottom-GWU) This gem is the country's only textile museum. Galleries spread over two floors hold exquisite fabrics and carpets. Exhibits revolve around a theme – say Asian textiles depicting dragons or Kuba cloth from the Democratic Republic of the Congo – and rotate a few times a year. Bonus: the museum shares space with George Washington University's Washingtonia trove of historic maps, drawings and ephemera.

Watergate Complex   NOTABLE BUILDING
(Map p262; 2600 Virginia Ave NW; Ⓜ Orange, Silver, Blue Line to Foggy Bottom-GWU) Designed by Italian architect Luigi Moretti and DC-based landscape architect Boris Timchenko and constructed between 1963 and 1971, this five-building curvilinear riverfront complex encompasses apartments, fountains, terraces, boutiques, the refurbished Watergate Hotel (p275), and the office towers that made 'Watergate' a byword for political scandal after it broke that President Nixon's 'plumbers' had bugged the headquarters of the 1972 Democratic National Committee here.

⊙ Downtown & Penn Quarter

The neighborhood has its share of DC's top museums and historic sites. They tend to cluster in the area's southern end, near the Mall. This is where you'll find the National Archives and Newseum. Ford's Theatre and the Reynolds Center for American Art & Portraiture hover a few blocks north. All of these sights are in close, walkable proximity. Each will require a good hour or two of your time.

★**National Archives**   LANDMARK
(Map p262; ☎866-272-6272; www.archives.gov/museum; 700 Pennsylvania Ave NW, Penn Quarter; ⊙10am-5:30pm; Ⓜ Green, Yellow Line to Archives) FREE It's hard not to feel a little in awe of the big three documents in the Archives: the Declaration of Independence, the Constitution and the Bill of Rights, plus a copy of Magna Carta. Taken together, it becomes clear just how radical the American experiment was. The archival bric-a-brac of the Public Vaults

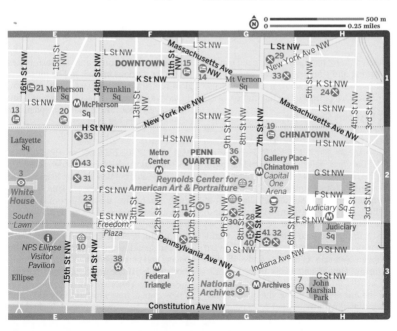

White House Area & Downtown

◎ Top Sights

1	National Archives	G3
2	Reynolds Center for American Art & Portraiture	G2
3	White House	E2

◉ Sights

4	FDR Memorial Stone	G3
5	Ford's Theatre	G2
6	International Spy Museum	G2
7	Newseum	H3
8	Textile Museum	C2
9	Watergate Complex	B2
10	White House Visitor Center	E3

◐ Activities, Courses & Tours

	DC Brew Tours	(see 2)
11	Old Town Trolley Tours	F2

◉ Sleeping

12	Club Quarters	D1
13	Hay-Adams Hotel	E1
14	Henley Park Hotel	G1
15	Hostelling International – Washington DC	F1
16	Hotel Hive	B2
17	Hotel Lombardy	C1
18	Hotel RL	D1
19	Pod DC Hotel	G2
20	Sofitel Lafayette Square	E1
21	St Regis Washington	E1
22	Watergate Hotel	A2
23	Willard InterContinental Hotel	E2

◈ Eating

24	A Baked Joint	H1
25	Central Michel Richard	F3
26	Equinox	D1
27	Founding Farmers	C1
28	Jaleo	G3
29	Kinship	G1
30	Minibar	G2
31	Old Ebbitt Grill	E2
32	Rasika	G3
33	Shouk	G1
34	Sichuan Pavilion	D1
35	Woodward Table	E2
	Woodward Takeout Food	(see 35)
36	Zaytinya	G2

◉ Drinking & Nightlife

37	Compass Coffee	G2
	Off the Record	(see 13)
	Round Robin	(see 23)
	Top of the Gate	(see 22)

◎ Entertainment

38	Capitol Steps	F3
39	Kennedy Center	A2
40	Shakespeare Theatre Company	G3
	Washington National Opera	(see 39)
41	Woolly Mammoth Theatre Company	G3

◉ Shopping

42	The Indian Craft Shop	D3
43	White House Gifts	E2
	White House Historical Association Museum Shop	(see 10)

makes a flashy rejoinder to the main exhibit. In spring and summer, you can reserve tickets (www.recreation.gov) for $1.50 and use the fast-track entrance on Constitution Ave.

★ **Reynolds Center for American Art & Portraiture** MUSEUM
(Map p262; ☑ 202-633-1000; www.americanart.si.edu; cnr 8th & F Sts NW, Penn Quarter; ⊙ 11:30am-7pm; Ⓜ Red, Yellow, Green Line to Gallery Pl-Chinatown) FREE The Reynolds Center is one of DC's finest museums. This Smithsonian venue combines the National Portrait Gallery and the American Art Museum into one whopping collection of American art that's unmatched anywhere in the world. Keep an eye out for famed works by Edward Hopper, Georgia O'Keeffe, Andy Warhol, Winslow Homer and loads more celebrated artists. Be sure to hit the **Luce Center** on the 3rd and 4th floors: the open storage area stuffed with more than 3000 paintings,

sculptures, miniatures and folk-art pieces makes for glorious browsing. The museum's glass-roofed inner courtyard on the 1st floor, dotted with trees and marble benches, is another lovely spot. Bring your own picnic or order sandwiches at the cafe.

Newseum MUSEUM
(Map p262; ☑ 202-292-6100; www.newseum.org; 555 Pennsylvania Ave NW, Penn Quarter; adult/child $25/15; ⊙ 9am-5pm Mon-Sat, from 10am Sun; ⓐ; Ⓜ Green, Yellow Line to Archives) This six-story, highly interactive news museum is worth the admission price. You can delve into the major events of recent years (the fall of the Berlin Wall, September 11, Hurricane Katrina), and spend hours watching moving film footage and perusing Pulitzer Prize–winning photographs. If nothing else, stroll up to the museum's entrance, where the front pages of newspapers from around the world – and every US state – are displayed. Tickets are

usable for two consecutive days, so you can always return. Start at the top level (Level 6), with its awesome terrace views of Pennsylvania Ave up to the Capitol, and work your way down. Level 4 has twisted wreckage from the September 11 attacks and haunting final images from Bill Biggart's camera (Biggart was the only journalist to be killed that day). Level 3 holds a memorial to journalists killed in pursuit of the truth. Level 2 has video stations where kids read news stories from a teleprompter and 'report' the news in front of a DC backdrop. The concourse level displays FBI artifacts from prominent news stories, such as the Unabomber's cabin and gangster Whitey Bulger's fishing hat.

Ford's Theatre   HISTORIC SITE
(Map p262; 202-347-4833; www.fords.org; 511 10th St NW, Penn Quarter; 9am-4:30pm; Red, Orange, Silver, Blue Line to Metro Center) FREE
On April 14, 1865, John Wilkes Booth assassinated Abraham Lincoln here. Timed-entry tickets provide access to the site, which has four parts: the theater itself (where you see the box seat Lincoln was sitting in), the basement museum (displaying Booth's pistol, his muddy boot etc), Petersen House (across the street, where Lincoln died) and the aftermath exhibits. Arrive early (by 8:30am) because tickets do run out or reserve online ($3 fee) to ensure admittance. National Park Service rangers are on hand to tell the story.

The theater still holds performances, and sometimes the venue is closed to the public. It's always smart to check the schedule before heading out. Ford's posts it online, or you can call the box office to make sure the site is open. Also, not all entry tickets provide admittance to all four parts of the experience, due to occasional scheduling conflicts. Be sure to check before booking. Allow 1½ hours to see it all.

International Spy Museum   MUSEUM
(Map p264; 202-393-7798; www.spymuseum.org; 800 F St NW, Penn Quarter; adult/child $23/15; 9am-7pm mid-Apr–mid-Aug, 10am-6pm rest of year; ; Red, Yellow, Green Line to Gallery Pl-Chinatown) One of DC's most popular museums, the International Spy Museum is flashy, over the top, and probably guilty of overly glamming up a life of intelligence-gathering. But who cares? You basically want to see Q's lab, and that's what the Spy Museum feels like. Check out James Bond's tricked-out Aston Martin, the KGB's lipstick-concealed pistol and more. Kids go crazy for this spot, but be warned: lines form long and early. Ease the wait somewhat by reserving online.

There are all kinds of artifacts and interactive displays. You can try to identify disguises, listen to bugs and spot hidden cameras throughout the museum. A lot of the exhibits are historical in nature, focusing on the Cold War in particular (a re-creation of the tunnel under the Berlin Wall is an eerie winner). The museum also offers several tours, such as 'Spy in the City' ($15), a sort of GPS-driven scavenger hunt across DC. Expect even more intrigue when the museum moves to its new, twice-as-big digs at L'Enfant Plaza sometime in 2019.

Logan Circle, U Street & Columbia Heights
While none of DC's top-draw sights rise in the area, many historical, religious and natural attractions beckon – and most of them are free. The African American Civil War Memorial, beside the U St Metro station, is worth a peek, while President Lincoln's Cottage lies a few miles northeast. Nearby, religious sights such as the Franciscan Monastery and Basilica of the National Shrine of the Immaculate Conception cluster in Brookland. Further east, the National Arboretum and Kenilworth Aquatic Gardens offer excellent refuges to escape the crowds.

★United States National Arboretum   GARDENS
(202-245-2726; www.usna.usda.gov; R St NE; 8am-5pm; Orange, Silver, Blue Line to Stadium-Armory, then bus B2) FREE The greatest green space in Washington unfurls almost 450 acres of meadowland, sylvan theaters and a pastoral setting that feels somewhere between bucolic Americana countryside and a classical Greek ruralscape. Highlights include the Bonsai & Penjing Museum (exquisitely sculpted mini trees), the National Herb Garden (lots of hot peppers) and the otherworldly Capitol Columns Garden (studded with Corinthian pillars that were once part of the Capitol building). All are near the R St entrance.

African American Civil War Memorial   MONUMENT
(Map p266; www.afroamcivilwar.org; cnr U St NW & Vermont Ave NW; 24hr; Green, Yellow Line to U St) Standing at the center of a granite plaza, this bronze memorial depicting rifle-bearing troops is DC's first major art piece by black sculptor Ed Hamilton. The statue is surrounded on three sides by the Wall of Honor, listing the names of 209,145 black troops who fought in the Union Army, as well as

Dupont Circle & Logan Circle

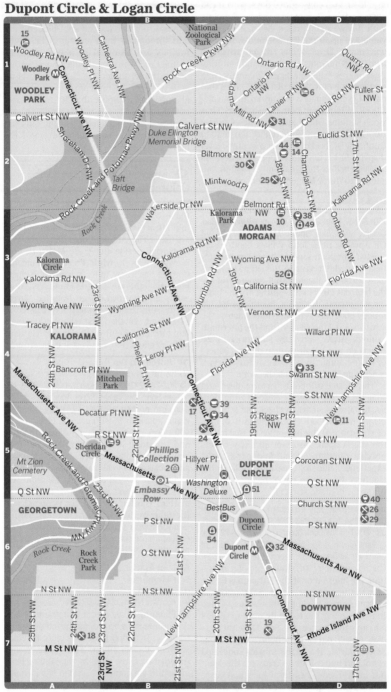

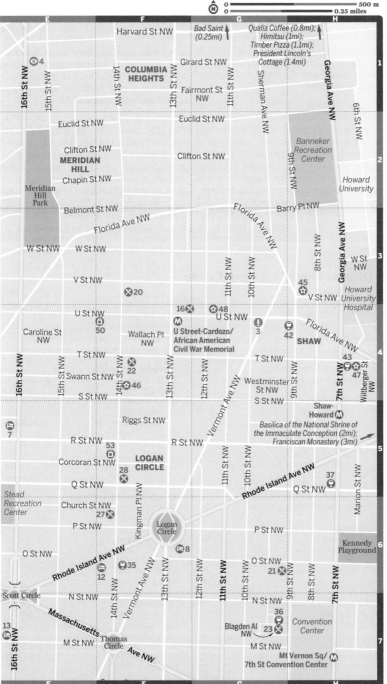

0   500 m
0   0.25 miles

Harvard St NW

Bad Saint
(0.25mi)

Qualia Coffee (0.8mi);
Himitsu (1mi);
Timber Pizza (1.1mi);
President Lincoln's
Cottage (1.4mi)

4

16th St NW

15th St NW

14th St NW

COLUMBIA
HEIGHTS

Girard St NW

13th St NW

11th St NW

Sherman Ave NW

Georgia Ave NW

6th St NW

1

Fairmont St
NW

Euclid St NW

Euclid St NW

Banneker
Recreation
Center

Howard
University

9th St NW

Clifton St NW

MERIDIAN
HILL

Clifton St NW

2

Chapin St NW

Meridian
Hill
Park

Belmont St NW

Barry Pl NW

Florida Ave NW

Florida Ave NW

W St NW

W St NW

V St NW

8th St NW

Georgia Ave NW

W St
NW

3

20

45

V St NW

Howard
University
Hospital

U St NW

16   48

11th St NW

10th St NW

50

U St NW

Caroline St
NW

Wallach Pl
NW

U Street-Cardozo/
African American
Civil War Memorial

3

42

SHAW

Florida Ave NW

16th St NW

15th St NW

14th St NW

T St NW

22

13th St NW

12th St NW

T St NW

43

47

7th St NW

Wiltberger St
NW

Swann St NW

46

Westminster
St NW

9th St NW

S St NW

S St NW

Shaw-
Howard

Riggs St NW

Vermont Ave NW

Basilica of the National Shrine of
the Immaculate Conception (2mi);
Franciscan Monastery (3mi)

7

R St NW

53

R St NW

11th St NW

10th St NW

5

Corcoran St NW

LOGAN
CIRCLE

28

Rhode Island Ave NW

37

Marion St NW

Q St NW

Q St NW

Stead
Recreation
Center

Church St NW

27

Logan
Circle

P St NW

P St NW

Kennedy
Playground

6

Rhode Island Ave NW

O St NW

8

O St NW

21

8th St NW

7th St NW

9th St NW

35

12

Scott Circle

N St NW

N St NW

36

Convention
Center

13

16th St NW

Massachusetts

14th St NW

Vermont Ave NW

13th St NW

12th St NW

11th St NW

10th St NW

Blagden Al
NW

23

Thomas
Circle

M St NW

Ave NW

M St NW

Mt Vernon Sq/
7th St Convention Center

7

E   F   G   H

---

the 7000 white soldiers who served alongside them.

To look up individual names and find their location on the memorial, check the website's 'Colored Troops Search.' To reach the plaza, depart the Metro station via the 10th St exit (follow the 'memorial' signs as you leave the train).

Mexican Cultural Institute CULTURAL CENTER
(Map p266; 202-728-1628; www.institute ofmexicodc.org; 2829 16th St NW; 10am-6pm Mon-Fri, noon-4pm Sat; Green, Yellow Lines to Columbia Heights) FREE The Mexican Cultural Institute looks locked up and imposing, but don't be deterred. The gilded beaux-arts mansion is open to the public and hosts excellent art and cultural exhibitions related to Mexico. You might see a show on Diego Rivera's art, Mayan religious artifacts or Octavio Paz's writings. Ring the doorbell for entry.

◉ Dupont Circle & Kalorama

While Dupont doesn't hold any top-tier sights, it has an excellent modern-art museum, plus several historic-house museums and galleries. Architecture fans will find lots to look at thanks to all of the embassies and other notable buildings. Everything is spread throughout the district.

★ Embassy Row ARCHITECTURE
(Map p266; www.embassy.org; Massachusetts Ave NW, btwn Observatory & Dupont Circles NW; Red Line to Dupont Circle) Stroll northwest along Massachusetts Ave from Dupont Circle (the actual traffic circle) and you pass more than 40 embassies housed in mansions that range from elegant to imposing to discreet. Tunisia, Chile, Turkmenistan, Togo, Haiti – flags flutter above heavy doors and mark the nations inside, while dark-windowed sedans ease out of driveways ferrying diplomats to

Dupont Circle & Logan Circle

and fro. The district has another 130 embassies sprinkled throughout, but this is the main vein.

★ **Phillips Collection** MUSEUM
(Map p266; ✆202-387-2151; www.phillipscollection.org; 1600 21st St NW; Tue-Fri free, Sat & Sun $10, ticketed exhibitions per day $12; ◷10am-5pm Tue, Wed, Fri & Sat, to 8:30pm Thu, noon-7pm Sun; Ⓜ Red Line to Dupont Circle) The first modern-art museum in the country (opened in 1921) houses a small but exquisite collection of European and American works. Renoir's *Luncheon of the Boating Party* is a highlight, along with pieces by Gauguin, Van Gogh, Matisse, Picasso, Rothko and many other greats. The permanent collection is free on weekdays. Download the free app or dial ✆202-595-1839 for audio tours through the works. Famous works sometimes rotate into the museum's ticketed exhibitions (in which case admission fees apply). The Phillips' Sunday chamber-music series has been making sweet sounds since 1941; concerts start at 4pm October through May, and tickets cost $40.

National Geographic Museum MUSEUM
(Map p266; ✆202-857-7700; www.nationalgeographic.org/dc; 1145 17th St NW; adult/child $15/10; ◷10am-6pm; Ⓜ Red Line to Farragut North) The museum at National Geographic Society headquarters can't compete with the Smithsonian's more extensive offerings, but it can be worth a stop, depending on what's showing. Exhibits change periodically. The society also hosts films, concerts and lectures by famed researchers and explorers; most programs have a fee.

◉ Georgetown

Historic homes and gardens are Georgetown's stock in trade, with a couple of atmospheric cemeteries thrown in for good measure. They're all in relatively close proximity to each other. Many sights are closed on Monday.

★ **Dumbarton Oaks** GARDENS, MUSEUM
(Map p270; ✆202-339-6401; www.doaks.org; 1703 32nd St NW; museum free, gardens adult/child $10/5; ◷museum 11:30am-5:30pm Tue-Sun, gardens 2-6pm; 🚍Circulator) The mansion's 10 acres of enchanting formal gardens are straight out of a storybook. In springtime the blooms are stunning. The mansion itself is worth a walk-through to see exquisite Byzantine and pre-Columbian art (including El Greco's *The Visitation*) and the library of rare books that date as far back as 1491.

In 1944 diplomatic meetings took place here that laid the groundwork for the UN. The trustees of Harvard University operate the house, so Harvard students, faculty and staff get in free. From November to mid-March the gardens are free to all (and they close at 5pm). The garden entrance is at R and 31st Sts NW.

Georgetown Waterfront Park PARK
(Map p270; www.georgetownwaterfrontpark.org; Water St NW, btwn 30th St & Key Bridge; 🦽; 🚍Circulator) This park is a favorite with couples on first dates, families on an evening stroll and power players showing off their yachts. Benches dot the way, where you can sit and watch the rowing teams out on the Potomac River. Alfresco restaurants cluster near the harbor at 31st St NW. They ring a terraced plaza filled with fountains (which become an ice rink in winter). The docks are also here for boats that ply the Potomac to Alexandria, VA, and Capitol Hill's Wharf.

Georgetown University UNIVERSITY
(Map p270; ✆202-687-0100; www.georgetown.edu; cnr 37th & O Sts NW; 🚍Circulator) Georgetown is one of the nation's top universities, with a student body that's equally hard-working and hard-partying. Founded in 1789, it was America's first Roman Catholic university. Notable Hoya (derived from the Latin *hoya saxa,* 'what rocks') alumni include Bill Clinton, as well as many international royals and heads of state. Near the campus' east gate, medieval-looking **Healy Hall** impresses with its tall, Hogwarts-esque clock tower. Pretty **Dahlgren Chapel** and its quiet courtyard hide behind it.

Exorcist Stairs FILM LOCATION
(Map p270; 3600 Prospect St NW; 🚍Circulator) The steep set of stairs dropping down to M St is a popular track for joggers, but more famously it's the spot where demonically possessed Father Karras tumbles to his death in horror-film classic *The Exorcist* (1973). Come on foggy nights, when the stone steps really are creepy as hell.

◉ Upper Northwest DC

Three of the major sights in this part of the city (Hillwood Estate, Museum & Gardens; National Zoo; Rock Creek Park) can be accessed via the Metro. To reach the Washington National Cathedral and Kreeger Museum, you'll need to take buses from Dupont Circle; it's an easy walk along residential streets between the two.

Georgetown

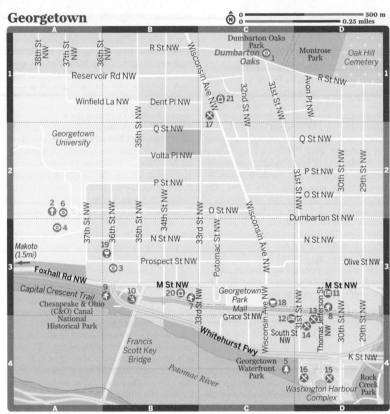

★**Washington National Cathedral** CHURCH (Map p272; ☎202-537-6200; www.cathedral.org; 3101 Wisconsin Ave NW, Cathedral Heights; adult/ child 5-17yr $12/8, Sun free; ☺10am-5pm Mon-Fri, 10am-4pm Sat, 12:45-4pm Sun; ☐N2, N3, N4, N6 from Dupont Circle) Built between 1907 and 1990, this huge neo-Gothic cathedral blends the spiritual with the profane in its architecture. Most of its colored stained-glass windows celebrate religious themes, although the 'Scientists and Technicians' window with its embedded lunar rock is an exception. The exterior gargoyles depict everything from Darth Vader to a Missouri bear. Specialty tours are available; check online for details. The excellent cafe **Open City** (www.opencitycathedraldc. com; brunch dishes $4-11, sandwiches $8-10; ☺7am-6pm; ☎) is in the cathedral's grounds.

★**Hillwood Estate,**
Museum & Gardens MUSEUM, GARDENS
(Map p272; ☎202-686-5807; www.hillwood museum.org; 4155 Linnean Ave NW, Forest Hills; adult/student/child 6-18yr $18/10/5; ☺10am-5pm Tue-Sat; ⓜRed Line to Van Ness-UDC) The former estate of Marjorie Merriweather Post of Post cereal fame, this lavish 1920s mansion showcases her extraordinary collections of Russian imperial art (icons, paintings, jewelry, Fabergé eggs) and French 18th-century decorative artwork. Wandering through the mansion is fascinating – the state-of-the-art 1950s kitchen, modern staff quarters and opulent, objet-laden entertaining and living areas give a wonderful insight into her privileged life and role as a notable society hostess.

★**Kreeger Museum** MUSEUM
(Map p272; ☎202-337-3050; www.kreegermuse um.org; 2401 Foxhall Rd NW, Foxhall Crescent; adult/ student $10/8; ☺10am-4pm Tue-Sat, closed Aug; ⓜRed Line to Farragut North or Dupont Circle, then bus D6) One of DC's top attractions for architecture buffs and those with an interest in 20th-century art, this museum is housed in a stunning 1963 International Style building

Georgetown

WASHINGTON, DC ACTIVITIES

designed by American architect Philip Johnson. Clad in travertine, it features a distinctive roofline, light-saturated interior salons and an expansive sculpture terrace that is home to works by artists including Jean Arp and Henry Moore. Inside, artworks from the top-drawer personal collection of David and Carem Kreeger are displayed.

National Zoo ZOO
(Map p272; ☑202-633-4888; www.nationalzoo.si.edu; 3001 Connecticut Ave NW, Woodley Park; ☺9am-6pm mid-Mar–Sep, to 4pm Oct–mid-Mar, grounds 8am-7pm mid-Mar–Sep, to 5pm Oct–mid-Mar; Ⓜ Red Line to Cleveland Park or Woodley Park) **FREE** Home to more than 1800 animals and more than 300 species in natural habitats, the National Zoo is famed for its giant pandas Mei Xiang, Tian Tian and Bei Bei. Other highlights include the African lion pride, Asian elephants, and orangutans swinging 50ft overhead from steel cables and interconnected towers (aka the 'O Line').

Rock Creek Park PARK
(Map p272; www.nps.gov/rocr; ☺sunrise-sunset; Ⓜ Red Line to Friendship Heights; Red, Green, Yellow Line to Fort Totten; then bus E4 from either) At 1700-plus acres, Rock Creek is twice the size of New York's Central Park and feels wilder. Terrific trails for hiking, biking and horseback riding extend the entire length, and the boundaries enclose Civil War forts, dense forest and wildflower-strewn fields.

Beach Drive is undergoing extensive renovation and various sections will be closed to vehicles over the course of several years. Visit www.nps.gov/rocr to learn more.

🏃 Activities

Hiking & Cycling

Everyone runs on the Mall. Rock Creek Park has 15 miles of unpaved trails. A good map is *Map N: Trails in the Rock Creek Park Area,* published by the Potomac Appalachian Trail Club (www.patc.net). Better yet, join the welcoming District Running Collective (www.districtrunningcollective.com) on its Wednesday group run through the city.

C&O Canal Towpath CYCLING
(Map p270; www.nps.gov/choh; 1057 Thomas Jefferson St NW; ☐Circulator) The shaded hiking-cycling path – part of a larger national historic park – runs alongside a waterway built in the mid-1800s to transport goods to West Virginia. Step on at Jefferson St for a lovely green escape from the crowd. (Note the canal and environs are being restored and enhanced over the next several years, so you might run into construction along the way; check the latest updates before setting off.) In its entirety, the gravel path runs for 185 miles from Georgetown to Cumberland, MD. Lots of cyclists do the 14-mile ride from Georgetown to Great Falls, MD. The tree-lined route goes over atmospheric wooden bridges and past waterwheels and old lock houses. It's mostly flat, punctuated by occasional small hills. The park's website and Bike Washington (http://bikewashington.org) has trail maps.

Capital Crescent Trail CYCLING
(Map p270; www.cctrail.org; Water St; ☐Circulator) Stretching between Georgetown and Bethesda, MD, the constantly evolving Capital Crescent Trail is a fabulous (and very

popular) jogging and biking route. Built on an abandoned railroad bed, the 11-mile trail is paved and is a great day trip. It has beautiful lookouts over the Potomac River, and winds through woodsy areas and upscale neighborhoods. In Georgetown, the trail begins under the Key Bridge on Water St (which is what K St becomes as it moves west along the waterfront); the trailhead is clearly marked. In Bethesda, it starts at the Wisconsin Ave Tunnel, on Wisconsin Ave just south of Old Georgetown Rd (it's clearly marked here too, and accessible from Bethesda Metro station). The trail also links up with the C&O Canal Towpath (p271) and trails through Rock Creek Park.

Big Wheel Bikes CYCLING
(Map p270; ☎ 202-337-0254; www.bigwheel bikes.com; 1034 33rd St NW; per 3hr/day $21/35; ⏰ 11am-7pm Tue-Fri, 10am-6pm Sat & Sun; ☷ Cir-

Upper Northwest DC

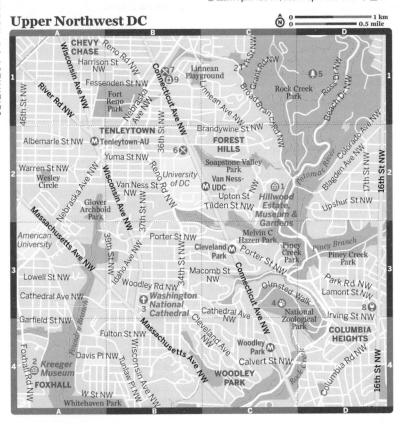

Upper Northwest DC

culator) Big Wheel has a wide variety of two-wheelers to rent, and you can spin onto the C&O Canal Towpath (p271) practically from the front door. Staff members also provide the lowdown on the nearby Capital Crescent Trail (p271) and Mount Vernon Trail (p347). There's a three-hour minimum with rentals. For an extra $10 you can keep your bike overnight.

Boating

Kayaks and canoes cruise the waters of both the Potomac River and the Anacostia River. Convenient boathouses that rent vessels are in Georgetown, the Navy Yard, the Wharf and Upper Northwest DC. Staff at these facilities provide instruction if you need it.

Key Bridge Boathouse   WATER SPORTS
(Map p270; ☑202-337-9642; www.boatingindc.com/boathouses/key-bridge-boathouse; 3500 Water St NW; ⊙hours vary mid-Apr–Oct; ⬜Circulator) Located beneath the Key Bridge, the boathouse rents canoes, kayaks and stand up paddleboards (prices start at $16 per hour). In summer it also offers guided, 90-minute kayak trips ($45 per person) that glide past the Lincoln Memorial as the sun sets. If you have a bike, the boathouse is a mere few steps from the Capital Crescent Trail.

Tidal Basin Boathouse   BOATING
(Map p254; ☑202-479-2426; www.boatingindc.com/boathouses/tidal-basin; 1501 Maine Ave SW; 2-/4-person boat rental $18/30; ⊙10am-6pm mid-Mar–Sep; ⬜Circulator, ⓂOrange, Silver, Blue Line to Smithsonian) Rents paddleboats to take out on the Tidal Basin. Make sure you bring a camera as there are great views from the water.

Ballpark Boathouse   KAYAKING
(Map p260; ☑202-337-9642; www.boatingindc.com/boathouses/ballpark-boathouse; Potomac Ave SE; single/double kayak per hr $16/22; ⊙noon-8pm Thu & Fri, from 9am Sat & Sun mid-May–mid-Sep; ⓂGreen Line to Navy Yard) Rent a kayak and glide along the Anacostia River., where you might spy a heron spearfishing for its lunch. Guided tours (per person $45, 90 minutes) take off at sunset each evening.

⚲ Tours

Bike & Roll   CYCLING
(Map p254; ☑202-842-2453; www.bikeandrolldc.com; 955 L'Enfant Plaza SW; tours adult/child from $44/34; ⊙9am-8pm, reduced hours spring & fall, closed early Dec–mid-Mar; ⓂOrange, Silver, Blue, Yellow, Green Line to L'Enfant Plaza) This branch of the bike-rental company (from $16 per two hours) is the one closest to the Mall.

> **ⓘ CYCLING THE MALL**
> Bicycles are welcome on the Mall, and two-wheeling is a great way to navigate the lengthy expanse. **Capital Bikeshare** (☑877-430-2453; www.capitalbikeshare.com; per 1/3 days $8/17) has several stations around the area. Handy ones are by the Smithsonian Metro, Lincoln Memorial, Maryland and Independence Aves SW (near the National Air and Space Museum) and Jefferson and 14th Sts SW (near the Washington Monument). No companies rent bikes on the Mall proper, though Bike & Roll at L'Enfant Plaza isn't too far away.

In addition to bike rental, it also provides tours. Three-hour jaunts wheel by the main sights of Capitol Hill and the National Mall. The evening rides to the monuments are particularly good.

DC Brew Tours   BUS
(Map p262; ☑202-759-8687; www.citybrewtours.com/dc; 801 F St NW, Penn Quarter; tours $70-99; ⓂRed, Yellow, Green Line to Gallery Pl-Chinatown) Visit three to four breweries by van. Routes vary but could include DC Brau, Atlas, Capital City and Port City, among others. Five-hour jaunts feature tastings of 15-plus beers and a light meal. The 3½-hour forgoes the meal and pares down the brewery tally. Departure is from outside the Reynolds Center. Tours go daily, at various times.

DC by Foot   WALKING
(Map p254; ☑202-370-1830; www.freetoursbyfoot.com/washington-dc-tours) Guides for this pay-what-you-want walking tour offer engaging stories and historical details on different jaunts covering the National Mall, Lincoln's assassination, Dupont Circle's ghosts and many more. Most takers pay around $10 to $15 per person. Reserve in advance to guarantee a spot.

DC Metro Food Tours   WALKING
(☑202-851-2268; www.dcmetrofoodtours.com; per person $56-67) These walkabouts explore the culinary riches of various neighborhoods, stopping for multiple bites along the way. Offerings include Capitol Hill, U St, Little Ethiopia, Georgetown and Alexandria, VA. Most last from three to 3½ hours. Departure points vary.

Old Town Trolley Tours   BUS
(Map p262; ☑202-832-9800; www.trolleytours.com; 1001 E St NW, Penn Quarter; adult/child

$40/30; Ⓜ Red, Orange, Silver, Blue Line to Metro Center) This open-sided bus offers hop-on, hop-off exploring of some 25 major sights around the Mall, Arlington and Downtown. The company also offers a 'monuments by moonlight' tour and the DC Ducks tour, via an amphibious vehicle that plunges into the Potomac. Buy tickets at the **Washington Welcome Center** (1001 E St NW), at Union Station, or online.

✯✯ Festivals & Events

Independence Day   CULTURAL
(☉ Jul 4) Huge crowds gather on the Mall to watch marching bands parade and hear the Declaration of Independence read from the National Archives steps. Later the National Symphony Orchestra plays a concert on the Capitol's steps, followed by mega-fireworks.

National Cherry Blossom Festival   CULTURAL
(www.nationalcherryblossomfestival.org; ☉late Mar-mid-Apr) The star of DC's annual calendar celebrates spring's arrival with boat rides in the Tidal Basin, evening walks by lantern light, cultural fairs and a parade. The three-week event commemorates Japan's gift of 3000 cherry trees in 1912. It's DC at its prettiest.

★ Snallygaster   BEER
(www.snallygasterdc.com; tickets $35) Beloved by beer geeks, this outdoor fest held next to Nationals Park features a terrific selection of 400 brews (some quite rare), dance punk bands and food trucks. Held on a Saturday in mid- to late September.

Smithsonian Folklife Festival   CULTURAL
(www.festival.si.edu; ♿; 🚌 Circulator, Ⓜ Orange, Silver, Blue, Green, Yellow Lines to L'Enfant Plaza) This fun family event, held over 10 days in late June and early July, celebrates international and US cultures. It features folk music, dance, crafts and ethnic fare, and highlights a diverse mix of countries and regions. It takes place at the Mall's east end.

🛏 Sleeping

🛏 White House Area & Foggy Bottom

Hotel RL   HOTEL $
(Map p262; 📞 202-223-4320; www.redlion.com/washington-dc; 1823 L St NW; r from $89; Ⓟ ➿ ❄ @ 🛜 🐾; Ⓜ Red, Orange, Silver, Blue Line to Farragut North or Farragut West) Hotel RL styles itself as a boutique choice, but it's too worn for that category. Still, it has a bouncy vibe and quirky edge, with free bike hire and gym

passes, a games room and a space in the lobby where performances and lectures are staged. Rooms are large, and have a kitchenette; free coffee is available downstairs each morning. Note that multinight minimum stays sometimes apply.

★ Sofitel Lafayette Square   HOTEL $$
(Map p262; 📞 202-730-8800; www.sofitelwashingtondc.com; 806 15th St NW; r $199-730, ste $260-1500; Ⓟ ➿ ❄ @ 🛜 🐾; Ⓜ Orange, Silver, Blue Line to McPherson Sq) We rarely give establishments a 10 out of 10 score, but that's what this splendid hotel deserves. Not as large as its five-star DC competitors, it has a classy and calm ambience and offers exemplary levels of service. Decor is decidedly Parisian and everything about the rooms (beds, bathrooms, amenities, facilities) is top-notch, especially in the luxury rooms and suites.

★ Hotel Hive   DESIGN HOTEL $$
(Map p262; 📞 202-849-8499; www.hotelhive.com; 2224 F St NW; r $99-299, loft r $149-329; ❄ 🛜 🐾; Ⓜ Orange, Silver, Blue Line to Foggy Bottom-GWU) There's plenty of buzz around DC's first micro-hotel. The 83 rooms are small (twin and bunk-bed rooms are tiny, and don't have closets – opt for a king loft if possible). Clever design features include under-bed luggage storage and a small work desk. A hip bar and branch of the trendy **&pizza** eatery are downstairs, and there's a rooftop bar, too. For on-the-go types who don't mind the lack of space and hostel vibe, it's good value for the location (right by the George Washington University campus, and a short walk to the Mall). Bargain hunters can save even more money by choosing rooms that are below the lobby and viewless, or above the bar and noisier.

Club Quarters   HOTEL $$
(Map p262; 📞 202-463-6400; www.clubquarters.com/washington-dc; 839 17th St NW; r $110-450; Ⓟ ➿ ❄ @ 🛜; Ⓜ Orange, Silver, Blue Line to Farragut West) Club Quarters is a favorite with business travelers on the go. Rooms are small and without views, lacking any semblance of charm or quirk, but the bed is comfortable, the desk workable, the wi-fi fast enough and the coffee maker well stocked. Oh, and the prices are reasonable in an area where they're usually sky-high.

Hotel Lombardy   BOUTIQUE HOTEL $$
(Map p262; 📞 202-828-2600; www.hotellombardy.com; 2019 Pennsylvania Ave NW; r $109-299; Ⓟ ➿ ❄ 🛜; Ⓜ Orange, Silver, Blue Line to Foggy Bottom-GWU) The Lombardy first welcomed guests in the 1970s, when its intimate Venetian-style decor (shuttered doors, warm

gold walls) was an instant hit with visiting Europeans. The well-maintained rooms are in need of a refresh – furnishings are worn and bathrooms dated. Opt for an upper-floor room on the east side of the building. The restaurant is disappointing.

★ **Hay-Adams Hotel** HERITAGE HOTEL $$$
(Map p262; ☑ 202-638-6600; www.hayadams. com; 800 16th St NW; r from $400; P ✱ @ 🛜 🏊; Ⓜ Orange, Silver, Blue Line to McPherson Sq) One of the city's great heritage hotels, the Hay is a beautiful old building where 'nothing is overlooked but the White House.' It has the best rooms of the old-school luxury genre in the city, sporting elegant decor, top-quality fittings, hugely comfortable beds and luxe bathrooms. Facilities include a gym, restaurant and popular basement bar (p285).

★ **Watergate Hotel** DESIGN HOTEL $$$
(Map p262; ☑ 202-827-1600; www.thewater gatehotel.com; 2650 Virginia Ave NW; r/ste from $399/669; P ✱ @ 🛜 ☕ 🏊; Ⓜ Orange, Silver, Blue Line to Foggy Bottom-GWU) The 2016 unveiling of this iconic hotel's redesign had DC's smart set all aflutter, and the general consensus seems to be that Ron Arad's sleek interior treats Luigi Moretti's 1965 design with the respect it deserves. Public areas have plenty of pizzazz (the Next Whisky Bar in the lobby is a knockout) and the spacious rooms successfully meld comfort and style.

Willard InterContinental Hotel HISTORIC HOTEL $$$
(Map p262; ☑ 202-628-9100; www.washington. intercontinental.com; 1401 Pennsylvania Ave NW; r/ste from $300/600; P ⊖ ✱ @ 🛜 🏊; Ⓜ Red, Orange, Silver, Blue Line to Metro Center) The Willard is where MLK wrote his 'I Have a Dream' speech; where the term 'lobbyist' was coined (by President Grant to describe political wranglers trolling the lobby); and where many presidents have lain their heads. The 335 spacious rooms are slowly being renovated: premium options overlook the Washington Monument. Families appreciate the kids concierge and program. Breakfast costs $34.

St Regis Washington HOTEL $$$
(Map p262; ☑ 202-638-2626; www.stregiswash ingtondc.com; 923 16th St NW; r/ste from $350/550; P ✱ @ 🛜 🏊; Ⓜ Orange, Silver, Blue Line to McPherson Sq) The neo-renaissance St Regis is one of the grandest hotels in the city. What else can you say about a building designed to resemble nothing less than an Italian palace? Rooms are as gilded as you'd expect, with hand-carved armoires, double-basin marble sinks and luxe Italian bed linen.

🛏 Capitol Hill & South DC

William Penn House HOSTEL $
(Map p260; ☑ 202-543-5560; www.william pennhouse.org; 515 E Capitol St; dm $45-55; ⊖ ✱ @; Ⓜ Orange, Silver, Blue Line to Capitol South or Eastern Market) This friendly Quaker-run guesthouse with garden offers clean, well-maintained dorms, though it could use more bathrooms. There are 30 beds in total, including two 10-bed dorms, two four-bed dorms and one two-bed room. The facility doesn't require religious observance, but there is a religious theme throughout, and it prefers guests who are active in progressive causes. Rates include continental breakfast.

The curious and spiritually minded can rise for the 7:30am worship service.

★ **Kimpton George Hotel** HOTEL $$$
(Map p260; ☑ 202-347-4200; www.hotelgeorge. com; 15 E St NW; r $269-429; P ⊖ ✱ @ 🛜 🏊; Ⓜ Red Line to Union Station) Nods to namesake George Washington are pervasive at this hotel, which is the hippest lodging on the Hill. Rooms exude a cool, creamy-white Zen and feature large bathrooms, Colonial-inspired work desks, fun presidential pop art and wallpaper adorned with Washington's cursive-written inaugural address. The handy location puts you between Union Station and the Capitol.

🛏 Downtown & Penn Quarter

★ **Hostelling International – Washington DC** HOSTEL $
(Map p262; ☑ 202-737-2333; www.hiwashing tondc.org; 1009 11th St NW, Downtown; dm $33-55, d $110-150; ⊖ ✱ @ 🛜; Ⓜ Red, Orange, Silver, Blue Line to Metro Center) Top of the budget picks, this large, friendly hostel attracts a laid-back international crowd and has loads of amenities: lounge rooms, a pool table, a 60in TV for movie nights, free tours of various neighborhoods and historic sites, free continental breakfast, and free wi-fi.

★ **Pod DC Hotel** DESIGN HOTEL $$
(Map p262; ☑ 202-847-4444; www.thepodhotel. com; 627 H St NW, Downtown; d $140-240; ✱ 🛜; Ⓜ Red, Yellow, Green Line to Gallery Pl-Chinatown) The Pod is a micro-hotel with teeny rooms. But that's not necessarily bad, especially if you crave hipness at a reasonable price. Under-bed luggage storage and a work desk are among the clever design features. There's a comfort food diner and whiskey bar, a rooftop bar with free happy hour snacks, and savvy young staff presiding over it all. The vibe

is a bit like a hostel. It's a stone's throw from the Metro station and Chinatown Gate, and while there are plenty of people around, this stretch of street feels a tad sketchy at night.

★**Henley Park Hotel**   BOUTIQUE HOTEL **$$**
(Map p262; ☑202-638-5200; www.henleypark. com; 926 Massachusetts Ave NW, Downtown; d $150-270; P◉❄@🛜; Ⓜ Green, Yellow Line to Mt Vernon Sq/7th St-Convention Center) This beautiful Tudor-style structure used to be an apartment building for Senators and Congressmen. The rooms – decked in tasteful plaids, paisleys, and dark wood furniture – are as elegant as the edifice. The property has tons of character, with a charming bar and restaurant serving afternoon tea. Some noise seeps in from the street outside, but overall it's excellent value.

🛏 Logan Circle, U Street & Columbia Heights

★**Chester Arthur House**   B&B **$$**
(Map p266; ☑877-893-3233; www.chesterarthur house.com; 23 Logan Circle NW; r $185-225; ◉❄🛜; Ⓜ Green, Yellow Line to U St) Snooze in one of four rooms in this beautiful Logan Circle row house, located a stumble from the restaurant boom along P and 14th Sts. The 1883 abode is stuffed with crystal chandeliers, antique oil paintings, oriental rugs and a mahogany paneled staircase, plus ephemera from the hosts' global expeditions.

Kimpton Mason & Rook Hotel   HOTEL **$$**
(Map p266; ☑202-742-3100; www.masonan drookhotel.com; 1430 Rhode Island Ave NW; r $189-399; P◉❄@🛜🐾; Ⓜ Orange, Silver, Blue Line to McPherson Sq) 🐾 Snuggled into a tree-lined neighborhood near trendy 14th St, Mason & Rook feels like your urbane friend's chic apartment. The lobby resembles a handsome living room, with comfy seating, bookshelves and eclectic art. The large guest rooms invite lingering with plush fabrics, rich dark wood and leather decor, and marble bathrooms with walk-in rain showers.

🛏 Dupont Circle & Kalorama

★**Akwaaba**   B&B **$$**
(Map p266; ☑202-328-3510; www.dcakwaaba.com; 1708 16th St NW; r $175-285; P◉❄🛜; Ⓜ Red Line to Dupont Circle) Part of a small chain of B&Bs that emphasizes African American heritage in its properties, DC's Akwaaba outpost fills a handsome, late-19th-century mansion. Rooms are themed from literary abstractions ('Inspiration,' which has fine, airy ceilings and

a slanting skylight) to authors ('Zora,' an all-red room that's as romantic as can be). The cooked breakfast gets rave reviews, and the Dupont vibe is at your doorstep.

★**Kimpton Carlyle Hotel**   HOTEL **$$**
(Map p266; ☑202-234-3200; www.carlylehotel dc.com; 1731 New Hampshire Ave NW; r $179-349; P◉❄@🛜🐾; Ⓜ Red Line to Dupont Circle) In-the-know business travelers, families and couples make their way to the overlooked Carlyle, set amid embassies. The art-deco gem offers quiet, handsomely furnished rooms with crisp white linens, luxury mattresses, 37in flat-screen TVs and kitchenettes (in some). As part of the snazzy Kimpton brand, guests have access to freebies such as bicycles to use, an evening wine happy hour and yoga mats in rooms. Families can get cribs and roll-away beds for children. Pet owners can get beds and treats for Fido.

Embassy Circle Guest House   B&B **$$**
(Map p266; ☑202-232-7744; www.dcinns.com; 2224 R St NW; r $200-350; ◉❄🛜; Ⓜ Red Line to Dupont Circle) Embassies surround this 1902 French country–style home, which sits a few blocks from Dupont's nightlife hubbub. The 11 big-windowed rooms are decked out with Persian carpets and original art on the walls; they don't have TVs, though they do each have wi-fi. Staff feed you well throughout the day, with a hot organic breakfast, afternoon cookies and an evening wine-and-beer soirée.

Embassy Circle's sister property – **Woodley Park Guest House** (Map p266; ☑202-667-0218; 2647 Woodley Rd NW, Woodley Park; r $180-250, without bath $130-165; P❄@🛜; Ⓜ Red Line to Woodley Park) in further-flung northwest DC – is also a hot spot.

★**The Jefferson**   HOTEL **$$$**
(Map p266; ☑202-448-2300; www.jeffersondc. com; 1200 16th St NW; r from $450; P◉❄@🛜🐾; Ⓜ Red Line to Farragut North) The elegant, two-winged 1923 mansion has an ornate porte-cochère, beaux-arts architecture and a luxurious interior full of crystal and velvet, all meant to evoke namesake Thomas Jefferson's digs when he lived in Paris. Favored by diplomatic visitors, the hotel's antique-furnished rooms boast cushy beds, marble bathrooms, tobacco and earth tones, and Gilded Age class.

The 99-room property regularly places near the top of Washington's best-hotel lists. The on-site cocktail bar is superb for a nightcap while listening to the gentleman piano player.

🛏 Adams Morgan

HighRoad Hostel HOSTEL **$**
(Map p266; 📞202-735-3622; www.highroadhos
tels.com; 1804 Belmont Rd NW; dm $42-60; 🌐🐾🛜;
Ⓜ Red Line to Woodley Park-Zoo/Adams Morgan)
HighRoad's Victorian row-house exterior belies its modern interior. The dorms come in various configurations, from four to 14 beds – some co-ed, others gender-specific. All have stark white walls, gray metal bunks and black lockers. There's a fancy (though small) community kitchen and common room with a fireplace, chandelier and a jumbo, Netflix-wired TV. Nighthawks will groove on nearby 18th St's bounty. Free movie nights, pasta dinners, outings to local bars and other group activities take place several times a week.

Adam's Inn B&B **$**
(Map p266; 📞202-745-3600; www.adamsinn.com; 1746 Lanier Pl NW; r $119-199, without bath $99-160; 📶🐾🌐@🛜; Ⓜ Red Line to Woodley Park-Zoo/Adams Morgan) Tucked on a shady residential street, this 27-room inn is known for its personalized service, fluffy linens and handy location just a few blocks from 18th St's global smorgasbord. Inviting, homey rooms sprawl through two adjacent townhouses and a carriage house. The common areas have a nice garden patio, and there's a general sense of sherry-scented chintz. Breakfast is DIY continental style.

The Line Hotel DC DESIGN HOTEL **$$**
(Map p266; 📞202-588-0525; www.thelinehotel.
com/dc; 1770 Euclid St NW; r $229-399; 📶🌐@🛜;
Ⓜ Red Line to Woodley Park-Zoo/Adams Morgan) Opened in early 2018, the Line breathes fresh energy into an old church. It's as on-trend as you can get, with three restaurants and two bars by local celebrity chefs, 24-hour room service and an internet radio station that broadcasts from the lobby. The 220 rooms are airy, white-walled visions of low-key cool, sporting vintage radios, sculptural dangling lights and hardwood floors.

🛏 Georgetown

Graham Georgetown BOUTIQUE HOTEL **$$**
(Map p270; 📞202-337-0900; www.thegra
hamgeorgetown.com; 1075 Thomas Jefferson St NW; r $275-375; 📶🐾🌐@🛜; 🚌Circulator) Set smack in the heart of Georgetown, the Graham occupies the intersection between stately tradition and modernist hip. Good-sized rooms have tasteful silver, cream and chocolate decor with pops of ruby and geometric accents. Even the most basic rooms have linens by Liddell Ireland and L'Occitane bath amenities, which means you'll be as fresh, clean and beautiful as the surrounding Georgetown glitterati.

Rosewood Washington, D.C. BOUTIQUE HOTEL **$$$**
(Map p270; 📞202-617-2400; www.rosewood
hotels.com; 1050 31st St NW; d $395; 📶🐾@🛜🏊) Perched on the C&O Canal, this hidden Georgetown gem is the epitome of modern elegance. Spacious guest rooms, in a soothing neutral palette with pewter and gold accents, are fitted with custom-wood furnishings, hardwood floors and original contemporary art. The service, needless to say, is impeccable. Head to the rooftop terrace to enjoy cocktails and bites, or relax in the infinity pool.

🍴 Eating

A homegrown foodie revolution has transformed the once-buttoned-up DC dining scene. Driving it is the bounty of farms at the city's doorstep, along with the booming local economy and influx of worldly younger residents. Small, independent, local-chef-helmed spots now lead the way. And they're doing such a fine job that Michelin deemed the city worthy of its stars.

🍴 National Mall

Hank's Oyster Bar on the Wharf SEAFOOD **$$**
(Map p254; 📞202-817-3055; https://hanksoyster
bar.com/the-wharf; 701 Wharf St SW; mains $18-28; ⏱11:30am-10pm Mon-Thu, to 11pm Fri, 11am-11pm Sat, to 10pm Sun; Ⓜ Green Line to Waterfront-SEU, Ⓜ Orange, Silver, Yellow, Green Line to L'Enfant Plaza) Chef Jamie Leeds has built a name for herself in DC, with several restaurants showcasing 'urban beach food,' and others focusing on pasta and cocktails. Her latest enterprise brings coastal favorites and New England beach classics to the Wharf. Oysters are the mainstay of course, though the lobster roll is a taste of summer on cloud-soft bread.

Del Mar SPANISH **$$$**
(Map p254; 📞202-525-1402; www.delmardc.
com; 791 Wharf St SW; mains $36-130; ⏱4-10pm Mon, 11:30am-10pm Tue-Thu, to 10:30pm Fri & Sat, 11am-10pm Sun; Ⓜ Green Line to Southwest-SEU, Ⓜ Orange, Blue, Silver, Yellow, Green Line to L'Enfant Plaza) Treat yourself to an impeccable meal at Michelin-star-winning Del Mar, Fabio and Maria Trabocchi's latest culinary vision. Spanish cuisine is celebrated here, with an emphasis on seafood (Maria is from Mallorca). The Mediterranean-style setting is as outstanding as the food, including

custom-made furniture, hand-painted tiles and one-of-a-kind artworks. If you get only one dish, make it the paella.

✖ Capitol Hill & South DC

Capitol Hill has long been an outpost for the DC burger bar, the type of unpretentious spot where you roll up your sleeves and knock back a side of beer with your patty. Hip, upscale eateries have colonized the neighborhood, especially along Pennsylvania Ave, Barracks Row (ie 8th St SE, near the Marine Barracks) and around the Navy Yard and Wharf. H St NE, east of Union Station, has seen lots of action. The formerly beat-up area continues to transform with scads of fun, offbeat restaurants and bars stretching from 4th to 14th Sts NE.

★ChiKo
ASIAN **$**

(Map p260; ☑202-558-9934; www.chikodc.com; 423 8th St SE; mains $9-18; ⊗5-11pm Mon-Thu, to midnight Fri & Sat, to 10pm Su; Ⓜ Orange, Silver, Blue Line to Eastern Market) ChiKo stands for Chinese and Korean, and it fuses the cuisine with low-key style. Dishes such as pork and kimchi potstickers and chilled acorn noodles wow the foodie masses: it's high-brow fare at a budget price. The restaurant is fast-casual in set-up: order at the counter, then try to score one of the handful of picnic tables in the fluorescent-lit room.

Toki Underground
ASIAN **$**

(Map p260; ☑202-388-3086; www.tokiunderground.com; 1234 H St NE; mains $13-15; ⊗11:30am-2:30pm & 5-10pm Mon-Thu, to midnight Fri & Sat; Ⓜ Red Line to Union Station then streetcar) Spicy ramen noodles and dumplings sum up Toki's menu. Steaming pots obscure the busy chefs, while diners slurp and sigh contentedly. It takes limited reservations, so there's typically a wait. Use the opportunity to explore the surrounding bars; Toki will text when your table is ready. The restaurant isn't signposted; look for the Pug bar, and Toki is above it.

Good Stuff Eatery
BURGERS **$**

(Map p260; ☑202-543-8222; www.goodstuffeatery.com; 303 Pennsylvania Ave SE; burgers $7-9; ⊗11am-10pm Mon-Sat; 🐾; Ⓜ Orange, Silver, Blue Line to Capitol South or Eastern Market) 🍴 Spike Mendelsohn (of *Top Chef* TV fame) is the cook behind Good Stuff, a popular burgers-shakes-and-fries spot. You can top off fries at the 'dipping bar' of various sauces, and the toasted-marshmallow milkshake comes with an honest-to-god toasted marshmallow. The ambience is that of a fast-food joint,

and seats are at a premium weekend nights, when Cap Hill youth descend on the place.

★Ambar
BALKAN **$$**

(Map p260; ☑202-813-3039; www.ambarrestaurant.com; 523 8th St SE; small plates $7-13; ⊗11am-2pm & 4-10pm Mon-Thu, 11am-11pm Fri, 10am-11pm Sat, 10am-10pm Sun; Ⓜ Orange, Silver, Blue Lines to Eastern Market) Ambar buzzes, especially at happy hour, when the convivial, European-style restaurant slings heaps of small plates. Roasted pepper and eggplant, smoked trout and pickled peppers, braised cabbage, brandy-soaked mussels – intriguing Balkan dishes hit the table one after the other to be shared between friends. Serbian beer, Moldovan whites and Bulgarian reds flow ialongside. Many diners take advantage of Ambar's $49 deal for unlimited small plates and selected drinks.

Ethiopic
ETHIOPIAN **$$**

(Map p260; ☑202-675-2066; www.ethiopicrestaurant.com; 401 H St NE; mains $14-20; ⊗5-10pm Tue-Thu, from noon Fri-Sun; 🖉; Ⓜ Red Line to Union Station) In a city with no shortage of Ethiopian joints, Ethiopic stands above the rest thanks to its warm, stylish ambience. Top marks go to the various *wats* (stews) and the signature *tibs* (sautéed meat and veg), derived from tender lamb that has sat in a bath of herbs and hot spices. Vegans get lots of love here too.

Ted's Bulletin
AMERICAN **$$**

(Map p260; ☑202-544-8337; www.tedsbulletincapitolhill.com; 505 8th St SE; mains $12-20; ⊗7am-10:30pm Sun-Thu, to 11:30pm Fri & Sat; 🐾; Ⓜ Orange, Silver, Blue Line to Eastern Market) Plop into a booth in the art-deco-meets-diner ambience, and loosen the belt. Beer biscuits and sausage gravy for breakfast, meatloaf with ketchup glaze for dinner and other hipster spins on comfort foods hit the table. You've got to admire a place that lets you substitute pop tarts for toast. Breakfast is available all day and pulls big crowds on weekends.

★Rose's Luxury
AMERICAN **$$$**

(Map p260; ☑202-580-8889; www.rosesluxury.com; 717 8th St SE; small plates $13-16, family-style plates $28-36; ⊗5-10pm Mon-Sat; Ⓜ Orange, Silver, Blue Line to Eastern Market) Michelin-starred Rose's is one of DC's most buzzed-about eateries. Crowds fork into worldly Southern comfort food as twinkling lights glow overhead and candles flicker around the industrial room. Rose's doesn't take reservations, but ordering your meal at the upstairs bar can save time (and the cocktails are delicious).

✕ White House Area & Foggy Bottom

★ Woodward Takeout Food
AMERICAN $

(Map p262; ☑202-347-5355; www.woodward table.com; 1426 H St NW; sandwiches $6-12; ⊗7:30am-2:30pm Mon-Fri; ⓂOrange, Silver, Blue Line to McPherson Sq) Woodward Takeout is the small, mostly carryout adjunct to the popular **Woodward Table** (pizzas $17-20, mains $19-23; ⊗11:30am-10:30pm; ☑) restaurant. Jump in the line with all of the office workers to order a gourmet lunch sandwich, pizza slice, pasta or salad. Breakfast is busy too, with egg-laden sandwiches on crumbly biscuits, salted chocolate croissants and a daily doughnut.

★ Sichuan Pavilion
CHINESE $$

(Map p262; ☑202-466-7790; www.sichuan-pavilion .com; 1814 K St NW; mains lunch $10-18, dinner mains $12-35; ⊗11:30am-9:30pm; ⓂOrange, Silver, Blue Line to Farragut West) Many Chinese come to this few-frills restaurant to feast on fiery, aromatic Sichuan classics. Around the world, piquant Sichuan (or Szechuan) cuisine is often toned down for Western customers, but these guys keep it real for all their clientele, Asian or not. Menu highlights include fried string beans and the *ma-po tofu* laden with fermented black beans and fiery peppercorns.

★ Old Ebbitt Grill
AMERICAN $$

(Map p262; ☑202-347-4800; www.ebbitt.com; 675 15th St NW; mains $18-32; ⊗7:30am-1am Mon-Fri, from 8:30am Sat & Sun, happy hour 3-6pm & 11pm-1am; ⓂRed, Orange, Silver, Blue Line to Metro Center) Established in DC in 1856, this legendary tavern has occupied prime real estate near the White House since 1983. Political players and tourists pack into the wood-paneled interior, where thick burgers, succulent steaks and jumbo lump crab cakes are rotated out almost as quickly as the clientele. Pop in for a cocktail and oysters during happy hour.

★ Equinox
MODERN AMERICAN $$$

(Map p262; ☑202-331-8118; www.equinoxrestau rant.com; 818 Connecticut Ave NW; mains $31-38; ⊗11:30am-2pm & 5:30-9pm Mon-Fri, 5:30-10:30pm Sat, to 9pm Sun; ☑; ⓂOrange, Silver, Blue Line to Farragut West) ⌀ Chef Todd Gray has long eschewed imported ingredients in favor of meat, fish, fowl, vegetables and fruit sourced from farms in the Shenandoah Valley and Chesapeake Bay, and the food served at this stylish restaurant is a delectable testament to his enlightened approach. Dishes are seasonal and up to 50% plant-based (Sunday brunch is 100% plant-based). Love it.

✕ Downtown & Penn Quarter

★ Shouk
ISRAELI $

(Map p262; ☑202-652-1464; www.shouk.com; 655 K St NW, Downtown; mains $10; ⊗11am-10pm; ☑; ⓂGreen, Yellow Line to Mt Vernon Sq/7th St-Convention Center) Fast and casual, Shouk creates big flavor in its vegan menu of Israeli street food, served with craft beer and tap wines. A crazy-good burger made of chickpeas, black beans, lentils and mushrooms gets stuffed into a toasty pita with pickled turnips, arugula and charred onions. The mushroom-and-cauliflower pita and sweet-potato fries with cashew *labneh* (creamy 'cheese') are lip smacking.

★ A Baked Joint
CAFE $

(Map p262; ☑202-408-6985; www.abakedjoint. com; 440 K St NW, Downtown; mains $5-11; ⊗7am-3pm Mon-Wed, to 10pm Thu & Fri, 8am-10pm Sat, to 6pm Sun; ⓂRed, Yellow, Green Line to Gallery Pl-Chinatown) Order at the counter then take your luscious, heaped-on-housemade-bread sandwich – perhaps the fried egg and goat's cheese on a fluffy biscuit, or the Nutella and banana on whole-wheat sourdough – to a bench or table in the big, open room. Natural light streams in the floor-to-ceiling windows. Not hungry? It's also a great place for a well-made latte.

Rasika
INDIAN $$

(Map p262; ☑202-637-1222; www.rasikarestau rant.com; 633 D St NW, Penn Quarter; mains $14-28; ⊗11:30am-2:30pm Mon-Fri, 5:30-10:30pm Mon-Thu, 5-11pm Fri & Sat; ☑; ⓂGreen, Yellow Line to Archives) Rasika is as cutting edge as Indian food gets. The room resembles a Jaipur palace decorated by modernist art-gallery curators. Top marks go to the *murgh mussalam,* a plate of juicy tandoori chicken with cashews and quail eggs; and the deceptively simple *dal* (lentils), with just the right kiss of sharp fenugreek. Vegetarians will feel a lot of love here.

Zaytinya
MEDITERRANEAN $$

(Map p262; ☑202-638-0800; www.zaytinya.com; 701 9th St NW, Penn Quarter; meze $8-14; ⊗11am-10pm Mon & Sun, to 11pm Tue-Thu, to midnight Fri & Sat; ☑; ⓂRed, Yellow, Green Line to Gallery Pl-Chinatown) One of the culinary crown jewels of chef José Andrés, ever-popular Zaytinya serves superb Greek, Turkish and Lebanese meze in a long, noisy dining room with soaring ceilings and all-glass walls. It's a favorite after-work meet-up spot for wine, cocktails, and a nibble.

WASHINGTON, DC EATING

★ **Central Michel Richard** AMERICAN $$$
(Map p262; ☎202-626-0015; www.cen
tralmichelrichard.com; 1001 Pennsylvania Ave NW,
Penn Quarter; mains $24-34; ⏱11:30am-2:30pm
Mon-Fri, 5-10pm Mon-Thu, to 10:30pm Fri & Sat,
11am-2:30pm Sun; Ⓜ Orange, Silver, Blue Line to
Federal Triangle) Michel Richard was one of
Washington's first star chefs. He died in
2016, but his namesake Central blazes on-
ward. It's a special dining experience, eating
in a four-star bistro where the food is old-
school, comfort-food favorites with a twist:
perhaps lobster burgers, a sinfully complex
meatloaf, or fried chicken that redefines
what fried chicken can be.

Kinship AMERICAN $$$
(Map p262; ☎202-737-7700; www.kinshipdc.
com; 1015 7th St NW, Downtown; mains $25-32;
⏱5:30-10pm; Ⓜ Yellow, Green Line to Mt Vernon
Sq/7th St-Convention Center) Round up your
friends and enjoy a convivial night at this
Michelin-starred restaurant by James Beard
Award–winning chef Eric Ziebold. Pick and
choose across the menu's five categories echoing the chef's passions: ingredients (surf
clams, Rohan duck), history (classics), craft
(using culinary techniques), indulgence
(caviar, white truffles) and 'For the Table.'

The roast chicken from the last category,
stuffed with a lemon-garlic-brioche mixture,
is to die for.

Minibar AMERICAN $$$
(Map p262; ☎202-393-0812; www.minibarby
joseandres.com; 855 E St NW, Penn Quarter; tast-
ing menu from $275; ⏱6pm & 8:30pm Tue-Sat;
Ⓜ Green, Yellow Line to Archives) Whimsical
Minibar is a two-Michelin-starred foodie
nirvana, where 12 lucky people get wowed
by animal bits spun into cotton candy and
cocktails frothed into clouds. The tasting
menu, determined by chef José Andrés, is
delicious and never dull. There's a sense of
madcap experimentation among the 20-plus
courses, as you'd expect from a molecular
gastronomist. Reservations are tough to get.

Bookings become available the first Mon-
day of the month for the following 60 days.
If you don't score a reservation, or if you're
looking to sample Andrés' famous food but
in more casual environs, try his other local
restaurants such as **Jaleo** (Map p262; ☎20
2-628-7949; www.jaleo.com; 480 7th St NW, Penn
Quarter; tapas $9-18; ⏱11am-10pm Mon, to 11pm
Tue-Thu, to midnight Fri, 10am-midnight Sat, to
10pm Sun; Ⓜ Green, Yellow Line to Archives) and
Zaytinya (p279).

🍴 Logan Circle, U Street & Columbia Heights

★ **Ben's Chili Bowl** AMERICAN $
(Map p266; ☎202-667-0909; www.benschilibowl.
com; 1213 U St NW; mains $6-10; ⏱6am-2am Mon-
Thu, to 4am Fri, 7am-4am Sat, 11am-midnight Sun;
Ⓜ Green, Yellow Line to U St) Ben's is a DC institu-
tion. The main stock in trade is half-smokes,
DC's meatier, smokier version of the hot dog,
usually slathered with mustard, onions and
the namesake chili. For nearly 60 years presi-
dents, rock stars and Supreme Court justices
have come to indulge in the humble diner,
but despite the hype, Ben's remains a true
neighborhood establishment. Cash only. To
place your order, join the locals clustered at
the counter and gabbing over sweet iced tea.

Timber Pizza PIZZA $
(☎202-853-9746; www.timberpizza.com; 809
Upshur St NW; pizzas $12-16; ⏱5-10pm Tue-Sun;
Ⓜ Green, Yellow Lines to Georgia Ave-Petworth)
Bon Appetit magazine crowned Timber
one of the best new restaurants in America
in 2017, while the James Beard Foundation
nominated the chef as a rising star. So yeah,
the wood-fired pizzas are pretty damn good,
especially alongside a pitcher of local beer.
It's a wee space, with no reservations, so be
prepared to wait.

Chercher ETHIOPIAN $
(Map p266; ☎202-299-9703; www.chercherres
taurant.com; 1334 9th St NW; mains $11-17; ⏱11am-
11pm Mon-Sat, noon-10pm Sun; ☝; Ⓜ Green, Yellow
Line to Mt Vernon Sq/7th St-Convention Center)
Ethiopian expats have been known to com-
pare Chercher's food to their grandma's home
cooking. It prepares terrific *injera* (spongy
bread) for dipping into hot spiced *wats*
(stews). Vegetarians will find lots to devour.
There's beer and honey wine from the moth-
erland, and spices you can buy to go.

Union Market MARKET $
(www.unionmarketdc.com; 1309 5th St NE; mains
$6-11; ⏱11am-8pm Tue-Fri, from 8am Sat & Sun;
Ⓜ Red Line to NoMa) The cool crowd hobnobs
at this food hall, where culinary entrepre-
neurs sell their banana-ginger chocolates,
herbed goat's cheeses and smoked meats.
Among the stalls featuring prepared foods,
everything from Burmese milkshakes to
Indian dosas to Korean tacos boggle taste
buds. Craft beers and coffee provide added
sustenance. Tables dot the sunlit warehouse,
and many locals make an afternoon of it
here, nibbling and reading.

★**Himitsu**   JAPANESE **$$**

(www.himitsudc.com; 828 Upshur St NW; small plates $12-18; ⊙5-10pm Tue-Thu, to 11pm Fri & Sat; ⓂGreen, Yellow Lines to Georgia Ave-Petworth) Himitsu gets heaped with praise by foodie tastemakers (*Bon Appetit* magazine, James Beard Foundation) and no wonder. It's hard not to fall for chili-spiked seafood *crudos* (raw fish) and candied pumpkin seed-topped eggplant, served with cocktails and exquisite care in a comfy, 24-seat room. No reservations, so give the host your cell number, then wait in a nearby bar.

★**Compass Rose**   INTERNATIONAL **$$**

(Map p266; ☑202-506-4765; www.compass rosedc.com; 1346 T St NW; small plates $8-16; ⊙5pm-2am Mon-Thu, to 3am Fri & Sat, from 1am Sun; ⓂGreen, Yellow Line to U St) Compass Rose feels like a secret garden, set in a discreet townhouse a whisker from 14th St's buzz. The exposed brick walls and sky-blue ceiling give it a casually romantic air. The menu is a mash-up of global comfort foods, so dinner might entail Korean *galbi* (short ribs), Lebanese *kefta* (ground lamb and spices) and Georgian *khachapuri* (cheese-filled bread).

★**Busboys & Poets**   CAFE **$$**

(Map p266; ☑202-387-7638; www.busboys andpoets.com; 2021 14th St NW; mains $12-21; ⊙7am-midnight Mon-Thu, to 2am Fri, from 8am Sat & Sun; 🛜🍴; ⓂGreen, Yellow Line to U St) Busboys & Poets is one of U St's linchpins. Locals pack the place for coffee, boozy brunches, books and a progressive vibe that makes San Francisco feel conservative. The lengthy, vegetarian-friendly menu spans sandwiches, pizzas and Southern fare like shrimp and grits. Tuesday night's open-mike poetry reading ($5 admission, from 9pm to 11pm) draws big crowds. The cafe's slate of events also includes story slams, film screenings and discussion series. The front bookstore, which stocks loads of social justice works and titles by local authors, is an inspiring browse.

Bad Saint   FILIPINO **$$**

(www.badsaintdc.com; 3226 11th St NW; mains $20-32; ⊙5:30-10pm Mon, Wed & Thu, to 11pm Fri, 5-11pm Sat, from 5pm Sun; ⓂGreen, Yellow Line to Columbia Heights) Lines form early at this wee, 24-seat restaurant. It doesn't take reservations, so expect to wait. The reward is Filipino flavors like none you've laid lips on before. The menu changes often, but you might enjoy dishes such as *kalderetang kordero* (lamb neck, sunchoke and baby carrot stew) or *ginisang tulya* (clam and coconut milk stew). It's always amazing.

Estadio   SPANISH **$$**

(Map p266; ☑202-319-1404; www.estadio-dc.com; 1520 14th St NW; tapas $7-17; ⊙5-10pm Mon-Thu, 11:30am-2pm & 5-11pm Fri, 11am-2pm & 5-11pm Sat, 11am-2pm & 5-9pm Sun; ⓂGreen, Yellow Line to U St) Estadio buzzes with a low-lit, date-night vibe. The tapas menu is as deep as an ocean trench. There are three variations of *ibérico* ham and a delicious foie gras, scrambled egg and truffle open-faced sandwich. Wash it down with some traditional *calimocho* (red wine and Coke). No reservations after 6pm, which usually means a wait at the bar.

Masseria   ITALIAN **$$$**

(☑202-608-1330; www.masseria-dc.com; 1340 4th St NE; prix-fixe menus $92-135; ⊙5:30-9:30pm Tue-Thu, to 10pm Fri, 5-10pm Sat; ⓂRed Line to NoMa) Chef Nicholas Stefanelli's Michelin-star-winning Italian oasis flourishes in the industrial neighborhood near Union Market. A festive outdoor terrace and two cozy interior rooms convey the tranquil allure of a southern Italian evening – as does the prix-fixe-only menu. Innovative dishes range from linguine with spicy sauce or beef tripe and lobster stew to venison with wild mushrooms and chestnuts.

Le Diplomate   FRENCH **$$$**

(Map p266; ☑202-332-3333; www.lediplomate dc.com; 1601 14th St NW; mains $23-35; ⊙5-11pm Mon-Thu, to midnight Fri, 9:30am-midnight Sat, from 9:30am Sun; ⓂGreen, Yellow Line to U St) This charming French bistro is one of the hottest tables in town. DC celebrities galore cozy up in the leather banquettes and at the sidewalk tables. They come for an authentic slice of Paris, from the *coq au vin* (wine-braised chicken) and aromatic baguettes to the vintage curios and nudie photos decorating the bathrooms. Make reservations.

✗ Dupont Circle & Kalorama

★**Bub & Pop's**   SANDWICHES **$**

(Map p266; ☑202-457-1111; www.bubandpops. com; 1815 M St NW; sandwiches half/whole $10/18; ⊙8am-4pm Mon-Fri, 11am-4pm Sat; ⓂRed Line to Dupont Circle) A chef tired of the fine-dining rat race opened this gourmet sandwich shop with his parents. Ingredients are made in-house from scratch – the meatballs, pickles, mayonnaise and roasted pork. Congenial mom Arlene rules the counter and can answer questions about any of it. The sandwiches are enormous, and best consumed hot off the press in the bright aqua-and-red room.

Un Je Ne Sais Quoi
BAKERY $

(Map p266; 202-721-0099; www.facebook.com/
unjenesaisquoipastry; 1361 Connecticut Ave NW;
pastries $2.50-5; 7:30am-7pm Mon-Thu, 7:30am-
8pm Fri, 10am-8pm Sat; Red Line to Dupont
Circle) The smell of rich coffee envelops you
when you enter this little bakery, where a
couple of French expats bake *merveilleux*,
their signature pastry plumped with layers
of meringue and ganache. It's like biting
into a glorious cloud. Tarts, eclairs and other
sweets are equally exquisite.

Dolcezza
GELATO $

(Map p266; 202-299-9116; www.dolcezzage
lato.com; 1704 Connecticut Ave NW; gelato $6-8;
7am-10pm Mon-Thu, 7am-11pm Fri, 8am-11pm
Sat, 8am-10pm Sun; ; Red Line to Dupont
Circle) The local mini-chain Dolcezza whips
up the District's best gelati. Some flavors
are unusual, such as blueberry lavender
and Thai coconut milk, and change with the
seasons. Traditionalists can always get their
licks with chocolate, salted caramel and
peppermint. Good coffee, vintage-chic decor
and free wi-fi add to the pleasure.

★ Bistrot du Coin
FRENCH $$

(Map p266; 202-234-6969; www.bistrotducoin.
com; 1738 Connecticut Ave NW; mains $20-30;
11:30am-midnight Mon-Wed, 11:30am-1am Thu
& Fri, noon-1am Sat, noon-midnight Sun; Red
Line to Dupont Circle) This lively and much-
loved neighborhood favorite has roll-up-
your sleeves, working-class French fare. The
kitchen sends out consistently good onion
soup, classic *steak-frites* (grilled steak and
French fries), cassoulet, open-face sandwich-
es and nine varieties of its famous *moules*
(mussels). Regional wines from around the
motherland accompany the food by the
glass, carafe and bottle. Make reservations.

Duke's Grocery
GASTROPUB $$

(Map p266; 202-733-5623; www.dukesgrocery.
com; 1513 17th St NW; mains $12-16; 11am-10pm
Mon & Tue, 11am-1am Wed & Thu, 11am-2am Fri,
10am-2am Sat, 10am-10pm Sun; ; Red Line to
Dupont Circle) 'A taste of East London in East
Dupont' is Duke's tagline, and that means
black pudding for brunch, curried chicken
for lunch, and the famed burgers and cocktails anytime. Set over two floors in a snug
row house, its genial vibe invites linger-
ing, so sometimes it's hard to score a table
among the groups of chit-chatty friends and
couples on low-maintenance dates.

★ Little Serow
THAI $$$

(Map p266; www.littleserow.com; 1511 17th St NW;
set menu $49; 5:30-10pm Tue-Thu, to 10:30pm

Fri & Sat; Red Line to Dupont Circle) Set in a
cavern-like green basement, Little Serow
has no phone, no reservations and no sign
on the door. It only seats groups of four or
fewer (larger parties will be separated), but
despite all this, people line up around the
block. And what for? Superlative northern
Thai cuisine. The single-option menu, which
consists of six or so hot-spiced courses,
changes weekly.

★ Dabney
AMERICAN $$$

(Map p266; 202-450-1015; www.thedabney.com;
122 Blagden Alley NW, Downtown; small plates $14-23;
5:30-10pm Tue-Thu, to 11pm Fri & Sat, 5-10pm Sun;
Green, Yellow Line to Mt Vernon Sq/7th St-Conven
tion Center) Chef Jeremiah Langhorne studied
historic cookbooks, discovering recipes that
used local ingredients and lesser-explored
flavors in his quest to resuscitate mid-Atlantic cuisine lost to the ages. Most of the dishes
are even cooked over a wood-burning hearth,
as in George Washington's time. Langhorne
gives it all a modern twist – enough to earn
him a Michelin star. You'll need to order
two or three small plates to make a meal.
The warm, wood-clad spot is tucked away
in Blagden Alley. From 9th St NW look for
the 'Blagden' street sign and follow the brick
lane in past the mural-painted buildings and
garages. Bonus: the restaurant's basement
houses **Dabney Cellar** (6pm-midnight Wed-
Sat), an equally impressive wine bar.

Blue Duck Tavern
AMERICAN $$$

(Map p266; 202-419-6755; www.blueduck
tavern.com; 1201 24th St NW; mains $30-46;
6:30am-2:30pm & 5:30-10:30pm Sun-Thu, to
11pm Fri & Sat; ; Red Line to Dupont Circle)
A reliable rave winner, the Michelin-starred
Blue Duck creates a rustic kitchen ambience
in the midst of an uber-urbanized corridor
of M St. The changing menu draws from
farms across the country, mixing mains such
as venison tartare and suckling pig sourced
from Pennsylvania, crab cakes from nearby
Chesapeake Bay and grits from Virginia.
Weekend brunch is a big to-do.

Komi
FUSION $$$

(Map p266; 202-332-9200; www.komires
taurant.com; 1509 17th St NW; set menu $150;
5:30-10pm Tue-Sat; Red Line to Dupont Circle)
There is an admirable simplicity to Komi's
changing menu, which is rooted in Greece
and influenced by everything – but primarily genius. Dinner comprises 12 or so dishes; say suckling pig, scallops and truffles, or
roasted baby goat. Komi's cozy space doesn't
take groups larger than four, and you need

to reserve in advance. Call a month before your desired dining date.

✖ Adams Morgan

★ Donburi   JAPANESE $

(Map p266; ☑ 202-629-1047; www.donburidc.com; 2438 18th St NW; mains $11-13; ☺ 11am-10pm; Ⓜ Red Line to Woodley Park-Zoo/Adams Morgan) Hole-in-the-wall Donburi has 15 seats at a wooden counter where you get a front-row view of the slicing, dicing chefs. *Donburi* means 'bowl' in Japanese, and that's what arrives steaming hot and filled with, say, panko-coated shrimp atop rice and blended with the house's sweet-and-savory sauce. It's a simple, authentic meal. There's often a line, but it moves quickly. No reservations.

Donburi has another venue in Dupont Circle that's larger, but the Adams Morgan location is the atmospheric original.

★ Tail Up Goat   MEDITERRANEAN $$

(Map p266; ☑ 202-986-9600; www.tailupgoat. com; 1827 Adams Mill Rd NW; mains $18-27; ☺ 5:30-10pm Mon-Thu, 5-10pm Fri-Sun; Ⓜ Red Line to Woodley Park-Zoo/Adams Morgan) With its pale-blue walls, light wood decor and lantern-like lights dangling overhead, Tail Up Goat exudes a warm, island-y vibe. The lamb ribs are the specialty – crispy and lusciously fatty, with grilled lemon, figs and spices. The housemade breads and spreads star on the menu too – say, flaxseed sourdough with beets. No wonder Michelin gave it a star.

Mintwood Place   AMERICAN $$

(Map p266; ☑ 202-234-6732; www.mintwood place.com; 1813 Columbia Rd NW; mains $18-30; ☺ 5:30-10pm Tue-Thu, to 10:30pm Fri & Sat, to 9pm Sun, plus 10:30am-2:30pm Sat & Sun; Ⓜ Red Line to Woodley Park-Zoo/Adams Morgan) In a neighborhood known for jumbo pizza slices and Jell-O shots, Mintwood Place is a romantic anomaly. Take a seat in a brown-leather booth or at a reclaimed-wood table under twinkling lights. Then sniff the French-American fusion dishes that emerge from the wood-burning oven. The *flamme-kueche* (onion and bacon tart), chicken-liver mousse and escargot hush puppies show how it's done.

✖ Georgetown

★ Baked & Wired   BAKERY $

(Map p270; ☑ 703-663-8727; www.bakedand wired.com; 1052 Thomas Jefferson St NW; baked goods $3-6; ☺ 7am-8pm Mon-Thu, to 9pm Fri, 8am-9pm Sat, to 8pm Sun; ▤ Circulator) This cheery cafe whips up beautifully made coffees, bacon cheddar buttermilk biscuits and enormous cupcakes (like the banana and peanut-butter-frosted Elvis). It's a fine spot to join university students and cyclists coming off the nearby trails for a sugar buzz. When the weather permits, patrons take their treats outside to the adjacent grassy area by the C&O Canal.

★ Simply Banh Mi   VIETNAMESE $

(Map p270; ☑ 202-333-5726; www.simplybanh midc.com; 1624 Wisconsin Ave NW; mains $7-10; ☺ 11am-7pm Tue-Sun; 🖋; ▤ Circulator) There's nothing fancy about the small, below-street-level space, and the compact menu sticks mostly to sandwiches and bubble tea. But the brother-sister owners know how to take a crusty baguette, stuff it with delicious lemongrass pork or other meat (or tofu), and make your day. They're superattentive to quality and to customer needs (vegan, gluten-free etc).

Farmers Fishers Bakers   AMERICAN $$

(Map p270; ☑ 202-298-8783; www.farmersfishers bakers.com; 3000 K St NW, Washington Harbour; mains $15-29; ☺ 7:30-10pm Mon-Wed, to 11pm Thu, to midnight Fri, 9am-midnight Sat, to 10pm Sun; ▤ Circulator) The folksy cow above the front door might tip you off. Or the larder-designed corner lined with farm-canned goods. This eco-chic restaurant on the Georgetown waterfront – sibling to the acclaimed **Founding Farmers** (Map p262; ☑ 202-822-8783; www.wearefoundingfarmers.com; 1924 Pennsylvania Ave NW; breakfast dishes $6-15; mains $12-37; ☺ 7am-10pm Mon, to 11pm Tue-Thu, to midnight Fri, 9am-midnight Sat, to 10pm Sun; 🖋; Ⓜ Orange, Silver, Blue Line to Foggy Bottom-GWU or Farragut West) 🖋) – is all about paying homage to Americana. The menu roams from honey pot-fried chicken to jambalaya. And everything is fresh, fresh, fresh.

★ Fiola Mare   SEAFOOD $$$

(Map p270; ☑ 202-628-0065; www.fiolamaredc. com; 3050 K St NW, Washington Harbour; mains $28-54; ☺ 5-10pm Mon, 11:30am-2:30pm & 5-10pm Tue-Fri, 11:30am-2pm & 5-10:30pm Sat, 11am-2pm & 5-10pm Sun; ▤ Circulator) Fiola Mare delivers the chichi Georgetown experience. It flies in fresh fish and crustaceans from Maine and Tasmania daily. The yacht-bobbling river view rocks. The see-and-be-seen multitudes are here. It's DC at its luxe best. Try it at lunchtime on a weekday, when $20 or so gets you an Italian-style seafood main and a drink in the bar area. Make reservations.

Chez Billy Sud
FRENCH $$$

(Map p270; ☏202-965-2606; www.chezbillysud.
com; 1039 31st St NW; mains $25-38; ⊙5-10pm
Mon, 11:30am-2pm & 5-10pm Tue-Thu, 11:30am-
2pm & 5-11pm Fri, 11am-2pm & 5-11pm Sat, 11am-
2pm & 5-10pm Sun; ▣Circulator) An endearing
little bistro tucked away on a residential
block, Billy's mint-green walls, gilt mirrors
and wee marble bar exude laid-back ele-
gance. Mustachioed servers bring baskets
of warm bread to the white-linen-clothed
tables, along with crackling pork and pista-
chio sausage, golden trout, tuna niçoise sal-
ad and plump cream puffs.

Makoto
JAPANESE $$$

(☏202-298-6866; www.sakedokoromakoto.com;
4822 MacArthur Blvd NW, 1st fl; 8-course set menu
$135; ⊙6:30-8:30pm Tue-Thu, to 9:30pm Fri,
6-9:30pm Sun; ▣D5 or D6) The napkins look
like origami. The wasabi is freshly grated.
You leave your shoes at the door. And the
food – a chef's-choice tasting menu – is exquisite, with dishes such as fava-bean-encrusted
halibut and shrimp with cherry-blossom-leaf
sauce. There's no mucking about: this is traditional stuff prepared with the height of
focus and technique. The restaurant is tiny,
with barely 30 seats, and you must reserve in
advance. Note there's a business-casual dress
code (no athletic gear allowed).

✖ Upper Northwest DC

★ Bread Furst
BAKERY $

(Map p272; ☏202-765-1200; www.breadfurst.
com; 4434 Connecticut Ave NW, Van Ness/Forest
Hills; sandwiches $8-10, cakes $6; ⊙7am-7pm
Mon-Fri, 8am-5pm Sat & Sun; ⊛; ⓜRed Line to Van
Ness-UDC) 🏊 Watch the bakers hand-shape
artisanal breads and traditional pastries at
this bustling bakery. Owner Mark Fursten-
berg was dubbed 'Outstanding Baker of the
US' by the James Beard Foundation in 2017
– sample a delicious sandwich or baguette,
brownie, cake, pastry or muffin to see why.
Challah is available on Fridays.

★ Comet Ping Pong
PIZZA $

(Map p272; ☏202-364-0404; www.cometping
pong.com; 5037 Connecticut Ave NW, Chevy Chase;
pizzas $9-19; ⊙5-9:30pm Mon-Thu, 11:30am-
10:45pm Fri & Sat, 11:30am-9:30pm Sun; ⊕; ⓜRed
Line to Van Ness-UDC) Proving that DC is more
than a city of suits and corporate offices, Com-
et Ping Pong offers a fun and festive counterpoint to most of the city's eateries, with ping-
pong tables, an industrial-chic interior and
delicious pizza cooked in a wood-burning
oven. Reservations not required.

🍷 Drinking & Nightlife

🍸 Capitol Hill & South DC

★ Copycat Co
COCKTAIL BAR

(Map p260; ☏202-241-1952; www.copycatcompa
ny.com; 1110 H St NE; ⊙5pm-2am Sun-Thu, to 3am
Fri & Sat; ⓜRed Line to Union Station then streetcar)
When you walk into Copycat it feels like a
Chinese fast-food restaurant. That's because
it is (sort of) on the 1st floor, where Chinese
street-food nibbles are available. Fizzy drinks
and egg-white-topped cocktails fill glasses
upstairs, in the dimly lit, speakeasy-meets-
opium-den-vibed bar. Staff are unassuming
and gracious in helping newbies figure out
what they want from the lengthy menu.

★ Tune Inn
BAR

(Map p260; ☏202-543-2725; 331 Pennsylvania Ave
SE; ⊙8am-2am Sun-Thu, to 3am Fri & Sat; ⓜO-
range, Silver, Blue Line to Capitol South or Eastern
Market) Tune Inn has been helping the thirsty
since 1947. Mounted deer heads stare from
the wall and watch over old-timers knocking
back Budweisers at the bar. Meanwhile, Hill
staffers, off-duty cops and other locals scarf
greasy-spoon grub and all-day breakfasts in
the vinyl-backed booths.

Bluejacket Brewery
BREWERY

(Map p260; ☏202-524-4862; www.bluejacketdc.
com; 300 Tingey St SE; ⊙11am-1am Sun-Thu, to
2am Fri & Sat; ⓜGreen Line to Navy Yard) Beer-
lovers' heads will explode in Bluejacket. Pull
up a stool at the mod-industrial bar, gaze at
the silvery tanks bubbling up the ambitious
brews, then make the hard decision about
which of the 20 tap beers you want to try.
A dry-hopped kolsch? Sweet-spiced stout? A
cask-aged farmhouse ale? Four-ounce tasting pours help with decision-making.

Granville Moore's
PUB

(Map p260; ☏202-399-2546; www.granvillemoor
es.com; 1238 H St NE; ⊙5pm-midnight Mon-Thu,
5pm-1am Fri, 11am-1am Sat, 11am-midnight Sun;
ⓜRed Line to Union Station then streetcar) Besides
being one of DC's best places to grab *frites*
and a steak sandwich, Granville Moore's has
an extensive Belgian beer menu that should
satisfy any fan of low-country boozing. With
its raw, wooden fixtures and walls that look
as if they were made from daub and mud,
the interior resembles a medieval barracks.
The fireside setting is ideal on a winter's eve.

Little Miss Whiskey's Golden Dollar
BAR

(Map p260; www.littlemisswhiskeys.com; 1104 H St
NE; ⊙5pm-2am Sun-Thu, to 3am Fri & Sat; ⓜRed
Line to Union Station then streetcar) If Alice had

returned from Wonderland so traumatized that she needed a stiff drink, we imagine she'd pop down to Little Miss Whiskey's. She'd love the whimsical-meets-dark-nightmares decor. And she'd probably have fun with the club kids partying on the upstairs dancefloor on weekends. She'd also adore the weirdly fantastic back patio. The excellent beer and whiskey menu and savvy staff make this feel like a bartender's bar.

🍷 White House Area & Foggy Bottom

★ **Top of the Gate** ROOFTOP BAR
(Map p262; www.thewatergatehotel.com/dine-and-drink/top-of-the-gate; 2650 Virginia Ave NW, Watergate Hotel, Foggy Bottom; ice skating adult/child 5-12yr $20/10; ⏰5pm-midnight Sun-Thu, to 1am Fri & Sat summer, 5-10pm Wed-Fri, 1-10pm Sat & Sun winter; Ⓜ Red Line to Foggy Bottom-GWU) The downstairs whiskey bar at the sleek Watergate Hotel is impressive, but it pales in comparison with the hotel's rooftop bar and lounge, which offers ice skating in winter and, blissfully balmy river breezes in summer and spectacular views all year round.

★ **Round Robin** BAR
(Map p262; 🕿202-628-9100; http://washington.intercontinental.com/food-drink/round-robin-bar; 1401 Pennsylvania Ave NW, Willard InterContinental Hotel; ⏰noon-1am Mon-Sat, to midnight Sun; Ⓜ Red, Orange, Silver, Blue Line to Metro Center) Dispensing drinks since 1850, the bar at the Willard hotel is one of DC's most famous watering holes. The small, circular space is done up in Gilded Age accents, all dark wood walls, marble bar and velvet curtains,

and while it's touristy, you'll still see officials here likely determining your latest tax hike over a mint julep or single malt Scotch.

The bar claims to be the place where the mint julep was introduced to DC courtesy of planter and statesman Henry Clay.

★ **Off the Record** BAR
(Map p262; 🕿202-638-6600; www.hayadams.com/dining/off-the-record; 800 16th St NW, Hay-Adams Hotel; ⏰11:30am-midnight Sun-Thu, to 12:30am Fri & Sat; Ⓜ Orange, Silver, Blue Line to McPherson Sq) Table seating, an open fire in winter and a discreet basement location in one of the city's most prestigious hotels, right across from the White House – it's no wonder DC's important people submerge to be seen and not heard (as the tagline goes) here. Experienced bartenders swirl martinis and manhattans for the suit-wearing crowd. Enter through the hotel lobby.

🍷 Downtown & Penn Quarter

★ **Columbia Room** COCKTAIL BAR
(Map p266; 🕿202-316-9396; www.columbiaroomdc.com; 124 Blagden Alley NW, Downtown; ⏰5pm-12:30am Tue-Thu, to 1:30am Fri & Sat; Ⓜ Green, Yellow Line to Mt Vernon Sq/7th St-Convention Center) Serious mixology goes on at Columbia Room, the kind of place that sources spring water from Scotland, and uses pickled cherry blossom and barley tea among its ingredients. But it's done in a refreshingly nonsnooty environment. Choose from three areas: the festive Punch Garden on the outdoor roof deck, the comfy, leather-chair-dotted Spirits Library, or the 14-seat, prix-fixe Tasting Room.

COFFEE IN THE CAPITAL

DC has been getting its caffeine on. Local mini-chains such as **Filter** (Map p266; 🕿202-234-5837; www.filtercoffeehouse.com; 1726 20th St NW; ⏰7am-7pm Mon-Fri, 8am-7pm Sat & Sun; Ⓜ Red Line to Dupont Circle) and **Peregrine Espresso** (Map p260; 🕿202-629-4381; www.peregrineespresso.com; 660 Pennsylvania Ave SE; ⏰7am-8pm Mon-Sat, 8am-8pm Sun; 🛜; Ⓜ Orange, Silver, Blue Line to Eastern Market) use beans from small-batch roasters and get hard-core with their brewing techniques. Peregrine pays the knowledge forward by offering DIY brewing classes. Petworth's **Qualia Coffee** (🕿202-248-6423; www.qualiacoffee.com; 3917 Georgia Ave NW; ⏰7am-7pm Mon-Fri, 8am-6pm Sat & Sun; Ⓜ Green, Yellow Line to Georgia Ave-Petworth) roasts its own beans and offers bimonthly tasting sessions. **Compass Coffee** (Map p262; www.compasscoffee.com; 650 F St NW, Penn Quarter; ⏰6am-9pm; 🛜; Ⓜ Red, Yellow, Green Line to Gallery Pl-Chinatown) is a local, fast-growing roaster. The city's Ethiopian community shows how it's done too: **Sidamo Coffee & Tea** (Map p260; 🕿202-548-0081; www.sidamocoffeeandtea.com; 417 H St NE; ⏰7am-7pm Mon-Fri, 8am-6pm Sat, 8am-5pm Sun; 🛜; Ⓜ Red Line to Union Station) is one of several family-run shops that roasts beans and puts on traditional Ethiopian coffee ceremonies.

FIVE NEIGHBORHOODS FOR A NIGHT OUT

After a day of museums and monuments, it's time to let loose. Bohemian jazz clubs? Wee-hour half-smokes? Dive bars for nighthawks? DC has several buzzy neighborhoods to make it happen. In these places, the hot spots even line up in a walkable row.

Logan Circle North of downtown in trendy Logan Circle, 14th St NW bursts with wine bars, beer bars, tapas bars and oyster bars. Churchkey glows with the requisite hipness. DC's political glitterati cozy up nearby at Le Diplomate.

U Street NW Just north of Logan Circle, U St is DC's richest nightlife zone. DJ-savvy groovesters hit the dance floor at U Street Music Hall. Late-night half-smokes await at Ben's Chili Bowl.

H Street NE Pie cafes, noodle shops and beer gardens roll out east of Union Station. Little Miss Whiskey's Golden Dollar sets the frisky standard with hallucinogenic decor and boogaloo-spinning DJs. H Street Country Club pours beer alongside a DC-themed mini-golf course.

Barracks Row In Capitol Hill along 8th St SE, locals line up for shabby-chic Rose's Luxury and Chinese-Korean fusion at ChiKo. They also sip Balkan wines at convivial Ambar and see what's on at the Fridge street-art gallery.

Columbia Heights The main vein is 11th St NW. In good weather the patio benches at Wonderland Ballroom fill with neighborhoodies hoisting brews. It's the same scene up the road at wine-pouring Room 11 and beer-and-pool bar Meridian Pint.

🍷 Logan Circle, U Street & Columbia Heights

★ Primrose WINE BAR
(📞 202-248-4558; www.primrosedc.com; 3000 12th St NE; ⊙5-10pm Mon, Wed & Thu, to 11pm Fri & Sat, to 9:30pm Sun; Ⓜ Red Line to Brookland-CUA) Stepping into Primrose is like being in Paris and finding the quintessential cafe hidden down a tiny lane. The ostrich-feathered chandeliers, turquoise bar, rustic wood tables and lengthy wine list set the mood. Fifteen wines, all from France or Virginia, come by the glass. *Coq au vin* (wine-braised chicken), steak *frites* and cheeses galore are on the menu if you're hungry.

★ Atlas Brew Works BREWERY
(📞 202-832-0420; www.atlasbrewworks.com; 2052 West Virginia Ave NE, Suite 102; ⊙4-10pm Mon-Thu, to 11pm Fri, 11am-11pm Sat, from 11am Sun; 🚇D4) An awesome, welcoming spot filled with local beer buffs. With its concrete floor, exposed air ducts and hodgepodge of tables, the taproom may not look like much, but when the knowledgeable bartenders fill your flight of glasses with the brewery's gose, saison and other suds, you might as well give in to being here all afternoon.

★ Right Proper Brewing Co BREWERY
(Map p266; 📞202-607-2337; www.rightproper brewery.com; 624 T St NW; ⊙5pm-midnight Mon-Thu, 11:30am-1am Fri & Sat, 11:30am-11pm Sun; Ⓜ Green, Yellow Line to Shaw-Howard U) Right Proper Brewing Co makes sublime ales in a building where Duke Ellington used to play pool. It's the Shaw district's neighborhood clubhouse, a big, sunny space filled with folks gabbing at reclaimed wood tables. The tap lineup changes regularly as the brewers work their magic, but crisp farmhouse ales are an oft-flowing specialty.

Right Proper also has a larger **production house** (📞202-526-5904; 920 Girard St NE; ⊙4-9pm Mon-Fri, from noon Sat & Sun; Ⓜ Red Line to Brookland-CUA or Rhode Island) and tasting room in the Brookland neighborhood, a couple of miles northeast.

★ Raven BAR
(Map p272; 📞202-387-8411; 3125 Mt Pleasant St NW; ⊙4pm-2am Mon & Tue, from 2pm Wed & Thu, 2pm-3am Fri & Sat, from 1pm Sun; Ⓜ Green, Yellow Line to Columbia Heights) The best jukebox in DC, a dark interior crammed with locals and lovers, that neon lighting that casts you under a glow Edward Hopper should rightly have painted, and a tough but friendly bar staff are the ingredients in this shot, which, when slammed, hits you as DC's best dive by a mile. Cash only.

Dacha Beer Garden BEER GARDEN
(Map p266; ☑202-350-9888; www.dachadc.com; 1600 7th St NW; ⊙4-10:30pm Mon-Thu, to midnight Fri, noon-midnight Sat, from noon Sun, reduced hours winter; Ⓜ Green, Yellow Line to Shaw-Howard U) Happiness reigns in Dacha's freewheeling beer garden. Kids and dogs bound around the picnic tables, while adults hoist glass boots filled with German brews. When the weather gets nippy, staff bring blankets and stoke the fire pit. And it all takes place under the sultry gaze of Elizabeth Taylor (or a mural of her, which sprawls across the back wall).

Churchkey BAR
(Map p266; ☑202-567-2576; www.churchkey dc.com; 1337 14th St NW; ⊙4pm-1am Mon-Thu, to 2am Fri, 11:30am-2am Sat, from 11:30am Sun; Ⓜ Orange, Silver, Blue Line to McPherson Sq) Coppery, mod-industrial Churchkey glows with hipness. Fifty beers flow from the taps, including five brain-walloping, cask-aged ales. If none of those please you, another 500 types of brew are available by bottle (including gluten-free suds). Churchkey is the upstairs counterpart to **Birch & Barley** (www.birchandbarley.com; mains $17-29; ⊙5:30-10pm Tue-Thu, to 11pm Fri, 11am-3pm & to 11pm Sat, 11am-3pm & 5:30-9pm Sun), a popular nouveau comfort-food restaurant, and you can order much of its menu at the bar.

Dupont Circle & Kalorama

★**Bar Charley** BAR
(Map p266; ☑202-627-2183; 1825 18th St NW; ⊙5pm-12:30am Mon-Thu, 4pm-1:30am Fri, 10am-1:30am Sat, 10am-12:30am Sun; Ⓜ Red Line to Dupont Circle) Bar Charley draws a mixed crowd from the neighborhood – young, old, gay and straight. They come for groovy cocktails sloshing in vintage glassware and ceramic tiki mugs, served at very reasonable prices by DC standards. Try the gin and gingery Suffering Bastard. The beer list isn't huge, but it is thoughtfully chosen with some wild ales. Around 60 wines are available too.

If you're hungry, Charley serves steaks and globe-trotting small plates (poutine, curried mussels). The drinks are the prize here, though.

★**Board Room** BAR
(Map p266; ☑202-518-7666; www.boardroom dc.com; 1737 Connecticut Ave NW; ⊙4pm-2am Mon-Thu, 4pm-3am Fri, noon-3am Sat, noon-2am Sun; Ⓜ Red Line to Dupont Circle) Grab a table, pull up a stool and crush your opponent at Hungry Hungry Hippos. Or summon spirits with a ouija board. Board Room lets you flash back to childhood via stacks of board games. Battleship, Risk, Operation – name it, and it's available to rent for $2. Around 20 beers flow from the taps and are available by pitcher to stoke the festivities.

Adams Morgan

★**Songbyrd Record Cafe & Music House** CAFE
(Map p266; ☑202-450-2917; www.songbyrddc. com; 2477 18th St NW; ⊙8am-2am Sun-Thu, to 3am Fri & Sat; 🛜; Ⓜ Red Line to Woodley Park-Zoo/Adams Morgan) By day hang out in the retro cafe, drinking excellent coffee, munching sandwiches and browsing the small selection of soul and indie LPs for sale. You can even cut your own record in the vintage recording booth ($15). By night the party moves to the DJ-spinning bar, where beer and cocktails flow alongside burgers and tacos, and indie bands rock the basement club.

★**Dan's Cafe** BAR
(Map p266; ☑202-265-0299; 2315 18th St NW; ⊙7pm-2am Tue-Thu, to 3am Fri & Sat; Ⓜ Red Line to Woodley Park-Zoo/Adams Morgan) This is one of DC's great dive bars. The interior looks sort of like an evil Elks Club, all unironically old-school 'art,' cheap paneling and dim lights barely illuminating the unapologetic slumminess. It's famed for its whopping, mix-it-yourself drinks, where you get a ketchup-type squirt bottle of booze, a can of soda and bucket of ice for $20. Cash only.

Dan's isn't marked, as the sign fell by the wayside a while ago, so keep an eye on the surrounding street addresses.

Georgetown

★**Ching Ching Cha** TEAHOUSE
(Map p270; ☑202-333-8288; www.chingching cha.com; 1063 Wisconsin Ave NW; ⊙11am-8pm Thu-Mon; 🚎Circulator) Airy, Zen-like Ching Ching Cha is a world away from the shopping mayhem of M St. Stop in for a leisurely pot of rare tea (it brews more than 70 varieties) and snacks such as steamed dumplings, coconut tarts, or a 'tea meal,' with three little dishes along the lines of green squash and miso salmon.

IVY CITY DISTILLERIES

An industrial former rail yard, Ivy City sat forlorn for years. Then booze makers began moving in, drawn by vast warehouse spaces and cheap rent. Coffee roasters, performance venues and rooftop restaurants followed. Now the gritty neighborhood is very much an off-the-beaten-path destination.

Booze hounds can take a DIY distillery crawl, hitting four makers plus a brewery in less than a mile; most offer tours and tastings. Here's the lineup, from northeast to southwest:

Jos A Magnus & Co (☎202-450-3518; www.josephmagnus.com; 2052 W Virginia Ave NE; ⊗4-10pm Wed & Thu, to midnight Fri, noon-midnight Sat, noon-7pm Sun; 🚌D4) Makes bourbon, gin and vodka and has a jazzy bar. Bonus: it occupies the same building as Atlas Brew Works (p286).

New Columbia Distillers (www.greenhatgin.com; 1832 Fenwick St NE) Known for its Green Hat Gin and free tastings, but it's open on Saturday only.

Republic Restoratives (☎202-733-3996; www.republicrestoratives.com; 1369 New York Ave NE; ⊗5-11pm Thu & Fri, from noon Sat, noon-5pm Sun; 🚌D4) Vodka, bourbon and rye whiskey are the specialties at this women-owned distillery that has an attached cocktail bar.

One Eight Distilling (www.oneeightdistilling.com; 1135 Okie St NE) Another Saturday-only tasting room, when you can sample the housemade gin, vodka and whiskey.

★**Tombs**   PUB
(Map p270; ☎202-337-6668; www.tombs.com; 1226 36th St NW; ⊗11:30am-1:30am Mon-Thu, to 2:30am Fri & Sat, 9:30am-1:30am Sun; 🚌Circulator) Every college of a certain pedigree has 'that' bar – the one where faculty and students alike sip pints under athletic regalia of the old school. The Tombs is Georgetown's contribution to the genre. If it looks familiar, think back to the '80s: the subterranean pub was one of the settings for the film *St Elmo's Fire*.

☆ Entertainment

☆ National Mall

Anthem   CONCERT VENUE
(Map p254; ☎202-888-0020; www.theanthemdc.com; 901 Wharf St SW; ⊗box office noon-7pm; Ⓜ Orange, Silver, Blue, Yellow, Green Line to L'Enfant Plaza or Green Line to Waterfront) The Anthem opened in 2017 and has quickly become one of DC's best live-music venues. The 6000-capacity hall books acts from Judas Priest to Lorde to Big Sean, though rock is the mainstay genre. Most tickets are general admission to stand on the floor. Get in line early on show day, and you could be front row for your favorite band.

Jazz in the Garden   LIVE MUSIC
(Map p254; ☎202-842-6941; www.nga.gov/jazz; cnr Constitution Ave & 7th St NW; ⊗5-8:30pm Fri late May-late Aug; 🚌Circulator, Ⓜ Green, Yellow Line to Archives) **FREE** Lots of locals show up for these free outdoor jazz, blues and world-music concerts at the National Gallery of Art Sculpture Garden (p257). Bring a blanket and picnic food, and supplement with beverages from the on-site Pavilion Cafe (p257).

Discovery Theater   THEATER
(Map p254; ☎202-633-8700; www.discoverytheater.org; 1100 Jefferson Dr SW, Ripley Center; tickets $6; 👶; 🚌Circulator, Ⓜ Orange, Silver, Blue Line to Smithsonian) In the basement of the Ripley Center, the Smithsonian's Discovery stages delightful puppet shows and other live educational performances for children aged two to 11 years.

Pearl Street Warehouse   LIVE MUSIC
(Map p254; ☎202-380-9620; www.pearlstreetwarehouse.com; 33 Pearl St SW; ⊗8:30am-1am Tue & Wed, to 2am Thu-Sat, to midnight Sun; Ⓜ Orange, Silver, Blue, Yellow, Green Line to L'Enfant Plaza or Green Line to Waterfront) This small Wharf venue has a rootsy feel, like it could be set in Austin or Nashville. Blues, country and rock bands take the stage, including the occasional big name. Tickets typically cost between $10 and $20. The attached diner serves breakfast, burgers and beer.

☆ Capitol Hill & South DC

★ Nationals Park   STADIUM
(Map p260; ☎202-675-6287; www.mlb.com/na
tionals; 1500 S Capitol St SE; ☎; Ⓜ Green Line
to Navy Yard) The major-league Washington
Nationals play baseball at this spiffy stadium beside the Anacostia River. Don't miss
the mid-fourth-inning 'Racing Presidents'
– an odd foot race between giant-headed
caricatures of George Washington, Abraham Lincoln, Thomas Jefferson and Teddy
Roosevelt. Hip bars and eateries and playful green spaces surround the ballpark, and
more keep coming as the area gentrifies.

Catch a game if you can. The Nats act as
a strong social glue among DC's transients
and natives. And tickets can be cheap, starting at around $18.

Folger Theatre   THEATER
(Map p260; ☎202-544-7077; www.folger.edu/
folger-theatre; 201 E Capitol St; tickets from $30;
Ⓜ Orange, Silver, Blue Line to Capitol South) The
250-seat, Renaissance-style theater attached
to the Folger Shakespeare Library stages
classic and modern interpretations of the
bard's plays, as well as new works inspired
by Shakespeare. Literary readings (including the PEN/Faulkner series) and great
programs for children are also all part of
the venue's repertoire. With its three-tiered
wooden balconies, half-timbered facade and
sky canopy, the theater evokes an inn courtyard, where troupes often staged plays in
Shakespeare's day.

☆ White House Area & Foggy Bottom

★ Kennedy Center   PERFORMING ARTS
(Map p262; ☎202-467-4600; www.kennedy
-center.org; 2700 F St NW; ⊙ box office 10am-9pm
Mon-Sat, noon-9pm Sun; ☎♿; Ⓜ Orange, Silver,
Blue Line to Foggy Bottom-GWU) Overlooking
the Potomac River, the magnificent Kennedy Center hosts a staggering array of performances; more than 2000 each year in venues including the Concert Hall – home to the
National Symphony (www.kennedy-center.
org/nso) – and Opera House, home to the
National Opera (www.kennedy-center.org/
wno). Free performances are staged on the
Millennium Stage daily at 6pm as part of
the center's 'Performing Arts for Everyone'
initiative.

LGBTQ+ DC

DC is one of the most gay-friendly cities in the USA. It has an admirable track record
of progressivism and a bit of a scene to boot. The rainbow stereotype here consists of
well-dressed professionals and activists working in politics on LGBT issues such as gay
marriage (legal in DC since 2010). The community concentrates in Dupont Circle, but U
Street, Shaw, Capitol Hill and Logan Circle also have lots of gay-friendly businesses.

Capital Area Gay & Lesbian Chamber of Commerce (www.caglcc.org) Sponsors
lots of networking events around town.

LGBT DC (https://washington.org/lgbtq) The DC tourism office's portal, with events,
neighborhood breakdowns and a travel resource guide.

Metro Weekly (www.metroweekly.com) Free weekly news magazine. Aimed at a younger demographic than its rival, the *Washington Blade*.

Washington Blade (www.washingtonblade.com) Free weekly gay newspaper. Covers
politics and has lots of business and nightlife listings.

Top bars include the following:

Larry's Lounge (Map p266; ☎202-483-1483; 1840 18th St NW; ⊙4pm-2am Mon-Thu, to 3am
Fri & Sat, 2pm-2am Sun; 🐾; Ⓜ Red Line to Dupont Circle) Neighborhood tavern that's perfect
for people-watching and stiff drinks.

JR's (Map p266; ☎202-328-0090; www.jrsbar-dc.com; 1519 17th St NW; ⊙4pm-2am Mon-Thu,
4pm-3am Fri, 1pm-3am Sat, 1pm-2am Sun; Ⓜ Red Line to Dupont Circle) Dupont Pub where a
young, well-dressed crowd kicks back and sings show tunes.

Nellie's (Map p266; ☎202-332-6355; www.nelliessportsbar.com; 900 U St NW; ⊙5pm-1am
Mon-Thu, 3pm-3am Fri, 10:30am-3am Sat, from 10:30am Sun; Ⓜ Green, Yellow Line to Shaw-
Howard U) Drinkers amass for sports-tuned TVs and the sweet roof deck.

☆ Downtown & Penn Quarter

★ Woolly Mammoth Theatre Company
THEATER

(Map p262; ☎202-393-3939; www.woollymammoth.net; 641 D St NW, Penn Quarter; average ticket $67; Ⓜ Green, Yellow Line to Archives) Woolly Mammoth is the edgiest of DC's experimental groups. For most shows, $20 'stampede' seats are available at the box office two hours before performances. They're limited in number, and sold first-come, first-served, so get there early.

Shakespeare Theatre Company
THEATER

(Map p262; ☎202-547-1122; www.shakespearetheatre.org; 450 7th St NW, Penn Quarter; average ticket $85; Ⓜ Green, Yellow Line to Archives) The nation's foremost Shakespeare company presents masterful works by the Bard, as well as plays by George Bernard Shaw, Oscar Wilde, Eugene O'Neill and other greats. The season spans about a half-dozen productions annually, plus a free summer Shakespeare series on-site for two weeks in late August.

Capitol Steps
COMEDY

(Map p262; ☎202-397-7328; www.capsteps.com; Ronald Reagan Bldg, 1300 Pennsylvania Ave NW, Penn Quarter; tickets from $36; ⊙shows 7:30pm Fri & Sat; Ⓜ Orange, Silver, Blue Line to Federal Triangle) This singing troupe claims to be the only group in America that tries to be funnier than Congress. Many of the performers are former congressional staffers, so they know their political stuff, although sometimes it can be overly corny. The satirical, bipartisan jokes poke fun at both sides of the spectrum.

☆ Logan Circle, U Street & Columbia Heights

★ Black Cat
LIVE MUSIC

(Map p266; ☎202-667-4490; www.blackcatdc.com; 1811 14th St NW; tickets $10-25; Ⓜ Green, Yellow Line to U St) The Black Cat is the go-to venue for music that's loud and grungy with a punk edge. The White Stripes, Arcade Fire and Foo Fighters have all thrashed here. The action divides between tiny and intimate Backstage, downstairs, and the upstairs Mainstage, which is still small enough to see what the band is guzzling.

If you're not up for a show, head to the Red Room bar for the jukebox, billiards, pinball and strong cocktails. A vegetarian cafe is also on-site.

U Street Music Hall
CLUB

(Map p266; ☎202-588-1889; www.ustreetmusichall.com; 1115 U St NW; tickets $10-25; ⊙hours vary; Ⓜ Green, Yellow Line to U St) Two local DJs own and operate the basement club; it looks like a no-frills rock bar, but it has a pro sound system, a cork-cushioned dance floor and other accoutrements of a serious dance club. Alternative bands also thrash a couple of nights per week to keep it fresh. Shows start between 7pm and 10pm.

Howard Theatre
THEATER

(Map p266; ☎202-803-2899; www.thehowardtheatre.com; 620 T St NW; Ⓜ Green, Yellow Line to Shaw-Howard U) Built in 1910, Howard Theatre was the top address when U St was known as 'Black Broadway.' Duke Ellington, Ella Fitzgerald and other famed names lit the marquee. Now big-name comedians and blues, gospel and jazz acts fill the house. There's a photo op out front with the steel-and-granite statue of Ellington pounding the keys of a swirling treble clef.

9:30 Club
LIVE MUSIC

(Map p266; ☎202-265-0930; www.930.com; 815 V St NW; tickets $20-35; Ⓜ Green, Yellow Line to U St) The 9:30, which can pack 1200 people into a surprisingly compact venue, is the grand-daddy of the live-music scene in DC. Pretty much every big name that comes through town ends up on this stage at some point. Headliners usually begin between 10:30pm and 11:30pm.

Shopping

🏛 Capitol Hill & South DC

★ Capitol Hill Books
BOOKS

(Map p260; ☎202-544-1621; www.capitolhillbooks-dc.com; 657 C St SE; ⊙11:30am-6pm Mon-Fri, from 9am Sat & Sun; Ⓜ Orange, Silver, Blue Line to Eastern Market) A trove of secondhand awesomeness, this shop has so many books that staff have to double-stack them on the shelves. Superb notes by the cantankerous clerks help guide your selection. Categories are, er, unconventional, including 'Hinduism and Bobby Knight' and 'Sideshows and Carnivals.' The section on US presidents is huge (Chester Arthur books! An entire shelf of Truman books!).

REI Washington DC
Flagship Store SPORTS & OUTDOORS
(Map p260; 202-543-2040; www.rei.com/
stores/washington-dc.html; 201 M St NE; ⊙10am-
9pm Mon-Sat, 11am-7pm Sun; MRed Line to
NoMa-Gallaudet U) Who says Washington isn't
an adventure city? This 51,000-sq-ft building in the revitalizing NoMa neighborhood
– outdoor retailer REI's fifth flagship store
– proves it. Peruse an enormous array of outdoor gear and clothing, sign up for a guided
local hike, attend a navigation-skills event,
or simply sip coffee at the in-house cafe (or
around the outdoor fire pit).

One of the coolest things about the massive store is the Adventure Station, where
national park staff and/or volunteers are on
hand to help you plan your next outdoor adventure in the DC area. And there's history
to boot. The store occupies the historic Uline
Arena, also called the Washington Coliseum,
best known for hosting the Beatles' first
American concert in 1964. President Dwight
D Eisenhower's inaugural ball in 1953, as
well as countless professional hockey and
basketball games, also took place here. History buffs will be happy to know that hints
of the past remain, including one hallway
with original basketball flooring and old stadium seating mounted to the wall.

Flea Market MARKET
(Map p260; www.easternmarket.net; 7th St SE,
btwn C St & Penn Ave; ⊙10am-5pm Sat & Sun;
MOrange, Silver, Blue Line to Eastern Market) On
weekends an outdoor flea market sets up
on a two-block stretch of 7th St SE, adjacent
to Eastern Market. Vendors sell all kinds of
cool art, antiques, furniture, maps, prints,
global wares, clothing, crafts and curios.
Sunday is the bigger day, with more stalls.

Eastern Market MARKET
(Map p260; 202-698-5253; www.easternmarket
-dc.org; 225 7th St SE; ⊙7am-7pm Tue-Fri, to 6pm
Sat, 9am-5pm Sun; MOrange, Silver, Blue Line to
Eastern Market) One of the icons of Capitol
Hill, this roofed bazaar sprawls with delectable chow and good cheer, especially
on the weekend. Built in 1873, it is the last
of the 19th-century covered markets that
once supplied DC's food. The South Hall
has a bakery, a dairy, a fishmonger, butchers, flower vendors, and fruit and vegetable
sellers.

⌂ White House Area & Foggy Bottom

White House Gifts GIFTS & SOUVENIRS
(Map p262; 202-737-9500; www.whitehouse
gifts.com; 701 15th St NW; ⊙8am-9pm Mon-Sat,
9am-8pm Sun; MRed, Orange, Silver, Blue Line to
Metro Center) Though not to be confused with
the official White House gift **shop** (Map p262;
http://shop.whitehousehistory.org; 1450 Pennsylvania Ave NW; ⊙7:30am-4pm; MOrange, Silver, Blue
Line to Federal Triangle) in the White House Visitor Center, this store sells official souvenirs
alongside less-orthodox offerings. So while
you can still find the certified White House
Christmas ornament among the stock, you'll
also see caricature Trump bottle openers
and the Political Inaction Figures paper-
doll set.

The Indian Craft Shop ARTS & CRAFTS
(Map p262; 202-208-4056; www.indiancraft
shop.com; 1849 C St NW, Dept of Interior;
⊙8:30am-4:30pm Mon-Fri; MOrange, Silver, Blue
Line to Farragut West) Representing more than
45 tribal groups in the US, this compact
shop sells basketry, weavings, pottery, bead-
work, sand paintings and fetish carvings
made by Native Americans. The high-quality
pieces don't come cheap. The shop is hidden
inside the Department of the Interior; show
photo ID to enter the building.

⌂ Logan Circle, U Street & Columbia Heights

★Miss Pixie's ANTIQUES
(Map p266; 202-232-8171; www.misspixies.com;
1626 14th St NW; ⊙11am-7pm; MGreen, Yellow Line
to U St) Bright and festive with classic pop
tunes playing in the background, Miss Pixie's
is a great browse. It's piled high with relics
of the past, from stuffed leather armchairs
to 1960s lawn ornaments. You'll find dishes,
rocking chairs, farm tables, black-and-white
photos, and plenty of other curiosities. New
items arrive on Wednesday nights and hit
the shelves by Thursday morning.

Good Wood ANTIQUES
(Map p266; 202-986-3640; www.goodwooddc.
com; 1428 U St NW; ⊙noon-7pm Mon-Sat, to 5pm
Sun; MGreen, Yellow Line to U St) Even if you're
not in the market for a midcentury armoire,
Good Wood is well worth a visit. The warm,
atmospheric space holds a cool selection of
antiques, including handcrafted chairs and

tables, elegant lamps and wall hangings, plus modern decorative items such as candles and glassware.

Dupont Circle & Kalorama

★ Kramerbooks   BOOKS
(Map p266; ☑ 202-387-1400; www.kramers.com; 1517 Connecticut Ave NW; ☺ 7:30am-1am Sun-Thu, to 3am Fri & Sat; Ⓜ Red Line to Dupont Circle) This flagship independent – which leapt into First Amendment history when it refused to release Monica Lewinsky's book-buying list to Ken Starr's snoops – features first-rate literature, travel and politics sections. The big, sunny bookstore attaches to the fun-loving **Afterwords Cafe** (☑ 202-387-3825; mains $18-22; ☺ 7:30am-1am Sun-Thu, to 3am Fri & Sat), where a frisky crowd flirts over drinks and pages into the wee hours.

Author readings and other literary events take place several nights each week.

★ Second Story Books   BOOKS, MUSIC
(Map p266; ☑ 202-659-8884; www.secondstory books.com; 2000 P St NW; ☺ 10am-10pm; Ⓜ Red Line to Dupont Circle) Packed with dusty secondhand tomes, atmospheric Second Story also sells used CDs (mostly jazz and classical), antiquarian books and old sheet music. The prices are decent and the choices are broad (particularly in the realm of history and Americana). Be sure to browse the sidewalk bins, which have books from 50¢ to $2.

Adams Morgan

Brass Knob   ANTIQUES
(Map p266; ☑ 202-332-3370; www.thebrassknob. com; 2311 18th St NW; ☺ 10:30am-6pm Mon-Sat, noon-5pm Sun; Ⓜ Red Line to Woodley Park-Zoo/ Adams Morgan) This unique two-floor shop sells 'rescues' from old buildings: fixtures, lamps, tiles, mantelpieces and mirrors. The store's raison d'être, though, is the doorknob: brass, wooden, glass, elaborate, polished and antique. If you need to accent your crib like the interior of the best old DC row houses, look no further. Staff can help you find whatever you need.

Meeps   VINTAGE
(Map p266; ☑ 202-265-6546; www.meepsdc.com; 2104 18th St NW; ☺ noon-7pm Sun & Mon, to 8pm Tue-Sat; Ⓜ Red Line to Dupont Circle) There's this girl you know: extremely stylish and never seems to have a brand name on her body. Now, picture her wardrobe. Mod dresses, cowboy shirts, suede jackets, beaded purses, leather boots, Jackie O sunglasses and denim jumpsuits: there's Meeps mapped out for you. The store also carries a selection of clever, locally designed T-shirts.

Georgetown

Oliver Dunn, Moss & Co   ANTIQUES
(Map p270; ☑ 202-338-7410; 1657 Wisconsin Ave NW; ☺ 11am-5pm Tue-Sat; 🚌 Circulator) The lengthy name comes from two businesses under one roof. Located in a cute row house in the thick of Book Hill (Georgetown's antique-laden block of shops), this spot spreads posh linens, Scandinavian textiles, French signs and concrete garden ornaments through six rooms and into the back yard.

Cady's Alley   HOMEWARES
(Map p270; www.cadysalley.com; 3314 M St NW; ☺ 8am-6pm Mon-Sat, from noon Sun; 🚌 Circulator) Not a store per se, Cady's Alley is a small cobblestone lane lined with ubercool (and often expensive) clothing and interior-design boutiques selling everything from little black dresses to concept furniture. It runs parallel to M St NW, between 33rd and 34th Sts NW; you can enter off M St.

Upper Northwest DC

Politics and Prose Bookstore   BOOKS
(Map p272; ☑ 202-364-1919; www.politics-prose. com; 5015 Connecticut Ave NW, Chevy Chase; ☺ 8am-10pm Mon-Sat, to 8pm Sun; 🛜; Ⓜ Van Ness-UDC, then bus L1 or L2) A much-loved DC literary hub, this independent bookstore carries an excellent selection of fiction and nonfiction, has knowledgeable staff and is fiercely supportive of local authors. It's known for hosting readings and book clubs. The basement coffeehouse and wine bar (sandwiches $9 to $10) hosts cultural and music events, and offers happy hour from 4pm to 7pm Monday to Friday.

ℹ️ Information

Destination DC (☑ 202-789-7000; www. washington.org) DC's official tourism site, with the mother lode of online information.

NPS Ellipse Visitor Pavilion (Map p262; ☑ 202-208-1631; www.nps.gov; ☺ 7:30am-4pm; Ⓜ Orange, Silver, Blue Line to Federal Triangle) Has a staffed information desk and sells snacks; located at the northeast corner of the Ellipse, south of the White House.

Smithsonian Visitor Center (Map p254; 📞 202-663-1000; www.si.edu/visit; 1000 Jefferson Dr SW; ⏰ 8:30am-5:30pm; 🚻; 🚇 Circulator, Ⓜ Orange, Silver, Blue Line to Smithsonian) Located in the castle, it is a great resource with a staffed information desk and everything you ever wanted to know about the museum programs.

🅞 Getting There & Away

Most visitors arrive by air. The city has two airports: Dulles International Airport is larger and handles most of the international flights, as well as domestic flights. Ronald Reagan Washington National Airport handles domestic services plus some flights to Canada. Reagan is more convenient, as it's closer to the city and has a Metro stop. Baltimore's airport is a third, often-cheaper option. It's connected to DC by commuter rail, though it's not handy if you're arriving at night.

Buses are a popular means of getting to DC from nearby cities such New York, Philadelphia and Richmond, VA. Tickets are cheap, the routes are direct to the city center, and the buses usually have free wi-fi and power outlets.

It's also easy to reach DC by train from major east-coast cities. The fast, commuter-oriented Acela train links Boston, New York and Philly to DC's Union Station.

Flights, cars and tours can be booked online at lonelyplanet.com/bookings.

AIR

Ronald Reagan Washington National Airport (DCA; www.flyreagan.com) is 4.5 miles south of downtown in Arlington, VA. It has free wi-fi, several eateries and a currency exchange (National Hall, Concourse Level).

Dulles International Airport (IAD; 📞 703-572-2700; www.flydulles.com) is in the Virginia suburbs 26 miles west of DC. It has free wi-fi, several currency exchanges and restaurants throughout the terminals. Famed architect Eero Saarinen designed the swooping main building. The Metro Silver Line is slated to reach Dulles in 2020, providing a transfer-free ride at long last.

Baltimore/Washington International Thurgood Marshall Airport (p431) is 30 miles northeast of DC in Maryland.

BUS

Cheap bus services to and from Washington, DC, abound. Most charge $25 to $30 for a one-way trip to NYC (it takes four to five hours). Many companies use Union Station as their hub; other pick-up locations are scattered around town, but are always accessible by Metro. Tickets usually need to be bought online, but can sometimes be purchased on the bus itself if there are still seats available.

BestBus (Map p266; 📞 202-332-2691; www. bestbus.com; cnr 20th St & Massachusetts Ave NW; 🚻; Ⓜ Red Line to Dupont Circle) Several trips to/from NYC daily. The main bus stop is by Dupont Circle; there's another at Union Station.

BoltBus (Map p260; 📞 877-265-8287; www. boltbus.com; 50 Massachusetts Ave NE; 🚻; Ⓜ Red Line to Union Station) It goes to NYC multiple times each day, and to other East Coast cities. Lateness and spotty wi-fi can be issues. It uses Union Station as its terminal.

Greyhound (📞 202-589-5141; www.greyhound. com; 50 Massachusetts Ave NE; 🚻; Ⓜ Red Line to Union Station) Provides nationwide service. The terminal is at Union Station.

Megabus (📞 877-462-6342; http://us.mega bus.com; 50 Massachusetts Ave NE; 🚻; Ⓜ Red Line to Union Station) Offers the most trips to NYC (around 15 to 20 per day), as well as other East Coast cities; arrives at/departs from Union Station. Buses run behind schedule fairly often.

Peter Pan Bus Lines (📞 800-343-9999; www. peterpanbus.com; 50 Massachusetts Ave NE; 🚻; Ⓜ Red Line to Union Station) Travels throughout the northeastern USA; has its terminal at Union Station.

Vamoose Bus (📞 212-695-6766; www.va moosebus.com; 1801 N Lynn St; $60) Service between NYC and Arlington, VA (the stop is near the Rosslyn Metro station).

Washington Deluxe (Map p266; 📞 866-287-6932; www.washny.com; 1610 Connecticut Ave NW; 🚻; Ⓜ Red Line to Dupont Circle) Good express service to/from NYC. It has stops at both Dupont Circle and Union Station.

CAR & MOTORCYCLE

I-495 – aka the Capital Beltway – circles the city. It connects with I-95 on the outskirts, which goes northeast to Baltimore, MD, and southwest to Virginia. Hwy 50 rolls right through DC on its east–west cross-country route; it becomes New York Ave and Constitution Ave in the city. Expect lots of traffic whatever road you take.

TRAIN

Magnificent, beaux-arts Union Station (p261) is the city's rail hub. There's a handy Metro station (Red Line) here for transport onward in the city.

Amtrak (www.amtrak.com) arrives at least once per hour from major East Coast cities. Its Northeast Regional trains are cheaper but slower (about 3½ hours between NYC and DC).

Amtrak's Acela Express trains are more expensive but faster (2¾ hours between NYC and DC; 6½ hours between Boston and DC). The express trains also have bigger seats and other business-class amenities.

MARC trains (www.mta.maryland.gov) arrive frequently from downtown Baltimore (one hour) and other Maryland towns, as well as Harpers Ferry, WV.

TO/FROM THE AIRPORT
Dulles International Airport

➤ The Silver Line Express bus run by Washington Flyer (www.washfly.com) operates every 15 to 20 minutes from Dulles (main terminal, arrivals level door 4) to the Wiehle-Reston East Metro station between 6am and 10:40pm (from 7:45am weekends). Total time to DC's center is 60 to 75 minutes; total bus-Metro cost is around $11.

➤ Metrobus 5A (www.wmata.com) runs every 30 to 40 minutes from Dulles to Rosslyn Metro (Blue, Orange and Silver Lines) and on to central DC (L'Enfant Plaza) between 5:50am (6:30am weekends) and 11:35pm. Total time to the center is around 60 minutes; total fare is $7.50.

➤ The Supershuttle (www.supershuttle.com) door-to-door shared-van service goes downtown for $30. It takes 30 to 60 minutes and runs from 5:30am to 12:30am.

➤ Taxi rides to the city center take 30 to 60 minutes (depending on traffic) and cost $62 to $73. Follow the 'Ground Transportation' or 'Taxi' signs to where they queue.

Ronald Reagan Washington National Airport

➤ The airport has its own Metro (www.wmata.com) station on the Blue and Yellow Lines. Trains (around $2.65) depart every 10 minutes or so between 5am (from 7am weekends) and 11:30pm (to 1am Friday and Saturday); they reach the city center in 20 minutes. It connects to the concourse level of terminals B and C.

➤ The Supershuttle (www.supershuttle.com) door-to-door shared-van service goes downtown for $16. It takes 10 to 30 minutes and runs from 5:30am to 12:30am.

➤ Rides to the city center take 10 to 30 minutes (depending on traffic) and cost $19 to $26. Taxis queue outside the baggage-claim area at each terminal.

Baltimore-Washington International Thurgood Marshall Airport

➤ Metrobus B30 (www.wmata.com) runs from BWI to the Greenbelt Metro station (last stop on the Green Line); it departs every 60 minutes from bus stops on the lower level of the international concourse and concourse A/B. The total bus-Metro fare is about $12. Total trip time is around 75 minutes.

➤ The Supershuttle (www.supershuttle.com) door-to-door shared-van service goes to downtown DC for $37. The ride takes 45 minutes to an hour and runs from 5:30am to 12:30am.

➤ A taxi to DC takes 45 minutes or so and costs $90. Taxis queue outside the baggage-claim area of the Marshall terminal.

➤ Both Maryland Rail Commuter (MARC; www.mta.maryland.gov) and Amtrak (www.amtrak.com) trains travel to DC's Union Station. They depart from a terminal 1 mile from BWI; a free bus shuttles passengers there. Trains leave once or twice per hour, but there's no service after 9:30pm (and limited service on weekends). It takes 30 to 40 minutes; fares start at $7. MARC typically is cheaper than Amtrak.

ⓘ Getting Around

The Metro is the main way to move around the city. Buy a rechargeable SmarTrip card at any Metro station. You must use the card to enter *and* exit station turnstiles.

Metro Fast, frequent, ubiquitous (except during weekend track maintenance). It operates between 5am (from 7am weekends) and 11:30pm (1am on Friday and Saturday). Fares are from $2 to $6 depending on distance traveled. A day pass costs $14.75.

DC Circulator bus Useful for the Mall, Georgetown, Adams Morgan and other areas with limited Metro service. Fare is $1.

Bicycle Capital Bikeshare stations are everywhere; a day pass costs $8.

Taxi Relatively easy to find (less so at night), but costly. Ridesharing companies are used more in the District.

Delaware

POP 952,065

Best Places to Eat

➡ Henlopen City Oyster House (p300)

➡ Agave (p298)

➡ Dogfish Head Brewings & Eats (p300)

➡ Iron Hill Brewery (p303)

➡ Off the Hook (p301)

➡ Blue Hen (p300)

Best Places to Stay

➡ Cottages at Indian River Marina (p301)

➡ Hotel du Pont (p303)

➡ Hotel Rehoboth (p300)

➡ Avenue Inn & Spa (p300)

➡ Dogfish Inn (p298)

Why Go?

Tiny Delaware, the nation's second-smallest state (96 miles long and less than 35 miles across at its widest point), is overshadowed by its neighbors – and often overlooked by visitors to the region. And that's too bad, because Delaware has a lot more on offer than just tax-free shopping and chicken farms.

Long, white sandy beaches, cute colonial villages, a cozy countryside and small-town charm characterize the state that happily calls itself the 'Small Wonder.' It's also the home state of former vice president and US senator Joe Biden, a resident of Wilmington.

When to Go
Wilmington

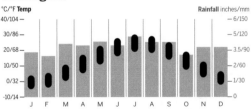

Jun Rock out at the Firefly Music festival in Dover.

Jul Beach season is in full swing along the coast with fireworks on the 4th.

Dec For grand and colorful holiday cheer, visit the Du Pont estate in the Brandywine Valley.

Delaware Highlights

1 Brandywine Valley (p303) Digging into Du Pont family history on grand estates, and living large in a vast scenic valley linking Delaware and Pennsylvania.

2 Cape Henlopen State Park (p297) Scanning for birds, cycling the trails and taking in the coastal views.

3 Delaware Art Museum (p302) Admiring the fantastic collection in this Wilmingto n gallery.

4 Rehoboth Beach (p299) Strolling the boardwalk, relaxing on the beach and savoring great meals in this family- and gay-friendly resort.

5 Old State House (p305) Learning the history of the quirky former state capitol building in Dover and checking out the surrounding historic sights.

6 Dogfish Head Brewings & Eats (p300) Tasting craft beer at welcoming microbreweries like this one; others can be found across the state

7 Dewey Beach (p301) Living the party life with the young professionals who've fled DC to kick it on the coast in summer.

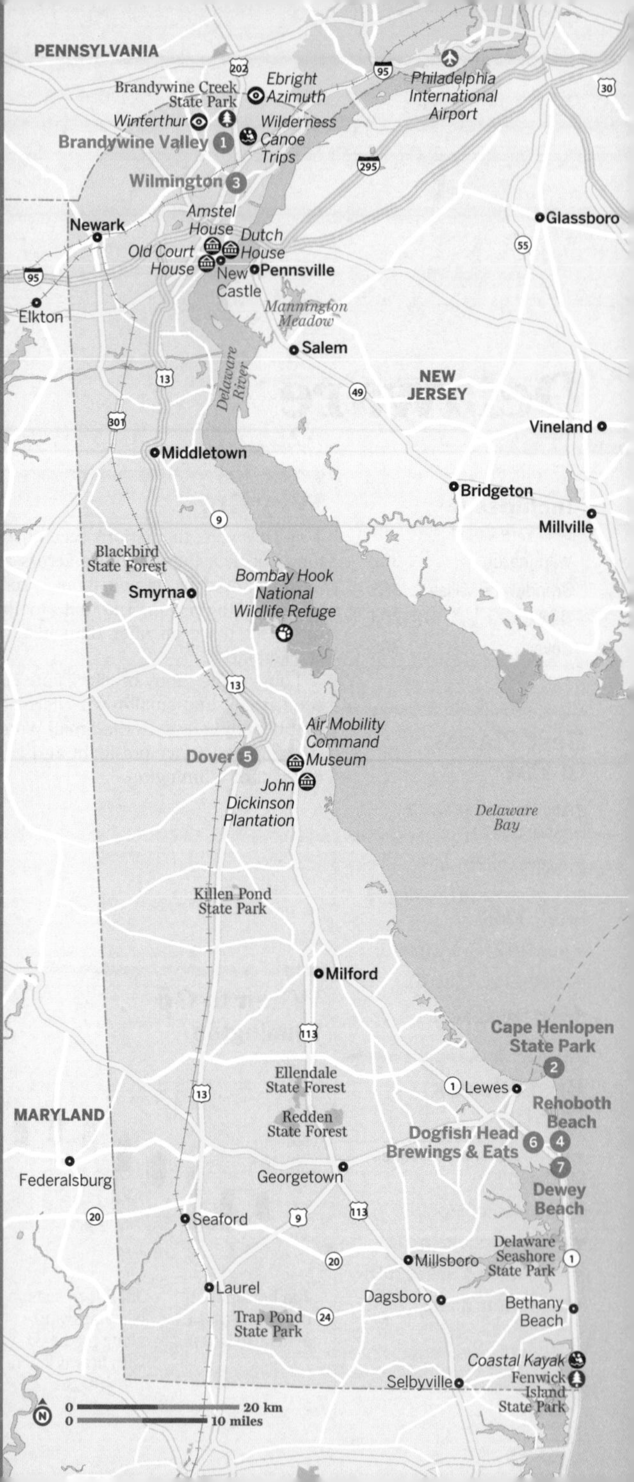

History

In colonial days, Delaware was the subject of an aggressive land feud between Dutch, Swedish and British settlers. The first two imported classically northern European middle-class concepts, the third a plantation-based aristocracy – which is partly why Delaware remains a typically mid-Atlantic cultural hybrid today.

The little state's big moment came on December 7, 1787, when Delaware became the first colony to ratify the US Constitution, thus becoming the first state in the Union. It remained in that union throughout the Civil War, despite supporting slavery. During this period, as throughout much of the state's history, the economy drew on its chemical industry. DuPont, the world's second-largest chemical company, was founded here in 1802 as a gunpowder factory by French immigrant Eleuthère Irénée du Pont. Low taxes drew other firms (particularly credit-card companies) in the 20th century, boosting the state's prosperity.

ℹ Getting There & Away

The coastal cities are 120 miles from both Washington, DC and Baltimore. Wilmington is in the northern reaches of the state, 75 miles northeast of Baltimore via I-95 and 30 miles south of Philadelphia via I-95 – and just a few miles from the Pennsylvania state line. Amtrak runs nine routes through Wilmington. The closest major airport to Wilmington is Philadelphia International Airport.

Delaware Coast

With gorgeous coastal views and beach towns for every personality, Delaware's 28 miles of sandy Atlantic beaches are a great reason to linger here. They're also easy to reach from Washington, DC, Baltimore and NYC. Head to Lewes for the walkable downtown, filled with history and great restaurants. Gay-friendly Rehoboth also works well for families and those seeking upscale distractions, from pampering spas to fine cocktails. South of Rehoboth, wild Dewey is the place to get your beach party on while Bethany is made for lazy days on the sand. Pretty beaches and state parks stretch between the towns – ending at the Maryland border – and connect the ocean and the bays. Cycling the parks and kayaking the salt marshes are top outdoor activities. Most businesses and services are open year-round. Off-season (outside of June to August), price bargains abound.

ℹ Getting There & Away

The beaches are all about 120 miles from both Washington, DC and Baltimore, MD. NYC is 210 miles north. In summer (late May through early September), BestBus (www.bestbus.com) runs routes from DC (2½ hours) and NYC (4½ hours) to Rehoboth and Dewey.

Lewes

🗺 302 / POP 2955

In 1631, the Dutch gave this whaling settlement the pretty name of Zwaanendael (Valley of the Swans), before promptly getting massacred by local Nanticokes. The name was changed to Lewes (loo-iss) when William Penn gained control of the area. Today it's an attractive seaside gem with a mix of English and Dutch architecture – and loads of great restaurants. Pretty Cape Henlopen State Park is only 2.5 miles from downtown.

◉ Sights & Activities

Cape Henlopen State Park   STATE PARK
(☑ 302-645-8983; www.destateparks.com/park/cape-henlopen; 15099 Cape Henlopen Dr; Mar-Nov per car out-of-state/in-state $10/5, Dec-Feb free; ⊙ 8am-sunset; P 🚻) One mile east of Lewes, more than 4000 acres of dune bluffs, pine forests and wetlands are preserved at this lovely state park that's popular with bird-watchers, beachgoers and campers.

> ### CYCLING THE JUNCTION & BREAKWATER TRAIL
>
> For a scenic ride between Rehoboth and Lewes, rent a bicycle and hit the 6-mile **Junction & Breakwater Trail** (www.leweschamber.com). Named after the former rail line that operated here in the 1800s, this smooth, graded greenway travels through wooded and open terrain, over coastal marshes and past farmland. Pick up a map from the Rehoboth visitor center or from **Atlantic Cycles** (☑ 302-226-2543; www.atlanticcycles.net; 18 Wilmington Ave; half/full day from $16/24; ⊙ 8am-3pm in season), also in Rehoboth, which offers inexpensive rentals. In Lewes, try **Lewes Cycle Sports** (☑ 302-645-4544; www.lewescyclesports.com; 526 E Savannah Rd; single-speed cruiser day/week $25/52; road bike $55/95; ⊙ 9am-5pm Mon & Tue, 10am-3pm Wed, 9am-5pm Fri & Sat, 10am-4pm Sun) at the Beacon Motel.

There's also a 3.5-mile paved loop cycling trail. You can see clear to Cape May from the observation tower. **North Shores beach** draws many gay and lesbian couples. Campsites ($40 to $59) and cabins ($130) are also available. The admission fee is cash only.

Zwaanendael Museum MUSEUM

(📞302-645-1148; https://history.delaware.gov/museums; 102 Kings Hwy; ⊙10am-4:30pm Tue-Sat, 1:30-4:30pm Sun Apr-Oct, 10am-4:30pm Wed-Sat Nov-Mar) FREE According to a staffer, you won't find exhibits about the town's first settlers – 32 Dutchmen – because they were all massacred by a local tribe in the mid-1600s. Alrighty then. What you will find is an exhibit spotlighting the fate of the HMS *deBraak*, a ship that sank in Delaware Bay in 1798. Oh, and there's a Fijian merman upstairs.

Quest Fitness Kayak KAYAKING

(📞302-745-2925; www.questkayak.com; 514 E Savannah Rd; kayak hire per 2/8hr $25/50; ⊙from 8am, close hours vary May-Sep, reservation only

Oct-Apr) For aquatic action, Quest Fitness Kayak operates a kayak-rental stand next to the Beacon Motel. It also runs scenic paddle tours around the Cape ($65) and a pints-and-paddles trip that ends with a tour and tasting at Dogfish Head Brewery ($65).

Sleeping & Eating

Dogfish Inn MOTEL $$$

(📞302-644-8292; www.dogfish.com/inn; 100 Savannah Rd; r $189; cottage ste $395; P❀⊛🛜🐾) We dig your summer-camp style Dogfish, but why d'ya make yourself so tough to love? Rooms at this two-story motel come with a local treasure map, nifty beach supplies and a complimentary beer growler. But there's the rub – there's no beer!

Agave MEXICAN $$

(📞302-645-1232; www.agavelewes.com; 137 2nd St; mains $12-24; ⊙noon-8:45pm Mon-Thu, to 9:45pm Fri & Sat, 3-8:45pm Sun) The margaritas are flowing and the guacamoles preening at this upscale but convivial Mexican spot that

Delaware Coast

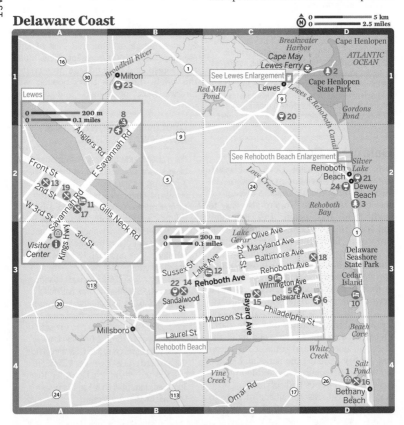

packs 'em in for housemade mole sauce, filet-stuffed fajitas and sweet ancho ribs. Agave has grown from 30 seats to more than 100 in 10 years. Everyone around us was ordering the chipotle mayo–slathered corn on the cob too – we may have missed out!

Touch of Italy   ITALIAN $$
(☑302-827-2730; www.touchofitaly.com; 101 2nd St; mains $13-28; ☺10:30am-9pm Sun-Thu, to 10pm Fri & Sat) They might just hand you a free frosted cookie from the bakeshop if your timing is right at this cozy Italian restaurant where you can while away an afternoon with red wine and a fresh mozzarella-and-tomato hero, or tuck in at night for veal parmigiana, meat lasagne or a prosciutto pizza.

Striper Bites   SEAFOOD $$
(☑302-645-4657; www.striperbites.com; 107 Savannah Rd; lunch mains $11-19, dinner mains $11-32; ☺11:30am-9pm Mon-Thu, to 10pm Fri & Sat) The delicious crab bisque is topped with a hunk of crab meat at this welcoming seafood restaurant where the nautical theme trends toward stylish, not salty. Seafood entrees from seared scallops to panko-encrusted halibut are on the menu as well as sandwiches and salads. Small bar too.

 Drinking & Nightlife

Crooked Hammock Brewery   MICROBREWERY
(☑302-644-7837; www.crookedhammockbrewery.com; 36707 Crooked Hammock Way; ☺11am-1am) If Dave is behind the bar, you will have no problems navigating the 12 drafts on tap at this cavernous place where a ping-pong table, photos of customers and a lazy hammock or two add to the sense of fun. There are hints of coconut and Hawaiian sunshine in the popular Wai Ola ale, also sold by the can. Good food too, from sandwiches and burgers to a few seafood mains ($11 to $22).

ℹ️ **Information**

In a historic building, the **visitor center** (☑302-645-8073; www.leweschamber.com; 120 Kings Hwy; ☺10am-4pm Mon-Fri year-round, 9am-3pm Sat & 10am-2pm Sun Jun-Sep) provides useful insight into attractions and outings in the surrounding area.

ℹ️ **Getting There & Away**

Cape May–Lewes Ferry (☑800-643-3779; www.capemaylewesferry.com; 43 Cape Henlopen Dr; round trip per motorcycle/car $43/51, adult/child 6-13yr $14/7) runs daily 90-minute ferries across Delaware Bay to New Jersey from the terminal, 1 mile from downtown Lewes. For foot passengers, a seasonal shuttle bus ($5) operates between the ferry terminal and Lewes. Reservations recommended. The town sits on the coast just off the Coastal Hwy/Rte 1.

Delaware Coast

Rehoboth Beach

☑302 / POP 1119

As the closest stretch of sand to Washington, DC (121 miles), Rehoboth Beach is often dubbed 'the Nation's Summer Capital.' It is both a family-friendly and gay-friendly destination. To escape the chaos of busy Rehoboth Ave (and the heavily built-up outskirts), wander into the side streets downtown. There you'll find a mix of gingerbread houses, tree-lined streets, posh restaurants and kiddie amusements, plus a wide beach fronted by a mile-long boardwalk.

🏃 **Activities**

Funland   AMUSEMENT PARK
(☑302-227-1921; www.funland.com; 6 Delaware Ave; 1/20 tickets 40¢/$8; ☺10am-11pm

OFF THE BEATEN TRACK

STEAMPUNK TREEHOUSE

Get your camera ready for a photo of the futuristic Steampunk Treehouse, a functional piece of art perched in an artificial tree on the grounds of the **Dogfish Head Craft Brewery & Tasting Room** (☑302-684-1000; www. dogfish.com; 6 Cannery Village Ctr, Milton; ⊘11am-7pm Mon-Sat, noon-7pm Sun) in Milton. Constructed of recycled and reclaimed materials by California artist Sean Orlando and the Five Ton Crane Arts Group, the treehouse made its debut at the Burning Man festival in Black Rock City, NV in 2007. It found a home in Milton in 2010. The total height of the piece is about 40ft. The interior, sadly, is open only to employees of the brewery. The tasting room inside the brewery has 27 rotating taps.

Milton is 12 miles west of Lewes via Hwy 1 and Cave Neck Rd.

mid-May–mid-Sep; ♿) Bring the family to this 20-ride amusement park in operation since the 1960s. Most rides are geared to younger kids and run the gamut from a carousel to the new Superflip that swings you 360 degrees. Rides require anywhere from one to six tickets. There's also an arcade.

🛏 Sleeping

Nice indie motels and hotels are located near the boardwalk. Prices skyrocket on summer weekends, with many places requiring a two-night minimum. Cheaper lodging options are located on Rte 1.

Hotel Rehoboth   BOUTIQUE HOTEL **$$$**
(☑302-227-4300; www.hotelrehoboth.com; 247 Rehoboth Ave; r $359; P❄@🛜🏊) This boutique hotel has gained a reputation for great service and luxurious amenities, including a free shuttle to the beach. Complimentary wine and cheese reception in the evening.

Avenue Inn & Spa   SPA HOTEL **$$$**
(☑800-433-5870; www.avenueinn.com; 33 Wilmington Ave; r from $299) Rooms sport a crisp and unfussy beach style at this relaxing property just one block from the boardwalk. Complimentary perks like afternoon wine and cheese followed by fresh cookies in the evening contribute to the hospitable vibe. Spa services include deep-tissue massage, organic facials and a lavender body wrap.

🍴 Eating

Thrasher's French Fries   AMERICAN **$**
(www.thrasherfries.com; 7 Rehoboth Ave; small fries $5) Well of course you're going to stroll the boardwalk with a container of piping hot, perfectly greasy french fries! Cooked in peanut oil, these hot potatoes have wowed regional beachgoers since 1929. No ketchup served – just vinegar.

Blue Hen   AMERICAN **$$**
(☑302-278-7842; www.thebluehenrehoboth.com; 33 Wilmington Ave; mains $14-32; ⊘noon-late Thu-Mon) From the same team behind the lauded Henlopen City Oyster House, this fresh-on-the-scene restaurant is winning accolades in its own right. At press time the Blue Hen had just earned a Best New Restaurant semi-finalist nomination from the James Beard Foundation. Inside the eatery's farmhouse-chic digs, chef Julia Robinson whips up gourmet comfort fare, including deviled eggs with chicken cracklins and lobster pot pie.

Chesapeake & Maine   GASTROPUB **$$**
(☑302-226-3600; www.dogfish.com; 316 Rehoboth Ave; mains $15-29; ⊘4-9pm Mon-Thu, to 10pm Fri & Sat, 1am-3pm & 4-9pm Sun) The bar at Chesapeake & Maine sparkles with style and top-notch service. Beer-making powerhouse Dogfish Head owns the place, and the acclaimed cocktails here are mixed with spirits produced by Dogfish Head Distilling Co, soon moving its operations next door. The raw bar and the seafood dishes are sourced from Chesapeake Bay and coastal Maine.

Chesapeake & Maine earned a James Beard semi-finalist nomination for Best Bar Program in 2017.

★**Henlopen City Oyster House**   SEAFOOD **$$$**
(☑302-260-9193; www.hcoysterhouse.com; 50 Wilmington Ave; mains $11-38; ⊘dinner from 5pm) Seafood lovers won't want to miss this elegant but inviting spot, where an enticing raw bar and mouth-watering seafood dishes draw crowds (arrive early; no reservations). Good microbrews, cocktails and wine selections round out the appeal. The menu changes every day. Happy hours runs from 3pm to 5pm, lunch is served in the off-season.

🍸 Drinking & Nightlife

★**Dogfish Head Brewings & Eats**   PUB
(☑302-226-2739; www.dogfish.com; 320 Rehoboth Ave; mains $12-25; ⊘11am-11pm Sun-Thu, to 1am Fri & Sat, to 2pm Sun) There's a long list of beers available at this iconic brewery, which also serves tasty pizzas, burgers, crab cakes

and other pub fare. They all go perfectly with the award-winning IPAs. Kids menu available with $6 meals. The restaurant is fresh from a $4 million rebuild – which is right next door to its former home of 22 years. Dogfish is a regional draw.

The famous 120 Minute IPA is released in April and November. Live music on Friday and Saturday nights.

ⓘ Getting There & Away

BestBus (www.bestbus.com) offers bus services from DC ($40, 2½ hours) and NYC ($49, 4½ hours) to Rehoboth; running Friday to Sunday in summertime only (late May through early September). Also stops in Dewey Beach.

The Jolly Trolley (www.jollytrolly.com) connects Rehoboth and Dewey beaches, and makes frequent stops along the way. A round-trip costs $5, and the trolley runs from 8am to 2am June through August. Cash only.

Dewey Beach

🏄 302 / POP 300

Less than 2 miles south on Hwy 1 from Rehoboth Beach is the tiny hamlet of Dewey Beach. Unapologetically known as 'Do Me' Beach for its (heterosexual) hook-up scene and hedonistic nightlife, Dewey is a major party beach.

⊙ Sights

Delaware Seashore State Park STATE PARK
(🖉302-227-2800; www.destateparks.com/park/del aware-seashore; 39415 Inlet Rd; Mar-Nov per car out-of-state/in-state $10/5; Dec-Feb free; ⊙8am-sunset; P) A windswept slice of dunes possessed of a wild, lonely beauty. The 3-mile round-trip Burton Island Trail begins at the northern tip of the Indian River Marina, offering

views of upland forest, salt marshes and Indian River and Rehoboth Bays. Camping is available year-round (campsite $40 to $50).

🛏 Sleeping

Hotels and motels can be found along the Coastal Hwy through town, plus there are oodles of condo and house rentals.

★**Cottages at Indian
River Marina**   COTTAGE $$$
(🖉302-227-3071; www.destateparks.com/camping/ cottages; 39415 Inlet Rd; per week peak/shoulder/ off-season $1900/1250/850, 2 days off-season $200-300; P❄) These cottages, located in Delaware Seashore State Park 6 miles south of Dewey Beach, are some of our favorite local vacation rentals. Not for the decor per se, but for the patios and unadulterated views across the pristine beach to the water. Each cottage has two bedrooms and a loft.

🍺 Drinking & Nightlife

Starboard   BAR
(🖉302-227-4600; www.thestarboard.com; 2009 Coastal Hwy; ⊙8:30am-1am Wed-Sat, to 8pm Sun May-Sep, hours vary Oct & mid-Mar–Apr, closed Nov–mid-Mar) Around since the early 1960s, this fun-loving beach bar draws 'em in for its Bloody Mary bar on Suicide Sundays. Live music most nights they're open. It's not right on the beach, but you probably won't care after a few cocktails in the sunshine.

Dewey Beer Co   MICROBREWERY
(🖉302-227-1182; www.deweybeerco.com; 2100 Coastal Hwy; ⊙noon-9pm Sun-Thu, to 9:30pm Fri, 11am-9:30pm Sat) The beer tanks stand right behind the bar at this welcoming brewpub, so you know your brews are oh-so-fresh. They also pair well with the delicious seafood and sandwiches on the menu, which

---

WORTH A TRIP

BETHANY BEACH

To escape the hubbub in Rehoboth Beach and Dewey Beach, make your way to pretty Bethany Beach. Scan for birds from the nature trail at the **Bethany Beach Nature Center** (🖉302-537-7680; www.inlandbays.org; 807 Garfield Pkwy; ⊙10am-3pm Wed-Fri; trail dawn to dusk; P) FREE then tuck in for a fantastic seafood lunch at nearby **Off the Hook** (🖉302-829-1424; www.offthehookbethany.com; 769 Garfield Pkwy; lunch mains $13-16, dinner mains $20-27; ⊙11:30am-9pm Sun-Thu, to 10pm Fri & Sat). For a quiet beach day, relax at **Fenwick Island State Park** (🖉302-227-2800; www.destateparks.com/park/fenwick-island; Rte 1; Mar-Nov per car out-of-state/in-state $10/5, Dec-Feb free; ⊙sunrise-sunset; P), a barrier island just north of the Maryland border. Based in the park, **Coastal Kayak** (🖉302-539-7999; http://coastalkayak.com; 36840 Coastal Hwy/DE-1; tours $50-55, half-day kayak rental from $35, half-day SUP rental $45, 2hr sailing rental from $80; ⊙9am-6pm Jun-Aug) leads wetlands tours and rents kayaks for self-guided exploring.

WORTH A TRIP

SYMRNA

It may be a speck on the map but a handful of quality stops make Smyrna worthy of a detour on a drive between Wilmington and Dover. For prime wildlife watching in a coastal setting of marshes and maritime forest, head 8 miles east from Smyrna to **Bombay Hook National Wildlife Refuge** (☑302-653-9345; www.fws.gov/refuge/Bombay_Hook; 2591 Whitehall Neck Rd; per vehicle/pedestrian or cyclist $4/2; ☉sunrise-sunset; visitor center 8am-4pm Mon-Fri, also Sat & Sun spring & fall; ℗). Here you can drive the wildlife loop trail and scan for shorebirds and red foxes. On the way back stop for lunch and a hoppy beer at **Brick Works Brewing and Eats** (☑302-508-2523; www.brickworksde.com; 230 S Dupont Blvd; mains $10-28; ☉11am-10pm Sun-Thu, to 11pm Sat & Sun) just before town. Cap off your detour with a trip downtown to **Painted Stave Distilling** (☑302-653-6834; www.paintedstave.com; 106 W Commerce St; ☉6-9pm Thu, 5-10pm Fri, noon-6pm Sat, 1-5pm Sun), housed in an old movie theater. Word of mouth is strong for this venture, where the names of many of the spirits give a nod to famous films. Delaware is known for its love of scrapple – a term for scraps of edible pork – and Painted Stave pays homage to the meat with a scrapple-flavored vodka called Off the Hoof. Hmmm. Tastings and tours are available. Smyrna is 11 miles north of Dover via US 13.

changes daily. The vibe is easygoing and the bar area is an easy place to hang out in.

❶ Getting There & Away

Dewey is about 120 miles from both Washington, DC and Baltimore, MD. You can typically get to the beach in less than three hours from either place.

BestBus (www.bestbus.com) offers bus service from DC ($40, 2¼ hours) and NYC ($49, 4½ hours) to Dewey (late May through early September only).

The Jolly Trolley (www.jollytrolly.com) connects Rehoboth and Dewey beaches. A round-trip costs $5, and the trolley runs from 8am to 2am June to August. Cash only.

Wilmington

☑302 / POP 71,442

A unique cultural milieu (African Americans, Jews and Caribbeans) and an energetic arts scene make this city worth a visit. Wilmington is also a good launchpad for exploring the scenic Brandywine Valley, 6 miles north, and its many historic homes, gardens and mills. Much of the current grandeur traces back to the Du Pont family, whose legacy began with a gunpowder mill on the banks of the Brandywine River. The 1.3-mile downtown riverfront along the Christina River is a nice place for a patio meal and a stroll. And no description of Wilmington is complete without mentioning hometown politician Joe Biden, former vice-president and US senator, who regularly rode Amtrak between Wilmington and Washington, DC. After his tenure as vice-president ended in 2017, he rode Amtrak home.

◉ Sights

Delaware Art Museum　　　　MUSEUM
(☑302-571-9590; www.delart.org; 2301 Kentmere Pkwy; adult/child 7-18yr $12/6, 4-8pm Thu & Sun free; ☉10am-4pm Wed & Fri-Sun, to 8pm Thu; ℗) Exhibits work of the local Brandywine School, including Edward Hopper, John Sloan and three generations of Wyeths. The museum's fantastic collection of original works by illustrator Howard Pyle, a native of Wilmington, is showcased in six galleries.

Ebright Azimuth　　　　NATURAL FEATURE
(Ebright Rd, at Ramblewood Dr) FREE At 447.65 ft, the highest point in Delaware does not share lofty views or pose a challenge for access. In fact, you can drive there, park on a cross street and walk to it in about five steps. There's a marker and a bench, and it's fun for a photo. The marker is just south of the Pennsylvania state line.

Delaware Center for the Contemporary Arts　　　　MUSEUM
(☑302-656-6466; www.decontemporary.org; 200 S Madison St; ☉noon-5pm Tue & Sun, noon-7pm Wed, 10am-5pm Thu-Sat; ℗) FREE Consistently displays innovative exhibitions across seven galleries. Many of the works are for sale.

⊨ Sleeping

Inn at Wilmington　　　　HOTEL $$
(☑302-479-7900; www.innatwilmington.com; 300 Rocky Run Pkwy; r $119; ste $179-229; ℗❄@✿) This good-value option sits inside a nondescript hotel building – reminiscent of most midlevel national chains – 5 miles north of

downtown. Decor is well-loved but also well-kept, and rooms come with a mini-fridge and microwave. Hot breakfast buffet included. Not far from Brandywine Valley attractions.

★**Hotel du Pont** HOTEL **$$$**
(☎302-594-3100; www.hoteldupont.com; 42 W 11th St, cnr Market & 11th Sts; r $439-459; ste $899; P ❄ ☎) Under new ownership in 2017 after 100 years as a Du Pont–owned property, there is only one word to describe this revamped hotel: opulent. The premier hotel in the state, the Du Pont is luxurious and classy enough to satisfy its namesake (one of America's most successful industrialist families). The spot exudes an art-deco majesty that Jay Gatsby would have embraced.

Eating

Mrs. Robino's ITALIAN **$**
(☎302-652-9223; www.mrsrobinos.com; 520 N Union St; mains $10-15; ⏱11am-8:30pm Mon-Thu, 11am-9pm Fri, noon-10pm Sat, noon-8:30pm Sun) It feels like mama's house at Mrs. Robino's, where warm service, hearty Italian fare and happy families are highlights. Open since 1940, the restaurant is tucked inside three adjoining row houses. You'll get two courses for $10 on Tuesdays.

Iron Hill Brewery PUB FOOD **$$**
(☎302-472-2739; www.ironhillbrewery.com; 620 Justison St; mains $12-30; ⏱11:30am-11pm Mon-Fri, from 11am Sat & Sun) The spacious and airy multilevel Iron Hill Brewery is set in a converted brick warehouse on the riverfront. Satisfying microbrews pair nicely with the hearty pub fare.

Drinking & Nightlife

Two Stones Pub CRAFT BEER
(☎302-439-3231; www.twostonespub.com; 2502 Foulk Road; ⏱11:30am-1pm Mon-Sat, 10am-1pm Sun) The bartenders make this craft-beer bar something special, answering questions with friendly aplomb and making all feel welcome. Settle in at the long bar and take your pick of local and regional beers from the 24 on tap – be sure to try one of Two Stones' own beers. We liked the easy-drinking 2SP Delco Lager. The pub food here is also fantastic.

Stanley's Tavern BAR
(☎302-475-1887; www.stanelys-tavern.com; 2038 Foulk Rd; ⏱11am-1am Mon-Sat, 10am-1am Sun) It's sports, sport, sports on the television screens at this upbeat and beloved neighborhood bar, sprawled across several rooms in a building that's been a watering hole since 1935. It's an all-ages crowd in the dining room for the burgers, boardwalk fries and American fare. Everyone's here or on the way.

Information

The **visitor center** (☎800-489-6664; www.visitwilmingtonde.com; 100 W 10th St; ⏱9am-5pm Mon-Thu, 8:30am-4:30pm Fri) is downtown.

Getting There & Away

Just off I-95, Wilmington is midway between Washington, DC and New York City, about two hours from either city. **Greyhound** (☎302-655-6111; www.greyhound.com; 101 N French St) stops downtown. Amtrak (www.amtrak.com) trains leave from the **Joseph R. Biden Jr Railroad Station** (☎800-872-7245; www.amtrak.com; 100 S French St) and connect Wilmington with DC (1½ hours), Baltimore (45 minutes) and New York (two hours).

Brandywine Valley

After making their fortune, the French-descended Du Ponts turned the Brandywine Valley into a sort of American Loire Valley. It remains a nesting ground for the wealthy and ostentatious to this day. A few miles north of downtown Wilmington, the Delaware section is just one part of the 350-sq-mile valley, which straddles the Brandywine River into Pennsylvania (p243).

Sights

Hagley Museum & Library MUSEUM
(☎302-658-2400; www.hagley.org; 200 Hagley Creek Rd; adult/child 6-14yr $15/6; ⏱10am-5pm mid-Mar–early Nov, to 4pm early Nov–mid-Mar; P) The Du Pont family got its start here in 1802 making...gunpowder. In the museum, check out the exhibits about the family's early history then join a guided tour to explore the grounds, the garden and various buildings beside the Brandywine River, including the Georgian-style ancestral home. The complex was known as the Eleutherian Mills. Tours last about two hours. To see the museum only, and not the grounds, the fee is $7.

Brandywine Creek State Park STATE PARK
(☎302-577-3534; www.destateparks.com/park/brandywine-creek; 41 Adams Dam Rd; Mar-Nov per vehicle in-state/out-of-state $4/8, Dec-Feb free; ⏱8am-sunset; nature center 8am-4pm Mon-Fri; P) This state park is the gem of the area. A green space this size would be impressive anywhere, but is doubly so considering how

close it is to prodigious urban development. Nature trails and shallow streams wend through the park. Come here to watch the annual hawk migrations, flying north in the spring (March to May) and south in the fall (September to November).

Winterthur   HISTORIC SITE
(☑302-888-4600; www.winterthur.org; 5105 Kennett Pike/Rte 52; adult/child 2-11yr $20/6; ⊙10am-5pm Tue-Sun Mar-Dec, closed Jan & Feb) Six miles northwest of Wilmington is the 175-room country estate of industrialist Henry Francis du Pont and his collection of antiques and American arts, one of the world's largest. Nice gardens too.

☞ Tours

Wilderness Canoe Trips   CANOEING
(☑302-654-2227; www.wildernesscanoetrips.com; 2111 Concord Pike; solo kayak from $53, tandem kayak or canoe trip from $63, tube $23) Call this outfit for information about paddling or tubing down the dark-green and slow-moving Brandywine Creek. Paddlers will be shuttled to the starting point. All trips end at Bransywine Creek State Park. Trips are not guided.

❶ Getting There & Away

Greyhound stops at the Wilmington Transportation Center (p303). Amtrak trains also leave from here and connect Wilmington with DC (1½ hours), Baltimore (45 minutes) and New York (two hours).

New Castle
☑302 / POP 5372

As cute as a colonial kitten, New Castle is a web of cobble-stoned streets and beautifully preserved 18th-century buildings lying near a riverfront (that said, the surrounding area is unfortunately a bit of an urban wasteland). Sights include the Old Court House, the arsenal on the Green, churches and cemeteries dating back to the 17th century, and historic houses.

◉ Sights

Amstel House   MUSEUM
(☑302-322-2794; www.newcastlehistory.org; 2 E 4th St; adult/child 6-12yr $6/2, with Dutch House $10/3; ⊙10am-4pm Wed-Sat, from noon Sun Apr-Dec) One of three museums overseen by the New Castle Historical Society, this house is a surviving remnant of 1730s colonial opulence. Guided tours available April through December.

Dutch House   MUSEUM
(☑302-322-2794; www.newcastlehistory.org; 32 E 3rd St; adult/child 6-12yr $6/2, with Amstel House $10/3; ⊙10am-4pm Wed-Sat, from noon Sun Apr-Dec) A small example of a working residence dating from the late 1600s. Tours offered at 1pm and 3pm.

Old Court House   MUSEUM
(☑302-323-4453; http://history.delaware.gov; 211 Delaware St; ⊙10am-4:30pm Tue-Sat, 1:30-4:30pm Sun) FREE Built in 1732, and now a state-operated museum, this was the first court and state capitol in Delaware. The state colonial assembly met here from 1732 until 1777. Open year-round.

▣ Sleeping & Eating

Terry House B&B   B&B $
(☑302-690-2275; www.terryhouse.com; 130 Delaware St; r $90-110; P❋🐾) The owner of the five-room Terry House B&B will sometimes play the piano for guests while they enjoy a full breakfast. That's a treat for sure, but we're more impressed by the historical grounds and the supremely cozy rooms; there's nothing like stepping from a historical village into historical accommodations.

Dog House   AMERICAN $
(☑302-328-5380; 1200 N Dupont Hwy; mains under $10; ⊙10:30am-midnight) This unassuming countertop diner on the outskirts of New Castle might be the best dining option in town. Don't be fooled by the name; while this place does hot dogs and does them exceedingly well (the chili dogs are a treat), it also whips out mean subs and cheesesteaks that could pass muster in Philly.

Jessop's Tavern   AMERICAN $$
(☑302-322-6111; www.jessops-tavern; 114 Delaware St; mains $12-24; ⊙11:30am-9pm Mon-Thu, to 10pm Fri & Sat, to 8pm Sun) Tonight we're going to party like its 1679. On the Bill of Fare you'll find Dutch pot roast, a 'Pilgrim's Feast' (oven-roasted turkey with all the fixings) and Belgian beers, all served in a colonial atmosphere. Offers 21 beers on draft – 13 Belgian and eight craft. The building dates from 1674.

❶ Information

Stop by the **visitor center** (☑302-322-2794; www.newcastlehistory.org; 30 Market St; ⊙9:30am-4:30pm Mon-Sat, 11:30am-4pm Sun Apr-Dec, Sat & Sun only Jan-Mar) for a walking-tour map showing historic sights downtown. Called the Arsenal, the visitor-center building served as an ammunition storage facility during the War of 1812.

ⓘ Getting There & Away

New Castle borders the Delaware River. Hwy 9 connects New Castle with Wilmington, which is 7 miles north.

Dover

📃 302 / POP 37,786

Dover's city center is quite attractive; the row-house-lined streets are peppered with restaurants and shops, while broadleaf trees spread their branches over pretty little lanes. Most museums and historic sites are downtown near the capitol, with a couple just south of downtown off Rte 1. Dover Air Force Base is 4 miles south of downtown.

◉ Sights

Old State House   MUSEUM
(📞302-744-5054; http://history.delaware.gov/museums; 25 The Green; ⏱9am-4:30pm Mon-Sat, 1:30-4:30pm Sun) **FREE** Take a moment to enjoy the short docent-led tour of this small but interesting former state capitol building. Built in 1791 and since restored, the Old State House contains art galleries and in-depth exhibits about the First State's history and politics. We learned here that every state house in the USA has a portrait of George Washington!

Johnson Victrola Museum   MUSEUM
(📞302-739-3262; https://history.delaware.gov/museums; 375 S New St; ⏱9am-4:30pm Wed-Sat) Throw your doubts aside. This small niche museum is pretty darn cool. Delaware native Eldridge Reeve Johnson founded the Victor Talking Machine Company, and this collection spotlights his life's work. Knowledgeable docents will crank up a 1903 Victrola for you and spin an old tune on a 78-rpm recording. Dog lovers can learn the story of Nipper the Victrola dog.

First State Heritage Park
Welcome Center & Galleries   MUSEUM
(📞302-739-9194; www.destateparks.com/heritagepark; 121 Martin Luther King Blvd N; ⏱8am-4:30pm Mon-Fri, 9am-4:30pm Sat, 1:30-4:30pm Sun; 🅿) **FREE** Delve into the history of Delaware at First State Heritage Park, which also serves as a welcome center for the city of Dover, the state of Delaware and the adjacent state house. This so-called 'park without boundaries' includes 19 historic sites within a few blocks of one another. Start out at the Welcome Center & Galleries, which has exhibitions exploring Delaware's history. You can

Dover

◉ Sights
1 First State Heritage Park Welcome
    Center & Galleries............................B3
2 Johnson Victrola Museum..................A3
3 Old State House...................................B3

🛏 Sleeping
4 Home2 Suites.......................................B2
5 State Street Inn....................................A2

🍴 Eating
6 Flavors of India.................................... B1

🍷 Drinking & Nightlife
7 Golden Fleece.......................................A3
8 Governor's Cafe A2

pick up more info about other key attractions nearby along with a walking map.

John Dickinson Plantation   MUSEUM
(📞302-739-3277; http://history.delaware.gov/museums; 340 Kitts Hummock Rd; ⏱10am-4:30pm Tue-Sat year-round, 1:30-4:30pm Sun Apr-Sep; 🅿) **FREE** A restored 18th-century home of the founding father of the same name, also known as the Penman of the Revolution for his eloquent written arguments for independence. Dickinson is perhaps not as well known as some colonial statesmen because

he did not sign the Declaration of Independence. He was a cautious and contemplative man, they say, but he did sign the Constitution. On-site colonial-era demonstrations – weaving, knitting, fabric dyeing – are held on Saturdays.

Air Mobility Command Museum   MUSEUM
(☑ 302-677-5938; www.amcmuseum.org; 1301 Heritage Rd; ☺ 9am-4pm Tue-Sun; P) FREE If you're into aviation, you'll enjoy this museum; the nearby airfield holds more than 30 restored vintage cargo and freight planes, including C-130s, a Vietnam War–era C-7 and a WWII–era 'Flying Boxcar.' Guided tours avaliable.

Dover Air Force Base (AFB) is a visible symbol of American military muscle and a poignant reminder of the cost of war. This is the location of the Department of Defense's largest mortuary, and traditionally the first stop on native soil for the remains of American service members killed overseas.

Festivals & Events

★ **Firefly Music Festival**   MUSIC
(☑ 312-253-6545; www.fireflyfestival.com; 1131 N Dupont Hwy, The Woodlands; ☺ mid-Jun) Four-day music festival with current indie rock headliners plus an iconic old-timer or two. Past headliners include the Killers, Arctic Monkeys, Kendrick Lamar, Eminem and Bob Dylan. Held at the Woodlands at Dover International Speedway.

Sleeping

State Street Inn   B&B $
(☑ 302-734-2294; www.statestreetinn.com; 228 N State St; r $100-135; ❉ ☎) The four cute bedrooms in this Tudor Revival home in the Victorian Dover historic district are each named for their predominant color scheme. All are on the 2nd floor. Under new ownership in 2017, the inn offers an unbeatable central location within walking distance of downtown. There's an exercise room inside and a putting green out back.

Home2 Suites   HOTEL $$
(☑ 302-674-3300; http://home2suites3.hilton.com; 222 S Dupont Hwy; ste $139-169; P ❉ ☎ ❉ ❉) This new all-suites hotel is a short drive – or a half-mile walk – from downtown. Well-suited for multiday stays, suites are modern, spacious and have full kitchenettes. There's also a combo laundry-fitness area. Hot breakfast included.

Eating & Drinking

Restaurant 55   BURGERS $
(☑ 302-535-8102; www.myrestaurant55.com; 2461 S State St; mains $10-15; ☺ 11am-2pm Tue-Fri, 4-9pm Tue-Thu, 4-10pm Fri, noon-10pm Sat, noon-8pm Sun) An all-ages crowds muscles in for the black-and-bleu burger and other gourmet patties at this hopping restaurant not far from Dover Air Force Base. Regional craft beer from Dogfish Head, Dewey Beer and Evolution keeps the grown-ups happy.

Flavors of India   INDIAN $$
(☑ 302-677-0121; www.flavorofindiade.com; 348 N Dupont Hwy; mains $12-19; ☺ 11am-10pm; P ☑ ❉) To say this place is an unexpected delight would be an understatement. First: it's in a Super 8 Motel off the highway. Second: it's great. The standards – vindaloos and kormas and tikka masalas – are all wonderful. Goat *palakwala* (goat curry with a spinach base)? Amazing. Also by far the best vegetarian option in the area.

Governor's Cafe   COFFEE, WINE
(☑ 302-747-7531; www.governorscafe.com; 144 Kings Hwy SW; ☺ 7:30am-10pm Mon-Fri, 10am-10pm Sat, 10am-8pm Sun) In a rambling 1850s house across the street from the Governor's Mansion, this inviting place is a talented multi-tasker. Pop in early to grab a coffee and a pastry to go. Come by in the afternoon to nibble cheese and read on the porch. Sip a cocktail in the cozy bar after work. Or tuck in at night for wine and a civilized meal.

Mains range from chicken-salad wrap to crab cakes ($7 to $10).

Golden Fleece   PUB
(☑ 302-674-1776; www.goldenfleecetavern.com; 132 W Loockerman St; mains $4-11; ☺ 6pm-1am Sat-Thu, from 4pm Fri) The best bar in Dover also serves up some good food – that you can order from the local pizza joint. First priority is maintaining the atmosphere of an old English pub, which meshes well with the surrounding red-brick Dover historical center. Has an outdoor patio for summer nights.

ℹ Getting There & Away

Dover is 50 miles south of Wilmington via Rte 1. US 301 connects Dover and Baltimore, which is 85 miles west. DART Bus 301 runs between Wilmington and the Dover Transit Center (www.dartfirststate.com), which is a half-mile from downtown Dover. The one-way fare is $6. **Greyhound** (☑ 800-231-2222; www.greyhound.com; 654 N Dupont Hwy) buses stop 2 miles north of downtown.

Maryland

POP 6,052,177

Best Places to Eat

➡ Blacksmith Bar & Restaurant (p328)

➡ Woodberry Kitchen (p319)

➡ Thames St Oyster House (p318)

➡ Vin 909 (p324)

➡ Out of the Fire (p326)

➡ Helmand (p318)

Best Places to Stay

➡ Sagamore Pendry (p317)

➡ Back Creek Inn (p338)

➡ Historic Inns of Annapolis (p323)

➡ HI Baltimore Hostel (p316)

Why Go?

The nickname 'America in Miniature' perfectly captures Maryland: this small state possesses all of the best bits of the country, from the Appalachian Mountains in the west to sandy white beaches in the east. A blend of northern street smarts and Southern down-home appeal gives this border state an appealing identity crisis. Its main city, Baltimore, is a sharp, demanding port town; the Eastern Shore jumbles art-and-antique-minded city escapees and working fishermen; and the DC suburbs are packed with government and office workers seeking green space, and the poor seeking lower rents. Yet it all somehow works – scrumptious blue crabs, Natty Boh beer and lovely Chesapeake country being the glue that binds it all. This is also an extremely diverse and progressive state, and was one of the first in the USA to legalize gay marriage.

When to Go
Baltimore

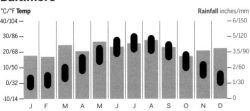

Apr Baseball season kicks off and Baltimore Orioles fans head to Camden Yards (p319).

Jul Prime beach season in Ocean City (p330); July 4 is celebrated across the state.

Oct Head to the mountains for colorful foliage and a scenic railroad ride.

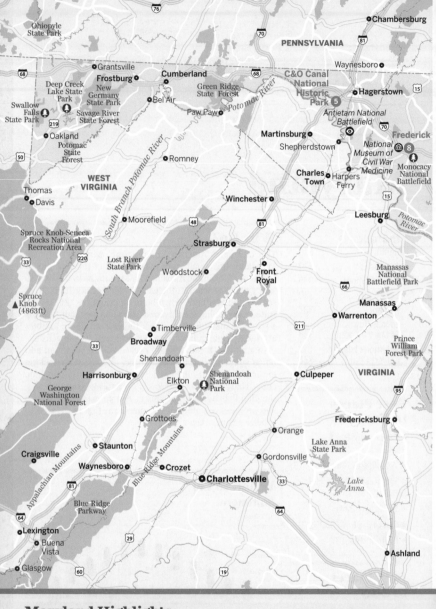

Maryland Highlights

1 **Chesapeake Bay Seafood** (p331) Cracking steamed crabs at one of the seafood joints along the bay.

2 **Baltimore** (p310) Considering art at one of the city's terrific museums, such as the edgy American Visionary Art Museum.

3 **Assateague Island** (p329) Enjoying the sun and searching for birds.

4 **Annapolis** (p320) Drinking beer at a waterfront bar while watching the sailboats and yachts pull into Ego Alley.

York

Philadelphia

Gettysburg
Hanover

Camden

95

83

Wilmington

Gunpowder Falls
State Park

Newark
New
Castle

Westminster

1

Havre De
Grace

Elkton

NEW
JERSEY

New
Windsor

Bel Air

Salem

Vineland

Mount
Airy

Loch Raven
Reservoir
Park

95

Aberdeen

Middletown

Bridgeton

Millville

70

Sykesville

Patapsco Valley
State Park

Elk Neck
State Park

Joppatowne

Patuxent
River
State Park

2 Baltimore

301

Ellicott
City

Fort McHenry
National Monument
& Historic Shrine

Chestertown

Dover

Delaware
Bay

270

Gaithersburg

Baltimore/Washington
International Thurgood
Marshall Airport

301

Rockville

95

DISTRICT OF
COLUMBIA

Annapolis

Bowie

4

1 Chesapeake Bay

Milford

WASHINGTON, DC

495

St Michaels

50

Arlington

Chesapeake Bay
Maritime Museum

Cannonball
House

404

DELAWARE

Alexandria

Rebecca
T Ruark

7 St Michaels &
Tilghman Island

Easton

Lewes

Woodbridge

Cedarville
State Forest

Huntingtown

Federalsburg

Georgetown

Rehoboth
Beach

Indian
Head

Waldorf

Harriet Tubman
Underground
Railroad National
Historical Park &
Visitor Center

Cambridge

Seaford

50

La Plata
Gilbert
Run Park

Hughesville

Blackwater
National
Wildlife Refuge

113

301

Calvert
Cliffs
State Park

Salisbury

Calvin B Taylor
House Museum

Newburg

Leonardtown
Wharf Park

Crapo

50

Berlin

6

St Marys River
Watershed Park

Lexington
Park

Whitehaven

Ward Museum of
Wildfowl Art

Assateague
State Park

Ocean
City

Westmoreland
State Park

Historic St
Mary's City

Princess
Anne

Assateague Island
National Seashore

Ridge

Point
Lookout
State Park

13

Pokomoke
City

3 Assateague
Island

Tappahannock

Janes Island
State Park

Crisfield

Chincoteague National
Wildlife Refuge

ATLANTIC
OCEAN

360

VIRGINIA

0   50 km
0   25 miles

N

1

95

Delaware River

5 **C&O Canal National
Historic Park** (p334) Cycling
along a scenic and historic
towpath beside the Potomac
River.

6 **Berlin** (p328) Exploring
the shops, restaurants and
historic hotels in Berlin and
other charming small towns.

7 **St Michaels & Tilghman
Island** (p325) Hopping

aboard a sailboat for a sunset
cruise.

8 **Frederick** (p332)
Strolling Carroll Creek Park
then enjoying First Saturday
festivities.

History

George Calvert established Maryland as a refuge for persecuted English Catholics in 1634 when he purchased St Mary's City from the local Piscataway tribe, with whom he initially tried to coexist. Puritan refugees drove both Piscataway and Catholics from control and shifted power to Annapolis; their harassment of Catholics produced the Tolerance Act, a flawed but progressive law that allowed freedom of any (Christian) worship in Maryland – a North American first.

A commitment to diversity has always characterized this state, despite a mixed record on slavery. Although state loyalties were split during the Civil War, a Confederate invasion was halted here in 1862 at Antietam. Following the war, Maryland harnessed its black, white and immigrant work force, splitting the economy between Baltimore's industry and shipping, and the later need for services in Washington, DC. Today the answer to 'What makes a Marylander?' is 'all of the above': the state mixes rich, poor, foreign-born, urban sophisticates and rural villages like few other states do.

BALTIMORE

410, 443, 667 / POP 614,664

Once among the most important port towns in America, Baltimore – or 'Bawlmer' to locals – is a city of contradictions. It remains a defiant, working-class city tied to its nautical past, but in recent years has earned acclaim for impressive, up-to-the-minute entrepreneurial ventures, from new boutique hotels and edgy exhibits at world-class museums to forgotten neighborhoods now bustling with trendy food courts and farm-to-table restaurants. But don't worry, traditionalists – local culture and hometown sports, from lacrosse to baseball, remain part of the appeal.

For travelers, a visit to B'more (another nickname) should include one trip to the waterfront, whether it's the Disney-fied Inner Harbor, the cobblestoned streets of portside Fells Point or the shores of Fort McHenry, birthplace of America's national anthem, 'The Star-Spangled Banner.' As you'll discover, there's an intense, sincere friendliness here, which is why Baltimore lives up to its final, most accurate nickname: 'Charm City.'

⊙ Sights

⊙ Harbor Place & Inner Harbor

This is where most tourists start and, unfortunately, end their Baltimore sightseeing. The Inner Harbor is a big, gleaming waterfront-renewal project of shiny glass, air-conditioned malls and flashy bars that manages to capture the maritime heart of this city, albeit in a safe-for-the-whole-family kinda way. The neighborhood is home to an amazing aquarium and several impressive historic ships, but these worthy sights are just the tip of Baltimore's iceberg.

National Aquarium   AQUARIUM
(Map p312; ☑410-576-3800; www.aqua.org; 501 E Pratt St, Piers 3 & 4; adult/child $40/25; ☺9am-5pm Sun-Thu, to 8pm Fri, to 6pm Sat, varies seasonally; ☑) Standing seven stories high and capped by a glass pyramid, this is widely considered to be America's best aquarium, with almost 20,000 creatures from more than 700 species, a rooftop rainforest, a multistory shark tank and a vast re-creation of an Indo-Pacific reef that is home to blacktip reef sharks, a green sea turtle and stingrays. There's also a reconstruction of the Umbrawarra Gorge in Australia's Northern Territory, complete with 35ft waterfall, rocky cliffs and free-roaming birds and lizards.

The largest exhibit contains seven bottlenose dolphins kept in captivity, though at press time the aquarium was planning to retire them to an oceanside sanctuary (freeing them to the wild is not an option, since they lack survival skills) by 2020. These dolphins no longer perform in shows. Kids will love the 4D Immersion Theater (admission costs an additional $5). There are loads of unique, behind-the-scenes tours, as well as dolphin and shark sleepovers. Go on weekdays (right at opening time) to beat the crowds.

Historic Ships in Baltimore   MUSEUM
(Map p312; ☑410-539-1797; www.historicships. org; 301 E Pratt St, Piers 1, 3 & 5; adult/student/ child from $15/13/7; ☺10am-5pm, hours vary seasonally; ☑) Ship lovers can tour four historic ships: a coast guard cutter that saw action in Pearl Harbor, a 1930 lightship, a submarine active in WWII and the USS *Constellation* – one of the last sail-powered warships built (in 1797) by the US Navy. You can opt for a two- or four-vessel admission ticket. If you only see two, include the four-deck USS *Constellation*, which spotlights the stories

of past crew members. Admission to the 1856 Seven Foot Knoll Lighthouse, on Pier 5, is free.

◉ Downtown & Little Italy

You can easily walk from downtown Baltimore to Little Italy, but follow the delineated path: there's a rough housing project along the way.

National Great Blacks in Wax Museum
MUSEUM
(☎410-563-3404; www.greatblacksinwax.org; 1601 E North Ave; adult/student/child $15/14/12; ⊗9am-5pm Tue-Sat, from noon Sun) This simple but thought-provoking African American history museum has exhibits spotlighting Frederick Douglass, Jackie Robinson, Dr Martin Luther King Jr and Barack Obama, as well as lesser-known figures such as explorer Matthew Henson. It also covers slavery, the Jim Crow era and African leaders – all told in surreal but informative fashion through Madame Tussaud–style wax figures. Unflinching exhibits about the horrors of slave ships and lynchings are graphic and may not be suitable for younger children.

Extended hours in July and August. For a compelling first-person introduction to the museum, listen to NPR's *This American Life* Episode 627: 'Suitable for Children,' which aired in October 2017 and is archived online (www.thisamericanlife.org).

Star-Spangled Banner Flag House & 1812 Museum
MUSEUM
(Map p312; ☎410-837-1793; www.flaghouse.org; 844 E Pratt St; adult/child $9/7; ⊗10am-4pm Tue-Sat; ♿) This historic home, built in 1793, is where Mary Pickersgill sewed the gigantic flag that inspired America's national anthem. Costumed interpreters and 19th-century artifacts transport visitors back in time to dark days during the War of 1812; there's also a hands-on discovery gallery for kids.

Jewish Museum of Maryland
MUSEUM
(Map p312; ☎410-732-6400; www.jewishmuseummd.org; 15 Lloyd St; adult/student/child $10/6/4; ⊗10am-5pm Sun-Thu) Maryland has traditionally been home to one of the largest, most active Jewish communities in the country, and this is a fine place to explore their experience in America. The exhibit *Voices of Lombard Street: A Century of Change in East Baltimore* skillfully showcases the Jewish immigrant experience in Jones Falls and along the Lombard Stand commercial district. The museum also hous-

SMALL MUSEUMS

Baltimore does niche museums very well. If you like digging into a specific topic, you'l find a range of good options.

B&O Railroad Museum (Map p312; ☎410-752-2490; www.borail.org; 901 W Pratt St; adult/child $20/12; ⊗10am-4pm Mon-Sat, from 11am Sun; P♿) See the 60ft turntable in the 1884 Roundhouse.

Babe Ruth Museum (Map p312; ☎410-727-1539; www.baberuthmuseum.com; 216 Emory St; adult/child $10/5; ⊗10am-5pm, closed Mon Oct-Mar) Learn the Great Bambino's life story.

Evergreen Museum (☎410-516-0341; http://museums.jhu.edu; 4545 N Charles St; adult/child $8/5; ⊗11am-4pm Tue-Fri, from noon Sat & Sun; P) Peruse the fine-art collection of a savvy 19th-century millionaire collector.

Edgar Allan Poe House & Museum (Map p312; ☎410-462-1763; www.poeinbaltimore.org; 203 N Amity St; adult/student/child $5/4/free; ⊗11am-4pm Thu-Sun) Explore the home of the macabre poet and writer.

es two wonderfully preserved historical synagogues. Call or check the museum's website for the scheduled hours of synagogue tours.

Edgar Allan Poe's Gravesite
CEMETERY
(Map p312; ☎410-706-2072; www.westminsterhall.org; 519 W Fayette St, cnr N Greene St, Westminster Hall; ⊗grounds 8am-dusk) Horror writer Edgar Allan Poe was buried twice on the grounds of Westminster Hall. His body was first deposited in an unmarked grave behind the church after his death in 1849. In 1875, his remains were moved to the northwest corner of the property, where they are now marked by a sturdy four-sided monument. Note the engraved birthday – it's incorrect. Poe was born on January 19, not January 20.

◉ Mt Vernon

Just north of downtown, this progressive and walkable neighborhood is dotted with museums. Inviting indie bars and restaurants line N Charles St. The towering Washington Monument anchors the neighborhood.

★ Walters Art Museum
MUSEUM
(Map p312; ☎410-547-9000; www.thewalters.org; 600 N Charles St; ⊗10am-5pm Wed & Fri-Sun, to

Baltimore

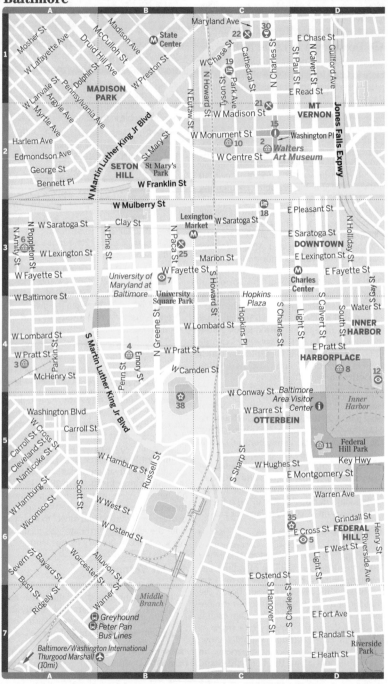

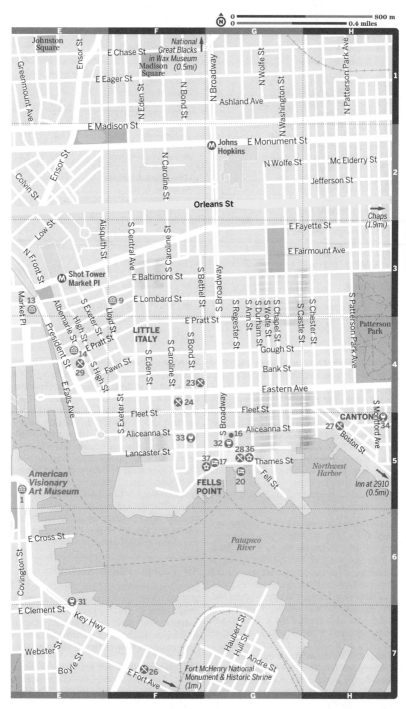

MARYLAND

National
Great Blacks
in Wax Museum
Madison (0.5mi)
Square

Johnston
Square

E Chase St

E Eager St

E Madison St

Johns
Hopkins

E Monument St

Mc Elderry St

Jefferson St

Orleans St

Chaps
(1.9mi)

E Fayette St

E Fairmount Ave

Shot Tower
Market Pl

E Baltimore St

E Lombard St

E Pratt St

LITTLE
ITALY

Gough St

Bank St

Eastern Ave

23

24

Fleet St

Fleet St

CANTON

Aliceanna St

Aliceanna St

27

Lancaster St

33

32

16

28 36

Thames St

Northwest
Harbor

American
Visionary
Art Museum

37 17

20

FELLS
POINT

Fell St

Inn at 2910
(0.5mi)

Patapsco
River

E Cross St

E Clement St

Key Hwy

31

Webster
St

Boyle St

E Fort Ave

26

Fort McHenry National
Monument & Historic Shrine
(1mi)

Baltimore

9pm Thu) **FREE** The magnificent Chamber of Wonders re-creates the library of an imagined 17th-century scholar, one with a taste for the exotic. The abutting Hall of Arms and Armor displays the most impressive collection of medieval weaponry you'll see this side of *Game of Thrones*. In sum, don't pass up this excellent, eclectic museum. It spans more than 55 centuries, from ancient to contemporary, with top-notch displays of Asian treasures, rare and ornate manuscripts and books, and a comprehensive French paintings collection.

Washington Monument MONUMENT
(Map p312; ☏410-962-5070; www.mvpconservancy.org; 699 Washington Pl; adult/child $6/4; ◷10am-5pm Wed-Sun) For the best views of Baltimore, climb the 227 marble steps of the 178ft-tall Doric column dedicated to America's founding father, George Washington. The monument was designed by Robert Mills, who also created DC's Washington Monument, and is looking better than ever following a $6-million restoration project. The ground floor contains a museum about Washington's life. To climb the monument, buy a ticket on-site or reserve online. Spaces are limited. The 1st-floor gallery is free.

Maryland Historical Society MUSEUM
(Map p312; ☏410-685-3650; www.mdhs.org; 201 W Monument St; adult/child $9/6; ◷10am-5pm Wed-Sat, from noon Sun) With more than 350,000 objects and seven million books and documents, this is among the world's largest collections of Americana. Highlights include one of two surviving Revolutionary War officer's uniforms, photographs from the Civil Rights movement in Baltimore, and Francis Scott Key's original manuscript of 'The Star-Spangled Banner' (displayed at the top of the hour). The 10ft-tall replica mastodon – the original was preserved by artist and Maryland native Charles Wilson Peale – is impressive. A few original bones are displayed.

◉ Federal Hill & Around

On a bluff overlooking the harbor, Federal Hill Park lends its name to the comfortable neighborhood that's set around **Cross St Market** (Map p312; www.southbaltimore.com; 1065 S Cross St, btwn Light & Charles Sts; ◷7am-7pm) and comes alive after sundown.

★**American Visionary Art Museum** MUSEUM
(AVAM; Map p312; ☏410-244-1900; www.avam.org; 800 Key Hwy; adult/child $16/10; ◷10am-6pm

Tue-Sun) Housing a jaw-dropping collection of self-taught (or 'outsider' art), AVAM is a celebration of unbridled creativity free of pretension. Across two buildings and two sculpture parks, you'll find broken-mirror collages, homemade robots and flying apparatuses, elaborate sculptural works made of needlepoint, and gigantic model ships painstakingly created from matchsticks. The whimsical automatons in the Cabaret Mechanical Theater are worth a closer look. And don't miss the famous Flatulence Post and its, er, 'fart art' in the Basement Gallery.

Fort McHenry National
Monument & Historic Shrine   HISTORIC SITE
(☑410-962-4290; www.nps.gov/fomc; 2400 E Fort Ave; adult/child $10/free; ⊙9am-5pm; Ⓟ) On September 13 and 14, 1814, this star-shaped fort successfully repelled a British navy attack during the Battle of Baltimore. After a long night of bombs bursting in the air, shipbound prisoner Francis Scott Key saw, 'by dawn's early light,' the tattered flag still waving. Inspired, he penned 'The Star-Spangled Banner,' which was set to the tune of a popular drinking song.

⊙ Fells Point & Canton

Once the center of Baltimore's shipbuilding industry, the historic cobblestoned neighborhood of Fells Point is now a gentrified mix of 18th-century homes and restaurants, bars and shops. The neighborhood has been the setting for several films and TV series, most notably *Homicide: Life on the Street*. Further

east, the slightly more sophisticated streets of Canton fan out, with its grassy square surrounded by great restaurants and bars.

⊙ Hampden, Remington & North Baltimore

The 'Hon' expression of affection – an oft-imitated, never-quite-duplicated 'Bawlmerese' peculiarity – originated in Hampden, an area straddling the line between working class and hipster-creative class. Spend a lazy afternoon browsing kitsch, antiques and vintage clothing along the Avenue (aka W 36th St). To get to Hampden, take I-83 N, merge onto Falls Rd (northbound) and take a right onto the Avenue. The prestigious **Johns Hopkins University** (Map p316; ☑410-516-8000; www.jhu.edu; 3400 N Charles St) is nearby. South of Johns Hopkins, just east of I-83, new restaurants and housing developments mark rapidly gentrifying Remington, a walkable neighborhood with a demographic similar to that of Hampden.

Baltimore Museum of Art   MUSEUM
(Map p316; ☑443-573-1700; www.artbma.org; 10 Art Museum Dr; ⊙10am-5pm Wed-Sun) ⒻⓇⒺⒺ Works by Van Gogh, Renoir, Degas, Georgia O'Keeffe and Andy Warhol fill the galleries, and the museum hosts thought-provoking temporary exhibits with a contemporary spin. At lunchtime, though, we're not sure whether folks are flowing in for the impressive Matisse collection or the upscale American fare at ever-so-chic **Gertrude's**, the busy on-site cafe (www.gertrudesbaltimore.com).

MARYLAND BALTIMORE

BALTIMORE FOR CHILDREN

Most attractions are centered on the Inner Harbor, including the National Aquarium (p310), perfect for pint-sized visitors as well as pre-teens and teenagers. Kids can run wild o'er the ramparts of Fort McHenry National Monument & Historic Shrine, too, while older children will appreciate the history.

Maryland Science Center (Map p312; ☑410-685-2370; www.mdsci.org; 601 Light St; adult/child $25/19; ⊙10am-5pm Mon-Fri, to 6pm Sat, 11am-5pm Sun, longer hours in summer) is an awesome attraction featuring a three-story atrium, tons of interactive exhibits on dinosaurs, outer space and the human body, and the requisite IMAX theater ($4 extra). This one works well for the whole family.

Two blocks north is the converted fish market of **Port Discovery** (Map p312; ☑410-727-8120; www.portdiscovery.org; 35 Market Pl; $16; ⊙9:30am-4:30pm Tue-Fri, 10am-5pm Sat, noon-5pm Sun, also open Mon Jun-Aug; ♿), which has a tree house, an Egypt-inspired archaeology site and an artist's studio. It's geared to younger kids, so you can wear them out here – especially if they spend time climbing and sliding in the multi-level tree house.

At **Maryland Zoo in Baltimore** (Map p316; ☑410-396-7102; www.marylandzoo.org; 1 Safari Pl, Druid Hill Park; adult/child $19/15; ⊙10am-4pm daily Mar-Dec, Fri-Mon only Jan & Feb; Ⓟ♿), lily-pad-hopping adventures with Billy the Bog Turtle and grooming live animals are all in a day's play. Older kids may enjoy the zookeeper chats – and the reptiles!

North Baltimore

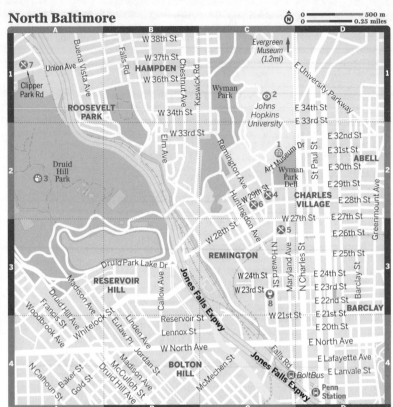

Tours

Baltimore Ghost Tours WALKING
(Map p312; 877-293-1571; www.baltimoreghost
tours.com; per person $15; 7pm Fri & Sat Mar-
Nov) Offers several walking tours exploring
the spooky and bizarre side of Baltimore.
The popular Fells Point ghost walk departs
from Max's on Broadway (731 S Broadway).

Festivals & Events

Preakness Stakes SPORTS
(410-542-9400; www.preakness.com; 5201 Park
Heights Ave) Held the third Saturday in May
at Pimlico, this long-running thoroughbred
horse race is the second of three races comprising the Triple Crown, occurring between
the Kentucky Derby and Belmont Stakes.

HONfest CULTURAL
(www.honfest.net; Jun) FREE Put on your
best 'Bawlmerese' accent and head to Hampden for this celebration of kitsch, beehive
hairdos, rhinestone glasses and other Baltimore eccentricities.

Artscape ART
(www.artscape.org; 140 W Mt Royal Ave, Patricia &
Arthur Modell Performing Arts Center; mid-Jul)
FREE America's largest free arts festival,
lasting three days, features art displays, live
music and theater and dance performances.

Sleeping

HI Baltimore Hostel HOSTEL $
(Map p312; 410-576-8880; www.hiusa.org/bal
timore; 17 W Mulberry St, Mt Vernon; dm $30-31;
P❄@🛜) Located in a beautifully restored
1857 mansion, the HI Baltimore has dorms
with four, eight and 12 beds. Helpful management, a nice location between Mt Vernon
and downtown, and a filigreed classical-chic
look make this one of the region's best hostels. The front desk is open 24 hours. Breakfast is included. Parking is $8 per night.

North Baltimore

Hotel Brexton　　　　　　　HOTEL **$$**
(Map p312; ☑443-478-2100; www.hotelbrex
ton.com; 868 Park Ave, Mt Vernon; r $159-219;
P❋🕲🖥) This redbrick 19th-century land-
mark has recently been reborn as an appeal-
ing, if not overly lavish, hotel. Rooms offer a
mix of wood floors or carpeting, comfy mat-
tresses, mirrored armoires and framed art
prints on the walls. Curious historical foot-
note: Wallis Simpson, the woman for whom
Britain's King Edward VIII abdicated the
throne, lived in this building as a young girl.

Admiral Fell Inn　　　　　　HOTEL **$$**
(Map p312; ☑410-522-7380; www.admiralfell.
com; 888 S Broadway, Fells Point; r from $200;
P❋◉🕲🖥) This old sailors' hotel has been
converted into a lovely inn with Federal-style
furniture and four-poster beds. It has the
best of both of Baltimore's worlds, with historical and nautical details on the one hand,
and ample modern amenities on the other.
Rooms fronting Thames St can be loud late at
night, when Fells Point is in full party mode.

★**Sagamore Pendry**　BOUTIQUE HOTEL **$$$**
(Map p312; ☑443-552-1400; www.pendryho
tels.com; 1715 Thames St, Fells Point; r/ste from
$399/759; P🕲❋🖥) Hunkered command-
ingly on the historic Recreation (Rec) Pier,
this new luxury property is a game changer,
bringing a big dose of charm and panache
to Baltimore's favorite party neighborhood.
With local art on the walls, nautical and
equestrian touches in the common areas,
and an 18th-century cannon on display
(unearthed during construction), the hotel
embraces Charm City's culture and history.

✕ Eating

Handlebar Cafe　　AMERICAN; MEXICAN **$**
(Map p312; ☑443-438-7065; www.handle
barcafe.com; 511 S Caroline St, Fells Point; mains

breakfast $7-13, lunch & dinner $8-15; ◷7am-2am
Tue-Sun, to 3pm Mon) Owned by X-Games
champ Marla Streb, this friendly bike shop
and bistro – adorned with mountain bikes
and gear-themed decor – serves burritos and
wood-fired pizzas behind its big garage door.
Craft beer, live music and an indoor sprint
series too. The vibe is so darn cool even the
clumsiest goof in town will be considering a
career in trick dirt biking.

Ekiben　　　　　　　　　FUSION **$**
(Map p312; ☑410-558-1914; www.ekibenbalti
more.com; 1622 Eastern Ave, Fells Point; mains $9-
12; ◷11am-3:30pm & 4:30-10pm Mon-Thu, to 11pm
Fri & Sat) The 'spicy bird bun' at this Asian fu-
sion box of deliciousness is a sight to behold,
and then devour: a giant piece of curry-fried
chicken practically leaping from the pillowy
embrace of a soft steamed bun. Buns and
bowls are the draw at this tiny spot in Fells
Point. With just a few tables and stools, it's
best for takeout.

Sip & Bite　　　　　DINER; GREEK **$**
(Map p312; ☑410-675-7077; www.sipandbite.com;
2200 Boston St, Canton; mains breakfast $7-12,
lunch & dinner $8-27; ◷7:30am-5am) Yes, you
do want the grilled crab cake with two eggs,
hash browns and toast. And no...don't even
say the word 'diet.' No question, a hearty, ap-
pealingly greasy breakfast or late-night feast
is the way to go at this small Greek-run din-
er that's been open since 1948. Craft beers
and pop art give a nod to a new generation.

R House　　　　　　　　FOOD HALL **$**
(Map p316; ☑443-347-3570; http://r.housebalti
more.com; 301 W 29th St, Remington; mains $4-16;
◷8am-11pm Sun-Wed, to midnight Thu-Sat) This
sleek spot is home to 10 gourmet food stalls
featuring a global array of cuisine from up-
and-coming Baltimore chefs. Take your pick
of *poke*, tacos, arepas, breakfast sandwich-
es, crab cakes and more. With 350 seats, a
center-of-the-action bar, loads of glowing
publicity and local support, this revamped
warehouse is the place to be.

Dooby's Coffee　　　　　　CAFE **$**
(Map p312; ☑410-609-3162; www.doobys.com;
802 N Charles St, Mt Vernon; mains breakfast $5-13,
lunch & dinner $11-14; ◷7am-9:30pm Mon-Thu, to
10pm Fri, 8am-10pm Sat, 8am-4pm Sun; 🖥) This
hip but unpretentious place is equal parts
sunny cafe and creative eating and drinking
spot. Come in the morning for tasty pastries
and egg-and-pepper-jack sandwiches. At
lunchtime or dinner, dive into for Korean-
style rice bowls and toasted sandwiches. It's

ANNE TYLER

Baltimore writer and literary critic Anne Tyler, a native of the city, has set most of her 20-plus novels in the neighborhoods surrounding Johns Hopkins. *The Accidental Tourist* (1985) was turned into an Oscar-winning film starring William Hurt, Kathleen Turner and Geena Davis, and *Breathing Lessons* (1988) won the Pulitzer Prize for Fiction.

a short stroll from the Washington Monument (p314).

Chaps
BARBECUE $

(☑410-483-2379; www.chapspitbeef.com; 5801 Pulaski Hwy; mains $5-19; ⊙10:30am-10pm) This is the go-to stop for pit beef, Baltimore's take on barbecue – thinly sliced top round grilled over charcoal. Park and follow your nose to smoky mouthwatering goodness, and get that beef like a local: shaved onto a kaiser roll with a raw onion slice on top, smothered in 'tiger sauce' (a creamy blend of horseradish and mayonnaise).

Papermoon Diner
DINER $

(Map p316; ☑410-889-4444; www.papermoon diner24.com; 227 W 29th St, Remington; mains $10-25; ⊙7am-9pm Sun, Mon, Wed & Thu, to 10pm Fri & Sat) This brightly colored, quintessential Baltimore diner is decorated with thousands of old toys, creepy mannequins and other quirky knickknacks. The real draw here is the anytime breakfast – fluffy buttermilk pancakes, crispy bacon, and crab-and-artichoke-heart omelets. Wash it down with a caramel-and-sea-salt milkshake.

Lexington Market
FAST FOOD $

(Map p312; www.lexingtonmarket.com; 400 W Lexington St, Mt Vernon; ⊙6am-6pm Mon-Sat) Around since 1782, Mt Vernon's Lexington Market is one of Baltimore's true old-school food markets. It's a bit shabby on the outside, but the food is great. Don't miss the crab cakes at Faidley's seafood stall, because my goodness, they are amazing – maybe the best in the city. There are several parking garages nearby.

Vaccaro's Pastry
ITALIAN $

(Map p312; ☑410-685-4905; www.vaccarospas try.com; 222 Albemarle St, Little Italy; desserts $4-9; ⊙9am-10pm Sun-Thu, to midnight Fri & Sat) Open for more than 60 years, Vaccaro's serves some of the best desserts and coffee in town. The cannolis are legendary.

★Thames St Oyster House
SEAFOOD $$

(Map p312; ☑443-449-7726; www.thamesstreet oysterhouse.com; 1728 Thames St, Fells Point; mains $12-29; ⊙5-9:30pm Sun-Thu, to 10:30pm Fri & Sat, plus 11:30am-2:30pm Wed-Sun) A Fells Point icon, this vintage dining and drinking hall serves some of Baltimore's best seafood. Dine in the polished upstairs dining room with waterfront views, take a seat in the backyard, or plunk down at the bar in front (which stays open till midnight) and watch the drink-makers and oyster-shuckers in action. The lobster rolls are recommended too. Raw bar open until 10:30pm Sunday to Thursday, until 11:30pm Friday and Saturday.

★Helmand
AFGHANI $$

(Map p312; ☑410-752-0311; www.helmand.com; 806 N Charles St, Mt Vernon; mains $14-25; ⊙5-10pm Sun-Thu, to 11pm Fri & Sat) The Helmand is a longtime favorite for its *kaddo borawni* (pumpkin in yogurt-garlic sauce), vegetable platters and flavorful beef-and-lamb meatballs, followed by cardamom ice cream. If you've never tried Afghan cuisine, this is a great place to do so.

Parts & Labor
AMERICAN; SANDWICHES $$

(Map p316; ☑443-873-8887; www.partsand laborbutchery.com; 2600 N Howard St, Remington; mains lunch $10-24, dinner $10-35; ⊙11am-9pm) We like your steampunk style and your hospitality, Parts & Labor. And those snout-to-tail cuts of meat, from fancy bologna to chorizo sausage, are darn fine too. A neighborhood kickstarter in gentrifying Remington, this hip eatery is also a butcher shop. If you're famished, order the 'dad bod' sandwich: smoked ham, pit beef, krakowska sausage, barbecue, onion and 'tiger sauce.'

Faidley
SEAFOOD $$

(Map p312; ☑410-727-4898; www.faidleyscrab cakes.com; 203 N Paca St, Lexington Market; lump crab cakes $15; ⊙10am-5pm Mon-Wed, to 5:30pm Thu-Sat) Here's a fine example of a place that the press and the tourists 'discovered' long ago, yet whose brilliance hasn't been dimmed by the publicity. Faidley is best known for its crab cakes, in-claw meat, backfin (body meat) or all lump (the biggest chunks of body meat). Tuck in at a stand-up counter with a cold beer and know happiness. The surrounding neighborhood is a bit rough, but safe enough during daylight hours.

LP Steamers
SEAFOOD $$

(Map p312; ☑410-576-9294; www.locustpoint steamers.com; 1100 E Fort Ave, South Baltimore; mains $8-27; ⊙11:30am-9:30pm Sun-Thu, to 10pm

Fri & Sat) LP is the best in Baltimore's seafood stakes: working class, teasing smiles and the freshest crabs on the southside. Stop by on your way back from Fort McHenry National Monument (p315).

Dukem ETHIOPIAN $$
(Map p312; ☑410-385-0318; www.dukemres taurant.com; 1100 Maryland Ave, Mt Vernon; mains $7-34; ☺11am-10pm) Dukem is a standout among Baltimore's many Ethiopian places. Delicious mains, including spicy chicken, lamb and vegetarian dishes, all sopped up with spongy injera flatbread.

★**Woodberry Kitchen** AMERICAN $$$
(Map p316; ☑410-464-8000; www.woodberry kitchen.com; 2010 Clipper Park Rd, Woodberry; mains brunch $13-23, dinner $21-45; ☺5-10pm Mon-Thu, to 11pm Fri & Sat, to 9pm Sun, plus brunch 10am-2pm Sat & Sun) The Woodberry takes everything the Chesapeake region has to offer, plops it into a former flour mill and creates culinary magic. The menu is a playful romp through the best of regional produce, seafood and meats, from Maryland rockfish with Carolina Gold grits to Shenandoah Valley lamb with collard greens, and hearty vegetable dishes plucked from nearby farms. Reserve ahead.

🍸 Drinking & Nightlife

Brewer's Art PUB
(Map p312; ☑410-547-6925; www.thebrewersart. com; 1106 N Charles St, Mt Vernon; ☺4pm-1:45am Mon-Fri, from noon Sat & Sun) In a vintage early-20th-century mansion, Brewer's Art serves well-crafted Belgian-style microbrews to a laid-back Mt Vernon crowd. There's tasty pub fare (mac 'n' cheese, cheeseburgers) in the bar, and upscale American cuisine in the elegant back dining room. Head to the subterranean drinking den for a more raucous crowd. During happy hour (4pm to 7pm) house drafts are just $4.

Verde COCKTAIL BAR
(Map p312; ☑410-522-1000; www.verdepizza.com; 641 S Montford Ave, Canton; ☺5-10pm Tue-Thu, to 11pm Mon & Fri, noon-11pm Sat, 11am-10pm Sun) The cocktail game is strong at this trattoria in Canton, also known for its wood-fired pizza. Adding a touch of old-school class? The long marble-topped bar. Elderberry wild kombucha and gin are the key ingredients in the winningly named cocktail 'The piano has been drinking.'

One-Eyed Mike's BAR
(Map p312; ☑410-327-0445; www.oneeyed mikes.com; 708 S Bond St, Fells Point; ☺noon-2am

Mon-Thu, from 11am Fri-Sun) Santa Claus sent us a shot of Grand Marnier during a December jaunt to this cozy gastropub where bottles of the orange-flavored liqueur line the shelves. You too can buy a lifetime membership ($175) to the bar's Grand Marnier Club, more than 2900 strong, and your bottle will be forever reserved. Good cheer and top-notch pub grub are draws too.

Cannon Room COCKTAIL BAR
(Map p312; ☑443-552-1400; www.pendryhotels. com; 1715 Thames St, Fells Point; ☺5pm-2am) The curved roof of this 20-seat whiskey bar, which is tucked in the deep recesses of the Sagamore Pendry (p317), was designed to resemble an oversized whiskey barrel. Look down to see the namesake cannon, which basks in the spotlight beneath a glass-panel floorboard. The cannon dates from the 1700s and was discovered during construction.

Clavel BAR
(Map p316; ☑443-900-8983; www.barclavel.com; 225 W 23rd St, Remington; ☺5pm-1am Mon-Sat, 10am-3pm Sun) Celebrating agave is the stated mission at this sultry gathering spot, where mescal flights and a mescal library are on the menu. Complement that flight with a few of chef Carlos Raba's traditional Mexican tacos, expertly simmered and seasoned with moles, chiles and salsa. They may be the best in town.

Max's Taphouse CRAFT BEER
(Map p312; ☑410-675-6297; www.maxs.com; 737 S Broadway, Fells Point; ☺11am-2am; ☎) A neighborhood bar and then some, this convivial Fells Point institution lures 'em in with 102 rotating taps and more than 1500 bottles. Look for Baltimore favorites from Brewer's Art and Union Craft Brewing, plus plenty of Belgian ales. On-the-ball bartenders keep things moving.

Little Havana BAR
(Map p312; ☑410-837-9903; www.littlehavanas. com; 1325 Key Hwy, Federal Hill; ☺11:30am-midnight Mon-Thu, to 2am Fri & Sat, 11am-midnight Sun) A good after-work spot and a great place to sip mojitos on the waterfront deck, this converted brick warehouse is a major draw on warm, sunny days (especially around weekend brunch time).

☆ Entertainment

★**Oriole Park at Camden Yards** STADIUM
(Map p312; ☑888-848-2473; www.orioles.com; 333 W Camden St, Downtown) The Baltimore Orioles play here, arguably the best ballpark

MARYLAND BALTIMORE

in America, from April through September. Daily tours of the stadium are offered April through November; tours cost $9 for adults, $6 for children under 15 years of age.

8 x 10
LIVE MUSIC

(Map p312; 410-625-200; www.the8x10.com; 10 E Cross St, Federal Hill) It's bigger than 8ft-by-10ft, but this bi-level club in Federal Hill still feels intimate – even when rocking out with jam bands, DJs and great local musicians. For music lovers, this is your place.

Horse You Came In On
LIVE MUSIC

(Map p312; 410-327-8111; www.thehorsebaltimore.com; 1626 Thames St, Fells Point; 11am-1:30am) Live music daily beginning around 1pm. With its drink specials and cowboy-saddle bar stools, the Horse is an unabashed tourist trap, but with enough history for a worthwhile stop. Established in 1775, it's the oldest bar in Baltimore, and they say writer Edgar Allan Poe quaffed his last drink here before his death. Quoth the Raven: We're not so sure.

Cat's Eye Pub
LIVE MUSIC

(Map p312; 410-276-9866; www.catseyepub.com; 1730 Thames St, Fells Point; 2pm-2am Mon-Thu, from noon Fri-Sun) If you prefer your music venues more scruffy than hip, then step inside this old-timer – open since 1975 – across from Rec Pier. From blues to rock, there's live music nightly and during the afternoon Friday through Sunday.

❶ Information

On Light St in the Inner Harbor, the **Baltimore Area Visitor Center** (Map p312; 877-225-8466; www.baltimore.org; 401 Light St, Inner Harbor; 10am-5pm, closed Mon Jan & Feb;) provides more than 200 brochures, guides and maps, plus you'll find cellphone charging stations and free wi-fi. Also sells the **Harbor Pass** (adult/child $54/41), which gives admission to four major area attractions.

❶ Getting There & Away

The **Baltimore/Washington International Thurgood Marshall Airport** (BWI; 410-859-7111; www.bwiairport.com; 7035 Elm Rd;) is 10 miles south of downtown via I-295.

Departing from a terminal 2 miles southwest of Inner Harbor, **Greyhound** (Map p312; 443-371-0692; www.greyhound.com; 2110 Haines St) has numerous buses from Washington, DC ($8 to $18, roughly every 45 minutes, one hour), and from New York ($11 to $52, 15 per day, four hours). You can also try **Peter Pan Bus Lines**

(Map p312; 800-343-9999; www.peterpanbus.com; 2110 Haines St, Carroll-Camden), which runs buses from the Greyhound station ($27, three hours 40 minutes). The **BoltBus** (Map p316; 877-265-8287; www.boltbus.com; 1578 Maryland Ave; one-way tickets $11-23;) ($11 to $23) has five to 10 buses a day to/from NYC; it departs from a street-side location outside of Penn Station in north Baltimore.

MARC operates weekday commuter trains between **Penn Station** (https://mta.maryland.gov/marc-train; 1500 N Charles St, Charles North) and Union Station in Washington, DC ($8, about one hour), on the Penn Line. The Brunswick Line runs from Union Station to Frederick and Harpers Ferry, WV. Amtrak (www.amtrak.com) trains serve the East Coast and beyond.

Supershuttle (www.supershuttle.com) provides a BWI van service to the Inner Harbor from $16.

❶ Getting Around

Light rail (http://mta.maryland.gov/light-rail) runs from BWI airport to Lexington Market, Mt Vernon and Penn Station. Train frequency is every 10 to 15 minutes. MARC trains run hourly on weekdays (and six to nine times daily on weekends) between Penn Station and BWI for $8. Check Maryland Transit Administration (https://mta.maryland.gov) for all local transportation schedules and fares.

Baltimore Water Taxi (410-563-3900; www.baltimorewatertaxi.com; Inner Harbor; daily pass adult/child $14/6; 10am-midnight May-Aug, shorter hours rest of the year) docks at all harborside attractions and neighborhoods.

The free green-and-purple **Charm City Circulator** (410-350-0456; www.charmcitycirculator.com) shuttles travel four routes, three of them to tourist spots in downtown-area neighborhoods. The Purple Route connects the Inner Harbor, Mt Vernon and Federal Hill. The Green Route runs through Fells Point. The Banner Route runs from the Inner Harbor to Fort McHenry.

ANNAPOLIS

410, 443, 667 / POP 39,418

Annapolis is as charming as state capitals get. The Colonial architecture, cobblestones, flickering lamps and brick row houses are worthy of Victorian author Charles Dickens, but the effect isn't artificial: this city has preserved, rather than created, its heritage.

Perched on Chesapeake Bay, Annapolis revolves around the city's rich maritime traditions. It's home to the US Naval Academy, whose 'middies' (midshipmen students) stroll through town in their starched white uniforms. Sailing is not just a hobby here but a way of life, and the city docks are crammed with vessels of all shapes and sizes. With its historic sights, water adventures and great dining and shopping, Annapolis is worthy of more than a day trip – try for at least two if you can.

◉ Sights

US Naval Academy   UNIVERSITY
(◪ visitor center 410-293-8687; www.usnabsd.com/for-visitors; Randall St, btwn Prince George & King George Sts; ⊙ visitor center 9am-5pm Mar-Dec, to 4pm Mon-Fri Jan & Feb) The undergraduate college of the US Navy is one of the most selective universities in America. Book tours (adult/child $11.50/9.50; 75 minutes) at the Armel-Leftwich Visitor Center (p324) and immerse yourself in all things Academy-related. Come for the formation weekdays at 12:05pm sharp, when the 4000 students conduct a 20-minute military marching display in the yard. Photo ID is required for entry. If you've got a thing for American naval history, revel in the well-done **Naval Academy Museum** (◪410-293-2108; www.usna.edu/Museum/index.php; 118 Maryland Ave; ⊙9am-5pm Mon-Sat, from 11am Sun) **FREE**. The visitor entrance for pedestrians is located at Gate 1 on Prince George St (at Craig St), within easy walking distance of the historic downtown.

Maryland State House   HISTORIC BUILDING
(◪410-260-6445; http://msa.maryland.gov/msa/mdstatehouse/html/home.html; 99 State Circle; ⊙9am-5pm) **FREE** The country's oldest state capitol in continuous legislative use, the grand 1772 State House also served as national capital from 1783 to 1784. Notably, General George Washington returned his commission here as Commander-in-Chief of the Continental Army in 1783 after the Revolutionary War, ensuring that governmental power would be shared with Congress. The exhibits and portraits here are impressive and include Washington's copy of his speech resigning his commission. Pick up a self-guided tour map on the 1st floor. Photo ID is required at the entrance, where you'll pass through metal detectors. The upside-down giant acorn atop the building's dome stands for wisdom. The Maryland Senate is in session from January to April.

Hammond Harwood House   MUSEUM
(◪410-263-4683; www.hammondharwoodhouse.org; 19 Maryland Ave; adult/child $10/5; ⊙noon-5pm Tue-Sun Apr-Dec) Of the many historical homes in town, the Hammond Harwood House, dating from 1774, is the one to visit. It has a superb collection of decorative arts, including 18th-century furniture, paintings and ephemera, and is one of the finest existing British Colonial homes in America. Knowledgeable guides help bring the past to life on 50-minute house tours (held at the top of the hour). Even if you don't have time for a tour, take a moment to stroll past. Thomas Jefferson called the ornate front door the 'most beautiful door in America.' We think it is rather nice too.

Banneker-Douglass Museum   MUSEUM
(◪410-216-6180; http://bdmuseum.maryland.gov; 84 Franklin St; ⊙10am-4pm Tue-Sat) **FREE** A short stroll from the State House, this small but worthwhile museum highlights the history and achievements of Marylanders of African American ancestry. Permanent exhibits cover US Supreme Court justice Thurgood Marshall, explorer Matthew Henson and public intellectual Frederick Douglass, while temporary exhibitions run the gamut from forays into the Civil Rights era to

MARYLAND ANNAPOLIS

EASTPORT VERSUS ANNAPOLIS: SLAUGHTER ACROSS THE WATER

Fans of the NBC comedy *Parks & Recreation* are familiar with the rivalry between snobby Eagleton and scruffy Pawnee. There's a similar competition between Annapolis and neighboring Eastport, a scrappy community that sits just across Spa Creek from the Annapolis historic district. The rivalry came to a head in 1998 when the Public Works Department closed the short bridge connecting the two communities for a construction project, leaving Eastport stranded and neglected. Over beers, a few indignant Eastporters created the Maritime Republic of Eastport (www.themre.org) and asserted their independence from the city. Every November, to prove who's boss and earn bragging rights, the communities hold a fierce tug-of-war match, using an 1800ft-long rope. This instrument of war is stretched from City Dock to the Eastport peninsula, with Spa Creek in between. The winner is determined after seven different matches between Annapolis and Eastport teams. During the 20th-anniversary tug in 2017, Eastport won 4–3. The real winners? The local charities supported by the popular competition.

Annapolis

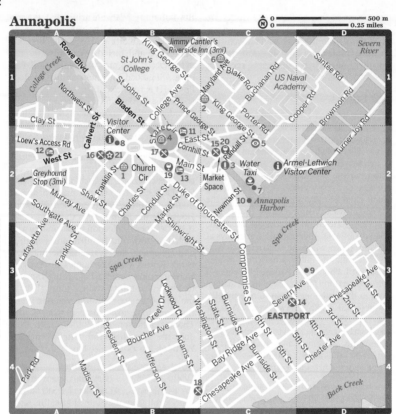

today's crop of great African American artists, musicians and writers. Check out the stained-glass artwork, part of the attached 1875 Mt Moriah African Methodist Episcopal Church.

Kunta Kinte–Alex Haley
Memorial   MONUMENT
(City Dock, off Market Space) Beside City Dock, the Kunta Kinte–Alex Haley Memorial marks the spot where Kunta Kinte – ancestor of *Roots* author Alex Haley – was brought in chains from Africa. The statues here depict Haley sharing the story of his ancestor with three children.

☞ Tours

Four Centuries Walking Tour   WALKING
(☑ 410-268-7601; www.annapolistours.com; 26 West St; 2¼hr tour adult/child $20/10) A costumed docent leads this great introduction to all things Annapolis. The 10:30am tour

leaves from the visitor center; the 1:30pm tour from the information booth at City Dock. There's a slight variation in sights visited by each, but both cover the country's largest concentration of 18th-century buildings, influential African Americans and colonial spirits who don't want to leave.

The associated one-hour **Pirates of the Chesapeake Cruise** (☑ 410-263-0002; www.chesapeakepirates.com; 311 3rd St; $22; ☼ daily mid-Apr–Aug, Sat & Sun only Sep & Oct; ☝) is good 'yar'-worthy fun, especially for the kids.

Cruises on the Bay   CRUISE
(☑ 410-268-7601; www.cruisesonthebay.com; City Dock; 40min cruise adult/child $17/6; ☼ late Mar–mid-Nov) The best way to explore the city's maritime heritage is on the water. Watermark, which also operates the Four Centuries Walking Tour (p322), offers a variety of cruise options, with frequent departures.

Annapolis

Woodwind   CRUISE
(☎410-263-7837; www.schoonerwoodwind.com; 80 Compromise St; adult/child 2hr sail $43/29, sunset cruise $46/29; ⊙Tue-Sun mid-Apr–Oct) This beautiful 74-ft schooner offers two-hour day and sunset cruises. Or splurge for the Woodwind 'boat & breakfast' package (rooms $319, including breakfast), one of the more unique lodging options in town.

⭐ Festivals & Events

Annapolis Cup Croquet   SPORTS
(www.sjc.edu/annapolis/events/croquet; College Ave, St John's College; ⊙mid-Apr) St John's College and the Naval Academy face off for the coveted winner's cup in this simultaneously wacky and oh-so-serious croquet match that's entertained nattily dressed spectators for more than 30 years. Midshipmen wear croquet whites while the Johnnies wear attire related to an annual theme. Held on the front lawn at St John's, which currently leads the series.

🛏 Sleeping

ScotLaur Inn   GUESTHOUSE $
(☎410-268-5665; www.scotlaurinn.com; 165 Main St; r $119-149; P✱☎) The folks from Chick & Ruth's Delly (p323) offer 10 rooms above the restaurant, each with wrought-iron beds, floral wallpaper and private bath. The quarters are small but have a cozy and familial atmosphere (the guesthouse is named after the owners' children Scott and Lauren, whose photos adorn the hallways). Breakfast included. Two-night minimum stay on weekends.

Historic Inns of Annapolis   HOTEL $$
(☎410-263-2641; www.historicinnsofannapolis.com; 58 State Circle; r from $209; P✱☎) The Historic Inns comprise three different boutique guesthouses, each set in a heritage building in the heart of old Annapolis: the Maryland Inn, the Governor Calvert House and the Robert Johnson House. Common areas are packed with period details, and the best rooms boast antiques, fireplaces and attractive views (the cheapest can be small). Check in at Governor Calvert House.

Loew's Annapolis   HOTEL $$$
(☎410-263-7777; www.loewshotels.com/annapolis; 126 West St; r from $309; P✱@☎🐾) Rooms and suites pop with fresh modern style inside this red-brick redoubt on West St, about a 15-minute walk to the water. With 17 suites and a craft-beer bar on-site, the hotel works well for a girls weekend or other group getaway. Self-parking is a steep $23 per night and valet parking is $26. Pet fee is $50 per stay.

🍴 Eating

Vida Taco Bar   MEXICAN $
(☎443-837-6521; www.vidatacobar.com; 200 Main St; tacos $4-6; ⊙5-10pm Tue-Thu, noon-11pm Fri & Sat, noon-9pm Sun) The crowd is stylish – and getting its drink on – at this convivial spot serving fantastic street tacos and strong margaritas.

Chick & Ruth's Delly   DINER $
(☎410-269-6737; www.chickandruths.com; 165 Main St; mains breakfast & lunch $8-15, dinner $5-23; ⊙6:30am-11:30pm Sun-Thu, to 12:30am Fri & Sat; 🐾) A cornerstone of Annapolis, the-squeeze-'em-in-tight Delly bursts with affable quirkiness and a big menu, heavy on

MARYLAND ANNAPOLIS

sandwiches and breakfast fare. Patriots can relive grade-school days reciting the Pledge of Allegiance weekdays at 8:30am and Saturdays and Sundays at 9:30am. Breakfast served all day.

★ Vin 909   AMERICAN $$
(☑410-990-1846; www.vin909.com; 909 Bay Ridge Ave; small plates $12-20; ☺5:30-10pm Wed & Thu, to 11pm Fri, 5-11pm Sat, 5-9pm Sun, plus noon-3pm Wed-Sat, closes at 9pm Tue & Sun in winter) Perched on a little wooded hill and boasting intimate but enjoyably casual ambience, Vin is the best thing happening in Annapolis for food. Farm-sourced goodness features in the form of duck confit, dry-aged Angus-beef sliders and homemade pizzas with toppings such as wild-boar meatballs or honey-braised squash with applewood bacon.

Iron Rooster   BREAKFAST $$
(☑410-990-1600; www.ironroosterallday.com; 12 Market Space; mains breakfast & lunch $9-20, dinner $10-25; ☺7am-10pm Mon-Sat, to 8pm Sun) From the crab-cake Benedict layered with lump crab, poached eggs and hollandaise to the buttermilk fried chicken and waffles with black-pepper pan gravy, everything sounds good at this rustic-chic enclave near Dock St that brings in appreciative breakfast crowds. Other highlights include gourmet pop tarts and the bacon Bloody Mary.

Breakfast is available all day, with burgers and gourmet comfort food on the menu at lunch and dinner.

Boatyard Bar & Grill   SEAFOOD $$
(☑410-216-6206; www.boatyardbarandgrill.com; 400 4th St, Eastport; mains $10-27; ☺7:30am-midnight Mon-Fri, from 8am Sat & Sun; ⚓) This bright, nautically themed restaurant with a big central bar is a festive and welcoming spot for crab cakes, fish and chips, oysters, fish tacos and other seafood. Happy hour (3pm to 7pm Monday to Friday) draws in the crowds with $3 drafts. Patty's Fatty's oysters are $1 on Sundays.

It's a short drive (or 10-minute walk) from the City Dock, across the Spa Creek Bridge.

🍸 Drinking & Nightlife

Fox's Den   PUB
(☑443-808-8991; www.foxsden.com; 179 B Main St; ☺5-11pm Mon, Wed & Thu, to midnight Fri, 4pm-midnight Sat, 4-11pm Sun) Head underground for microbrews and craft cocktails, all served in a snug gastropub in the thick of the Main St action. Hopping on Mondays when the brick-oven pizzas are $10.

McGarvey's Saloon & Oyster Bar   BAR
(☑410-263-5700; www.mcgarveysannapolis.com; 8 Market Space; ☺11:30am-2am Mon-Sat, from 10am Sun) Join the chatty crowd at the bar at this locals' spot near City Dock for an evening of good cheer. There's been a bar here since 1871. Domestic bottles are $2 and oyster shooters $1 during happy hour (4pm to 7pm Monday to Friday). Food can be hit or miss – get dinner elsewhere.

☆ Entertainment

Rams Head On Stage   LIVE MUSIC
(☑410-268-4545; www.ramsheadonstage.com; 33 West St; tickets $15-135) Settle in at tables to watch performances by well-known bands and musicians, from Dave Davies to Lee Ann Womack to Keller Williams. Small bites ($10 to $15), wine, cocktails and beer are served. The venue is next door to **Rams Head Tavern** (☑410-268-4545; www.ramsheadtavern. com; mains lunch & dinner $10-30, brunch $10-16; ☺11am-2am Mon-Sat, from 10am Sun), which has a separate menu.

❶ Information

There's a **visitor center** (☑410-280-0445; www.visitannapolis.org; 26 West St; ☺9am-5pm) on West St and a seasonal information booth at City Dock (open 9am to 5pm March to October). For information about tours and sights at the Naval Academy, stop by the expansive **Armel-Leftwich Visitor Center** (☑410-293-8687; www.usnabsd.com/for-visitors; 52 King George St, Gate 1, City Dock entrance; tours adult/child $11.50/9.50; ☺9am-5pm Mar-Dec, to 4pm Jan & Feb) on the Yard near the waterfront.

❶ Getting There & Away

Annapolis is 26 miles from Baltimore and 30 miles from Washington, DC. Check https://mta. maryland.gov for light rail and bus route options connecting Baltimore/Washington International Thurgood Marshall Airport (p320) and Baltimore with Annapolis.

Greyhound (☑800-231-2222; www.grey hound.com; 275 Harry S Truman Pkwy) runs daily buses ($8 to $10) to Washington, DC, from a pick-up and drop-off stop 5 miles west of the historic downtown.

❶ Getting Around

For information about metered parking and parking garages in the historic district, visit www.annapolisparking.com. Meter rates are

$2 per hour with a maximum of two hours per spot and are enforced 10am to 7:30pm Monday through Saturday and noon to 7:30pm Sunday.

The free **Circulator** (www.annapolisparking. com; ⊙ 7:30am-11pm Mon-Sat, 8am-8pm Sun) bus loops every 20 minutes between four parking garages scattered across the historic district. Helpful if you don't want the hassle of traffic near the waterfront.

A **water taxi** (☑ 410-263-0033; www. cruisesonthebay.com; City Dock; fares $3-8; ⊙ 9:30am-11pm Mon-Thu, to midnight Fri, 9am-midnight Sat, 9am-11pm Sun mid-May– Aug) runs between downtown and Eastport from mid-May through August.

EASTERN SHORE

Just across the Chesapeake Bay Bridge, nondescript suburbs give way to unbroken miles of bird-dotted wetlands, serene waterscapes, endless cornfields, sandy beaches and friendly villages. The Eastern Shore retains its charm despite the growing influx of gentrifiers and day-trippers. This area revolves around the water: working waterfront communities still survive off Chesapeake Bay and its tributaries, and boating, fishing, crabbing and hunting are integral to local life. Come here to explore nature by trail, boat or bicycle, to read on the beach, to delve into regional history and, of course, to enjoy the delicious seafood.

ℹ Information

Chesapeake Heritage & Visitor Center
(☑ 410-604-2100; www.findyourchesapeake. com; 429 Piney Narrows Rd, Kent Narrows; ⊙ 10am-4pm)

ℹ Getting There & Away

The region is best explored by car. Baltimore is 70 miles from Easton and 150 miles from Ocean City. Greyhound stops in Easton and Salisbury.

St Michaels & Tilghman Island

☑ 410, 443, 667

The prettiest little village on the Eastern Shore, St Michaels lives up to its motto as the 'Heart and Soul of the Chesapeake Bay.' Hugging US 33, it's a mix of old Victorian homes, quaint B&Bs, boutique shops and working docks, where escapees from Washington, DC, mix with salty-dog watermen.

During the War of 1812, inhabitants rigged up lanterns in a nearby forest and blacked out the town. British naval gunners shelled the trees, allowing St Michaels to escape destruction. The building now known as the **Cannonball House** (Mulberry St, St Michaels) was the only structure to have been hit.

At the end of the road at the end of the peninsula, and over the US 33 drawbridge, tiny Tilghman Island still runs a working waterfront, where local captains take visitors out on graceful sailing vessels.

⊙ Sights

Chesapeake Bay Maritime Museum   MUSEUM
(☑ 410-745-2916; www.cbmm.org; 213 N Talbot St, St Michaels; adult/child $15/6; ⊙ 9am-5pm May-Oct, 10am-4pm Nov-Apr; 🅐) Throughout its indoor-outdoor exhibits, the Chesapeake Bay Maritime Museum delves into the deep ties between Shore folk and America's largest estuary. Learn about a 19th-century lighthouse-keeper's life while exploring inside the relocated 1879 lighthouse.

☞ Tours

Lady Patty Classic Yacht Charters   BOATING
(☑ 410-886-1127; www.ladypatty.com; 6176 Tilghman Island Rd, Tilghman Island; cruises adult/child from $45/25; ⊙ tours Wed-Mon May-Oct) Runs two-hour sails on the Chesapeake on a 1935 racing yacht. Think teak, bronze and wind-drive prowess – these trips are for the pure thrill of sailing.

Rebecca T Ruark   CRUISE
(☑ text 410-829-3976; www.skipjack.org; Dogwood Harbor, off US 33; 2hr cruise adult/child $30/15; ⊙ 11am-1pm & 6-8pm daily May-Oct) For old-fashioned fun, hop aboard this 1886 skipjack, a traditional oyster-dredging boat, for a sunset sail. It's the oldest one on the Chesapeake Bay and is now a historic landmark. Cash or check only.

🛏 Sleeping & Eating

Parsonage Inn   INN $$
(☑ 410-745-8383; www.parsonage-inn.com; 210 N Talbot St, St Michaels; r $220-290; 🅿🅐🛜) Classic Victorian-era decor is brightened here and there with unexpected splashes of color – is that a green Hawaiian quilt? – inside the red-brick Parsonage Inn. Breakfast is a focus, and you might find deconstructed Scotch eggs on the menu. Close to the Maritime Museum.

WORTH A TRIP

EASTON & OXFORD

Easton, founded in 1710, is both a quintessential Shore town and anything but. Its historic center, seemingly lifted from the pages of a children's book, is wedding-cake cute, locals are friendly and the antique shops and galleries are well stocked. That's because this isn't what Shore people would call a 'working water town,' which is to say, a town that relies on Bay seafood to live. Rather, Easton relies on the Bay for tourism purposes. It has retained the traditional appearance of a working water town by being a weekend retreat for folks from DC, Baltimore and further afield.

Ten miles southwest is Oxford, a small village with a history tracing back to the 1600s and a fine spread of leafy streets and waterfront homes. Although you can drive there via US 333, it's well worth taking the old-fashioned ferry from Bellevue. At sunset there are memorable views.

For a fantastic dinner in a welcoming service, don't miss **Out of the Fire** (⌨410-770-4777; www.outofthefire.com; 22 Goldsborough St; mains lunch $12-22, dinner $16-28; ⏰11:30am-2pm Tue-Sat, 5-9pm Tue-Thu, to 10pm Fri & Sat; ✏) ⚲ in downtown Easton. This welcoming spot turns sustainable ingredients into delicious food that bridges the globe, but is often influenced by the Chesapeake Bay.

Ava's Pizzeria & Wine Bar   PIZZA; ITALIAN **$$**
(⌨410-745-3081; www.avaspizzeria.com; 409 S Talbot St, St Michael's; pizzas $12-19, mains $11-21; ⏰11:30am-9:30pm Sun-Thu, to 10pm Fri & Sat) From the dough to the mozzarella, it's all made in-house at this popular pizzeria where the pies are cooked in an 800°F oven. Serves 15 wines by the glass and offers a strong lineup of regional draft beers. It's usually pretty crowded.

Crab Claw   SEAFOOD **$$**
(⌨410-745-2900; www.thecrabclaw.com; 304 Burns St, St Michaels; mains $9-31; ⏰11am-10pm mid-Mar–Oct) The Crab Claw serves up tasty Maryland blue crabs to splendid views over the harbor. Avoid the Waterman's seafood sampler, unless you're a fan of deep-fried seafood. It's next door to the Chesapeake Bay Maritime Museum (p325).

⚲ Drinking & Nightlife

Carpenter Street Saloon   BAR
(⌨410-745-5111; www.carpenterstreetsaloon.com; 113 S Talbot St; ⏰8am-2am) Get your grog on with the locals at this bar inside the oldest commercial building in town, built in 1887.

❶ Getting There & Away

St Michaels and Tilghman Island border US 33 on a narrow, zigzagging peninsula. US 33 leads west toward the towns from Easton. Baltimore is 80 miles from St Michaels and Tilghman Island is another 12 miles or so along the peninsula.

If you have a friend with a boat docked on the Chesapeake Bay, this is the time to ask for a ride – both towns have docks. They are also part of

Talbot County, which has more than 600 miles of shoreline.

Cambridge

⌨410 / POP 12,468
First settled in 1684, Cambridge is one of the oldest cities in the country. Situated on the Choptank River, it has historically been a farming town. The city center has historic buildings fashioned in Federal Style; it may not be quite as picture-perfect as Easton, but the populace is less transplant-heavy and more authentically of the Shore (and it's diverse to boot – almost 50-50 split between white and African American). In Dorchester County, Cambridge is also the closest city to the new visitor center at the Harriet Tubman National Historical Park and its neighbor the Blackwater National Wildlife Refuge.

With level roads unfurling through a striking coastal landscape filled with farms, marshes and waterways, the county is an inviting cycling destination, and hosts two Ironman triathlons annually. Bird-watching and paddling are popular too.

◉ Sights

Harriet Tubman Underground Railroad National Historical Park & Visitor Center   MONUMENT
(⌨410-221-2290 ext 5070; www.nps.gov/hatu; 4068 Golden Hill Rd, Church Creek; ⏰9am-5pm; ⓟ) FREE This new visitor center and historic site honors Harriet Tubman, 'the Moses of her people' who led black slaves to freedom

on the Underground Railroad, the pipeline that sent escaped slaves north. She was born on nearby Greenbrier Rd. The visitor center is a helpful orientation point for exploring the Harriet Tubman Underground Railroad Byway, which stops here and at 35 other related sites on the Eastern Shore. It's co-managed by the National Park Service and Maryland state parks.

Blackwater National
Wildlife Refuge   WILDLIFE RESERVE
(☑ 410-228-2677; www.fws.gov/blackwater; 2145 Key Wallace Dr; wildlife drive per vehicle/pedestrian or cyclist $3/1; ⊙ refuge sunrise-sunset, visitor center 8am-4pm Mon-Fri, 9am-5pm Sat & Sun; ℗) The Atlantic Flyway is the main route birds take between northern and southern migratory trips, and the Blackwater National Wildlife Refuge was established to give our feathered friends a rest stop. This enormous expanse of marsh and pine forest contains a third of Maryland's wetland habitat. Thousands upon thousands of birds call the refuge home, or stop there on their migratory routes. Driving or cycling the paved 4.5-mile wildlife drive is perhaps the seminal wildlife experience on the Eastern Shore.

🛏 Sleeping & Eating

Hyatt Regency Chesapeake Bay   RESORT $$$
(☑ 410-901-1234; www.hyatt.com; 100 Heron Blvd, Cambridge; r/ste from $339/539; ℗ ❀ ⚛ ➰ ❀) With sprawling grounds, a waterside perch, indoor and outdoor pools, a spa and an 18-hole golf course, this pretty resort works well for family vacations and small-group getaways. Rooms have breezy, unfussy style and come in a variety of configurations, including a few types of suites. There are several restaurants on-site. The lobby view of the Choptank River is gorgeous.

The pet fee is $150. The resort fee is $30 per day from April through September and $25 per day from October through March.

High Spot Gastropub   AMERICAN $$
(☑ 410-228-7420; www.thehighspotgastropub.com; 305 High St; mains lunch $11-18, dinner $15-21; ⊙ 11am-midnight) Wash down your Duck Fat Burger – a steakhouse grind topped with a fried egg, mushrooms, bacon and smoked gouda – with a draft from the short but interesting list of local craft brews. The supper menu expands to include gourmet comfort fare such as chicken and waffles or steak-tip poutine. The small bar is good for solo travelers.

ℹ Information

Dorchester County Visitor Center (☑ 410-228-1000; www.visitdorchester.org; 2 Rose Hill Pl, Cambridge; ⊙ 8:30am-5pm) Along the Choptank River.

ℹ Getting There & Away

The city borders US 50/Ocean Gateway and is located 15 miles south of Easton. You'll want a car to explore the sights near Cambridge.

Salisbury

☑ 410, 443, 667 / POP 33,114

The biggest city in the region, Salisbury is a good base camp if you want to explore the southern reaches of the Eastern Shore or don't want to stay in Ocean City, 30 miles east. It lacks the charm of small towns like Berlin and Easton, but a host of good restaurants and bars make it a solid choice for an overnight stay.

Officially established in 1732 and now the seat of Wicomoco County, Salisbury is the headquarters for Perdue Farms, one of the largest chicken-processing companies in the country. Downtown borders the Wicomoco River and is dotted with restaurants, bars and indie shops. Salisbury University is a short drive south of downtown.

⊙ Sights

Ward Museum of Wildfowl Art   MUSEUM
(☑ 410-742-4988; www.wardmuseum.org; 909 S Schumaker Dr; adult/child $7/3; ⊙ 10am-5pm Mon-Sat, from noon Sun; ℗) This museum is built around a little-known but fascinating art form that was largely perfected by two brothers who rarely left their small town. In the early 20th century, Stephen and LT Ward – natives of nearby Crisfield – spent a lifetime carving and painting waterfowl decoys that are wonderful in their realism and attention to detail. The Ward Museum exhibits the works of the Brothers Ward, as well as decoy art gathered from around the world.

🛏 Sleeping & Eating

Hampton Inn Salisbury   HOTEL $$
(☑ 410-334-3080; www.hamptoninn3.hilton.com; 121 E Naylor Mill Rd; r $219; ℗ ❀ @ ⚛ ➰ ❀) Yes, it's a nondescript chain hotel, but we like the accommodating front desk, its proximity to US 50 (the road to the beach!) and the slightly bold color scheme in the rooms. Hot breakfast included.

MARYLAND BERLIN

Acorn Market SANDWICHES; SALADS $

(📞 410-334-2222; www.theacornmarket.com; 150 W Market St; mains $7-11; ⏱ 7am-3pm Mon-Fri, from 9am Sat) This order-at-the-counter gourmet sandwich shop is great for grabbing a picnic lunch to go if you're driving east to Ocean City on US 50 Business. The tasty 'hen house' comes with sliced eggs and crispy bacon, but you can take your pick of turkey, ham, chicken salad, the caprese (with local heirloom tomatoes) and more. Great daily soups, too.

Evolution Craft Brewing AMERICAN $$

(📞 443-260-2337; www.evolutioncraftbrewing. com; 201 E Vine St; mains lunch $12-22, dinner $14-28; ⏱ 11:30am-midnight Mon-Wed, to 12:30am Thu-Sat, 10am-midnight Sun) Evo's citrusy Lot No 3 IPA appears on taps across the state, but folks show up for the hearty servings of gourmet pub food as much as the beer at this cavernous restaurant, formerly an ice plant. Deviled eggs, big salads, messy burgers and various seafood dishes pass by your table as you review the menu; all look delicious!

Enjoy a flight and fill your growler in the attached tasting room (3pm to 8pm Monday to Thursday, noon to 8pm Friday to Sunday).

Berlin

📞 410, 443, 667 / POP 4608

Imagine a typical small-town-America main street, then cute that vision up by a few points, and you've come close to the Eastern Shore village of Berlin. Most of the buildings here are handsomely preserved, and antique shops litter the area. Several great restaurants dot the easily walkable downtown. The city is a convenient and appealing launchpad for exploring Assateague Island, Ocean City and the surrounding Eastern Shore.

◉ Sights & Activities

Calvin B Taylor
House Museum HISTORIC BUILDING

(📞 410-641-1019; www.taylorhousemuseum.org; 208 N Main St; ⏱ 1-4pm Mon, Wed, Fri & Sat Jun-Oct) Built in 1832, this green-shuttered Federal-style house evokes everyday smalltown life in the 1800s and 1900s through period furnishings and exhibits spotlighting town notables, from house namesake and banker Calvin B Taylor to racehorse Man o'War. You'll spend more time than expected checking out local artifacts and knickknacks in the small 2nd-floor gallery.

Ayers Creek Adventures CANOEING; KAYAKING

(📞 888-602-6288; www.ayerscreekadventures. com; 8628 Grey Fox Ln; guided trips adult/child from $40/30; 🚣) This family-owned company leads eco-minded tours through the coastal marshes and forested wetlands near Berlin and Ocean City. Paddling newbies will do just fine. Leave the kids at home for the full moon paddles, though, which are followed by a bonfire with snacks and wine. Also rents canoes and kayaks (half-day canoe/single-person kayak/tandem kayak $30/40/45).

🛏 Sleeping

Holland House B&B $$

(📞 410-641-1956; www.hollandhousebandb.com; 5 Bay St; r $175; 🅿❄🛜) A doctor's home in the early 1900s, this inviting six-bedroom house is just 1½ blocks from Main St. There are several common areas for relaxing and the popular Blacksmith restaurant and bar is next door. The owners have extensive knowledge about the town's history and outdoor activities in the region. A full breakfast is included.

Atlantic Hotel HOTEL $$

(📞 410-641-3589; www.atlantichotel.com; 2 N Main St; r $170-270, ste $350; 🅿❄🛜) This handsome, Gilded Age lodger gives guests the time-warp experience with all the modern amenities. The smaller rooms can be cramped, so spring for a larger room if you have a few extra bucks. Great front porch with a fine view of Main St.

🍴 Eating & Drinking

Island Creamery ICE CREAM $

(📞 410-973-2839; www.islandcreamery.net; 120 N Main St; one scoop $5; ⏱ 11am-9pm Mon-Thu, to 10pm Fri-Sun) A spin-off from uber-popular Island Creamery in Chincoteague (p365), this tiny ice-cream shop pulls in crowds hungry for its big scoops with bold flavors, from the bourbon caramel crunch to the vanilla butterscotch to the cotton candy party.

★ Blacksmith Bar &
Restaurant AMERICAN $$

(📞 410-973-2102; www.blacksmithberlin.com; 104 Pitts St; mains lunch $9-14, dinner $11-27; ⏱ 11:30am-9:30pm Mon-Sat) Folks across the Eastern Shore recommend this cozy and congenial spot, which began life as a blacksmith shop and now serves hearty portions of delicious farm-to-table comfort food. Servers soon feel like friends – in a non-annoying way – while the low ceiling and thick walls evoke a warm roadside tavern. The jumbo lump crab cakes with herbed potatoes are divine.

You'll find several Eastern Shore beers on tap and a creative list of cocktails at the welcoming bar. If you just want a quick bite to eat with your beer, the empanada with slow-cooked beef is a tasty choice.

Fins Ale House & Raw Bar SEAFOOD $$
(☑ 410-641-3000; www.facebook.com/FinsAle-HouseBerlin; 119 N Main St; mains lunch $10-24, dinner $12-29; ⊙11:30am-9pm Mon-Thu, 11am-9:30pm Fri & Sat, 10am-9pm Sun) The lump crab cake is so good you might consider packing up and moving to Berlin. Based on the happy crowds here, others may have had the same idea. It's not on the water, but considerate service, big windows, a cozy patio and enticing seafood dishes make Fins the next best thing to a seafood shack by the ocean.

Burley Oak Brewing Co MICROBREWERY
(☑ 443-513-4647; www.burleyoak.com; 10016 Old Ocean City Blvd; ⊙11am-11pm Mon-Thu, to 2am Fri & Sat, to 9pm Sun) At first glance this rustic place looks like a forgotten party barn. But step inside. With 20 innovative beers on tap, live music on weekends and a bearded hipster or two (plus a few local parents escaped from the kids) this is the hippest watering hole in town. The Homegrown Session IPA is made from 100% local barley.

🛍 Shopping

**Assateague Island
Surf Shop** SPORTS & OUTDOORS
(☑ 410-973-2632; www.assateagueislandsurfshop.com; 8315 Stephen Decatur Hwy; ⊙9am-6pm Feb-Dec, closed Tue-Thu Jan; 🛜🐾) You'll find 'I love ASS' socks for sale at this amiable beach shop that sits on the road to (Ass)ateague. Stop here for beach gear and outdoor apparel as well as chic duds. The comfy cafe serves coffee, smoothies and sandwiches ($10).

❶ Getting There & Away

Berlin sits near the junction of Hwy 113 and US 50, about 8 miles southwest of Ocean City. The town is 140 miles southeast of Baltimore and 140 miles east of Washington, DC.

Assateague Island

The Assateague Island seashore, a perfectly barren landscape of sand dunes and beautiful, secluded beaches, is just 8 miles south but a world away from Ocean City. This undeveloped barrier island is populated by a herd of wild horses, made famous in the book *Misty of Chincoteague*.

The 37-mile-long island is divided into three sections: Assateague State Park in Maryland, federally administered Assateague Island National Seashore and Chincoteague National Wildlife Refuge (p365) in Virginia. For an overview, check out the Plan your Visit section of the National Park Service website (www.nps.gov/asis) or pick up the *Assateague Island National Seashore* pamphlet, which has a helpful map.

As well as swimming and sunbathing, recreational activities include birding, hiking, kayaking, canoeing, camping, crabbing and fishing. There are no food or drink services on the Maryland side of the island in the off-season. Don't forget insect repellent: the mosquitoes and biting horseflies can be ferocious!

◉ Sights

**Assateague Island
National Seashore** PARK
(☑ 410-641-1441; www.nps.gov/asis; 7206 National Seashore Ln, Berlin; vehicle access per week $20; ⊙visitor center 9am-5pm Mar-Dec, closed Tue & Wed Jan & Feb; 🅿) A low-key barrier island, Assateague is a place to relax. In the Maryland section of the national seashore, you can cycle along a 4-mile road, hike nature trails, paddle a kayak, check out the exhibits at the visitor center, catch a ranger talk or simply chill out on the beach. You might even spot some of the famed wild horses (p330). If you enter the park as a pedestrian or cyclist, admission is free. Camping is allowed year-round.

Assateague State Park STATE PARK
(☑ 410-641-2918; http://dnr.maryland.gov; 6915 Stephen Decatur Hwy; $6 Jun-Aug, $5 Sep-May; ⊙day-use areas 7am-sunset, campground late Apr-Oct; 🅿🐾) The Maryland-run section of Assateague Island stretches for 2 miles along the coast and is tucked within the boundaries of the national seashore. Come here to sunbathe, surf, picnic, kayak, camp (campsites $28 to $39) and generally just relax in a cool barrier-island setting. Pets are allowed in certain areas; check specifics online. Do not approach, touch or feed the wild horses (p330), which you may see while visiting. They are unpredictable wild animals. Lifeguards are on duty 10am to 5pm June through August. State residents get discounted entry.

MARYLAND ASSATEAGUE ISLAND

WILD HORSES OF ASSATEAGUE

There's a good chance you'll see a few of the island's famous wild horses on the Maryland side of the park. Managed by the National Park Service, the horses are free-roaming and you can often see them chowing down on grass beside park roads. You may also glimpse a few along the Life of the Forest and Life of the Marsh Trails, or simply galloping past a parking lot!

Although popular rumor says they are descended from the survivors of nearby shipwrecks, it is more likely that they are the descendants of horses kept here by locals in the 1600s who did not want to pay taxes on the animals. Take as many photos as you like, but do not approach, touch or feed the horses. If you do so, you risk incurring a $100 fine and you may also find yourself seeking first aid for a painful kick or a bite.

In Virginia, the horses are privately owned. The last Wednesday of July they are herded from the island through Chincoteague Bay to Chincoteague, where the foals are sent to auction. Their journey is covered in the famous children's book *Misty of Chincoteague*, written in 1947.

🏃 Activities

Nature Trails HIKING
(www.nps.gov/asis; Assateague Island National Seashore) There are three separate half-mile trails in the Assateague Island National Seashore (p329), each exploring a different type of coastal landscape: the Life of the Marsh Trail, the Life of the Forest Trail and the Life of the Dunes Trail. All are scenic and easy, although the Dunes Trail is sand-covered and a bit harder on the calves.

Assateague Outfitters CYCLING; WATER SPORTS
(www.mdcoastalbays.org/rentals; 13002 Bayside Dr; per hr bicycles/stand-up paddleboards/canoes $6/20/22, kayaks $15-20; ☉10am-4pm Sat & Sun mid-Apr–May & Sep–mid-Oct, 9am-6pm Jun-Aug) Rents bicycles, kayaks, canoes and stand-up paddleboards near the bay on Assateague Island National Seashore (p329). You can buy pre-made sandwiches, snacks and camping supplies here. Also operates a separate beach hut selling beach gear and snacks.

🛏 Sleeping

Assateague Island
Campground CAMPGROUND $
(☏ ranger station 410-641-1441 ext 3, reservations 877-444-6777; www.recreation.gov; Assateague Island National Seashore; campsites $30; ℗) ⚐
You can camp on the Maryland side of the island. The national seashore facilities are basic – chemical toilets, cold showers and drinking water – but decently comfortable. We recommend just bringing your tent and waking up to the wind – who can object to a morning with an Atlantic sunrise and wild horses (p330) cantering by the waves?

ℹ Information

Assateague Island National Park Visitor Center (☏ 410-641-1441 ext 1; www.nps.gov/asis; 11800 Marsh Ln, Berlin; ☉9am-5pm Mar-Dec, closed Wed Jan & Feb; 🏃) Learn about the ecology of barrier islands, watch a film about the island's wild horses (p330), touch a horseshoe crab in the touch tank or simply sit on a rocking chair and take in the marshy view.

ℹ Getting There & Away

The best way to reach the island is by car. The park is 150 miles southeast of Baltimore and 150 miles east of Washington, DC.

ℹ Getting Around

If you're feeling athletic, you can leave your car at the visitor center then hike or bike across the half-mile Verrazano Bridge to the island. From there pedal south on Bayberry Dr to its end point, about 9 miles round-trip from the visitor center.

OCEAN CITY

☏ 410, 443, 667 / POP 7041

Two words describe 'the OC' from June through August: party central. This is where you'll experience the American seaside resort in its wildest glory. Some might call it tacky. Others might call it, well, fun. Here you can take a spin on nausea-inducing thrill rides, buy a T-shirt with obscene slogans and drink to excess at cheesy theme bars. The center of action is the 2.5-mile-long boardwalk, which stretches from the inlet to 27th St. The beach is attractive, but you'll have to contend with heavy traffic and noisy crowds; the beaches north of the boardwalk are much quieter. How busy is it?

They say Ocean City welcomes eight million visitors annually, with most of them arriving in summer – in a town with a year-round population of just over 7000!

◉ Sights

Ocean City Life-Saving Station Museum MUSEUM
(☑️410-289-4991; www.ocmuseum.org; 813 S Atlantic Ave; adult/child $5/3; ⏰10am-4pm May & Oct, to 6pm Jun-Sep, 10am-4pm Wed-Sun Apr & Nov) This small but engaging museum sits inside an 1891 life-saving station at the southern end of the boardwalk. Here, the station keeper and six to eight 'surfmen' lived and responded to emergency calls from ships in distress. Exhibits include stories about nearby shipwrecks and a display spotlighting rescue gear, including a 26ft-long rescue boat, which would look rather small and fragile in a storm!

Trimpers Rides AMUSEMENT PARK
(☑️410-289-8617; www.trimpersrides.com; S 1st St & Boardwalk; unlimited afternoon rides $26; ⏰1pm-midnight Mon-Fri, from noon Sat & Sun, hours vary seasonally) If you really want to engage in tacky seaside fun to the fullest possible extent, hit up Trimpers Rides, one of the oldest of old-school amusement parks. Have some fries with vinegar, play the games and enjoy people-watching. Tickets are 60¢ each, with a varying number required per ride.

🛏 Sleeping

King Charles Hotel GUESTHOUSE $$
(☑️410-289-6141; www.kingcharleshotel.com; 1209 N Baltimore Ave, cnr 12th St; r $185-209 May-early

Oct; 🅿️❄️📶) This place could be a quaint summer cottage, except it happens to be a short stroll to the heart of the boardwalk action. It has aging but clean rooms with small porches attached, and it's quiet (ie it's not a party hotel).

Courtyard Ocean City Oceanfront HOTEL $$$
(☑️410-289-5008; www.marriott.com; Two 15th St; r from $509; 🅿️❄️@📶🏊) The ocean views are sublime from this sleek number, one of the swankiest Courtyards we've seen. On the boardwalk, the hotel greets guests with a bright modern lobby. Rooms are spacious and sport mini-fridges and microwaves. An $8 breakfast voucher is included for the on-site Captain's Table – on Friday night you might catch the happy sounds of pianist Phil Perdue. The hotel is open year-round. Rates can hover around $100 in the off-season.

🍴 Eating & Drinking

Layton's Family Restaurant DINER $
(☑️410-289-6635; https://laytons1601.wixsite. com/laytons16restaurant; 1601 Philadelphia Ave; mains $5-15, doughnuts $1.25; ⏰6am-2pm; 🚼) Celebrating its 50th birthday in 2018, Layton's is the place to enjoy an old school breakfast. Join the crowds for diner standards and specialties, such as the crab and eggs, that spotlight the region's coastal bounty. In a hurry? Order a doughnut to-go at the counter. From glazed to chocolate peanut, they're hard to resist! Also serves burgers and sandwiches.

Liquid Assets MODERN AMERICAN $$
(☑️410-524-7037; https://la94.com; 9301 Coastal Hwy, cnr 94th St; mains $13-36; ⏰11:30am-11pm

---

MARYLAND BLUE CRABS

Eating at a crab shack, where the dress code stops at shorts and flip-flops, is the quintessential Chesapeake Bay experience. Folks in these parts take their crabs seriously, and can spend hours debating the intricacies of how to crack a crab, the proper way to prepare crabs and where to find the best ones. There is one thing Marylanders can agree on: they must be blue crabs (scientific name: *Callinectes sapidus*, or 'beautiful swimmers'). Sadly, blue crab numbers have suffered with the continuing pollution of the Chesapeake Bay, and many crabs you eat here are imported from elsewhere.

Steamed crabs are prepared very simply, using beer and Old Bay seasoning. One of the best crab shacks in the state is near Annapolis at **Jimmy Cantler's Riverside Inn** (☑️410-757-1311; www.cantlers.com; 458 Forest Beach Rd; mains $10-32; ⏰11am-10pm Sun-Thu, to 11pm Fri & Sat), located 4 miles northeast of the Maryland State House, across the Severn River Bridge; here, eating a steamed crab has been elevated to an art form – a hands-on, messy endeavor, normally accompanied by corn on the cob and ice-cold beer. Another fine spot is across the bay at **Red Roost** (☑️410-546-5443; www.theredroost.com; 2670 Clara Rd, Whitehaven; mains $17-40; ⏰5:30-9pm Mon-Thu, to 10pm Fri, noon-10pm Sat, to 9pm Sun mid-Mar–Oct).

Sun-Thu, to midnight Fri & Sat) Like a diamond in the rough, this bistro and wine shop is hidden in a strip mall in north OC. The menu is a refreshing mix of innovative seafood, grilled meats and regional classics. The small bar area is a convivial place to be early in the evening, and the pan-steamed mussels are a hit with the drinking crowd.

Seacrets BAR
(☑ 410-524-4900; www.seacrets.com; 117 49th St; ⊙ 11am-midnight, vary seasonally) A Jamaican-themed, rum-soaked bar straight out of MTV's *Spring Break*. You can drift around in an inner tube while sipping a drink and people-watching at OC's most famous meat-market. When it comes to the wildest beach-party bar, this is the one against which all other claimants must be judged. The distillery, which opened in 2016, seems a bit superfluous.

❶ Information

For information about things to do in Ocean City, stop by the **visitor center** (☑ 800-626-2326; www.ococean.com; 4001 Coastal Hwy, at 40th St; ⊙ 8am-4:30pm Mon-Sat, 9am-3pm Sun) on the Coastal Hwy.

❶ Getting There & Away

Ocean City is 140 miles southeast of Baltimore via Hwy 10 and US 50. **Greyhound** (☑ 800-231-222; www.greyhound.com; 101 S Division St, S Division St Transit Ctr) currently stops 30 miles west of Ocean City in Salisbury, where you can transfer to a local shuttle running to the southern end of the boardwalk.

❶ Getting Around

The **Coastal Hwy Beach Bus** (☑ 410-723-2174; http://ococean.com/explore-oc/getting-around-oc; day passes $3; ⊙ 24hr Apr-early Nov, vary early Nov-Mar) travels up and down the length of the beach around the clock year-round. There's also a **tram** (☑ 410-289-5311; http://ococean.com/explore-oc/getting-around-oc; tickets per ride $3, day passes $6; ⊙ 11am-midnight Jun-Aug) that runs along the boardwalk (https://oceancitymd.gov/oc) from June through September. For details about off-season transit and schedules, visit www.shoretransit.org.

WESTERN MARYLAND

The western spine of Maryland is mountain country. The Appalachian peaks soar to 3000ft above sea level, and the surrounding valleys are packed with rugged scenery and Civil War battlefields. This is Maryland's playground, where hiking, cycling, skiing, rock climbing and white-water rafting draw the outdoor-loving crowd. Two long-distance hiking and biking trails are particularly noteworthy: the Great Allegheny Passage and the C&O Canal towpath, both offering an invigorating mix of history, scenery and adventure.

Passionate local chefs are embracing the region's bounty, and you'll find fantastic farm-to-table fare in the larger towns. Plenty of welcoming microbreweries too.

When trip planning, remember that the narrow Maryland panhandle is bordered by Virginia, West Virginia and Pennsylvania. If you're exploring Civil War battlefields or looking for larger towns for an overnight stay, check our regional map for options that may be just a few miles over state lines.

Frederick

Central Frederick is, well, perfect. Its historic, pedestrian-friendly center of red-brick row houses is filled with a diverse array of restaurants and shops. The engaged, cultured arts community is anchored by the excellent Weinberg Center for the Arts. The meandering Carroll Creek runs through it all, flanked by a lovely park with art and gardens. Unlike other communities in the region with historic districts, this is a mid-sized city, an important commuter base for thousands of federal government employees and a biotechnology hub in its own right. For travelers, Frederick makes a great central base for exploring Brunswick, Mt Airy and the regional Civil War battlefields.

◉ Sights

Antietam National Battlefield HISTORIC SITE
(☑ 301-432-5124; www.nps.gov/anti; 5831 Dunker Church Rd, Sharpsburg; 3-day passes per person/vehicle $5/10; ⊙ grounds sunrise-sunset, visitor center 9am-5pm) The site of the bloodiest day in American history is now, ironically, supremely peaceful, quiet and haunting – and uncluttered, save for plaques and statues. On September 17, 1862, General Robert E Lee's first invasion of the north was stalled here in a tactical stalemate that left more than 23,000 dead, wounded or missing – more casualties than America had suffered in all its previous wars combined. Check out the exhibits in the visitor center then walk or drive the grounds. Poignantly, many of the battlefield graves are inscribed with German

and Irish names, a roll call of immigrants who died fighting for their new homeland.

The visitor center shows a short film (playing on the hour and half-hour) about the events that transpired here. It also sells books and materials, including self-guided driving and walking tours of the battlefield.

Antietam is 25 miles west of Frederick and just 5 miles northeast of Shepherdstown, WV.

Carroll Creek Park PARK
(www.visitfrederick.org) Originally a flood control project, this mile-long walking path stretches along Carroll Creek between S Bentz St and S East St, all just south of the historic downtown. Today it's dotted with gardens, fountains and public art, including a trompe l'oeil design of stone and ivy that's painted on the concrete S Carroll St Bridge – the realistic, 3D-style details are mesmerizing.

**Monocacy National
Battlefield** NATIONAL PARK
(☑301-662-3515; www.nps.gov/mono; 5201 Urbana Pike; ⊘ grounds 7am-sunset, visitor center 9am-5pm; P) FREE The crucial but little known Battle of Monocacy occurred during the last Confederate invasion of the north, which began when Confederate General Jubal Early pushed toward Washington, DC, with 15,000 troops. A Union force of 6600, led by General Lew Wallace, clashed with the rebels here on July 9, 1864, delaying their march by one day. This delay gave Union reinforcements time to organize, ultimately saving the nation's capital. Hiking trails and a driving tour stop by key battle sights.

**National Museum of
Civil War Medicine** MUSEUM
(☑301-695-1864; www.civilwarmed.org; 48 E Patrick St; adult/student/child $9.50/7/free; ⊘10am-5pm Mon-Sat, from 11am Sun) The National Museum of Civil War Medicine gives a fascinating, and sometimes gruesome, look at the health conditions soldiers and doctors faced during the war, as well as important medical advances that resulted from the conflict.

🛏 Sleeping

Hollerstown Hill B&B B&B $
(☑301-228-3630; www.hollerstownhill.com; 4 Clarke Pl; r $149; P❄🐾) The elegant, friendly Hollerstown has four pattern-heavy rooms, two resident dogs, a doll collection and a fancy billiards room. This lovely Victorian sits right in the middle of the historic downtown area of Frederick, so you're within easy

walking distance of all the goodness. No children under 16.

Hilton Garden Inn HOTEL $$
(☑240-566-1501; http://hiltongardeninn3.hilton.com; 7226 Corporate Ct; r/ste $149/169; P@🐾🖥) Three miles south of downtown and close to Monocacy National Battlefield, this branch of the national chain wins points for its quiet rooms that come with microwaves, mini-fridges and Keurig coffee makers.

🍴 Eating & Drinking

Volt AMERICAN $$
(☑301-696-8658; www.voltrestaurant.com; 228 N Market St; dinner mains $20-31, brunch $15-16; ⊘5:30-9:30pm Tue-Sun, 11:30am-2pm Sat & Sun) Let's class it up a bit, shall we? Step inside an 1800s brownstone mansion in the heart of the historic district for a white-linen dinner of regionally sourced meats, produce and seafood dishes from executive chef and regional restauranteur Bryan Voltaggio. The three-course dinner option is $45. Business-casual attire is recommended.

Brewer's Alley PUB FOOD $$
(☑301-631-0089; www.brewers-alley.com; 124 N Market St; mains $9-19; ⊘11:30am-11:30pm Mon & Tue, to midnight Wed & Thu, to 2:30am Fri & Sat, noon-11:30pm Sun; 🐾) This bouncy brewpub is one of our favorite places in Frederick for several reasons. First, the beer: house-brewed, plenty of variety, delicious. Second, the burgers: enormous, half-pound monstrosities of staggeringly yummy proportions. Third, the rest of the menu: excellent Chesapeake seafood plus Frederick county farm produce and meats. The small patio is pleasant on sunny days.

Flying Dog Brewery MICROBREWERY
(☑301-694-7899; www.flyingdogbrewery.com; 4607 Wedgewood Blvd; ⊘3-8pm Wed-Fri, from noon Sat, noon-6pm Sun) Oh Flying Dog, we'll forgive your vaguely misogynistic beer names – Raging Bitch, Pearl Necklace – because your brews are so darn good and your staff is as helpful as can be. Stop here for a large selection of year-round and seasonal craft beers, the festive vibe and the patio. Beers are $6 by the glass or $8 for a four-beer flight. There's usually a food truck parked near the patio.

⭐ Entertainment

Weinberg Center for the Arts THEATER
(☑301-600-2828; www.weinbergcenter.org; 20 W Patrick St) Check the calendar for the schedule

WORTH A TRIP

POTOMAC RIVER & THE C&O RAILROAD
....

The Potomac River begins in the Allegheny Mountains of West Virginia, picking up force as it flows 380 miles through Maryland and Virginia on its way to the Chesapeake Bay. Laborers began constructing the Chesapeake & Ohio Canal along the river in the 1800s, setting up a system in which harnessed mules would trudge along a towpath, pulling boats upstream. A vibrant and economically important transportation route was born. Today, the National Park Service manages the C&O Canal National Historic Park (p334), a 184.5-mile hiking and cycling route that rolls along the towpath, passing historic sites and charming small towns.

A good starting point for exploring the towpath is the **Great Falls Tavern Visitor Center** (⤢ 301-767-3714; www.nps.gov/choh; 11710 MacArthur Blvd, Potomac; ⊙ 9am-4:30pm Wed-Sun; 🚻) 🐾, where you can take family-friendly boat rides. From here you can also walk to the Great Falls Overlook, a little over a half-mile one way, for a stunning view of the namesake falls.

of classic and silent movies, live music ranging from banjo to funk and an intriguing speaker series – featuring the likes of autism spokesperson and professor Temple Grandin or actor Mark Ruffalo – supported by an engaged and cultured arts community.

ℹ️ Getting There & Away

Frederick is accessible via Greyhound (www.greyhound.com) and **MARC** (⤢ MARC train 800-325-7245; https://mta.maryland.gov/marc-train; 100 S East St) trains (Monday to Friday) at the transit center located one block north of the **visitor center** (⤢ 301-600-4047; www.visitfrederick.org/visit/visitor-center; 151 S East St; ⊙ 9am-5:30pm). The MARC train Brunswick Line connects Frederick with Harpers Ferry, WV, Silver Spring, MD, and Washington, DC.

Cumberland

⤢ 240, 301 / POP 19,978

At the Potomac River, the frontier outpost of Fort Cumberland (not to be confused with the Cumberland Gap between Virginia and Kentucky) was the pioneer gateway across the Alleghenies to Pittsburgh and the Ohio River. With the completion of the C&O Canal and the arrival of the railroad in the 1800s, the city became a commercial hub, transporting goods and natural resources down the river to Georgetown.

Cumberland today has expanded into the outdoor recreation trade to guide visitors into the region's rivers, forests and mountains. The heart of the outdoor scene is Canal Pl, where two long-distance hike-and-bike paths meet: the C&O Canal towpath and the Great Allegheny Passage. Their

junction point is just a few steps from the depot for the popular scenic railroad. Canal Pl is also just a short stroll from the pedestrian-friendly streets of downtown.

⊙ Sights & Activities

**C&O Canal National
Historic Park**   NATIONAL PARK
(⤢ headquarters 301-739-4200; www.nps.gov/choh; 13 Canal St, Western Maryland Railway Station; ⊙ sunrise-sunset) FREE A marvel of engineering, the C&O Canal was designed to stretch alongside the Potomac River from the Chesapeake Bay to the Ohio River. Construction on the canal began in 1828 but was halted here in 1850 by the Appalachian Mountains. The park's protected 184.5-mile corridor includes a 12ft-wide towpath, now a hiking and bicycling trail, which stretches from here to Georgetown in DC. The Cumberland Visitor Center has displays chronicling the importance of river trade in eastern seaboard history.

At the visitor center, look for the helpful *Towpath to Town* brochure, which shares lodging and restaurant options in eight small canal towns along the route.

Allegany Museum   MUSEUM
(⤢ 301-777-7200; http://alleganymuseummd.org; 3 Pershing St; ⊙ 10am-4pm Tue-Sat, from 1pm Sun, closed Jan–mid-Mar) FREE Set in the old courthouse, this is an intriguing place to delve into Cumberland's past, with exhibits by local folk artist and woodcarver Claude Yoder; an old moonshine still; 1920s firefighting gear; a c 1880 photograph of downtown; and beautifully garbed mechanized puppets and other curiosities.

**Cumberland Visitor
Center & Museum** MUSEUM
(☑301-722-8226; www.nps.gov/choh; 13 Canal St,
Western Maryland Railway Station; ☺9am-5pm;
ⓟ) The national historic park visitor center
stocks numerous brochures about the C&O
Canal towpath and related attractions. A
mock Paw Paw Tunnel connects the visitor
center with the C&O Canal Museum, which
chronicles the importance of river trade in
eastern seaboard history. You'll also find a
replica canal boat, boat-building tools and
other related items on display.

The visitor center shares brochure space
with Allegheny Tourism, so you can pick up
self-guided walking-tour maps of Cumberland's historic downtown as well as pam-
phlets about regional attractions.

**Great Allegheny Passage –
Cumberland** CYCLING
(www.gaptrail.org; Canal Pl) From its trailhead
in Pittsburgh, PA, this biking-and-hiking
trail runs 150 scenic miles to its terminus in
Cumberland. Here it meets the 184.5-mile
C&O Canal towpath. This dedicated trail is
free of cars.

Cumberland Trail Connection CYCLING
(☑301-777-8724; www.ctcbikes.com; 14 Howard St,
Canal Pl; per half-day/day/week from $20/35/175;

☺8am-7pm Apr-Oct, 10:30am-6pm Nov-Mar)
Conveniently located near the start of the
C&O Canal towpath, this outfit rents bicycles (cruisers, touring bikes and mountain
bikes), and also arranges shuttle service anywhere from Pittsburgh to DC. Does bike repair, too. Check the website for a basic map
of the towpath.

🚩 Tours

Western Maryland Scenic Railroad TOURS
(☑800-872-4650; www.wmsr.com; 13 Canal St;
adult/child $46/30; ☺generally 11:30am Fri & Sat,
1pm Sun mid-Apr–Oct, hours & trips vary seasonally)
Passengers can catch steam-locomotive
rides, traversing forests and steep ravines,
to the Frostburg depot, a 3½-hour round-
trip from its Cumberland terminus outside
the Cumberland Visitor Center, near the
start of the C&O Canal. In Frostburg, you
can explore a carriage museum and walk to
downtown restaurants during the one-hour
layover before climbing back aboard.

🛏 Sleeping & Eating

Fairfield Inn & Suites HOTEL $$
(☑301-722-0340; www.marriott.com; 21 N Wine-
ow St; r $154; ⓟ❄@🛜🏊) This modern
and recently renovated property bordering
the C&O Canal towpath is a prime spot for

MARYLAND CUMBERLAND

DEEP CREEK LAKE

Deep in western Maryland, plunked into a blue valley at the end of a series of tree-ridged mountains, is the state's largest man-made lake: Deep Creek. With some 69 miles of shoreline stretching through the hills in the surrounding Garrett County, there are a lot of outdoor activities here, as well as several small towns scattered about where you can find lodging and food.

Hikers can enjoy waterfalls, thick woods and great camping in **Swallow Falls State Park** (☑301-387-6938; http://dnr.maryland.gov/publiclands; 2470 Maple Glade Rd; per person $5 Jun-Aug and Sat & Sun May, Sep & Oct, per vehicle $5 rest of year; ☺8am-sunset Mar-Oct, from 10am Nov-Feb; ⓟ🚻🏊), while fishing, boating, kayaking and stand-up paddleboard-ing are popular distractions at the lake. The lake is easily accessed from **Deep Creek Lake State Park** (☑301-387-5563; http://dnr.maryland.gov/publiclands; 898 State Park Rd, Swanton; per vehicle $5 Jun-Aug, per person $5 Sep-May; ☺8am-sunset; ⓟ🚻🏊), where you'll find an inviting woodsy campground.

The five-day **Autumn Glory Festival** (www.visitdeepcreek.com; ☺mid-Oct) draws leaf peepers in October. Every room has a view of the lake at pleasant **LakeStar Lodge** (☑301-387-5596; www.lakestarlodge.com; 2001 Deep Creek Dr, McHenry; r $179; ⓟ❄🛜🏊). Wash down delicious wood-fired flatbreads with a refreshing craft ale at rustic **Mountain State Brewing** (☑301-387-3360; www.mountainstatebrewing.com; 6690 Sang Run Rd; sandwiches $9-13, pizzas $12-26; ☺11am-9pm Sun-Thu, to 10pm Fri & Sat), the lone Maryland outpost of the popular West Virginia microbrewery.

All just a short drive from the West Virginia border, it's a scenic place to relax and/or play between Baltimore and Morgantown, WV.

cyclists. The included continental buffet breakfast will energize you for your ride. It's also an easy walk to the Western Maryland Scenic Railroad (p335) depot as well as downtown. Rooms come with a microwave and mini-fridge.

Queen City Creamery & Deli   DINER $
(☑301-777-0011; www.queencitycreamery.com; 108 W Harrison St; mains $4-9, one scoop custard $3; ⊙7am-9pm Mon-Thu, to 10pm Fri, 8am-10pm Sat, to 8am-9pm Sun, vary seasonally) This retro soda fountain is like a 1940s time warp, with creamy shakes and homemade frozen custard, thick sandwiches and belly-filling breakfasts.

Baltimore Street Grill   AMERICAN $$
(☑301-724-1711; www.facebook.com/bstgrill; 82 Baltimore St; mains lunch $7-15, dinner $7-31; ⊙11am-10pm Mon-Sat, bar open to 2am Wed-Sat) At lunchtime, everyone at the bar seems to know one other at this narrow and cozy neighborhood spot that serves up good pub fare, including burgers, sandwiches, pizzas and a few Cajun specialties. It's an easy walk from the C&O Canal towpath.

❶ Getting Around

The **Amtrak station** (☑800-872-7245; www.amtrak.com; 201 E Harrison St) is close to downtown. Cumberland is on the daily Capitol Limited route that links Washington, DC, and Chicago. Pittsburgh is 100 miles northwest of the city. Greyhound buses also stop at the station. From the eastern part of Maryland, Cumberland can be reached by following I-70 west to I-68 west.

SOUTHERN MARYLAND

Tucked between the nation's capital, the Potomac River and the Chesapeake Bay, this little-known region is a patchwork of marsh, fields and forests spread across three counties. It's also home to the state's oldest European settlements and stunning riverscape vistas – all an hour or so from Washington, DC. The Religious Freedom Byway, a state scenic drive, spotlights the struggles of Protestant and Catholic settlers in the region. Their religious conflicts are engagingly explained in Historic St Mary's City, a sprawling living history museum near the southern tip of the peninsula. Nobody seems to be thinking much about religion near the waterfront in the tiki hut bar on Solomons

Island. Kayakers should head to one of the coastline water trails of the tidal Potomac.

❶ Getting There & Away

The region will need to be explored by car. The northernmost county in the region is Charles County. It begins 35 miles south of DC. Historic St Mary's City is 70 miles south of DC and located in St Mary's County south of La Plata. Solomons Island is across the Patunxet River to the east.

Leonardtown & St Mary's County

The seat of St Mary's county has worked hard to maintain its small-town atmosphere. The central square (Fenwick & Washington St) is the closest thing this community has to a town green. Look for a rock in front of the nearby circuit courthouse (Courthouse Dr & Washington); legend has it that Moll Dwyer, a local 'witch', froze to death while kneeling on said rock and cursed the town with her dying breath. Her faint knee imprints are supposedly still visible in the stone.

Maryland's status as a border state between the North and South is evident in the square's onsite World War I memorial, divided into 'white' and 'colored' sections. The sprawling Historic St Mary's City recreates the state's first capital, which was once a busy port town. Scattered parks and islands, plus a few paddling trails, round out the appeal.

◉ Sights & Activities

The Potomac River and Chesapeake Bay meet off the coast of St Mary's County, which covers the tip of the peninsula. Home to creeks, marshes and miles and miles of coastline, St Mary's is well suited for kayaking. There are numerous water trails here, and you'll find one for every skill level. For a list of paddling trails and local outfitters, visit the county website at www.visitstmarysmd.com or stop by the Old Jail.

Historic St Mary's City   MUSEUM
(HSMC; ☑800-762-1634, 240-895-4990; www.stmaryscity.org; 18751 Hogaboom Lane, St Mary's City; adult/children 6-18yr $10/6; ⊙10am-4pm Tue-Sat mid-Mar–Jun & Sep-Nov, Wed-Sun Jul & Aug; 🅿🚻) In the 1600s, St Mary's City was a busy port and served as the state's first capital. Today, the spot is a living history museum romantically positioned among the sur-

rounding forests, fields and farmlands along the river. The reconstructed buildings and costumed docents really make the past feel relevant. Given its distance from anything resembling a crowd, HSMC feels more colonial than similar places like Williamsburg.

Leonardtown Wharf Park WATERFRONT
(☑301-475-9791; www.visitstmarysmd.com; 22510 Washington St, Leonardtown) Stretch your legs by the waterfront and admire the large compass rose design at the wharf. There's a small playground, and you can rent kayaks and stand-up paddleboards here Thursdays through Sundays ($35 for three hours).

Point Lookout State Park STATE PARK
(☑301-872-5688; www.dnr.maryland.gov/public lands; 11175 Point Lookout Rd, Scotland; per vehicle $5, summer per person $7; ⏰6am-sunset; Ⓟ🚻) 🏊 The western shore of Maryland – that is, the western peninsula created by Chesapeake Bay – terminates here, in a preserved space of lagoons, pine woods and marshes managed by Point Lookout State Park. There's a playground for kids and a sandy beach that's OK for swimming, but watch out for jellyfish in summer; they're not deadly, but their stings hurt.

During the Civil War, the Union Army imprisoned thousands of Confederate POWs here, overseen by black soldiers. Swampy conditions and harsh treatment by guards led to the death of some 4000 Confederates. A controversial shrine to their memory has been built, and legends persist of Confederate ghosts haunting local swamps at night.

Old Jail Museum & Visitor Center HISTORIC BUILDING
(☑301-475-2467; 11 Courthouse Dr, Leonardtown; ⏰10am-5pm Fri & Sat) Completed in 1876, this small jail replaced the 1858 jail – which was apparently quite easy to escape. The Old Jail is two stories high and the cells were on the 2nd floor. The jailor and his family lived on the 1st floor. Inside the granite-and-brick structure you can see a few pieces of old furniture and exhibits about country history. The jail doubles as a visitor center.

Pac Paddle Sports KAYAKING
(☑410-394-2770; www.pacpaddle.com; 22510 Washington St, Leonardtown; 3hr kayak $35-45, 3hr SUP $35; ⏰11am-6pm Thu-Sun seasonally) Rents kayaks and stand-up paddle boards at Leonardtown Wharf Park and other locations in the county. Open seasonally.

SOUTHERN MARYLAND: WATER TRAILS

Six designated water trails explore the marshes and rivers running alongside the St Mary's peninsula coastline and the Potomac River. Levels range from easy to difficult. Check the county website (www.visitstmarysmd.com) or pick up the *Water Trails* brochure at the Old Jail for trailheads and trail descriptions. An access point for the McIntosh Run trail is at Leonardtown Wharf.

🛏 Sleeping & Eating

Woodlawn B&B $$
(☑301-872-0555; www.woodlawn-farm.com; 16040 Woodlawn Ln, Ridge; r $140-240; Ⓟ🐾) Seven well-kept suites, all individually decked out with rustic charm (think boxwood gardens, fireplaces and vanity chests) and modern amenities (such as glassed-in showers and Jacuzzis with views of the water) characterize the lodging at this farm, which has been converted into an excellent rural resort in the cornfields of southern St Mary's county.

Heritage Chocolates DESSERTS $
(☑240-587-3123; www.heritagechocolateshop. com; 22669 Washington St, Leonardtown; box of 4 chocolates $4.50; ⏰10am-8pm Mon-Sat, noon-7pm Sun) Why yes, I would like a handcrafted sea-salt caramel in a cute little box. And go ahead and throw in a cashew turtle. And an almond cluster. And a raspberry cream. And actually, forget the box. I'll eat them here. Overlooking the town square, this chocolate shop is a pleasant place to eat gourmet chocolate and sip coffee.

Courtney's Seafood Restaurant SEAFOOD $
(☑301-872-4403; www.courtneysseafoodrestau rant.com; 48290 Wynne Rd, Ridge; lunch mains $6-14, dinner mains $6-29; ⏰8am-9pm; Ⓟ) This fish shack, which isn't that far in exterior decor from a bomb shelter (it doesn't get significantly better inside), is run by Tom Courtney, local fisherman and all around surly character. So what's to love? Fish, crabs and oysters. Tom catches them, his wife cooks them, and everything is fresh and tasty.

⊕ Getting There & Away

Leonardtown is 60 miles south of Washington, DC and about 90 miles south of Baltimore. You will need a car to check out the sites.

Solomons Island & Calvert County

Solomons is a seaside (but not a beachy) town of antique shops, cafes, diners and one of the most famous bars in the state: the Tiki Bar. The town sits on a peninsula that is flanked by the Patuxent River and the Chesapeake Bay. Several parks with hiking trails – and one with good fossil-hunting – border these waterways. Solomons sits within Calvert County and easily connects to St Mary's County via the Thomas Johnson Bridge.

⊙ Sights

One of the favorite activities of Southern Maryland families is coming to Clavert Cliffs State Park, strolling across the sand and plucking out fossils and sharks' teeth from the pebbly debris near the base of the cliffs, at the end of the Red Trail. Note that you are allowed to hunt and collect fossils on the beach, but you cannot dig into the cliffs or hunt below the cliffs. Check the website for the location of the beach and other specifics. More than 600 species of fossils have been identified at the park.

Calvert Cliffs State Park   STATE PARK
(☑ 301-743-7613; www.dnr.maryland.gov/public lands; 9500 HG Trueman Rd, Lusby; per vehicle $7; ⊙ sunrise-sunset; Ⓟ 🚻 📷) 🚶 In Southern Maryland, skinny Calvert County scratches at the Chesapeake Bay and the Patuxent River. This is a gentle landscape ('user-friendly' as a local ranger puts it) of low-lying forests, estuarine marshes and placid waters, but there is one rugged feature: the 10- to 20-million-year-old Calvert cliffs. These burnt-umber pillars stretch along the coast for some 24 miles, and form the seminal landscape feature of Calvert Cliffs State Park, where they front the water and a peb-bly, honey-sand beach scattered with driftwood and drying beds of kelp.

🛏 Sleeping

Back Creek Inn   B&B $$
(☑ 410-326-2022; www.backcreekinnbnb.com; 210 Alexander Lane, Solomons; r $125-180, cottage $230; Ⓟ 🛜) This lovely B&B is positioned over the eponymous Back Creek – and can be reached by sea or by car. Pretty rooms are named after herbs, and couples can enjoy extra privacy in the adjacent cottage. Owner Carol is a warm hostess, and amenities on offer include bicycles for exploring and a fire pit. Breakfast expands to a buffet on Sundays.

🍴 Eating & Drinking

CD Cafe   AMERICAN $$
(☑ 410-326-3877; www.thecdcafe.com; 14350 Solomons Island Rd, Solomons; mains $11-26; ⊙ 11:30am-3:30pm & 5:30-9:30pm Mon-Sat, to 9pm Sun; 🍴) Intensely fresh seafood and produce characterize the menu at this sunny spot, where natural light, friendly service, crisp salads and tasty pastas are the order of the day. The fresh flounder sandwich is a seafood-lover's delight, while the shepherd's pie is hearty and filling on a chilly day.

Tiki Bar   BAR
(☑ 410-326-4075; www.tikibarsolomons.com; 85 Charles St, Solomons; ⊙ noon-2am Apr-Oct) We're not entirely sure why the bar is so famous; it's got a sandy beach, some Easter Island heads and Tiki torches (and very strong drinks), and that's about it. Nonetheless people come from as far away as DC and Baltimore to drink here on weekends, and the bar's grand opening for the summer season literally attracts thousands of tourists to Solomons Island.

⊕ Getting There & Away

Solomons Island is 65 miles Southwest of Washington, DC and about 85 miles south of Baltimore. The best way to get here? By car or by boat.

Virginia

POP 8.5 MILLION

Best Places to Eat

➡ The Shack (p370)

➡ L'Opossum (p355)

➡ Fat Canary (p363)

➡ Lucky (p374)

➡ Inn at Little Washington (p360)

Best Places to Stay

➡ Hornsby House Inn (p364)

➡ Quirk Hotel (p354)

➡ Georges (p373)

➡ South Street Inn (p359)

➡ HI Richmond (p354)

Why Go?

The Commonwealth of Virginia is steeped in history and tradition. It's the birthplace of America, where English settlers established the first permanent colony in the New World in 1607. Since that time, the state has played a lead role in nearly every major American drama, from the Revolutionary and Civil War to the Civil Rights movement and the attacks of September 11, 2001.

Virginia's natural beauty is also diverse. Chesapeake Bay and the wide sandy beaches kiss the Atlantic Ocean. Pine forests, marshes and rolling green hills form the soft curves of the central Piedmont region, while the rolling Blue Ridge mountains and stunning Shenandoah Valley line its back.

There's loads for the visitor to enjoy, including world-class tourist attractions such as Colonial Williamsburg, a wealth of outdoor activities, a foot-tapping mountain-music scene and an ever-growing network of wine, beer and spirit trails.

When to Go
Richmond

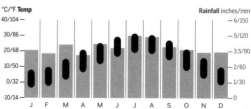

May Wild flowers and spring blooms brighten cycling trails and scenic drives.

Jul Fourth of July celebrations across the state, plus music festivals galore.

Oct Check out the colorful fall foliage on scenic mountain drives along Skyline Dr and the Blue Ridge Pkwy.

Virginia Highlights

1 **Historic Triangle** (p361) Tracing America's roots in Colonial Williamsburg, Jamestown and Yorktown.

2 **Shenandoah National Park** (p356) Cruising along

Skyline Drive and hiking to the summit of a commanding peak.

3 **Charlottesville** (p357) Marveling at Thomas Jefferson's architectural

genius at the University of Virginia and nearby Monticello.

4 **Alexandria** (p344) Wandering the pretty streets of the historic Old Town district then cycling the

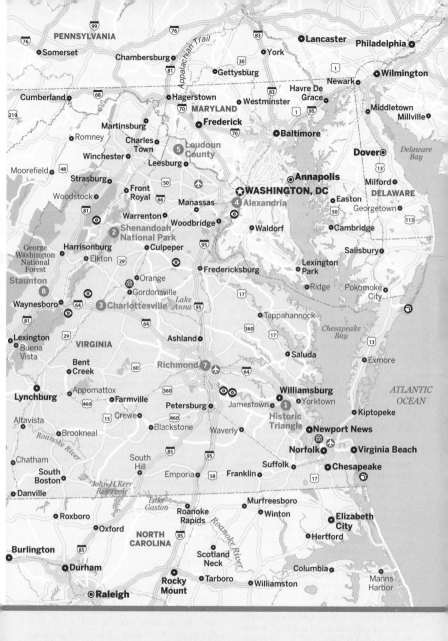

PENNSYLVANIA

Somerset

Chambersburg

York ●Lancaster

Philadelphia

Cumberland

Hagerstown

MARYLAND

Westminster

Havre de
Grace

Newark

●Wilmington

Middletown
Millville

Romney

Martinsburg

Frederick

●Baltimore

Dover●

Delaware
Bay

Charles
Town

Moorefield

Winchester

Leesburg

Loudoun
County

Milford

DELAWARE

Strasburg

Woodstock

Front
Royal

Manassas

★WASHINGTON, DC

Annapolis

Easton

Georgetown

Harrisonburg

Warrenton

Woodbridge

Alexandria

Waldorf

Cambridge

George
Washington
National
Forest

Elkton

Culpeper

Fredericksburg

Salisbury

Staunton

Orange

Lexington
Park

Pokomoke
City

Waynesboro

Gordonsville

Lake
Anna

Ridge

Charlottesville

VIRGINIA

Ashland

Tappahannock

Chesapeake
Bay

Lexington

Buena
Vista

Bent
Creek

Richmond

Saluda

Exmore

Lynchburg

Appomattox

Farmville

Williamsburg

Petersburg

Jamestown

Yorktown

ATLANTIC
OCEAN

Altavista

Crewe

Waverly

Historic
Triangle

Kiptopeke

Brookneal

Blackstone

Newport News

Chatham

South
Hill

Norfolk

Virginia Beach

South
Boston

Emporia

Franklin

Suffolk

Chesapeake

Danville

John H. Kerr
Reservoir

Lake
Gaston

Murfreesboro

Winton

Elizabeth
City

Roxboro

Roanoke
Rapids

Hertford

Oxford

NORTH
CAROLINA

Columbia

Manns
Harbor

Burlington

Scotland
Neck

Durham

Rocky
Mount

Tarboro

Williamston

●Raleigh

George Washington Memorial
Parkway.

5 Loudoun County (p350)
Following a wine trail along the
backroads of Virginia's famous
horse country.

6 Floyd (p375) Tapping your
feet to bluegrass music at
the Friday Night Jamboree at
Floyd Country Store.

7 Richmond (p350)
Exploring Downtown and

visiting the impressive
museums.

8 Staunton (p368)
Catching a Shakespeare
matinee then checking out
Staunton's foodie culture.

History

Humans have occupied Virginia for at least 5000 years. Several thousand Native Americans were already here in May 1607 when Captain James Smith and his crew sailed up Chesapeake Bay and founded Jamestown, the first permanent English colony in the New World. Named for Queen Elizabeth I – aka the 'Virgin Queen' – the territory originally occupied most of America's eastern seaboard. By 1610 most of the colonists had died from starvation in their quest for gold, until John Rolfe (husband of Pocahontas) discovered Virginia's real riches: tobacco.

A feudal aristocracy grew out of tobacco farming, and many gentry scions became Founding Fathers, including native son George Washington. In the 19th century the slave-based plantation system grew both in size and incompatibility with the industrializing north; Virginia seceded in 1861 and became the epicenter of the Civil War. Following its defeat, the state walked a tense cultural tightrope, accruing a layered identity that included older aristocrats, a rural and urban working class, waves of immigrants and, today, the tech-heavy suburbs of DC. The state revels in its history, yet still wants to pioneer the American experiment; thus, while Virginia reluctantly desegregated in the 1960s, today it houses one of the most ethnically diverse populations of the New South.

❶ Getting There & Away

The largest regional airports include **Washington Dulles International Airport** (IAD; www.metwashairports.com; 🕿) in Northern Virginia, **Richmond International Airport** (RIC; ☏ 804-226-3000; www.flyrichmond.com; 1 Richard E Byrd Terminal Dr; 🕿) in Richmond, Norfolk International Airport (p366) in and around, and Roanoke-Blacksburg Regional Airport (p368) in Southwest Virginia. American, United and Delta serve Charlottesville Albemarle Airport (p360) in the Piedmont region.

Amtrak stops in Richmond at Main St Station (p357) and Staples Mill Rd Station (p357). There are also train stations or platforms in Charlottesville (p360), Staunton (p370), Roanoke (p375), Williamsburg (p363) and Newport News. In and around Northern Virginia, Amtrak stops in Fredericksburg (p349) and near Manassas National Battlefield Park (p344).

NORTHERN VIRGINIA

Affluent, laid-back and green in both senses of the word, Northern Virginia (NoVa) is DC's equally refined neighbor. Located just across from the picket fence of the Potomac River, many NoVa communities are basically suburbs of Washington, attached by the Metro. Others are a short drive away. There are plenty of reasons to visit, including historic towns, districts and estates; Civil War sites; important monuments and memorials; and an ever-growing portfolio of wineries.

Arlington

☏ 703 / POP 230,050

Sitting just across the Potomac River from DC, Arlington is best known as the home of the Arlington National Cemetery and the Pentagon. Other than these two – admittedly major – draws, there's not much to attract the visitor. The once-vibrant music and club strip on Wilson Blvd has been decimated in recent times as buildings are torn down to make way for sleek new high-rise apartment and office towers.

◉ Sights

★**Pentagon** NOTABLE BUILDING
(https://pentagontours.osd.mil/tours; Arlington; ⊙memorial 24hr, tours by appointment 10am-4pm Mon-Thu, noon-4pm Fri; Ⓜ Blue, Yellow Line to Pentagon) South of Arlington Cemetery is the Pentagon, the largest office building in the world and the headquarters of the US Department of Defense, the Army, Navy and Air Force. Outside the building is the **Pentagon Memorial** (www.pentagonmemorial.org; ⊙24hr) FREE; 184 illuminated benches honor each person killed in the September 11, 2001, terrorist attack on the Pentagon. To get inside the building, you'll have to book a free guided one-hour tour on the website and provide appropriate photo ID. Make reservations 14 to 90 days in advance.

★**Arlington National Cemetery** CEMETERY
(☏ 877-907-8585; www.arlingtoncemetery.mil; Memorial Ave; ⊙8am-7pm Apr-Sep, to 5pm Oct-Mar; Ⓜ Blue Line to Arlington Cemetery) FREE Arlington is the somber final resting place for more than 400,000 military personnel and their dependents. The 624-acre grounds contain the dead of every war the USA has fought since the Revolution. Highlights include the Tomb of the Unknown Soldier, with its elaborate changing-of-the-guard ceremony (every hour on the hour October through March; every half-hour April through September), and the grave of John F Kennedy and his family, marked by an eternal flame.

Departing from the **Welcome Center** (Memorial Dr), hop-on, hop-off **bus tours** (📞202-750-9636; www.arlingtontours.com; adult/child $13.50/6.75; ⏰8:30am-6pm Apr-Sep, to 4pm Oct-Mar) are an easy way to visit the cemetery's main sights. Other points of interest include the **Shuttle Challenger Memorial** (off Memorial Dr); the **USS Maine Memorial** (off McPherson Dr), marked by the battleship's

huge mast; the controversial **Confederate Memorial** (off McPherson Dr) that honors war dead from the Civil War's breakaway states; and the tomb of DC city planner **Pierre L'Enfant** (off Sherman Dr). The **Iwo Jima Memorial** (Ord & Weitzel Dr), displaying the famous raising of the flag over Mt Suribachi, is on the cemetery's northern fringes and is included in the bus tour.

Arlington

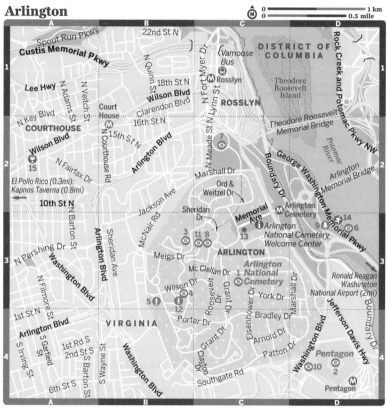

VIRGINIA ARLINGTON

Arlington

344

OFF THE BEATEN TRACK

MANASSAS BATTLEFIELD PARK

The site of two major Confederate victories early in the Civil War, **Manassas National Battlefield Park** (☑703-361-1339; www.nps.gov/mana; 6511 Sudley Rd, off I-66; ☺park dawn-dusk, visitor center 8:30am-5pm) **FREE** today is a curving green hillscape, sectioned into fuzzy fields of tall grass and wildflowers by split-rail wood fences. Start your tour at the Henry Hill Visitor Center to watch the orientation film and pick up park and trail maps. Daily guided tours are offered in summer.

Much of the cemetery was built on the grounds of **Arlington House** (☑703-235-1530; www.nps.gov/arho; Sherman Dr; ☺9:30am-4:30pm) **FREE**, the former home of Robert E Lee and his wife Mary Anna Custis Lee, a descendant of Martha Washington. When Lee left to lead Virginia's army in the Civil War, Union troops confiscated the property to bury their dead.

George Washington Memorial Parkway
PARKWAY

(☑703-289-2500; www.nps.gov/gwmp) The 25-mile Virginia portion of the highway honors its namesake with recreation areas and memorials all the way south to his old estate at Mount Vernon. It's lined with remnants of George Washington's life and works, such as his old Patowmack Company canal (in Great Falls National Park) and parks that were once part of his farmlands (Riverside Park, Fort Hunt Park). The 18.5-mile-long Mount Vernon Trail (p347) parallels the parkway.

Kennedy Gravesites
TOMB

(off Sheridan Dr, Arlington National Cemetery; Ⓜ Blue Line to Arlington Cemetery) An eternal flame flickers beside this simple but moving gravesite – the final resting place for President John F Kennedy and Jacqueline Kennedy Onassis. Arlington National Cemetery Tours buses stop nearby.

✖ Eating & Drinking

El Pollo Rico
LATIN AMERICAN $

(☑703-522-3220; www.elpolloricorestaurant.com; 932 N Kenmore St; chicken with sides $8-17; ☺11am-10pm; Ⓜ Silver, Orange Line to Clarendon/Virginia Sq-GMU) *Polla a la brasa* (rotisserie chicken)

fiends queue outside the door of this no-frills Peruvian chicken joint every night, keen to feast on its tender, juicy, flavor-packed birds served with succulent (highly addictive) dipping sauces, crunchy fries and sloppy 'slaw.

Kapnos Taverna
GREEK $$

(☑703-243-4400; www.kapnostaverna.com; 4000 Wilson Blvd, Ballston; mezze & spreads $10-24; ☺11:30am-3 & 5-10pm Mon-Thu, to 11pm Fri, 11am-3pm & 5-11pm Sat, 11am-3pm & 5-9pm Sun; ☑; Ⓜ Silver, Orange Line to Ballston-MU) It may be too sleek to qualify as an old-school taverna, but this buzzy hot spot from chef and restaurateur Mike Isabella still inspires thoughts of Greece with its rich coastal and traditional dishes, not to mention the loud atmosphere. Try a variety of mezzes and spreads and then chicken, fish or lamb shoulder to share with your table.

Whitlow's on Wilson
BAR

(☑703-276-9693; www.whitlows.com; 2854 Wilson Blvd; ☺11am-2am Mon-Fri, 9am-2am Sat & Sun; Ⓜ Silver, Orange Line to Clarendon) Occupying almost an entire block just east of Clarendon Metro, Whitlow's on Wilson has something for everyone: burgers, brunch and comfort food on the menu; happening happy hours and positive pickup potential; plus 12 brews on tap, a pool table, a jukebox, live music and an easygoing atmosphere. Head to the rooftop tiki bar in warmer months.

❶ Getting There & Away

Arlington borders I-66 and is partially encircled by I-495, which loops around DC.

Alexandria

☑703 / POP 155,810

The charming town of Alexandria is 5 miles and 250 years away from Washington. Once a salty port, Alexandria – known as 'Old Town' to locals – is today a posh collection of red-brick homes, cobblestone streets, gas lamps and a waterfront promenade near the Potomac River. It's often described as one of the best-preserved historical districts in the nation. Boutiques, outdoor cafes and bars pack the main thoroughfare, making the town a fine afternoon or evening jaunt. Two miles north of Old Town, the residential Del Ray neighborhood is a pleasant place to stroll, especially along the eatery-lined Mt Vernon Ave. Alexandria is also a jumping-off spot for excursions to Mount Vernon.

Alexandria

N 0 ——————— 400 m
  0 ——————— 0.2 miles

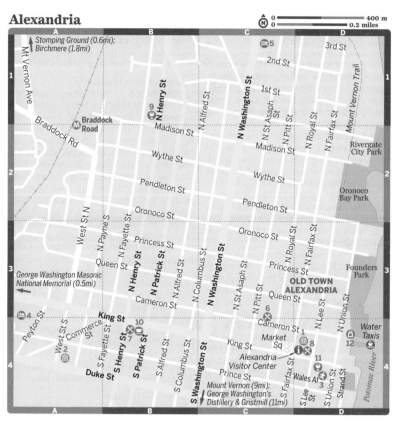

Alexandria

◎ Sights
1 Carlyle House D4
2 Freedom House Museum A4

◎ Activities, Courses & Tours
3 Bike & Roll D4

◎ Sleeping
4 Lorien Hotel & Spa A3
5 Old Colony Inn C1

◎ Eating
Brabo Tasting Room .... (see 4)

6 Caphe Banh Mi C3
7 Hank's Oyster Bar B4
8 Sonoma Cellars D4

◎ Drinking & Nightlife
9 Captain Gregory's B1
10 Killer ESP B4
11 Pizzeria Birreria Paradiso D4

◎ Shopping
12 Torpedo Factory Art Center D4

◎ Sights

★**Mount Vernon**   HISTORIC SITE
(☏703-780-2000; www.mountvernon.org; 3200
Mount Vernon Memorial Hwy; adult/child 6-11yr
$20/12; ◷9am-5pm Apr-Oct, to 4pm Nov-Mar;
Ⓜ Yellow Line to Huntington, then Fairfax Connector
bus 101) One of America's most visited histor-

ic sites, Mount Vernon was the beloved home
of George and Martha Washington, who
lived here from the time of their marriage
in 1759 until George's death in 1799. Regular
guided tours of the furnished main house
give a fascinating insight into the Washing-
tons' daily life, and self-guided tours of the

outbuildings and gardens estate offer plenty of opportunities to interact with actors offering first-person narratives of working and living on the 18th-century plantation.

From April to October, the Mount Vernon entrance ticket also includes entry to Washington's nearby **distillery and gristmill** (adult/child 6-11yr $5/3, free with Mount Vernon ticket; ⊙10am-5pm Apr-Oct); a free shuttle bus travels between these and the estate.

To avoid inevitable queues at the entrance to Mount Vernon, purchase your ticket online ahead of your visit (you'll save money too!). A number of tours and performances are offered daily, including the popular one-hour 'Enslaved People of Mount Vernon' tour ($4). Some tours sell out, so it's best to book these online ahead of your visit. Audio-guide tours of the estate cost $7 and can be shared within a group.

Be sure to allow at least one hour to browse the object-rich exhibits and view the immersive 4D 'Revolutionary War Experience' spectacular in the Donald W Reynolds Museum and Education Center. Kids will love the 'Hands on History' activity room here, too.

Mount Vernon is 16 miles south of DC, off the Mount Vernon Memorial Hwy. By public transportation, take the Metro (Yellow Line) to Huntington, then switch to Fairfax Connector bus 101. **Grayline** (☑202-779-9894; www.graylinedc.com; adult/child 6-11yr $75/40; ⊙Tue-Sat late Jan-Dec), **OnBoard Tours** (☑301-839-5261; www.onboardtours.com; adult/child incl Mount Vernon $80/70; ⊙Apr-Sep) and **USA Guided Tours** (☑202-733 7376; www.usaguidedtours.com; adult/child 3-12yr incl Mount Vernon $79/69) run bus tours from DC.

Several companies offer seasonal boat trips to Mount Vernon; **Potomac Riverboat Company** (☑877-511-2628; www.potomacriverboatco.com; return adult/child 6-11yr incl Mount Vernon from $42/22; ⊙Apr-Oct) has boats that depart from the Alexandria City Marina and **Spirit Cruises** (☑866-302-2469; www.spiritcruises.com; return adult/child 6-11yr incl Mount Vernon $50/45; ⊙Mar-Oct) has the *Spirit of Mount Vernon*, which departs from the SW Waterfront in DC.

Carlyle House
HISTORIC BUILDING

(☑703-549-2997; www.novaparks.com; 121 N Fairfax St; adult/child 5-12yr $5/3; ⊙10am-4pm Tue-Sat, noon-4pm Sun; Ⓜ Blue, Yellow Line to King St-Old Town) If you have time for just one historic house tour in Alexandria, make it this one. The house dates from 1753 when merchant and city founder, John Carlyle, built the most lavish mansion in town (which in those days

was little more than log cabins and muddy lanes). The Georgian Palladian–style house is decorated with paintings, historic relics and period furnishings that help bring the past to life. Visits are by one-hour guided tour.

Freedom House Museum
MUSEUM

(☑708-836-2858; www.visitalexandriava.com; 1315 Duke St; ⊙10am-3pm Mon-Fri, guided tours & weekends by appointment only; Ⓜ Blue, Yellow Line to King St-Old Town) **FREE** This demure Federal-style row house holds a tragic story. At a time when Alexandria was the nation's second-largest slave center (after New Orleans), a flourishing slave-trading business occupied this building and adjoining space. A well-presented basement museum, developed by the Northern Virginia Urban League, powerfully tells the stories of the thousands of enslaved people who passed through. Personal video narratives and artifacts are on view in a heartbreaking setting.

Up to 150 slaves were kept in the holding pen outside (since torn down). Among those likely held here was Solomon Northup, a free black man who in 1841 was kidnapped from Washington and sold into bondage in the south. His story was portrayed in the film *Twelve Years a Slave*. There's no admission, but donations are encouraged. The museum isn't signed; look for the Franklin and Armfield Slave Office information panel.

George Washington
Masonic National Memorial
MONUMENT

(☑703-683-2007; www.gwmemorial.org; 101 Callahan Dr at King St; adult/child under 13yr $15/free; ⊙9am-5pm; Ⓜ Blue, Yellow Line to King St-Old Town) Alexandria's most prominent landmark features a fine view from the observation deck of its 333ft tower. Modeled after Egypt's Lighthouse of Alexandria, it honors the first president (who was initiated into the Masons in Fredericksburg in 1752 and later became Worshipful Master of Alexandria Lodge No 22). After paying admission, you can explore exhibits on the 1st and 2nd floors, but to visit the tower and see Washington-family artifacts, you must take a 60-minute guided tour.

Tours depart at 9:30am, 11am, 1pm, 2:30pm and 4pm. If you ask one too many questions about masonic symbolism and the *National Treasure* movies, a trapdoor will open and drop you into the parking lot. We jest; it's all quite welcoming and fascinating.

Tickets to the observation deck are free and general admission is discounted to $10 for holders of the Alexandria Museum Pass.

🏃 Activities

★ Mount Vernon Trail
CYCLING

(www.nps.gov; ⊙6am-10pm; Ⓜ Arlington Cemetery, Ronald Reagan Washington National Airport & Rosslyn) The 18-mile-long Mount Vernon Trail is a paved riverside path that is a favorite with local cyclists. From the Francis Scott Key Bridge, it follows the Potomac River south past Roosevelt Island, Arlington National Cemetery and Ronald Reagan Washington National Airport, through Old Town Alexandria, all the way to Mount Vernon.

Sights along the way include **Lady Bird Johnson Park** (www.nps.gov; ⊙6am-10pm; Ⓜ Arlington Cemetery), which commemorates the First Lady who tried to beautify the capital via greenery-planting campaigns; swathes of tulips and daffodils bloom here in spring. Gravelly Point, just north of the airport, provides a vantage point for watching the planes take off and land. Roaches Run Waterfowl Sanctuary lets you check out naturally airborne creatures including ospreys and green herons.

The trail is mostly flat, except the long climb up the hill to George Washington's house at the end. The scenery is magnificent – DC skylines and all – and the historical component is certainly unique.

Bike & Roll
CYCLING

(☎202-842-2453; www.bikethesites.com; 1 Wales Alley; per 2hr/day from $16/40; ⊙10am-6pm Wed-Sun mid-Mar–Oct; Ⓜ Blue, Yellow Line to King St-Old Town) Rent a bike and hop on the Mount Vernon Trail one block south. You'll have to call ahead, though, since bikes are available only by reservation (no walk-ins). Ask about package deals (including picnic provisions, admission fees and one-way boat trips) to George Washington's estate. The shop is located off Strand St. Kids' bikes are also available (per hour/day $10/25).

🛏 Sleeping

Old Colony Inn
MOTEL $

(☎703-739-2222; www.oldcolonyinnalexandria. com; 1101 N Washington St; r from $67; 🅿🐾🛜❄; Ⓜ Blue, Yellow Line to Braddock Rd) Offers good-value rooms, proximity to Old Town, a fitness center and complimentary breakfasts. There's also a free shuttle service to Reagan airport, the Old Town (just under a mile away) and to the Metro station.

Lorien Hotel & Spa
HOTEL $$

(☎703-894-3434; www.lorienhotelandspa.com; 1600 King St; r $199-399; 🅿🐾❄🛜❄; Ⓜ Blue, Yellow Line to King St-Old Town) Hidden behind

King St shopfronts, this is Alexandria's best accommodation option. Recently renovated rooms are comfortable and well sized, but it's the added extras here that matter: a communal wine hour in the early evening, complimentary morning coffee in the foyer, spa treatments (massages $115 to $250), a gym and a steam room. Meals can be enjoyed in the attached **Brabo Tasting Room** (☎703-894-5252; www.braborestaurant.com; sandwiches $14-16, mains $13-22; ⊙7-10:30am & 11:30am-10pm Mon-Thu, to 11pm Fri, 8-11am & 11:30am-11pm Sat, to 10pm Sun).

🍴 Eating

Stomping Ground
BREAKFAST $

(☎703-567-6616; www.stompdelray.com; 309 Mt Vernon Ave; mains $7-12; ⊙7am-3pm Tue-Sat, 9am-3pm Sun; Ⓜ Blue, Yellow Line to Braddock St-Old Town) Did somebody say biscuit? Oh yes they did. And make that a scratch-made buttermilk biscuit piled with fillings of your choice (Benton's bacon, eggs, veggie frittata, avocado and many more) and with gouda grits on the side. Or just stop by this stylish Del Ray spot for coffee and to work on your laptop. Order and collect at the counter.

Caphe Banh Mi
VIETNAMESE $

(☎703-549-0800; www.caphebahnmi.com; 407 Cameron St; dishes $5-12; ⊙11am-3pm & 5-9pm Mon-Fri, 11am-9pm Sat, 11am-8pm Sun; Ⓜ Blue, Yellow Line to King St-Old Town) Stop in this neighborhood favorite for delicious banh mi sandwiches, big bowls of pho, pork-belly steamed buns and other simple but well-executed Vietnamese dishes. The small but cozy space always draws a crowd, so go early to beat the dinner rush. Drinks include beer and bubble tea.

Sonoma Cellars
CALIFORNIAN $$

(☎703-566-9867; www.mysonomacellar.com; 703 King St; mains $14-24; ⊙4-10pm Mon, to 11pm Tue-Fri, 10am-11pm Sat, to 10pm Sun; Ⓜ Blue, Yellow Line to King St-Old Town) Drinking California wines (particularly those from Napa and Sonoma) is de rigueur at this West Coast outpost. Duck in for a glass of chardonnay and a cheese and charcuterie plate ($18 to $22), or settle in for the evening to graze on tacos, quesadillas, burgers and salads piled with sun-drenched produce. In warmer weather, most action occurs in the rear courtyard.

Hank's Oyster Bar
SEAFOOD $$

(☎703-739-4265; www.hanksoysterbar.com; 1024 King St; mains $18-31; ⊙11:30am-midnight Mon-Fri, from 11am Sat & Sun; Ⓜ Blue, Yellow Line to King St-Old Town) Get your oyster fix during happy hour (3pm to 7pm and 10pm to midnight Monday to Friday) when the briny critters are only $1.25 apiece at this outpost of the popular Dupont Circle business. If you're not sure which oysters to pick from the long list, opt for a sampler. There are also seafood and meat dishes on offer.

 Drinking & Nightlife

★ **Captain Gregory's**   COCKTAIL BAR
(www.captaingregorys.com; 804 N Henry St; ⊙5:30-11:30pm Wed & Thu, to 1am Fri & Sat, to 10:30pm Sun; Ⓜ Blue, Yellow Line to Braddock Rd) This nautical-themed speakeasy is hidden inside a Sugar Shack doughnut shop, which explains the decadent gourmet doughnuts on the menu. As for drinks, from Anais Needs a Vacay to Moaning Myrtles Morning Tea, the names are as diverse as the ingredients. Think flavored liqueurs, infused spirits and a range of fruit and spices. The cocktail menu changes frequently. Reservation recommended.

Killer ESP   CAFE
(1012 King St; ⊙7am-9pm Sun-Thu, to 11pm Fri & Sat; 🛜; Ⓜ Blue, Yellow Line to King St-Old Town) Killer by name and execution, this hipster haven serves Alexandria's best coffee. Enjoy an espresso, drip, cold brew or pour-over example with a gluten-free cookie ($2), French pastry ($2) or empanada ($5). Tables out front, comfy couches out back.

Pizzeria Birreria Paradiso   BAR
(☑703-837-1245; www.eatyourpizza.com; 124 King St; pizzas $13-21; ⊙11:30am-10pm Mon-Thu, to 11pm Fri & Sat, noon-10pm Sun; Ⓜ Blue, Yellow Line to King St-Old Town) Sure, the focus is pizza, but the beer list here is outstanding. With 14 brews on draft, 190 or so bottle varieties and one rotating cask selection, you won't lack for options. It's a comfy spot for hopheads to sit back and indulge in small-batch suds chased with piping-hot pizza from a wood-fired stone oven.

 Entertainment

Birchmere   LIVE MUSIC
(☑703-549-7500; www.birchmere.com; 3701 Mt Vernon Ave; tickets $30-100; ⊙box office 5-9pm, shows 7:30pm; Ⓜ Blue, Yellow Line to Pentagon City) This 50-year-old place, hailing itself as 'America's Legendary Music Hall,' hosts a wide range of fare, from old-time folk musicians to country, blues and R&B stars. The lineup also features the odd burlesque show, indie rock bands and the occasional one-person comedy act.

 Shopping

★ **Torpedo Factory Art Center**   ARTS & CRAFTS
(☑703-746-4570; www.torpedofactory.org; 105 N Union St; ⊙10am-6pm Fri-Wed, to 9pm Thu; Ⓜ Blue, Yellow Line to King St-Old Town) The former munitions factory today houses studios in which 165 artists and craftspeople sell their creations directly to the customer. There are also seven galleries. It is a distinctive setup, and there's a good chance you'll head home with a reasonably priced, one-of-a-kind painting, textile or piece of jewelry.

ℹ️ **Information**

Visitor Center (☑703-838-6494; www.visit alexandriava.com; 221 King St; ⊙10am-6pm Sun-Wed, to 8pm Thu-Sat Apr-Sep, to 5pm Oct-Mar; Ⓜ Blue, Yellow Line to King St-Old Town) Pick up a visitor guide and brochures; also sells the Alexandria Museum Pass and tickets for guided tours.

ℹ️ **Getting There & Away**

To get to Alexandria from downtown DC, take the Metro (Blue and Yellow Lines) to the King St-Old Town station. A free **trolley** (www.dashbus.com/trolley; ⊙10am-10:15pm Sun-Wed, to midnight Thu-Sat; Ⓜ Blue, Yellow Line to King St-Old Town) makes the 1-mile journey from the metro station to the waterfront and then back again.

Seasonal **water taxis** (☑703-684-0580; www.potomacriverboatco.com; one way adult/child from $12/8.50; ⊙Mar-Sep) travel between Alexandria's wharf and the Wharf District in DC. There's also a seasonal service between Georgetown and Alexandria. Tour boats travel to/from the Mount Vernon estate during the summer season, too.

ℹ️ **Getting Around**

Street parking in the Old Town costs $1.75 per hour (two hour maximum). Parking in the Market Sq carpark costs $2.50 per hour (maximum $10).

Alexandria Transit Company (DASH; www.dashbus.com) buses service the district. Single fares cost $1.60 and can be purchased on buses. SmarTrip passes can be used.

Capitol Bikeshare (☑877-430-2453; www.capitalbikeshare.com) has over 30 stations across Alexandria, including one in Market Sq.

Fredericksburg

☑540 / POP 28,300

Fredericksburg is a pretty town with a downtown area that's almost a cliché of small-town Americana. George Washington grew up here, and the Civil War exploded in the streets and surrounding fields. Today the historic district surrounding William St provides opportunities for atmospheric ambles, with colonial-era architecture to admire, intimate museums to visit and plenty of eating and drinking options to sample.

◉ Sights

Fredericksburg & Spotsylvania
National Military Park   HISTORIC SITE
(☑ 540-693-3200; www.nps.gov/frsp; 1013 Lafayette Blvd; ☺ Fredericksburg & Chancellorsville visitor centers 9am-5pm, hours vary at other exhibit areas) **FREE** More than 13,000 Americans were killed during the Civil War in four battles fought in a 17-mile radius covered by this park: Fredericksburg, Chancellorsville, the Wilderness and Spotsylvania Courthouse. Today they are maintained by the National Park Service. Check its website for the locations of various visitor centers, and for staffing, which may be seasonal. Orientation films (adult/child under 10 years $2/ free) are screened at the Fredericksburg and Chancellorsville visitor centers every 30 minutes, and audioguides can be hired.

At Chancellorsville (9001 Plank Rd) you can track Stonewall Jackson's battle maneuvers and see where he was mortally wounded by friendly fire.

Ellwood Manor   HISTORIC SITE
(☑ 540-786-2880; www.fowb.org; Rte 20, just west of Rte 3; ☺ 10am-5pm early Jun-Aug, Sat & Sun only Apr-early Jun & Aug-Nov) **FREE** This fascinating home sits on the grounds of the Wilderness Battlefield. Perhaps best known as the burial site for Confederate general Stonewall Jackson's amputated arm – there is a marker – the manor (c 1790) here once anchored a 5000-acre estate and has undergone a full interior restoration in recent times. Step inside to learn the interesting history of the house on a docent-led guided tour.

James Monroe Museum &
Memorial Library   HISTORIC SITE
(☑ 540-654-1043; http://jamesmonroemuseum. umw.edu; 908 Charles St; adult/child 6-17yr $6/2; ☺ 10am-5pm Mon-Sat, from 1pm Sun, closes 4pm Dec-Feb) The museum's namesake was the nation's fifth president. US history buffs will delight in the small and eclectic collection of Monroe memorabilia, including the desk on which he wrote the famous Monroe Doctrine. His diplomatic court suit, worn at the coronation of Napoleon and dating from 1785 or so, is also on display.

🍴 Sleeping & Eating

Richard Johnston Inn   B&B $$
(☑ 540-899-7606; www.therichardjohnstoninn. com; 711 Caroline St; r $160-225; P ✳ 🛜 🐾) In an 18th-century brick mansion, this cozy B&B scores points for its downtown location, handsome communal areas and rear garden. Room rates drop mid-week. The same friendly team operates the 1890 Caroline House annexe a short distance away, which offers three larger rooms ($225 to $300); its Sawyer Scott Suite is particularly nice. Breakfast (included) can be vegan or gluten-free by arrangement.

Legume Kitchen and Bar   VEGETARIAN $$
(☑ 540-371-1116; www.legumerestaurant.com; 715 Caroline St; mains $14-21; ☺ 11am-9pm Tue-Thu, to 10pm Fri & Sat, 11am-3pm & 4-8pm Sun; 🍽) The dishes aren't solely vegetarian at this modern bistro on the main entertainment drag, but there are loads of options to make vegetarians, vegans and gluten-free diners happy. Choose from an array of curries, pastas and sandwiches. The rear bar and patio serves $3 tacos all day on Tuesday, hosts live music on weekends and is a popular meeting spot.

Confident Rabbit   FRENCH $$
(☑ 540-371-9999; www.theconfidentrabbit.com; 309 William St; lunch mains $9-14, dinner mains $14-27; ☺ 11:30am-2:30pm & 5-10pm Tue-Sat, to 9pm Sun) Classic French bistro cuisine and a raw bar where fresh Chesapeake Bay oysters are shucked are the draws at this modern and extremely stylish eatery in downtown Fredericksburg. Grab a bar stool or banquette and feast on a selection of small plates (rillettes, charcuterie, salads), a succulent steak, or seasonal fish. At lunch, the duck burger reigns supreme.

❶ Getting There & Away

Virginia Railway Express (www.vre.org; $11.90, 1½ hours) and Amtrak (from $20, 1¼ hours) trains depart from the **Fredericksburg train station** (www.amtrak.com; 200 Lafayette Blvd) with service to DC. Greyhound has buses to/ from DC ($10 to $24, 1½ hours, four or five per day) and Richmond ($10 to $30, one hour, two or three per day). The **Greyhound station** (☑ 540-373-2103; www.greyhound.com; 1400 Jefferson Davis Hwy; ☺ ticket office 7am-2pm & 4-7:30pm Mon-Fri, 7am-noon Sat & Sun) is roughly 2 miles west of the historic district; buses travel to/from Washington, DC (tickets from $12, 1½ hours, five per day). Fredericksburg borders I-95 midway between Washington, DC, and Richmond, VA. It's about 55 miles north to DC and 60 miles south to Richmond.

WORTH A TRIP

LOUDOUN WINE TRAIL

There are more than 40 wineries and vineyards in Loudoun County, which is also known as DC's Wine Country. The soil and climate are well suited to white varietals – viognier and chardonnay thrive – but decent reds are also produced here. There are six regional clusters: Snicker's Gap, Mosby, Harmony, Waterford, Loudoun Heights and Potomac. Loudoun Heights and Snicker's Gap are particularly impressive. Many of the wineries have restaurants, and most sell cheese and charcuterie plates or picnic provisions. Top choices for a visit include **Bluemont Vineyard** (☑540-554-8439; www.bluemontvineyard. com; 18755 Foggy Bottom Rd, Bluemont; tastings $15; ☺11am-6pm Sat-Thu, to 8pm Fri, reduced hours winter; ☺), **Breaux Vineyards** (☑540-668-6299; www.breauxvineyards.com; 36888 Breaux Vineyards Lane, Hillsboro; tastings $15; ☺11am-6pm mid-Mar–Oct, to 5pm Nov-early Mar; ☺), **Otium Cellars** (☑540-338-2027; www.otiumcellars.com; 18050 Tranquility Rd, Pur-cellville; tastings $10; ☺11am-5pm Mon & Thu, to 10pm Fri, to 9pm Sat, to 5pm Sun), **Sunset Hills VIneyard** (☑540-882-4560; www.sunsethillsvineyard.com; 38295 Fremont Overlook Lane, Purcellville; tastings $10; ☺noon-5pm Mon-Thu, to 6pm Fri, 11am-6pm Sat & Sun; ℙ) ∂ and **Tarara Vineyard** (☑703-771-7100; www.tarara.com; 13648 Tarara Lane; tastings $10-20; ☺11am-5pm Mon-Thu, to 6pm Fri-Sun, closed Tue & Wed Nov-Mar; ☺).

Go to loudounfarms.org/craft-beverages/wine-trail/ for an interactive map. There's plenty more information at www.visitloudoun.org/things-to-do/wine-country/.

THE PIEDMONT

Nestled between the Blue Ridge Mountains and the coastal plain, this central tract of Virginia is a mix of forest and gently sloping hills with well-drained, mineral-rich soil – perfect conditions in which to cultivate grapes. More than 100 wineries are located here, alongside rural villages, grand colonial estates, microbreweries, cideries and distilleries. The history-rich cities of Charlottesville and Richmond are popular bases for exploring the region.

❶ Getting There & Away

The Piedmont region is flanked by I-81 and I-64. The area is best explored by car. Charlottesville anchors the region and has an airport (p360), Amtrak (p360) station and Greyhound (p360) station. On Fridays you'll likely join a few UVA students hopping the train to Washington, DC.

Richmond

☑804 / POP 223,170

Richmond has woken up from a very long nap – and we like it. The capital of the Commonwealth of Virginia since 1780, and the capital of the Confederacy during the Civil War, it's long been an old-fashioned city clinging too tightly to its Southern roots. But an influx of new and creative young residents is energizing and modernizing the community.

Today the 'River City' shares a buzzing food-and-drink scene and an active arts community. The rough-and-tumble James River has also grabbed more of the spotlight, drawing outdoor adventurers to its rapids and trails. Richmond is also an undeniably handsome town and easy to stroll, full of red-brick row houses, stately drives and leafy parks.

◉ Sights

The three attractions that together comprise the American Civil War Museum (White House of the Confederacy, Historic Tredegar and American Civil War Museum – Appomattox) can be visited on individual tickets, but it can often make sense to purchase a combination pass. Two of these are available: the **Richmond Experience Package** (adult/child 6-17yr $18/9), which gives entrance to the three Richmond attractions; and the **Civil War Experience Package** ($26/12), which gives entry to all four. Package tickets can be purchased online or at the individual site ticket offices.

★**Virginia State Capitol** NOTABLE BUILDING
(☑804-698-1788; www.virginiacapitol.gov; 1000 Bank St, Capitol Sq, Court End; ☺9am-5pm Mon-Sat, 1-5pm Sun) **FREE** Designed by Thomas Jefferson, the capitol building was completed in 1788 and houses the oldest legislative body in the Western Hemisphere – the Virginia General Assembly, established in 1619. Free one-

hour guided tours of the historic building are available between 10am and 4pm Monday to Saturday, and between 1pm and 4pm on Sunday; a self-guided tour is also available. Temporary exhibits are staged in the underground galleries near the visitor entrance.

★ **Virginia Museum of Fine Arts** MUSEUM
(VMFA; ☏804-340-1405; www.vmfa.museum; 200 N Blvd, Museum District; ☉10am-5pm Sat-Wed, to 9pm Thu & Fri) FREE Richmond is a cultured city, and this splendid art museum is the cornerstone of the local arts scene. Highlights of its eclectic, world-class collection include the Sydney and Frances Lewis Art Nouveau and Art Deco Galleries, which include furniture and decorative arts by designers including Eileen Gray, Josef Hoffmann and Charles Rennie Mackintosh. Other galleries house one of the largest Fabergé egg collections on display outside Russia, and American works by O'Keefe, Hopper, Henri, Whistler, Sargent and other big names.

★ **Poe Museum** MUSEUM
(☏804-648-5523; www.poemuseum.org; 1914-16 E Main St, Shockoe Bottom; adult/child 7-17yr $8/6; ☉10am-5pm Tue-Sat, from 11am Sun) Contains the world's largest collection of manuscripts and memorabilia of poet and horror writer Edgar Allan Poe, who lived and worked in Richmond. Exhibits include the first printing of 'The Raven', Poe's vest, his pen knife and a work chair with the back cut off – they say his boss at the *Southern Literary Messenger* wanted Poe to sit up straight. Pesky know-it-all. Stop by on the fourth Thursday of the month for the Poe-themed Unhappy Hour (6pm to 9pm April to October; $8).

St John's Episcopal Church CHURCH
(☏804-648-5015; www.historicstjohnschurch.org; 2401 E Broad St, Church Hill; tours adult/child 7-18yr $8/6; ☉10am-4pm Mon-Sat, from 1pm Sun) It was here that firebrand Patrick Henry uttered his famous battle cry – 'Give me Liberty, or give me Death!' – during the rebellious 1775 Second Virginia Convention. The short but informative tour is given by guides dressed in period costume and traces the history of the church and of the famous speech. Above the pulpit, the rare 1741 sounding board and its sunburst are worth a closer look. Henry's speech is re-enacted at 1pm on Sundays in summer.

Hollywood Cemetery CEMETERY
(☏804-648-8501, tour reservations 804-649-0711; www.hollywoodcemetery.org; 412 S Cherry St, entrance cnr Albemarle & Cherry Sts; ☉8am-

6pm) FREE Perched above the James River rapids, this tranquil cemetery contains the gravesites of two US presidents (James Monroe and John Tyler), the only Confederate president (Jefferson Davis) and 18,000 Confederate soldiers. Guided walking tours are conducted at 10am Monday through Saturday April to October, and Saturdays only in November (adult/child under 13 years $15/5). For a self-guided walk, check the virtual tour offered on the website.

Historic Tredegar MUSEUM
(☏804-649-1861; https://acwm.org; 500 Tredegar St, Gambles Hill; adult/child 6-17yr $10/5; ☉9am-5pm) Part of the multisite American Civil War Museum, this fascinating exhibit – housed inside an 1861 iron works that at its height employed 800 free and slave laborers – explores the causes and course of the Civil War from the Union, Confederate and African American perspectives.

Monument Avenue STREET
(btwn N Lombardy St & Roseneath Rd, Fan District) Famous southerners including JEB Stuart, Robert E Lee, Matthew Fontaine Maury, Jefferson Davis and Stonewall Jackson are memorialized in statue form along this beautiful tree-lined boulevard in northeast Richmond. The latest addition is a statue of African American tennis champion Arthur Ashe – heaven knows how he would have felt about being included in such company. Snarky students at the nearby University of Richmond have been known to refer to the avenue's historic inhabitants as the 'largest collection of second place trophies in America.'

 Activities

For white-water rafting, head to the James River. It is said Richmond is the only major urban area home to Class II to IV rapids.

Virginia Capital Trail CYCLING
(www.virginiacapitaltrail.org) Open to cyclists and pedestrians, this 52-mile paved trail, completed in 2015, links Richmond with Jamestown and outer Williamsburg, passing several plantations along the way. Check the helpful website for a map showing parking areas, restrooms, bike shops, restaurants and lodging. There are loads of historic sights and markers along the way. Starts at the junction of S 17th and Dock Sts.

Riverside Outfitters CANOEING
(☏804-560-0068; www.riversideoutfitters.net; Brown's Island, Downtown; per hr kayak/SUP boards/bike rental $15/15/10; ☉9am-5pm Mon-Fri

Richmond

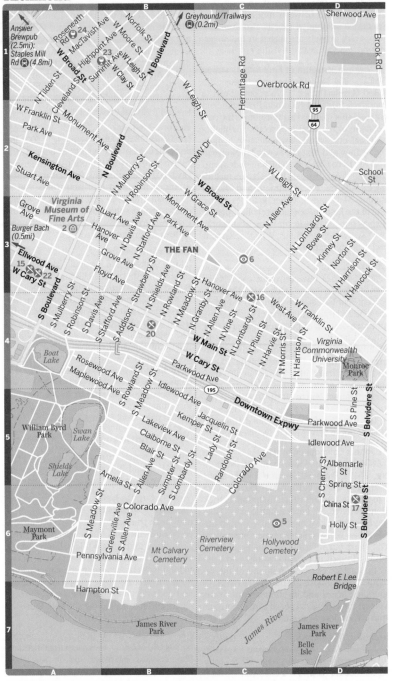

Answer Brewpub (2.5mi); Staples Mill Rd (4.8mi)

Greyhound/Trailways (0.2mi)

Sherwood Ave

Brook Rd

Roseneath Rd — 24
MacTavish Ave
Highpoint Ave
W Moore St
Norfolk St
23
Summit Ave
W Leigh St
W Clay St
N Boulevard
W Broad St

Hermitage Rd

Overbrook Rd

N Tilden St
Cleveland St
Monument Ave

W Leigh St

95
64

W Franklin St

Park Ave

W Leigh St

School St

Kensington Ave

Stuart Ave

N Boulevard

N Mulberry St
N Robinson St

DMV Dr

W Broad St

W Grace St

N Allen Ave

N Lombardy St

Bowe St
Kinney St
Norton St
N Harrison St
N Hancock St

Grove Ave

Virginia Museum of Fine Arts
2

Stuart Ave
N Davis Ave
N Stafford Ave

Monument Ave
Park Ave

THE FAN

6

Burger Bach (0.5mi)

Hanover Ave
Grove Ave
Floyd Ave

Ellwood Ave
15   22
W Cary St

S Boulevard
S Mulberry St
S Robinson St
S Davis Ave
S Stafford Ave
S Addison St

Strawberry St
N Shields Ave
N Rowland St
N Meadow St
N Granby St

Hanover Ave
N Allen Ave
N Vine St
N Lombardy St
N Plum St
N Harvie St
N Morris St
N Harrison

16

West Ave

W Franklin St

Virginia Commonwealth University

Monroe Park

20

W Main St

W Cary St

Parkwood Ave

S Belvidere St

Boat Lake

Rosewood Ave
Maplewood Ave

S Meadow St
S Rowland St

Idlewood Ave

195

Downtown Expwy

S Pine St

Parkwood Ave

William Byrd Park

Swan Lake

Shields Lake

S Lakeview Ave
Claiborne St
Blair St

Kemper St
Jacquelin St
Lady St
Randolph St

Idlewood Ave

S Cherry St

Albemarle St

Spring St

China St   17

S Belvidere St

Amelia St
S Allen Ave
Sumpter St
S Lombardy St

Colorado Ave

Holly St

Maymont Park

S Meadow St
Greenville Ave
S Allen Ave

Colorado Ave

Pennsylvania Ave

Mt Calvary Cemetery

Riverview Cemetery

5

Hollywood Cemetery

Robert E Lee Bridge

Hampton St

James River Park

James River

James River Park

Belle Isle

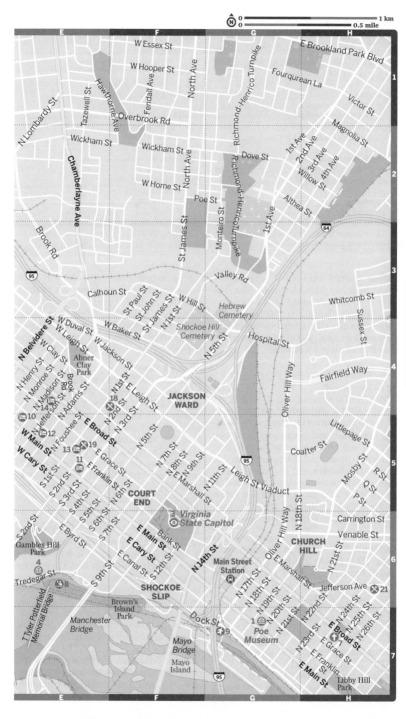

Richmond

Nov-Mar, extended hours rest of year) Rent a kayak, stand-up paddleboard or bike. The shop is on Brown's island across the street from Historic Tredegar at 500 Tredegar St. These folks also offer guided rafting ($59 to $84) and kayaking ($59 to $69) trips, which launch from various locations.

🛏 Sleeping

★ HI Richmond   HOSTEL $
(☑804-729-5410; www.hiusa.org; 7 N 2nd St; dm $30-45, r $85-110, non-members add $3; ⊜🕸🛜)
🖊 Inside the 1940s Otis Elevator Co building, this stylish and ecofriendly downtown option is one of the best hostels you'll ever encounter. Rooms and dorms are clean and bright, with lockers and charging stations; linen and towels are supplied. Communal facilities – free washing machines and driers, lounge with pool table and television, large and well-equipped kitchen – are excellent.

Graduate   BOUTIQUE HOTEL $$
(☑804-644-9871; www.graduatehotels.com/richmond; 301 W Franklin St; r from $139; 🅿🛜🛎)
The Richmond branch of a popular budget boutique chain, this hip hotel has a cafe on the ground floor, a seasonal bar on the rooftop and spacious rooms with an attractive decor and good amenities. Sadly, the hotel's internet service is really slow.

Linden Row Inn   HOTEL $$
(☑804-783-7000; www.lindenrowinn.com; 100 E Franklin St; r from $139, ste $289; 🅿🕸@🛜) This antebellum gem has 70 attractive rooms (with period Victorian furnishings) spread among neighboring Greek Revival town houses in an excellent downtown location. Friendly Southern hospitality, reasonable prices and thoughtful extras (free passes to the YMCA, free around-town shuttle service) sweeten the deal. There'a also an on-site cafe.

★ Quirk Hotel   BOUTIQUE HOTEL $$$
(☑804-340-6040; www.destinationhotels.com/quirk-hotel; 201 W Broad St, Monroe Ward; r $170-450, ste $330-680; 🅿⊜🕸🛜🛎) From the moment you stroll into the big-windowed lobby, which houses a glam bar and restaurant, this downtown boutique choice impresses. The high ceilings and maple floors in rooms are a direct link to the building's past life as a luxury department store. Beds, bathrooms and amenities are excellent. The hotel's popular rooftop bar is open late April to late October.

Jefferson Hotel   HISTORIC HOTEL $$$
(☑804-649-4750; www.jeffersonhotel.com; 101 W Franklin St; r from $315; 🅿⊜🕸🛜🛎🛎) The vision of tobacco tycoon and Confederate major Lewis Ginter, the beaux arts–style hotel was completed in 1895. Rooms sport an old-fashioned but inviting decor and are extremely comfortable; amenities and facilities are good. According to rumor (probably untrue), the magnificent grand staircase in the lobby served as the model for the famed stairs in *Gone with the Wind*. Even if you don't stay here, it's worth having a peek inside. Pick up a hotel walking-tour brochure at the concierge desk. A statue of the hotel's

namesake, Thomas Jefferson, anchors the lobby. Afternoon tea is served beneath Tiffany stained glass in the Palm Court lobby (from 3pm Friday to Sunday), and cocktails are shaken or stirred at the grand Lemaire Bar.

✕ Eating

★ Perly's
DELI $

(☎ 804-912-1560; www.perlysrichmond.com; 111 E Grace St, Monroe Ward; brunch dishes $7-14, sandwiches $9-13; ⏰ 8am-9pm Mon-Sat, to 3pm Sun) Generations of locals have enjoyed Yiddish specialties at Perly's (it dates from 1962) and we think you should, too. Choose from treats including corned beef hash, cinnamon babka, knish and latkes at brunch (which runs till 3pm daily) and opt for one of the sandwiches at lunch. There's booth and bar seating, and a friendly retro vibe.

★ Sugar & Twine
CAFE $

(☎ 804-204-1755; www.sugartwine.com; 2928 W Cary St, Carytown; pastries $2-3, sandwiches $5-6; ⏰ 7am-8pm Mon-Sat, to 6pm Sun; 🛜 🍴) Let's face it: contemporary coffee culture hasn't made inroads in Virginia yet. Fortunately, stylish cafes like this one are in the vanguard. We like everything about Sugar & Twine: the excellent espresso coffee, delicious pastries, tasty sandwiches (some vegan and veggie; gluten-free bread available), free wi-fi and friendly staff.

★ Kuba Kuba
CUBAN $

(☎ 804-355-8817; www.kubakuba.info; 1601 Park Ave, Fan District; sandwiches $8-10, mains $13-20; ⏰ 9am-9:30pm Mon-Thu, to 10pm Fri & Sat, to 8pm Sun; 🍴) Kuba Kuba feels like a bodega straight out of Old Havana, with roast pork dishes, Spanish-style omelets and panini offered at rock-bottom prices. Finish with a dessert and good espresso coffee.

Sub Rosa
BAKERY $

(☎ 804-788-7672; www.subrosabakery.com; 620 N 25th St, Church Hill; pastries $1.25-4.50; ⏰ 7am-6pm Tue-Fri, 8am-5pm Sat & Sun; 🚌 44 & 45) In the residential Church Hill neighborhood, this wood-fired bakery serves some of the best baked goods in the south. Some of the treats on offer are Turkish – flaky *börek* stuffed with cheese, meat or greens and sweet *poğaça* (buns). Make your choice at the counter and enjoy it with a well-made coffee or Moroccan mint tea. Indoor and outdoor seating.

Mama J's
AMERICAN $

(☎ 804-225-7449; www.mamajskitchen.com; 415 N 1st St, Jackson Ward; mains $8-15, sandwiches $5-9; ⏰ 11am-9pm Mon-Thu, to 10pm Fri & Sat, to 9pm Sun) The fried catfish may not look fancy, but it sure tastes like heaven. Set in the historic African American neighborhood of Jackson Ward, Mama J's serves delicious fried chicken and legendary fried catfish, along with collard greens, mac 'n' cheese, candied yams and other fixings. The service is friendly and the lines are long. Come early to beat the crowds.

Sidewalk Cafe
AMERICAN, GREEK $

(☎ 804-358-0645; www.sidewalkinthefan.com; 2101 W Main St, Fan District; mains $11-18, sandwiches $ 9-10, brunch dishes $8-13; ⏰ 11am-2am Mon-Fri, from 9:30am Sat & Sun) A much-loved local haunt, Sidewalk Cafe feels like a dive bar (year-round Christmas lights, wood-paneled walls, kitschy artwork), but the food is first-rate. There's outdoor seating on the sidewalk, daily specials (eg Taco Tuesdays) and legendary weekend brunches.

Burger Bach
PUB FOOD $

(☎ 804-359-1305; www.theburgerbach.com; 10 S Thompson St, Carytown; mains $9-13; ⏰ 11am-10pm Sun-Thu, to 11pm Fri & Sat; ❄ 🍴 🐾) 🐾 We give Burger Bach (pronounced 'batch') credit for being the only restaurant found in the area that self-classifies as a New Zealand–inspired burger joint. And that said, why yes, it does serve excellent lamb burgers, although the locally sourced beef, chicken and vegetarian options are awesome, too. There's a choice of 16 different sauces for the fresh-cut fries.

Daily Kitchen & Bar
MODERN AMERICAN $$

(☎ 804-342-8990; www.thedailykitchenandbar.com; 2934 W Cary St, Carytown; lunch mains $9-16, dinner mains $12-26; ⏰ 7am-10pm Sun-Thu, to midnight Fri & Sat; 🍴) 🐾 In the heart of Carytown, the Daily is a great dining and drinking choice no matter the time of day. Stop by for lump crab omelets at breakfast, blackened mahi-mahi BLT at lunch and seared scallops by night. Extensive vegan options, first-rate cocktails, a buzzing dining room and expansive terrace all seal the deal.

★ L'Opossum
AMERICAN, FRENCH $$$

(☎ 804-918-6028; www.lopossum.com; 626 China St, Oregon Hill; mains $22-36; ⏰ 5pm-midnight Tue-Sat) We're not exactly sure what's going on at this gastronomic laboratory, but it works. The name of the place is terrible. And dishes come with names that are self-consciously hip and verging on offensive ('Vegan Orgy on Texan Beach'). What ties it together? The culinary prowess of award-winning chef David Shannon and his attentive and talented

SHENANDOAH NATIONAL PARK
....

One of the most spectacular national parks in the country, **Shenandoah National Park** (☎540-999-3500; www.nps.gov/shen; Skyline Dr; 1-week pass per car $25; ☺year-round) is a showcase of natural color and beauty: in spring and summer the wildflowers explode, in fall the leaves burn bright red and orange, and in winter a cold, starkly beautiful hibernation period sets in. White-tailed deer are a common sight and, if you're lucky, you might spot a black bear, bobcat or wild turkey. The park lies just 75 miles west of Washington, DC.

Your first stop should be the **Dickey Ridge Visitor Center** (www.nps.gov/shen; Mile 4.6, Skyline Dr; ☺9am-5pm Mon-Fri, to 6pm Sat & Sun, closed late Nov-early Apr), close to the northern end of Skyline Drive, or the **Harry F Byrd Visitor Center** (www.nps.gov/shen; Mile 51, Skyline Dr; ☺9am-5pm late Mar-late Nov, 9:30am-4pm Fri-Sun late Nov-late Mar). Both places have exhibits on flora and fauna, as well as maps and information about hiking trails and activities.

The surrounds are mighty easy on the eyes, set against a backdrop of the dreamy Blue Ridge Mountains, ancient granite and metamorphic formations that are more than one billion years old. The park itself was founded in 1935 as a retreat for East Coast urban populations. It is an accessible day-trip destination from DC, but you should aim to stay longer if you can. The 500 miles of hiking trails, 75 scenic overlooks, 30 fishing streams, seven picnic areas and four campgrounds are sure to keep you entertained. If not, horseback riding is also offered!

Skyline Drive is the breathtaking road that follows the main ridge of the Blue Ridge Mountains and winds 105 miles through the center of the park. It begins in Front Royal at the western end of I-66, and ends in the southern part of the range at Rockfish Gap near I-64. Mile markers at the side of the road provide a reference. Miles and miles of blazed trails wander through the park.

The most famous trail in the park is a 101-mile stretch of the **Appalachian Trail** (AT), a 2175-mile route crossing through 14 states. Access the trail from Skyline Drive, which roughly runs parallel. Aside from the AT, Shenandoah has over 400 miles of hiking trails in the park. Options for short hikes include **Compton Peak** (Mile 10.4; 2.4 miles return; easy to moderate), **Traces** (Mile 22.2; 1.7 miles return; easy), **Overall Run** (Mile 22.2; 6 miles return; moderate) and **White Oak Canyon** (Mile 42.6; 4.6 miles return; strenuous). The climb to **Hawksbill Mountain Summit** (Mile 46.7; 2.1 miles return; moderate), the park's highest peak (4050ft), offers an unforgettable view of the mountain landscape from a rustic stone observation platform.

One of the best day hikes in the state is the trek to the summit of **Old Rag Mountain**. This extremely tough, full-day 9.2-mile circuit trail culminates in an adventurous rocky scramble – one that's suitable only for the physically fit. Your reward is the summit of Old Rag Mountain, not to mention the fantastic views along the way. The trailhead is accessed from outside the park, off Rte 600.

You'll need your own wheels to explore the park, which is easily accessed from several exits off I-81. Amtrak (www.amtrak.com) runs train services between DC and Staunton. There is a gas station at Big Meadows Wayside.

staff. Make a reservation or get here early to snag a seat at the bar.

 Drinking & Nightlife

New craft breweries and a cider house or two are bringing lively crowds to the rapidly developing Scott's Addition neighborhood north of Broad St. For a full list of breweries across the city and their locations, check out the map for the Richmond Beer Trail (www.visitrichmondva.com/drink/richmond-beer-trail). Neighborhood pubs are the draw in

the Fan and Carytown districts, just west of downtown.

Blue Bee Cider   DISTILLERY
(☎804-231-0280; www.bluebeecider.com; 1320 Summit Ave, Scott's Addition; ☺1-8pm Mon-Fri, noon-9pm Sat, to 7pm Sun) Stop in for a taste of a rotating list of top-notch, small-batch ciders. Recipes range from crisp, apples-only varieties to berry- or hop-infused blends. Blue Bee often collaborates with other local distillers and brewers – the sweet and spicy

Firecracker, made with a ginger *eau de vie* from Catoctin Creek Distilling Co, is a standout example. Ample outdoor seating makes Blue Bee a summer afternoon hot spot.

Answer Brewpub   MICROBREWERY
(📞804-282-1248; http://theanswerbrewpub.com; 6008 W Broad St; ☺4pm-midnight Mon-Wed, noon-midnight Thu-Sat, noon-10pm Sun) Killer IPAs, very strange fruited sours (a cross between tart beer and fruit smoothie) and a hip Asian nightclub vibe make this brewpub one of the most unusual and popular drinking dens in Richmond. There are 56 taps, two bars, and a stage area for live music

Veil Brewing   MICROBREWERY
(www.theveilbrewing.com; 1301 Roseneath Rd, Scott's Addition; ☺4-9pm Tue-Thu, to 10pm Fri, noon-10pm Sat, noon-6pm Sun) One of the most popular craft breweries in the emerging Scott's Addition neighborhood, Veil is known for its hop-forward beers, plenty of which are offered on draft at the taproom.

☆ Entertainment

Byrd Theater   CINEMA
(📞804-353-9911; www.byrdtheatre.com; 2908 W Cary St, Carytown; tickets from $4) You can't beat the price at this classic 1928 cinema, which shows second-run films and longtime favorites. Wurlitzer-organ concerts precede the Saturday night shows.

❶ Getting There & Away

Amtrak trains stop at the **Staples Mill Rd station** (www.amtrak.com; 7519 Staples Mill Rd), 7 miles north of town (accessible to downtown via bus 27). More convenient but less frequent trains stop downtown at the **Main St Station** (www.amtrak.com; 1500 E Main St). Richmond is serviced by the Northeast Regional, Carolinian, Palmetto, Silver Star and Silver Meteor lines, all of which link the city frequently with Washington, DC (tickets from $28, 2¼ to 2½ hours).

Buses stop at the **Greyhound/Trailways Bus Station** (📞804-254-5910; www.greyhound.com; 2910 North Blvd, The Diamond; ☺24hr).

❶ Getting Around

A new **bike share program** (www.rvabikes.com) has recently been launched in the city. A one-way, 45-minute trip pass costs $1.75 and a day pass costs $6. Download the bike share app from the website for station locations.

Greater Richmond Transit Company (www.ridegrtc.com) runs local buses. Tickets cost $1.50 and exact change is needed. The company is currently constructing a bus rapid transit line called the GRTC Pulse (often abbreviated as the Pulse) that will link Willow Lawn with Rockett's Landing via Broad St and Main St. Street car parking costs $1.25 per hour.

Charlottesville

📞434 / POP 46,910
Set in the shadow of the Blue Ridge Mountains, Charlottesville is regularly ranked as one of the USA's best places to live. This culturally rich town is home to the architecturally resplendent University of Virginia (UVA), which attracts Southern aristocracy and artsy lefties in equal proportions. The UVA grounds, Main St and the pedestrian downtown mall area overflow with students, professors and tourists, endowing 'C-ville' with a lively, cultured and diverse atmosphere.

◉ Sights

★ Monticello   HISTORIC SITE
(📞434-984-9800; www.monticello.org; 931 Thomas Jefferson Pkwy; adult/child 5-11yr $22/9; ☺8:30am-6pm Mon-Fri, to 7pm Sat & Sun, hours vary seasonally) The house at Monticello is an architectural masterpiece designed and inhabited by Thomas Jefferson, founding father and third US president, who spent 40 years building his dream home. It was finally completed in 1809. Today it is the only home in America designated a Unesco World Heritage Site. The centerpiece of a plantation that once covered 5000 acres, it can be visited on guided tours (ground floor only) and its grounds and outbuildings can be explored in themed and self-guided tours.

The 45-minute 'Slavery at Monticello' walking tour (included in ticket price) is the highlight of any trip. Guides don't gloss over the complicated past of the man who declared that 'all men are created equal' in the Declaration of Independence, while owning slaves and likely fathering children with slave Sally Hemings. Jefferson and his other family are buried in a small wooded plot near the home.

Two tours per day visit the upstairs rooms of the house ($60, child under five years free); these are popular so must be booked in advance.

A high-tech exhibition center delves deeper into Jefferson's world – including exhibits on architecture, enlightenment through education, and the complicated idea of liberty. Frequent shuttles run from the visitor center to the hilltop house, or you can walk along a wooded footpath.

VIRGINIA CHARLOTTESVILLE

Monticello is about 4.5 miles northwest of downtown Charlottesville.

★ **University of Virginia**   UNIVERSITY
(☎434-924-0311; www.virginia.edu; Charlottesville) Thomas Jefferson founded the University of Virginia, and designed what he called an 'Academical Village' embodying the spirit of communal living and learning. At the heart of this 'village' is the Lawn, a large gently sloping grassed field fringed by columned pavilions, student rooms, the Stand-ford White–designed Old Cabell Hall (1898) and Jefferson's famous Rotunda, modelled on Rome's Pantheon. Together, the original Neoclassical and Palladian-style university buildings and Jefferson's Monticello comprise a Unesco World Heritage Site. Free, student-led guided tours (www.uvaguides.org) of the original university and lawn depart daily from the Rotunda at 10am, 11am and 2pm during the school year (September to April).

Charlottesville

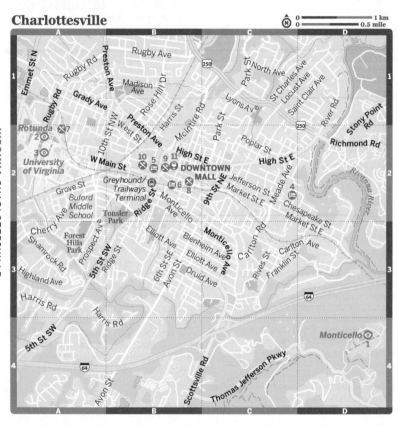

Charlottesville

CROZET

West of Charlottesville, close to the southern entrance to Skyine Dr and the northern entrance to the Blue Ridge Parkway, the small town of Crozet is set in attractive countryside covered in farms, fruit orchards and vineyards. The town itself is unremarkable – although it does host a branch of the excellent Charlottesville-based **Mudhouse Coffee Roasters** (☑434-823-2240; www.mudhouse.com; 5793 The Square; ☺7am-7pm Mon-Thu, to 8pm Fri-Sun) – but the immediate area rewards exploration. Spectacularly sited wineries such as **Grace Estate** (☑434-823-1486; www.graceestatewinery.com; 5273 Mount Juliet Farm, Crozet; tasting $9; ☺11am-5:30pm Wed, Thu & Sun, to 9pm Fri & Sat), **King Family Vineyards** (☑434-823-7800; www.kingfamilyvineyards.com; 6550 Roseland Farm, Crozet; tastings $10, tour $20; ☺10am-5:30pm Thu-Tue, to 8:30pm Wed; 🐾) and **Pippin Hill** (☑434-202-8063; www.pippinhillfarm.com; 5022 Plank Rd, North Garden; tastings $10; ☺11am-5pm Sun & Tue-Fri, to 4:30pm Sat) 🐾 are close by, as is the idyllically peaceful **Our Lady of the Angels** (☑434-823-1452; www.olamonastery.org; 3365 Monastery Dr, Millington; ☺cheese sales 9-11am & 2-4pm Mon-Sat) monastery, where the nuns produce wheels of heavenly gouda cheese, and the welcoming **Blue Mountain Brewery** (☑540-456-8020; www.bluemountainbrewery.com; 9519 Critzer's Shop Rd, Afton; ☺11am-10pm Mon-Sat, to 9pm Sun), home of beers such as the powerful Full Nelson. Crozet is 12 miles west of downtown Charlottesville, via US 250 and VA 240.

★**Rotunda** NOTABLE BUILDING

(☑434-924-7969; www.rotunda.virginia.edu; 1826 University Ave; ☺9am-5pm) The centerpiece of UVA is the Jefferson-designed Rotunda, modelled after Rome's Pantheon and constructed between 1822 and 1832. It has always functioned as a library. Free guided tours of the original university and lawn area are offered daily at 10am, 11am and 2pm during the school year (September to April) and start in the Rotunda.

★**Montpelier** HISTORIC BUILDING

(☑540-672-2728; www.montpelier.org; 11350 Constitution Hwy, Montpelier Station; adult/child 6-14yr $22/8; ☺9am-5pm Apr-Oct, 10am-4pm Nov-Mar) Thomas Jefferson gets all the attention in these parts, but it's worth branching out and visiting James Madison's Montpelier, a spectacular estate 25 miles northeast of Charlottesville (off Hwy 20). Madison was a brilliant but shy man, who devoted himself to his books; he was almost single-handedly responsible for developing and writing the US Constitution. Guided tours shed a light on his life as well as his gifted and charismatic wife Dolley, plus other residents of the estate.

🛌 Sleeping

Fairhaven GUESTHOUSE $

(☑434-933-2471; www.fairhavencville.com; 413 Fairway Ave; r $55-90; P❄🐾🎱🐾) This friendly and welcoming guesthouse is a great deal if you don't mind sharing facilities (there's just one bathroom for the three rooms). Each room has wood floors, with comfy beds and a cheerful color scheme, and guests can use the kitchen, living room or backyard. It's about a 1-mile walk to the pedestrian mall.

★**Residence Inn by Marriott** HOTEL $$

(☑434-220-0075; www.marriott.com; 315 W Main St; studio $149-299, 1-bed apt $189-399, 2-bed apt $229-499; P❄🐾🎱🐾) We're not usually chain-hotel fans, but this excellent place deserves serious praise. Its location couldn't be better, and its clean, comfy and well-equipped studios and apartments make great bases for a Charlottesville stay. Facilities include a pool, bar, gym, and coin-operated laundry, and there's a free shuttle service within a 10-mile radius (including the airport).

★**South Street Inn** B&B $$

(☑434-979-0200; www.southstreetinn.com; 200 W South St; r $135-325, ste $195-355; P❄🎱) Having gone through previous incarnations as a girls' finishing school, a boarding house and a brothel, this elegant 1856 building, with its picture-perfect front porch, now houses a heritage-style B&B with 11 well-sized and beautifully presented rooms; there are extra rooms in an attached cottage. Breakfast is served in the library, as is complimentary wine and cheese every evening.

🍴 Eating

★**Bodo's Bagels** BAGELS $

(☑434-293-6021; www.bodosbagels.com; 1609 University Ave; bagels $0.80-4; ☺7am-8pm Mon-Fri, 8am-4pm Sat & Sun) Students and university staff are regulars at this Charlottesville

> **OFF THE BEATEN TRACK**
>
> ### INN AT LITTLE WASHINGTON
>
> This Relais and Chateaux **property**
> (✆540-675-3800; www.theinnatlittle
> washington.com; cnr Middle & Main Sts,
> Washington; dinner prix fixe $218, optional
> wine pairing $125; ⏱6-9pm Mon, Wed &
> Thu, 5-9pm Fri-Sun) has one of the best
> restaurants in the state – you may need
> to sell a kidney before you can make a
> reservation. Diners have their pick of
> three tasting menus, one of which is
> vegetarian. Treats like caviar and Japa-
> nese Wagyu beef are par for the course.
> After your meal, it makes sense to over-
> night in the super-swish rooms.

institution, lured by its wonderful bagels and its location on UVA Corner. Choose from a large array of options. Also offers sandwiches. Eat in or order to go.

Mudhouse Coffee Roasters CAFE $
(✆434-984-6833; www.mudhouse.com; 213 W Main St; pastry $3; ⏱7am-10pm Mon-Thu, to 11pm Fri & Sat, to 7pm Sun; ☎) Its mantra is 'Beautiful coffee. Thoughtfully sourced. Carefully roasted.' and we can attest to the fact that this cafe on the pedestrian mall practices what it preaches. Excellent coffee (espresso and drip) and delicious pastries are enjoyed in stylish surrounds or at tables on the mall.

Citizen Burger AMERICAN $
(✆434-979-9944; www.citizenburgerbar.com; 212 E Main St; burgers $7-21; ⏱11:30am-10:30pm Sun-Thu, to 11:30pm Fri & Sat; ✐) The ethos at this hugely popular burger joint on the pedestrian mall is commendably local and sustainable (organically raised, grass-fed cows, Virginia-made cheeses and beers). Don't miss the truffle fries. The bar stays open after meal service finishes.

★**Oakhart Social** MODERN AMERICAN $$
(✆434-995-5449; www.oakhartsocial.com; 511 W Main St; small plates $8-14, pizza $15; ⏱5pm-midnight Tue-Sun, to 2am Fri & Sat) Seasonally inspired small plates and wood-fired pizzas emerge from the kitchen of this hipster haunt at a great rate, keeping its loyal crew of regulars fed and happy. On warm nights, the front patio is a perfect cocktail-sipping spot, and the bar is a great spot for solo diners.

★**Public Fish & Oyster** SEAFOOD $$$
(✆434-995-5542; www.publicfo.com; 513 W Main St; mains $19-26; ⏱4-9pm Sun & Mon, to 9:30pm Tue-Thu, to 10pm Fri & Sat) This bright and in-

viting space will catch your eye, but it's the skillfully seasoned seafood dishes that will keep you ordering plates of freshly shucked oysters, mussels and other maritime delights. If you're a raw oyster virgin, this is the place to change that story. The twice-cooked Belgian fries with sea salt are fantastic.

Drinking & Nightlife

Whiskey Jar COCKTAIL BAR
(✆434-202-1549; www.thewhiskeyjarcville.com; 227 W Main St; lunch mains $10-15, dinner mains $12-32; ⏱11am-midnight Mon-Thu, to 2am Fri & Sat, 11am-3pm Sun) On the pedestrian mall, the Whiskey Jar offers a huge (more than 125 varieties!) whiskey selection in a rustically hip setting – wooden furniture with waitstaff wearing plaid and drinks in Mason jars. Also serves neo-Southern comfort food, including great barbecue.

❶ Getting There & Away

Amtrak (www.amtrak.com; 810 W Main St; ⏱ticket office 6am-9:30pm) Two daily trains to Washington, DC (from $27, 2¾ hours).

Charlottesville Albemarle Airport (CHO; ✆434-973-8342; www.gocho.com) Ten miles north of downtown; offers nonstop flights along the East Coast and to Chicago.

Greyhound/Trailways Terminal (✆434-295-5131; www.greyhound.com; 310 W Main St; ⏱ticket office 8am-10pm) Runs two daily buses to Richmond (from $13, 1¼ hours), three to Roanoke (from $18, 2½ hours) and two to Washington, DC (from $18, three hours).

HISTORIC TRIANGLE

This is America's birthplace. Nowhere else in the country has such a small area played such a pivotal role in the course of the nation's history. The nation's roots were planted in Jamestown, the first permanent English settlement in the New World; the flames of the American Revolution were fanned at the colonial capital of Williamsburg; and America finally won its independence from Britain at Yorktown. You'll need at least two days to do the Triangle any justice.

❶ Getting There & Away

The Historic Triangle surrounds I-64. The largest regional airport is Norfolk International Airport (p366) followed by **Newport News/Williamsburg International Airport** (PHF; www.flyphf.com). Williamsburg is serviced by Amtrak, and local WATA buses (www.gowata.org) link it with Jamestown ($1.50).

Williamsburg

📞 757 / POP 15,210

If you visit only one historic town in Virginia, make it Williamsburg – home to Colonial Williamsburg, one of the largest, most comprehensive living-history museums in the world. If any place is going to get kids into history, this is it, but it's plenty of fun for adults too. The actual town of Williamsburg, Virginia's capital from 1699 to 1780, is a stately place that can sometimes verge on being twee. Fortunately, the campus of the College of William & Mary adds a decent dash of youth culture.

◉ Sights

Williamsburg, Jamestown and Yorktown are linked by the scenic Colonial Parkway (www.nps.gov/colo/parkway), a highway managed by the National Park Service.

★**Colonial Williamsburg**　　HISTORIC SITE
(📞888-974-7926; www.colonialwilliamsburg.org; adult/child 6-12yr day $41/21, multi-day $51/26; ⊗8:45am-5pm) The restored capital of England's largest colony in the New World is a must-see attraction for visitors of all ages. This is not some phony, fenced-in theme park: Colonial Williamsburg is a living, breathing, working history museum with a painstakingly researched environment that brilliantly evokes 1700s America. It contains 88 original 18th-century buildings and several hundred faithful reproductions, as well as an impressive museum complex. Townsfolk and 'interpreters' in period dress go about their colonial jobs, emulating daily life.

The park doesn't gloss over America's less glorious moments. Today's re-enactors debate and question slavery (52% of the population of 18th-century Williamsburg were slaves), women's suffrage, the rights of indigenous Americans and whether or not it is even moral to engage in revolution.

Walking around the historic district and patronizing the shops and taverns is free, but entry to building tours and most exhibits is restricted to ticketholders. Expect crowds, lines and overtired children, especially in summer. There are a number of taverns and a bakery where visitors can eat, and there's also a bakery in the Art Museums complex.

To park and to purchase tickets, follow signs to the visitor center (p363), found north of the historic district between Hwy 132 and Colonial Pkwy; kids can also hire out period costumes here for $25 per day. A program detailing the day's events will be given to you with your ticket, which helps when planning your time at the site. Parking at the visitor center is free; shuttle buses run frequently between it and the historic district, or you can walk along the tree-lined footpath. You can also buy tickets at the Merchants Square information booth (p363).

★**Art Museums**　　MUSEUM
(www.colonialwilliamsburg.com/art-museums; Francis St; adult/child 6-12yr $13/6.50, free with Colonial Williamsburg ticket; ⊗10am-7pm Mar-Dec, to 5pm Jan & Feb) Entered through Colonial Williamsburg's former public hospital, this complex is home to two equally splendid museums: the DeWitt Wallace Decorative Arts Museum and the Abby Aldrich Rockefeller Folk Art Museum. The decorative arts museum is home to the world's largest collection of Southern furniture and one of the largest collections of British ceramics

VIRGINIA WILLIAMSBURG

APPOMATTOX

At the McLean House in the town of Appomattox Court House, General Robert E Lee surrendered the Army of Northern Virginia to General Ulysses S Grant, in effect ending the Civil War. The **Appomattox Court House National Historic Park** (📞434-352-8987; www.nps.gov/apco; 111 National Park Dr; ⊗9am-5pm) FREE comprises over two dozen restored buildings; a number are open to visitors, and set with original and period furnishings from 1865. Highlights include the parlor of the McLean House, where Lee and Grant met; the Clover Hill Tavern, used by Union soldiers to print 30,000 parole passes for Confederate soldiers; and the dry-goods-filled Meeks General Store.

At the nearby **American Civil War Museum - Appomattox** (📞434-352 5791; https://acwm.org; 159 Horseshoe Rd; adult/child 6-17yr $12/6; ⊗10am-5pm; 🅿), photographs, documents and audiovisual presentations tell the story of the lead-up to the end of the Civil War and the start of America becoming a reunified nation. Look for the uniform coat and sword that Robert E Lee wore to the surrender.

outside England. The folk art museum has one of the largest collections of American folk art in the world – portraits, quilts, toys, musical instruments and much more.

College of William & Mary HISTORIC BUILDING
(www.wm.edu; 200 Stadium Dr) Chartered in 1693, the College of William & Mary is the second-oldest college in the country and retains the oldest academic building in continued use in the USA, the **Sir Christopher** Wren Building. The school's alumni include Thomas Jefferson, James Monroe and comedian Jon Stewart. A free campus audio tour and interactive map are available online.

🛏 Sleeping & Eating

Williamsburg Woodlands Hotel & Suites HOTEL **$**
(☎757-220-7960; www.colonialwilliamsburg.com; 105 Visitor Center Dr; r/ste from $89/119; P ✳)

Williamsburg

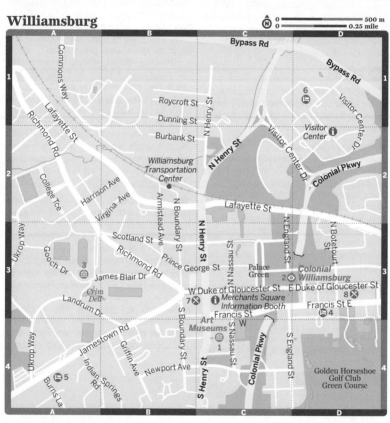

Williamsburg

🛰🖥) This good-value option has dowdy but comfortable rooms and is located near the main visitor center in Colonial Williamsburg. The splash park, games (minigolf, table tennis), kids club and complimentary breakfast make it a hit with families. Can feel a little more impersonal than other local lodging options.

Williamsburg White House B&B $$
(📞757-229-8580; www.awilliamsburgwhitehouse.com; 718 Jamestown Rd; r $119-199, ste $129-399; 🅿😊❄🛰) This romantic, beautifully furnished B&B is located across from the campus of the College of William & Mary, just a few blocks' walk from Colonial Williamsburg. It's a favorite spot of visiting politicos and bigwigs. Guests love the lavish breakfast and the afternoon drinks and nibbles served in the Diplomatic Reception Room. Book ahead, as there are only six rooms.

Colonial Williamsburg Historic Lodging – Colonial Houses GUESTHOUSE $$
(📞757-220-7978; www.colonialwilliamsburg.com; 136 E Francis St; r from $169) For true 18th-century immersion, guests can stay in one of 26 original colonial houses inside the historic district. Accommodations range in size and style, though the best have period furnishings, canopy beds and wood-burning fireplaces.

Cheese Shop DELI $
(📞757-220-0298; www.cheeseshopwilliamsburg.com; 410 W Duke of Gloucester St, Merchants Square; sandwiches $5.50-8; 🕙10am-8pm Mon-Sat, 11am-6pm Sun) This gourmet deli showcases some flavorful sandwiches and antipasti, plus baguettes, pastries, ready-made meals, wine, beer and wonderful cheeses. Order a sandwich and a glass of wine – at different counters – then enjoy your meal and the people-watching from the patio.

★**Fat Canary** MODERN AMERICAN $$$
(📞757-229-3333; www.fatcanarywilliamsburg.com; 410 W Duke of Gloucester St, Merchants Square; mains $28-40; 🕙5-9:30pm, closed Mon Jan & Feb) The best restaurant in the historic triangle, this friendly and stylish place offers top-notch service, excellent wines and a menu of Modern American cuisine with Asian and Italian accents. We love the fact that local produce is a focus, that orders of half serves are accepted and that the list of wine by the glass features interesting choices.

King's Arms Tavern MODERN AMERICAN $$$
(📞866-348-9022; www.colonialwilliamsburg.com; 416 E Duke of Gloucester St; lunch mains $14-16, dinner mains $25-40; 🕙11:30am-2:30pm & 5-8pm Thu-Mon Mar-Dec) This traditional tavern serves early American cuisine such as game pie – venison, rabbit and duck braised in port-wine sauce. Of the four restaurants within Colonial Williamsburg, it is the most elegant. You might hear live flute music with your meal, and staff will share history about colonial dining habits. Book ahead for dinner; vegetarians should dine elsewhere.

ℹ Information

Merchants Square Information Booth (www.colonialwilliamsburg.com; W Duke of Gloucester St; 🕙9am-5pm) In town.

Visitor Center (📞888-965-7254, 757-220-7645; www.colonialwilliamsburg.com; 101 Visitor Center Dr; 🕙8:45am-9pm) When you get into town, start your trip at this Colonial Williamsburg center.

ℹ Getting There & Around

Amtrak (www.amtrak.com) trains travel twice a day to Washington, DC (from $34, four hours) and Richmond (from $16, 50 minutes).

From the **transportation center** (📞757-229-8750; 468 N Boundary St, cnr Boundary & Lafayette Sts; 🕙7:30am-10pm), Williamsburg Area Transit Authority buses travel around town and to/from Jamestown ($1.50). For schedules and ticketing information see www.gowata.org.

Parking in the downtown carparks is free, but is limited to one hour between 9am and 6pm.

Jamestown
📞757

On May 14, 1607, a group of 104 English men and boys settled on this swampy island, bearing a charter from the Virginia Company of London to search for gold and other riches. Instead they found starvation and disease. By January 1608, only about 40 colonists were still alive and had resorted to cannibalism to survive. The colony pulled through the 'Starving Time' with the leadership of Captain James Smith and help from Powhatan, a local Native American leader. In 1619, the elected House of Burgesses convened, forming the first democratic government in the Americas. Today, two sites share the story of this early settlement.

◉ Sights

★**Historic Jamestowne** HISTORIC SITE
(📞757-856-1250; www.historicjamestowne.org; 1368 Colonial Pkwy; adult/child under 16yr $14/free; 🕙9am-5pm) Run by the NPS, this fascinating

VIRGINIA JAMESTOWN

place is the original Jamestown site, established in 1607 and home of the first permanent English settlement in North America. The settlement's ruins were rediscovered in 1994; visitors can take a free guided tour of the excavations (daily 11am, also 2pm on weekends and between April and September). On arrival, view the orientation film and then head to the Archaearium, an archaeology museum with more than 4000 artifacts and a 'World of Pocahontas, Unearthed' exhibit. Ask one of the docents to share the real story – not the Disney version – of the relationship between Pocahontas and John White, a British soldier and explorer who was the leader of the Virginia Colony based in Jamestown from 1608 to 1609 and was the first English explorer to map the Chesapeake Bay area. The plaque on White's statue here in the site isn't complimentary, calling him 'an arrogant and boastful man.'

Entry is discounted to $7 for visitors with a ticket receipt for Yorktown Battlefield and to $5 if you have a National Parks pass. There's a cafe on site.

Jamestown Settlement HISTORIC SITE
(🔋888-593-4682; www.historyisfun.org; 2110 Jamestown Rd; adult/child 6-12yr $17/8, incl American Revolutionary Museum at Yorktown $23/12; ⊙9am-5pm, to 6pm mid-Jun–mid-Aug; 🅿🛆) Popular with kids, the state-run Jamestown Settlement reconstructs the 1607 James Fort; a Native American village; and full-scale replicas of the first ships that brought the settlers to Jamestown, along with living-history fun. Multimedia exhibits and costumed interpreters bring the 17th century to life. This one can get uncomfortably busy with elementary school field trips, so arrive early during the school year.

❶ Getting There & Away

The best way to get to Jamestown is by car. Amtrak (www.amtrak.com) stops at the Williamsburg Transportation Center (p363) twice a day en route to Washington, DC ($46, four hours) and Richmond ($22, 90 minutes), both on the Northeast Regional route. From the transportation center, Williamsburg Area Transit Authority buses (www.gowata.org) travel to/from Jamestown ($1.50).

Yorktown

🔋757 / POP 195
On October 19, 1781, British General Cornwallis surrendered to George Washington here, effectively ending the American Rev-

olution. Overpowered by massive American guns on land and cut off from the sea by the French, the British were in a hopeless position. Although Washington anticipated a much longer siege, the devastating barrage quickly overwhelmed Cornwallis, who surrendered within days.

The actual town of Yorktown is a pleasant waterfront village overlooking the York River, with a sandy beach, a scattering of shops, and a few restaurants and pubs. For more information, go to www.visityorktown.org.

◉ Sights

Yorktown Battlefield HISTORIC SITE
(🔋757-898-2410; www.nps.gov/york; 1000 Colonial Pkwy; adult/child under 16yr $7/free; ⊙9am-5pm; 🅿🛆) Yorktown Battlefield, run by the NPS, is the site of the last major battle of the American Revolution. Start your tour at the visitor center and check out the orientation film and the display of Washington's original tent, then drive the 7-mile Battlefield Rd Tour, which takes you past the major highlights. Don't miss a walk through the last British defensive sites, Redoubts 9 and 10, reached via Ballard St. Entry is free if you have a ticket receipt for Historic Jamestowne (p363).

American Revolution Museum at Yorktown MUSEUM
(🔋757-887-1776; www.historyisfun.org; 200 Water St; adult/child 6-12yr $12/7, incl Jamestown Settlement adult/child $23/12; ⊙9am-5pm, to 6pm mid-July–mid-Aug; 🅿🛆) Formerly the Yorktown Victory Center, this new and expanded exhibition space and living history museum vividly describes the build-up to the Revolutionary War, the war itself and daily life on the home front. The thrilling *Siege* is a nine-minute 4D movie spotlighting the Battle of Yorktown. Lots of significant artifacts are here too, including an early printing of the Declaration of Independence. At the re-created military encampment outside, costumed Continental soldiers share details about life in a Revolutionary War camp.

🛏 Sleeping & Eating

⭐**Hornsby House Inn** B&B $$
(🔋757-369-0200; www.hornsbyhouseinn.com; 702 Main St; r $130-250; 🅿🛆) Close to Yorktown's beach and eateries, this house was built by the current owner's grandfather in 1933 and retains its old-fashioned ambiance. That's not to say that it is dated or dowdy, because nothing could be further from the truth – we love the elegant ground-floor lounge and

CHINCOTEAGUE ISLAND

This long, flat peninsula on Virginia's Eastern Shore is separated geographically by the Chesapeake Bay, but is also quite removed from the rest of Virginia in terms of its culture, which is slow-paced and distinctively maritime. The main pleasure on the Shore is exploring the backroads leading to the waterfronts – either the rough Atlantic or placid Chesapeake Bay. Sampling the fresh harvest from local oyster beds and clam shoals is a highlight.

The entire peninsula is known as Chincoteague, as is its main town, which is close to adjoining Assateague Island in Maryland. In the lush **Chincoteague National Wildlife Refuge** (☑757-336-6122; www.fws.gov; 8231 Beach Rd; vehicle pass $20; ⊘5am-10pm May-Sep, 6am-6pm Nov-Mar, to 8pm Apr & Oct; P♿) you can look for the wild horses (p330). Don't miss a scoop of ice cream from **Island Creamery** (☑757-336-6236; www.islandcreamery. net; 6243 Maddox Blvd; one scoop $4; ⊘11am-10pm daily late May–mid-Sep, to 9pm Mon-Fri, 10pm Sat & Sun mid-Sep–late May) or a taco from **Pico Taqueria** (☑757-785-9920; www.pico taqueria.com; 6382 Maddox Blvd; tacos $3.50-4; ⊘11am-8pm mid-Apr–early Oct) roadside stand.

During the annual Chincoteague Pony Swim (www.chincoteague.com), in July, wild ponies are moved annually from Assateague Island to Chincoteague Island to auction the foals. The event was notably covered in Marguerite Henry's novel *Misty of Chincoteague*.

Tiny Tangier Island is in the Chesapeake Bay, off Chincoteague's west shore.

the six large, light, and elegantly furnished rooms (most accessed by stairs).

Yorktown Pub   SEAFOOD **$$**
(☑757-886-9964; www.yorktownpub.com; 540 Water St; sandwiches $6-14, mains $23-27; ⊘11am-midnight Sun-Thu, to 1:30am Fri & Sat) Most of the local action in Yorktown occurs at this pub by the beach. Serving good pub grub (including loads of local seafood) and staging live music on Friday and Saturday nights, it's as popular in winter as it is in the warmer weather due to the open fire and warm welcome offered by the staff.

❶ Getting There & Away

There is no public transport to Yorktown, so you'll need a car to visit. A free trolley loops between historic sites and the village every 20 to 35 minutes (11am to 5pm mid-March to December; extended hours June to August).

HAMPTON ROADS

Hampton Roads (named not for asphalt, but for the confluence of the James, Nansemond and Elizabeth Rivers and Chesapeake Bay) has always been prime real estate. The Powhatan Confederacy fished these waters and hunted this part of the Virginia coast for thousands of years before John Smith arrived in 1607. Today the area is known for congestion – particularly around the Chesapeake Bay Bridge Tunnel – and a cultural mishmash of history, the military and the arts.

❶ Getting There & Away

Norfolk International Airport (p366) is the primary airport for the region. I-64 is the main interstate. Expect slowdowns around the Hampton Roads Bridge-Tunnel, which links Newport News and Norfolk. If the electronic traffic signs suggest using the I-664 detour, take it.

Amtrak's Northeast Regional train service connects Newport News with Washington, DC; Richmond; and Williamsburg. Greyhound buses connect Norfolk with Virginia Beach; Richmond; and Washington, DC.

Norfolk

☑757 / POP 245,120

It's home to the world's largest naval base, so it's not surprising that Norfolk has long had a reputation as a rowdy port town filled with drunken sailors. However, in recent years the city has worked hard to clean up its image through development and by focusing on its burgeoning arts scene, which is spearheaded by the impressive Chrysler Museum of Art. The downtown Ghent District is where most of the town's cultural and entertainment action occurs, and the recently opened nearby Waterside District, a dining and entertainment complex on the Elizabeth River, is worth a visit.

◉ Sights

★**Chrysler Museum of Art**   MUSEUM
(☑757-664-6200; www.chrysler.org; 1 Memorial Pl; ⊘10am-5pm Tue-Sat, noon-5pm Sun) **FREE**
A glorious setting for an eclectic collection

VIRGINIA NORFOLK

of artifacts from ancient Egypt to the present day, including works by Henri Matisse, Albert Bierstadt, Georgia O'Keeffe, Jackson Pollock and Andy Warhol, and an expansive collection of glass objects spanning 3000 years. Don't miss the collection of Tiffany blown glass.

Naval Station Norfolk   MUSEUM
(📱757-444-7955; www.cnic.navy.mil/norfolksta; 9079 Hampton Blvd, near Gate 5; adult/child 3-11yr $10/5; ⊙hours vary) The world's largest navy base, and one of the busiest airfields in the country. Hampton-based company Tidewater Touring works with the base to offer 45-minute bus tours conducted by naval personnel; tours must be booked in advance (hours vary). Photo ID is required for adults.

Nauticus   MUSEUM
(📱757-664-1000; www.nauticus.org; 1 Waterside Dr; adult/child 4-12yr $16/11.50; ⊙10am-5pm daily Jun-Aug, 10am-5pm Tue-Sat, noon-5pm Sun Sep-May) This massive, interactive, maritime-themed museum has exhibits on undersea exploration, aquatic life of the Chesapeake Bay and US Naval lore. The museum's highlight is clambering around the decks and inner corridors of the USS *Wisconsin*. Built in 1943, it was the largest (887ft long) and last battleship built by the US Navy.

🛏 Sleeping

Residence Inn Norfolk Downtown   HOTEL $$
(📱757-842-6216; www.marriott.com; 227 W Brambleton Ave; r/ste $142-209, 1-bed ste $209-259; 🅿@🛜🏊🐾) A short stroll to the Granby St eating strip, this Marriott hotel offers spacious but slightly worn studios and suites with small kitchenettes. Facilities include a fitness center. Breakfast is included in the room rate.

Main Hotel   HOTEL $$$
(📱757-763-6200; www.3hilton.com; 100 E Main St; r $236-400; 🅿❄🛜🏊) The rooms are swanky at this new member of the Hilton family, which is located near the Nauticus Center. Rooms with a river view cost more, but you may not need to book one – just settle in for a drink and river view at the rooftop lounge **Grain**, one of the hotel's three dining-drinking establishments. It's popular – book well in advance.

🍴 Eating & Drinking

Cure   CAFE $
(📱757-321-0044; www.curenorfolk.com; 503 Botetourt St; sandwiches $8-10, cheese board $12; ⊙8am-10pm Mon-Wed & Sat, 7am-10pm Thu & Fri,

8am-8pm Sun; 🛜) This neighborhood cafe on the edge of the historic district serves tasty and creative sandwiches along with good coffee. Later in the day, craft beer, cocktails and wine supplant the coffee action and can be enjoyed with a cheese or charcuterie board.

⭐**Press 626 Wine Bar**   MODERN AMERICAN $$
(📱757-282-6234; www.press626.com; 626 W Olney Rd; sandwiches $10-14, mains $10-26; ⊙11am-11pm Mon-Fri, 5-11pm Sat, 10:30am-2:30pm Sun; 🍴) Embracing the Slow Food movement, this charming place in the Ghent district has a small but well-judged menu, with something to suit most tastes and budgets. The cheese and charcuterie plates are particularly good. Its wine selection is global and interesting, and its popular program of events includes wine seminars.

Luna Maya   MEXICAN $$
(📱757-622-6986; www.lunamayarestaurant.com; 2010 Colley Ave; mains $13-19; ⊙4:30-10pm Tue-Sat; 🍴) Friendly service and awesome burritos set this hip place apart from the competition on busy Colley Ave. Not to mention the tasty margaritas and an extensive selection of vegetarian and vegan dishes for the non-carnivores in your group.

⭐**Smartmouth Brewing Company**   BREWERY
(📱757-624-3939; www.smartmouthbrewing.com; 1309 Raleigh Ave; ⊙4:30-9pm Wed-Fri, noon-9pm Sat, 1-5pm Sun; 🍺) In the Chelsea arts district, this indoor-outdoor tasting room and brewery has an inviting neighborhood feel, plus there's usually a food truck handy. If you like *hefeweizens* (wheat beer), give the seasonal Sommer Fling a try (April to December). There are free brewery tours every hour between 1pm and 5pm on Saturdays.

ℹ Getting There & Away

The region is served by **Norfolk International Airport** (NIA; 📱757-857-3351; www.norfolkairport.com; 2200 Norview Ave; 🛜), 7 miles northeast of downtown Norfolk. **Greyhound** (📱757-625-7500; www.greyhound.com; 701 Monticello Ave) runs buses to Virginia Beach (from $6, 40 minutes); Richmond (from $17, two to 2½ hours); and Washington, DC ($20, 5¼ hours).

VIRGINIA BEACH

📱757 / POP 452,600

With 35 miles of sandy beaches, a 3-mile concrete oceanfront boardwalk and nearby outdoor activities, it's no surprise that Virginia Beach is a prime tourist destination. The city

JAMES RIVER PLANTATIONS

The grand homes of Virginia's slaveholding aristocracy were a clear sign of the era's class divisions. A string of them, including **Berkeley Plantation** (☎804-829-6018; www.berkeley plantation.com; 12602 Harrison Landing Rd, Charles City; adult/child 6-16yr $12/7; ◷9:30am-4:30pm, reduced hours Jan & Feb) and **Shirley Plantation** (☎800-829-5121; www.shirley plantation.com; 501 Shirley Plantation Rd, Charles City; adult/child 7-16yr $12.50/8.50; ◷9:30am-4pm early Mar-Dec), line scenic Hwy 5 on the north side of the river, though only a few are open to the public. If traveling along Hwy 5, make time for a meal and glass of wine at **Upper Shirley Vineyards** (☎804-829-9463; www.uppershirley.com; 600 Shirley Plantation Rd; mains $16-25, tasting $11; ◷11am-5pm Wed-Mon, closed Mon Dec-Feb), which sits prettily on a bend of the river. For cyclists, the new Virginia Capital Trail (p351) linking Richmond and Williamsburg travels beside Rte 5, near the Shirley and Berkeley Plantations.

has worked hard to shed its reputation as a rowdy 'Redneck Riviera,' and hey, the beach *is* wider and cleaner now and there are fewer louts. Beach aside, you'll find lovely parks and nature sites beyond the crowded high-rises lining the shore. In summer, expect thick crowds, heavy traffic and high prices.

◉ Sights

**Virginia Aquarium &
Marine Science Center**   AQUARIUM
(☎757-385-3474; www.virginiaaquarium.com; 717 General Booth Blvd; adult/child 3-11yr $25/20; ◷9am-5pm) This is an aquarium done right. In various habitats, you can see a great array of aquatic life, including sea turtles, river otters and Komodo dragons.

First Landing State Park   NATURE RESERVE
(☎757-412-2300; www.dcr.virginia.gov; 2500 Shore Dr; per vehicle $7-9; ◷8am-dusk) Shake off the Virginia Beach flash at this lower key 2888-acre woodland, which has 20 miles of hiking trails and 1.5 miles of beach, plus opportunities for camping, cycling, fishing, kayaking and swimming.

**Back Bay National
Wildlife Refuge**   NATURE RESERVE
(☎757-301-7329; www.fws.gov; 4005 Sandpiper Rd; per vehicle/pedestrian Apr-Oct $5/2, free Nov-Mar; ◷sunrise-sunset) This 9250-acre wildlife and migratory-bird marshland habitat is most stunning during the December migration season. The refuge's visitor center is open from 8am to 4pm weekdays, 9am to 4pm weekends.

⌂ Sleeping & Eating

First Landing State Park   CAMPGROUND $
(☎800-933-7275; www.dcr.virginia.gov; Cape Henry; tent & RV sites $28-41, cabins from $74; ◷early Mar-early Dec; ℗) You couldn't ask for a pret-

tier campground than the one at this bay-front state park, though the cabins have no water view.

Hilton Virginia Beach Oceanfront   HOTEL $$
(☎757-213-3000; www.hiltonvb.com; 3001 Atlantic Ave; r from $122; ℗@☏☒) One of the premier places to stay on the beach, this 21-story hotel offers spacious and comfortable oceanfront rooms with large balconies that open out to the beach and Neptune Park below. Facilities include a fitness center and two pools: an outdoor rooftop infinity pool and an indoor alternative. In summer, rooms are cheaper mid-week than on weekends.

Esoteric   AMERICAN $$
(☎757-822-6008; www.esotericvb.com; 501 Virginia Beach Blvd; mains $12-31; ◷4-10pm Mon-Wed, to 11pm Thu, to midnight Fri, noon-midnight Sat) The menu at this joint lives up to its name, including everything from hummus to dolmades, tacos to gnocchi. At lunch, the gourmet sandwiches and craft beer are a winning combination. The husband-and-wife team behind grow some of their produce in the attached garden, and embrace local food producers as collaborators. Bravo.

Blue Pete's   SEAFOOD $$
(☎757-426-2278; www.bluepetespungo.com; 1400 N Muddy Creek Rd; mains $11-32; ◷5-10pm Mon-Thu, 5pm-midnight Fri, noon-midnight Sat, noon-10pm Sun) Perched over a peaceful creek near Back Bay, Blue Pete's has an enchanting woodland setting and a wide-ranging and well-priced menu: oysters, gumbo, she-crab soup, brisket sandwiches, pastas and crab cakes.

❶ Information

Visitor Center (☎1-800-822-3224; www.visit virginiabeach.com; 2100 Parks Ave; ◷9am-5pm, to 7pm mid-Jun–Aug) Friendly visitor center; has loads of info on Virginia Beach.

VIRGINIA VIRGINIA BEACH

❶ Getting There & Away

Greyhound (☏ 757-422-2998; www.greyhound.com; 971 Virginia Beach Blvd) runs buses daily to Richmond (from $13, 3¼ hours), which also stop in Norfolk and Hampton; transfer in Richmond for services to Washington, DC, Wilmington, NYC and beyond. Buses depart from Circle D Food Mart, 1 mile west of the boardwalk.

Hampton Roads Transit runs the Virginia Beach Wave trolley (tickets $2), which plies Atlantic Ave in summer.

SHENANDOAH VALLEY

Local lore says Shenandoah was named for a Native American word meaning 'Daughter of the Stars.' True or not, there's no question this is God's country, and one of the most beautiful places in America. The 200-mile-long valley and its Blue Ridge Mountains are packed with picturesque small towns, wineries, microbreweries, preserved battlefields and caverns. This was once the western border of colonial America, settled by Scots-Irish frontiersmen who were Highland Clearance refugees. Outdoor activities such as hiking, cycling, camping, fishing, horseback riding and canoeing abound, and hitting the road on the famed Skyline Drive is an unforgettable experience, particularly in the fall when the palette of the forest canopy ranges from russet red to copper-tinged orange.

❶ Getting There & Away

The best way to explore is by car. The I-81 and I-64 are the primary interstates here. The largest airport is **Roanoke-Blacksburg Regional Airport** (☏ 540-362-1999; www.roanokeairport.com; 5202 Aviation Dr NW). Amtrak stops at the train station (p370) in Staunton and the Virginia Breeze (p373) bus service to/from Washington, DC, stops at Arlington, Front Royal, Staunton and Lexington (tickets $15 to $50).

Staunton
☏ 540 / POP 24,363

This small-town beauty has much going for it, including a historic and walkable town center, a fantastic foodie scene, great microbreweries, regular live music downtown and a first-rate theater. Add to this an abundance of outdoor activities nearby and you may find yourself looking into local real estate when you get here.

◉ Sights

Ox-Eye Vineyard Tasting Room WINERY
(☏ 540-849-7926; www.oxeyevineyards.com; 44 Middlebrook Ave; tasting $7; ⊙ noon-6pm Mon-Thu, to 7pm Fri, 10am-7pm Sat, noon-5pm Sun) Ox-Eye is known for its cool climate reds and whites (particularly its dry rieslings, Lemberger and pinot noir). Its wharf district tasting room occupies a handsome building dating from 1904 and is a pleasant stop when wandering through town. Light fare ($5.50 to $8) is available to enjoy with your tasting.

Frontier Culture Museum MUSEUM
(☏ 540-332-7850; www.frontiermuseum.org; 1290 Richmond Rd; adult/student/child 6-12yr $12/11/7; ⊙ 9am-5pm mid-Mar–Nov, 10am-4pm Dec–mid-Mar) The excellent Frontier Culture Museum is cooler than its name might suggest. On the 100-plus acre grounds you'll find authentic historic buildings from Germany, Ireland and England, plus re-created West African dwellings and a separate area of

---

DON'T MISS

LURAY CAVERNS

If you can only fit one cavern into your Shenandoah itinerary, head 25 miles south from Front Royal to the world-class **Luray Caverns** (☏ 540-743-6551; www.luraycaverns.com; 970 US Hwy 211 W, Luray; adult/child 6-12yr $27/14; ⊙ 9am-7pm daily mid-Jun–Aug, to 6pm Sep-Nov & Apr–mid-Jun, to 4pm Mon-Fri, to 5pm Sat & Sun Dec-Mar) and hear the 'Stalacpipe Organ' – hyped as the largest musical instrument on earth. On busy weekends tours can feel like a cattle call, but the stunning underground formations make up for all the elbow-bumping. To save time at the entrance, buy your ticket online ahead of time, then join the entry line. Also here is a Ropes Adventure Park (adult/child $9/6) and a Garden Maze ($8/6). For a down-home breakfast, drive six miles south of Luray to **Hawksbill Diner** (☏ 540-778-2006; www.facebook.com/thehawksbilldiner; 1388 E Main St/Hwy 340 Business, Stanley; breakfast dishes $2-6, sandwiches $2-7, dinner mains $6-11; ⊙ 6am-5pm Mon-Thu, to 8pm Fri & Sat; 🅿). Though the place is full of chatting locals who all seem to know each other, staff offer strangers a warm welcome. There's country and western on the jukebox, old signs on the walls and a menu replete with traditional diner fare.

Staunton

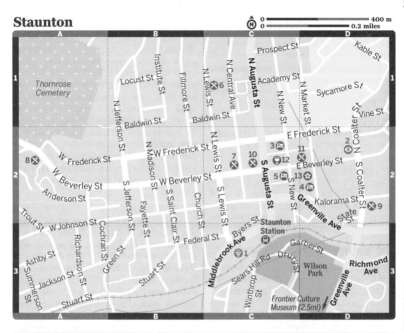

Staunton

◎ Sights
1 Ox-Eye Vineyard Tasting Room...........C3
2 Woodrow Wilson Presidential
   Library...D2

🛏 Sleeping
3 Frederick House.................................C2
4 Stonewall Jackson Hotel...................D2
5 Storefront...C2

✕ Eating
6 Chicano Boy.......................................C1

7 Farmhouse Kitchen & Wares.............C2
8 Newtown Bakery.................................A2
9 Shack...D2
10 Split Banana Co..................................C2
11 Zynodoa...D2

🍷 Drinking & Nightlife
12 Yelping Dog..C2

✪ Entertainment
13 Blackfriars Playhouse.........................D2

American frontier dwellings. Costumed interpreters (aided by bleating livestock) do an excellent job showing what life was like for the disparate ancestors of today's Virginians.

Woodrow Wilson
Presidential Library   HISTORIC SITE
(☎540-885-0897; www.woodrowwilson.org; 18 N Coalter St; adult/student/child 6-12yr $14/7/5; ◉9am-5pm Mon-Sat, from noon Sun Mar-Oct, to 4pm Nov-Feb) History buffs should check out the Woodrow Wilson Presidential Library near downtown. Stop by and tour the hilltop Greek Revival house where Wilson grew up, which has been faithfully restored to its original 1856 appearance. 'Behind the Scenes' guided tours ($40) Tuesdays and Thursdays at 2pm; 'Wilson and Slavery' tour ($25) first and third Friday of month at 11:30am.

🛏 Sleeping

Storefront   APARTMENT $$
(☎804-218-5656; www.the-storefront-hotel.com; 14 S New St; r Sun-Thu $115, Fri-Sun $159) It dubs itself a very small hotel, but this hip getaway is really a narrow building with one two-story apartment. The front door opens onto a sitting area and bar. Upstairs you'll find a kitchen and bedroom. Two-night minimum stay Friday and Saturday.

Frederick House   B&B $$
(☎540-885-4220; www.frederickhouse.com; 28 N New St; r $135-155, ste $170-230; 🅿❄🛜📶🐾)

Owners Ross and Brooke Williams work hard to ensure that guests at their downtown guesthouse are happy. Rooms are scattered throughout five historical residences with 23 varied rooms and suites – all with private bathrooms and some with air-con. The nicest rooms are in Patrick House (request room 26). Breakfast is included in the price.

Stonewall Jackson Hotel   HOTEL **$$**
(☑ 540-885-4848;   www.stonewalljacksonhotel. com; 24 S Market St; r $119-250; P ✴ 🛜 ♨ 🐾) Once a showcase of the restrained Southern style of the classical Commonwealth, Staunton's best-known hotel is looking dowdy these days and is in sore need of a full makeover. That said, rooms are comfortable enough, rates are reasonable and there's an on-site gym, indoor pool and bar.

✖ Eating

★ Chicano Boy   MEXICAN **$**
(☑ 540-569-2105;   www.chicanoboytaco.com; 240 N Central Ave, suite 6; tacos $9, burritos $10; ◷ 11am-2pm & 5-9pm Tue-Sat; ✎ 🐾) It's hard to beat the value offered by this taquería's $7 lunch deal, which delivers a drink, a dip and two tacos. Prices don't rise much at dinner, when tacos, including the Al Pastor (pork marinated in chilli and pineapple), vegetarian (sweet potato and black bean) and vegan (soy protein, tomato, olives, capers), run out the door. Eat in or take out.

★ Newtown Bakery   BAKERY, PIZZERIA **$**
(☑ 540-885-3799;   www.newtownbaking.com; 960 W Beverley St; sandwiches $6-9, pizzas $10-14; ◷ 7:30am-3pm & 5-9pm Wed-Fri, 8am-2pm & 5-9pm Sat; P ✎ 🐾) This is the type of place that every small town needs. It bakes its own European-style bread and pastries; serves soup and sandwiches at lunch; and cranks up the wood-fired pizza oven at night to offer piping hot, super-tasty pies. Coffee is from the Staunton Coffee Company, and wine and beer are available, too. Love it.

Farmhouse Kitchen & Wares   CAFE **$**
(☑ 540-712-7791;   www.farmhousekitchenand wares.com; 101 W Beverly St; breakfast dishes $6-11, sandwiches $9-12.50; ◷ 8am-3pm Mon-Sat) The delicious gourmet sandwiches are piled high at this country-chic cafe, where you can also purchase any of the stylish cookware on display. Homemade breakfasts too.

Split Banana Co.   ICE CREAM **$**
(☑ 866-492-3668; www.thesplitbanana.com; 7 W Beverley St; one scoop $2.70; ◷ noon-11pm; 🐾) This locals' favorite ice-cream parlor has delicious flavors, served up in a charmingly old-fashioned setting. Open late.

★ The Shack   AMERICAN **$$**
(☑ 540-490-1961;   www.theshackva.com;   105 S Coalter St; brunch mains $12-22, dinner 3-/4-course prix-fixe $45/55; ◷ 5-9pm Wed-Sat, 10:30am-2pm Sun; ✎) It may be cooked and served in a small and unadorned space (hence the name), but the dishes served here are among the best in the state. Chef Ian Boden, a two-time James Beard semi-finalist, makes the most of seasonal local produce in his menu, which is inspired by his mountain roots and Eastern European Jewish heritage. Good wine list.

Zynodoa   SOUTHERN US **$$$**
(☑ 540-885-7775; www.zynodoa.com; 115 E Beverley St; mains $21-34; ◷ 5-9:30pm Sun-Tue, to 10:30pm Wed-Sat; ✎) Local farms and wineries are the backbone of Zynodoa's larder, and the chef delivers his predominantly Southern dishes (vegetable succotash, cornmeal-crusted wild blue catfish, apple cider–braised pork, Rappahannock River fried oysters) in a sleekly designed dining room. Its location makes it a favoured destination for pre-theatre dinners.

🍷 Drinking & Entertainment

Yelping Dog   WINE BAR
(☑ 540-885-2275; www.yelpingdogwine.com; 9 E Beverly St; ◷ 11am-9pm Tue-Thu, to 10pm Fri & Sat, noon-6pm Sun) An inviting wine bar in the thick of the downtown action, the Yelping Dog has its priorities right: wine, cheese and charcuterie. It also serves craft beer. If you're on the fence about ordering one of the gourmet grilled cheese sandwiches ($9 to $10), go ahead and fall off. They're delicious. Live music some Saturday nights.

★ Blackfriars Playhouse   THEATER
(☑ 540-851-1733;   www.americanshakespeare center.com; 10 S Market St; tickets $29-49) Don't leave Staunton without catching a show at the Blackfriars Playhouse, where actors from the American Shakespeare Center perform in a re-creation of Shakespeare's original indoor theater. The acting is up-close and engaged, and brave guests can grab a seat on the side of the stage.

ℹ Getting There & Away

Staunton sits beside I-81, not far from its junction with I-64 E. **Amtrak** (www.amtrak.com; 1 Middlebrook Ave) trains stop here three times per week on their way to/from Charlottesville and Washington, DC.

Lexington

📞 540 / POP 7045

The fighting spirit of the South is visually encapsulated by the sight of cadets from the Virginia Military Institute (VMI) strutting their stuff at Friday's full dress parade. The institute is one of Lexington's two major historic institutions, the other being Washington & Lee University (W&L). Two Civil War generals, Robert E Lee and Stonewall Jackson, lived here and are buried in town, and Lexington has long been a favorite stop for Civil War enthusiasts. Today you're as likely to see hikers, cyclists and paddlers using Lexington as a launchpad for adventures in the nearby Blue Ridge Mountains, where the Blue Ridge Parkway and the Appalachian Trail overlook the valley, as well as on the James River. The opening of new hotels, bars

Lexington

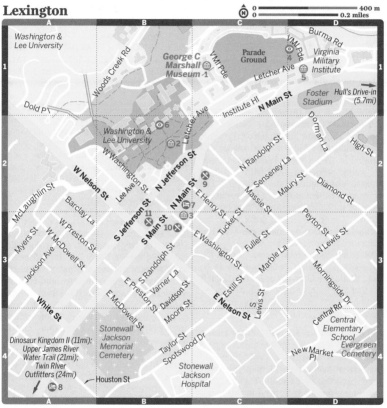

VIRGINIA LEXINGTON

Lexington

and restaurants has re-energized the city in recent years – it's a great Shenandoah base.

◎ Sights

★ George C Marshall Museum   MUSEUM

(🖉540-463-2083; www.marshallfoundation.org/museum; VMI Parade; adult/student/child under 13yr $5/2/free; ⊙11am-4pm Tue-Sat) Many visitors to Lexington give this museum in the grounds of the Virginia Military Institute (VMI) a miss. We counsel you not to do the same, as its subject matter and exhibits are totally engrossing. Chief of staff of the US army during WWII, Marshall was described by Winston Churchill as 'the organiser of the Allied victory.' A 1901 graduate of VMI, he is perhaps best known as the creator of the $13 billion Marshall Plan for post-WWII European reconstruction.

Washington & Lee University   UNIVERSITY

(🖉540-458-8400; www.wlu.edu) Named for George Washington and Robert E Lee, this pretty and preppy liberal arts college was founded in 1749. George Washington saved the young school in 1796 with a gift of $20,000. Confederate general Robert E Lee served as president after the Civil War in the hopes of unifying the country through education. Visitors today can stroll along the striking red-brick Colonnade and visit Lee Chapel & Museum (p372).

Note that doors on the garage stall of the university president's house will likely be open. While president of the school, Lee left the door ajar for his wandering horse Traveller. Today, tradition keeps them open in case Traveller's ghost wanders home.

Stonewall Jackson House   HISTORIC BUILDING

(🖉540-464-7704; www.stonewalljackson.org; 8 E Washington St; adult/child 6-17yr $8/6; ⊙9am-5pm Mon-Sat, from 1pm Sun) One of the most revered generals of the south, Thomas Jonathon 'Stonewall' Jackson lived in this handsome brick Federal-style town house with his wife and five slaves from 1851 to 1861, while he taught at nearby VMI. The house is remarkably well preserved, and 45-minute guided tours providing fascinating insight into Jackson's life and times. His body (all but his left arm, anyway) is buried in the cemetery a few blocks away.

Virginia Military Institute   UNIVERSITY

(VMI; www.vmi.edu; Letcher Ave) You'll either be impressed or put off by the extreme discipline of the cadets at Virginia Military Institute, the only university to have sent its entire graduating class into combat (plaques to student war dead are touching and ubiquitous). The VMI Museum (🖉540-464-7334; www.vmi.edu/museum; 415 Letcher Ave; $5; ⊙9am-5pm) houses the stuffed carcass of Stonewall Jackson's horse among its artifacts and the George C Marshall Museum honors the creator of the Marshall Plan for post-WWII European reconstruction. Contact the museum for a free 45-minute cadet-guided tour, offered at noon during term time. A full-dress parade takes place most Fridays at 4pm during the school year.

Lee Chapel & Museum   MUSEUM

(🖉540-458-8768; www.wlu.edu/lee-chapel-and-museum; Washington & Lee University; adult/child $5/3; ⊙9am-4pm Mon-Sat, 1-4pm Sun Nov-Mar, to 5pm Apr-Oct) This picturesque chapel inters Robert E Lee (1807–70). After Lee's death, Virginia sculptor Edward Valentine created its life-size 'Recumbent Lee' statue. A small museum displays Lee's office, and his horse Traveller is buried outside.

Washington & Lee University has a single-sanction honor system, and students must withdraw if convicted by a student jury of lying, cheating or stealing. Honor trials are held in the chapel.

Dinosaur Kingdom II   AMUSEMENT PARK

(🖉540-464-2253; www.dinosaurkingdomii.com; 5781 S Lee Hwy, Lexington; adult/child 3-12yr $10/3; ⊙11am-5pm Sat & Sun May & Sep-early Nov, 10am-6pm Jun-Aug; 🎡) One of the wackiest attractions yet from artist and creative wunderkind Mark Cline, this kitschy theme park transports visitors to an alternate reality: a forested kingdom where Union soldiers are attempting to use life-size dinosaurs as weapons of mass destruction against Confederate forces during the Civil War. Even President Lincoln is here, trying to lasso a flying pteranodon. The Styrofoam and fiberglass creations are lifelike enough to amaze younger kids, and the offbeat historic juxtapositions will entertain even the grouchiest of adults. The park is about 12 miles south of Lexington on S Lee Hwy/Rte 11.

Activities

Upper James River Water Trail   CANOEING

(www.upperjamesriverwatertrail.com; Botetourt) This new 74-mile paddling trail follows the James River as it flows through the foothills of the Blue Ridge Mountains toward Richmond and the coast. The trail is divided into various sections taking between one and seven hours to traverse by canoe or kayak.

Twin River Outfitters
CANOEING; TUBING

(☑540-254-8012; https://canoevirginia.net; 640 Lowe St, Buchanan; paddling trips from $34; ☺9am-5pm Apr-Oct) Scan for eagles and deer as you paddle or tube down the James River on the new Upper James River Paddling Trail with this popular outfitter, owned by twin brothers. Mileage and travel times vary, as does difficulty. A shuttle ride is included in the price.

🛏 Sleeping

Grace House
B&B $$

(☑571-286-8411; www.gracehouselexva.com; 506 S Main St; r from $140; P 🛜) There are plenty of upmarket B&Bs in Virginia, but few are as stylish as this one. In an 1890 building that once functioned as Grace Presbyterian Church, it offers four elegant guest rooms with attached or adjoining private bathrooms. There's also a comfortable guest lounge.

★Georges
BOUTIQUE HOTEL $$$

(☑540-463-2500; www.thegeorges.com; 11 N Main St; r $170-310, ste $310-460; P ✳🛜) Set in two historic buildings on opposite sides of Main St, Georges has 18 classy rooms featuring high-end furnishings and luxury linens. The great location, friendly service and delicious breakfast (included in the room rate) make it Lexington's best accommodation option, and put it in the running for the accolade of best in the Shenandoah, too.

🍴 Eating

Pure Eats
AMERICAN $

(☑540-462-6000; www.pure-eats.com; 107 N Main St; burgers $7-12, doughnuts $1.25; ☺8am-8pm) In a former filling station, Pure Eats doles out delicious housemade doughnuts and egg-and-cheese biscuits in the morning; later in the day, burgers are the popular choice. Also sells local craft brews, milkshakes made with local milk and ice cream from a local creamery.

★Red Hen
FRENCH $$$

(☑540-464-4401; www.redhenlex.com; 11 E Washington St; mains $22-28; ☺5-9:30pm Tue-Sat; 🍴) 🍷 Reserve well ahead for a memorable meal at Red Hen, an intimate restaurant occupying an 1890 building just off Main St. The limited menu features a creative, French-focused menu showcasing fine local produce. Great cocktails, too.

BEER IN THE BLUE RIDGE

Traveling south, the **Shenandoah Beerwerks Trail** (http://beerwerkstrail.com/trail-map) wends its way from Harrisonville to just past Lexington and incorporates 14 breweries. Most of these places have taprooms, some host hipster-ish eateries or food trucks, and all offer good cheer. For gorgeous mountain views, try the hill-topping **Great Valley Farm Brewery** (60 Great Valley Ln, Natural Bridge; www.greatvalleyfarmbrewery.com) just south of Lexington.

Southern Inn
AMERICAN $$$

(☑540-463-3612; www.southerninn.com; 37 S Main St; mains $16-35; ☺11:30am-10pm Mon-Sat, 10am-9pm Sun) There's an old-fashioned feel at this popular eatery on Lexington's main drag. The food could be better (though our most recent meal featured excellent produce, dishes were poorly executed), but the surrounds and staff are welcoming.

🍸 Drinking & Entertainment

Taps
BAR

(☑540-463-2500; www.thegeorges.com; 11 N Main St, Georges; ☺3-10pm Mon-Thu, 11am-11pm Fri & Sat) This cozy place in Georges doubles as Lexington's living room, with students, professors and other locals hanging out on the fancy couches or at the small bar. Come here for craft beer, fine cocktails and local gossip. There's also a short pub-grub menu (sandwiches $9 to $11).

Hull's Drive-in
CINEMA

(☑540-463-2621; www.hullsdrivein.com; 2367 N Lee Hwy/US 11; adult/child 5-11yr $7/3; ☺gates open 6:30pm Fri & Sat Mar-Oct; 🚗) For old-fashioned amusement, catch a movie at this 1950s drive-in movie theater, set 5.5 miles north of Lexington. Movies start 20 minutes after sunset. Concession stand sells burgers, popcorn, sno-cones

❶ Getting There & Away

Lexington sits at the junction of I-81 and I-64. The closest airport is Roanoke-Blacksburg Regional Airport (p368), which is 55 miles south. The **Virginia Breeze** (☑877-462-6342; www.catchthevabreeze.com; tickets $15-50) bus service from DC travels here daily via Front Royal, Harrisonburg and Staunton and continues to Christianburg and Blacksburg before returning along the same route.

BLUE RIDGE HIGHLANDS & SOUTHWEST VIRGINIA

The Blue Ridge Highlands and the Roanoke Valley are two of the most attractive regions in the state, with farm-dotted valleys unfurling between the Blue Ridge and Allegheny mountains. The Blue Ridge Parkway and Appalachian Trail roll across the mountains, home to scenic rivers, streams and lakes. Old-time music can be heard regularly, and wineries and craft breweries offer tastings in small towns and on mountain slopes. The most rugged part of the region – and the state – is the southwestern tip of Virginia, where mountain music was born. Turn onto any side road and you'll plunge into dark strands of dogwood and fir, and see fast streams and white waterfalls. You might even hear banjos twanging and feet stomping in the distance.

❶ Getting There & Away

To explore the byways and country roads, you will need a car. The primary interstate here is I-81, running north–south through the western edge of the state. The Blue Ridge Parkway runs parallel to I-81, but it is much slower going.

Roanoke is served by Amtrak, with daily services linking it to New York (tickets from $75, 9½ hours) and Washington, DC (tickets from $37, five hours). The major airport in the region is the Roanoke-Blacksburg Regional Airport (p368).

Roanoke

📞540 / POP 98,660

Illuminated by the giant star atop Mill Mountain, Roanoke is the largest city in the Roanoke Valley and is the self-proclaimed 'Capital of the Blue Ridge.' Close to the Blue Ridge Parkway and the Appalachian Trail, it's a convenient base camp for exploring the great outdoors. An expanding greenway system, a burgeoning arts scene and a slowly growing portfolio of farm-to-table restaurants have energized the city in recent years, flipping Roanoke from sleepy to almost hip.

◉ Sights & Activities

★ **O. Winston Link Museum** MUSEUM
(📞540-982-5465; http://roanokehistory.org; 101 Shenandoah Ave NE; adult/child 3-11yr $6/5; ◷10am-5pm Tue-Sat) Trainspotters aren't the only ones who will find this museum fascinating. It is home to a large collection of photographs, sound recordings and film by O Winston Link (1914–2001), a New Yorker who in the 1950s spent nine months recording the last years of steam power on the Norfolk and Western Railway. The gelatin silver prints of Link's black-and-white photographs are hugely atmospheric – many were shot at night, a rarity at the time.

Taubman Museum of Art MUSEUM
(📞540-342-5760; www.taubmanmuseum.org; 110 Salem Ave SE; ◷10am-5pm Wed-Sat, noon-5pm Sun, to 9pm 3rd Thu & 1st Fri of month; 🅿) FREE
The jewel in Roanoke's cultural crown, this impressive museum is set in a sculptural steel-and-glass edifice. Inside, you'll find a small permanent collection strong in 19th- and 20th-century American works including Norman Rockwell's crowd-pleasing *Framed* (1946) and Winslow Homer's *Woodchopper in the Adirondacks* (c 1870). Four temporary exhibition galleries host everything from craft to video to installation art.

McAfee Knob HIKE
(off Rte 311, Appalachian Trail) This dramatic rock ledge is one of the most photographed sights on the Appalachian Trail, offering a sweeping view of Catawba Valley and surrounding mountains. The ledge is a 4.4-mile climb from the trailhead, which is 16 miles northwest of downtown Roanoke. To get there, take I-581 N to I-81 S, following the latter to Exit 141. From there, take Hwy 419 N to Rte 311. It's 5.5 miles to the trailhead parking lot atop Catawba Mountain.

🛏 Sleeping & Eating

Hotel Roanoke HOTEL $$$
(📞540-985-5900; www.hotelroanoke.com; 110 Shenandoah Ave NW; r from $129; 🅿🅰🛜🏊) This Tudor-style grand dame has presided over this city at the base of the Blue Ridge Mountains for more than a century. Now part of the Hilton Group, it's in desperate need of refurbishment. Rooms are adequate only; service can be lackadaisical. A covered elevated walkway links the hotel with downtown precinct.

Texas Tavern DINER $
(📞540-342-4825; www.texastavern-inc.com; 114 W Church Ave; burgers $1.50-2.75, chile $1.90; ◷24hr) Wait. What? A hamburger or hot dog for only $1.50? Yep, the food is cheap and tasty at the legendary Texas Tavern, a boxcar-sized diner that opened in 1930. The infamous cheesy western is a burger topped with a fried egg, cheese, relish, pickles and onions.

★ **Lucky** MODERN AMERICAN $$
(📞540-982-1249; www.eatatlucky.com; 18 Kirk Ave SW; mains $18-30; ◷5-9pm Mon-Wed, to 10pm

THE CROOKED ROAD

When Scots–Irish fiddle-and-reel joined with African American banjo-and-percussion, American mountain or 'old-time' music was born, spawning such genres as country and bluegrass. The latter genre still dominates the Blue Ridge, and Virginia's Heritage Music Trail, the 330-mile-long Crooked Road (www.myswva.org/tcr), takes you through nine sites associated with that history, along with some eye-stretching mountain scenery. It's well worth taking a detour and joining the music-loving fans of all ages who kick up their heels (many arrive with tap shoes) at these festive jamborees. During a live show you'll witness elders connecting to deep cultural roots and a new generation of musicians keeping that heritage alive and evolving. Top venues include the **Blue Ridge Music Center** (☑276-236-5309; www.blueridgemusiccenter.net; 700 Foothills Rd/Mile 213, Blue Ridge Pkwy; ⊙10am-5pm late May-late Oct, 10am-5pm Thu-Mon early May-late May) near Galax, the **Floyd Country Store** (☑540-745-4563; www.floydcountrystore.com; 206 S Locust St; ⊙10am-5pm Mon-Thu, to 10:30pm Fri, to 6pm Sat, 11am-6pm Sun) on Friday nights and the **Carter Family Fold** (☑276-386-6054; www.carterfamilyfold.org; 3449 AP Carter Hwy/SR 614, Hiltons; adult $10-15, 6-11yr $2; ⊙7:30pm Sat; 📶) on Saturday nights.

Thu-Sat) Lucky has excellent cocktails (try 'The Cube') and a seasonally inspired menu of small plates (hickory-smoked porchetta, roasted oysters) and heartier mains (buttermilk fried chicken, morel and asparagus gnocchi). It also operates the equally wonderful Italian restaurant **Fortunato** (www.fortunatoroanoke.com) a few doors down, where the wood-fired pizzas are the stuff of dreams and poems.

 Drinking

Ballast Point   BREWERY
(☑540-591-3059; www.ballastpoint.com; 555 International Pkwy, Daleville; ⊙11am-9pm Mon-Thu, 11am-11pm Fri & Sat, 10am-9pm Sun) You'll find bold brews and rugged views at this new outpost of the famed San Diego brewery. Folks from miles around gather on the patio to sip one of the 35 beers on tap, with local mountains as the backdrop. The brewery, which also serves gourmet pub fare, is 18 miles north of downtown Roanoke off I-81.

🛍 **Shopping**

⭐**Black Dog Salvage**   ANTIQUES
(☑540-343-6200; www.blackdogsalvage.com; 902 13th St SW; ⊙9am-5pm Mon-Sat, noon-5pm Sun) As seen on the cable show *Salvage Dogs*, the folks at this sprawling antique shop sell doors and doorknobs, light fixtures, wrought iron, and vintage plumbing and hardware, Basically, it's filled with architecturally unique old house parts and fixtures that have been reclaimed and re-purposed, plus random antiques. Stop by, it's a welcoming place filled with unexpected treasures.

ℹ **Getting There & Away**

Amtrak operates daily services between Roanoke and New York (tickets from $75, 9½ hours) on the Northeast Regional line. These leave from the downtown **train station** (www.amtrak.com; 55 Norfolk Avenue SW) and travel via Washington, DC (tickets from $37, five hours).

The airport (p368) is 5 miles north of downtown and serves the Roanoke and Shenandoah Valley regions. If you're driving, I-81 and I-581 link to the city. The Blue Ridge Parkway is just 5 miles from downtown.

Abingdon

☑276 / POP 8080
One of the most photogenic towns in Virginia, Abingdon retains fine Federal and Victorian architecture in its historic district. The regional theater in the center of town is a state-wide draw, as is the magnificent Virginia Creeper Trail. Popular with cyclists and hikers, this leafy path down from the mountains unfurls along an old railroad bed.

🏃 **Activities**

Virginia Creeper Trail   CYCLING, HIKING
(www.vacreepertrail.com) This 33.4-mile cycling and hiking trail on an old railroad corridor rolls through the Mount Rogers National Recreation Area, connecting lofty Whitetop with Damascus and eventually Abingdon. Local bike companies rent out bikes and provide shuttle services.

Virginia Creeper Trail Bike Shop   CYCLING
(☑276-676-2552; www.vacreepertrailbikeshop.com; 201 Pecan St; per 2hr/day $15/25; ⊙9am-5pm Sun-Fri, 8am-6pm Sat mid-Mar–mid-Nov)

WORTH A TRIP

BLUE RIDGE PARKWAY

Where Skyline Drive (p356) ends, the **Blue Ridge Parkway** (www.nps.gov/blri) picks up. Managed by the national park service, this pretty-as-a-picture drive stretches from the southern Appalachian ridge in Shenandoah National Park (at Mile 0) to North Carolina's Great Smoky Mountains National Park (at Mile 469).

Most facilities along the the Blue Ridge Parkway, including picnic areas, visitor centers and museum-style exhibits, such as the historic farms at Humpback Rocks, officially open on Memorial Day weekend (the last weekend in May). That said, some facilities are open year-round, and private concessionaires along the parkway maintain their own hours; we have listed these where applicable. You can also check on updated opening hours and facility renovations at www.nps.gov/blri/planyourvisit. During winter, portions of the parkway may be snowed out; check online for updates. There are numerous private camping sites, and four public **campgrounds** (☑877-444-6777; www.recreation.gov; tent & RV sites $20; ☻May-late Oct), located at Mile 60.8, Mile 85.6, Mile 120.4 and Mile 161.1, on the Virginia side of the Blue Ridge Parkway.

Campgrounds along the parkway are open from May to October; book online. Demand is higher on weekends and holidays. While there are no electrical hookups at parkway campsites, you will find restrooms, potable water and picnic tables. You're often at a pretty high elevation (over 2500ft), so even during summer it can get chilly up here.

The Blue Ridge Parkway can feel crowded in spring and summer, when thousands of motorists hit the road, but there are so many pull-offs and picnic areas you rarely feel too hemmed in. Just remember this is a scenic route; don't be the jerk who tailgates on the parkway. Expect people to drive slowly up here. Honestly, it's a good idea to follow suit; this road has lots of narrow twists and turns. You can take your RV on the parkway. The lowest tunnel clearance is 10ft 6in near the park's terminus in Cherokee, NC.

Rents bikes near the Virginia Creeper trailhead. Will also shuttle you and a bike to destinations along the trail (adult/child under 13 years $15/12), with a slight discount if you also rent its bikes. You can park at the shop.

🛏 Sleeping & Eating

Alpine Motel MOTEL $
(☑276-628-3178; www.alpinemotelabingdon.com; 882 E Main St; r $49-69; P❋☎) Low room rates are the only reason to consider this somewhat depressing option on the highway east of the historic center. Large and musty rooms have wheezing air-con units and 1970s-era bathrooms. A basic breakfast is included.

Martha Washington Inn & Spa HOTEL $$$
(☑276-628-3161; www.themartha.com; 150 W Main St; r $175-265, ste $385-595; P❋@☎☀) This is the region's best-known historic hotel, a handsome Victorian-era hulk set amid formal gardens. The rocking chairs on the front porch are a pleasant place to relax, as is the library with its open fire. Rooms are comfortable but faded; food in the restaurant could be a lot better. Rates include breakfast. A compulsory resort fee ($16 per room per night) is levied on top of the room rate.

★ Rain AMERICAN $$$
(☑276-739-2331; www.rainabingdon.com; 283 E Main St; lunch mains $9-10, dinner mains $18-32; ☻11am-2pm & 4-9pm Tue-Sat, reduced hours Jan; P) Culinary influences here roam from Mexico, Asia and Mediterranean Europe but arrive with aplomb in contemporary America. The food is excellent, and extremely well priced for its quality, especially at lunch. Service is attentive and the lounge bar stays open after meals service. Good one.

☆ Entertainment

Barter Theatre THEATER
(☑276-628-3991; www.bartertheatre.com; 127 W Main St; ☻box office 9am-5pm Tue-Sat, from 1pm Sun) Founded during the Depression, Barter Theatre earned its name from audiences trading food for performances. Actors Gregory Peck and Ernest Borgnine cut their teeth on Barter's stage.

❶ Getting There & Away

Abingdon borders I-81 near the Virginia–Tennessee border, 366 miles southwest of Washington, DC, and about 180 miles northwest of Charlotte, NC. Regional airports include Asheville Regional Airport in Asheville, NC, and Roanoke-Blacksburg Regional Airport (p368) in Roanoke.

West Virginia

POP 1.82 MILLION

Best Places to Eat

➡ Press Room (p384)

➡ Pies & Pints (p391)

➡ Thyme Bistro (p389)

➡ Secret Sandwich Society (p391)

➡ Blue Moon Cafe (p383)

➡ Tari's (p384)

Best Places to Stay

➡ Greenbrier (p393)

➡ General Lewis Inn (p393)

➡ Bavarian Inn (p383)

➡ Brass Pineapple (p395)

Why Go?

For rugged East Coast adventuring with a gorgeous mountain backdrop, set your car toward wild and wonderful West Virginia, a state often overlooked by both American and foreign travelers. It doesn't help that the state can't seem to shake its negative stereotypes. That's too bad, because West Virginia is one of the prettiest states in the Union. With its line of unbroken green mountains, raging white-water rivers and snowcapped ski resorts, this is an outdoor-lovers' paradise.

Created by secessionists, the people here still think of themselves as hardscrabble sons of miners, and that perception isn't entirely off. But the Mountain State is also gentrifying and, occasionally, that's a good thing: the arts are flourishing in the valleys, where some towns offer a welcome break from the state's constantly evolving outdoor activities. Charleston is the capital and the state's largest city – and its population is under 50,000.

When to Go
Charleston

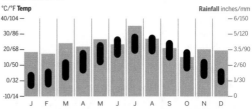

May Look for bright spring blooms on southern West Virginia trail.

Jun Summer festivals bring folks together for art, food, craft beer and live music.

Oct Cruise past the colorful fall foliage and raft the Gauley River during dam release.

West Virginia Highlights

1 **New River Gorge National River** (p389) Tackling the white-water on a rafting adventure.

2 **Harpers Ferry National Historic Park** (p380) Stepping into the town's dramatic Civil War–era past in a well-preserved collection of museums and historic structures.

3 **Greenbrier** (p393) Touring the secret Cold War–era bunker at one of the country's poshest resorts.

4 **Berkeley Springs State Park** (p384) Soaking in the mineral waters that have soothed sore muscles for centuries.

5 **Purple Fiddle** (p389) Tapping your toes to live bluegrass tunes in the tiny town of Thomas.

6 **Dolly Sods Wilderness** (p385) Hiking through mountain forests in one of the most remote regions in the Mid-Atlantic.

7 **Fayetteville** (p391) Embracing all that is good in a top-notch mountain town, from the cafes to the outdoor sports to the great restaurants.

8 **NROCKS Outdoor Adventure** (p386) Climbing craggy rock fins on a fixed-anchor *via ferrata* course.

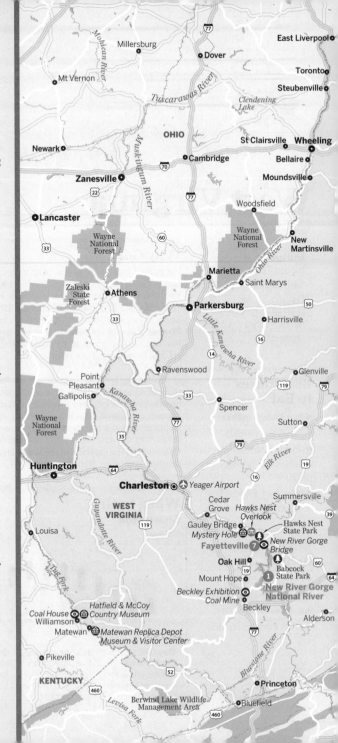

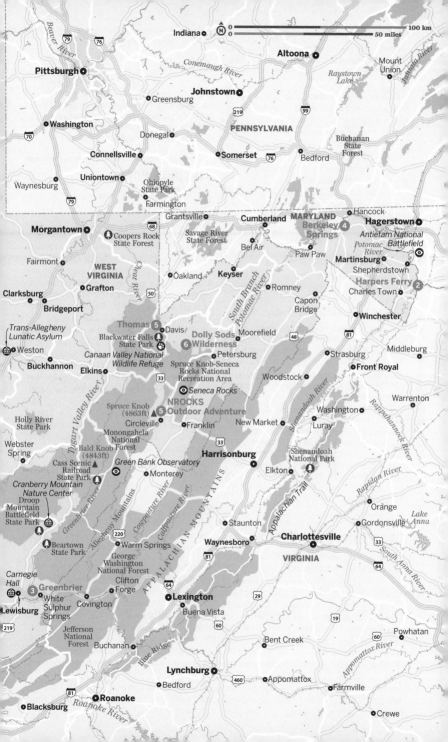

History

Virginia was once the biggest state in America, divided between the plantation aristocracy of the Tidewater and the mountains of what is now West Virginia. The latter were settled by tough farmers who staked out independent freeholds across the Appalachians. Always resentful of their Eastern brethren and their reliance on cheap (ie slave) labor, the mountaineers of West Virginia declared their independence from Virginia when the latter tried to break off from America during the Civil War.

Yet the scrappy, independent-at-all-costs stereotype was challenged in the late 19th and early 20th centuries, when miners formed into cooperative unions and fought employers in some of the bloodiest battles in American labor history. That mix of chip-on-the-shoulder resentment toward authority and look-out-for-your-neighbor community values continues to characterize West Virginia today.

🛈 Getting There & Away

West Virginia's Eastern Panhandle begins about 60 miles northwest of Washington, DC, and it's a fairly easy drive from the busy metropolitan area – but expect traffic.

Amtrak and MARC trains stop at the station (p382) in Harpers Ferry. Charleston has a small airport (p396).

For the national forest and the southern reaches of the state, you will need a car to explore and will likely be accessing most mountain towns and parks on two-lane roads. So although the mileage looks short, the distance will take longer to cover than on the interstate. Cell phone coverage can be very spotty on mountain roads, so check your directions – and maybe write them down – before starting your trip.

EASTERN PANHANDLE

The most accessible part of West Virginia has always been a mountain getaway for DC types – the region is just 70 miles west of the capital-area sprawl. Here, Civil War–era history, soothing hot springs, leafy scenery and outdoor recreation on trails and rivers work together for visitors, offering an easy package of experiences than can be enjoyed on one long weekend.

One tricky part of travel in the panhandle is the practically overlapping proximity of three states – West Virginia, Virginia and Maryland – with Pennsylvania lying in wait just north. When planning, get out your maps to make sure you've spotted all attractions in the multistate region.

🛈 Getting There & Away

I-81 is the major interstate through the region. There's a train station (p382) in Harpers Ferry served by Amtrak (www.amtrak.com) daily and MARC (http://mta.maryland.gov) commuter trains Monday through Friday, both connecting to Union Station in Washington, DC.

Harpers Ferry

📖 304, 681 / POP 213

History lives on in this attractive town, set with steep cobblestoned streets, and framed by the Shenandoah Mountains and the confluence of the rushing Potomac and Shenandoah Rivers. The lower town functions as an open-air museum, with more than a dozen buildings that you can explore to get a taste of 19th-century, small-town life. Exhibits narrate the town's role at the forefront of westward expansion, American industry and, most famously, the slavery debate – in 1859 old John Brown tried to spark a slave uprising here and was hanged for his efforts; the incident rubbed friction between North and South into the fires of Civil War.

The upper town is dotted with cafes and B&Bs. Harpers Ferry sits beside the Appalachian Trail across the Potomac from the C&O Canal bike path, so there are lots of outdoorsy types filling the coffee houses and hostels. The town is touristy for sure, but it has a fun and energetic vibe.

◉ Sights

After picking up your park pass at the visitor center, start your exploring at the small museum and information desk in the **Master Armorers House** (📞 304-535-6029; www.nps. gov/hafe; Shenandoah St; ⊗ 9am-5pm) **FREE** in the lower town, near the riverfront.

Harpers Ferry National Historic Park PARK (📞 304-535-6029; www.nps.gov/hafe; 171 Shoreline Dr; per person on foot or bicycle $5, vehicle $10; ⊗ trails sunrise-sunset, visitor center 9am-5pm; 🅿 ♿) Historic buildings and museums are accessible to those with passes, which can be found, along with parking and shuttles, north of town at the Harpers Ferry National Historic Park Visitor Center off Hwy 340. Parking is incredibly limited in Harpers Ferry proper so plan to park at the visitor center and catch the frequent shuttle. It's a short and scenic ride.

The Point   NATURAL FEATURE

(www.npd.gov/hafe; Potomac St) At the southern end of Potomac St, just a few steps from the lower town, take in a view of three states – Maryland, Virginia, West Virginia – from the confluence of the Potomac and Shenandoah Rivers.

John Brown Museum   MUSEUM

(www.nps.gov/hafe; Shenandoah St; ⊙9am-5pm) **FREE** Across from Arsenal Sq and one of the park's museums, this three-room gallery gives a fine overview (through videos and period relics) of the events surrounding John Brown's famous raid.

Jefferson Rock   NATURAL FEATURE

(off Church St, Appalachian Trail) A slab of rock marks the spot where the woods open up to a fine river vista. Known as Jefferson Rock, the formation is named for President Thomas Jefferson. Jefferson stopped here in 1783 and had this to say about the view: 'The passage of the Patowmac through the Blue Ridge is perhaps one of the most stupendous scenes in Nature.' It is pretty darn sweet.

**Black Voices: African
American History**   MUSEUM

(www.nps.gov/hafe; High St; ⊙9am-5pm) **FREE** Part of the national park, this worthwhile, interactive exhibit has narrated stories of hardships and hard-won victories by African Americans from the times of enslavement through the Civil Rights era. Across the street is the Storer College exhibit, which gives an overview of the ground-breaking educational center and Niagara movement that formed in its wake.

Storer College Campus   HISTORIC SITE

(www.nps.gov/hafe; Fillmore St) Founded immediately after the Civil War, Storer College grew from a one-room schoolhouse for freed slaves to a respected college open to all races and creeds. It closed in 1955. You can freely wander the historic campus, reachable by taking the path to upper town, past St Peter's church, Jefferson Rock and Harper Cemetery.

John Brown Wax Museum   MUSEUM

(☑304-535-6342; www.johnbrownwaxmuseum. com; 168 High St; adult/child 6-12yr $7/5; ⊙10am-4:30pm daily mid-Mar–mid-Dec, Sat & Sun only late Dec & early Mar, closed Jan–mid-Mar) Not to be confused with the National Park–run museum, this private wax museum is a kitschy (and rather overpriced) attraction that pays tribute to the man who led an ill-conceived slave rebellion here. The exhibits are very

> ## APPALACHIAN TRAIL CONSERVANCY
>
> The 2160-mile Appalachian Trail is headquartered at this tremendous **resource** (ATC; ☑304-535-6331; www.appalachian trail.org; 799 Washington St, cnr Washington & Jackson Sts, Harpers Ferry; ⊙9am-5pm) for hikers, which offers a chance for conversation, information, trail updates and restrooms. Less-ambitious travelers will appreciate the free and helpful Harpers Ferry map – ask at the information desk – which provides a summary of several area day hikes, including the 1.5-mile loop around Harpers Ferry that begins here. The hiker lounge has wi-fi, a computer and a free phone – which sits beside a giant sign reminding hikers to call their mothers.

old-school; nothing says historical accuracy like scratchy vocals, jerky animatronics and dusty old dioramas. But younger kids seem to dig it – maybe because some of the scenes are a bit horrifying.

Keep an eye out for the wax replica of museum's founder – he's tucked among the historic figures in one of the dioramas.

 Activities

**C&O Canal National
Historic Park**   CYCLING, HIKING

(www.nps.gov/choh) The 184.5-mile towpath passes along the Potomac River on the Maryland side. From the historic downtown you can reach it via the Appalachian Trail across the Potomac Bridge. Check www.nps. gov/hafe for additional access points to the towpath and a list of bike-rental companies.

River Riders   ADVENTURE SPORTS; CYCLING

(☑304-535-2663; www.riverriders.com; 408 Alstadts Hill Rd; guided kayaking trip per person $74; ⊙8am-6pm Jun-Aug, hours vary rest of year) The go-to place for rafting, canoeing, tubing, kayaking and multiday cycling trips, plus cycle rental (two hours is $34 per person). There's even a 1200ft zip-line.

O Be Joyfull   WALKING

(☑732-801-0381; www.obejoyfull.com; 110 Church St, Thomas Hall at St Peter's Church; tours adult/child 8-12yr $34/15) Offers eye-opening historical daytime walking tours (lasting three to four hours) around Harpers Ferry.

Harpers Ferry

Sleeping & Eating

HI-Harpers Ferry Hostel
HOSTEL **$**

(☑301-834-7652; www.hiusa.org; 19123 Sandy Hook Rd, Knoxville; dm $25; ☺mid-Apr–mid-Nov; P❋@☎) This friendly hostel has plenty of amenities, including a kitchen, laundry and lounge area with games and books. It's popular with cyclists on the C&O Canal towpath and hikers on the Appalachian Trail, both nearby. Breakfast is included. It's 2 miles from downtown Harpers Ferry, on the Maryland side of the Potomac River.

Add $3 to the rate if you're not a member of Hostelling International or the National Youth Hostel Association.

Jackson Rose
B&B **$$**

(☑304-535-1528; www.thejacksonrose.com; 1167 W Washington St; r weekday/weekend $140/160, closed Jan & Feb; P❋☎) This marvelous 18th-century brick residence with stately gardens has three attractive guestrooms, including a room where Stonewall Jackson lodged briefly during the Civil War. Antique furnishings and vintage curios are sprinkled about the house, and the cooked breakfast is excellent. It's a 600m walk downhill to the historic district. No children under 12.

Cannonball Deli
SANDWICHES **$**

(☑304-535-1762; 148 High St; sandwiches $4-11; ☺10am-6pm) From the High St entrance near the national park, head underground for tasty subs, gyros and sandwiches. On a pretty day, walk through the tiny kitchen to the back deck, which has a view of Potomac St and the railroad. Convenient to the C&O cycling path just across the Potomoc Bridge.

Drinking & Nightlife

Guide Shack Cafe
COFFEE **$**

(☑304-995-6022; www.guideshackcafe.com; 1102 Washington St; ☺6:30am-6:30pm Mon-Fri, 7pm Sat & Sun; ☎) Of course there's a mini climbing wall in the back of this coffee shop: the place is a short walk from both the Appalachian Trail and the C&O Canal cycling path. Stop for a bit of conversation and the sweet and creamy iced coffee.

Beans in the Belfry
AMERICAN **$**

(☑301-834-7178; www.beansinthebelfry.com; 122 W Potomac St, Brunswick; sandwiches $7; ☺8am-9pm Mon-Thu, to 10pm Fri & Sat, to 7pm Sun; ☎❖) This converted red-brick church about 6 miles east of Harpers Ferry, WV, shelters mismatched couches and kitsch-laden walls. The menu features coffee and light fare (chili, sandwiches, quiche), and there's a tiny stage where live folk, blues and bluegrass bands strike up several nights a week. Sunday jazz brunch ($18) is a hit. A cool spot and worth the drive.

ℹ Getting There & Away

Amtrak (www.amtrak.com) trains run from the **Harpers Ferry Station** (www.amtrak.com; Potomac St) to Washington's Union Station (daily, 90 minutes) on the Capitol Limited route. MARC trains (http://mta.maryland.gov) run to Washington's Union Station several times per day (Monday to Friday) on the Brunswick Line.

Shepherdstown

☑304, 681 / POP 1578

Shepherdstown is a charmer. This is the oldest town in West Virginia, founded in 1762,

and its historic district is packed with Federal-style brick buildings that are heart-rendingly cute. It's also one of many artsy college towns in the West Virginia mountains that balance a significant amount of natural beauty with a quirky, bohemian culture.

The bulk of the best preservation can be found along (and within walking distance of) German St. The historic center is also close to Shepherd University; the student presence can be felt pretty strongly in town, but it's balanced out by plenty of pick-up-driving West Virginia locals.

The city is a good base for exploring Harpers Ferry, plus the Antietam National Battlefield just over the state line in Maryland. It's also a nice place to unwind after adventuring on the C&O towpath or the Potomac River.

🏃 Activities

Pedal & Paddle   CYCLING; KAYAKING
(☏304-876-3000; www.thepedalpaddle.com; 115 W German St; rental bike/kayak 4hr from $35/45; ⊙11am-7pm Mon-Fri, 10am-7pm Sat, 10am-5pm Sun Apr-Dec, noon-6pm Tue-Sat Jan & Feb) What? A no-attitude bike shop? We love it! Stop here to rent a bike before cycling the C&O towpath or checking out the local battlefields and countryside. You can also rent kayaks, canoes and inner tubes. Packages include shuttle service for various cycling trips and river runs on the Potomac (paddle/pedal trips from $49/54).

🛏 Sleeping & Eating

★ **Bavarian Inn**   HOTEL **$$**
(☏304-876-2551; www.bavarianinnwv.com; 164 Shepherd Grade Rd; r from $185, ste $355;

P✳🛜🏊) The Bavarian takes the Euro-mountaineering theme and runs with it all the way up the Alps. The exterior looks like a chalet, and the rooms have an attractively severe, clean, comfortable and efficient air that's, forgive us the stereotype, kind of German. A nice break from the trails. Short walk to downtown.

There's fine dining on-site at the Potomac room, or just grab a beer and pub grub at the revamped Rathskeller.

Blue Moon Cafe   DELI **$**
(☏304-876-1920; www.facebook.com/bluemoon wv; 200 E High St; mains $9-16; ⊙11am-9pm) There's a lot to love about this deli, with its collegiate and hippie staff, huge outdoor patio, indoor pub-like dining area and excellent menu of healthy and not-so-healthy salads and sandwiches. The sandwich menu is intimidatingly large, but everything is delicious. It's kind of scruffy, but therein lies the Blue Moon's counter-culture charm.

Betty's   DINER **$**
(☏304-876-6080; 114 E German St; breakfast & lunch mains $2-23; ⊙6am-4pm Mon-Sat, 7am-2pm Sun) The bacon is crispy and the service slow at this scrappy diner, which is busting at its well-worn seams with everyone in town in the morning. They claim to serve the best sausage gravy in the world. Social media here is listening in on the neighboring table or the crowds hunched by the door.

Press Room NEW AMERICAN **$$**
(☑304-876-8777; http://shepherdstown.info/eat/press-room; 129 W German St; mains $17-30; ◷5-9pm Mon, Wed & Thu, to 10pm Fri & Sat, 10:30am-2pm, 4-8pm Sun) This oft-recommended spot is housed in an old newspaper building, but the hospitable vibe and cozy decor evoke the home of a close friend. Fresh and seasonal New American fare is on the menu, and we bet you'll be pleased with whatever you pick. The restaurant is a bit coy with its online details – but that's why we're here.

Drinking & Entertainment

Lost Dog Coffee COFFEE
(☑304-876-0871; www.lostdogcoffee.com; 134 E German St; ◷6:30am-6pm Mon-Fri, 7:30am-6pm Sat & Sun) Is that the inviting scent of roasting coffee? Add in walls lined with knickknacks, local art and a mounted deer head, and we say, hello perfect indie coffee shop.

Town Run Tap House BAR
(☑304-876-0502; www.townruntaphouse.com; 202 E Washington St; ◷3:30pm-midnight Tue & Wed, 11am-midnight Thu-Sat, 11am-4pm Sun) Sometimes the thought of stepping into another glossy gastropub serving hoppy craft brews and duck fat fries can make one feel the world has lost its quirky edges. Town Run is not one of those places. Down by the railroad tracks, this cavernous old warehouse welcomes families and dogs, and impresses with its classic arcade games.

O'Hurley's General Store LIVE MUSIC
(☑304-876-6907; www.facebook.com/ohurleygeneralstore; 205 E Washington St; ◷10am-5pm Mon, 10am-7pm Tue-Sat, 11am-6pm Sun) **FREE** Not quite bluegrass. Not quite Scottish. Let's just call it music you might hear on *Outlander* from a band of traveling minstrels. But whatever the tune is at the weekly Thursday night jam (7:30pm), it's engaging. Grab a seat and listen close to a variety of instruments and musicians. The rest of the week, the store sells old-time mountain crafts and wares.

ℹ Information

Stop by the **visitors center** (☑304-876-2786; www.shepherdstown.info; 201 S Princess St; ◷10am-4pm) for a walking tour map covering historic buildings downtown.

ℹ Getting There & Away

Shepherdstown is 10 miles east of Martinsburg and I-81, 12 miles north of Harpers Ferry and just 4 miles west of Sharpsburg, MD, home to Anti-etam National Battlefield (p332). You will want a car to explore the region.

Berkeley Springs

☑304, 681 / POP 543

America's first spa town (George Washington relaxed here) is an odd jumble of spiritualism, artistic expression and pampering spa centers. Farmers in pickups sporting Confederate flags and acupuncturists in tie-dye smocks regard each other with bemusement on the roads of Bath (still the official name).

🏃 Activities

Berkeley Springs State Park SPA
(☑304-258-2711; www.berkeleyspringssp.com; 2 S Washington St; 30min bath $27, 1hr massage $99-111; ◷10am-6pm) Don't let the locker-room appearance deter you from the Berkeley Springs State Park's Roman Baths – it's the cheapest spa deal in town. Fill your water bottle with some of the magic stuff at the fountain outside the door – it's mineral-filled and it's free! In the summer, kids will enjoy the spring-fed (but chlorinated) outdoor swimming pool (adult/child under 12 years $5/3) in the middle of the green.

🛏 Sleeping

Cacapon Resort State Park CABIN **$**
(☑304-258-1022; www.cacaponresort.com; 818 Cacapon Lodge Dr; r/cabin from $89/79; **P**✳ 🛜🐾) Cacapon State Park has simple lodge accommodations plus modern and rustic cabins (some with fireplaces) in a peaceful wooded setting, 9 miles south of Berkeley Springs (off Hwy 522). There's hiking, lake swimming, horseback riding, a restaurant and a golf course. Wi-fi available in the lodge but not the cabins.

Pet fee is $20 per day per pet.

Country Inn of Berkeley Springs HOTEL **$$**
(☑304-258-1200; www.thecountryinnwv.com; 110 S Washington St; r/ste from $119/169; **P**✳🛜) The Country Inn, right next to the park, offers luxurious treatments and comfortable but not overly fancy rooms. You'll also find lodging package deals. There's a good restaurant on hand.

🍴 Eating & Drinking

★ **Tari's** FUSION **$$$**
(☑304-258-1196; www.tariscafe.com; 33 N Washington St; lunch mains $10-15, dinner mains $21-30;

⊙11am-9pm Mon-Sat, to 8pm Sun; 🅿) 🖋 Tari's is a very Berkeley Springs sort of spot, with fresh local food and good vegetarian options served in a laid-back atmosphere with all the right hints of good karma abounding. Dig into the jumbo lake crab cakes with a side of fries at dinner.

Berkeley Springs Brewing Co BREWERY
(📞304-258-3369; www.berkeleyspringsbrewing company.com; 91 Sugar Hollow Rd; ⊙noon-9pm Thu-Sat, to 7pm Sun) Local mineral water is the secret ingredient in these craft beers, served in a welcoming strip-mall location about 2 miles south of the springs. Enjoy a post-soak brat while sipping a Cacapon Kolsch.

ⓘ Getting There & Away

Berkeley Springs is 40 miles west of I-95, about 90 minutes from the Washington, DC metro area.

MONONGAHELA NATIONAL FOREST

Almost the entire eastern half of West Virginia is marked green parkland on the map, and most of that goodness falls under the auspices of this stunning national forest. Established in 1920 with just 7200 acres, the forest today covers more than 900,000 acres across 10 counties. The region, also known as the Potomac Highlands, is the adventure capital of the state. Within its boundaries are wild rivers, striking rock formations and the highest peak in the state, Spruce Knob. More than 850 miles of trails include the nearly 330-mile Allegheny Trail and the 78-mile rails-to-trails Greenbrier River Trail (p387). The surreal landscapes at Seneca Rocks attract rock climbers.

The towns of Thomas and Davis, in the northern reaches of the region, are good basecamps for Canaan Valley and Dolly Sods. Seneca Rocks is centrally located within the forest region. Snowshoe Mountain Resort is a good launchpad in the south.

ⓘ Information

The **National Forest Service Headquarters** (📞304-636-1800; www.fs.usda.gov/mnf; 200 Sycamore St, Elkins; ⊙8am-4:45pm Mon-Fri) distributes recreation directories for hiking, cycling and camping.

The **Seneca Rocks Discovery Center** (📞304-567-2827; www.fs.usda.gov/mnf; Hwy 28/55, at Hwy 33; ⊙9am-4:30pm daily mid-May–Aug, Wed-Sun Sep & Oct, Fri-Sun Apr–mid-May) is

---

DON'T MISS

DOLLY SODS WILDERNESS

Red spruce trees, windswept boulders, valley views and boggy forests set a striking scene in the northern reaches of the remote **Dolly Sods Wilderness** (📞304-636-1800; www.fs.usda.gov; Fire Road 19, Davis; 🅿) **FREE** atop the Allegheny Plateau. The alpine landscape evokes the mountain scenery of northern Canada, and with 47 miles of trails crisscrossing its 17,371 acres, Dolly Sods is a prime spot for a day-long or weekend adventure. You can build your own loop hike from the Beaver Dam or Bear Rocks trailheads.

There are 11 primitive first-come first-served sites at the Red Creek Campground (campsites $11 per night).

---

also a good spot for information about regional outdoor activities.

The **visitor center** (www.canaanvalley.org; 410 Wiliam Ave; ⊙9am-5pm) in Davis is helpful too, especially for the northern reaches of the forest.

ⓘ Getting There & Away

To explore this remote and rugged region, you will need a car. Thomas is 68 miles southeast of Morgantown. Snowshoe is 230 miles from Washington, DC.

Canaan Valley

Anchored by a posh state park with a ski resort, mountain-flanked Canaan Valley is a lovely spot for year-round adventure. The region particularly shines in winter, with skiing, snowboarding, tubing and great cross-country skiing. In summer and fall, the lofty trails of the legendary Dolly Sods bring day-trippers as well as campers for the otherworldly landscapes and big views. Welcoming breweries and eclectic live music in nearby Thomas and Davis are fine post-adventuring rewards.

⊙ Sights & Activities

Canaan Valley National Wildlife Refuge WILDLIFE RESERVE
(📞304-866-3858; www.fws.gov; 6263 Appalachian Hwy; 🅿) **FREE** The 0.4-mile one-way Freedland Boardwalk Trail meanders through wetlands, a shrubland, a beaver pond and a limestone spring. Views of Canaan Valley, hugged by the Allegheny Mountains, are a

gorgeous backdrop as you walk. The trailhead is beside Freedland Rd, across from White Grass. The 16,550-acre refuge is home to shrub and bog wetlands, forests and a range of wildlife, from salamanders to turkeys and bears. You'll find exhibits about the refuge at the visitor center.

White Grass SNOW SPORTS
(📞304-866-4114; www.whitegrass.com; 643 Weiss Knob Ski Rd; adult/child under 12yr $20/5) More than 15 miles of groomed cross-country trails of varying difficulty wind through through wooded slopes. Also offers classes.

Canaan Valley Resort SKIING
(📞304-866-4121; www.canaanresort.com; 230 Main Lodge Rd; lift tickets adult/youth 6-12yr/child $68/44/free; ♿) It's a winter sports extravaganza at this state park: downhill skiing on 47 slopes, cross-country skiing, snowboarding, snow tubing, snowshoeing and ice skating. Après-ski, parents can relax in the spa or one of the lounges while the kids hit the game rooms. In summer, come here to hike, bike and golf.

❶ Getting There & Away

Canaan Valley Resort is 12 miles south of Davis via Hwy 32. You will need a car to explore the area.

Snowshoe & Pocahontas County

Anchored by Snowshoe Mountain Resort and home to a national scenic byway, a hard-working steam train and several long distance hiking and biking trails, Pocahontas County is the adventure-loving heart of the Monongahela National Forest. A world-renowned radio observatory adds science and astronomy to the mix.

◉ Sights

Green Bank Observatory OBSERVATORY
(📞304-456-2150; www.greenbankobservatory. org; 155 Observatory Rd; tours adult/under 11yr $6/ free; ⏰8:30am-7pm Jun-Aug, 8:30am-7pm Sep & Oct, 10am-6pm Thu-Mon Nov-May; ♿⛔) FREE The enormous Green Bank Telescope is a radio telescope, so you won't be looking at the stars through any lenses here. But you can learn about radio astronomy and get a closer look at the telescope – the dish's surface could hold two football fields. Because the dish is so powerful and finely attuned to catch radio waves, the surrounding 13,000-sq-mile region has been designated a National Radio Quiet Zone to minimize interference. So expect trouble using cell phones! The SETI tour takes you on a search for life among the stars.

Cass Scenic Railroad State Park STATE PARK
(📞304-456-4300; www.wvstateparks.com; 242 Main St, Cass; adult/child 4-11yr $66/56; ♿⛔) A lumber mill town in the early 1900s, Cass today is best known as the launch point for the Cass Scenic Railroad (www.mountainrailwv. com). On the popular Bald Knob trip, one of the steam trains here – possibly a 100-year-old Shay locomotive – chugs to an overlook atop the state's third-highest point. Themed trips are offered throughout the year. Pick up a walking-tour map for the town in the visitor center.

CLIMBING SENECA ROCKS

A striking rock formation rising 900ft above a fork of the Potomac River, **Seneca Rocks** (📞304-567-2827; www.fs.usda.gov/mnf; Hwy 28/55; ⏰sunrise to sunset; ⛔) is one of the most recognizable natural features in the state. Rock climbers have scaled the sandstone walls here since the mid-1930s. Today there are more than 370 mapped climbing routes. Hikers can walk 1.5 miles to an observation platform near the top of the formation. There are two climbing schools in the area. For more information about the region and the Monangahela National Forest stop by the Seneca Rocks Discovery Center (p385) – where the big-windowed view of the formation is superb.

If you're not ready to commit to rock climbing, consider a *via ferrata* climb at **NROCKS Outdoor Adventure** (📞877-435-4842; www.nrocks.com; 141 Nelson Gap Rd, Circleville; $115) down the road. The thrills begin the moment you clip into your harness for this rugged adventure, a fixed-anchor guided climb that scrambles up and across over a double-fin rock formation. One highlight is the crossing of a suspension bridge 150ft above a canyon. Guides are upbeat and fun but professional, and tours last from 3½ to five hours. You don't need to be an athlete to complete the climb, but the trip will be more fun if you're in reasonably good shape and have a little upper body strength. Climbers must be at least 13 years old.

Cranberry Mountain Nature Center MUSEUM
(☑304-653-4826; www.fs.usda.gov/mnf; cnr
Hwys 150 & 39/55; ⊙9am-4:30pm Thu-Mon mid-
Apr–mid-Oct; ⓟ) The scat exhibit hanging
on the wall is quite eye-catching, as are the
live snakes inhabiting several terrarriums at
this nature center in the southern end of the
forest. The nature center has scientific information about the forest and the surrounding 750-acre bog ecosystem, the largest of
its kind in the state. Live snake shows held
most Sundays at 1pm.

🏃 Activities & Tours

Greenbrier River Trail CYCLING; HIKING
(www.wvstateparks.cpm; off WV 66, Cass) Cass
Scenic Railroad State Park is the northern
terminus of this 78-mile hiking and biking
trail on a former railroad right-of-way, beginning in Caldwell (p392).

Cranberry Glades Boardwalk Trail HIKING
(www.fs.usda.gov/mnf; Fire Road 102, off Rte 150)
A half-mile boardwalk trails meanders
through a mesmerizing swath of peat bogs,
home to orchids and carnivorous plants.
You'll want to photograph the sprawling –
and spongy – wetlands. There is interpretive
signage along the way. Check with the nature centerabout dates for guided tours.

**Snowshoe Mountain
Resort** SKIING; MOUNTAIN BIKING
(☑877-441-4386; www.snowshoemtn.com; 10
Snowshoe Dr; lift tickets adult/13-17yr/6-12yr
$69/52/50; ⓜ) The largest ski resort in
the region, Snowshoe attracts skiers and snow-
boarders from across the country with 59
trails across three ski areas. Twelve trails are
open for night skiing. In summer, mountain
bikers hurtle down wooded terrain on more
than 35 trails. You can visit Snowshoe and
enjoy the facilities without staying overnight. Lodging options range from large
cabins with expansive mountain views to
condos just steps from the slopes. In the central village, the Junction restaurant is open
year-round. There's also a play area on the
resort lake.

Highland Scenic Highway SCENIC DRIVE
(☑304-653-4826; www.fs.usda.gov/mnf; Hwy
150) This 43-mile National Scenic Byway
unfurls across the leafy heights of the Allegheny Highlands and Plateau, passing four
overlooks with expansive mountain and
valley views. It's an exhilarating drive that
soars toward the sky, rising from 2235ft to
over 4500ft. The highway rolls north on

Rte 39/55 from Richwood to the Cranberry
Nature Center. From there, hop onto the 22-
mile parkway section on Hwy 150.

Picnic tables and restrooms are located
at each overlook. Note that the parkway section is not maintained in winter and is typically closed December through March. More
than 150 miles of trail can be accessed from
the highway.

🛏 Sleeping

Allegheny Springs LODGE $$
(☑877-441-4386; www.snowshoemtn.com; Snow-
shoe Dr, The Village, Snowshoe Mountain Resort; r
from $180; ⓟ❄📶❄) Well hello there, lobby
lounge. Comfy chairs, a big stone hearth –
we like your rugged style. Studios and con-
do units in this flagship property are in the
thick of the mountaintop action and steps
from the slopes and several restaurants. For
the glossiest digs, reserve a condo unit in the
Brigham Collection.

🍴 Eating & Nightlife

Foxfire Grille AMERICAN $$
(☑304-572-5555; www.foxfiregrille.com; Snow-
shoe Dr, The Village, Snowshoe Mountain Resort;
mains $9-39; ⊙11am-10pm, hours vary seasonally)
Pop into the lively bar for a post-run beer
and the Buffalo Chicken Dip, or settle in by
the big windows to watch the sunset while
digging into hearty mains, from burgers and
ribs to steak. The tasty Rancher Steak Salad
is pretty filling too. Located in the Village.

Old Spruce Tavern BAR
(☑304-572-1020; www.oldsprucetavern.com; 10
Snowshoe Dr, The Village, Snowshoe Mountain Resort;
⊙noon-midnight, hours vary seasonally) On top of
the mountain (like the rest of Snowshoe resort), this place is tiny, so on busy nights it
can feel as if you're bumping elbows with
every skier on the mountain. Let's call it energized mayhem (and a bit of a sausage-fest).
But it's fun after a day on the slopes. The Old
Spruce Draft House is a few steps away and
serves only West Virginia craft beer.

ℹ Getting There & Away

Snowshoe is 230 miles west of Washington, DC
via I-68 and several state highways. Expect the
trip to take about 4½ hours. Green Bank Observatory is about 75 miles northwest of Staunton, VA
on Hwy 250 west and Hwy 92 south. You will need
a car to explore the area. Note that cell-phone
reception can be spotty to nonexistent outside of
towns and resort areas in this region, so you may
want to write down directions before heading out.

Thomas & Davis

📞 304, 681 / POP 1017

A visit to the mountain towns of Thomas and Davis, packed with microbreweries, good restaurants and indie shops, is a great addition to a weekend spent hiking and exploring the surrounding national forest. Thomas isn't much more than a blip on the map, but the music scene has injected a newfound energy and cool, with live music played more than 300 nights annually. Just 3 miles east, equally tiny Davis is Thomas' partner in fun. Both are home to a compelling mix of longtime locals and big-city transplants, the latter bringing entrepreneurial energy and a love of the outdoors.

◎ Sights

Blackwater Falls State Park   STATE PARK
(📞304-259-5216; www.blackwaterfalls.com; 1584 Blackwater Lodge Rd; 🅿) **FREE** The falls tumble into an 8-mile gorge lined by red spruce, hickory and hemlock trees. With more than 24 miles of trails, there are loads of hiking options; look for the Pendleton Point Overlook, which perches over the deepest, widest point of the Canaan Valley. There's an inviting lodge here as well as cabins and campsites ($25 per night).

🛏 Sleeping & Eating

Your best bets in Thomas and Davis are B&Bs, motels or rooms in the lodge at Blackwater Falls State Park (p388). Rooms get a bit more posh at Canaan Valley Resort (p386) down the road.

Billy Motel   MOTEL **$**
(📞304-851-6125; www.thebillymotel.com; 1080 William Ave, Davis; r $100; 🅿 ❉ 🛜) The 10 rooms pop with bright colors and fresh modern style inside this classic motor court. The cozy lobby has a fireplace and a lounge bar, which serves cocktails on Friday and Saturday nights.

Cooper House Bed & Cocktail   B&B **$**
(📞304-851-4553; www.cooperhousebandc.com; 114 East Ave, Thomas; r $100-120; ❉ 🛜) Proprietor Joy Malinowski brings the spark to this creaky but inviting house that's within stumbling distance of the Purple Fiddle (p389). There's a fun communal vibe, but don't worry, the four bedrooms each have their own bathroom. Guests can enjoy a cocktail in the common area. Breakfast at local spots is encouraged in this support-your-neighbor community. Scruffy the dog will probably greet you at the door.

Hellbender Burritos   MEXICAN **$**
(📞304-259-5557; www.hellbenderburritos.com; 457 William Ave, Davis; mains $6-9; ⊙11:30am-9pm Wed, Thu & Sun, to 10pm Fri & Sat) They stuff the big burritos here Mountain-State style – think blue cheese dressing, Fritos, homemade pulled pork and other stuff that may not be Mexican but sure tastes good. There's even a PB&J burrito for the kiddies. Lots of vegetarian options too. Grab a table upstairs or head down to the bar.

🍺 Drinking & Entertainment

Mountain State Brewing Co   MICROBREWERY
(📞304-463-4500; www.mountainstatebrewing.com; 1 Nelson Blvd, Thomas; ⊙6pm-midnight Thu-Fri, 3pm-midnight Sat, 1-7pm Sun) The $4 flight of six beers may be the best deal going in the state. And staff might even throw in a sample of sangria, because heck, why not? On a cold night the Coal Miner's Daughter Oatmeal Stout hits the spot. The wood-hewn tasting room feels like a camp lodge in the deep woods.

WORTH A TRIP

BEARTOWN & DROOP MOUNTAIN STATE PARKS

Fantastical rock formations. Civil War history. And pretty trails though thick forest. Yep, if you're driving between Lewisburg and the Monongahela National Forest, take a moment to stretch your legs in two small state parks that have a lot to offer. Tiny **Beartown** (📞304-799-4087; www.wvstateparks.com; 4800 Watoga Rd; ⊙Apr-Oct; 🅿) **FREE** is a lush wonderland of moss-covered boulders crisscrossed by a half-mile wooden boardwalk. Just north is **Droop Mountain Battlefield** (📞304-653-4254; www.droopmountainbattlefield.com; 683 Droop Park Rd, Hillsboro) **FREE** where trails pass a mountain bog, Civil War sights and a wooden lookout tower with a broad view of the surrounding mountains. Both parks are free. Beartown is 25 miles north of Lewisburg via US 219. Drive an additional 2 miles on Hwy 219 to reach the battlefield.

WESTON & THE TRANS-ALLEGHENY LUNATIC ASYLUM

So you think you can handle a good scare? You might change your mind during a ghost tour of the **Trans-Allegheny Lunatic Asylum** (☑ 304-269-5070; www.trans-allegheny lunaticasylum.com; 71 Asylum Dr; 90min tour $30; ⊙ noon-6pm Tue-Fri & Sun, from 10am Sat Apr-Oct; P ♿) in Weston, 60 miles south of Morgantown. The striking hospital, made of hand-cut sandstone and stretching a quarter of a mile, admitted its first patient in 1864. It reached its overcrowed peak in the 1950s, when it was home to 2400 patients. Guided tours of the facility include a history tour, a criminally insane tour, and various ghost tours – one with an overnight stay. Despite the insensitive name of the facility, which was later renamed Weston State Hospital, the history tours take a thoughtful look at the often inhumane medical practices that occurred here. Guides share lots of fascinating stories about the patients and staff. The hospital closed in 1994.

After your tour, enjoy a hearty meal at **Thyme Bistro** (☑ 304-269-7177; www.facebook. com/ThymeBistro; 125 Main Ave, Weston; lunch mains $11-15, dinner mains $10-40; ⊙ 11am-3pm, 5-9pm Tu-Fri, 5-9pm Sat), one of the best restaurants in the state. The memorable flavors here create the magic, a result of fresh and locally sourced ingredients, buttery sautees and the oh-so-cheesy toppings.

Stumptown Ales MICROBREWERY
(☑ 304-259-5570; www.stumptownales.com; 390 William Ave, Davis; ⊙ 5-9pm Mon-Wed, 5-10pm Thu & Fri, noon-10pm Sat, 1-7pm Sun) The saws on the wall and the 21ft-long, red-oak bar give a nod to the region's logging past. And the tasty hop-forward beers give a kick to the taste buds at this welcoming taproom.

Purple Fiddle LIVE MUSIC
(☑ 304-463-4040; www.purplefiddle.com; 96 East Ave, Thomas; ⊙ 11am-8pm Sun-Thu, to midnight Fri & Sat) One of those great mountain stores where bluegrass culture and hipster day-trippers from the urban South and Northeast mash up into a stomping good time. There's live music every night; you may want to purchase tickets for weekend shows in advance. The artsy Fiddle is an unexpected surprise out here, and a fun one at that. Also serves soup and good sandwiches ($8 to $10).

ⓘ Getting There & Away

Thomas is 65 miles southeast of I-79 at Morgantown. Davis is 3 miles east of Thomas. The towns are 170 miles west of Washington, DC. You will need a car to explore the area.

NEW RIVER & THE GREENBRIER VALLEY

This part of the state has carved out a viable stake as the adventure-sports capital of the eastern seaboard, with wild white-water rafting, terrific mountain biking, lots of leafy trails; and inviting small towns holding it all together. Home to minerals springs and five golf courses, the swanky Greenbrier resort brings big spenders to the region.

ⓘ Getting There & Away

Fayetteville is 22 miles north of Beckley off I-64. Amtrak stops along the New River Valley on the Cardinal route, which runs between Washington, DC and Chicago. Stops include **White Sulphur Springs** (www.amtrak.com; 315 W Main St, White Sulphur Springs) (p391), outside Beckley. The best way to explore the region is by car.

New River Gorge National River

The New River is actually one of the oldest in the world, and the primeval forest gorge it runs through is one of the most breathtaking in the Appalachians. The National Park Service (NPS) protects a stretch of the New River that falls 750ft over 50 miles, with a compact set of rapids up to Class V concentrated at the northernmost end. The region is an adventure mecca, with world-class white-water runs and challenging single-track trails. Rim and gorge hiking trails offer beautiful views. One of four NPS visitor centers, the Canyon Rim visitor center (p390) just south of the bridge has information about scenic drives, river outfitters and other outdoor adventures.

⊙ Sights

New River Gorge Bridge BRIDGE
(www.nps.gov/neri; Hwy 19; P) FREE Completed in 1977, the New River Gorge Bridge is the

WEST VIRGINIA NEW RIVER GORGE NATIONAL RIVER

third-highest bridge in the US and the longest single-arch bridge in the Western Hemisphere. Made from 22,000 tons of structural steel, it rises 876ft above the New River and stretches 3030ft across the gorge. For the best view of the span, head to the overlooks behind the Canyon Rim Visitor Center or join a Bridgewalk tour. The bridge is open to pedestrians and BASE jumpers on Bridge Day, a festival held annually on the third Saturday of October. The bridge shortened the time needed to cross the gorge – from 40 minutes to less than a minute.

Hawks Nest State Park   STATE PARK
(☑304-658-5212; www.hawksnestsp.com; 49 Hawks Nest Park Rd; lodge r $99-124, ste $124-154; ℗) There are hiking trails, a nature center and an aerial tram (open May to October; adult/child $7/5), which runs from the lodge down to the river's edge. The layout of the lodge is a little confusing, but the comfy rooms offer fabulous views over the gorge. Book early for the fall foliage display.

Hawks Nest Overlook   VIEWPOINT
(www.wvstateparks.com; Hwy 60; ℗) FREE An 80yd paved trail leads to a lofty view of the New River. The photogenic rock wall surrounding the overlook was built by the Civilian Conservation Corps in the 1930s. It's worth the short walk from the parking lot to get there. It's a quarter-mile south of the main lodge at Hawks Nest State Park.

Babcock State Park   STATE PARK
(☑304-438-3004; www.babcocksp.com; 486 Babcock Rd; cabins $69-144, campsites $25-28; ℗) FREE Babcock State Park has hiking, canoeing, horseback riding, and camping and cabin accommodations. The park's highlight is its photogenic Glade Creek Grist Mill. The cabins and campground are open from mid-April through late October.

Mystery Hole   MUSEUM
(☑304-658-9101; www.mysteryhole.com; 16724 Midland Trail, Ansted; adult/child $7/6; ⊙10:30am-5:30pm Wed-Sun Jun-Aug, Sat & Sun only Sep, Fri-Sun May & Oct; ℗✈) See gravity and the known limits of tackiness defied at the Mystery Hole, one of the great attractions of roadside America. Everything inside this madhouse *tilts at an angle!* It's 1 mile west of Hawks Nest State Park.

🏃 Activities & Tours

Long Point Trail   HIKING
(www.nps.gov/neri; Newtown Rd, off Gatewood Rd) At just over 3 miles for the round-trip, this trail leads to a rocky outcrop with big views of the New River Gorge and the New River Gorge Bridge. This is a great short hike and the outcrop is perfect for a picnic.

Adventures on the Gorge   ADVENTURE
(☑855-379-8738; www.adventuresonthegorge.com; 219 Chestnutburg Rd, Lansing; guided rafting trips per person from $119; ✈) How many experiences does this reputable outfit offer? Well, their catalog is 63 pages long and covers everything from white-water rafting on the New and Gauley Rivers to ziplining, rappelling, rock-climbing and more. It has a wide array of cabins (including some with Jacuzzis), plus campsites and several restaurants, including Smokey's Steakhouse (open May to October; mains $18 to $36) near the rim of the gorge. Campsites are $15, while cabins start at $89 per night.

★ Bridgewalk   WALKING
(☑304-574-1300; www.bridgewalk.com; 57 Fayette Mine Rd; $69; ⊙9am-4pm) Wow. The bird's-eye view of the New River from the catwalk running below the river's namesake bridge is amazing. And it's eerie to hear traffic rattling by overhead. If you're not afraid of heights – you're 851ft above the river – this is a recommended bucket-list adventure. The tours, which last two to three hours, are guided and very informative. Expect to walk 1.25 miles.

🎉 Festivals & Events

Bridge Day Festival   SPORTS
(www.officialbridgeday.com; Hwy 19; ⊙Oct) On the third Saturday in October, hundreds of BASE jumpers parachute from the 876ft-high New River Gorge Bridge. Includes live music in Fayetteville the same weekend.

ℹ Information

For information about history, geology and recreation, stop by the Canyon Rim Visitor Center (☑304-574-2115; www.nps.gov/neri; 162 Visitor Center Rd, Lansing; ⊙9am-5pm; ✈), one of four NPS visitor centers along the New River. A short trail behind the building leads to a leaf-framed view of the bridge.

ℹ Getting There & Away

There is an airport (p396) in Charleston, 70 miles northwest. Amtrak stops at three places in the NPS region on the Cardinal route, which runs between Chicago, Washington, DC and New York City. One of these stops is the Prince Depot (p391), which is 23 miles south of Fayetteville near Beckley. Greyhound (www.greyhound.com) stops in Beckley at 360 Prince St.

Fayetteville

🏛 304, 681 / POP 2898

Packed tight with good restaurants and watering holes, pint-sized Fayetteville acts as a jumping-off point for New River thrill-seekers. Definitely plan to stop here for a meal if you're adventuring in the area. It's an artsy mountain enclave as well.

Activities

New River Bikes   CYCLING
(🏛304-574-2453; www.newriverbikes.com; 221 N Court St; bike hire per day $35, tours $79-110; ⊙10am-6pm Mon, Tue, Thu & Fri, to 4pm Sat) Mountain biking is superb on the graded loops of the Arrowhead Trails. You can hire wheels or take a guided trip through this outfit in Fayetteville.

Hard Rock   CLIMBING
(🏛304-574-0735; www.hardrockclimbing.com; 131 S Court St; half/full day with 2-person min from $80/150) For rock climbers, Hard Rock offers trips and training courses.

🛏 Sleeping & Eating

River Rock Retreat Hostel   HOSTEL $
(🏛304-574-0394; www.riverrockretreatandhostel. com; cnr Lansing-Edmond & Fayette Station Rds; dm $30; P❄🐾) Less than 1 mile north of the New River Gorge Bridge, this is a well-run hostel with basic, clean rooms and plenty of common space. No host on-site, but owner Joy Marr is a wealth of local information.

★**Secret Sandwich Society**   AMERICAN $
(🏛304-574-4777; www.secretsandwichsociety. com; 103 Keller Ave; mains $10-15; ⊙11am-9pm Sun-Thu, to 10pm Fri & Sat) If you're a connoisseur of sandwiches, or just super hungry, this easygoing spot is a must. The eatery has sandwiches slathered in tasty toppings, delicious burgers, hearty salads and a changing lineup of local microbrews. Eat on the pleasant deck for a fine breeze.

★**Pies & Pints**   PIZZA $$
(🏛304-574-2200; www.piesandpints.net; 219 W Maple Ave; pizzas $9-25; ⊙11am-9pm Sun-Thu, to 10pm Fri & Sat) Oooh baby. Let's talk about the Gouda Chicken. Topped with gourmet cheese, chipotle crema, apple-smoked bacon and grilled yard bird, this decadent pizza is darn-near heaven. The flagship location of the popular West Virginia and Ohio pizza-and-craft-beer mini-chain, this is a place where folks come to celebrate after a good time in the great outdoors. From ales and IPAs to sours, the craft beer list is impressive, with selections both local and national.

Cathedral Café   CAFE $$
(🏛304-574-0202; www.facebook.com/cathedral cafe; 134 S Court St; lunch mains $8-11, dinner mains $11-20; ⊙7:30am-4pm Sun-Thu, to 9pm Fri & Sat; 🖥🐾) Start the day with breakfast and coffee under stained-glass windows at this inviting cafe and former church. Local staff all seem to either work in, or know someone who works in, the local adventure-tourism industry, so it's a good spot to figure out what's going on in the New River Gorge area.

Drinking & Nightlife

Charlie's Pub   BAR
(🏛304-574-1078; 190 S Court St; ⊙from 4pm) A rafting guide named Sketchy recommended this place, which is tucked beneath a bakery building a short drive from downtown. We'd say it's half hipsters and half old salts, and the latter might get chatty. Two pool tables and a jukebox. Doesn't get going until 11pm. The entrance is in the back.

ℹ Getting There & Away

You will need a car to check out the regional attractions.

Amtrak (www.amtrak.com) stops on Wednesday, Friday and Sunday at the **Prince Depot** (🏛800-872-7245; www.amtrak.com; 5034 Stanaford Rd, Prince), 23 miles south of Fayetteville on the Cardinal route linking NYC, Washington, DC and Chicago. It's a fairly remote stop and there are no rental-car companies on-site. You will need to arrange for pick-up by a friend or a taxi.

Lewisburg

🏛 304, 681 / POP 3949

With a walkable and historic downtown dating from the late 1700s, now filled with boutiques, indie shops, antique stores, fantastic restaurants and a Carnegie performance hall, Lewisburg is a destination small town in its own right. But its proximity to the posh Greenbrier resort as well as unique state parks, striking natural attractions and a slew of places ready-made for outdoor fun makes Lewisburg an appealing base camp for exploring southern West Virginia. Prime outdoor activities near here include fishing, kayaking, cycling and hiking.

WORTH A TRIP

HATFIELD & MCCOY COUNTRY & THE MINE WARS

The legendary family feud between the Hatfields and McCoys began soon after the Civil War and developed along the banks of the Tug River in the mountainous terrain between the towns of Williamson and Matewan (Mate-wan) in southern West Virginia. The Hatfields, led by patriarch 'Devil Anse,' lived in West Virginia for the most part, while the McCoys tended to live in Kentucky, just across the river. It's a complicated saga, involving a land dispute, a stolen pig, an illicit love affair and lots of murders. The feud has been a well-known story in American folklore for generations, but the success of the 2012 *Hatfields & McCoys* miniseries on the History Channel – starring Kevin Costner as Devil Anse – kicked the story back into the spotlight. It also boosted regional tourism. For a driving map to key sites in the feud, stop by the **Coal House** (☑304-235-5240; www.tugvalleychamber.com; 73 E 2nd St; ☺9:30am-5pm Mon-Fri) visitor center in Williamson or the **Matewan Replica Depot Museum** (☑304-426-6744; www.historicmatewan.com; 100 Bridge St; ☺9am-5pm Mon-Sat, 11am-5pm Sun; ℗) in Matewan. You'll find more details about the conflict in the **Hatfield & McCoy Country Museum** (☑304-601-3066; https://hatfieldmccoycountrymuseum.com; 801 Alderson St, Williamson; $5; ☺9am-5pm Tue-Sat Apr-Nov) in Williamson.

Coal mining boomed across the region in the early 1900s, and the rapidly burgeoning industry fueled, literally, America's emergence as a world power. Miners, however, worked under terrible and very dangerous conditions. Many were immigrants, African Americans and men from poor regional families, and they were taken advantage of by the mining companies. In 1907 a mine explosion in Monongah, WV, killed at least 362 miners; it remains the worst mining disaster in US history. That same year, a total of 3241 coal miners were killed on the job. The companies also controlled the towns where the miners and their families lived, often paying them in scrip that could only be used at company stores. Conditions were rife for conflict, and the Mine Wars period between 1912 and 1921 saw numerous violent confrontations. Major incidents included the Matewan Massacre (1920) and the Battle of Blair Mountain (1921). In Matewan, the **Mine Wars Museum** (336 Mate St; www.wvminewars.com) spotlights this turbulent era. For more background, watch the acclaimed movie *Matewan,* written and directed by John Sayles. At the **Beckley Exhibition Coal Mine** (☑304-256-1747; www.beckley.org/gen eral-information-coal-mine; 513 Ewart Ave, Beckley; adult/child $20/12; ☺10am-6pm Apr-Oct) between Fayetteville and Charleston, visitors can ride a train 1500ft into a former coal mine.

Williamson is 80 miles south of Charleston. If you plan to do a weekend of exploring, consider an overnight stay at the **Mountaineer Hotel** (☑304-235-2222; www.mountain eerhotel.com; 31 E 2nd St; r/ste from $65/85; ℗❋🛜) in downtown Williamson. The gourmet sandwiches at nearby **34:Ate** (☑304-235-3488; www.facebook.com/34ate; 210 Pike St; mains $7-10; ☺11am-3pm Mon-Fri) work well for a picnic. If you're feeling adventurous, rent an ATV and hit the **Hatfield-McCoy Trails** (☑800-592-2217; www.trailsheaven.com; permit $50), which cover more than 600 rugged miles.

👁 Sights & Activities

Carnegie Hall
HISTORIC BUILDING

(☑304-645-7917; www.carnegiehallwv.com; 611 Church St; ☺10am-4pm Mon-Sat) **FREE** Industrialist Andrew Carnegie helped fund this 1902 Colonial Revival performance hall, one of only four Carnegie music halls still in continuous use. Stop by to see local art, the West Virginia Music Hall of Fame exhibit or to watch one of the monthly live-music performances (tickets typically cost $19 to $25).

Greenbrier Trail
CYCLING

(www.greenbrierrivertrail.com; Stonehouse Rd, Caldwell) Open to hikers and cyclists, this popular rail trail links Caldwell, on the outskirts of Lewisburg, with tiny Cass (p387), which sits 78 miles north near Cheat Mountain. The trail is packed gravel most of the way and dotted with picnic tables and benches. Trees, mountains and the Greenbrier River also hug this scenic path. Passes through Greenbrier and Pocahontas Counties.

📖 Sleeping & Eating

★ General Lewis Inn   INN $$
(📞304-645-2600; www.generallewisinn.com; 1236 E Washington St; r $125-200; ste $275; 🅿️❄️🛜) Creaky floors, four-poster beds and Persian rugs evoke thoughts of ghosts at this white-columned inn built around an 1830s home and a newer wing, which opened in 1928 as an inn. There's an on-site dining room and a casual lobby lounge serving local beer and spirits. Doors to unoccupied rooms remain open, so stop by to check them out.

Jim's Drive-In   BURGERS, HOT DOGS $
(📞304-645-2590; 479 W Washington St; mains $4-8; ⊙10am-5pm Mon & Tue, to 2:30pm Wed, to 6pm Thu-Sat) What? Is this a carhop situation? Oh yes it is. Pull up. Park. And scour the menu of burgers, hot dogs, barbecue and french fries as you wait for your server to walk to your window. The English hot dog comes on a toasted and buttered bun. Wash it all down with an Oreo milkshake. Cash only.

Stardust Cafe   AMERICAN $$
(📞304-647-3663; www.stardustcafewv.com; 1023 E Washington St; mains lunch $10-16, dinner $15-34; ⊙11am-3pm Mon-Sat, 5-8:30pm Mon-Thu, 5-9:30 Fri & Sat) 🍴 The magic in the signature Trust Me Salad is the homemade granola. Or maybe it's the just-right mix of chevre and avocado. Oh heck, maybe it's the hearty bowl of organic greens piled high with grilled chicken. Salads and gourmet sandwiches keep shoppers well-fueled at lunch. The mood and the fare – pasta, steaks, fish – get a little fancier at night.

🍷 Drinking & Nightlife

Smooth Ambler Spirits Distillery   DISTILLERY
(📞304-497-3123; www.facebook.com/smoothambler; 745 Industrial Park Rd; ⊙tasting room 2-5pm Mon-Fri, 11am-3pm Sat) Stop by the tasting room to sample handcrafted West Virginia whiskeys and other spirits, including gin, vodka and bourbon. The production area is visible from the tasting room, and you can learn more about the whiskey-making process during a free tour (2pm and 4pm Friday, noon and 2pm Saturday). Head 5.5 miles north on Hwy 19 from downtown.

ℹ️ Getting There & Away

Downtown Lewisburg sits at the junction of two busy highways, Hwy 219 and Hwy 60. The best way to explore the region is by car.

The Greenbrier resort in White Sulphur Springs is 9 miles east of Lewisburg via Hwy 60 or I-64. Amtrak (www.amtrak.com) stops in White Sulphur Springs on Sundays, Wednesdays and Fridays on the Cardinal route, which links New York City, Washington, DC, and Chicago.

CHARLESTON

📞304, 681 / POP 49,138

The capital of West Virginia, Charleston is tiny, with a population just under 50,000 at last count. But what it lacks in size, it makes up for with passion and civic pride. And have you seen the view? This compact place is nestled below the gorgeous Appalachians and flanked by the scenic Kanawha River. The striking gold-plated dome of the state

---

DON'T MISS

GREENBRIER RESORT BUNKER TOUR

Construction workers and locals were sworn to secrecy during the construction of this bunker at the posh **Greenbrier** (📞855-453-4858; www.greenbrier.com; 300 W Main St; r/ste/cottage from $318/478/518; 🅿️❄️🛜🏊) in White Sulphur Springs in the 1950s during the height of the Cold War. Built as an emergency relocation center for members of Congress in the event of a nuclear war, the bunker sits partly inside a hillside adjacent to the resort. The facility has a 25-ton blast door, 18 dorms, a clinic, a cafeteria and meeting rooms. The bunker was kept secret for 30 years, but is now open to the public for 90-minute **guided tours** (📞844-223-3173; www.greenbrier.com; adult/child 10-18yr $39/20; ⊙9:30am-3:30pm).

Travelers have enjoyed the mineral springs in White Sulphur Springs since the 1770s. The resort itself has impressed presidents and celebrities since the 1830s. Today this striking white, luxury property holds more than 710 rooms and suites. Common areas pop with the bright designs of famed decorator Dorothy Draper. The five golf courses are also a draw, plus there are more than 55 recreational activities from which to choose.

Nine miles west, you can stretch your legs and explore the shops and restaurants in downtown Lewisburg.

capitol building – it's hard to miss – is purely unnecessary, but kind of fun. The city was hit with some deserved bad press in 2014 after a chemical spill in the adjacent Elk River forced residents to shut off their water for days. But in the ensuing years a creative class of young citizens has injected optimistic energy into the city, opening new restaurants and shops in emerging neighborhoods to much acclaim and appreciation.

◉ Sights & Activities

West Virginia State Museum   MUSEUM
(☑304-558-0220; www.wvculture.org; 1900 Kanawha Blvd E; ⊙9am-5pm Tue-Sat) FREE The

voice of billionaire governor Jim Justice welcomes guests to this engaging museum, where a path winds past exhibit areas spotlighting key moments and eras in the history of the Mountain State. Stop here for background about frontier life, John Brown's Raid, the mining industry and the mine wars.

State Capitol Building   HISTORIC BUILDING
(☑304-558-4839; www.wvlegislature.gov; 1900 Kanawha Blvd E, State Capitol Complex; ⊙8am-6pm Mon-Fri; 9am-6pm Sat, noon-6pm Sun; ℗) FREE The 293ft-tall dome of the state capitol building is coated in 23.5-karat gold

Charleston

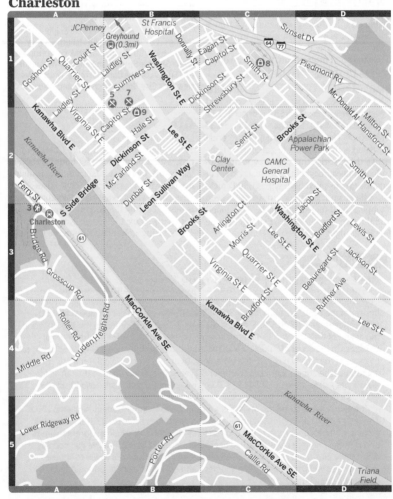

leaf – and it sure does sparkle on a sunny day. Completed in 1932, the building was designed by architect Cass Gilbert, who also designed the Supreme Court Building in Washington, DC. Tours of the capitol start every half-hour from the 1st-floor rotunda (9am to noon and 1pm to 3pm weekdays).

Sunrise Carriage Trail   HIKING
(MacCorkle Ave SE; ⊘dawn-dusk) Stretch your legs on a climb up the woodsy Sunrise Carriage Trail, a 0.65-mile pedestrian path near downtown that switchbacks to the former hilltop estate of governor William McCormick. To get to the base of the trail, cross

the Kanawha River on the South Side Bridge then turn right into the parking area.

👉 Tours

JQ Dickinson Salt-Works   FOOD
(☎304-925-7918; www.jqdsalt.com; 4797 Midland Dr, Malden; ⊘shop 1am-4pm Mon-Fri, tours 10am-4pm Tue-Sat mid-Apr–Nov) FREE Brother-and-sister team Lewis Payne and Nancy Bruns, who are seventh-generation salt-producers, reopened the family salt works in 2013. Their small-batch salt is a favorite of gourmet chefs nationwide. Stop in for a tour or to buy a jar of the chunky salt – good stuff! Malden is about 6 miles south of Charleston.

🛏 Sleeping & Eating

Brass Pineapple   B&B **$$**
(☎304-344-0748; www.brasspineapple.com; 1611 E Virginia St; r $179-199; P🐕) Just a half-block from the state capitol, this well-appointed Victorian-era home is a comfy base camp for exploring Charleston and the region. And you will start your daily explorations with a made-from-scratch full breakfast. Tea and sweets are served in the afternoon.

Ellen's Homemade Ice Cream   ICE CREAM **$**
(☎304-343-6488; www.ellensicecream.com; 225 Capitol St; 1 scoop $4; ⊘11am-8pm Mon-Thu, to 10pm Fri & Sat, to 5pm Sun; 🐾) Photos of kids adorn the walls at this bright ice-cream shop where the homemade flavors include Dutch chocolate, mocha almond and Oreo. Specialty flavors available daily. Lots of couches and chairs for relaxing.

Charleston

◎ Sights
1 State Capitol Building F5
2 West Virginia State Museum..............F5

🏃 Activities, Courses & Tours
3 Sunrise Carriage Trail A3

🛏 Sleeping
4 Brass Pineapple E5

🍴 Eating
5 Black Sheep Burrito & Brews..............B1
6 Bluegrass Kitchen...............................E4
7 Ellen's Homemade Ice Cream............B1

✪ Entertainment
Mountain Stage........................(see 2)

🛍 Shopping
8 Capitol Market....................................C1
9 Taylor Books.......................................B2

COOPERS ROCK STATE FOREST

One of the most photogenic spots in all of West Virginia is the main overlook at **Coopers Rock** (☑304-594-1561; www.wvstateparks.com; 61 County Line Dr, Bruceton Mills; P⚙) **FREE**. Picture a stone-and-log fence wrapped around a sandstone clifftop. That clifftop is perched above a big view of the Cheat River Gorge and the forested slopes beside it. Pretty darn awesome. The drive through the forest to get there is gorgeous too, particularly in fall when the leaves are changing color. Don't miss the **Rock City Trail** (0.7 miles one way), which barrels through a wonderland of boulders. There are 25 campsites, all with electrical hook-ups ($25 per night).

After your visit, head to Morgantown, the home of West Virginia University. For a burger and beer, step into **Mario's Fishbowl** (☑304-292-2511; www.mariosfishbowl.com; 704 Richmond Ave; ⊙11am-midnight Mon-Thu, to 1am Fri & Sat, to 10pm Sun) – pushing open the door is like walking into the best party in town. A bar since 1963, with the knickknackery to prove it, this place is named for its last owner and its goblet-sized drinking glasses.

Black Sheep Burrito & Brews MEXICAN $
(☑304-343-2739; www.blacksheepwv.com; 702 Quarrier St; mains $4-12; ⊙11am-10pm Mon-Wed, to 11pm Thu-Sat, to 9pm Sun) The Flock of Tacos – your choice of three tacos – is the dish to order at this breezy craft beer pub and Mexican joint that's a favorite of lawyers, cool kids and; well, just about anyone. A margarita with your meal on the patio is a nice way to spend an afternoon. And those margaritas are big!

Bluegrass Kitchen AMERICAN $$
(☑304-346-2871; www.bluegrasswv.com; 1600 E Washington St; mains dinner $7-14, brunch $13-24; ⊙3:30-9pm Mon-Thu, 3:30-10pm Fri, 10am-10pm Sat) 🌱 The West Virginia beers on tap pair well with just about anything on the menu at this welcoming spot, from the half-pound local beef burger topped with pimento cheese to the pickle-brined fried chicken to the organic tostada with guacamole. Fare is regional, herb-infused and often vegetarian. Look for shrimp and grits and homemade biscuits with gravy at brunch.

☆ Entertainment

Mountain Stage LIVE MUSIC
(☑304-556-4900; www.mountainstage.org; cnr Greenbrier St & E Washington St, Culture Center Theater; ⊙7pm Sun) This two-hour live NPR radio broadcast showcases a range of up-and-coming national talent, from folk and blues to indie to world music. Most shows are held at the performance hall at the West Virginia State Museum on the grounds of State Capitol Complex.

🛍 Shopping

Capitol Market MARKET
(☑304-344-1905; www.capitolmarket.net; 800 Smith St; ⊙10am-6pm Mon-Sat, to 5pm Sun) Shelves groan under regional jams and jellies, Holl's Swiss Chocolates and a long row of local produce at this indoor-outdoor market on the site of the old railyard for the Kanawha and Michigan railroad. You'll also find several restaurants and eateries, a coffee shop and tourist information. This is a great place to pick up locally made and sourced gifts.

Taylor Books BOOKS
(☑304-342-1461; www.taylorsbooks.com; 226 Capitol St; ⊙7am-8pm, 7am-10pm Fri, 9am-10pm Sat, 9am-5pm Sun; 🐾) In the heart of the downtown shopping district, this bustling yet intimate gathering place rolls four elements into one: indie bookstore, coffee shop, music venue and art gallery. And it works.

❶ Getting There & Away

Charleston sits at the junction of I-64, I-77 and I-79. The **airport** (☑304-344-8033; www2.yeagerairport.com; 100 Airport Rd) is 4 miles northeast of town, and is served by American, Delta, Spirit and United. The **Amtrak Station** (☑304-342-6766; www.amtrak.com; 350 MacCorkle Ave) borders the South Side Bridge, just across the Kanawha River from downtown. It is served three times per week by the Cardinal line connecting New York City with Chicago. The **Greyhound** (☑304-357-0056; www.greyhound.com; 300 Reynolds St) bus stop is just west of downtown.

WEST VIRGINIA CHARLESTON

Understand New York & the Mid-Atlantic

New York & the Mid-Atlantic Today

The USA's political landscape today is turbulent, and protests are common, with those on the left resisting the nation's sudden (and sharp) turn to the right. News organizations are hungry for content; decisions made by Congress, the Supreme Court and President Trump in Washington, DC, generate a daily deluge of political commentary, which exacerbates the conflicts. Hot topics include the ballooning divide between rich and poor, gun control, the environment and sexual harassment.

Best on Film

Taxi Driver (1976) Martin Scorsese's story of a troubled Vietnam veteran turned taxi driver.
Mr Smith Goes to Washington (1939) Jimmy Stewart gets a crash course in DC politics and corruption.
All the President's Men (1976) Two journalists uncover the Watergate scandal.
Hidden Figures (2016) The mathematical brilliance of three African American women helps NASA launch the first American into space.
Matewan (1987) True story of a labor union organizer during the West Virginia mining wars.

Best in Print

The Amazing Adventures of Cavalier & Clay (Michael Chabon; 2000) Touches upon Brooklyn, escapism and the nuclear family.
Twelve Days of Terror (Richard Fernicola, 2016) Spotlights shark attacks that caused Shore-wide panic in 1916.
Factory Man (Beth Macy; 2014) The history of Virginia's furniture industry through the story of a factory owner.
Lost in the City (Edward P Jones; 1992) Critically acclaimed short stories set in 1960s and '70s African American DC.
Homicide: A Year on the Killing Streets (David Simon; 1991) Nonfiction book behind NBC TV show *Homicide: Life on the Street*.

State Politics: Red, Blue & Purple

New York

New York routinely votes Democrat and is a dyed-in-the-wool 'blue state' with several pockets of conservative communities around upstate New York, the wealthier parts of Long Island and sections of New York City. Despite Democrats typically controlling the governor's mansion and both houses of its state congress, moderate conservatives (usually socially liberal and fiscally conservative) have a sway in state politics. In general you'll find lots of places in New York where conventional party-politics lines have blurred. There is also an overwhelming perception that state and local politics tend to be corrupt and easily swayed by the influence of Wall St and monied real-estate developers. Many New Yorkers on both sides of the political aisle view the state capital, Albany, in a negative light. They point to the lack of attention paid to public-works projects (the state's roads are notably bad and NYC's subway is in a state of disrepair) as evidence of state politicians' lack of interest in actually governing.

Pennsylvania

Pennsylvania continues to baffle outsiders who are trying to put their fingers on the state's political pulse. While the state voted for Democrats for six straight presidential elections, it narrowly broke for Donald Trump in 2016. Then, in a move that truly provoked some head scratches, the deeply conservative 18th district, which came in strong for Trump in 2016, elected Democratic candidate Conor Lamb to the US House of Representatives in 2018.

Ultimately, these incidents are not as unpredictable as they may first appear. Both Trump and Lamb made strong appeals to the state's neglected manufacturing class, which has been gutted by the continuing erosion of the American working class. The union members who went blue for Barack Obama cottoned on to Trump's

'America First' rhetoric, but when the promise of a revitalized economy was never realized in coal-and-steel country, they threw their lot in with Lamb, a moderate Democrat who made his political play couched in union rhetoric but without Trump's nativism.

One positive development? A state Supreme Court decision in 2018 to reduce gerrymandering – the practice of dividing districts along party lines for an advantage at the polls.

Virginia

After statewide elections in November 2017, the Republican Party's advantage in the Virginia House of Delegates dropped from 66–34 to 51–49, with Democrats picking up 15 seats. The parties would have been at parity in the lower chamber if a lottery-style tiebreaker to select the delegate from Newport News had broken for the Democratic candidate. Democratic candidates also won all three executive offices. With no elections until 2019, Republicans remained in control of the Virginia Senate 21–19.

The election was a wake-up call for Republicans, who have controlled the Virginia House of Delegates since 2001. Many political analysts consider Virginia a bellwether for national elections. Residents of fast-growing Northern Virginia tend to vote blue, for Democrats, while residents of rural counties in the south and southwest tend to vote red, for Republicans. With midsized cities like Richmond beginning to tilt blue, and rural red counties losing residents, Virginia may find itself a solidly blue state in 2019. Let's go with purple for now.

March for Our Lives & Gun Control

An estimated 800,000 protesters attended the March for Our Lives gun-control demonstration in Washington, DC, on March 25, 2018, putting it in the running for the largest single-day demonstration ever in the nation's capital.

Mass shootings in the Mid-Atlantic over the last decade range from the murder of 32 people at Virginia Tech in Blacksburg, VA, by gunman and student Seung-Hui Cho in 2007 to a school shooting at Great Mills High School in Southern Maryland that injured two students and left the gunman dead; the latter occurred just days before the DC demonstration.

On average, 32 Americans are murdered by guns every day, and another 148 wounded. Despite evidence (such as a 2013 study published in the *American Journal of Medicine*) that more guns equal more murders, and the comparatively low rates of death by firearms in countries with strict gun laws, American legislators have been unwilling to enact even modest gun-control laws. The reason in part: gun lobbies such as the National Rifle Association (NRA) wield lots of power, contributing more than $35 million annually to state and national political campaigns. A recent Pew Research poll found that 52% of Americans

CURRENCY: **US DOLLAR ($)**

TIME: **UTC/EASTERN STANDARD TIME (GMT MINUS FIVE HOURS)**

POPULATION: **17,984,089**

belief systems
(% of population)

47 Protestant

21 Roman Catholic

2 Jewish

2 Mormon

28 Other

if the Mid-Atlantic were 100 people

61 would be white
18 would be Latino
13 would be African American
6 would be Asian American
2 would be other

population per sq km

USA   AUSTRALIA   CANADA

≈ 3 people

said it was more important to protect gun rights than to control gun ownership.

NYC Gentrification

When visiting anywhere in New York it's important to keep in mind that many of the popular tourist destinations did not always look the way they do now. Gentrification, or the process of making a place more refined and appealing, has brought a lot of growth and revitalization to parts of the state, but it has also seen communities driven out of their historic homes, and entire neighborhoods and towns rendered unrecognizable to the people who used to live in them. The issue is especially fraught in many Brooklyn neighborhoods, where black communities are being edged out of apartments as developers entice young middle and upper-class white professionals to move in by creating large condo buildings that offer spectacular amenities for a fraction of the rent of Manhattan, gradually raising rents across the neighborhood.

Pipeline Blues

The Appalachian Trail Conservancy (ATC) and 39 other eco-minded groups aren't happy with the pending construction of the Mountain Valley Pipeline, which will carry fracked natural gas across West Virginia and Virginia. Though the 303-mile pipeline will bring temporary jobs during its construction, the ATC and other groups are worried about potential environmental harms and other detrimental effects. One fear is that the above-ground pipeline will scar scenic views from the Appalachian Trail, which the pipeline will track for 90 miles. They also warn that the pipeline will cross numerous water sources, many of them on land prone to seismic activity, erosion and landslides. At the time of writing, construction had begun in West Virginia; legal challenges were holding it up in Virginia.

Income Inequality

On February 22, 2018, 20,000 teachers across West Virginia began a walkout over low pay. Their protests would keep more than 277,000 students out of school for just over a week. The teachers argued that they had not been compensated for cost of living increases over the years and often could not afford to pay their health-care bills. Nine days later billionaire Governor Jim Justice and the state legislature – after much stonewalling – agreed to a 5% pay increase.

Before the strike, West Virginia – a very fiscally conservative state – ranked 48th in average teacher pay across all states. The strike highlights the problems faced today by low-income workers across the Mid-Atlantic and the rest of the country. The income gap between rich and poor continues to widen in the US. The top 1% of the population earns about 20% of the income (up from 9% in 1976), while the poor are getting poorer: the median wage earner takes home 11% less than in 1999.

History

The modern story of America began in 1607 when a determined band of colonists built a fort on the banks of the James River, VA. Named Jamestown, this small community would become the New World's first permanent English settlement. Ever since, residents of the Mid-Atlantic have witnessed – and sparked – transformational moments in American history: wars against the British, the creation of a new nation, slavery and its abolishment, the Civil War and Reconstruction, and the labor and Civil Rights movements.

First Inhabitants

Among North America's most significant prehistoric cultures were the Mound Builders, who inhabited the Mississippi, Kanawha and Potomac river valleys from around 3000 BC to AD 1200. They left behind enigmatic piles of earth that were tombs for their leaders and possibly tributes to their gods. There are nearly 50 mounds west of Charleston, WV. Most were built between 500 BC and AD 200 by the Adena people.

Before the first European colonists sailed up from Chesapeake Bay, most Native Americans living nearby spoke the Algonquian language, with others speaking Siouan or Iroquoian. In the early 1600s many of the the Algonquian-speaking tribes in the Tidewater region near Jamestown, VA were led by Chief Powhatan. The Piscataway tribe of the Algonquian made their home near the confluence of the Potomac and Anacostia Rivers.

Two centuries later, the regional tribes were all but gone. European explorers left diseases in their wake to which indigenous peoples had no immunity. More destructive than any other factor – war, slavery or famine – disease epidemics devastated Native American populations by anywhere from 50% to 90%.

Jamestown & Early Colonies

In 1606 three ships owned by the Virginia Company of London – the *Susan Constant, Godspeed* and *Discovery* – set sail for the New World to establish a profit-making colony. In May of the following year, this group

TIMELINE	1607	1634	1776
	The Jamestown settlement, the first permanent English colony in North America, is founded on marshland in present-day Virginia. The first few years are hard, with many dying from sickness and starvation.	With a goal of religious freedom for all, the first British colony in Maryland is founded at St Mary's City, which becomes the state's first capital.	At the Second Continental Congress, delegates from the 13 colonies converge in Philadelphia and sign the Declaration of Independence, formally breaking political bonds with Great Britain.

The New World (2005), directed by Terrence Malick, is a brutal but passionate film that retells the tragic story of the Jamestown colony and the pivotal peace-making role of Pocahontas, a daughter of Chief Powhatan.

of 104 men and boys selected a spot along the James River in current-day Virginia as the site for their new colony, which they named Jamestown in honor of King James I. It would become the first permanent European settlement in the New World.

Earlier English settlements had ended badly, and Jamestown almost did, too: the noblemen had chosen a swamp, planted their crops late and died from disease and starvation. The Powhatan tribe provided the settlement with enough aid to survive but relations between the colonists and the tribe deteriorated.

The first recorded white contact with the Piscataway to the north was in 1608 by the English Captain John Smith, who set out from the Jamestown colony to explore the upper Potomac. Relations with the peaceful Piscataway were amicable at first, but soon turned ruinous for the Native Americans, who suffered from European diseases. By 1700 the few remaining Piscataway migrated out of the region to Iroquois territory in Pennsylvania and New York.

For Jamestown and America, 1619 proved a pivotal year: the colony established the House of Burgesses, a representative assembly of citizens to decide local laws, and it received its first boatload of 20 African slaves. The Royal Colony of Virginia came into being in 1624.

That same year, the Dutch West India Company sent 110 settlers to begin a trading post in the new land. They settled in Lower Manhattan and called their colony New Amsterdam, touching off bloody battles with the unshakable Lenape. It all came to a head in 1626, when the colony's first governor, Peter Minuit, became the city's first – but certainly not the last – unscrupulous real-estate agent, by purchasing Manhattan's 14,000 acres from the Lenape for 60 guilders ($24) and some glass beads.

In 1634, fleeing the English Civil War, Lord Baltimore established the Catholic colony of Maryland at St Mary's City, where residents included a Spanish Jewish doctor, a black Portuguese sailor and Margaret Brent, the first woman to request the right to vote in North American politics (she was refused). Delaware was settled as a Dutch whaling colony in 1631, practically wiped out by Native Americans, and later resettled by the British.

Capitalism & End of Colonialism

By the late 1600s, expansive agricultural estates lined both sides of the Potomac and James Rivers. These tidewater planters became a colonial aristocracy, dominating regional affairs. Their most lucrative crop was the precious sot-weed – tobacco – which was tended by African indentured servants and slaves. The river ports of Alexandria and Georgetown became famous for their prosperous commercial centers.

1781	1791–4	1814	1848
Delaware becomes the first of the 13 original states to sign the US Constitution, earning it the nickname The First State.	Angry frontiersmen in western Pennsylvania instigate the Whiskey Rebellion after the federal government levies an excise tax on spirits. The uprising is put down by President George Washington.	The British burn Washington, DC, during the War of 1812. Francis Scott Key pens the *Star-Spangled Banner* after witnessing the British Navy bombard Fort McHenry in Baltimore.	Women's rights activists hold the first Seneca Falls Convention, sparking a greater push for women's rights.

Over the 17th and 18th centuries, slavery in America was slowly legalized into a formal institution to support this plantation economy. By 1800, one out of every five people was a slave.

Britain mostly left the American colonists to govern themselves. Town meetings and representative assemblies, in which local citizens (that is, white men with property) debated community problems and voted on laws and taxes, became common. By the end of the Seven Years' War in 1763, Britain was feeling the strains of running an empire: it had been fighting France for a century and had colonies scattered all over the world. It was time to clean up bureaucracies and share financial burdens.

The colonies, however, resented English taxes and policies. In 1774, representatives from 12 of the 13 colonies convened the First Continental Congress in Philadelphia's Carpenter's Hall to air complaints and prepare for the inevitable war ahead. During the Second Virginia Convention – held at Richmond's St John's Church – the following year, attorney and orator Patrick Henry urged his fellow statesmen to form a militia to defend against the British. He ended his speech with the battle cry, 'Give me liberty, or give me death!'

Revolution & Founding Fathers

George Washington, a wealthy Virginia farmer, was chosen to lead the American army after British troops skirmished with armed colonists in Massachusetts in the spring of 1775. Trouble was, Washington lacked gunpowder and money (the colonists resisted taxes even for their own military), and his troops were a motley collection of poorly armed farmers, hunters and merchants, who regularly quit and returned to their farms due to lack of pay. On the other side, the British 'Redcoats' represented the world's most powerful military. The inexperienced General Washington had to improvise constantly, sometimes wisely retreating, sometimes engaging in 'ungentlemanly' sneak attacks.

Meanwhile, the Second Continental Congress tried to articulate what exactly they were fighting for. In January 1776, Thomas Paine published the wildly popular *Common Sense*, which passionately argued for independence from England. Soon, independence seemed not just logical, but noble and necessary, and on July 4, 1776, the Declaration of Independence was finalized and signed. Largely written by Virginian Thomas Jefferson, it elevated the 13 colonies' particular gripes against the monarchy into a universal declaration of individual rights and republican government.

France allied with the revolutionaries in 1778, and they provided the troops, material and sea power that helped win the war. The British surrendered at Yorktown, VA, in 1781. Two years later Washington resigned his commission as commander in chief of the Continental Army in the Maryland State House in Annapolis, thereby returning power to the

Despite popular belief (asserted even by some congressmen), Washington, DC, was not built on a swamp. When surveying the capital, L'Enfant found fields, forests and bluffs. Some marshy areas near the river were prone to tidal fluctuations and periodic floods, but most of the new federal city was not swampy.

1861	1865	1868–1914	1870
Virginia secedes from the Union. In July, Confederate rebels defeat Union troops in the Battle of Manassas in Northern Virginia, the first major land battle of the Civil War.	Confederate General Robert E Lee surrenders to Ulysses S Grant at Appomattox Court House in Virginia on April 9, 1865. The war's end is marred by President Lincoln's assassination five days later.	Millions of immigrants flood into the US from Europe and Asia, fueling the age of cities. Baltimore is the USA's third busiest port of entry, with 1.2 million immigrants entering at the Locust Point piers.	Freed black men are given the vote, but the South's segregationist 'Jim Crow' laws (which remain until the 1960s) effectively disenfranchise African Americans from every meaningful sphere of daily life.

people and establishing the bedrock of American democracy. The Treaty of Paris formally recognized the 'United States of America.'

New York City functioned as the nation's capital from 1785 to 1790. State delegates gathered in Philadelphia in 1787 and drafted the Constitution: the US government was given a stronger federal center, with checks and balances between its three major branches. To guard against the abuse of centralized power, a citizen's Bill of Rights was approved in 1791.

Scots-Irish & the Wilderness Road

English settlers along the Atlantic coast may have established the country's governmental framework and its earliest traditions, but it's arguable that the Scots-Irish immigrants who arrived en masse during the 1700s came to represent America's id: self-sufficient, tough and often feisty.

Migrants from the lowlands of Scotland who settled in northern Ireland throughout the 1600s, the Scots-Irish were primarily tenant farmers. Many were also Presbyterians. In the early 1700s, to escape high rents and low pay, thousands began immigrating to America, many of them arriving in Philadelphia. The newcomers began traveling south in search of farmland, tracking the Allegheny and Blue Ridge mountains on the Wilderness Road, also known as the Great Wagon Road. From 1717 to 1775, a period known as the Great Migration, they – along with a number of German settlers – cleared the forests and built family farms, which stretched from Pennsylvania south through Maryland, Virginia, the Carolinas and into Georgia. By the start of the Revolutionary War, about 200,000 Scots-Irish had made America their home.

Civil War Films

....

Civil War (documentary; Ken Burns)
....
Glory (Edward Zwick)

Gods & Generals (Ronald Maxwell)
....
Gettysburg (Ronald Maxwell)
....
Gone With the Wind (Victor Fleming)

Today, the mountainous region settled by the Scots-Irish is known as Appalachia, with all of West Virginia and parts of western Virginia included in its unofficial boundaries. Though the remote region has battled everything from economic hardship to drug addiction, not to mention derogatory stereotypes associated with the isolated poor, it is home to rich cultural traditions celebrating family, hard work and the rugged but gorgeous landscape.

Civil War: Manassas to Appomattox

From 1861 to 1865, the Civil War fractured the nation, putting its very existence at risk. Numerous battlefields dot Virginia and Maryland, which saw much of the fighting. One reason for their central role? The location of the Mason-Dixon line, created in 1767 as a result of border disputes between Maryland, Delaware and Pennsylvania. The line eventually separated the industrial North from the agrarian, slave-holding South, which included Virginia.

The US Constitution hadn't ended slavery, but it did give Congress the power to approve (or not) slavery in new states. Public debates raged

1896	1912-1921	1919	1920
In Plessy versus Ferguson, the US Supreme Court rules that 'separate but equal' public facilities for blacks and whites are legal, arguing that the Constitution addresses only political, not social, equality.	During the West Virginia Mine Wars, clashes between miners and coal companies culminate in the Battle of Blair Mountain in 1921, the largest armed uprising in the US since the Civil War.	Bootlegging flourishes in the southern Appalachian Mountains after the passage of the 18th Amendment, which bans alcohol. The amendment is repealed in 1933.	The 19th Amendment to the Constitution grants women the right to vote.

constantly over the expansion of slavery, particularly since this shaped the balance of power between the industrial North and the agrarian South. Even many northern politicians feared that ending slavery with the stroke of a pen would be ruinous. Limit slavery, they reasoned, and in the competition with industry and free labor, slavery would wither without inciting a violent slave revolt – a possibility that was constantly feared. Indeed, in 1859, radical abolitionist John Brown tried (unsuccessfully) to spark such an uprising at Harpers Ferry, WV.

The economics of slavery were undeniable. In 1860, there were more than four million slaves in the US, most held by southern planters; these planters grew 75% of the world's cotton, accounting for over half of US exports. Thus, the Southern economy supported the nation's economy, and it required slaves.

In the South, even the threat of federal limits was too onerous to abide, and as President Lincoln took office, 11 states seceded from the Union and formed the Confederate States of America. The Mid-Atlantic area in particular split along its seams: Virginia seceded from the Union, while its impoverished western farmers, long resentful of genteel plantation owners, seceded from Virginia to form West Virginia. Maryland stayed in the Union, but its white slave owners rioted against Northern troops, while thousands of black Marylanders joined the Union Army.

War began in April 1861, when the Confederacy attacked Fort Sumter in Charleston, South Carolina. A month later, Richmond, VA, was selected as the capital of the new Confederacy. On July 21, 1861, Union and Confederate soldiers clashed at the First Battle of Bull Run (known in the South as First Manassas) in Northern Virginia, the first major land battle of the war. A surprise victory by the Confederate rebels erased any hopes of a quick conclusion to the war.

As fighting progressed, Lincoln recognized that if the war didn't end slavery outright, victory would be pointless. In 1863, his Emancipation Proclamation expanded the war's aims and freed all slaves. In April 1865, after abandoning Richmond and with prospects dimming as he retreated from Union forces, Confederate General Robert E Lee surrendered to Union General Ulysses S Grant in Appomattox, VA. The Union had been preserved, but at a staggering cost of more than 600,000 lives.

Political Biographies

Washington (Ron Chernow)

Thomas Jefferson (RB Bernstein)

Lincoln (David Herbert Donald)

Mornings on Horseback (David McCullough)

The Bridge (David Remnick)

Team of Rivals (Doris Kearns Goodwin)

HISTORY WORLD WARS, THE GREAT DEPRESSION & THE NEW DEAL

World Wars, the Great Depression & the New Deal

WWI saw a surge of immigration in Washington, DC. The administration of war had an unquenchable thirst for clerks, soldiers, nurses and other military support staff. By war's end, the population of the nation's capital was more than half a million.

1920s–1960s	1941–45	1954	1963
The '20s see the beginning of an African American cultural boom; U St, which eventually became home to more than 300 black businesses and entertainment options, is known as 'Black Broadway.'	America deploys 16 million troops and suffers 400,000 deaths in WWII. On D-Day (June 6, 1944), 19 of 30 soldiers from Bedford, VA, are killed, the highest per capita loss of any US community that day.	The Supreme Court rules that segregation in public schools is 'inherently unequal' and orders desegregation 'with all deliberate speed.' The fight to integrate schools spurs the Civil Rights movement.	Dr Martin Luther King Jr leads the Civil Rights march on the National Mall. He delivers his 'I Have a Dream' speech at Lincoln Memorial before a crowd of 200,000.

The 1920s brought prosperity to DC and other parts of the country, but the free-spending days wouldn't last. The stock market crash of 1929 heralded the dawn of the Great Depression, the severe economic downturn that had catastrophic implications for many Americans. As more and more lost their jobs and went hungry, people turned to Washington for help.

In 1932, Democrat Franklin D Roosevelt was elected president on the promise of a 'New Deal' to rescue the US from its crisis, which he did with resounding success. The Civilian Conservation Corps (CCC), also known as Roosevelt's Tree Army, hired young single men to build and improve state and national parks across the country. More than 1200 CCC workers built trails and laid the foundation for Skyline Drive at Shenandoah National Park, VA, which was officially established on December 26, 1935.

The Great Depression didn't really end until the arrival of WWII, when Washington, DC, again experienced enormous growth. A burgeoning organizational infrastructure supported the new national security state. The US Army's city-based civilian employee roll grew from 7000 to 41,000 in the first year of the war. The world's largest office building, the Pentagon, was built across the river as command headquarters. National Airport (today Ronald Reagan Washington National Airport) opened in 1941.

On December 7, 1941, Japan launched a surprise attack on Hawaii's Pearl Harbor, killing over 2000 Americans and sinking several battleships. Germany also declared war on the US, and America joined the Allied fight against Hitler and the Axis powers. From that moment, the US put almost its entire will and industrial prowess into the war effort. Fighting went on for more than two years in both the Pacific and in Europe.

The Allies dealt the fatal blow to Germany with the massive D-Day invasion of France on June 6, 1944. The impact of the invasion was acutely felt by the 3000 citizens of Bedford, VA. Thirty local boys were in the first wave of soldiers approaching Omaha Beach and 19 of them were killed in action – the highest per capita death toll for D-Day for any community in America.

Germany surrendered in May 1945. Nevertheless, Japan continued fighting. Newly elected President Harry Truman – ostensibly worried that a US invasion of Japan would lead to unprecedented carnage – chose to drop experimental atomic bombs, created by the government's top-secret Manhattan Project, on Hiroshima and Nagasaki in August 1945. The bombs devastated both cities, killing over 200,000 people. Japan surrendered days later, and the nuclear age was born.

1964	1969–71	1969	1972
Congress passes the Civil Rights Act, outlawing discrimination on the basis of race, color, religion, sex or national origin. First proposed by John F Kennedy, it was one of President Johnson's greatest achievements.	As the war in Vietnam claims thousands of American lives, many citizens come to Washington to protest. More than 500,000 march in 1969; protests continue in 1970 and 1971.	American astronauts land on the moon, fulfilling President Kennedy's unlikely 1961 promise to accomplish this feat within a decade. It's the culmination of the space race.	Five burglars working for President Nixon are arrested breaking into the Democratic campaign headquarters at the Watergate Hotel. The ensuing scandal and investigation leads to Nixon's resignation in 1974.

Civil Rights Movement

With its continent unscarred and its industry bulked up by WWII, America entered an era of growing affluence. However, African Americans remained segregated, poor and generally unwelcome at the party. Echoing the 19th-century abolitionist Frederick Douglass (who was born into slavery on the eastern shore of Maryland), the Southern Christian Leadership Coalition (SCLC), led by African American preacher Dr Martin Luther King Jr, aimed to end segregation and 'save America's soul'; to realize colorblind justice, racial equality and fairness of economic opportunity for all.

Beginning in the 1950s, King preached and organized nonviolent resistance in the form of bus boycotts, marches and sit-ins, mainly in the South. White authorities often met these protests with water hoses and police batons, and demonstrations sometimes dissolved into riots. Washington, DC, hosted key events in the national Civil Rights movement. In 1963 King led the March on Washington to lobby for passage of the Civil Rights Act. His stirring 'I Have a Dream' speech, delivered before 200,000 people on the steps of the Lincoln Memorial, was a defining moment of the campaign. With the passage of the 1964 Civil Rights Act, African Americans spurred a wave of legislation that swept away racist laws and laid the groundwork for a more just and equal society.

The assassination of King in Memphis in 1968, however, sent the nation reeling. Riots erupted in Washington, DC, Baltimore, MD, Wilmington, DE, and in more than 100 other American cities. DC exploded in two nights of riots and arson (centered on 14th and U Sts NW in the Shaw district). Twelve people died, over 1000 were injured, and hundreds of mostly African American-owned businesses were torched. White residents fled the city en masse, and downtown DC north of the Mall (especially the Shaw district) faded into decades of economic slump. The legacy of segregation has proved difficult to overcome over ensuing decades.

In an encouraging turn, Richmond, VA (former capital of the Confederacy) welcomed attorney Douglas Wilder to its Executive Mansion in 1989. Wilder was the first African American to be elected governor in the US.

NYC Activism

A spirit of activism has been strong in New York City since the 1800s, but the city really made its mark on social change in the 20th century. The modern LGBT rights movement was kickstarted in 1969 at New York City's Stonewall Inn, when drag queen Marsha P Johnson fought back against police officers harassing patrons at the gay bar. In the 1980s and '90s, the NYC HIV/AIDS activist group Act Up! fought tirelessly to stop a disease that was decimating their friends and family and being ignored by politicians at the time. They helped change the tide of the battle against the epidemic, saving thousands of lives in the process.

Forgotten-NY.com is Queens native Kevin Walsh's compendium of historical NYC, with not-found-elsewhere tales about everything from old subway stations to cemeteries.

1977-79	1989	1998	2001
After years of legal wrangling, New Jersey votes for casino gambling in 1977, and the first casino, Resorts, is completed in 1979, beginning a new era.	Attorney Douglas Wilder is elected governor of Virginia, becoming the country's first African American governor.	The Monica Lewinsky scandal breaks, with evidence of nine sexual encounters with the president. Bill Clinton becomes the first president since Andrew Johnson (in 1868) to be impeached.	On September 11, Al-Qaeda terrorists hijack four commercial airplanes, flying two into NYC's Twin Towers and one into the Pentagon (the fourth crashes in Pennsylvania); nearly 3000 people are killed.

Watergate

Washington, DC's most famous '70s scandal splashed across the world's newspapers when operatives of President Richard Nixon were arrested breaking into the Democratic National Committee headquarters at the Watergate Hotel. The ensuing cover-up and Nixon's disgraceful exit (in 1974, he became the first US president to resign from office) were not shining moments in presidential history.

September 11, 2001

On September 11, 2001, Islamic terrorists flew two hijacked planes into New York City's World Trade Center and another into the Pentagon in Washington, DC. A fourth plane crashes in Pennsylvania. This catastrophic attack united many Americans behind President George W Bush as he vowed revenge and declared a 'war on terror.' Bush soon attacked Afghanistan in an unsuccessful hunt for Al-Qaeda terrorist cells, then attacked Iraq in 2003 and toppled its anti-US dictator, Saddam Hussein. Meanwhile, Iraq descended into civil war. Following scandals and failures – torture photos from the US military prison at Abu Ghraib, the federal response in the aftermath of Hurricane Katrina and the inability to bring the Iraq War to a close – Bush's approval ratings reached historic lows in the second half of his presidency.

The White House: Obama & Trump

The 2008 election featured one of the most hotly debated presidential contests in American history. In the end, Barack Obama became the nation's first African American president. Obama had run on a platform of hope and change in an era of increasingly divisive American politics. Following the financial meltdown in 2008, the Obama administration pumped money into the flailing economy. He also took on the growing crisis in Afghanistan and the complicated issue of health care reform.

Obama's second term saw the country emerge from the Great Recession, as the president presided over a growing economy, rock-bottom gas prices and low unemployment. However, Congress put the screws on the federal budget, cutting spending and slashing jobs in Washington, DC. It also continued to meddle in the city's affairs, such as blocking a proposed ballot amendment to legalize retail marijuana sales.

The situation didn't improve in 2016, when the federal government shifted to the right after a hugely divisive election. Donald Trump took over in the White House, while Republicans took over both houses of Congress. Top of the new legislative agenda: cracking down on illegal immigration, dismantling Obama's health-care reforms and 'draining the swamp,' ie ridding the government of its old, business-as-usual practices.

2003	2008–09	2016	2017
After citing 'evidence' that Iraq possesses weapons of mass destruction, President George W Bush launches a preemptive war that will cost more than 4000 American lives and some $3 trillion.	Barack Obama becomes the first African American president; Vice President Joe Biden is from Wilmington, DE. The stock market crashes due to mismanagement by major American financial institutions.	After promising to put coal miners back to work, reality TV star Donald Trump wins almost 70% of the electoral vote in West Virginia. He's elected the 45th president (though not by popular vote).	In Washington, DC, an estimated 470,000 people attend the Women's March against the Trump administration.

People & Culture

The Mid-Atlantic is a compelling mix of big-city bankers and lawyers, DC legislators and lobbyists, small-town farmers and watermen, university students and beach bums, Democrats and Republicans. Southern hospitality is a highlight in the small towns of Virginia. Folks in the more insular small communities of West Virginia and the eastern shore of Maryland tend to warm up after checking you out first – just give a friendly hello to show you're harmless. Once you're in, the conversation flows.

Local Culture

The North–South tension long defined much of the central Mid-Atlantic, but the region has also swung between the cultures of aristocrats, miners, waterfolk, immigrants and the ever-changing rulers of Washington, DC. Since the Civil War, local economies have made the shift from agriculture and manufacturing to high technology and the servicing and staffing of the federal government.

Many African Americans settled this border region, either as slaves or escapees running for freedom in the North. Today African Americans still form the visible underclass of its major cities, but in the rough arena of the disadvantaged they compete with Latino immigrants, mainly from Central America. At the other end of the spectrum, ivory towers – in the form of world-class universities and research centers such as the National Institute of Health – attract intelligentsia from around the world. Local high schools are often packed with the children of scientists and consultants who staff some of the world's most prestigious think tanks.

All of this has spawned a culture that is, in turns, as sophisticated as a journalists' book club, as linked to the land as Virginia bluegrass festivals, and as hooked into the main vein of African American culture as Tupac Shakur, go-go, Baltimore club and DC Hardcore. And, of course, there's politics, a subject continually simmering under the surface here.

> According to the Pew Research Center, about a quarter of US adults (27%) say they think of themselves as spiritual but not religious. Dig into the numbers at www.pew research.org.

New York

According to stubbornly held stereotypes, New Yorkers differ from the denizens of the rest of the Mid-Atlantic. And their reputations frequently precede them. In New York City and Long Island, residents are known for their brash, no-nonsense attitudes. Hudson Valley, Catskills and Finger Lakes dwellers get pegged as earthy progressives, while those who call the north country home are regarded as more conservative. As with all generalizations, these oversimplified labels only scratch the surface of the diverse cultural veins that run through the state.

Progressive Roots

While parts of New York can seem quite conservative when compared to New York City, the state as a whole has a long history of progressive activism that has shaped attitudes and culture. There are many rural communities where the residents are generally committed to championing issues such as anti-racist and xenophobic activism, LGBT rights, union and workers' rights and environmental issues. Many newer farms in the state focus on organic, cruelty-free practices, as well as getting more people interested in sustainable and local food. All of this trickles down to culture in a variety of ways. Even small town dives brag about their fresh, locally sourced produce and it's not uncommon to see 'Everyone Welcome Here!' signs on establishments around the state. New Yorkers are generally happy to discuss issues even when there may be disagreements and you won't want for the sight of political lawn signs and bumper stickers while you drive around. It's important to keep in mind that the state's politics are particularly thorny, complicated and prone to corruption on both sides of the political aisle.

Queer Screen Classics

Torch Song Trilogy (1988)

The Boys in the Band (1970)

Paris Is Burning (1990)

Angels in America (2003)

Jeffrey (1995)

LGBT New Yorkers

New York City has long been seen as a safe haven for LGBT people from around the world. The liberal attitudes and diverse economic and cultural offerings fostered the growth of a large population of LGBT folks in the 20th century, especially concentrated in the West Village and Chelsea neighborhoods. HIV/AIDS was a huge blow to this community in the 1980s, but it weathered that storm and today remains a strong driving cultural force both in NYC and around the rest of the state. Several now-popular weekender destinations in the Hudson Valley owe part of their reputation to waves of LGBT home buyers that gradually changed the lay of the land. Other larger cities – Buffalo and Rochester – have their own longstanding LGBT communities. You'll also find strong representation in other smaller cities and towns, such as Albany and Ithaca.

Pennsylvania

In a country with an ever-widening gap between liberal blue and conservative red, purple Pennsylvania somehow embodies both ends of that political divide – as well as various internecine factions within those camps.

Pennsylvania Dutch

The Pennsylvania Dutch – a catch-all name for Lancaster County communities adhering to 'simple', low-tech lifestyles – are something of an anomaly amid the usual American urban–rural divide. The label is also dangerously simplistic: multiple schisms have split the community into countless ideological camps, ranging from hardcore Amish, who eschew all or most post-19th-century technology, to progressive Mennonites, who allow LGBT members to worship in church. There are 'simple' folks in Pennsylvania Dutch country who ride their horse and buggy to community meetings via GPS coordinates from a smart phone.

Even the term 'Pennsylvania Dutch' is a bit of a misnomer, referring to immigrants from Germany and Switzerland who migrated to Pennsylvania as religious refugees – 'Dutch' is a mistranslation of *Deutsch* (German). But beyond the theological and ideological divisions, all Pennsylvania Dutch communities emphasize modest dress, simple living, nonviolence and learning skilled trades.

Pennsyltucky

Few terms for Pennsylvania are used with both such affection and derision as 'Pennsyltucky.' This portmanteau of 'Pennsylvania' and 'Kentucky' refers to the deep-red, rural Bible Belt outside of the urban centers of Pittsburgh and Philadelphia (and to a lesser degree, Erie and the southeastern suburbs). Rural Pennsylvania is often deeply conservative and, at first glance, racially homogeneous, and Christianity is worn proudly on the sleeve. The area's Christian higher education institutions are known for feeding graduates into the ranks of the nation's Christian-conservative politicians.

Hunting and firearms hold great cultural sway in rural Pennsylvania; some public school districts expect many students to be absent at the start of deer-hunting season. While we want to avoid historical essentialism, there's a long legacy of resentment towards government 'intrusion' in western Pennsylvania – the Alleghenies were the center of the 1791 Whiskey Rebellion (p402), an armed insurrection that was provoked by the taxation of spirits and enraged the citizens of the then-frontier.

Yet the label Pennsyltucky belies a more complicated reality. The area's agricultural and manufacturing sectors, long a bedrock of local economies, have greatly benefited from undocumented labor, and even in isolated mountain towns you may see a rickety taco stand providing sustenance for a Latino work force. In addition, some of the rural resort areas near the Delaware Water Gap and the eastern seaboard cities have become politically liberal 'colonies' for migrants and retirees from big cities, while the city of Erie, in Pennsylvania's nominally conservative northwest, leans democratic.

New Jersey

As a fulcrum of industry and a font of raw materials, natural resources and jobs, New Jersey has always attracted settlers, from both inside and outside the United States. To this day it continues to be a cultural melting pot. Racially, the state is approximately 59% white, 18% Latino, 13% African American and 8% Asian.

Jewish Population

New Jersey has the second-largest Jewish population in the US, trailing only New York. Among its more notable citizens was department-store pioneer Louis Bamberger, who in addition to revolutionizing the way Americans shop, co-founded the Institute of Advanced Study at Princeton, a haven for Jewish scientists fleeing Germany in the 1930s. Among them: a fellow named Albert Einstein. Newark-born Philip Roth, the grandson of Jewish immigrants, went on to win the American Book Award and the Pulitzer Prize. Paul Auster, born in Newark a generation after Roth, has been honored abroad by France and Spain for his numerous novels.

Lifestyle

In general, the eastern USA has one of the world's highest standards of living, though there are some huge variances by region. Maryland sits near the top of the heap with a median household income of $73,760 (based on 2016 data); West Virginia dwells at the opposite end of the scale at $44,354. These amounts are in the high–low range not just for the Mid-Atlantic, but for the nation, upholding the pattern in which households in the Northeast earn the most, while those in the South earn the least.

High-school graduation rates are strong across the region, with 91% of Virginia high-school students graduating in four years. Rates are only slightly lower for high-school students in Maryland, Delaware and West Virginia. Washington, DC, has one of the lowest rates, with only 68% of high schoolers earning a degree after four years. But DC is not an intellectual vacuum (cue Congress jokes here): there are 20 colleges and universities packed into the capital city, many of them nationally acclaimed.

Sports

What really draws Americans together (sometimes slathered in blue body paint or with foam-rubber cheese wedges on their heads) is sports. In spring and summer there's baseball nearly every day, in fall and winter there's football, and through the long nights of winter there's plenty of basketball to keep the adrenaline going – those are the big three sports. Major League Soccer (MLS) is attracting an ever-increasing following. Ice hockey, once favored only in northern climes, has fans throughout the area. Women's basketball and soccer are also gaining traction nationwide, with multiple teams that play in pro leagues.

StoryCorps has collected and archived more than 75,000 interviews from people across America; they're preserved in the Library of Congress. Listen to folks tell their stories of discovery, family, identity, love and much more at www.storycorps. org.

ICONIC SPORTING VENUES

Yankee Stadium, NYC (p81) The Bronx's fabled baseball field, steeped in history and the ghost of Babe Ruth.

Madison Square Garden, NYC (p110) Not only do the Knicks dribble at the 'mecca of basketball,' but Ali boxed here and Elvis rocked here.

Camden Yards, Baltimore (p319) Opened in 1992, spurring the development of more fan-friendly and baseball-only ballparks across the country.

Baseball

Despite high salaries and its biggest stars being dogged by steroid rumors, baseball remains America's favorite pastime. It may not command the same TV viewership (and subsequent advertising dollars) as football, but baseball has 162 games over a season versus 16 for football.

Besides, baseball is better live than on TV – being at the ballpark on a sunny day, sitting in the bleachers with a beer and hot dog, and indulging in the seventh-inning stretch, when the entire park erupts in a communal sing-along of 'Take Me Out to the Ballgame.' The playoffs, held every October, still deliver excitement and unexpected champions.

Tickets to games are relatively inexpensive – seats average about $25 at most stadiums – and are easy to get for most games. Minor-league baseball games cost half as much, and can be even more fun, with lots of audience participation, stray chickens and dogs running across the field, and wild throws from the pitcher's mound. For information, see www.milb.com.

Football

Football is big, physical, and rolling in dough. With the shortest season and least number of games of any of the major sports, every match takes on the emotion of an epic battle, where the results matter and an unfortunate injury can deal a lethal blow to a team's playoff chances. It's also the toughest US sport, played in fall and winter in all manner of rain, sleet and snow. The rabidly popular Super Bowl is pro football's championship match, held in late January or early February. The other 'bowl' games are college football's title matches, held on and around New Year's Day.

In DC, the Washington Redskins have been disappointing fans for 25 years, having won their last Super Bowl in 1992; their neighbors, the Baltimore Ravens, won the national championship in 2013.

One dominant college football rivalry in the southern Mid-Atlantic is between the University of Virginia and Virginia Tech. And for years, students at West Virginia University in Morgantown would burn couches outdoors after football (and other) victories, but local police have cracked down on that tradition in recent years.

Best Sports Sites

Baseball:
www.mlb.com

Basketball:
www.nba.com

Football:
www.nfl.com

Hockey:
www.nhl.com

Car racing:
www.nascar.com

Soccer:
www.mlssoccer.com

Basketball

The most well-known teams in the region include the New York Knicks (where celebrities sit courtside despite a losing team on the court in recent years), the Washington Wizards and the Philadelphia 76'ers. The New York Liberty and the Washington Mystics are part of the Women's National Basketball Association.

College basketball also draws millions of fans, especially every spring when the March Madness playoffs roll around; it culminates in the Final Four, when the remaining quartet of teams competes for a spot in the championship game. The Cinderella stories and unexpected outcomes rival the pro league for excitement. The games are widely televised and bet upon – this is when Las Vegas bookies earn their keep.

Arts & Architecture

Filled with museums, galleries and concert halls, New York City and Washington, DC, anchor the Mid-Atlantic culturally and intellectually. Midsized cities like Philadelphia, PA, Richmond, VA, and Baltimore, keep the cultural scene vibrant across the region with innovative small museums, engaged local theaters and fantastic music venues, many of them outdoors.

Art

New York City: An Art Heavyweight

That New York claims some of the world's mightiest art museums attests to its enviable artistic pedigree. From Pollock and Rothko to Warhol and Rauschenberg, the city has nourished many of America's greatest artists and artistic movements.

Birth of an Arts Hub

In almost all facets of the arts, New York really got its sea legs in the early 20th century, when the city attracted and retained a critical mass of thinkers, artists, writers and poets. It was at this time that the home-grown art scene began to take shape. In 1905, photographer (and husband of Georgia O'Keeffe) Alfred Stieglitz opened 'Gallery 291,' a Fifth Ave space that provided a vital platform for American artists and helped establish photography as a credible art form.

In the 1940s, an influx of cultural figures fleeing the carnage of WWII saturated the city with fresh ideas – and New York became an important cultural hub. Peggy Guggenheim established the Art of this Century gallery on 57th St, a space that helped launch the careers of painters such as Jackson Pollock, Willem de Kooning and Robert Motherwell. These Manhattan-based artists came to form the core of the abstract-expressionist movement (also known as the New York School), creating an explosive and rugged form of painting that changed the course of modern art as we know it.

Current Scene

Today, the arts scene is mixed and wide-ranging. The major institutions – the Metropolitan Museum of Art (p72), the Museum of Modern Art (p65), the Whitney Museum of American Art (p64), the Guggenheim Museum (p73), the Met Breuer (p73) and the Brooklyn Museum (p77) – deliver major retrospectives covering everything from Renaissance portraiture to contemporary installation. The New Museum of Contemporary Art (p63), on the Lower East Side, is more daring, while countless smaller institutions, among them the excellent Bronx Museum (www.bronxmuseum.org), El Museo del Barrio (www.elmuseo.org) and the Studio Museum (www.studiomuseum.org) in Harlem, focus on narrower slices of art history.

New York remains the world's gallery capital, with more than 800 spaces showcasing all kinds of art all over the city. The blue-chip dealers can be found clustered in Chelsea and the Upper East Side. Galleries

In January 2018, the Metropolitan Museum of Art (p72) announced that it would begin charging admission to out-of-state visitors for the first time since 1970. The decision was a controversial one: while many recognized the museum's financial bind – only 8% of its income comes from government funds – others mourned the loss of the open-door policy that allowed universal access to a world-class art collection.

that showcase emerging and midcareer artists dot the Lower East Side, while prohibitive rents have pushed the city's more emerging and experimental scenes further out, with current hot spots including Harlem and the Brooklyn neighborhoods of Bushwick, Greenpoint, Clinton Hill and Bedford-Stuyvesant (Bed-Stuy).

Pennsylvania

Culture Capitals

Pennsylvania's two largest cities have always had their fingers on the cultural pulses of the eastern and western halves of the state. Their surrounding geographies have also had an enormous impact on the arts – the rushing streams of the Brandywine Valley and high cliffs of the Delaware Water Gap have had an impact on Philadelphia landscape painters, while the ruggedness of the Alleghenies has influenced Pittsburgh artists.

Philadelphia, a port city that has always been home to some of America's aristocratic elite, is well known for her excellent, traditionally oriented fine-arts institutions, such as the Philadelphia Museum of Art and the Barnes Collection. On the other hand, the City of Brotherly Love is a major port and point of entry for immigrants, and of late has been seen as a cheap alternative to New York City. This has prompted the genesis of an underground urban arts scene that underlies one of the more exciting arts scenes on the East Coast, led by creatives like Uncool Chuck and body painter Nebulus Flair.

Andy Warhol is the most famous artistic name to ever be associated with his hometown of Pittsburgh, which is a bit ironic considering Warhol left the 'Burgh for New York City and never really turned around. And yet: something about the Steel City – maybe the cheap cost of living and large empty spaces? – has made this town an exciting outpost of the contemporary arts scene, best accessed by institutions like the Mattress Factory.

Just outside Pittsburgh in the Laurel Highlands, you'll find two masterpieces by Frank Lloyd Wright, the nation's most iconic 20th-century architect. Kentuck Knob and Fallingwater are exemplars of the Prairie School of architecture, which emphasized clean lines, flat roofs and integration with nature.

Literature

Washington, DC's literary legacy is, not surprisingly, deeply entwined with US political history. The city's best-known early literature consists of writings and books that hammered out the machinery of US democracy. From Thomas Jefferson's *Notes on the State of Virginia* to James Madison's *The Federalist Papers* and Abraham Lincoln's historic speeches and proclamations, this literature fascinates modern readers.

Henry Adams (1838–1918), grandson of President John Adams, wrote the Pulitzer Prize–winning autobiography, *The Education of Henry Adams,* which provides a fascinating insider's account of Washington high society. Throughout the 20th century, Washington literature remained a political beast, defined by works such as Carl Bernstein and Bob Woodward's *All the President's Men* (1974).

Elsewhere in the region, Virginia-bred writer Tom Wolfe penned New Journalism classics *The Electric Kool-Aid Acid Test* and *The Right Stuff,* as well as the social-commentary novel *The Bonfire of The Vanities.* Thriller writer David Baldacci is a Virginian. Born in Newport News, VA, novelist William Styron wrote *The Confessions of Nat Turner,* an acclaimed fictionalized account of an 1831 Virginia slave revolt. Maryland writers include Tom Clancy, master of the spy thriller, and romance writer Nora Roberts.

Music

New York City: A Musical Metropolis

This is the city where jazz players such as Ornette Coleman, Miles Davis and John Coltrane pushed the limits of improvisation in the 1950s. It's where various Latin sounds – from cha-cha-cha to rumba to mambo – came together to form the hybrid we now call salsa, where folk singers such as Bob Dylan and Joan Baez crooned protest songs in coffeehouses, and where bands such as the New York Dolls and the Ramones tore up the stage in Manhattan's gritty downtown. It was the ground zero of disco. And it was the cultural crucible where hip-hop was nurtured and grew – then exploded.

The city remains a magnet for musicians to this day. The local indie-rock scene is especially vibrant: groups including the Yeah Yeah Yeahs, LCD Soundsystem and Animal Collective all emerged in NYC. Williamsburg is at the heart of the action, packed with clubs and bars, plus there are indie record labels and internet radio stations. The best venues for rock include the Music Hall of Williamsburg (www.musichallofwilliamsburg.com) and the Brooklyn Bowl (p110), as well as Manhattan's Bowery Ballroom (www.boweryballroom.com).

Washington, DC: Jazz to Go-Go

In the early 20th century, segregation of entertainment venues meant that black Washington had to create its own arts scene. Jazz, big band and swing flourished at clubs and theaters around DC, particularly in the Shaw district. Greats such as Duke Ellington, Pearl Bailey, Shirley Horn, Johnny Hodges and Ben Webster all got their start in the clubs of U St NW. Today, this district has been reborn, with new clubs and theaters opening in its historic buildings.

Go-go, which originated in the city in the 1970s, is an infectiously rhythmic dance music combining elements of funk, rap, soul and Latin percussion. These days, go-go soul blends with hip-hop and reggae's rhythm.

Mountain Music & Bluegrass

English immigrants brought their violins to America in the Colonial era, and their 'fiddles' soon joined forces with the African banjo. The music traveled west, eventually blending with the ballads and songs carried south by Scots-Irish and German settlers moving south from Pennsylvania along the Great Wagon Road. What emerged over time in the secluded Appalachian Mountains was fiddle-and-banjo hillbilly, also known

COUNTRY ROADS, TAKE ME HOME

Almost Heaven, West Virginia...Yep, even if you spend only a few hours in West Virginia, we guarantee you'll hear John Denver's catchy ode to the Mountain State drifting from a speaker somewhere. Penned by Denver and co-writers Bill Danoff and Taffy Nivert, the song reached number two on the Billboard charts in 1971 and put Denver on the country road to stardom. Although the song references places typically associated with Virginia – the Blue Ridge Mountains and the Shenandoah River – both are found in West Virginia, if only minimally (and, well, there is some debate about the Blue Ridge). Some argue that Denver really meant west-ern Virginia but changed the wording to protect the cadence. But the fact is, no one seems to care. The legislature made Denver's hit one of the state's official songs, and Mountaineers at West Virginia University belt out the tune at the end of every home football game. And the hashtag promoted by the state's tourism office? #AlmostHeaven, natch. So crank up the radio, roll down the car window and sing along. Take me home...

as old-time mountain music. Bluegrass, which allows electric amplification and spotlights prowess on individual instruments, soon followed. The genre known today as 'country music' is directly influenced by the sounds of Appalachia.

You can hear mountain music and bluegrass along the Crooked Road musical heritage trail in Virginia and in music venues across West Virginia. Virginia's Carter Family – who in later decades would receive the accolade 'First Family of Country Music' – became a household name after the Bristol Sessions in Bristol, VA, in 1927. This recording session would pave the way for their music to be shared with the world.

Architecture

New York

The trajectory of New York's architectural development is deeply rooted in the immigrant communities who have made the state their home and the economic boom that swept through the state after the construction of the Erie Canal in 1825. There are few corners of the state that do not have some kind of architectural claim to fame, and despite the pride surrounding New York's many heritage buildings, exciting new developments in home and commercial design are typically embraced.

Reaching Skyward

By the time New York settled into the 20th century, elevators and steel-frame engineering had allowed the city to grow up – literally. This period saw a building boom of skyscrapers, starting with Cass Gilbert's neo-Gothic 57-story Woolworth Building, built in 1913. To this day it remains one of the 50 tallest buildings in the United States.

Others soon followed. In 1930, the Chrysler Building (p69), the 77-story art deco masterpiece designed by William Van Alen, became the world's tallest structure. The following year, the record was broken by the Empire State Building (p69), a clean-lined moderne monolith crafted from Indiana limestone. Its spire was meant to be used as mooring mast for dirigibles (airships) – an idea that made for good publicity, but which proved to be impractical and unfeasible.

Washington, DC

Washington's architecture and city design are the products of its founding fathers and city planners, who intended to construct a capital city befitting a powerful nation. The early architecture of Washington, DC, was shaped by two influences: Pierre Charles L'Enfant's 1791 city plan, and the infant nation's desire to prove to European powers that its capital possessed political and artistic sophistication rivaling the ancient, majestic cities of the Continent.

L'Enfant Plan & Federal Period

The L'Enfant plan imposed a street grid marked by diagonal avenues, roundabouts and grand vistas. L'Enfant had in mind the magisterial boulevards of Europe. To highlight the primacy of the city's political buildings, he intended that no building would rise higher than the Capitol. This rule rescued DC from the dark, skyscraper-filled fate of most modern American cities.

In an effort to rival European cities, Washington's early architects – many of them self-taught 'gentlemen architects' – depended heavily upon the Classic Revival and Romantic Revival styles, with their ionic columns and marble facades. Federal-style row houses dominated contemporary domestic architecture, and still line the streets of Capitol Hill and Georgetown.

Conspiracy theories abound about the secret symbols planted in the nation's capital by its masonic architects. The evidence: draw lines along the avenues between major DC points and you get key Masonic symbols – the pentagram, square and compass. To delve deeper, read *The Secrets of Masonic Washington* by James Wasserman.

NYC: Must-See Buildings
....
Chrysler Building (Midtown)
....
Grand Central Terminal (Midtown)
....
Morris-Jumel Mansion (Washington Heights)
....
Empire State Building (Midtown)
....
Temple Emanu-El (Upper East Side)
....
New Museum of Contemporary Art (Lower East Side)

Landscapes & Wildlife

Mountains, rivers, forests, marshes, swamps and sandy coasts – you're spoiled for choice when it comes to scenic backdrops in the Mid-Atlantic. On footpaths, scenic byways and canoe trails across the region, you *will* see wildlife, from red foxes to black bears. You just need to get away from the urban centers – though usually you don't have to go far. State and national parks, dedicated to the conservation of the wilderness of the East, welcome you.

Landscapes

The eastern USA is a land of temperate, deciduous forests, and contains the ancient Appalachian Mountains, a low range that parallels the Atlantic Ocean. Between the mountains and the coast lies the country's most populated, urbanized region, particularly along the city-lined north-south corridor stretching from Boston south to New York City, Philadelphia, Baltimore and Washington, DC.

Wetlands, marshes and sandy beaches hug the Mid-Atlantic coast. Assateague Island, off the coasts of Maryland and Virginia, is a barrier island marked by sand dunes, salt marshes and maritime forests.

Geologists believe that roughly 460 million years ago the Appalachian Mountains were the highest on earth – higher even than the Himalayas are today.

New York: Meadowlands

Only 7 miles west of Manhattan, the Meadowlands is one of the largest wetlands ecosystems in the United States. Known for its ecological diversity, nearly 40% of the country's 800 bird species pass through or live here. And, of course, it was a dumping ground for every waste product you can imagine during the 19th and 20th centuries.

Long-term restoration projects by the Fish & Wildlife Service, as well as activist groups like Hackensack Riverkeeper, are slowly returning the area to a cleaner and more useful place. Many use it for kayaking and canoeing (swimming's still a bad idea), and it's hoped that one day the fish and crabs will be safe to eat.

Robert Sullivan's entertaining *The Meadowlands: Wilderness Adventures at the Edge of a City* is a witty book on one man's travails by canoe through the Hackensack Delta. Jim Wright's *The Nature of the Meadowlands*, published in conjunction with the New Jersey Meadowlands Commission, is a lovely picture book that tells the story in a more straightforward way.

New York: Mountain Ranges

Two mountain ranges define the landscape of upstate New York. In the north, the Adirondacks are a circle of 46 peaks, the highest being Mt Marcy at 5344ft. The fir and spruce forests that cover the slopes provide great coverage for the miles of hiking trails that snake up and down the region. Up in the range you'll find high altitude lakes, frozen solid in the winter and pristine blue in the summer.

To the southwest, the Catskills are known more for the leisure culture that was cultivated in the quaint towns and enormous lodges that dot their slopes. The mountains don't have the same rugged appeal as their larger neighbors to the north; instead you'll find pine-tree-covered hills and valleys cut through with winding seasonal roads perfect for taking in the incredible vistas.

New Jersey: Pine Barrens

So named by early settlers because they couldn't get traditional crops to grow, the 2000-square-miles (1.4 million acres) Pine Barrens.Pines are in fact a flourishing and unique ecosystem, and not somewhere to be rushed through en route to the Shore or Philadelphia.

The barrens were the site of murderous mayhem in both *The Sopranos* and *Boardwalk Empire*, but it is the living things like the pitch pine, cedar and oak that thrive in the sandy soils that make the Pines what they are. The Pine Barrens includes dwarf or 'pgymy' forests where the trees grow to only 4ft to 10ft in height (two are near Warren Grove and called the East Plains and West Plains).

The oldest and deepest aquifers in the state are here, because the loamy soil drains quickly. Joseph Wharton bought huge tracts of land here in the late 1800s, hoping to sell the water to Philadelphia; subsequent legislation, thankfully, prevented that.

The 1967 book *The Pine Barrens* by Princeton-born author John McPhee brought attention to the area again, and political pressure was brought to bear on those wanting to develop a massive airport here. Brendan Byrne was the New Jersey governor when much of the legislation protecting the Pines went into effect, and hence one of the state forests is named for him.

Pennsylvania: The Poconos

The most famous mountain range in the state is a favorite weekend spot for visitors from NYC, Philadelphia and beyond. Tourists come for many reasons: stunning views, brilliant fall foliage and the sheer, raw beauty of the Delaware Water Gap, a national park that marks the place where the Delaware River cuts a gorge through the mountains and separates Pennsylvania from New Jersey and New York. Beyond the obvious appeal of the mountains are flat tow paths and railway trails that follow former public right-of-ways. You can walk or cycle along these routes, many of which pass places that were integral to the formation of the USA, without having to worry about serious (or any) elevation gain.

Western Pennsylvania & the Pennsylvania Wilds

The Allegheny Mountains once formed the western frontier of the United States, and even today there are isolated mountain towns out in these valleys and hollows that seem to stand outside of time. The Laurel Highlands make for an interesting, chic escape from Pittsburgh. Pittsburgh itself is both cut through and surrounded by mountains and rivers; few cities seem so inextricably tied to their geography.

Head into the northwest corner of the state and you'll find the entire area blanketed by the half million acres of the Allegheny National Forest. West of here, one enters the Pennsylvania Wilds, a sparsely populated borderland that is on the edge of New York and is webbed with dozens of gorges, including the Pine Creek Gorge, ambitiously referred to as the 'Pennsylvania Grand Canyon.'

The eastern USA holds eight national sea-shores (including Assateague Island National Seashore in Maryland, and Virginia and Fire Island in New York), four national lakeshores, and 10 national rivers (including New River Gorge in West Virginia). The National Park Service (www.nps.gov) has the lowdown.

West Virginia

Mountainous West Virginia is home to two landscapes more commonly seen in northern climes. The Cranberry Glades botanical area protects acidic wetlands known as bogs; this spongy terrain is comprised of partially decayed plants known as peat. The Dolly Sods Wilderness is a high plateau topped by windswept, alpine plains littered with boulders and shrubby plant life.

Wildlife

For your best chance of seeing wildlife, travel to the region's state and national parks and its wildlife refuges. Virginia's Shenandoah National Park is home to more than 50 species of mammals, including the frequently-seen woodchucks, skunks, gray squirrels and white-tailed deer.

Land Mammals

Black Bears

Despite a decline in numbers, black bears prowl most parts of the region, especially in the Blue Ridge Mountains across Maryland, West Virginia and Virginia. Males can stand 7ft tall and weigh 550lb – but that depends on when you encounter them. In autumn they weigh up to 30% more than when they emerge from hibernation in the spring. Although they enjoy an occasional meaty snack, black bears usually fill their bellies with berries and other vegetation. They're opportunistic, adaptable and curious animals and can survive on very small home ranges. As their forests diminish, they're occasionally seen traipsing through nearby populated areas.

Deer

The white-tailed deer can be found everywhere in the region, from top to bottom. If you spend any time exploring the Blue Ridge Parkway and Skyline Drive in Shenandoah National Park, you will likely see a few deer nibbling grass beside the roadside.

Reptiles

There are 26 species of reptiles found in Shenandoah National Park, including snakes, turtles and one type of lizard. You'll find salamanders, snakes, toads and turtles in Bombay Hook National Wildlife Refuge on the Delaware coast.

ENVIRONMENTAL ISSUES: FRACKING

Pennsylvania used to be one of the major oil, gas and lumber states in the country, but the focus of resource extraction has gradually moved west. Even as this has happened, there have been numerous attempts to 'frack' – use pressurized liquid to fracture rock – to access more local gas reserves. These attempts have been vociferously opposed by local environmental groups in the state. The documentary *Gasland* explores some of the issues surrounding fracking from, initially, a Pennsylvania perspective.

Methane has become a serious greenhouse-gas issue in the state. The old jokes trace the origin of methane to cow flatulence, but humans produce the gas as well – and not just from our rear ends. Drilling or fracking in the 95%-methane Marcellus Shale could release enormous amounts of the gas, which is 80 times more damaging to the climate than carbon dioxide

On the plus side, a glut of private preserves operated by groups like the Nature Conservancy and local equivalents seem to be opening across the state. These small, private concessions are capable of protecting thousands of acres of land at a time, and often operate with the support of Pennsylvania's considerably active hunting community.

Snakes

There are three species of venomous snakes in Virginia – timber rattlesnakes, copperheads and water moccasins. Copperheads are found across the state. In addition to copperheads, Shenandoah National Park is home to timber rattlesnakes. Running into either species in the park is uncommon. If you do see one, give it space and don't pester it. You'll find timber rattlesnakes and copperheads in Maryland and West Virginia. Copperheads reside in Delaware but are rare.

Turtles

There are four species of turtles in Shenandoah National Park. The eastern box turtle is the one most commonly seen by visitors – check meadows and fields.

The diamondback terrapin is the Maryland state reptile and the mascot of the University of Maryland. They live in salt marshes and other brackish habitats along the East Coast. Terrapins have grayish skin, marked by black streaks and spots, and distinctive brown shells covered with diamond-shaped growths.

Birds

The bald eagle, the USA's national symbol since 1782, is the only eagle unique to North America. Its wingspan can reach more than 6.5ft across. The eagle has come off the endangered species list, having made a remarkable comeback from a low of 417 breeding pairs in 1963 to almost 9800 pairs today (that's in the lower 48 states; another 30,000-plus live in Alaska). You can see them along the James River, near the Blue Ridge Mountains and in Richmond, VA. You can also spot them in Blackwater National Wildlife Refuge on the eastern shore of Maryland.

Blackwater is one of several national wildlife refuges along the Mid-Atlantic coast. The refuges serve as stopovers for migrating wildfowl, such as ducks and geese, as well as shorebirds.

New Jersey is a birder's paradise; expect to see everything from shorebirds along the Atlantic Ocean and riverine waterways to birds of prey soaring over the Highlands, as well as thousands of warblers passing through on their spring or fall migration. A common sight is the American goldfinch, a bright yellow species that is the official state bird. Nearly 500 species have been recorded in the state, and Cape May in the far south in an international birding destination.

Winner of the 2015 Pulitzer Prize for nonfiction, *The Sixth Extinction* by Elizabeth Kolbert examines why species are disappearing from the planet at an alarming rate. It examines everything from the collapse in the population of golden frogs in the Panamanian rainforest to mass bat die-offs in Vermont, near the author's home.

Survival Guide

Directory A–Z

Accessible Travel

If you have a physical disability, the USA can be an accommodating place. The Americans with Disabilities Act (ADA) requires that public buildings, private buildings built after 1993 (including hotels, restaurants, theaters and museums) and public transit be wheelchair accessible. However, call ahead to confirm. Some local tourist offices publish detailed accessibility guides.

Phone companies offer relay operators, available via teletypewriter (TTY) numbers, for the hearing impaired. Most banks provide ATM instructions in Braille and via earphone jacks for hearing-impaired customers. Major airlines, Greyhound buses and Amtrak trains will assist travelers with disabilities; describe your needs when making reservations at least 48 hours in advance. Service animals (guide dogs) are allowed to accompany passengers; bring documentation.

Some car rental agencies, such as Budget and Hertz, offer hand-controlled vehicles and vans with wheelchair lifts at no extra charge, but you must reserve well in advance. Wheelchair Getaways (www.wheelchairget aways.com) rents accessible vans throughout the USA. In many cities and towns, public buses are accessible to wheelchair riders and will 'kneel' if you are unable to use the steps; just let the driver know that you need the lift or ramp.

Most cities have taxi companies with at least one accessible van, though you'll have to call ahead. Cities with underground transportation have varying levels of facilities such as elevators for passengers needing assistance – DC has the best network (every station has an elevator), while NYC has elevators in about a quarter of its stations.

Many national and some state parks and recreation areas have wheelchair-accessible paved, graded-dirt or boardwalk trails. US citizens and permanent residents with permanent disabilities are entitled to a free 'America the Beautiful' Access Pass: see www.nps.gov/findapark/passes.htm for details.

For tips and insight on traveling with a disability, check out online posts by Martin Heng, Lonely Planet's Accessible Travel Manager: twitter.com/martin_heng. Download Lonely Planet's free Accessible Travel guides from http://lptravel.to/AccessibleTravel.

Disabled Sports USA (www.dis abledsportsusa.org) Offers sport, adventure and recreation programs for those with disabilities. Publishes *Challenge* magazine.

Flying Wheels Travel (www. flyingwheelstravel.com) A full-service travel agency, highly recommended for those with mobility issues or chronic illness.

Mobility International USA (www.miusa.org) Advises USA-bound travelers on mobility issues, and promotes the global participation of people with disabilities in international exchange and travel programs.

New York City

Much of the city is accessible with curb cuts for wheelchair users. All major sites (the Met, the Guggenheim, and Lincoln Center) are accessible. Some, but not all, Broadway theaters are accessible.

Only about 100 of New York's 468 subway stations are fully accessible. In general, bigger stations have access, such as West 4th St, 14th St-Union Sq, 34th St-Penn Station, 42nd St-Port Authority Terminal, 59th St-Columbus Circle, and 66th St-Lincoln Center. For a list of accessible subway stations, visit http://web.mta.info/accessibility/stations.htm. Also visit www.nycgo.com/accessibility.

All of NYC's MTA buses are wheelchair accessible, and are often a better option than negotiating cramped subway stations. The city also provides paratransit buses for getting around town for the same price as a subway fare, though these aren't very practical as you must order them 24 hours in advance. Call **Access-a-Ride** (📞877-337-2017) to request transport.

More practical is simply ordering an accessible

taxi through **Accessible Dispatch** (☑646-599-9999; http://accessibledispatch. org); there's also an app that allows you to request the nearest available service.

Another excellent resource is the **Big Apple Greeter** (☑212-669-8198; www.bigapplegreeter.org) **FREE** program, which has more than 50 volunteers on staff with physical disabilities who are happy to show off their corner of the city.

Washington, DC

DC is well equipped for travelers with disabilities:

➡ Most museums and major sights are wheelchair accessible, as are most large hotels and restaurants.

➡ All Metro trains and buses are accessible to people in wheelchairs. All Metro stations have elevators, and guide dogs are allowed on trains and buses.

➡ All DC transit companies offer travel discounts for disabled travelers.

➡ Hindrances to wheelchair users include buckled-brick sidewalks in the historic blocks of Georgetown and Capitol Hill, but sidewalks in most other parts of DC are in good shape.

➡ All Smithsonian museums have free wheelchair loans and can arrange special tours for hearing-impaired visitors. See www.si.edu/ visit/visitorswithdisabilities.

Accommodations

Peak season is generally May to September, when lodging and campsites along the coast and in mountain parks can book up months in advance. Peak months at ski resorts are typically January and February.

B&Bs A good choice near historic sites.

Cabins & Cottages Cabins are abundant near the Blue Ridge Mountains; find cottages along the Delaware coast and near Virginia Beach.

Historic Inns Well done in small cities in the foothills of the Blue Ridge Mountains and near battle-fields and historic sights.

Hostels Available in larger cities and near the Appalachian Trail and the C&O towpath.

Hotels Found across the region; there's a wide range (including boutique hotels) in NYC, DC, Philadelphia, PA, northern Virginia, Baltimore, MD, and Richmond, VA.

Motels Find gems in touristy regions along the coast and in the mountain foothills.

B&Bs & Inns

These accommodations vary from small, comfy houses with shared baths (least expensive) to romantic, historic homes and mansions with private baths (most expensive). Those focusing on upscale romance may discourage children. Inns and B&Bs often require a minimum stay of two or three days on weekends, and reservations are essential. Always call ahead to confirm bathroom arrangements and policies regarding kids, pets, smoking etc.

Camping

Campsites at national and state parks typically come in three types:

Primitive Free to $10 per night; no facilities.

Basic $10 to $20; with toilets, drinking water, fire pits and picnic tables.

Developed $20 to $50; with more amenities such as showers, barbecue grills, recreational vehicle (RV) sites with hookups etc.

Make reservations for national parks and other federal lands through www.recreation.gov. Camping is usually limited to 14 days and can be reserved up to six months in advance. For some state park

---

424

campgrounds, you can make bookings through ReserveAmerica (www.reserveamerica.com).

Most privately owned campgrounds are geared to RVs, but will also have a small section available for tent campers. Expect amenities including swimming pools, laundry facilities, convenience stores and bars. Kampgrounds of America (www.koa.com) is a national network of private campgrounds; their camping cabins have air-conditioning and kitchens.

Hostels

Hostelling International USA (www.hiusa.org) runs several hostels in the Mid-Atlantic. Most have gender-segregated dorms, a few private rooms, shared baths and a communal kitchen. Overnight fees for dorm beds range from $30 to $55. You don't have to be a member, but non-members pay a slightly higher rate. Reservations are accepted (you can book online).

Hotels

Hotels in all categories typically include cable TV, wi-fi, private baths and a simple continental breakfast. Many midrange properties provide minibars, microwaves, hairdryers and swimming pools, while top-end hotels add concierge services, fitness and business centers, spas, restaurants and bars.

Motels

Motels – distinguishable from hotels by having rooms that open onto a parking lot – tend to cluster around interstate exits and along main routes into town. Many are inexpensive 'mom-and-pop' operations; breakfast is rarely included; and amenities might top out at wi-fi and a TV (maybe with cable). Although most motel rooms won't win any style awards, they can be clean and comfortable and offer good value. Ask to see a room first if you're unsure.

Booking Services

Lonely Planet (www.lonelyplanet.com/usa/new-york-city/hotels) offers accommodations reviews and an online booking service.

NEW YORK CITY

newyorkhotels.com (www.newyorkhotels.com) The self-proclaimed official website for hotels in NYC.

NYC (www.nycgo.com/hotels) Loads of listings from the NYC Official Guide.

WASHINGTON, DC

Bed & Breakfast DC (www.bedandbreakfastdc.com) One-stop shop for B&Bs and apartments.

WDCA Hotels (www.wdcahotels.com) Discounter that sorts by neighborhood, price or eco-friendliness.

Customs Regulations

For a complete list of US customs regulations, visit the official website for US Customs and Border Protection (www.cbp.gov).

Duty-free allowance per person is as follows:

➡ 1L of liquor (provided you are at least 21 years old)

➡ 100 cigars and 200 cigarettes (if you are at least 18)

➡ $200 worth of gifts and purchases ($800 if a returning US citizen)

➡ If you arrive with $10,000 or more in US or foreign currency, it must be declared

There are heavy penalties for attempting to import illegal drugs. Forbidden items include drug paraphernalia, items with fake brand names, and most goods made in Cuba, Iran, Myanmar (Burma) and Sudan. Fruit, vegetables and other food must be declared (whereby you'll undergo a time-consuming search) or left in the bins in the arrival area.

Electricity

Type A
120V/60Hz

Type B
120V/60Hz

Embassies & Consulates

➡ For a map showing embassy locations in Washington, DC, go to www. embassy.org.

➡ Embassies aren't open to the public, so you can't go inside – except during Passport DC (www. culturaltourismdc.org), an event in May when embassies have open houses the first and second Saturday of the month.

➡ Most countries have an embassy for the UN in New York City. Some countries have consulates in other large cities.

Food

The best seafood in the country is served on the Eastern Shore and in seafaring places such as Norfolk, VA, and Annapolis and Baltimore, MD. Oysters and crab cakes are a must. The farmlands of Virginia, Maryland and Pennsylvania produce a range of vegetables that make their way to chef's tables across the region. Ethnic cuisine shines in New York City, Washington, DC, and Northern Virginia.

See p38 for everything you need to know about eating in the region.

Health

The Mid-Atlantic, like the rest of the USA, has a high level of hygiene, so infectious diseases are not a significant problem. There are no required vaccines, and tap water is safe to drink.

Bring any medications you may need in their original containers, clearly labeled. Having a signed, dated letter from your physician that describes all of your medical conditions and medications (including generic names) is also a good idea.

Health Insurance

The United States offers possibly the finest health care in the world – the problem is that it can be prohibitively expensive. It's essential to purchase travel health insurance if your home policy doesn't cover you for medical expenses abroad. Check the Insurance section of the Lonely Planet website (www.lonelyplanet.com/travel-insurance) for more information.

Find out in advance if your insurance plan will make payments directly to providers or reimburse you later for overseas health expenditures.

Availability & Cost of Health Care

If you have a medical emergency, go to the emergency room of the nearest hospital.

If the problem isn't urgent, call a nearby hospital and ask for a referral to a local physician; this is usually cheaper than a trip to the emergency room.

Stand-alone, for-profit, urgent-care centers provide good service, but can be the most expensive option.

Pharmacies are abundantly supplied. However, some medications that are available over the counter in other countries require a prescription in the US. If you don't have insurance to cover the cost of prescriptions, they can be shockingly expensive.

Infectious Diseases

Most infectious diseases are acquired by mosquito or tick bites or through environmental exposure. The Centers for Disease Control and Prevention (www.cdc.gov) has further details.

Alpha-gal Syndrome An uncommon but increasingly diagnosed – and very severe – meat allergy that results from Lone Star tick bites. Occurring in Virginia and southeastern states, and may be spreading.

Giardiasis Intestinal infection. Avoid drinking directly from lakes, ponds, streams and rivers.

Lyme Disease Occurs mostly in the Northeast. Transmitted by deer ticks in late spring and summer. Perform a tick check after you've been outdoors.

West Nile Virus Mosquito-transmitted in late summer and early fall. Prevent by keeping covered (wear long sleeves, long pants, hats and shoes rather than sandals) and apply a good insect repellent, preferably one containing DEET, to exposed skin and clothing.

Zika Of gravest concern to pregnant women, this mosquito-borne virus can cause microcephaly (when the brain does not develop fully) in utero.

EATING PRICE RANGES

The following price ranges refer to a main course. Unless otherwise stated, drinks, appetizers, desserts, taxes and tips are not included.

$ less than $15
$$ $15–$30
$$$ more than $30

Miami made the news in 2016 for having the first outbreak of its kind in the US, with over 250 locally acquired cases reported in southern Florida. Although the disease was considered eradicated there in early 2017, epidemiologists warn that Zika could rebound with the arrival of warmer temperatures and heavier rainfall.

Environmental Hazards

Cold exposure This can be a problem, especially in the mountains. Keep all body surfaces covered, including the head and neck. Watch out for the 'Umbles' – stumbles, mumbles, fumbles and grumbles – which are signs of impending hypothermia.

Heat exhaustion Dehydration is the main contributor. Symptoms include feeling weak, headache, nausea and sweaty skin. Lay the victim flat with their legs raised, apply cool, wet cloths to the skin, and rehydrate.

Tap Water

Tap water is safe to drink everywhere in the Mid-Atlantic, except in some state or national parks where it is expressly indicated that tap water is not potable.

Internet Access

Travelers will have few problems staying connected in the tech-savvy USA.

➡ Wi-fi (in-room, with decent speed) is common in lodgings across the price spectrum.

➡ Many properties also have an internet-connected computer for public use.

➡ Many restaurants, bars and cafes (such as Starbucks) offer free wi-fi. Some cities have wi-fi connected parks and plazas.

➡ If you're not packing a laptop or other web-accessible device, try the public library. Most have public terminals (though they have time limits) and wi-fi. Occasionally out-of-state

residents are charged a small fee for use.

➡ If you're not from the US, remember that you may need an AC adapter for your laptop (if it's not 110/220 dual-voltage), plus a plug adapter for US sockets; both are available at large electronics shops, such as Best Buy.

➡ For a list of wi-fi hot spots, visit www.wififreespot.com.

New York City

Most public parks in the city now offer free wi-fi. Some prominent ones include the High Line, Bryant Park, Battery Park, Central Park, City Hall Park, Madison Square Park, Tompkins Square Park and Union Square Park (Brooklyn and Queens are also well covered). For other locations, check out www.nycgovparks.org/facilities/wifi.

Even underground subway stations now offer free wi-fi, offering a way to pass time or get work done while waiting for signal problems or other delays to be resolved. LinkNYC (www.link.nyc), rolled out in 2016 to replace anachronistic pay phones (once iconic symbols of the city and where Superman changed into his suit), has installed free internet-connected kiosks, replete with charging stations and wi-fi access. The network aims to install some 7500 of these structures throughout the five boroughs.

Legal Matters

Note that, if you are stopped by the police, there is no system of paying traffic tickets or other fines on the spot. The officer will explain your options to you; there is usually a 30-day period to pay fines by mail.

If you are arrested, never walk away from an officer. You are allowed to remain silent, and you are entitled to have access to an attorney. The legal system presumes you're innocent until proven

guilty. All persons who are arrested have the right to make one phone call. If you don't have a lawyer or family member to help you, call your embassy or consulate. The police will give you the number on request.

Drugs & Alcohol

Being 'carded' (ie asked to show photo ID to prove you're of legal drinking age, which is 21 years old) is standard practice everywhere.

In all states the blood-alcohol limit is 0.08%. Driving under the influence of alcohol or drugs is a serious offense, subject to stiff fines and even imprisonment.

In November 2014 DC voted to legalize marijuana. The law lets residents and visitors have up to 2oz for personal use. Selling marijuana is prohibited, as is smoking in public, so it boils down to a home-grow, home-use policy and lots of 'gift' giving. Marijuana remains illegal in parts of the city that are federal land, such as the National Mall and other National Park Service grounds. If you're caught in possession there, you could be arrested. Elsewhere across the region, pot policy varies from state to state, so it's prudent to know the local laws before lighting up.

Possession of illicit drugs, including cocaine, ecstasy, LSD, heroin and hashish, is a felony potentially punishable by lengthy jail sentences.

LGBTIQ+ Travelers

Big cities in the Mid-Atlantic tend to be the most tolerant, and many have long-standing gay communities. Charlottesville and other small cities with universities also tend to have more relaxed attitudes.

Attitudes

Most major US cities have visible and open LGBTIQ communities that are easy to connect with.

However, note that the level of public acceptance varies nationwide. In some places, there is absolutely no tolerance whatsoever, and in others acceptance is predicated on LGBTIQ people not 'flaunting' their sexual orientation or identity. Be aware that bigotry still exists here. In rural areas and conservative enclaves, it's unwise to be openly out, as verbal abuse and even violence can sometimes occur. When in doubt, assume that locals follow a 'don't ask, don't tell' policy. Prior to 2015, 37 states (and DC) allowed gay marriage. In 2015 the US Supreme Court declared same-sex marriage legal in all 50 states. This means that no state can ban same-sex couples from getting married.

Resources

The Queerest Places: A National Guide to Gay and Lesbian Historic Sites, by Paula Martinac, covers the country and is full of juicy details and history. Visit her blog at www.queerestplaces.com.

Advocate (www.advocate.com) Gay-oriented news website reporting on business, politics, arts, entertainment and travel.

Gay Travel (www.gaytravel.com) Online guides to dozens of US destinations.

National LGBTQ Task Force (www.thetaskforce.org) The national activist group's website covers news, politics and current issues.

Out Traveler (www.outtraveler.com) Gay-oriented travel articles.

Purple Roofs (www.purpleroofs.com) Lists gay-owned and gay-friendly B&Bs and hotels.

Gaycation (www.vice.com/en_us/topic/gaycation) VICE TV's excellent documentary series on same-sex issues in the US and beyond.

LGBT DC (https://washington.org/lgbtq) The DC tourism office's portal, with events, neighborhood breakdowns and a travel resource guide.

GBT Community Center (☎212-620-7310; www.gaycenter.org; 208 W 13th St, btwn Seventh & Greenwich Aves, West Village; suggested donation $5; ⏰9am-10pm Mon-Sat, to 9pm Sun; [S]A/C/E, L to 8th Ave-14th St; 1/2/3 to 14th St) In NYC, provides a ton of regional publications about gay events and nightlife, and hosts frequent special events.

Money

ATMs are widely available. Credit cards are accepted at most hotels, restaurants and shops.

ATMs

Most locals do not carry large amounts of cash for everyday use, relying instead on credit cards, debit cards and ATMs. Don't, however, plan to rely exclusively on credit cards, as some machines (notably at many gas stations) won't accept foreign cards. Smaller businesses may refuse to accept bills over $20.

ATMs are available 24/7 at most banks and in shopping centers, airports, grocery stores and convenience stores. Most ATMs charge a service fee of $3 or more per transaction and your home bank may impose additional charges.

For foreign visitors, ask your bank for exact information about using its cards in stateside ATMs. The exchange rate is usually as good as you'll get anywhere.

Credit Cards

Major credit cards are almost universally accepted. In fact, it's next to impossible to rent a car or make phone reservations without one. Visa and Mastercard are the most widely accepted.

Money Changers

Banks are usually the best places to exchange foreign currencies. Most large city banks offer currency exchange but banks in rural areas may not. Currency-exchange counters at the airport and in tourist centers typically have the worst rates; ask about fees and surcharges first. Traveled (www.travelex.com) is a major currency-exchange company but American Express (www.amercianexpress.com) travel offices may offer better rates.

Tipping

Tipping is not optional; only withhold tips in cases of outrageously bad service.

Airport and hotel porters $2 per bag, minimum $5 per cart.

Bartenders 10% to 15% per round, minimum $1 per drink.

Hotel housekeepers $2 to $5 daily, left under the card provided.

Restaurant servers 15% to 20%, unless a gratuity is already charged on the bill.

Taxi drivers 10% to 15%, rounded up to the next dollar.

Valet parking attendants At least $2 on return of keys.

Opening Hours

Typical opening times are as follows:

Banks 8:30am to 4:30pm Monday to Friday (and possibly 9am to noon Saturday)

Bars 5pm to midnight Sunday to Thursday, to 2am Friday and Saturday

Nightclubs 10pm to 3am Thursday to Saturday

Post offices 9am to 5pm Monday to Friday

Shopping malls 9am to 9pm

Stores 9am to 6pm Monday to Saturday, noon to 5pm Sunday

Supermarkets 8am to 8pm, some open 24 hours

Post

The US Postal Service (www.usps.com) is reliable and inexpensive. The postal rates for first-class mail within the USA are 50¢ for letters weighing up to 1oz (21¢ for each additional ounce) and

35¢ for postcards. International airmail rates are $1.15 for a 1oz letter or postcard.

Public Holidays

On the following national public holidays, banks, schools and government offices (including post offices) are closed, and transportation, museums and other services operate on a Sunday schedule. Holidays falling on a weekend are usually observed the following Monday.

New Year's Day January 1

Martin Luther King Jr Day Third Monday in January

Presidents' Day Third Monday in February

Memorial Day Last Monday in May

Independence Day July 4

Labor Day First Monday in September

Columbus Day Second Monday in October

Veterans Day November 11

Thanksgiving Fourth Thursday in November

Christmas Day December 25

Safe Travel

➡ Hurricane season along the Atlantic seaboard extends from June through November, but the peak season is late August through October.

➡ The chances of encountering a hurricane are slim, but if you do, take the threat of danger seriously and pay close attention to all alerts, warnings and evacuation orders.

➡ When in doubt, listen to radio and TV news reports; for more information on storms and preparedness, see the National Weather Service website (www.weather.gov).

New York City

New York City is one of the safest cities in the USA – in

2017 homicides fell to a record low of fewer than 300 and overall violent-crime statistics declined for the 27th straight year. Still, it's best to take a common-sense approach to the city.

➡ Don't walk around alone at night in unfamiliar, sparsely populated areas.

➡ Carry your daily walking-around money somewhere inside your clothing or in a front pocket rather than in a handbag or a back pocket.

➡ Be aware of pickpockets, particularly in mobbed areas like Times Square or Penn Station at rush hour.

➡ While it's generally safe to ride the subway after midnight, you may want to skip going underground and take a taxi instead, especially if traveling alone.

Washington, DC

➡ While DC isn't dangerous, it does have typical big-city crime issues (mostly theft). Use common sense and be aware of your surroundings, especially around H St NE, southeast DC and Anacostia.

Smoking

As of 2017, 24 states, the District of Columbia and many municipalities across the US were entirely smoke-free in restaurants, bars and workplaces; an additional 11 states had enacted 100% public smoking bans in at least one of these venues. You may still encounter smoky lobbies in chain hotels and budget-minded inns, but most other accommodations are smoke-free. For more detailed state-by-state info on smoking laws, see www.cdc.gov and www.no-smoke.org.

Telephone

The US phone system mixes regional service providers, competing long-distance carriers and several cell-phone companies. Overall, the sys-

tem is efficient. Calls from a regular landline or cell phone are usually cheaper than a hotel phone or pay phone.

Mobile Phones

Foreign phones operating on tri- or quad-band frequencies will work in the USA. Or purchase inexpensive cell (mobile) phones with a pay-as-you-go plan here.

Most of the USA's cell-phone systems are incompatible with the GSM 900/1800 standard used throughout Europe and Asia (though some convertible phones will work). iPhones will work fine – but beware of roaming costs, especially for data. Check with your service provider about using your phone here.

It might be cheaper to buy a prepaid SIM card for the USA, such as those sold by AT&T or T-Mobile, which you can insert into your international mobile phone to get a local phone number and voicemail.

You can also buy inexpensive, no-contract (prepaid) phones with a local number and a set number of minutes, which can be topped up as needed. Virgin Mobile, T-Mobile, AT&T and other providers offer phones starting at $30, with a package of minutes starting at around $40 for 400 minutes.

Electronics store chain Best Buy (www.bestbuy.com) sells prepaid phones, as well as international SIM cards. Online retailer Telestial (www.telestial.com) also sells SIM cards and cell phones; it rents phones, too.

Rural swaths of the East, especially in the mountains and various national parklands, don't pick up a signal. Check your provider's coverage map.

Phone Codes

All phone numbers within the USA consist of a three-digit area code followed by a seven-digit local number. Typically, if you are calling a number within the same area code, you only have to dial the seven-digit number (though if it doesn't work, try adding 1 + the area code at the beginning).

More information on dialing:

US country code ☑1

Making international calls Dial ☑011 + country code + area code + local number.

Calling other US area codes or Canada Dial ☑1 + area code + seven-digit local number.

Directory assistance nationwide ☑411

Toll-free numbers Dial ☑1+ 800 (or 888, 877, 866) + seven-digit number. Some toll-free numbers only work within the US.

Phonecards

Prepaid phonecards are a good solution for travelers on a budget. They are available from convenience stores, supermarkets and pharmacy chains. AT&T sells a reliable phonecard that is widely available.

Toilets

Toilets are of the standard Western sit-down variety, with urinals for men common in public places. That said, public toilets in the East aren't the most savory or squeaky-clean of places, and toilets in national and state parks are commonly of the pit variety: take some backup toilet paper, just in case.

New York City

Considering the number of pedestrians, there's a noticeable lack of public restrooms around the city. You'll find spots to relieve yourself in Grand Central Terminal, Penn Station and Port Authority Bus Terminal, and in parks, including Madison Square Park, Battery Park, Tompkins Square Park, Washington Square Park and Columbus Park in Chinatown, plus several places scattered around Central Park. The

good bet, though, is to pop into a Starbucks (there's one about every three blocks), a department store (Macy's, Century 21, Bloomingdale's) or a neighborhood park like Tompkins Square in the East Village or Bleecker Playground (at W 11th and Hudson) in the West Village.

Washington, DC

The Mall has 10 public bathrooms, including those at the Lincoln Memorial, Jefferson Memorial, Martin Luther King Jr Memorial and Washington Monument. You can also dash into any of the Smithsonian museums to use their facilities, though you'll have to go through the security line to enter the building.

Tourist Information

The official tourism website of the USA is www.visittheusa.com. It has links to every US state tourism office and website, plus loads of ideas for itinerary planning. All the states in the Mid-Atlantic have their own tourism websites.

Most cities and towns have some sort of tourist center that provides local information, typically operated by the convention and visitors bureau (CVB) or chamber of commerce. These entities tend to list only the businesses that are bureau/chamber members, so not all of the town's hotels and restaurants receive coverage – keep in mind that good, independent options may be missing.

Visas

Visitors from Canada, the UK, Australia, New Zealand, Japan and many EU countries do not need visas for stays of less than 90 days, with ESTA (Electronic System for Travel Authorization) approval. For other nations, see www.

travel.state.gov or www.usa.gov/visas-and-visitors. See p430 for information about entering the country.

Visa Waiver Program & ESTA

Admission requirements are subject to rapid change. The US State Dept (www.travel.state.gov) has the latest information, or check with a US consulate in your home country.

The Visa Waiver Program (VWP) allows nationals from 38 countries (including most EU countries, Japan, Australia and New Zealand) to enter the US without a visa for up to 90 days.

VWP visitors require a machine-readable passport and approval under the Electronic System For Travel Authorization (www.cbp.gov/esta) at least three days before arrival. There is a $14 fee for processing and authorization (payable online). Once approved, the registration is valid for two years.

In essence, ESTA requires that you register specific information online (name, address, passport info etc). You will receive one of three responses: 'Authorization Approved' (this usually comes within minutes; most applicants can expect to receive this response); 'Authorization Pending' (you'll need to check the status within the next 72 hours); or 'Travel not Authorized.' If the latter is the case, it means you will need to apply for a visa.

Those who need a visa – ie anyone staying longer than 90 days, or from a non-VWP country – should apply at the US consulate in their home country.

Canadians are exempt from the process. They do not need visas, though they do need a passport or document approved by the Western Hemisphere Travel Initiative (www.cbp.gov/travel/us-citizens/western-hemisphere-travel-initiative).

Transportation

GETTING THERE & AWAY

The Mid-Atlantic region is easily reached via busy air, bus and train networks. Flights, cars and tours can be booked online at www.lonely planet.com/bookings.

Entering the Country

Entering the USA can be pretty straightforward, though at the time of writing, the Trump administration was making changes to immigration policy. Before you travel, check to see if you're affected at www.usa.gov/visas-and-visitors.

If you are flying, the first airport that you land in is where you must go through immigration and customs, even if you are continuing on the flight to another destination.

You'll be asked to fill out the US customs declaration form, which is usually handed out on the plane. Have it completed before you approach the immigration desk. For the question, 'US Street Address,' give the address where you will spend the first night (a hotel address is fine).

The immigration officer will look at your customs form and passport, and have you register with the Dept of Homeland Security's Office of Biometric Identity Management. This entails having your fingerprints scanned and a digital photo taken.

The immigration officer may ask about your plans and whether you have sufficient funds. It's a good idea to list an itinerary, produce an onward or round-trip ticket and have at least one major credit card.

Travelers from some countries, ie Canada and Visa Waiver Program nations, can bypass the immigration desks and use self-service kiosks for automated passport control. Not all airports have this technology. See www.cbp.gov/travel for details on participating locations and for further eligibility requirements.

Once you go through immigration, you collect your baggage and pass through customs. If you have nothing to declare, you'll probably clear customs without a baggage search, but don't assume this.

Remember: your passport should be valid for at least six months longer than your intended stay in the US.

Air

➡ The Mid-Atlantic's busiest international gateways are New York City, Philadelphia, Baltimore and Washington, DC.

➡ Checks by the Transportation Security Administration (TSA) and US Customs and Border Protection (CBP) can mean lengthy delays at airports;

CLIMATE CHANGE & TRAVEL

Every form of transport that relies on carbon-based fuel generates CO_2, the main cause of human-induced climate change. Modern travel is dependent on aeroplanes, which might use less fuel per kilometer per person than most cars but travel much greater distances. The altitude at which aircraft emit gases (including CO_2) and particles also contributes to their climate change impact. Many websites offer 'carbon calculators' that allow people to estimate the carbon emissions generated by their journey and, for those who wish to do so, to offset the impact of the greenhouse gases emitted with contributions to portfolios of climate-friendly initiatives throughout the world. Lonely Planet offsets the carbon footprint of all staff and author travel.

you may still have an hour or two to go before you have bags in hand and are on your way.

➡ Allow at least three hours to check in for departing international flights.

Airports

The busiest regional airports are in the New York City area, Philadelphia, Baltimore, Dulles and Washington, DC:

NEW YORK CITY & AROUND

JFK International Airport (JFK; Map p126; ☎718-244-4444; www.kennedyairport.com; [S]A to Howard Beach or E, J/Z to Sutphin Blvd-Archer Ave then Airtrain to JFK)

LaGuardia Airport (LGA; Map p62; ☎718-533-3400; www.laguardiaairport.com; 🚌M60, Q70)

Newark Liberty International Airport (EWR; ☎973-961-6000; www.newarkairport.com)

PHILADELPHIA

Philadelphia International Airport (PHL; ☎215-937-6937; www.phl.org; 8000 Essington Ave, Southwest Philadelphia; 🚆Airport Line)

BALTIMORE

Baltimore/Washington International Thurgood Marshall Airport (BWI; ☎410-859-7111; www.bwiairport.com; 7035 Elm Rd; 📶)

WASHINGTON, DC

Ronald Reagan Washington National Airport (DCA; www.flyreagan.com)

DULLES

Washington Dulles International Airport (IAD; www.metwashairports.com; 📶)

NORFOLK, VA

Norfolk International Airport (NIA; ☎757-857-3351; www.norfolkairport.com; 2200 Norview Ave; 📶)

RICHMOND, VA

Richmond International Airport (RIC; ☎804-226-3000; www.flyrichmond.com; 1 Richard E Byrd Terminal Dr; 📶)

CHARLESTON, WV

Yeager Airport (☎304-344-8033; www2.yeagerairport.com; 100 Airport Rd)

Land

The eastern USA has more than 20 official border crossings with Canada in the north. It is relatively easy crossing from the USA into Canada; it's crossing *into* the USA that can pose problems if you haven't brought all your documents. Some borders are open 24 hours, but most are not.

A busy entry point with Canada is between Buffalo, NY and Niagara Falls, ON.

Bus

Greyhound (www.greyhound.com) and its Canadian equivalent, Greyhound Canada (www.greyhound.ca), operate the largest bus network in North America. There are direct connections between main cities in the USA and Canada, but you usually have to transfer to a different bus at the border (where it takes a good hour for all passengers to clear customs and immigration). Most international buses have free wi-fi on board.

Megabus (www.megabus.com) also has international routes between Toronto and eastern cities including New York City, Philadelphia, PA, Baltimore, MD, and Washington, DC. Tickets can be purchased online only.

Car & Motorcycle

If you're driving into the USA from Canada, bring the vehicle's registration papers, proof of liability insurance and your home driver's license. Canadian driver's licenses and auto insurance are typically valid in the USA, and vice versa.

If your papers are in order, taking your own car across the US–Canadian border is usually fast and easy, but occasionally the authorities of either country decide to search a car *thoroughly*. On weekends and holidays, especially in summer, traffic at the main border crossings can be heavy and waits long.

> **DEPARTURE TAX**
>
> Departure tax is included in the price of a ticket.

Train

Amtrak (www.amtrak.com) services most major cities in the Mid-Atlantic, including New York City, Philadelphia, PA, Pittsburgh, PA, Dover, DE, Baltimore, MD, Norfolk and Richmond, VA, with most services running from or through Washington, DC.

Canadian travelers can transit through New York's Penn Station to transfer to trains heading to the Mid-Atlantic region.

Sea

Baltimore, MD, and Norfolk, VA, are small hubs for cruise ships in the Mid-Atlantic. Popular destinations are Bermuda, the Bahamas and the Caribbean.

You can also travel to and from Norfolk on a freighter. These vessels usually carry between three and 12 passengers and, though considerably less luxurious than cruise ships, give a salty taste of sea life. For more information visit the Maris website (www.freightercruises.com).

New York City

Seastreak (www.seastreak.com) has daily commuter services between Atlantic Highlands and Highlands,

New Jersey and Pier 11 near Wall St and E 35th St; there are also summer services to Sandy Hook (return $46) in New Jersey. Martha's Vineyard (one way/round trip $165/240, five hours) in Massachusetts is accessible on summer weekends from E 35th St.

Cruise ships dock at the Manhattan Cruise Terminal in Hell's Kitchen on the west side of Manhattan at several piers from W 46th to 54th Sts.

If you're arriving in NYC by yacht, there are ports at an exclusive boat slip at the World Financial Center, and at a long-term slip at the 79th St Boathouse on the Upper West Side.

GETTING AROUND

Air

Flying is usually more expensive than traveling by bus, train or car, but it's the way to go when you're in a hurry.

Airlines in the Mid-Atlantic

Overall, air travel in the USA is very safe (much safer than driving out on the nation's highways). For comprehensive details by carrier, check out www.airsafe.com.

The main domestic carriers:

Alaska Airlines (www.alaskaair.com) Recently purchased Virgin America. Nationwide service. Flights between Washington, DC, airports and numerous western cities.

American Airlines (www.aa.com) Nationwide service.

Delta Air Lines (www.delta.com) Nationwide service.

Frontier Airlines (www.flyfrontier.com) Denver-based airline with nationwide service.

JetBlue Airways (www.jetblue.com) Nonstop connections between eastern and western

US cities, plus Florida and New Orleans.

Southwest Airlines (www.southwest.com) Service across the continental USA.

Spirit Airlines (www.spirit.com) Florida-based airline; serves many US gateway cities.

United Airlines (www.united.com) Nationwide service.

Bicycle

Regional bicycle touring is popular: winding back roads and scenic coastlines make for great itineraries. Some cities have designated bike routes. Renting a bicycle is easy throughout the Mid-Atlantic. Some things to keep in mind:

➡ Cyclists must follow the same rules of the road as vehicles, but don't expect drivers to always respect your right of way.

➡ Helmets are mandatory for cyclists in some states and towns (though there is no federal law that requires it). This usually applies to children under age 18.

➡ The Bicycle Helmet Safety Institute (www.bhsi.org/mandator.htm) has a thorough, state-by-state list of local rules.

➡ The Better World Club (www.betterworldclub.com) provides emergency roadside assistance for cyclists. Membership costs $40 per year, plus a $12 enrollment fee, and entitles you to two free pickups.

➡ The League of American Bicyclists (www.bikeleague.org) offers general tips, plus lists of local bike clubs and repair shops.

Some cities are more friendly to bicycles than others, but most have at least a few dedicated bike lanes and paths, and bikes usually can be carried on public transportation. Washington, DC, and Richmond, VA, have bike-share programs.

Boat

In eastern Maryland, consider getting from Point A to Point B by boat.

Water taxis are a fun way to travel between attractions along the waterfront in Annapolis and Baltimore:

Water Taxi (Map p322; ☎410-263-0033; www.cruisesonthebay.com; City Dock; fares $3-8; ⏰9:30am-11pm Mon-Thu, to midnight Fri, 9am-midnight Sat, 9am-11pm Sun mid-May–Aug), Annapolis

Baltimore Water Taxi (☎410-563-3900; www.baltimorewatertaxi.com; Inner Harbor; daily pass adult/child $14/6; ⏰10am-midnight May-Aug, shorter hours rest of the year), Baltimore

Taking a ferry can be an efficient and scenic alternative to backtracking:

Cape May-Lewes Ferry (Map p298; ☎800-643-3779; www.capemaylewesferry.com; 43 Cape Henlopen Dr; round-trip per motorcycle/car $43/51, adult/child 6-13yr $14/7), Lewes, MD

Oxford-Bellevue Ferry (☎410-745-9023; www.oxfordbellevueferry.com; 101 E Strand, end of US 333; one way car/additional passenger/pedestrian $12/1/3; ⏰9am-sunset mid-Apr–Oct, Sat & Sun only Nov), Oxford & Bellevue, MD

White's Ferry (☎301-349-5200; www.facebook.com/pg/WhitesFerry; 24801 Whites Ferry Rd, Dickerson; car/bicycle/pedestrian $5/2/1; ⏰5am-11pm), Dickerson, MD

New York City

NYC Ferry (www.ferry.nyc; one way $2.75) Operating in the East River only since May 2017 (it replaced the former East River Ferry service), these boats link Manhattan, Brooklyn, Queens and the Bronx. At only $2.75 a ride ($1 more to bring a bicycle on board) and with charging stations and mini convenience stores on board, it's an altogether more pleasurable commute than being stuck underground on the subway. It is rapidly becoming a popular and scenic way to reach beach spots in Rockaway, Queens.

NY Water Taxi (www.nywatertaxi.com) Has a fleet of zippy yellow boats that provide hop-on, hop-off services with a few stops around Manhattan (Pier 79 at W 39th St; World Financial Center and Pier 11 near Wall St) and Brooklyn (Pier 1 in Dumbo), plus a **ferry service** (Ikea Express; ☎212-742-1969; www.nywatertaxi.com/ikea; 500 Van Brunt St, behind Fairway, Red Hook; adult/child $5/free, Sat & Sun free) between Pier 11 and the Ikea store in Red Hook, Brooklyn. At $35 for an all-day pass, though, it's priced more like a sightseeing cruise than practical transport.

Staten Island Ferry (Map p66; www.siferry.com; Whitehall Terminal, 4 South St, at Whitehall St; ⏲24hr; [S]1 to South Ferry; R/W to Whitehall St; 4/5 to Bowling Green) [FREE] Bright orange and large, this free commuter-oriented ferry to Staten Island makes constant journeys across New York Harbor. Even if you simply turn around to reboard in Staten Island, the views of lower Manhattan and the Statue of Liberty make this a great sightseeing experience and one of the cheapest romantic dates in the city.

Bus

Greyhound (www.greyhound.com) is the major long-distance carrier, plowing along an extensive network throughout the USA, as well as to/from Canada. As a rule, buses are reliable, clean(ish) and comfortable, with air-conditioning, barely reclining seats, on-board lavatories and a no-smoking policy. Several buses have wi-fi. While some shorter-route buses run express, most stop every 50 to 100 miles to pick up passengers, and long-distance buses stop for meal breaks and driver changes.

Other carriers (most with wi-fi and power outlets on board):

BestBus (www.bestbus.com) Cheap fares between the nation's capital and NYC. Also runs seasonal buses from DC and NYC to Rehoboth Beach and Dewey Beach in Delaware.

BoltBus (www.boltbus.com) Fast, cheap routes between major Northeast and mid-Atlantic cities, including Washington, DC, Baltimore, MD, NYC, Boston, Philadelphia, Newark and Richmond.

Megabus (www.megabus.com) BoltBus' main competitor, with routes between main cities in the Northeast and also the Midwest, radiating from hubs in NYC or Chicago. Fares can be quite low; ticket bookings online only.

Peter Pan Bus Lines (www.peterpanbus.com) Serves more than 50 destinations in the Northeast, as far north as Concord, NH, and as far south as Baltimore, MD, and Washington, DC.

Trailways (www.trailways.com) Mostly in the Mid-Atlantic and Midwest states; may not be as useful as Greyhound for long trips, but fares can be competitive on shorter routes.

Most cities and larger towns have dependable local bus systems, though they are often designed for commuters and provide limited service in the evening and on weekends. Costs range from free to between $1 and $3 per ride.

Car & Motorcycle

For maximum flexibility and convenience, and to explore outside of the cities, a car is essential. If you're planning to stay within a larger city, however, a car may be an expensive hassle.

New York City

Unless you plan to explore far-flung corners of the outer boroughs, it's a bad idea to have a car in NYC. Driving in this city can be challenging with lots of one-way streets and heavy traffic, plus plenty of aggressive taxi drivers, unmindful pedestrians and swerving bicyclists.

If this doesn't deter you, keep in mind that parking garages can be quite expensive, and finding street parking can be maddeningly difficult. If you drive in from New Jersey, you'll also have to contend with high tolls. Unlike in most other parts of the US, turning right on a red light is not legal here.

Washington, DC

DC has some of the nation's worst traffic congestion. Bottlenecks are in the suburbs, where the Capital Beltway (I-495) meets Maryland's I-270 and I-95, and Virginia's I-66 and I-95. Avoid the beltway during early-morning and late-afternoon rush hours (about 6am to 9am and 3pm to 6pm). Clogged rush-hour streets in DC include the main access arteries from the suburbs: Massachusetts, Wisconsin, Connecticut and Georgia Aves NW, among others.

PARKING

Finding street parking is difficult downtown and in popular neighborhoods (Georgetown, Adams Morgan and the U St area are particular nightmares), but it's reasonably easy in less congested districts.

Note that residential areas often have a two-hour limit on street parking. If you stay longer, you run the risk of getting ticketed.

Parking garages in the city cost $15 to $35 per day. Some garages have early-bird specials (ie in before 8am or 10am and out by 6pm or so) that cut rates in half.

DC Parking (www.dcparking.org) has the lowdown, with tips by neighborhood.

Automobile Associations

The American Automobile Association (www.aaa.com)

has reciprocal membership agreements with several international auto clubs (check with AAA and bring your membership card from home). For its members, AAA offers travel insurance, tour books and a wide-ranging network of regional offices. AAA advocates politically for the auto industry.

A more ecofriendly alternative, the Better World Club (www.betterworldclub.com) donates 1% of revenue to assist environmental cleanup, offers ecologically sensitive choices for every service it provides, and advocates politically for environmental causes.

For either organization, the primary member benefit is 24-hour emergency roadside assistance anywhere in the USA. Both also offer trip planning, free travel maps, travel-agency services, car insurance and a range of travel discounts (on hotels, car rentals, attractions etc).

Driver's License

Foreign visitors can legally drive a car in the USA for up to 12 months using their home driver's license. However, an International Driving Permit (IDP) will have more credibility with US traffic police, especially if your home license doesn't have a photo or isn't in English. Your automobile association at home can issue an IDP, valid for one year, for a small fee. Always carry your home license together with the IDP.

To drive a motorcycle in the USA, you will need either a valid US state motorcycle license or an IDP specially endorsed for motorcycles.

Fuel

Gas stations are ubiquitous and many are open 24 hours a day. Small-town stations may be open only from 7am to 8pm or 9pm. Plan on spending roughly $2.50 per US gallon. At many stations, you must pay before you pump.

Many gas stations will accept credit cards at the pump but will require the confirmation of a US zip code once you swipe: again, you'll need to go inside and prepay. If your car takes less fuel than you authorize payment for, the difference will be automatically refunded to the card.

Insurance

Insurance is legally required. Without it, you risk legal consequences and possible financial ruin if there's an accident.

Car rental agencies offer liability insurance, which covers other people and property involved in an accident.

Collision Damage Waivers (CDW) reduce or eliminate the amount you'll have to reimburse the rental company if there's damage to the car itself.

Paying extra for all of this insurance increases the cost of a rental car by as much as $32 a day.

Some credit cards cover CDW for a certain rental period (usually less than 15 days), if you use the card to pay for the rental, and decline the policy offered by the rental company. Always check with your card issuer to see what coverage they offer in the USA.

Car Rental

To rent a car in the USA you generally need to be at least 25 years old, hold a valid driver's license and have a major credit card. Some companies will rent to drivers between the ages of 21 and 24 for an additional charge.

You should be able to get an economy-sized vehicle for about $30 to $75 per day. Child safety seats are compulsory (reserve them when you book) and cost about $14 per day.

Some national companies, including Avis, Budget and Hertz, offer 'green' fleets of hybrid rental cars (eg Toyota Priuses, Honda Civics), although you'll usually have to

pay a lot extra to rent a more fuel-efficient vehicle.

Online, Car Rental Express (www.carrentalexpress. com) rates and compares independent agencies in US cities; it's particularly useful for searching out cheaper long-term rentals.

Major national car rental companies:

Alamo (www.alamo.com)

Avis (www.avis.com)

Budget (www.budget.com)

Dollar (www.dollar.com)

Enterprise (www.enterprise. com)

Hertz (www.hertz.com)

National (www.nationalcar.com)

Rent-A-Wreck (www.rentawreck. com) Rents cars that may have more wear and tear than your typical rental vehicle but are actually far from wrecks.

Thrifty (www.thrifty.com)

Motorcycle & Recreational Vehicle Rental

If you dream of riding a Harley, EagleRider (www. eaglerider.com) has offices in major cities nationwide and rents other kinds of adventure vehicles, too. Be aware that motorcycle rental and insurance are expensive.

Companies specializing in RV and camper rentals:

Adventures on Wheels (www. wheels9.com)

Cruise America (www.cruise america.com)

Road Conditions & Hazards

Road conditions are generally very good, but keep in mind the following:

➡ Winter travel in general can be hazardous due to heavy snow and ice, which may cause roads and bridges to close periodically. The Federal Highway Administration (www.fhwa. dot.gov/trafficinfo) provides links to road conditions and construction zones for each state.

➡ If you're driving in winter or in remote areas, make sure your vehicle is equipped with four-season radial or snow tires, and emergency supplies in case you're stranded.

➡ Where deer and other wild animals frequently appear roadside, you'll see signs with the silhouette of a leaping deer. Take these signs seriously, particularly at night.

Road Rules

If you're new to US roads, here are some basics:

➡ Drive on the right-hand side of the road. On highways, pass in the left-hand lane.

➡ The maximum speed limit on most interstates is 65mph or 70mph; a couple of eastern states go up to 75mph. It then drops to around 55mph in urban areas. Pay attention to the posted signs. City street speed limits vary between 15mph and 45mph.

➡ The use of seat belts and child safety seats is required in every state. In some states, motorcyclists are required to wear helmets.

➡ Unless signs prohibit it, you may turn right at a red light after first coming to a full stop (note that NYC is an exception, where it's illegal to turn right on a red).

➡ At four-way stop signs, the car that reaches the intersection first has right of way. In a tie, the car on the right has right of way.

➡ When emergency vehicles (ie police, fire or ambulance) approach from either direction, pull over safely and get out of the way.

➡ In an increasing number of states, it is illegal to talk (or text) on a handheld cell phone while driving; use a hands-free device or pull over to take your call.

➡ The blood-alcohol limit for drivers is 0.08%. Penalties are very severe for 'DUI' –

Driving Under the Influence of alcohol and/or drugs.

➡ In some states it is illegal to carry 'open containers' of alcohol in a vehicle, even if they are empty.

Taxi & Ride-Sharing
New York City

Hailing and riding in a cab, once rites of passage in New York, are being replaced by the ubiquity of ride-hailing app services like Lyft and Uber. In fact, those two alone have over 50,000 cars operating in the five boroughs compared to the 13,580 yellow cabs. Still, most taxis in NYC are clean and, compared to those in many international cities, pretty cheap. When you get a driver who's a neurotic speed demon, which is often, don't forget to buckle up.

Taxi & Limousine Commission (TLC; www.nyc.gov/html/tlc/html/home/home.shtml) The taxis' governing body has set fares for rides (which can be paid with credit or debit card). It's $2.50 for the initial ride (first one-fifth of a mile), 50¢ for each additional one-fifth mile as well as per 60 seconds of being stopped in traffic, $1 peak surcharge (weekdays 4pm to 8pm), and a 50¢ night surcharge (8pm to 6am), plus an MTA State surcharge of 50¢ per ride. Tips are expected to be 10% to 15%, but give less if you feel in any way mistreated; be sure to ask for a receipt and use it to note the driver's license number. The TLC keeps a Passenger's Bill of Rights, which gives you the right to tell the driver which route you'd like to take, or ask your driver to turn off an annoying radio station. Also, the driver does not have the right to refuse you a ride based on where you are going. Tip: get in first, then say where you're going.

Private car These services are a common taxi alternative in the outer boroughs. Fares differ depending on the neighborhood

and length of ride, and must be determined beforehand, as they have no meters. These 'black cars' are quite common in Brooklyn and Queens, but it's illegal if a driver simply stops to offer you a ride – no matter what borough you're in. A couple of car services in Brooklyn include **Northside** (www.northsideservice.com, ☎718-387-2222) in Williamsburg and **Arecibo** (☎718-783-6465) in Park Slope.

Boro Taxis Green Boro Taxis operate in the outer boroughs and Upper Manhattan. These allow folks to hail a taxi on the street in neighborhoods where yellow taxis rarely roam. They have the same fares and features as yellow cabs, and are a good way to get around the outer boroughs (from, say, Astoria to Williamsburg, or Park Slope to Red Hook). Drivers are reluctant (but legally obligated) to take passengers into Manhattan as they aren't legally allowed to take fares going out of Manhattan south of 96th St.

Ride-sharing App-based car-hailing services have taken over the streets of the five boroughs. Now, with nearly five times as many cars as yellow cabs and growing, they're both convenient, indispensable for some, and of course adding to the already terrible traffic problem. Tipping is highly encouraged; drivers may give you a low rating if you stiff them.

Washington, DC

Taxis are relatively easy to find (less so at night), but costly. Ride-sharing companies are used more in the District.

Train

➡ Amtrak (www.amtrak.com) has an extensive rail system throughout the USA, with several long-distance lines traversing the nation east-west, and even more running north-south. These link America's biggest cities and many of its smaller ones. In some places, Amtrak's Thruway buses provide connections to and from the rail network.

→ Compared with other modes of travel, trains are rarely the quickest, cheapest or most convenient option, but they do turn the journey into a relaxing, social and scenic all-American experience.

→ Free wi-fi is available on many, but not all, trains. The wi-fi speed is fine for email and web browsing, but usually not suitable for streaming videos or music.

→ Smoking is prohibited on all trains.

→ Rail services are busiest in the Northeast corridor, where high-speed Acela Express trains run from Boston, MA, to Washington, DC (via New York City, Philadelphia and Baltimore, MD). Another busy route is NYC to Niagara Falls.

→ Many big cities have their own commuter rail networks. These trains provide faster, more frequent services on shorter routes. The Long Island Rail Road (www.mta. info/lirr), NJ Transit (www. njtransit.com), New Jersey PATH (www.panynj.gov/ path) and Metro-North Railroad (www.mta.info/ mnr) all offer useful services for getting around NYC and surrounds.

→ The largest subway systems in the region are in New York City, Philadelphia,PA, Washington, DC. Other Mid-Atlantic cities may have small, one- or two-line rail systems that mainly serve downtown areas.

→ Key towns connected by rail from DC include Baltimore, MD; Cumberland, MD; Wilmington, DE; Harpers Ferry, WV; and in VA: Manassas, Fredericksburg, Richmond, Williamsburg, Newport News and Charlottesville.

→ MARC trains (https://mta. maryland.gov/marc-train) travel daily between Union Station in Washington, DC, BWI and Baltimore's Penn Station. On weekdays the Brunswick line connects Union Station with downtown Frederick.

NYC Subway

The New York subway system, run by the Metropolitan Transportation Authority (www.mta.info), is iconic, cheap ($2.75 per ride, regardless of the distance traveled), round-the-clock and often the fastest and most reliable way to get around the city. It's also safer and (a bit) cleaner than it used to be. Free wi-fi is available in all underground stations.

It's a good idea to grab a free map from a station

attendant. If you have a smartphone, download a useful app (like the free City-mapper), with subway map and alerts of service outages. When in doubt, ask someone who looks like they know what they're doing. They may not, but subway confusion (and frustration) is the great unifier in this diverse city. And if you're new to the underground, never wear headphones when you're riding, as you might miss an important announcement about track changes or skipped stops.

Washington, DC Metro

Buy a rechargeable SmarTrip card at any Metro station. You must use the card to enter and exit station turnstiles.

The Metro – the main way to move around the city – is frequent and ubiquitous (except during weekend track maintenance). It operates between 5am (from 7am weekends) and 11:30pm (1am on Friday and Saturday). Fares cost from $2 to $6 depending on distance traveled. A day pass costs $14.75.

Buy a rechargeable SmarTrip card at any Metro station. You must use the card to enter and exit station turnstiles.

Behind the Scenes

SEND US YOUR FEEDBACK

We love to hear from travelers – your comments keep us on our toes and help make our books better. Our well-traveled team reads every word on what you loved or loathed about this book. Although we cannot reply individually to your submissions, we always guarantee that your feedback goes straight to the appropriate authors, in time for the next edition. Each person who sends us information is thanked in the next edition – the most useful submissions are rewarded with a selection of digital PDF chapters.

Visit **lonelyplanet.com/contact** to submit your updates and suggestions or to ask for help. Our award-winning website also features inspirational travel stories, news and discussions.

Note: We may edit, reproduce and incorporate your comments in Lonely Planet products such as guidebooks, websites and digital products, so let us know if you don't want your comments reproduced or your name acknowledged. For a copy of our privacy policy visit lonelyplanet.com/privacy.

WRITER THANKS

Amy C Balfour

Thank you Ed and Melissa Reid, Alicia Matthai, Liz Robinson, Karen Snyder, David Martin, Brian Martin, Mary McRoberts, Suzanne Morris, Mary Kathryn Field, Jen Barrow, Mo Persinger, and Stephanie Coleman and family. Special thanks to Melissa, Mary, Anna and Carlton, Baltimore hostesses *extraordinaire*. Melissa, you are a friend in deed. Connie Tyree, thanks for the hospitality! Many thanks to the supportive team at Lonely Planet. This book is dedicated to Dave Dekema, the best co-adventurer out there. Miss ya Dave!

Robert Balkovich

First and foremost, thank you to my destination editor, Trisha Ping, who has given me so many wonderful opportunities and is a continual joy to work with. I'd also like to thank my parents for letting me convince them to send me to art school in New York, my sister for keeping me grounded, all of my New York friends who gave me fantastic recommendations, and Chelsea for her thoughtful insights. Special thanks to my friend Jonathan for all the logistical help and encouragement.

Ray Bartlett

Thanks first and always to my family for making all this possible and for putting up with me. Thanks to Trisha P, editor extraordinaire, for giving this the green light, and to my coauthors for the help and camaraderie. Hugs and deepest gratitude to everyone who went out of their way to show me around their amazing city: Belinda, Jennifer, Mayanne, Chang, Rebecca, Alex B, Clay, Danniel and Rachelle, Madoon, to name a few. And a shout out to all the other incredible NYC denizens who made researching this book such an awesome voyage. Can't wait to be back.

Adam Karlin

Thanks to: my usual Lonely Planet editorial crew, co-authors Brian Kluepfel and Robert Balkovich, Mark Leeper for PA Dutch Country recommendations, Jonah Evans and Trish Kelly for excellent Pittsburgh advice, my folks for taking me around Pennsylvania from a young age, wife Rachel for letting me roam, daughter Sanda for constantly making me laugh, and son Isaac for arriving and bringing great joy to our lives.

Brian Kluepfel

To my wife and North Star, Paula Zorrilla. To Trisha at Lonely Planet, and Robert and Adam, my writing cohorts. To Marc in Atlantic City, Brooke in Montauk, and Tom K in Hoboken for local knowledge. To Joe Dawson, Laura Tafuri and Karen Ramos for cool beach recommendations. And to all the lovely toll-takers on the Garden State Parkway, some of whom I now know on a first-name basis.

Ali Lemer

Many thanks to Will Coley, Nicole Marsella, Adam Michaels, Regis St Louis and Trisha Ping, and to Professor Kenneth Jackson, who taught me more about NYC history than anyone. My work is dedicated to the memory of my father, Albert Lemer, a first-generation

New Yorker who inspired my enthusiasm for international travel as much as he kindled my love of our shared hometown – the greatest city in the world.

Virginia Maxwell

Thanks to DC locals Barbara Balman and Bob Bresnahan for their convivial company and insider tips; to Trisha Ping for giving me the gig and supplying interesting leads; to DC expert Karla Zimmerman; and to traveling companions Eveline Zoutendijk, George Grundy and Ryan Ver Berkmoes. At home in Australia, thanks and much love to Peter Handsaker, who coped with apartment-renovation chaos and didn't blame me for my absence (well, not too much).

Simon Richmond

Many thanks to the following people who generously shared their time and knowledge about the city: Jerry Silverman, Lindsay Ryan, Tish Byrne, Mason Wray and Rajeev Shankar.

Regis St Louis

Many thanks to David Fung and Kristie Blase for their warm hospitality, to Jayson Mallie and Glen Brown for their friendship, and Ali and the felines for hosting me in Williamsburg. Special thanks to the staff at Mount Sinai Queens Hospital ER room for help after the late-night bike accident. As always, thanks to Cassandra and our daughters, Magdalena and Genevieve, for their support.

Karla Zimmerman

Deep appreciation to all of the locals who spilled the beans on their favorite places. Special thanks to Kate Armstrong, Virginia Maxwell, Ryan Ver Berkmoes, Amy Schwenkmeyer and Bill Brockschmidt. Thanks most to Eric Markowitz, the world's best partner-for-life, who kindly indulges my Abe Lincoln fixation. You top my Best List.

ACKNOWLEDGMENTS

Climate map data adapted from Peel MC, Finlayson BL & McMahon TA (2007) 'Updated World Map of the Köppen-Geiger Climate Classification', Hydrology and Earth System Sciences, 11, 1633–44.

Cover photograph: Kayaking in the Adirondacks, New York State, Aurora Photos/AWL ©.

Illustrations p58–9 by Javier Zarracina.

THIS BOOK

This 1st edition of Lonely Planet's New York & the Mid-Atlantic was curated by Amy C Balfour, and researched and written by Amy, Robert Balkovich, Ray Bartlett, Michael Grosberg, Adam Karlin, Brian Kluepfel, Ali Lemer, Virginia Maxwell, Simon Richmond, Regis St Louis and Karla Zimmerman. This guidebook was produced by the following:

Destination Editor
Trisha Ping
Senior Product Editors
Grace Dobell, Vicky Smith
Product Editor Kate James
Senior Cartographer
Alison Lyall
Book Designer
Ania Bartoszek
Assisting Editors Pete Cruttenden, Jacqueline Danam, Emma Gibbs, Carly Hall, Jennifer Hattam, Victoria Harrison, Alison Morris, Rosie Nicholson, Lauren O'Connell, Monique Perrin, Tamara Sheward, Amanda Williamson, Simon Williamson
Assisting Cartographers
Hunor Csutoros, Julie Sheridan, Diana Von Holdt
Cover Researcher
Naomi Parker
Thanks to Ben Buckner, Brana Vladisavljevic

BEHIND THE SCENES

Index

Map Legend

Sights
- Beach
- Bird Sanctuary
- Buddhist
- Castle/Palace
- Christian
- Confucian
- Hindu
- Islamic
- Jain
- Jewish
- Monument
- Museum/Gallery/Historic Building
- Ruin
- Shinto
- Sikh
- Taoist
- Winery/Vineyard
- Zoo/Wildlife Sanctuary
- Other Sight

Activities, Courses & Tours
- Bodysurfing
- Diving
- Canoeing/Kayaking
- Course/Tour
- Sento Hot Baths/Onsen
- Skiing
- Snorkeling
- Surfing
- Swimming/Pool
- Walking
- Windsurfing
- Other Activity

Sleeping
- Sleeping
- Camping
- Hut/Shelter

Eating
- Eating

Drinking & Nightlife
- Drinking & Nightlife
- Cafe

Entertainment
- Entertainment

Shopping
- Shopping

Information
- Bank
- Embassy/Consulate
- Hospital/Medical
- Internet
- Police
- Post Office
- Telephone
- Toilet
- Tourist Information
- Other Information

Geographic
- Beach
- Gate
- Hut/Shelter
- Lighthouse
- Lookout
- Mountain/Volcano
- Oasis
- Park
- Pass
- Picnic Area
- Waterfall

Population
- Capital (National)
- Capital (State/Province)
- City/Large Town
- Town/Village

Transport
- Airport
- BART station
- Border crossing
- Boston T station
- Bus
- Cable car/Funicular
- Cycling
- Ferry
- Metro/Muni station
- Monorail
- Parking
- Petrol station
- Subway/SkyTrain station
- Taxi
- Train station/Railway
- Tram
- Underground station
- Other Transport

Routes
- Tollway
- Freeway
- Primary
- Secondary
- Tertiary
- Lane
- Unsealed road
- Road under construction
- Plaza/Mall
- Steps
- Tunnel
- Pedestrian overpass
- Walking Tour
- Walking Tour detour
- Path/Walking Trail

Boundaries
- International
- State/Province
- Disputed
- Regional/Suburb
- Marine Park
- Cliff
- Wall

Hydrography
- River, Creek
- Intermittent River
- Canal
- Water
- Dry/Salt/Intermittent Lake
- Reef

Areas
- Airport/Runway
- Beach/Desert
- Cemetery (Christian)
- Cemetery (Other)
- Glacier
- Mudflat
- Park/Forest
- Sight (Building)
- Sportsground
- Swamp/Mangrove

Note: Not all symbols displayed above appear on the maps in this book

Brian Kluepfel

New Jersey Brian had lived in three states and seven different residences by the time he was nine, and just kept moving, making stops in Berkeley, Bolivia, the Bronx and the 'burbs further down the line. His journalistic work across the Americas has ranged from the Copa America soccer tournament in Paraguay to an accordion festival in Québec. His titles for LP include *Venezuela, Costa Rica, Belize & Guatemala, Bolivia* and *Ecuador*. He writes a blog about Venezuelan baseball players and another regarding birds of many nations called www.brianbirdwatching.blogspot.com.

Ali Lemer

New York City Ali has been a Lonely Planet writer and editor since 2007, and has authored guidebooks and travel articles on Russia, NYC, Los Angeles, Melbourne, Bali, Hawaii, Japan and Scotland. A native New Yorker and naturalized Melburnian, Ali has also lived in Chicago, Prague and the UK, and has traveled extensively around Europe and North America.

Virginia Maxwell

Washington, DC, Virginia Although based in Australia, Virginia spends at least half of her year updating Lonely Planet destination coverage across the globe. The Mediterranean is her major area of interest – she has covered Spain, Italy, Turkey, Syria, Lebanon, Israel, Egypt, Morocco and Tunisia for Lonely Planet – but she also covers Finland, Bali, Armenia, the Netherlands, the USA and Australia. Follow her @maxwellvirginia on Instagram and Twitter.

Simon Richmond

Philadelphia Journalist and photographer Simon Richmond has specialised as a travel writer since the early 1990s, covering countries including Australia, China, India, Iran, Japan, Korea, Malaysia, Mongolia, Myanmar (Burma), Russia, Singapore, South Africa and Turkey. He has lived in the UK, Japan and Australia, and is now based back in the UK in Folkestone on the east Kent coast. His travel features have been published in newspapers and magazines around the world, including in the UK's *Independent, Guardian, Times, Daily Telegraph* and *Royal Geographical Society Magazine*, and in Australia's *Sydney Morning Herald* and *Australian* newspapers and *Australian Financial Review* magazine.

Regis St Louis

New York City Regis grew up in a small town in the American Midwest – the kind of place that fuels big dreams of travel – and he developed an early fascination with foreign dialects and world cultures. He spent his formative years learning Russian and a handful of Romance languages, which served him well on journeys across much of the globe. Regis has contributed to more than 50 Lonely Planet titles, covering destinations across six continents. His travels have taken him from the mountains of Kamchatka to remote island villages in Melanesia, and to many grand urban landscapes. When not on the road, he lives in New Orleans. Follow him @regisstlouis on Instagram.

Karla Zimmerman

Washington, DC Karla lives in Chicago, where she eat doughnuts and yells at the Cubs, and writes stuff for books, magazines and websites when she's not doing the first two things. She has contributed to 70-plus guidebooks and travel anthologies covering destinations in Europe, Asia, Africa, North America and the Caribbean. To learn more, follow her @karlazimmerman on Instagram and Twitter.

Contributing Writer Michael Grosberg

Our Story

A beat-up old car, a few dollars in the pocket and a sense of adventure. In 1972 that's all Tony and Maureen Wheeler needed for the trip of a lifetime – across Europe and Asia overland to Australia. It took several months, and at the end – broke but inspired – they sat at their kitchen table writing and stapling together their first travel guide, *Across Asia on the Cheap*. Within a week they'd sold 1500 copies. Lonely Planet was born.

Today, Lonely Planet has offices in Franklin, London, Melbourne, Oakland, Dublin, Beijing and Delhi, with more than 600 staff and writers. We share Tony's belief that 'a great guidebook should do three things: inform, educate and amuse'.

OUR WRITERS

Amy C Balfour

Delaware, Maryland, West Virginia Amy practiced law in Virginia before moving to Los Angeles to try to break in as a screenwriter. After a stint as a writer's assistant on *Law & Order,* she jumped into freelance writing, focusing on travel, food and the outdoors. She has hiked, biked and paddled across Southern California and the Southwest, and recently criss-crossed the Great Plains in search of the region's best burgers and barbecue. Books authored or co-authored include Lonely Planet's *Los Angeles Encounter, Los Angeles & Southern California, Caribbean Islands, California, California Trips, USA, USA's Best Trips* and *Arizona.* Amy's essays have appeared in the *Los Angeles Times* and *Southern Living,* and the travel anthologies *Go Your Own Way* and *The Thong Also Rises*.

Robert Balkovich

New York City, New York State Robert was born and raised in Oregon, but has called New York City home for almost a decade. When he was a child and other families were going to theme parks and grandma's house he went to Mexico City and toured Eastern Europe by train. He's now a writer and travel enthusiast seeking experiences that are ever so slightly out of the ordinary to report back on. Instagram: @oh_balky

Ray Bartlett

New York City Ray has been a travel writer for nearly two decades, bringing Japan, Korea, Mexico and many parts of the United States to life in rich detail for top-industry publishers, newspapers and magazines. His acclaimed debut novel, *Sunsets of Tulum,* set in Yucatán, was a Midwest Book Review 2016 Fiction pick. Among other pursuits, he surfs regularly and is an accomplished Argentine tango dancer. Follow him on Facebook (RayBartlettAuthor), Twitter (@kaisora dotcom) or Instagram (@kaisoradotcom).

Adam Karlin

Pennsylvania Adam has contributed to dozens of Lonely Planet guidebooks, covering an alphabetical spread that ranges from the Andaman Islands to the Zimbabwe border. As a journalist, he has written on travel, crime, politics, archeology and the Sri Lankan Civil War, among other topics. He has sent dispatches from every continent barring Antarctica (one day!) and his essays and articles have featured on the BBC and NPR, and in multiple non-fiction anthologies. Adam is based out of New Orleans, which helps explain his love of wetlands, food and good music. Learn more at http://walkonfine.com, or follow @adamwalkonfine on Instagram.

OVER PAGE MORE WRITERS

Published by Lonely Planet Global Limited
CRN 554153
1st edition – March 2019
ISBN 978 1 78701 737 5
© Lonely Planet 2019 Photographs © as indicated 2019
10 9 8 7 6 5 4 3 2 1
Printed in Singapore

Although the authors and Lonely Planet have taken all reasonable care in preparing this book, we make no warranty about the accuracy or completeness of its content and, to the maximum extent permitted, disclaim all liability arising from its use.